W9-BZV-888

COUNTRIES AND CONCEPTS

POLITICS, GEOGRAPHY, CULTURE

NINTH EDITION

Michael G. Roskin

Lycoming College

2700

Upper Saddle River, New Jersey 07458

Library of Congress Cataloging-in-Publication Data

Roskin, Michael
   Countries and concepts: politics, geography, culture/Michael G. Roskin.—9th ed.
      p. cm.
   Includes bibliographical references and index.
   ISBN 0-13-243255-2
   1. Comparative government.   I. Title.
JF51.R54 2006
320.3—dc22

2006016906

Editorial Director: Charlyce Jones Owen
Executive Editor: Dickson Musslewhite
Associate Editor: Rob DeGeorge
Editorial Assistant: Jennifer Murphy
Senior Marketing Manager: Emily Cleary
Marketing Assistant: Jennifer Lang
Director of Production and Manufacturing: Barbara Kittle
Senior Managing Editor: Lisa Iarkowski
Production Liaison: Joe Scordato
Production Assistant: Marlene Gassler
Prepress and Manufacturing Manager: Nick Sklitsis
Prepress and Manufacturing Assistant Manager: Mary Ann Gloriande
Director, Image Resource Center: Melinda Reo

Manager, Rights and Permissions: Zina Arabia
Manager, Visual Research: Beth Brenzel
Manager, Cover Visual Research and Permissions: Karen Sanatar
Image Permission Coordinator: Annette Linder
Photo Researcher: Beaura Kathy Ringrose
Cover Art Director: Jayne Conte
Cover Design: Bruce Kenselaar
Cover Photos: Michael G. Roskin
Interior Design: John Paul Mazzola
Composition/Full-Service Project Management: Kari Callaghan Mazzola and John Paul Mazzola
Printer/Binder: Von Hoffmann Corporation
Cover Printer: Phoenix Color Corp.

This book was set in 10/11.5 Goudy.

Copyright © 2007, 2004, 2001, 1998, 1995, 1992, 1989, 1986, 1982 by Pearson Education, Inc., Upper Saddle River, New Jersey 07458.
Pearson Prentice Hall. All rights reserved. Printed in the United States of America. This publication is protected by copyright and permission should be obtained from the publisher prior to any prohibited reproduction, storage in a retrieval system, or transmission in any form or by any means, electronic, mechanical, photocopying, recording, or likewise. For information regarding permission(s), write to: Rights and Permissions Department.

Pearson Prentice Hall™ is a trademark of Pearson Education, Inc.
Pearson® is a registered trademark of Pearson plc
Prentice Hall® is a registered trademark of Pearson Education, Inc.

Pearson Education LTD.
Pearson Education Singapore, Pte. Ltd
Pearson Education, Canada, Ltd
Pearson Education–Japan
Pearson Education Australia PTY, Limited

Pearson Education North Asia Ltd
Pearson Educación de Mexico, S.A. de C.V.
Pearson Education Malaysia, Pte. Ltd
Pearson Education, Upper Saddle River, NJ

10 9 8 7 6 5 4 3 2 1
ISBN 0-13-243255-2

CONTENTS

CHAPTER 3   BRITAIN: THE KEY INSTITUTIONS   30

CHAPTER 4   BRITISH POLITICAL CULTURE   46

CHAPTER 8   FRANCE: THE KEY INSTITUTIONS   100

CHAPTER 9   FRENCH POLITICAL CULTURE   116

CHAPTER 10   FRANCE: PATTERNS OF INTERACTION   132

CHAPTER 11   WHAT THE FRENCH QUARREL ABOUT   146

Part III   Germany   160

CHAPTER 12   GERMANY: THE IMPACT OF THE PAST   162

CHAPTER 19   RUSSIA: THE KEY INSTITUTIONS   278

CHAPTER 20   RUSSIAN POLITICAL CULTURE   294

CHAPTER 21   RUSSIA: PATTERNS OF INTERACTION   308

CHAPTER 22   WHAT RUSSIANS QUARREL ABOUT   322

Part V   Japan   336

CHAPTER 23   JAPAN: THE IMPACT OF THE PAST   338

Part VI   China   406

Part VII The Third World 478

FEATURE BOXES

Chapter 4

Chapter 5

Chapter 6

Chapter 7

Chapter 8

Chapter 9

Chapter 10

Chapter 11

Chapter 12

Chapter 13

Chapter 14

Chapter 15

Chapter 16

Chapter 17

Chapter 18

Chapter 19

Chapter 20

Chapter 21

Chapter 22

Chapter 23

Chapter 24

Chapter 25

Chapter 26

Chapter 27

Chapter 28

Chapter 29

Chapter 30

Chapter 31

Chapter 32

Chapter 33

Chapter 34

Chapter 35

A Note to Instructors

Instructor input has prompted some major changes in the ninth edition of *Countries and Concepts*. Mexico replaces Brazil, and Nigeria replaces South Africa. I did this with heavy heart, as I am fond of Brazil and South Africa and believe that they offer valuable lessons. But as I got into Mexico and Nigeria, I realized that their lessons—often parallel with the lessons of Brazil and South Africa—are as valuable and sometimes more timely. For example, Brazil used to illustrate "praetorianism" but has modernized out of it into democracy. Now Nigeria allows us to study in real time the tendency for military coups.

Some long-term adopters also suggested fuller treatment of China. In previous editions I covered China briefly as part of the Third World, but now this emerging giant clearly merits a longer and deeper review. Accordingly, China now roughly doubles in length from one large chapter to five shorter chapters, the same as for Britain, France, Germany, Russia, and Japan. Adopters also thought that it was time to cover the European Union, which now appears as a chapter following Germany.

Most of the material from previous editions continues. Political geography is somewhat expanded. Instructors agree that ignorance of geography is widespread; the subject seems to have been dropped from most school curricula. At the behest of Lycoming's education department—our students were doing poorly on the geography section of state teacher exams—I offered Political Geography at Lycoming. I heard similar concerns from other instructors, so *Countries and Concepts* tries to fill this gap by combining political with geographical material, and the two fields overlap. For example, the discussion of German institutions lends itself to a box on federalism.

Also continued are the chapter-opening questions, which prime students for the main points, and the running marginal glossaries, which help students build their vocabularies as they read. The definitions here are those of a political scientist; in other contexts one might find different definitions. The boxes still have running poster-heads—Geography, Democracy, Personalities, Political Culture, Key Concepts, or Comparison—to give them greater focus and continuity.

The structure and purpose of *Countries and Concepts* continue as before. The book analyzes four European nations, Japan, and now China at some length, and three Third World nations more briefly. It does not attempt to create young scholars out of college sophomores. It sees, rather, comparative politics as an important but usually neglected grounding in citizenship that we should be making available to our young people. I agree with the late Morris Janowitz (in his 1983 *The Reconstruction of Patriotism: Education for Civic Consciousness*) that civic education has declined in the United States and that this poses dangers for democracy. Our students are often ill-prepared in the historical, political, economic, geographical, and moral aspects of democracy, and to expose them to professional-level abstractions in political science ignores their civic education and offers material that is largely meaningless to them. An undergraduate is not a miniature graduate student.

Accordingly, the ninth edition of *Countries and Concepts* includes a good deal of fundamental vocabulary and concepts, buttressed by many examples. It is readable. Many students neglect assigned readings; with *Countries and Concepts*, they can't make the excuse that the reading is long or boring.

Some reviewers have noted that *Countries and Concepts* contains values and criticisms. This is part of my purpose. The two go together; if you have no values, you have no basis from which to criticize. Value-free instruction is probably impossible. If successful, it would produce value-free students, and that, I think, should not be the aim of the educational enterprise. If one knows something with the head but not with the heart, one really does not know it at all.

Is *Countries and Concepts* too critical? It treats politics as a series of ongoing quarrels for which no very good solutions can be found. It casts a skeptical eye on all political systems and all solutions proposed for political problems. As such, the book is not out to "get" any one country. All political systems are flawed; none approach perfection. Let us simply say so. *Countries and Concepts* rejects absurd theories of political systems as well-oiled machines or gigantic computers that never break down or make mistakes. Put it this way: If we are critical of the workings of our own country's politics—and many, perhaps most, of us are—why should we abandon the critical spirit in looking at other lands?

The ninth edition continues the loose theoretical approach of the previous editions with the simple observation that politics, on the surface at least, is composed of a number of human conflicts or quarrels. These quarrels, if observed over time, usually form patterns of some durability beyond the specific issues involved. What I call patterns of interaction are the relationships among politically relevant groups and individuals, what they call in Russian *kto-kovo*, who does what to whom. There are two general types of such patterns: (1) between elites and masses, and (2) among and within elites.

Before we can appreciate these patterns, however, we must first study the political culture of a particular country, which leads us to its political institutions and ultimately to its political history. Thus we have a five-fold division in the study of each country. We could start with a country's contemporary political quarrels and work backward, but it is probably better to begin with the underlying factors as a foundation from which to understand their impact on modern social conflict. This book goes from history to institutions to political culture to patterns of interaction to quarrels. This arrangement need not supplant other approaches. Instructors have had no trouble utilizing this book in connection with their preferred theoretical insights.

Inclusion of the Third World in a first comparative course is problematic. The Third World is so complex and differentiated that many (myself included) suspect that the concept should be discarded. The semester is only so long. But if students are going to take only one comparative course—all too often the case nowadays—they should get some exposure to the majority of humankind. We include, therefore, briefer treatment of three non-European systems: Mexico, Nigeria, and Iran. They are not "representative" systems—what Third-World countries are?—but are interesting in their three different relationships to democracy: (1) democracy struggling in Mexico after a long period of one-party rule; (2) the difficult founding of a stable democracy in coup-prone Nigeria; and (3) democracy blanketed by an Islamic revolution in Iran. These three systems provide a refreshing counterpoise to the more settled systems of Europe and Japan. Instructors can and do omit some or all of these Third-World systems—for lack of time or in order to focus more closely on other countries—but this does not break the continuity of the text.

Neither is the order of studying these nine countries fixed. In my own course I now teach Japan ahead of Russia to form four groups, each followed by an exam, to facilitate comparisons between countries with similar problems: (1) Britain and France, (2) Germany and Japan, (3) Russia and China, and (4) Mexico, Nigeria, and Iran. The book may lend itself to other groupings.

■ Supplements

Companion Website™

www.prenhall.com/roskin   This web site brings an on-line study guide to students. When students log on, they find a wealth of study and research sources. Chapter outline and summary information, true/false tests, fill-in-the-blank tests, and multiple-choice tests—all with immediate feedback and chapter page numbers—give students ample opportunity to review the material. The site also includes an archive of the maps found in the text, as well as links to sites pertaining to the countries covered in the text.

Instructor's Manual with Test Item File

For each chapter in the book, this supplement—available in print as well as downloadable format—contains a chapter summary, true/false questions, essay questions, and multiple-choice questions based on the material discussed in the text. (ISBN 0-13-243268-4)

Prentice Hall Test Generator

A computerized version of the test item file, this program allows full editing of the questions and the addition of instructor-generated test items. Other special features include random generation, scrambling question order, and test preview before printing. This program is available in Windows and Macintosh formats. (ISBN 0-13-225457-3)

Customized Readers

www.amongnations.com   Instructors can assemble their own readers based on the database of selections, *Among Nations: Readings in International Relations*.

Prentice Hall's sister company, Pearson Custom Publishing, has entered a partnership with the Council on Foreign Relations, bringing together expertise in on-line book-building technology with academic excellence. The Council formed a special editorial team—which includes *Foreign Affairs'* Managing Editor Gideon Rose—to select the most influential articles on International Relations from *Foreign Affairs* and other prominent publications in the discipline. Along with suggested tables of content for specific courses and Prentice Hall texts, the Editorial Board has provided optional pedagogical apparatus.

Whether classic or current, theoretical or real-world applications, selections from *Among Nations* will bring important new perspectives to the classroom. This is the only on-line book-building resource of articles from *Foreign Affairs*. *Among Nations* provides access to all 1,500 articles published since the inception of *Foreign Affairs* magazine in 1922.

■ Acknowledgments

I welcome your suggestions on any area of the book and its supplementary materials. Many have generously offered their comments, corrections, and criticism. Especially valuable were the comments of Stephen Chilton, University of Minnesota–Duluth; Danny Damron, Brigham Young University; Susan Matarese, University of Louisville; Robert L. Youngblood, Arizona State University; Eleanor E. Zeff, Drake University; Christian Soe, California State University at Long Beach; Cheryl L. Brown, University of North Carolina at Charlotte; Karl W. Ryavec, University of Massachusetts at Amherst; Frank Myers, State University of New York at Stony Brook; Ronald F. Bunn, University of Missouri–Columbia; Said A. Arjomand, State University of New York at Stony Brook; Larry Elowitz, Georgia College; Arend Lijphart, University of California at San Diego; Thomas P. Wolf, Indiana University, Southeast; Susan Matarese, University of Louisville; Hanns-D. Jacobsen, Free University of Berlin [on Germany]; Ko Shioya of *Bungei Shunju* [on Japan]; Carol Nechemias, Penn State, Harrisburg; Yury Polsky, West Chester University; Marcia Weigle, Bowdoin College [on Russia]; Morgan Barr, Dan O'Connell, and Ryan Costella [on China]; Jim Coyle and Lycoming colleague Mehrdad Madresehee [on Iran]; John Peeler of Bucknell University [on Mexico]; Tony Phillips, USAF Retired [on the new European Union chapter]; and Ed Dew of Fairfield University for his suggestion to include geography. Special thanks go to former German Chancellor Schröder and former Japanese Prime Minister Koizumi for holding elections early in time for this edition. And to a student in China—who must remain nameless—I say thanks and *Minzhu!* All errors, of course, are my own. Instructors may send professional comments and corrections to me at Lycoming College, Williamsport, PA 17701, or e-mail roskin@lycoming.edu. I am grateful for suggestions for subsequent editions.

Michael G. Roskin

COUNTRIES AND CONCEPTS

Chapter 1

THE CONCEPT
OF COUNTRY

W hat are we chiefly studying? **Nations**? The Latin root of nation means *birth,* but instead of blood ties, nation now means people with a sense of identity and often the same language, culture, or religion. This process is not always easy or natural. To build modern France, kings united several regions first by the sword and then by language and culture. The United States is a bizarre mix of peoples, processed over time into a set of common values.

Should we call these entities **states**? Obviously we are not using *state* in the sense of the fifty U.S. states, which lack **sovereignty**, because ultimately Washington's laws prevail. State means governmental institutions and laws. Historically, states preceded and often formed nations. Over the centuries, the French government, by decreeing use of a certain dialect and spelling and enforcing nationwide educational standards, molded a French consciousness. The French state invented the French nation. All states are to a certain degree **constructed**, somewhat artificial.

We might settle on *country*, which originally meant a rural area where people shared the same dialect and traditions but broadened in meaning until most use it as synonymous with nation or state. Some use *nation-state* to combine the psychological and structural elements, but the term did not catch on. Nation-states were often defined as having territory, population, independence, government, and other attributes, but none of them are clear-cut.

Territory would seem to be basic, but what about those who have a strong sense of being a people but lack real estate? For example, the Jews turned their sense of nationhood into Israel, and the Palestinians now define themselves as a nation that is ready for statehood. This brings up the next problem: What happens when territorial claims overlap? Which claim is just? History is a poor guide, as typically many tribes and invaders have washed over the land over the centuries. France's Alsatians, on the west bank of the Rhine River, speak German and have Germanic family names. But they also speak French and think of themselves as French. Should Alsace belong to France or Germany? Wars are fought over such questions.

Population is obviously essential. But many countries are **multinational**, with populations divided by language or **ethnicity**. Sometimes the nationalities are angry and wish to break away. Like

Questions to Consider

1. What is the difference between nation and state?
2. Why are standard definitions of nation-state inadequate?
3. What factors produced the modern state?
4. Where did nationalism originate?
5. What does the author mean by "quarrels"?
6. How do we define Europe's regions?
7. Does stable democracy need a certain level of economic development?
8. What is a political institution?
9. What is political culture?
10. How are generalizations and theories related?
11. Should we spend more time studying democracies than studying dictatorships? Why?
12. What is "redistribution" and why is it never settled?

nation Cultural element of country; people psychologically bound to one another. (See page 1.)

state Institutional or governmental element of country. (See page 1.)

sovereignty Last word in law in given territory; boss on your own turf. (See page 1.)

constructed Deliberately created but widely accepted as natural. (See page 1.)

multinational Country composed of several peoples with distinct national feelings. (See page 1.)

ethnicity Cultural characteristics differentiating one group from another. (See page 1.)

diplomatic recognition State announcing official contact with other state.

failed state Collapse of sovereignty, essentially no national governing power.

reification Taking theory as reality.

causality Proving that one thing causes another.

the ex-Soviet Union, ex-Yugoslavia was composed of several quarrelsome nationalities, most of whom (Slovenes, Croats, Macedonians, Bosnian Muslims) left the Yugoslav state, which, they believed, was unfairly dominated by the largest nationality, the Serbs. Yugoslavia is an example of a recent (1918) and artificial construct that did not jell as a nation-state. All countries, to be sure, are more or less artificial, but over time some, such as France, have psychologically inculcated a sense of common nationhood that overrides earlier regional or ethnic loyalties. Germany has done this more recently, and Spain is still working on it. In Nigeria the process has barely begun.

Independence means that the state governs itself as a sovereign entity. Colonies, such as Algeria under the French, become nation-states when the imperial power departs, as the French did in 1962. **Diplomatic recognition** by other countries, especially by the major powers, confirms a country's independence and helps its economy. China got a boost with U.S. recognition in 1972. Some countries, however, are more sovereign and independent than others. East European lands during the Cold War were Soviet satellites, less than sovereign since Moscow controlled their major decisions. Are Central American "banana republics" and Iraq, under U.S. supervision, truly sovereign and independent? Sovereign independence may be a convenient legal fiction.

Government is the crux of being a state. No government means anarchy, with the high probability that the country will fall apart or be conquered. Some call countries like Afghanistan, the Congo, and Somalia **failed states**. Sometimes government can precede states. The Continental Congress preceded and founded the United States. A government can be in exile, as was de Gaulle's Free French government during World War II. The mere existence of a government does not automatically mean that it effectively governs the whole country. In much of the Third World, the government's writ falls off as one travels from the capital. In several Mexican states drug lords fight Wild West style while the government can do little to bring the chaos under legal control.

In sum, nation-states are not as clear-cut as supposed; their realities are messy but interesting. This is one reason for using the admittedly vague term "country": It avoids **reification**, a constant temptation in the social sciences, but one we must guard against.

■ The Modern State

Whatever we call it—country, state, or nation-state—we must recognize that its current form is relatively recent. To be sure, we find states at the dawn of written history. (Ancient kingdoms, in fact, invented writing in order to tax and control.) But the modern state is only about half a millennium old and traces back to the replacement of old European feudal monarchies by what were called "new monarchies" and subsequently the "strong state." There are many factors in this shift; it is impossible to pinpoint which were the causes and which the consequences. **Causality** is always difficult to demonstrate in the social sciences, but the box on page 3 discusses changes that ushered in the modern state. Notice how they happened about the same time and how each reinforced the others in a package of incredible change.

By the end of the Thirty Years' War in 1648, the feudal system had been displaced by the modern state. **Feudalism** balanced power between monarch and nobles; it was loose and sloppy and did not tolerate strong national government. It was not oriented to change or expansion. The new monarchies were **absolutist**, concentrating all power in themselves, disdaining the old medieval constitution in which their powers balanced with nobles, and using new economic, administrative, and military tools to increase their power. Royalist philosophers extolled the strong monarch and coined the term *sovereignty*. In consolidating their powers, monarchs had the nation celebrated, giving rise to the concept of nationality, of belonging to a nation rather than merely being the subject of an hereditary ruler.

> **feudalism**   Political system of power dispersed and balanced between king and nobles.
>
> **absolutism**   Royal dictatorship that bypasses nobles.
>
> **secularization**   Diminishing role of religion in government and society.

The Rise of Nationalism

The French Revolution unleashed modern nationalism. As the armies of German princes closed in on the Revolution in 1792, the French people rallied *en masse* to repel the foe, believing they were defending both the Revolution and the *patrie* (fatherland), and the two concepts merged. France, the revolutionaries claimed, was destined to liberate and reform the rest of Europe. The concept of

Geography

WHAT MADE THE MODERN STATE?

Europe began to stir in the eleventh century (late Middle Ages), but the Renaissance, starting in the fourteenth century, accelerated growth in art, philosophy, science, commerce, and population across Europe. The political system changed from feudalism to absolutism as monarchs increased and centralized their power over the nobles. By the middle of the fifteenth century, Europe was set for a revolution:

1453   The Turks use cannons to crack open the walls of Constantinople. European monarchs quickly acquired the new weapon to subdue nobles and consolidate their kingdoms.

1454   Gutenburg prints with moveable type. Printing increased the rate of diffusion of information, speeding up all other processes and displacing Latin with local tongues. Printed materials helped the national capital govern outlying provinces.

1488   Portuguese round Africa, soon followed by . . .

1492   The New World opens. Countries with access to the sea (Spain, Portugal, England, France, the Netherlands) rushed to Asia, Africa, and the Americas for trade and colonies.

1494   Italian monk Luca Pacioli invents accounting, making it possible to control large businesses and thus encouraging growth.

1517   Luther nails his ninety-five theses to the church door and founds Protestantism. Soon Protestant kings split from Rome and set up national churches, as in England and Sweden.

1545   This led to the wars of religion, first the Schmalkaldic War of 1545–1555 and then the devastating Thirty Years' War of 1618–1648. These conflicts increased state power and curtailed the church's temporal power, leading to **secularization**.

1618–1648   During the Thirty Years' War, state administration greatly improves. Warring monarchs, desperate for money, needed reliable tax bases and tax collectors. France's Richelieu and Sweden's Oxenstierna founded modern, rational administration, to control and tax an entire country. The state got its own budget, separate from the royal household budget.

quarrels   As used here, important, long-term political issues.

power   Ability of A to get B to do what A wants.

a nation embodying everything good was thus born and spread throughout Europe by Napoleon's enthusiastic legions.

By its very nature, nationalism could not stay confined to the French soldiers, who soon turned into brutal and arrogant occupiers. All over Europe, local patriots rose up against them with the same kind of nationalistic feelings the French had introduced. The spillover of French nationalism thus gave rise to Spanish, German, and Russian nationalism. By the late nineteenth century, with German and Italian unification, most Europeans had either formed nationalistic states or desired to (for example, Poland). Thinkers such as Germany's Hegel and Italy's Mazzini extolled the nation as the highest level of human (or possibly divine) development.

The modern state and its nationalism did not stay in West Europe. Driven to expand, the Europeans conquered Latin America, Asia, and Africa. Only Japan and Turkey kept the Europeans out; Meiji Japan carried out a brilliant "defensive modernization." The European imperialists introduced nationalism to their subject peoples. By their very integration and administration of previously fragmented territories, the British in India, the French in Indochina, and the Dutch in Indonesia taught "the natives" to think of themselves as a nation that, of right, deserved to be independent. Now virtually the entire globe is populated by national states, each jealous of their sovereign independence and many of them fired by nationalism.

■ Looking for Quarrels

One way to begin the study of a political system is to ask what its people fight about. There is no country without political **quarrels**. They range from calm discussions over whether to include dental care in nationalized health insurance to angry conflicts over language rights to murderous civil wars over who should rule the country.

You can get a fair idea of a country's quarrels by talking with its people, interviewing officials, following the local media, and attending election rallies. This is how journalists work. Political scientists, however, go further. They want to know the whys and wherefores of these controversies, whether they are long-standing issues or short-term problems. Our next step, then, is to observe the quarrels over time. If the basic quarrel lasts a long time, we are onto an important topic. To explain the quarrel, we must dig into the country's past, its institutions, and its culture.

In this book, we look at nine countries, considering each in five sections, each focusing on a subject area. We start with the underlying causes of current quarrels:

- ■ The Impact of the Past
- ■ The Key Institutions
- ■ The Political Culture

We study the past, including the country's geography, in order to understand the present. We do not seek the fascinating details of history but the major patterns that have set up present institutions and culture. We study institutions to see how **power** is structured, for that is what institutions are: structures of power. We study culture to see how people look at their social and political system, how deeply they support it, and how political views differ among groups.

Moving from underlying factors to current politics brings us to the next two areas:

- ■ Patterns of Interaction
- ■ What People Quarrel About

Here we get more specific and more current. The previous sections are, respectively, about the traditions, rules, and spirit of the game; the patterns of interaction are how the game is actually played. We look here for recurring behavior. The last section, the specific quarrels, represents the stuff of politics, the kind of things you see in a country's newspaper.

political geography   How territory and politics influence each other.

elites   Those few persons with great influence.

mass   Most people, those without influence.

democracy   Political system of mass participation, competitive elections, and human and civil rights.

per capita   GDP divided by population, giving approximate level of well-being.

GDP   Gross Domestic Product, sum total of goods and services produced in country in one year.

■ The Impact of the Past

We look first at a country's geography. *Physical geography* concerns the natural features of the earth, whereas **political geography** studies what is largely human-made. There is, of course, a connection between the two, as physical limits set by nature influence the formation, consolidation, and governing mentality of political systems.

Next, moving on to history, was the country unified early or late? For the most part, countries are artificial—not natural—entities, created when one group or tribe conquered its neighbors and unified them by the sword. The founding of nations is usually a bloody business, and the longer ago it took place, the better. We look at Sweden and say, "What a nice, peaceful country." We look at Afghanistan and say, "What a horror of warlords battling each other." Long ago, however, Sweden resembled Afghanistan.

The unification and consolidation of a country leaves behind regional memories of incredible staying power. People whose ancestors were conquered centuries ago still act out their resentments in political ways, in the voting booth, or in civil violence. This is one way history has an impact on the present.

Becoming "modern" is a wrenching experience. Industrialization, urbanization, and the growth of education and communications uproot people from their traditional villages and lifestyles and send them to work in factories in cities. In the process, previously passive people become aware of their condition and want to change it. Mobilized by new parties, they start to participate in politics and demand economic improvement. This is a delicate time in the life of nations. If traditional **elites** do not devise some way to take account of newly awakened **mass** demands, the system may be heading toward revolution.

No country has industrialized in a nice way; it is always a process marked by low wages, bad working conditions, and, usually, political repression. The longer in the past this stage has happened, the more peaceful and stable a country is likely to be. We must look for the stage of development a country is in. A country just undergoing industrialization can expect domestic tensions of the sort that existed earlier in Europe.

Religion is a crucial historical question. Does the country have its church-state relationship settled? If not, it is a lingering political sore. Protestant countries had an easier time secularizing; their churches cut their ties to Rome, the state became stronger than the church early on, and the church stayed out of politics. In Roman Catholic countries, where the church had power in its own right, there was a long church-state struggle called the "clerical-anticlerical split," which is still alive in France and Mexico: Conservatives are more religious, and liberals and leftists are indifferent or hostile to religion. Iran now has the Muslim equivalent of a clerical-anticlerical split.

At a certain point in their development, countries become ready for **democracy**. Very few poor countries can sustain democracy, which seems to require a good-sized middle class to work right. Attempts to implant democracy in countries with **per capita GDPs** below $5,000 generally fail, but democracy usually takes root in countries that have per capita GDPs above $6,000. Notice in the

| COMPARING SOME BASIC FIGURES | | | | | |
| | Population | | Per Capita GDP | | Workforce | Infant Mortality |
	in Millions 2005	Annual Growth Rate	ppp* 2004	Growth 2004	in Agriculture	per 1,000 Live Births
Britain	60	0.28%	$29,600	3.2%	1.5%	5.2
France	61	0.37	28,700	2.1	2.7	4.3
Germany	82	0.00	28,700	1.7	1.0	4.2
Russia	143	−0.37	9,800	6.7	4.9	15.4
Japan	127	0.05	29,400	2.9	1.3	3.3
China	1,306	0.58	5,600	9.1	49.0	24.2
Mexico	106	1.17	9,600	4.1	18.0	20.9
Nigeria	129	2.37	1,000	6.2	36.3	98.8
Iran	68	0.86	7,700	6.3	11.2	41.6
United States	296	0.92	40,100	4.4	0.9	6.5

*Purchasing Power Parity, explained on page 399.

Source: World Bank, *CIA World Factbook*. Regard all such tables as approximate. Data can change wildly and from one source to another, especially figures from developing countries, which are often estimates. Statistical quirks throw off economic-growth figures. For example, Nigeria, with a low base, enjoyed a jump in oil revenues in 2005 that registers as a big percent increase and makes Nigeria look like fast-growing economy. Population growth includes immigration, important for the U.S. figure. Averages deceive: Chinese and Mexican figures, for instance, do not show the major gaps between rich and poor in income, population growth, and infant mortality. Even the U.S. labor force in agriculture can vary, depending on whether illegal or temporary Mexican workers are counted.

---

electoral franchise   Right to vote.

symbol   Political artifact that stirs mass emotions.

table above that several of our countries are in this borderline area. This is one way economics influences politics.

As we learned in Iraq, democracy implanted by foreigners may not always work. Countries have to be ready for it. Trying to start democracy too early often fails amid rigged elections, powerful warlords, and civil unrest. Democracy can also come too late. If the traditional elite waits too long, the masses may mobilize, turn radical, and fall into the hands of revolutionary demagogues. What happened in Russia in 1917 happened again in Iran in 1979. The gradual expansion of the **electoral franchise**, as in Britain, is probably best.

The widening of the franchise means the rise of political parties. On what was a party first based? Urban middle class, farmers, workers, or a denomination? When was it founded? What were its initial aims, and how has it changed over the years? Was the party strongly ideological? Left-wing parties argued that government should provide jobs, welfare, and education. Other parties, on the political center or right, either reject the welfarist ideas, compromise with them, or steal them. Gradually, the country becomes a welfare state with a heavy tax burden.

Finally, history establishes political **symbols** that can awaken powerful feelings. Flags, monarchs, religion, and national holidays and anthems often help cement a country together, giving citizens the feeling they are part of a common enterprise. To fully know a country, one must know its symbols, their historical origins, and their current connotation.

The Key Institutions

A political **institution** is a web of relationships lasting over time, an established structure of power. An institution may or may not be housed in an impressive building. With institutions we look for durable sets of human relationships, not architecture.

A good way to begin is to ask, "Who has the power?" When A commands, do B and C follow? Or do they ignore or counterbalance A? A nation's **constitution**—itself an institution—may give us some clues, but it does not always pinpoint real power centers. Britain's monarch and Germany's president are more for decoration than governing. The French constitution changed over time, giving more power to prime ministers and less to presidents.

Is the system presidential or parliamentary (see box on page 38)? Both systems have **parliaments**, but a presidential system has a president who is elected and serves separately from the legislature; the legislature cannot vote out the president. The United States and Mexico are presidential systems. In parliamentary systems, action focuses on the prime minister, who is a member of parliament delegated by it to form a government (another word for cabinet). The prime minister and his or her cabinet can be ousted by a vote of no-confidence in parliament. Americans used to assume presidential systems were better and more stable than parliamentary systems. Recent problems might make Americans aware of the advantages of a parliamentary system, which can easily oust a chief executive. Besides, parliamentary systems, with the proper refinements such as Germany's, can be quite stable.

How powerful is the legislature? In most cases it is less powerful than the executive, and its power is generally declining. Parliaments still pass laws, but most of them originate with the civil servants and cabinet and are passed according to party wishes. In most legislatures (but not in the U.S. Congress), party discipline is so strong that a member of parliament simply votes the way party whips instruct. Parliaments can be important without originating many laws. They represent

institution Established rules and relationships of power.

constitution Written organization of a country's institutions.

parliament National assembly that considers and enacts laws.

authoritarian Nondemocratic or dictatorial politics.

Democracy

WAVES OF DEMOCRACY

Harvard political scientist Samuel P. Huntington saw democracy spreading in three waves. The first wave, a long one, lasted from the American and French Revolutions through World War I. It gradually and unevenly spread democracy through most of West Europe. But between the two world wars, a "reverse wave" of communist and fascist **authoritarian** regimes pushed back democracy in Russia, Italy, Germany, Spain, Portugal, and Japan.

The second wave, a short one, lasted from the end of World War II until the mid-1960s. It brought democracy to most of West Europe plus the many Asian and African colonies that got their independence. Most of

Asia, Africa, and Latin America, however, quickly turned authoritarian.

Huntington's third wave began in the mid-1970s with the return of democracy to Portugal, Spain, and Greece and thence to Latin America and East Asia. In 1989, as Communist regimes collapsed, it took over much of East Europe and, with the 1991 Soviet collapse, Russia. Even Mexico's long-dominant party relaxed its grip to let an opposition party win the 2000 presidential election. On paper, most of the world's 194 countries are approximately democratic. But, warned Huntington, get ready for another reverse wave as some shaky democratic regimes revert to authoritarianism. Russia did precisely that.

political culture Values and attitudes of citizens on politics and society.

citizens, educate the public, structure interests, and, most important, oversee and criticize executive-branch activities.

Does the parliament have two chambers (bicameral) or one (unicameral)? Two chambers are necessary in federal systems to represent the territorial divisions, but they are often extra baggage in unitary systems. Most of the countries studied in this book have bicameral legislatures.

How many parties are there? Are we looking at a one-party system, such as China; a dominant-party system, such as Mexico; two-party systems, such as Britain and the United States; or multiparty systems, such as France and Germany? Party system is partly determined by a country's electoral system, of which there are two basic types, majoritarian and proportional. A majoritarian system, as in the United States and Britain, enables one party to have a majority in parliament. This encourages two-party systems. Proportional systems, where parliamentarians are elected according to the percentage of the vote their party won, as in Germany and Israel, rarely give one party control of parliament, so coalitions are necessary. Proportional representation encourages multiparty systems, which in turn may contribute to cabinet instability as coalition members quarrel.

How powerful is the country's permanent civil service, its bureaucracy? The bureaucracy today has eclipsed both cabinet and parliament in expertise, information, outside contacts, and sheer numbers. Some lobbyists no longer bother with the legislature; they go where the action is, to the important decision makers in the bureaucracy.

■ Political Culture

After World War II, political scientists shifted their emphasis from institutions to attitudes. The institutional approach had become suspect. On paper, Germany's Weimar constitution was a magnificent achievement after World War I, but it did not work in practice because too few Germans supported democracy. By the late 1950s a newly prominent **political culture** approach to comparative politics

Political Culture

THE CIVIC CULTURE STUDY

In a massive 1959 study, political scientists Gabriel Almond and Sidney Verba led teams that asked approximately one thousand people in each of five countries—the United States, Britain, West Germany, Italy, and Mexico—identical questions on their political values and attitudes. The Civic Culture study, which was a benchmark in cross-national research, discerned three types of political culture:

1. *Participant*, in which people know a lot about politics and feel they should participate in politics.
2. *Subject*, in which people are aware of politics but cautious about participating; they are more conditioned to obeying.

3. *Parochial*, meaning narrow or focused only on their immediate concerns, is one in which people are not even much aware of politics and do not participate.

Almond and Verba emphasized that each country is a mixture of these types, with perhaps one type dominating: participant in America, subject in West Germany and Italy, parochial in Mexico. A good mixture, which they found in America and Britain, produces what they called "the civic culture." Question: If Americans are so participant, why do they vote so little?

sought to explain systems in terms of peoples' attitudes. This is a two-way street, however, because attitudes determine government, and government determines attitudes. Americans became much more **cynical** in the wake of Vietnam and Watergate, while Germans became more committed democrats as their country achieved economic success and political stability.

cynical   Untrusting; belief that political system is wrong and corrupt.

legitimacy   Mass perception that regime's rule is rightful.

ideology   Belief system to improve society.

pragmatic   Without ideological considerations, based on practicality.

Legitimacy is basic to political culture. It originally meant that the rightful king was on the throne, not a usurper. Now it means a mass attitude that people think the government's rule is valid and that it should generally be obeyed. Governments are not automatically legitimate; they have to earn the respect of their citizens. Legitimacy can be created over a long time as a government endures and governs well. Legitimacy can also erode as unstable and corrupt regimes come and go, never winning the people's respect. One quick test of legitimacy is how many police officers a country has. With high legitimacy, it needs few police because people obey the law voluntarily. With low legitimacy, a country needs many police. Regimes attempt to shore up their legitimacy by manipulating symbols.

One symbol frequently manipulated is **ideology**. An ideology is a grand plan to save or improve the country (see box on page 10). Typically, leaders at the top of a system take their ideology with a grain of salt. But for mass consumption, the Soviets and Chinese cranked out reams of ideological propaganda (which, in fact, most of their people ignored.)

Most of the other political systems explored in this book are not so ideologically explicit, but all espouse various ideologies to greater or lesser degrees: German Social Democrats are committed to the welfare state, British Conservatives to free-market economics, and Chinese Communists to "socialism with Chinese characteristics." Does every system have some sort of ideology? Probably. A system run on purely **pragmatic** grounds—if it works, use it—would be nonideological, but such systems are rare. Even Americans, who pride themselves on being pragmatic, are usually convinced of the effectiveness of the free market (Republicans) or moderate government intervention (Democrats). Thus, one of our questions: How ideological or pragmatic is a particular system and its political parties?

Another contributor to political culture is a country's educational system. Nearly everywhere, education is the main path to elite status. Who gets educated and in what way helps structure who gets political power and what they do with it. No country has totally equal educational opportunity. Even where schooling is legally open to all, social-, economic-, and even political-screening devices work against some sectors of the population. Most countries have elite universities that produce a big share of their political leadership, at times a near monopoly. The elite views formed in such schools are a major determinant of a country's politics.

■ Patterns of Interaction

Here we come to what is conventionally called "politics": Who does what to whom? We look for the interactions of parties, interest groups, and bureaucracies. Elites play a major role in these interactions. Even democratic politics is usually the work of a few. Most people, most of the time, do not participate in politics. But there are various kinds of elites, some more democratic and dedicated to the common good than others. How much of these interactions are an elite game with little or no mass participation?

generalization Finding repeated examples and patterns.

theory Firm generalization supported by evidence.

Do groups come together to compete or strike deals? How do political parties persuade the public to support them? We look not for one-time events but for things that occur with some regularity. Finding such patterns is the beginning of making **generalizations**, and generalizing is the beginning of **theory**. Once we have found a pattern, we ask why. The answer will be found partly from what we have learned about each country in preceding chapters and partly from the nature of political life where struggle and competition are normal and universal.

Some interactions are open and public; others are closed and secretive. The interactions of parties and citizenry are mostly open. Every party tries to convince the public that their party is the one fit to govern. This holds equally true for democratic and authoritarian systems. Do they succeed? Whom do the parties aim for, and how do they win them over? By ideology? Promises? Common interests? Or by convincing people the other party is worse?

Key Concepts

WHAT IS "IDEOLOGY"?

Political ideologies can be an important part of political culture. They are belief systems—usually ending in *-ism*—that claim to aim at improving society. Believers in an ideology say: "If we move in this direction, things will be much better. People will be happier, catastrophe will be avoided, society will become perfected." An ideology usually contains four elements:

1. The *perception* that things are going wrong, that society is headed down the wrong path. Fanatic ideologies insist that catastrophe is just around the corner.
2. An *evaluation* or analysis of why things are going wrong. This means a criticism of all or part of the existing system.
3. A *prescription* or cure for the problem. Moderate ideologies advocate reforms; extremist ideologies urge revolution and overthrow of the present system.
4. An effort to form a *movement* to carry out the cure. Without a party or movement, the above points are just talk without serious intent.

Marxism-Leninism is a perfect example of ideology. First, we have Marx's perception that capitalism is unjust and doomed. Second, we have his analysis, that capitalism contains internal contradictions that bring economic depressions. Third, we have a Marxist prescription: Abolish capitalism in favor of collective ownership of the means of production—socialism. And fourth, especially with Lenin, we have the determined movement to form a strong Communist party—the "organizational weapon"—to put the cure into effect by overthrowing the capitalist system. (How well does environmentalism fit this fourfold pattern?)

Ideologies are usually based on a serious thinker, often an important philosopher. Communism traces back to Hegel, classic liberalism to John Locke. But the philosopher's original ideas become popularized, vulgarized, and often distorted at the hands of ideologists who are trying to mass-market them. Deep thoughts are turned into cheap slogans. Often the original philosopher would reject what was done in his name. Toward the end of his life, Marx worried about the distortions of his ideas by younger thinkers and sadly commented, "One thing is for sure, I am not a Marxist."

An important point about ideologies is that they are always defective; that is, they never deliver what they promise: perfect societies and happy humans. Classic liberalism produced an underclass, Marxism-Leninism produced brutal dictatorships, and Iran's Islamic fundamentalism produced rule by rigid and corrupt clerics.

The parties interact with each other, sometimes cooperatively but more often competitively. How do they denounce and discredit each other? Under what circumstances do they make deals? Is their competition murderous or moderate? Parties also interact with the government. In China, the Party nearly is the government. In more politically open countries, parties try to capture and retain governmental power. How do parties form coalitions? Who gets the top cabinet jobs? Once in power, is the party able to act, or is it immobilized by opposition forces?

Key Concepts

THE POLITICS OF SOCIAL CLEAVAGES

Most societies are split along one or more lines. Often these splits, or "cleavages," become the society's fault lines along which political views form. Here are some of the more politically relevant social cleavages.

Social Class Karl Marx thought social class determined everything, that it was the only important social cleavage. Whether one was bourgeois or proletarian determined most political orientations. Marx held that middle- and upper-class people were conservative; working-class people, progressive or radical. This oversimplifies, as some poor people are extremely conservative, and some middle-class intellectuals are radical.

Still, social class does matter in structuring attitudes. The working class does tend toward the left, but never 100 percent, and it tends to be the moderate left of social democracy rather than the radical left of communism. Such is the case of the German Social Democratic party. Social class by itself seldom explains all political orientations. Other factors—such as religion and region—are usually present. The question, as Joseph LaPalombara put it, is, "Class plus what?"

Geographic Region Most countries have regional differences that are often politically important. Once a region gets set in its politics it can stay that way for generations. Often the region remembers past conquests and injustices. Scotland still resents England, and likewise the south of France resents the north. The Muslim north and Christian south of Nigeria seriously dislike each other. We must study the regions of a nation, what their politics are, and how they got to be that way.

Religion Religious struggles played major roles in most nations' histories and in some countries are still important. You can predict with fair accuracy how a French person will vote by knowing how often he or she attends Mass. You can partly predict how a German will vote by knowing if he or she is Protestant or Catholic. In Iran, religion dominates politics. Religion accounts for the formation of more political parties than does social class.

Urban-Rural Urban dwellers tend to be more aware of politics, more participatory, and more liberal or leftist. This is especially true in the Third World, where the countryside remains backward while the cities modernize. China, for example, has a major urban-rural split in terms of living conditions, education, and political orientation. The 2004 U.S. election graphically illustrated our urban-rural split.

There are other politically relevant social cleavages. In some countries gender matters, as in the United States, where women vote more Democrat than men. Occupation, as distinct from social class, can also influence political attitudes. A miner and a farmer may have the same income, but the miner will likely be leftist and the farmer conservative. Age can be a political factor. Young people are usually more open to new ideas and more likely to embrace radical and even violent causes than older citizens. Germany's terrorists, China's Red Guards, and Iran's *hezbollahi* were all young.

Almost any social cleavage or category can become politically relevant. Ask yourself from where did you get your political views? Is it your age? Did you get them from your family? And why does your family hold these views? Is it their religion? Their ethnic group? Their regional tradition?

interest group   Association aimed at getting favorable policies.

Politics within the parties is important, as most parties have factions. In Japan, the factions of the leading party are more important than most of the other separate parties. Does the party have left and right wings? How do its leaders hold it together? Do they pay off factions with ministerial positions? Do factional quarrels paralyze the party? Could it split?

Parties also interact with **interest groups**. Some groups enjoy "structured access" to like-minded parties. In Europe, labor unions are often linked formally to labor parties. Here we need to know: Does the party co-opt the interest group, or vice versa? How powerful are interest-group views in determining party policy?

Interest groups often decide it is not worth working on the electoral-legislative side and instead focus their attention on bureaucracies. One of the key areas of politics is where bureaucracies and businesses interface. Are interest groups controlled by government, or vice versa? What kind of relationships do businessmen and bureaucrats establish? Which groups are the most influential? These important interactions are generally out of the public sight and often corrupt. Does money change hands?

■ What People Quarrel About

Here we move to current issues, the political struggles of the day. We start with economics, the universal and permanent quarrel over who gets what. Politics and economics are closely connected; one can make or break the other. (Political scientists should have a grounding in economics; take an economics course.)

First, we inquire if the economy of the country is growing. Rapidly or slowly? Why? Are workers lazy or energetic? Are managers inept or clever? How much of the economy is supervised and

Democracy

CRISIS OF DEMOCRACY?

Worldwide, social scientists worry that the attitudes in firmly established democracies are becoming more cynical about government. If the trend deepens, it could undermine the basis of democracy. Observers focus on two trends: (1) A falloff of roughly 10 percent in voting turnout from the 1950s to the 1990s. (2) Public-opinion polls that show Americans, Europeans, and Japanese all trust government and politicians less. Is democracy threatened?

Be careful of doomsters; their predictions are usually wrong. The voting falloff may be due in part to the lowering of the voting age in the early 1970s nearly

everywhere from 21 to 18. Young people vote less. Cynical opinions may be due to increased expectations that government must provide jobs, health, and happiness—hyped by politicians—that government cannot possibly deliver. Viewed in this light, democracy may have been too successful.

Democracy may be entering a new phase in which better-educated citizens know more and criticize more: "critical citizens." Citizen efforts to fight corruption, curb the influence of powerful interest groups, and reform defective institutions are widespread. And how will the Internet affect democracy?

planned by government? Is government interference a hindrance on the economy? If the economy is declining, will it lead to political upheaval (as in the Soviet Union)? Why are some countries economic success stories and others not? How big a role does politics play in economic growth?

> **redistribution**   Taxing better off to help worse off.

Other issues: Have unions and management reached durable understandings, or are strikes frequent? Have unions won laws on wages, benefits, and layoffs? Has this led to "labor-force rigidities" that slow growth? Does government try to influence wage increases? Do workers have any say in running their companies? How much imported labor is there? How much unemployment?

Once we have a realistic picture of the economic pie, we inquire who gets what slice. How equal—or unequal—is the distribution of income and wealth? Does the government redistribute incomes to make people more equal or does it let inequality grow? Does unequal distribution lead to social and political resentment? **Redistribution** is another name for a welfare system, and all advanced democracies are to some extent welfare states. How high and how progressive are taxes? How many and how generous are welfare benefits? Do people want more welfare and higher taxes or less welfare and lower taxes? Which people? If stuck with an overgenerous welfare system, can the government trim it?

There are, to be sure, noneconomic quarrels as well. Regionalism is persistent and growing. Britain, France, Russia, and Nigeria have breakaway regional movements. East and West Germany resent each other. Mexico's regions vote differently from one another. What are a country's regions? Which of them are discontent? Over what? How do they show discontent? Is there violence? Is there movement to decentralize or devolve power to the regions? One quarrel getting nastier throughout West Europe is what to do with the millions of immigrants, usually from Third World lands: Let in more or keep them out? Integrate them or send them home?

Comparison

THE IMPORTANCE OF BEING COMPARATIVE

"You cannot be scientific if you are not comparing," UCLA's late, great James Coleman used to tell his students. Countries are not unique; they are comparable with other countries. When we say, for example, the parliament of country X has become a rubber stamp for the executive, this is not a meaningful statement until we note it is also the tendency in countries Y and Z.

The "uniqueness trap" often catches commentators of the American scene off-guard. We hear statements such as: "The U.S. political system is breaking down." Compared to what? To France in 1958? To Russia in 1991? Or to the United States itself in 1861? Compared to these other cases, the United States today is in great shape. We hear statements like: "Taxes in this country are outrageous." But what percentage of GDP do Americans pay in taxes compared to Britons, French, and Germans? Our thinking on politics will be greatly clarified if we put ourselves into a comparative mood by frequently asking, "Compared to what?"

Key Terms

absolutism (p. 3)
authoritarian (p. 7)
causality (p. 2)
constitution (p. 7)
constructed (p. 2)
cynical (p. 9)
democracy (p. 5)
diplomatic recognition (p. 2)
electoral franchise (p. 6)
elites (p. 5)
ethnicity (p. 2)
failed state (p. 2)
feudalism (p. 3)
GDP (p. 5)
generalization (p. 10)
ideology (p. 9)
institution (p. 7)
interest group (p. 12)

legitimacy (p. 9)
mass (p. 5)
multinational (p. 2)
nation (p. 2)
parliament (p. 7)
per capita (p. 5)
political culture (p. 8)
political geography (p. 5)
power (p. 4)
pragmatic (p. 9)
quarrels (p. 4)
redistribution (p. 13)
reification (p. 2)
secularization (p. 3)
sovereignty (p. 2)
state (p. 2)
symbol (p. 6)
theory (p. 10)

Key Web Sites

Brief Country Data
cia.gov/cia/publications/factbook/index
Elections around the World
electionworld.org
European Union
europa.eu.int
National Leaders through History
rulers.org
Library of Congress Country Studies
lcwb2.loc.gov/frd/cs
Economist Country Briefings
economist.com/countries
Maps
lib.utexas.edu/libs/PCL/Map_collection

Further Reference

Dalton, Russell J. *Citizen Politics: Public Opinion and Political Parties in Advanced Industrial Democracies*, 3rd ed. New York: Chatham House, 2002.

de Blij, Harm. *Why Geography Matters: Three Challenges Facing America; Climate Change, the Rise of China, and Global Terrorism*. New York: Oxford University Press, 2005.

Fukuyama, Francis. *State-Building: Governance and World Order in the 21st Century*. Ithaca, NY: Cornell University Press, 2004.

Judt, Tony. *Postwar: A History of Europe since 1945*. New York: Penguin, 2005.

Lane, Jan-Erik, and Svante Ersson. *Culture and Politics: A Comparative Approach*, 2nd ed. Williston, VT: Ashgate, 2005.

Lane, Ruth. *The Art of Comparative Politics*. Needham Heights, MA: Allyn & Bacon, 1997.

Lijphart, Arend. *Electoral Systems and Party Systems: A Study of Twenty-Seven Democracies, 1945–1990*. New York: Oxford University Press, 1994.

Perry, Robert L., and John D. Robertson. *Comparative Analysis of Nations: Quantitative Approaches*. Boulder, CO: Westview, 2001.

Peters, B. Guy. *Comparative Politics: Theory and Method*. New York: New York University Press, 1998.

Rokkan, Stein. *State Formation, Nation-Building, and Mass Politics in Europe*. New York: Oxford University Press, 1995.

Slomp, Hans. *European Politics into the Twenty-First Century: Integration and Division*. Westport, CT: Praeger, 2000.

Stepan, Alfred. *Arguing Comparative Politics*. New York: Oxford University Press, 2001.

Wiarda, Howard J., ed. *New Directions in Comparative Politics*, 3rd ed. Boulder, CO: Westview, 2002.

Part I

GREAT BRITAIN

Key Web Sites

British Broadcasting Corporation
bbc.co.uk

Both Houses of Parliament
parliament.uk/commons

Prime Minister's Office
number-10.gov.uk

British Monarchy
royal.gov.uk

British Newspapers
times.co.uk
guardian.co.uk
telegraph.co.uk

ATLANTIC
OCEAN

SCOTLAND

NORTH
SEA

Glasgow

55°

Northern
Ireland

Belfast

REPUBLIC
OF
IRELAND

IRISH
SEA

Dublin

Liverpool

Manchester

WALES

Birmingham

ENGLAND

London

50°

ENGLISH CHANNEL

0   100 Miles

0   100 Kilometers

10°   5°   0°

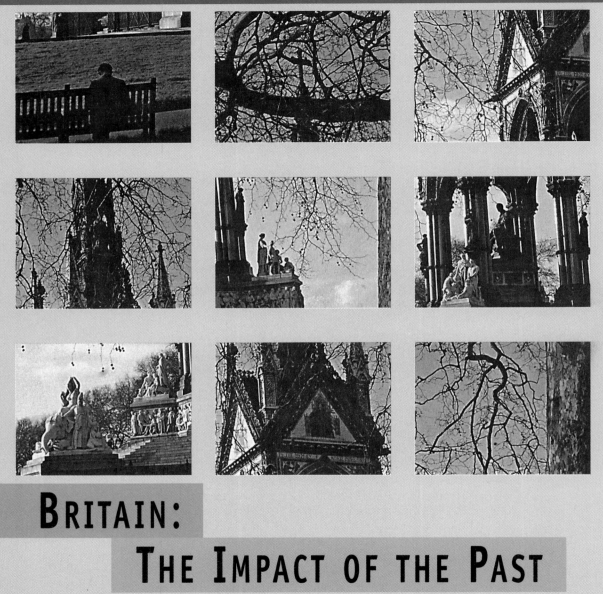

Chapter 2

BRITAIN:
THE IMPACT OF THE PAST

A Polish student I once knew at UCLA had to write a paper for her English class on what she most wished for her native land. She took the question as a geographical one and wrote: "I wish Poland be island like England." She would like to fix Poland's problem, its location on a plain between large, hostile neighbors (Germany and Russia) that has given it a sad history of invasion and partition.

England long ago was invaded many times. For a millennium and a half, waves of **Celts**, Romans, Angles and Saxons, Danes, and finally **Normans** washed upon Britain. One tribe of Celts, the Britons, gave their name to the entire island. Britishers, like most peoples, are not of one stock but of many.

The fierce Germanic tribesmen who rowed across the North Sea during the third to fifth centuries A.D. brought over Anglisch, what we call Old English, the language of the Angles, close to the Frisian of the Netherlands and German coast. "England" was simply the land of the Angles. The Angles and Saxons slowly moved across England, destroying towns and massacring inhabitants. The Celts were pushed back to present-day Wales and Scotland, which became a "Celtic fringe" to England. Some Celts fled to France and gave their name to Brittany. Preserving their distinct identity and languages (Cymric in Wales, Gaelic in Scotland), Britain's Celts never quite forgot what the newer arrivals did to them.

Other invaders followed. In the ninth century, Danish Vikings held much of eastern England (the Danelaw), but they were eventually absorbed. Another group of Vikings had meanwhile settled in France; these Norsemen (Normans) gave their name to Normandy. In 1066, with the English throne in dispute, William of Normandy put forward his own dubious claim to it and invaded with a force gathered from all over France. He defeated the English King Harold at the famous battle of Hastings, and England changed dramatically.

William the Conqueror replaced the entire Saxon ruling class with Norman nobles, who earned their **fiefdoms** by military service. At first the Norman conquerors spoke only French, so vast numbers of French words soon enriched the English language. Backed by military power, administration was better and tighter. William ordered a complete inventory of all lands and population in his new domain; the resulting Domesday Book provided a detailed tool for governance. The **Exchequer**—the name derived from the French word for a checkered counting table—became the king's powerful treasury minister, a title and office that still exists. Furthermore, since William and his descendants ruled both England and parts of France, England was tied for centuries to the affairs of the Continent.

Questions to Consider

1. How has geography influenced British development?
2. What does the Union Jack stand for?
3. What did the Magna Carta preserve?
4. What is the Common Law?
5. When did Parliament eclipse the monarch?
6. How did Puritanism influence democracy?
7. How did democracy come to Britain?
8. What was the difference between Hobbes and Locke?
9. How are Britain and Sweden so comparable?

■ Magna Carta

The Normans brought to England a political system that had first emerged on the **Continent**—*feudalism*. The feudal system was a contractual agreement between lords and vassals in which the lords would grant the vassals land and protection while the vassal would support the lord with military service. Feudalism appears when central authority breaks down and a money economy disappears, for then land and fighting ability take on tremendous importance. In Europe, the collapse of the Roman Empire meant kings could survive and thrive only if they had enough lords and knights to fight for them. The lords and knights in turn got land. Power here was a two-way street: The king needed the nobles and vice versa.

Celts   Pre-Roman inhabitants of Europe. (See page 19.)

Normans   Vikings who settled in and gave their name to Normandy, France. (See page 19.)

fiefdom   Land granted by a king to a noble in exchange for support. (See page 19.)

Exchequer   Britain's treasury ministry. (See page 19.)

the Continent   British term for mainland Europe, implying they are not part of it.

mixed monarchy   King balanced by nobles.

Magna Carta   1215 agreement to preserve rights of English nobles.

The **mixed monarchy** of the Middle Ages was a balance between king and nobles. The nobles of Aragon (in the northeast of Spain) expressed it bluntly in their oath to a new monarch: "We who are as good as you swear to you, who are no better than we, to accept you as our king and sovereign lord provided you observe all our statutes and laws; and if not, no."

Centuries of English history were dominated by the struggle to make sure the king did not exceed his feudal bounds and become an absolute monarch, which happened in most of Europe. This English struggle laid the foundation for limited, representative government, democracy, and civil rights, even though the participants at the time had no such intent.

The Great Charter the barons forced upon King John at Runnymede in 1215 is nothing so far-reaching or idealistic; it never mentions liberty or democracy. The barons and top churchmen simply wanted to stop the king from encroaching on feudal customs, rights, and laws by which they held sway in their localities. In this sense the **Magna Carta**, one of the great documents of democracy, was feudal and reactionary. Far more important than its content, however, was its effect of limiting the monarch's powers and making sure he stayed within the law.

The Magna Carta meant the king stayed in balance with the nobles, thus preventing either despotism or anarchy, the twin ills of the Continent, where countries either went to *absolutism*, as in France, or broke up into small principalities, as in Germany. British, and by extension, American

Geography

INVADABILITY

Britain is very hard to invade. The last successful invasion of England (by the Normans) was in 1066. The barrier that is posed by the English Channel has kept Spaniards, French, and Germans from conquering Britain. Politically, this has meant that England could develop its own institutions without foreign interference, a luxury not enjoyed by most Continental lands.

Militarily, it has meant that England rarely needed or had a large army, of great import in the seventeenth century when British kings were unable to tame Parliament because the monarch had few soldiers.

democracy owes a lot to the stubborn English barons who stood up for their feudal rights.

The Rise of Parliament

During the same century as the Magna Carta, English kings started calling to London, by now the capital, two to four knights from each shire (roughly a county) and a similar number of **burghers** from the towns to consult with the king on matters of the realm. These kings were not latent democrats but needed to raise taxes and get the support of those who had local power. The French holdings of English kings meant that they had to fight wars in France. These were expensive, and the only way to raise revenues to pay for them was by inviting local notables to participate, at least symbolically, in the affairs of state. Little did the kings know they were founding an institution in the thirteenth century that would overshadow the monarchy by the seventeenth century.

Parliament began as an extension of the king's court, but over the centuries took on a life of its own. Knights and burghers formed what we call a lower house, the House of **Commons**. Those of noble rank, along with the top churchmen, formed what we call an upper house, the House of **Lords**. In time, a leading member of the Commons, its Speaker, became its representative to the king. In order to conduct business unhampered, parliamentary privileges developed to prevent the arrest of members.

The House of Commons at this stage was not "representative," at least not in our sense. It represented only a few males who were locally wealthy or powerful. But more important than fair representation (which came in the nineteenth century), Parliament continued the blocking mechanism of the Magna Carta: It diffused power and prevented the king from getting too much. Parliament thus laid one of the foundations of democracy without knowing it.

burghers   Originally, town dwellers; by extension, the middle class; French *bourgeoisie.*

Parliament   When capitalized, Britain's legislature, now usually meaning the House of Commons.

Commons   Lower house of Parliament; the elected, important chamber.

Lords   Upper house of Parliament; less important than *Commons.*

Geography

THE UNITED KINGDOM

The full and official name of Britain is the United Kingdom of Great Britain and Northern Ireland. "Great Britain" refers to the whole island, which includes Wales and Scotland as well as England.

The British flag, the "Union Jack," stands for three saints representing different parts of the United Kingdom. The larger red cross is the Cross of St. George of England, the diagonal white cross is that of St. Andrew of Scotland, and the thinner, diagonal red cross is that of St. Patrick of Ireland. (Note this cross is off-center.) Now some English nationalists display just the English flag (red cross on a white field). In Edinburgh, capital of Scotland, most of the flags are now Scottish

(diagonal white cross on a blue field), an indication that the United Kingdom has grown less united. Symbols matter.

■ Henry VIII

Parliament got a major boost during the reign of Henry VIII (1509–1547), when Henry declared a partnership with Parliament in his struggle against Rome. In addition to growing tensions between the **Vatican** and London—the universal Church on the one hand and new religious ideas on the other—Henry needed the pope to grant him a divorce. His marriage to Catherine of Aragon had failed to produce the male heir Henry felt he needed to ensure stability after him. (Ironically, it was his daughter Elizabeth who went down in history as one of England's greatest monarchs.)

Vatican   Headquarters of the Roman Catholic church.

Anglican   Church of England, Episcopalian in America.

anticlerical   Favoring getting the Roman Catholic church out of politics.

Common Law   System of judge-made law developed in England.

precedent   Legal reasoning based on previous cases.

The pope refused—Catherine's Spanish relatives at that time controlled the papacy—so Henry summoned a parliament in 1529 and kept it busy for seven years, passing law after law to get England out of the Catholic church and the Catholic church out of England. The new **Anglican** church was at first identical to the Roman Catholic church (it turned Protestant later), but at its head was an Englishman, not the pontiff of Rome. The new church granted Henry his divorce in 1533. Henry married a total of six wives (and had two of them beheaded) but was not lusting for young brides; he was desperate for a male heir.

The impact of Henry's break with Rome was major. England was cut free from Catholic guidance and direction. Countries that stayed Catholic, such as France, Spain, and Italy, experienced wrenching splits for centuries between prochurch and **anticlerical** forces. England (and Sweden) avoided this nasty division because the state early on was stronger than the church and controlled it. This meant that in England it was far easier to *secularize* society and politics than in Roman Catholic countries, where the church was still an independent power.

Parliament became more important, as Henry needed it for his break with Rome. In 1543 Henry praised Parliament as an indispensable part of his government: "We be informed by our judges that we at no time stand so highly in our estate royal as in the time of parliament, wherein we as head and

Comparison

COMMON LAW

One of England's contributions to civilization is the **Common Law**, the legal system now also practiced in the United States, Canada, Australia, and other countries once administered by Britain (but not South Africa). Common Law grew out of the customary usage of the Germanic tribal laws of the Angles and Saxons, which stressed the rights of free men. It developed on the basis of **precedent** set by earlier decisions and thus has been called "judge-made law." After the Normans conquered England, they found the purely local nature of this law was too fragmented, so they set up central courts to systematize the local laws and produce a "common" law for all parts of England—hence the name.

Common Law is heavily case law and differs from code law, which is used by most of the Continent (and Scotland) and much of the world, that emphasizes fixed legal codes rather than precedent and case-study. Code law is essentially Roman Law that was kept alive in the Canon Law of the Catholic Church, revived by modernizing Continental monarchs, and updated in 1804 into the *Code Napoléon*. Compared to code law, Common Law is flexible and adapts gradually with new cases.

you as members are conjoined and knit together into one body politic."
Without knowing it, Henry started an institutional shift from monarch
to parliament. A century later Parliament beheaded an English king.

Royalists   Supporters of the king in English Civil War.

Parliamentarians   Supporters of Parliament.

landlocked   Country with no seacoast.

■ Parliament versus King

In the late fifteenth century several European monarchs expanded their powers and undermined
the old feudal *mixed monarchy*. The weakened power of Rome in the sixteenth century gave kings
more independence and introduced the notion that kings ruled by divine right, that is, that they received their authority directly from God without the pope as intermediary. Political theorists searched
for the seat of *sovereignty* and concluded it must lie in one person, the monarch. This gave rise to
absolutism. By 1660 absolute monarchs governed most lands of Europe—but not England.

The seventeenth century brought uninterrupted turmoil to England: religious splits, civil
war, a royal beheading, and a military dictatorship. The net winner, when the dust had settled,
was Parliament.

Trouble started when James I brought the Stuart dynasty from Scotland to take over the English throne after the death of Elizabeth I, the last Tudor, in 1603. James united the crowns of Scotland and England, but they remained separate countries until the 1707 Act of Union. James I carried
the absolutist notions then common throughout Europe; he did not like to share power and thought
that existing institutions should simply support the king. This brought him into conflict with Puritanism, an extreme Protestant movement that aimed to reform the "popish" elements out of the
Anglican church. James preferred the Anglican church to stay just the way it was, for it was one of
the pillars of his regime. With James's harassment, some Puritans ran away to Massachusetts.

By now Parliament had grown to feel equal with the king and, in the area of raising revenues,
superior. Hard up for cash, James tried to impose taxes without consent of Parliament, which grew
angry over the move. James's son, Charles I, took over in 1625, and fared even worse. He took England into wars with Spain and France; both were unsuccessful and increased the king's desperation
for money. Charles tried to play the role of a Continental absolute monarch, but the English people and Parliament would not let him.

When the **Royalists** fought the **Parliamentarians** in the English Civil War (1642–1648), the
latter proved stronger, for the Parliamentarian cause was aided by Puritans and the growing merchant
class. The Parliamentarians created a "New Model Army," which trounced the Royalists. (The king,
as was mentioned, had no standing army at his disposal.) Charles was captured, tried by Parliament,
and beheaded in 1649.

Geography

SEACOAST

A country with outlet to the sea has a major economic advantage over **landlocked** countries. Sea transport is cheap and does not require crossing neighboring countries. Usable natural harbors also help. Peter the Great battled for years to obtain Russian outlets on the Baltic and Black Seas. Atlantic Europe had an incredible advantage from the start. England's Atlantic orientation contributed to its empire, early industrialization, and prosperity.

Cromwell's Commonwealth

From 1649 to 1660 England had no king. Who, then, was to rule? The only organized force left was the army, led by Oliver Cromwell. Briefly, England became a **republic** called the **Commonwealth**, led by Cromwell. Discord grew. To restore order, Cromwell in 1653 was designated Lord Protector, a sort of uncrowned king, and imposed a military dictatorship on England. When Cromwell died in 1658, most Englishmen had had enough of turbulent republicanism and longed for stability and order. In 1660, Parliament invited Charles II, son of the beheaded king, to return from Dutch exile and reclaim the throne. The English monarchy was restored, but now Parliament was much stronger and demanded respect.

The "Glorious Revolution"

Charles II knew he could not be an absolute monarch; instead, he tried to manipulate Parliament discreetly, but religion tripped him up. Charles was pro-Catholic and secretly ready to proclaim allegiance to Rome. In 1673 he issued the Declaration of Indulgence, lifting laws against Catholics and non-Anglican Protestants. Parliament saw this act of tolerance toward minority religions as an illegal return to Catholicism and blocked it. Anti-Catholic hysteria swept England with fabricated stories of popish plots to take over the country.

republic   Country not headed by a monarch.
Commonwealth   A republic.
republican   In its original sense, favoring getting rid of monarchy.
Levellers   Radicals during English Civil War who argued for equality and "one man, one vote."

When Charles II died in 1685, his openly Catholic brother, James, took the throne as James II. Again, a Declaration of Indulgence was issued, and again Parliament took it as a return to both Catholicism and absolutism. Parliament dumped James II (but let him escape) and invited his Protestant daughter, Mary, and her Dutch husband, William, to be England's queen and king. This was the "Glorious Revolution" of 1688: A major shift of regime took place with scarcely a shot fired. (In 1690, William beat James in Ireland, but that was after the Revolution.) In 1689 a "Bill of Rights"—unlike its U.S. namesake—spelled out Parliament's relationship to the Crown: no laws or taxes without Parliament's assent.

Democracy

"ONE MAN, ONE VOTE"

Among the antiroyalists were **republicans**, called **Levellers**, who sought political equality. Soldiers in the New Model Army argued that people like themselves—tradesmen, artisans, and farmers—should have the vote. They were influenced in their thinking by Puritanism, which taught that all men were equal before God and needed no spiritual or temporal superiors to guide them. (This Puritan influence also powerfully impacted American democracy.)

One group of Levellers, meeting in Putney in 1647, even went so far as to advocate "one man, one vote." This radical idea was a good two centuries ahead of its time, and the more conservative forces of England, including Cromwell himself, rejected it out of hand. Still, the Putney meeting had introduced the idea of the universal franchise—that is, giving everybody the right to vote.

The majority of Englishmen approved. If it was not clear before, it was now: Parliament was supreme and could invite and dismiss monarchs. In 1714 Parliament invited George I from Hanover in Germany to become king; the present royal family is descended from him. Since that time, the British monarch has been increasingly a figurehead, one who reigns but does not rule.

prime minister Chief of government in parliamentary systems.

minister Head of a major department (ministry) of government.

Whigs Faction of Parliament that became Liberal party.

Tories Faction of Parliament that became Conservative party.

■ The Rise of the Prime Minister

One of the consequences of bringing George I to England was that he could not govern even if he wanted to. He spoke no English and preferred Hanover to London. So he turned to an institutional device that had been slowly developing and gave it executive power—the cabinet, composed of ministers and presided over by a first or prime minister. Headed by Sir Robert Walpole from 1721 to 1742, the cabinet developed nearly into its present form, but lacked two important present-day features: The **prime minister** could not pick his **ministers** (that was reserved for the king), and the cabinet was not responsible—meaning, in its original sense, "answerable"—to Parliament.

Absolutism had one last, temporary gasp. George III packed Commons with his supporters and governed with the obedient Lord North as prime minister. One unforeseen result: the U.S. Declaration of Independence, which sought to regain the traditional rights of Englishmen against a too-powerful king. Following this British defeat, William Pitt the Younger restored the cabinet and prime minister to power and made them responsible only to Commons, not to the king. This began the tradition—it has never been written into law—that the "government" consists of the leader of the largest party in the House of Commons plus other people he or she picks. As party chief, top member of Parliament, and head of government combined, the prime minister became the focus of political power in Britain.

■ The Democratization of Parliament

Parliament was supreme by the late eighteenth century, but it was not democratic or representative. In the country, the right to vote was limited to landowners. In the towns, often only a dozen or so men were eligible to vote, although in the cities the franchise was much wider.

In the eighteenth century, parties began to form. The labels **Whig** and **Tory** first appeared under Charles II, connoting his opposition and his supporters, respectively. Both were derisive names: The

Democracy

"POWER CORRUPTS"

Nineteenth-century British historian and philosopher Lord Acton distilled the lessons of centuries of English political development in his famous remark: "Power tends to corrupt; absolute power corrupts absolutely." Acton feared the human tendency to abuse power. His insight is absolutely accurate—check today's news—and underlies democratic thinking.

state of nature   Humans before civilization.

civil society   Humans after becoming civilized. Modern usage: associations between family and government.

conservatism   Ideology aimed at preserving existing institutions and usages.

original Whigs were Scottish bandits, and the original Tories were Irish bandits. At first these proto-parties were simply parliamentary caucuses, Tories representing the landed aristocracy, Whigs the merchants and manufacturers. Only in the next century did they take root in the electorate.

During the nineteenth century, a two-party system emerged. The Whigs grew into the Liberal party and the Tories into the Conservative party (still nicknamed Tories). Whatever their party label, parliamentarians were not ordinary people. The House of Lords was limited to hereditary peers. The House of Commons, despite its name, was the home of gentry, landowners, and better-off people. Elections were often won by bribing the few voters.

Personalities

HOBBES, LOCKE, BURKE

Thomas Hobbes lived through the upheavals of the English Civil War in the seventeenth century and opposed them for making people insecure and frightened. Hobbes imagined that life in "the **state of nature**," before "**civil society**" was founded, must have been terrible. Every man would have been the enemy of every other man, a "war of each against all." Humans would live in savage squalor with "no arts; no letters; no society; and which is worst of all, continual fear, and danger of violent death; and the life of man, solitary, poor, nasty, brutish, and short." To escape this horror, people would—out of self-interest—rationally join together to form civil society. Society thus arises naturally out of fear. People would also gladly submit to a king, even a bad one, in order to prevent anarchy.

John Locke saw the same upheavals but came to less harsh conclusions. Locke theorized that the original state of nature was not so bad; people lived in equality and tolerance with one another. But they could not secure their property: There was no money, title deeds, or courts of law, so their property was uncertain. To remedy this, they contractually formed civil society and thus secured "life, liberty, and property." Locke is to property rights as Hobbes is to fear of violent death. Americans are the children of Locke; notice the American emphasis on "the natural right to property."

Edmund Burke, a Whig member of Parliament, was horrified at the French Revolution, warning it would end up a military dictatorship (it did). The French revolutionists had broken the historical continuity,

Thomas Hobbes

John Locke

Edmund Burke

institutions, and symbols that restrain people from bestial behavior, argued Burke. Old institutions, such as the monarchy and church, must be pretty good because they have evolved over centuries. If you scrap them, society breaks down and leads to tyranny. Burke understood that **conservatism** means constant, but never radical, change. Wrote Burke: "A state without the means of some change is without the means of its conservation." Progress comes not from chucking out the old but from gradually modifying the parts that need changing while preserving the overall structure, keeping the form but reforming the contents.

By the time of the American and French revolutions in the late eighteenth century, however, Parliament noticed winds stirring in favor of expanding the electorate. People talked about democracy and the right to vote. Under the impact of the industrial revolution and economic growth, two powerful new social classes arose—the middle class and the working class. Whigs and Tories, both elite in their makeup, at first viewed demands for the mass vote with disdain and even horror; it reminded them of how democracy ran amok during the French Revolution.

Reform Acts   Series of laws expanding the British electoral franchise.

Gradually, though, it dawned on the Whigs that the way to head off revolution was to incorporate some ordinary Britons into politics and give them a stake in the system. Furthermore, they realized that the party that supported broadening the franchise would most likely win the new voters. After much resistance by Tories in Commons and by the entire House of Lords, Parliament passed the **Reform Act** of 1832, which allowed more of the middle class to vote but still only expanded the electorate by about half, to about 7 percent of adults. The Reform Act established the principle, though, that the Commons ought to be representative of, and responsive to, the broad mass of citizens, not just the notables. In 1867, it was the Conservatives' turn. Under Prime Minister Benjamin Disraeli, the Second Reform Act doubled the size of the electorate, giving about 16 percent of adult Britons the vote. In 1884, the Third Reform Act added farm workers to the electorate and thus achieved nearly complete male suffrage. Women finally got the vote in 1918.

The interesting point about the British electorate is that its growth was slow. New elements were added to the voting rolls only gradually, giving Parliament time to assimilate the forces of mass politics without going through an upheaval. The gradual tempo also meant citizens got the vote when they were ready for it. In some countries where the universal franchise—one person, one vote—was instituted early, the result was fake democracy, as crafty officials rigged the voting of people who did not understand electoral politics. Spain, for example, got universal suffrage in the

Comparison

THE ORIGINS OF TWO WELFARE STATES

Both Britain and Sweden are welfare states, Sweden more so than Britain. How did this come to be? In comparing their histories, we get some clues.

- Swedish King Gustav Vasa broke with Rome in the 1520s, a few years earlier than Henry VIII. In setting up churches that were dependent on their respective states—Lutheran in Sweden, Anglican in England—the two countries eliminated religion as a source of opposition to government.

- Because of this, politics in both lands avoided getting stuck in a clerical-anticlerical dispute over the role of the Church, as happened in France, Italy, and Spain. In Britain and Sweden, the main political split was along class lines, working class versus middle class.

- Britain and Sweden both developed efficient and uncorrupt civil services, an absolute essential for the effective functioning of welfare programs.

- Workers in both countries organized strong—but not Marxist—labor unions, the TUC in Britain and LO in Sweden.

- These two labor movements gave rise to moderate, worker-oriented parties, Labour in Britain and the Social Democrats in Sweden, which demanded, and over time got, numerous welfare measures passed. One big difference is the Social Democrats have been in power in Sweden for all but a few years since 1932 and have implemented a more thorough—and more expensive—welfare state.

welfare state Political system that redistributes wealth from rich to poor, standard in West Europe.

1870s, but election results were set in advance. By the time the British working class got the vote, they were ready to use it intelligently.

With the expansion of the voting franchise, political parties turned from parliamentary clubs into modern parties. They had to win elections involving thousands of voters. This meant organization, programs, promises, and continuity. The growth of the electorate forced parties to become vehicles for democracy.

The Rise of the Welfare State

By the beginning of the twentieth century, with working men having the right to vote, British parties had to pay attention to demands for welfare measures—public education, housing, jobs, and medical care—that the upper-crust gentlemen of the Liberal and Conservative parties had earlier minimized. Expansion of the electoral franchise led to the growth of the **welfare state**.

One force pushing for welfare measures was the new Labour party, founded in 1900. At first, Labour worked with the Liberals—the "Lib-Lab" coalition—but by the end of World War I, Labour pushed the Liberals into the weak third-party status they have languished in to this day. Unlike most Continental socialists, few British Labourites were Marxists. Instead, they combined militant trade unionism with intellectual social democracy to produce a pragmatic, gradualist ideology that sought to level class differences in Britain. As one observer put it, the British Labour party "owed more to Methodism than to Marx."

The British labor movement of the late nineteenth century was tough, a quality it long retained. Resentful of being treated like dirt, many working men went into politics with a militancy that still characterizes some of their heirs. In the 1926 General Strike, the trade unions attempted to bring the entire British economy to a halt to gain their wage demands. They failed.

Briefly and weakly in power under Ramsay MacDonald in the 1920s, Labour won resoundingly in 1945 and implemented an ambitious welfare program plus state takeover of utilities, railroads, coal mines, and much heavy manufacturing. Since then, the chief quarrel in British politics has been between people who like the welfare state and state ownership and people who do not.

Key Terms

Anglican (p. 22)

anticlerical (p. 22)

burghers (p. 21)

Celts (p. 20)

civil society (p. 26)

Common Law (p. 22)

Commons (p. 21)

Commonwealth (p. 24)

conservatism (p. 26)

Continent, the (p. 20)

Exchequer (p. 20)

fiefdom (p. 20)

landlocked (p. 23)

Levellers (p. 24)

Lords (p. 21)

Magna Carta (p. 20)

minister (p. 25)

mixed monarchy (p. 20)

Normans (p. 20)

Parliament (p. 21)

Parliamentarians (p. 23)

precedent (p. 22)

prime minister (p. 25)
Reform Acts (p. 27)
republic (p. 24)
republican (p. 24)
Royalists (p. 23)

state of nature (p. 26)
Tories (p. 25)
Vatican (p. 22)
welfare state (p. 28)
Whigs (p. 25)

Further Reference

Beloff, Max. *Wars and Welfare: Britain 1914–1945*. London: Edward Arnold, 1984.

Callaghan, John. *Socialism in Britain since 1884*. Cambridge, MA: Basil Blackwell, 1990.

Chrimes, S. B. *English Constitutional History*. London: Oxford University Press, 1967.

Clarke, Peter. *Hope and Glory: Britain 1900–1990*. New York: Penguin, 1996.

Colley, Linda. *Britons: Forging the Nation, 1707–1837*. New Haven, CT: Yale University Press, 1992.

Davies, Norman. *The Isles: A History*. New York: Oxford University Press, 1999.

Greenleaf, W. H. *The British Political Tradition*, 3 vols. London: Methuen, 1987.

Hibbert, Christopher. *Cavaliers & Roundheads: The English Civil War, 1642–1649*. New York: Scribner's, 1993.

Kishlansky, Mark. *A Monarchy Transformed: Britain, 1603–1714*. New York: Allen Lane/Penguin Press, 1997.

McKibben, Ross. *Classes and Cultures: England 1918–1951*. New York: Oxford University Press, 1998.

Thorpe, Andrew. *A History of the British Labour Party*. New York: St. Martin's, 1997.

Williams, Glyn, and John Ramsden. *Ruling Britannia: A Political History of Britain, 1688–1988*, 2nd ed. New York: Longman, 1990.

Chapter 3

BRITAIN:
THE KEY INSTITUTIONS

It is commonly said that Britain has no written constitution, but parts of the British constitution are written. It does not consist of a single document but is rather a centuries-old collection of Common Law, historic charters, **statutes** passed by Parliament, and, most important, established custom.

This **eclectic** quality gives the British constitution flexibility. With no single, written document to refer to, nothing can be declared "unconstitutional." Parliament—specifically the House of Commons—can pass any law it likes, letting the British political system change over time without a systemic crisis. The U.S. Supreme Court sometimes blocks changes as unconstitutional, rarely a problem in Britain.

The negative side to this was that Britain had little to guarantee human rights. In 1991, six men convicted as IRA bombers in 1975 were freed with the shameful admission that confessions had been beaten out of them and the police had rigged evidence. The European Court of Human Rights, located in Strasbourg, France, ruled against British justice in several such cases, a considerable embarrassment for Britain. In 2000, Britain adopted the European Convention on Human Rights as domestic law, finally giving Britons the equivalent of a U.S. Bill of Rights.

The British speak of "the **Crown**," an all-encompassing term meaning the powers of government in general. Originally, the Crown meant the king, but over the centuries it has broadened to include everyone helping the king or queen, such as Parliament, the cabinet, and civil servants. Let us consider some of these.

Questions to Consider

1. What did Bagehot mean by "dignified" as opposed to "efficient" offices? Examples?
2. How is Britain a "prime ministerial government"?
3. Does Britain have checks and balances?
4. Describe Blair's political positions.
5. When does Britain hold general elections?
6. What are the differences between presidential and parliamentary systems?
7. What did Blair do with Lords?
8. Describe the British electoral system.
9. What are Britain's main parties?

The Monarch

In Britain there is a clear distinction between "head of state" and "chief of government." In America this distinction is ignored because the two are merged into one in the presidency. In most of the rest of the world, however, there is a top figure without much power who symbolizes the nation, receives foreign ambassadors, and gives speeches on patriotic occasions. This person—often a figurehead—can be either a hereditary monarch or an elected president, although not a U.S.-style president. Britain, Sweden, Norway, Denmark, the Netherlands, Belgium, and Spain are monarchies. This does not mean they are undemocratic; it just means the head of state is a carryover from old days.

statute Ordinary law, usually for specific problem. (See page 31.)

eclectic Drawn from a variety of sources. (See page 31.)

Crown The powers of the British government. (See page 31.)

dignified In Bagehot's terms, symbolic or decorative offices.

efficient In Bagehot's terms, working, political offices.

A hereditary head of state can be useful. Above politics, a monarch can serve as psychological cement to hold a country together because he or she has no important role in government. Because the top position in the land—what royalist philosophers used to call the sovereign—is already occupied, there are no political battles over it. The nastiest struggles in the world are precisely over who is to be sovereign; in Britain, the issue has long been settled.

The great commentator on the British constitution, Sir Walter Bagehot, divided it into **dignified** and **efficient** parts. The monarch, as head of state, is a dignified office with much symbolic but no real political power. He or she "reigns but does not rule." The king or queen nominally appoints a cabinet of His or Her Majesty's servants (see box on page 34), but otherwise a monarch is more like an official greeter.

The "efficient" office in Britain is the chief of government, the prime minister—a working politician who fights elections, leads his or her party, and makes political deals. Despite the prestige of a prime minister, it does not have nearly the "dignity" that the monarch has. There is an advantage in the way Britain and other countries split the two positions. If the chief of government does something foolish or illegal, he or she will catch the public's ire, but the blame will fall on the individual prime minister, and respect will not diminish for the head of state, the "dignified" office. The system retains its legitimacy. Where the two offices are combined, as in the United States, and the president is involved in something crooked, the public gets disgusted at both the working politician and the nation's symbolic leader. "The British do not need to love their prime minister," said one diplomat. "They love their queen."

The 1997 death of Princess Di, ex-wife of Prince Charles, jolted Britain, including the royal family. Di was the only royal with the common touch; her charity work and love life upstaged the cold and remote House of Windsor. Amidst the outpouring of grief for Di came mutterings that the royal family really did not much care. Some even thought it might be time to dump the monarchy. But old dynasties know how to survive, and the Queen and Prince Charles quickly became more public and outgoing.

Prince Charles, Britain's future king and head of the state, in happier days with his then-wife, the late Princess Diana, and their children, Prince William, also a future king, and Prince Henry. The divorce of Charles and Diana in 1996 did not affect Charles's succession to the throne.

Although few would exchange the monarchy for a republic, some (including Queen Elizabeth herself) suggest reforms that would cut government funds for the royal house and make female heirs to the throne the equal of males. Look for a major decision point when Queen Elizabeth dies. Will Charles automatically accede to the throne? Even with his 2005 remarriage? To a commoner (herself divorced)? The last time this happened, in 1936, King Edward VIII abdicated, but a replay is unlikely; times have changed. Britain will likely retain a monarchy, but it may be a monarch with reduced financial support and political roles.

MP   Member of Parliament

junior minister   MP with executive responsibilities below cabinet rank.

portfolio   Minister's assigned ministry.

Cortes   Spain's parliament.

antithetical   Ideas opposed to one another.

■ The Cabinet

The British cabinet also differs from the U.S. cabinet. The former consists of members of Parliament (most in Commons, a few in Lords) who are high up in their parties and important political figures. Most have lots of experience, first as ordinary **MPs** (members of Parliament), then as **junior ministers**, and finally as cabinet ministers. The American cabinet, which now seldom meets and counts for little, usually consists of experts from businesses, law offices, and universities, mostly without political experience, who serve more as administrators than as policy innovators. British cabinet government has been declining since World War I, which required speedy, centralized decisions. Now the prime minister develops policy with a small personal staff and then informs the cabinet of it. British commentators fear the rise of a "command premiership" in this development.

Originally, the British cabinet consisted of ministers to the king. Starting in the seventeenth century, the cabinet became more and more responsible to Parliament and less and less to the king. A British minister is not necessarily an expert in his or her **portfolio** but is carefully picked by the

Democracy

THE LAST POLITICAL MONARCH

Unlike other European monarchs, King Juan Carlos of Spain retains some crucial political functions. Juan Carlos took over as head of state after Franco's death in 1975 and initiated and backstopped a process that turned Spain from dictatorship to democracy. He named a prime minister who dismantled the Franco structure, carried out Spain's first free elections in forty-one years, and drafted a new constitution—all with the open approval of the king.

Juan Carlos's real test as defender of democracy came in 1981 when some disgruntled officers attempted a coup; they held the entire **Cortes** at gunpoint. In military uniform, the king addressed the nation on television and ordered the troops back to their barracks. They complied, and democratic Spaniards of all parties thanked God for the king. Democracy and monarchy are not **antithetical**; one can support the other. *¡Viva el rey!*

fusion of powers   Connection of executive and legislative branches in parliamentary systems; opposite of U.S. separation of powers.

prime minister for political qualifications. Both major British parties contain several viewpoints and power centers, and prime ministers usually take care to see they are represented in the cabinet. When Prime Minister Thatcher ignored this principle by picking as ministers only Tories loyal to her and her philosophy, she was criticized as dictatorial and ultimately lost her job. Balancing party factions in the cabinet helps keep the party together in Parliament and in power.

Notice the British cabinet straddles the gap between "executive" and "legislative." The elaborate American separation of powers (adopted by the Founding Fathers from an earlier misperception of British government by Montesquieu) does not hold in Britain or in most of the world. The United Kingdom has a combining or **fusion of powers**. The British cabinet practices "collective responsibility," meaning they all stick together and, in public at least, support the prime minister. Occasionally, a minister resigns in protest over a major controversy.

In recent years, the cabinet has consisted of some twenty ministers, although this number and portfolio titles change. Commons routinely approves the prime minister's requests to add, drop, or combine ministries. Most countries function that way (not, of course, the United States). In the 2000s, the British cabinet consisted of the following "secretaries of state," or ministers:

Chancellor of the Exchequer (treasury)
Lord Chancellor (member of Lords, heads judiciary)
Foreign and Commonwealth Affairs
Home Development (internal governance, including police)
Environment, Food, and Rural Affairs
International Development
Work and Pensions
Transport, Local Government, and the Regions
Health
Northern Ireland

Democracy

THE QUEEN CHOOSES A NEW PRIME MINISTER

In May 1997 an old ritual was repeated. Ostensibly Queen Elizabeth II chose a new prime minister, but of course she really had no choice at all. Events unrolled according to the fiction that the prime minister is still chief advisor to the monarch. Britain's governing Conservative party saw their voter support erode due to some unpopular policies of Prime Minister Margaret Thatcher and the weak leadership of her successor, John Major, who had narrowly won the 1992 elections. Commons can go up to five years between elections, so in 1997 Major had to

call them. His Conservatives lost massively to a resurgent Labour party.

No longer leader of the party with a majority of the Commons seats, Major could not remain prime minister, so the day after elections he called on the Queen to formally resign as first minister to Her Majesty. (He continued as a member of parliament but was dumped as Tory leader.) That same day the Queen called Tony Blair, as leader of what was now the largest party in the Commons, to Buckingham Palace and "asked" him to form a new government. He accepted.

Wales
Scotland
Defense
Trade and Industry
Education and Skills
Culture, Media, and Sport

government   A particular cabinet, what Americans call "the administration."

In addition, the leaders of both Commons and Lords are in the cabinet, along with a chief secretary for the cabinet as a whole.

Below cabinet rank are more than thirty noncabinet "departmental ministers" and a similar number of "junior ministers" assigned to help cabinet and departmental ministers. All totaled, at any given time about a hundred MPs are also serving in the executive branch. The hope of being named to one of these positions ensures the loyalty and obedience of most younger MPs.

For all intents and purposes, in Britain (and in most parliamentary systems) cabinet equals **government**; the two terms are used interchangeably. One speaks of the "Blair government." (Only the United States uses the word "administration.") When the "government falls" it simply means

Key Concepts

PRIME MINISTERS INTO PRESIDENTS

Political scientists have for some time suggested that prime ministers are becoming more and more presidential. With Tony Blair, this theory gained credence, for Blair indeed concentrated and centralized power in his immediate office at the expense of the cabinet and Commons.

Blair no longer pretended to be "first among equals" in his cabinet, which met less often and decided issues less frequently. Like the U.S. cabinet secretaries, British ministers became more like top administrators. Instead, Blair tripled the size of the staff at 10 Downing Street, headed them with trusted advisors, and used them to make decisions, rather like the White House.

Continuing a trend, Blair spent less time in Commons. Prime Minister Churchill voted in 55 percent of Commons divisions in 1951. Prime Minister Wilson voted 43 percent of the time in 1974. Tony Blair voted 5 percent of the time in Commons in 1997.

Some called Blair a "control freak" who broke with British tradition in order to amass personal power. Maybe, but personality alone does not explain the long-term trend for prime ministers everywhere to become presidential. One key factor changing political systems worldwide: television, which centralizes election campaigns, emphasizes the top candidates, creates massive need for fundraising, bypasses parties and parliaments, and enables leaders to reach people directly. Blair was good on television. Other factors include the decline of legislatures, the growth of interest groups, and the tendency of voters to concentrate in the center of the political spectrum.

Things have changed for parliamentary systems; they cannot operate as before. Systems as different as Britain, France, Germany, and Japan have tended to "presidentialize" themselves as prime ministers gain power and start acting as if they have been directly elected. Everywhere, even in parliamentary systems, parties in elections showcase their leading personality as if he or she was a presidential candidate. Parliamentary systems will not turn completely into U.S.-type systems; all will retain distinctive characteristics. But neither will any of them return to the pure parliamentary model, which was never completely realistic. Even in parliamentary systems, power long ago began shifting to prime ministers, and this has continued. A strong prime minister begins to resemble a U.S.-type president.

the cabinet has resigned. Britain is often referred to as "cabinet government," although some call it "prime ministerial government."

■ The Prime Minister

The prime minister, PM for short (not to be confused with MP, which he or she also is), is the linch-pin of the British system. In theory, the PM's powers could be dictatorial. Because the prime minister picks and controls the cabinet and heads the largest party in Parliament, he or she should be able

Personalities

TONY BLAIR: A NEW MODEL PRIME MINISTER

Tony Blair, first elected prime minister in 1997 at age forty-three (Britain's youngest prime minister since 1812) continued a trend that some observers say has been underway since the 1960s: prime ministers acting more like presidents. Blair indeed centralized and con-centrated power in his immediate office at the expense of the cabinet and Commons (see box on page 35).

Blair did several things that made him look like his friend, President Bill Clinton. (Blair was also close to President Bush.) First, he recast the Labour party—which he called "New Labour"—into a reformist but not radical centrist party. Blair jettisoned uncritical support for unions, higher taxes, and the welfare state in favor of Clinton-type ideas on economic growth and getting people off welfare. With an upbeat personal-ity, he trounced the Conservatives and John Major, who had trouble leading a divided party, in the 1997 general elections to form the first Labour government since 1979.

Some called Blair's ideology—a "Third Way" be-tween capitalism and socialism—vague. Like Clinton, Blair had stolen much of the right's economic agenda but put a smiling face on it. Within two years, lead-ers across Europe wanted to be like Tony Blair, the man with a vision of a humane but flexible market-based system who refused to get stuck in yesterday's thinking.

Blair supported market economics but concentrat-ed on modernizing Britain's sometimes creaky institu-tions. He brought a shaky peace to Northern Ireland, devolved some powers to Scotland and Wales, reformed

Tony Blair

the House of Lords, gave Britain the equivalent of a U.S. Bill of Rights, and managed the economy well. He even considered changing Britain's electoral system in favor of proportional representation. He also cut a swath on the world stage by frequent visits with other chiefs and use of British forces in chaotic areas such as Iraq. By tackling problems that his predecessors ig-nored, Blair proved himself a new type of prime min-ister: a fresh-thinking optimist who won re-election in 2001 over the pessimistic Tories.

By 2003, Blair was in trouble, though, over British participation in the Iraq war, which some 80 percent of Britons, like other Europeans, opposed. Blair faced a revolt within Labour's ranks that included back-benchers and his own cabinet ministers, some of whom resigned in protest that he followed President Bush too uncritically. The Labour party and Blair won the 2005 elections but with a reduced majority. Blair's already-named successor: able Chancellor of the Ex-chequer Gordon Brown, whose eagerness to take over from Blair led to open friction.

to get nearly any measure passed. British parliamentarians are well-disciplined; party **whips** make sure their MPs turn out for **divisions** and vote the party line. Yet even with the reins of power held by one person, prime ministers do not turn into dictators, chiefly because general elections are never more than five years away.

Prime ministers are usually cautious about introducing measures that might provoke public ire. When John Major saw his popularity slipping, he knew he would lose if he "went to the country" with new elections, so he tried to stall, hoping his party's fortunes would rise before the five years were up. Typically, prime ministers introduce moderate, piecemeal measures to avoid offending key blocks of voters. Fear of losing the next election keeps most prime ministers (but not Thatcher) cautious.

Furthermore, a prime minister has to be careful of the major currents of opinion within party ranks. As in the United States, the two large British parties contain left, right, and center wings, as well as regional viewpoints, and a prime minister usually constructs the cabinet with top MPs representing several views within the majority party. In cabinet meetings the PM tries to fashion a consensus from the several stands.

Then the cabinet has to sell the policy to their MPs back in Commons. Party discipline is good but rarely total. The prime minister, through the chief whip, has a hold on the MPs. One who does not "take the whip" (follow the party line on a vote) risks losing his or her nomination for re-election—in effect, getting fired from Parliament. But this is a two-way street. If a party policy really bothers an MP, the member can threaten to quit and make a stink. Sometimes an MP "crosses the aisle" and joins the other party in protest (as did the young Winston Churchill). In 1995 one moderate Conservative MP was so upset by what he saw as right-wing domination of his party that he quit the Tories and ran (successfully) as a Labourite, a slap at party leadership.

If a PM fails badly, he or she can even be dumped by MPs. Occasionally both Labour and Conservative cabinets have to withdraw or water down their legislative proposals for fear of backbenchers' revolt within their own party. A backbenchers' revolt helped oust Thatcher in 1990. In 2005 forty-nine backbenchers revolted against a bill Blair said was necessary to fight terrorism. The vote was over how long police could detain without charges, but the underlying issue was Blair's Iraq policy.

whip Parliamentary party leader who makes sure members obey party in voting.

division Vote in the House of Commons.

WHO WAS WHEN: BRITAIN'S POSTWAR PRIME MINISTERS		
Clement Attlee	Labour	1945–1951
Winston Churchill	Conservative	1951–1955
Anthony Eden	Conservative	1955–1957
Harold Macmillan	Conservative	1957–1963
Alec Douglas-Home	Conservative	1963–1964
Harold Wilson	Labour	1964–1970
Edward Heath	Conservative	1970–1974
Harold Wilson	Labour	1974–1976
James Callaghan	Labour	1976–1979
Margaret Thatcher	Conservative	1979–1990
John Major	Conservative	1990–1997
Tony Blair	Labour	1997–

vote of no-confidence   Parliamentary vote to oust cabinet.

by-election   Special election for vacant seat in Parliament.

Labour backbenchers shot down Blair's bill, in effect saying: "Blair, time for you to go." Commons can oust a PM on a **vote of no-confidence**, but that is rare; it indicates the ruling party has split so badly its MPs are willing to give up power. Blair's 2005 loss was not a "motion of confidence" and so did not require him to resign. Loss of a big measure, such as the budget, would require the PM to resign.

The PM does have a potent political weapon: the power to call new elections whenever he or she wishes. By law, the Commons can go up to five years without a general election. **By-elections** when an

Democracy

PARLIAMENTARY VERSUS PRESIDENTIAL SYSTEMS

In a parliamentary system, like Britain, voters choose only a parliament, which in turn chooses (and can oust) the executive branch, headed by a prime minister. The executive is a committee of the legislature. In a presidential system, such as the United States, voters choose both a legislature and a chief executive, and the two are expected to check and balance each other. In a parliamentary system, they are not.

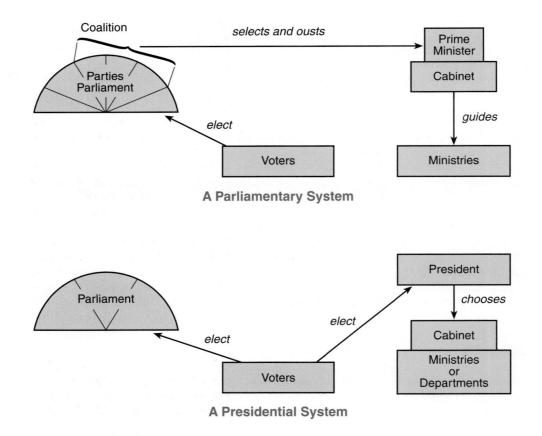

A Parliamentary System

A Presidential System

House of Commons in session. Notice how small it is.

MP dies or retires can come any time; they are closely watched as polit-ical barometers. A crafty prime minister calls for new general elections when he or she thinks the party will do best. A good economy and sunny weather tend to produce a happy electorate, one that will increase the seats of the incumbent party. In 1974 Britain held two general elections because Prime Minister Harold Wilson thought he could boost Labour's strength in the Commons (he did). In 2001 and 2005 Tony Blair called elections a year early to take advantage of good economic news and disarray in the Conservative party; he won handily. Public-opinion polls and by-elections help the prime minister decide when to ask the queen to dissolve Parliament and hold new elections.

Whitehall   Main British government offices.
Westminster   Parliament building.

Since 1735 British prime ministers have resided in an ordinary brick row house, No. 10 Down-ing Street. Except for a couple of London bobbies on guard outside, it looks like a private home. This is deceptive; behind the walls, Downing Street is actually the nerve center of **Whitehall**. Upstairs at No. 10, the prime minister has his or her apartment. On the ground floor, in the back, the cabi-net meets in a long white room. No. 10 connects to No. 12 Downing Street, the residence of the chief whip, the prime minister's parliamentary enforcer. They can visit without being seen from the street. Also connecting out of sight is No. 11 Downing Street, residence of the important Chancellor of the Exchequer, head of the powerful Treasury Ministry. Next door is the Foreign Office. At the corner of Downing Street, also connecting to No. 10, is the cabinet secretariat, responsible for com-munication and coordination among the departments.

Commons

One can look at the cabinet as a committee of the House of Commons sent from **Westminster** to near-by Whitehall to keep administration under parliamentary control. Another way is to view Commons as an electoral college that stays in operation even after it has chosen the executive (the cabinet). In

opposition Parties in parliament that are not in cabinet.

backbencher Ordinary MP with no executive responsibility.

Lockean theory, legislative power has primacy, but in practice Commons has rarely been free and independent and is becoming less so. Prime ministers lead and control Commons.

The two main parties in Commons—Conservative and Labour—face each other on long, parallel benches. The largest party is automatically Her Majesty's Government and the other Her Majesty's Loyal **Opposition**. The size of Commons explains a lot: It is very small, only 45 by 68 feet (14 by 21 meters) and was originally designed for only about 400 members. How then can it possibly hold the current membership of 646? Membership has increased over the years as Britain's population grows in some areas more than in others. Parliament in 2005 cut thirteen seats by combining some smaller constituencies. It is still crowded. Members have no individual desks, unlike most modern legislators. For an important vote, MPs pack in like sardines and sit in the aisles.

Keeping Commons small ensures that members face each other in debate a few yards apart. The parallel benches go well with the two-party system; the half-circle floor plan of most Continental legislatures facilitates pielike division into multiparty systems. But the main reason for the chamber's small size is that it was always small, ever since 1547 when Henry VIII first gave Commons the use of the St. Stephen's royal chapel. During World War II when Commons was damaged by German bombs, Prime Minister Winston Churchill ordered it rebuilt exactly the way it had been.

Each side of the oblong chamber has five rows of benches. The front row on either side is reserved for the leading team of each major party, the cabinet of the government party, and the "shadow cabinet" of the opposition. Behind them sit the **backbenchers**, the MP rank and file. A neutral Speaker, elected for life from the MPs, sits in a thronelike chair at one end. The Speaker, who never votes or takes sides, manages the floor debate and preserves order. In 1992, Commons elected its first woman Speaker, Labourite Betty Boothroyd.

Comparison

HOW MUCH ARE PARLIAMENTARIANS PAID?

Compared to other advanced democracies, British MPs are paid little and do not enjoy substantial allowances. And this is after a pay raise for MPs in 1996.

Many MPs work at other jobs, some as "consultants" for interest groups. This gives some a reputation for "sleaze" that they detest. Many MPs would like to stop or limit outside pay, but the cost of living in London is high, and MPs' salaries are totally inadequate. The huge allowances for U.S. representatives (senators can get almost $2 million) illustrate the strong constituency orientation of U.S. legislators: They need large, specialized staffs both to help the folks back home and to study current issues, functions that are not as highly developed in other parliaments.

Member of	Salary	Allowances
British House of Commons	$67,000	$72,000
French National Assembly	94,400	14,600
German Bundestag	89,000	110,700
Russian Duma	7,000	—
Japanese Diet	146,200	108,900
U.S. House of Representatives	133,600	887,000

A table in the center, between the party benches, is where legislation is placed (the origin of the verb "to table" a proposal). The Speaker calls the house to order at 11:30 A.M. and sessions can go on until 7:30 P.M. Unless "the whip is on"—meaning an MP had better be there because an important vote is expected—many MPs are busy elsewhere.

How Commons Works

Each year Parliament opens in November with a Speech from the Throne by the queen, another tradition. The MPs are ritually summoned by Black Rod, the queen's messenger, from Commons and file into the nearby House of Lords. (Neither monarchs nor lords may enter Commons.) From a gold-paneled dais in Lords, Her Majesty reads a statement outlining the policies "my government" will pursue. The speech has been written by the prime minister with the queen serving as announcer. A conservative king, George VI, read a Labour speech in 1945 promising extensive nationalization of industry.

Just as the queen takes her cues from the prime minister, so does Commons. Practically all legislation is introduced by the "government" (that is, the cabinet) and stands a high chance of passing nearly intact because of the party discipline discussed previously. What the PM wants, the PM usually gets. When a Labour government introduces bills into Commons, Labour MPs—unlike their American counterparts in Congress—rarely question them. Their job is to support the party, and individual conscience seldom gets in the way.

The task of challenging proposals falls to the opposition, seated on the Speaker's left. From the opposition benches come questions, denunciations, warnings of dire consequences, anything that might make the government look bad. A spirit of bipartisanship seldom gets in the way. Government MPs, particularly the cabinet and subcabinet ministers on the front bench, are duty-bound to defend the bills. In situations like these, the famous rhetorical ability of MPs produces debates matched by few other legislatures.

Although the rhetoric is brilliant and witty, the homework is weak. Because they are expected simply to obey their party, few MPs bother specializing. Traditionally, British parliamentary committees were also unspecialized; they went over the precise wording of bills but called no witnesses and gathered no data. The structure of legislative committees is an important key to their

Democracy

THE DECLINE OF LEGISLATURES

Commons is less important than it used to be. As in most of the world, legislatures, the great avenues of democracy are declining in power. Fewer people—especially young people—bother voting and fewer follow debates in Commons, which gets less media attention. The debates matter little; thanks to Britain's (over)disciplined parties, the prime minister almost always gets his or her way. The only way to jump-start Commons back into life would be to let

MPs ignore the whip and vote as they wish. A deliberate weakening of Britain's parties might make Commons exciting, unpredictable, and messy, like the U.S. Congress. A word of caution here: Capitol Hill has also been losing power to the White House. This may be an unstoppable world trend. Even so, legislatures are invaluable for scrutinizing executive power, holding it accountable, and occasionally ousting it. If they do this, they are still bulwarks of democracy.

select committee   Specialized committee of Commons focusing on one ministry.

life peers   Distinguished Britons named lords for their lifetimes only, does not pass on to children.

Law Lords   Britain's top judges, members of Lords.

power, and gradually some MPs saw the need for a more American type of committee system. In 1979, fourteen **select committees** were set up to scrutinize the workings of each ministry; they have the power to take written and oral evidence. The select committees, with permanent, stable membership, resemble to some extent U.S. Congressional committees.

Neither Tory nor Labour governments have been enthusiastic about specialized committees that can monitor and criticize executive functions. That may be part of the U.S. system of separation of powers, some have argued, but it has no place in the U.K. system of fusion of powers. In general, the British cabinet would like to use Commons to rubber-stamp its decisions. Fortunately, such rubber-stamping is not always the case, as we shall explore later.

Peerless Lords

In 1999, Parliament drastically reformed the House of Lords by kicking out most of its hereditary peers, thus turning it over to **life peers**. Since 1958 distinguished Britons in science, literature, politics, military service, business, and the arts have been named as Lords or Ladies of the Realm, but for their life only. The change did nothing to enhance Lords' weak powers. Lords now has some seven hundred peers (a number that changes with deaths and new appointments), most of them life peers, plus ninety-two hereditary peers and twenty-six top churchmen.

The British Parliament is nominally bicameral, but Commons has limited Lords' powers over the centuries, so that now when one says "Parliament," one really means Commons. Early on, Commons established supremacy in the key area of money: raising revenues, and spending them. (An echo of this is the U.S. provision that money bills originate in the lower chamber, the House of Representatives.) Britain's seventeenth-century battles centered on the power of Commons, and it emerged the winner; Lords gradually took a back seat. By 1867 Bagehot considered Lords a "dignified" part of the constitution.

Since Britain's unwritten constitution does not specify or make permanent the powers of the two chambers, it was legally possible for Commons to change Lords. Its powers now are severely limited. The 1911 Parliament Act allows Lords to delay legislation not more than thirty days on financial bills and two years (since 1949, one year) on other bills. Lords can amend legislation and send it back to Commons, which in turn can (and usually does) delete the changes by a simple majority. Every few years, however, Lords jolts the government by forcing Commons to take another look at bills passed without sufficient scrutiny. Lords, then, is somewhat more important than a debating club. It is the only British institution in a position to check the powers of a prime minister who has a large and disciplined majority in Commons. It is thus a weak analog to the U.S. Supreme Court, a "conscience of the nation." Lords is also able to debate questions too hot for elected officials—for example, laws concerning abortion and homosexuality.

Usually, fewer than three hundred lords turn up in the House of Lords; a quorum is three. A few lords are named to the cabinet or to other high political or diplomatic positions. The chamber is also home to the five **Law Lords**, life peers who are the top judges in the British court system to whom cases may be appealed. Now that Britain has a Human Rights Act (see page 75), a sort of embryonic constitution, the law lords can declare something "unconstitutional." The law lords may thus turn into a U.S.-style Supreme Court.

Most Britons agree that Lords is an **anachronism** ripe for reform but cannot agree on what to do with it. Blair's 1999 step depriving most hereditary peers of their seats made Lords meritocratic but not democratic. Blair once considered a more sweeping proposal: a 600-member House of Lords with 120 elected lords and the rest named by political parties and the government. Criticism from all parties and the media shot down the proposal. Many feared prime ministers would simply stack the new chamber with loyal supporters, giving the prime minister control of both houses and depriving Lords of its independence to criticize. Many Britons want to make Lords fully elected, like the U.S. Senate, but some fear that would dilute the legislative supremacy of Commons and turn Lords over to vote-seeking party politicians. Changing constitutions is tricky: When you change one thing, you change everything.

anachronism   Something from the past that does not fit present times.

"two-plus" party system   Two big parties and several small ones.

single-member district   Sends one representative to parliament.

FPTP   "First past the post," short way of saying "single-member districts with plurality win."

plurality   Largest quantity, even if less than a majority.

majoritarian   Electoral system that encourages dominance of one party in parliament, as in Britain and the United States.

Key Concepts

BRITAIN'S TWO-PARTY SYSTEM

Britain is usually described as a two-party system, but some third parties are important. Britain, like many democracies, is more accurately a **"two-plus" party system**. In 1979, for example, the withdrawal of support by the eleven Scottish Nationalists in Commons brought down the Callaghan government in a rare *vote of no-confidence*. The Liberal Democrats may get one vote in five, forcing the Labour and Conservative parties to change positions on some issues.

Britain's electoral system keeps two parties big and penalizes smaller parties. Britain, like the United States and Canada, uses **single-member districts** as the basis for elections. This old English system is simple: Each electoral district or constituency sends one person to the legislature, the candidate that gets the most votes even if less than a majority, sometimes called "first past the post" (**FPTP**). In 1992, for example, a Lib Dem in Scotland won with just 26 percent of the vote. This system of single-member districts with **plurality** victors tends to produce two large political parties. The reason: There is a big premium to combine small parties into big ones in order to edge out competitors. If one of the two large parties splits, which sometimes happens, the election is thrown to the other party, the one that hangs together. In countries with proportional representation there is not such a great premium on forming two large parties, and that contributes to multiparty systems.

The countries that inherited the British **majoritarian** system tend toward two large parties, one left, the other right, such as the U.S. Democrats and Republicans. Canada is an exception to this pattern, because its third parties are territorially concentrated, especially the separatist Bloc Québécois. New Zealand used the Anglo-American system, and it too yielded two large parties. It also left many New Zealanders discontent, because other viewpoints got ignored, so its parliament in 1993 adopted a new electoral law, modeled on Germany's hybrid system of half single-member districts and half PR. New Zealand soon developed a more complex party system.

■ The Parties

Commons works as it does because of the British party system. This is a fairly recent development; only since the time of the French Revolution (1789) has it been possible to speak of coherent parties in Britain. Parties are now the cornerstone of British government. If a party elects a majority of the MPs, that party controls Commons and forms the government.

British parties are more cohesive, centralized, and ideological than American parties. It is fair to say there are as many differences within the two big U.S. parties as between them. Now, however, like their U.S. counterparts, the two large British parties tend to converge to the center. Earlier, British Labourites, who sometimes called themselves Socialists, favored nationalization of industry, more welfare measures, and higher taxes. Conservatives urged less government involvement in society and the economy and lower taxes. Internal party differences arose from the degree to which party members supported these general points of view. Now, as we shall explore subsequently, differences between the two parties are muted.

In 1981, the moderate wing of the Labour party split off to form a centrist Social Democratic party. They argued that Labour had fallen under the control of leftist radicals. The Social Democrats faced the problem that besets Britain's third party, the struggling Liberals, namely, that single-member plurality districts severely penalize smaller parties.

The Liberal party illustrates how smaller parties suffer under the British system of electing MPs. In the last century the Liberals were one of the two big parties, but by the 1920s they had been pushed into a weak third place by Labour. Now, although the Liberals often win nearly 20 percent of the vote, they rarely get more than a few dozen Commons seats because their vote is territorially dispersed, so in few constituencies does it top Tories or Labourites.

proportional representation (PR) Electoral system of multimember districts with seats awarded by percentage parties win.

In 1983 and 1987, the Liberals and Social Democrats ran jointly as the "Alliance," and in 1988 they merged into the Liberal Democratic party. Because they are spread rather evenly, the "Lib Dems" still get shortchanged on parliamentary seats (see box on page 43). The Liberal Democrats would like to move away from the majoritarian system and toward **proportional representation** (PR), something Blair also mentioned. The leading proposal is to keep FPTP but "top off" seats to more accurately reflect nationwide party strengths. (The German system, by contrast, starts with PR but adds FPTP.)

Scottish and Welsh nationalist parties have had spurts of growth and decline. Their territorial concentration enables them to win a few seats in Westminster and many seats in the Scottish and Welsh assemblies instituted in 1999. We will explore patterns of interaction among the parties and the voters in Chapter 5.

Key Terms

anachronism (p. 43)

antithetical (p. 33)

backbencher (p. 40)

by-election (p. 38)

Cortes (p. 33)

Crown (p. 32)

dignified (p. 32)

division (p. 37)

eclectic (p. 32)

efficient (p. 32)

FPTP (p. 43)

fusion of powers (p. 34)

government (p. 35)

junior minister (p. 33)

Law Lords (p. 42)

life peers (p. 42)

majoritarian (p. 43)

MP (p. 33)

opposition (p. 40)

plurality (p. 43)

portfolio (p. 33)

proportional representation (p. 44)

select committee (p. 42)

single-member district (p. 43)

statute (p. 32)

"two-plus" party system (p. 43)

vote of no-confidence (p. 38)

Westminister (p. 39)

whip (p. 37)

Whitehall (p. 39)

Further Reference

Birch, Anthony H. *The British System of Government,* 10th ed. New York: Routledge, 1998.

Blackburn, Robert. *The Electoral System in Britain.* New York: St. Martin's, 1995.

Bogdanor, Vernon, ed. *The British Constitution in the Twentieth Century.* New York: Oxford University Press, 2003.

Foley, Michael. *The British Presidency: Tony Blair and the Politics of Public Leadership.* New York: St. Martin's, 2000.

Foster, Christopher. *British Government in Crisis.* Oxford: Hart, 2005.

Hennessey, Peter. *The Prime Minister: The Office and Its Holders since 1945.* New York: Palgrave, 2001.

Kavanagh, Dennis, and Anthony Selden. *The Powers behind the Prime Minister: The Hidden Influence of Number Ten.* New York: HarperCollins, 2000.

Lipsey, David. *The Secret Treasury.* New York: Viking, 2000.

Poguntke, Thomas, and Paul Webb, eds. *The Presidentialization of Politics: A Comparative Study of Modern Democracies.* New York: Oxford University Press, 2005.

Rentoul, John. *Tony Blair: Prime Minister.* London: Time Warner, 2002.

Riddell, Peter. *Parliament under Blair.* London: Politico, 2000.

Selden, Anthony. *Blair.* New York: Free Press, 2004.

Chapter 4

BRITISH POLITICAL CULTURE

"England is a snob country," one long-time American resident in London told me. She added: "And I'm a snob, so I like it here." Her candor touched one of the facets of British political life: the large and often invidious distinctions made between and by social classes.

Social class can be analyzed in two ways, objectively and subjectively. The objective approach uses data such as income and neighborhood to put people into categories. The subjective approach asks people to put themselves into categories. There are often discrepancies between the two, as when a self-made businessman, thinking of his humble origins, describes himself as **working class**, or when a poorly paid schoolteacher, thinking of her university degrees, describes herself as **middle class**. In Britain and in most industrialized democracies, the main politically relevant distinction is between working class and middle class.

__Questions to Consider__

1. How does a wage differ from a salary? In class terms?
2. What is the difference between objective and subjective?
3. What is a British "public" school?
4. How does an "Oxbridge" education form an elite?
5. What is "class voting" and has it declined?
6. What story does a map of the 2005 elections tell?
7. What sort of center-periphery tension does Britain have?
8. Have British parties always been pragmatic?
9. What do polls tell politicians about voters' ideology?
10. How did Northern Ireland become such a problem?

Objectively, class differences in Britain are no greater than in the rest of West Europe. The time has long passed when Disraeli could write that Britain was not one nation but two, the rich and the poor. Since then, the British working class has grown richer, the middle class bigger, and the small upper class poorer. But **subjectively** or psychologically, class differences remain. Working-class people live, dress, speak, and enjoy themselves differently than the middle class. Britons seem to like these differences and try to preserve them.

German sociologist Ralf Dahrendorf felt the key word in Britain is not class but **solidarity**. While there has been a leveling of objective class differences, Dahrendorf held, the idea of individual competition and improvement has not caught on in Britain as in other industrial countries. Rather than struggling to improve themselves individually, many Britons relish the feeling of solidarity they get by sticking with their old jobs, neighborhoods, and pubs. "Britain is a society in which the values of solidarity are held in higher esteem than those of individual success at the expense of others," Dahrendorf wrote. Whether one calls it class or solidarity, these divisions influence British politics. They contribute to the way Britons vote, color the attitudes of labor unions and of the Labour party, and—very importantly—give birth to Britain's elites through the education system.

■ "Public" Schools

Although many claim that since World War II Britain has become a **meritocracy**, having the right parents still makes a big difference. No society, including the United States, is purely merit-based. One way the British upper and upper-middle classes pass on their advantages is the **"public" school**—actually private and expensive—so called after their original purpose of training boys for public life in the military, civil service, or politics. Eton, Harrow, Rugby, St. Paul's, Winchester, and other famous academies have for generations molded the sons of better-off Britons into a ruling elite.

What a small minority of young Britons learn from ages thirteen to eighteen is more than their demanding curriculum. It is the personal style inculcated in public schools: self-confident to the point of arrogance, self-disciplined, bred to rule. Spy novelist John Le Carré recalled with distaste how his public schoolmates during World War II felt nothing but contempt for lower-class "oiks." In terms of class relations, added Le Carré decades later, "nothing, but absolutely nothing, has changed" since the 1940s.

The British private-school system generates an **old boy** network that assists graduates later in life. The years of floggings, vile food, and bullying by upper-classmen forge bonds among old schoolmates, and they often help each other get positions in industry and government. Most of Britain's elite have gone to private boarding schools, including over half of Conservative MPs. Fewer Labour MPs went to such schools, but Prime Minister Tony Blair was one. Ninety percent of Thatcher's ministers had been privately educated, 64 percent of Major's, but only 39 percent of Blair's.

Until the 1970s, most young Britons took a frightening exam at age eleven (the "11-plus") that selected the best into state-funded *grammar* schools but left most in *secondary modern* schools. In all but Northern Ireland, Labour governments phased out this selective system in favor of *comprehensive* schools for all, like U.S. high

social class   Layer or section of population of similar income and status. (See page 47.)

working class   Those paid an hourly wage, typically less affluent and educated. (See page 47.)

middle class   Professionals or those paid salaries, typically more affluent and educated. (See page 47.)

objective   Judged by observable criteria. (See page 47.)

subjective   Judged by feeling or intuition. (See page 47.)

solidarity   Feeling of cohesion within a social class. (See page 47.)

meritocracy   Promotion by brains and ability rather than heredity.

public school   In Britain, a private, boarding school, equivalent to a U.S. prep school.

old boy   Someone you knew at public school.

Democracy

WHAT TO DO WITH "PUBLIC" SCHOOLS?

The British Labour party long sought to do away with the country's private boarding schools. Labourites regarded them as undemocratic, part of a class system that benefits a privileged few. Many Conservative politicians have attended "public" schools, but few Labour politicians have. Conservatives want to maintain the schools, arguing that they train the best people and imbue them with a sense of public service.

In actual practice, Labour governments essentially let the private boarding schools alone while they upgrade the quality of publicly supported "comprehensive" schools. Blair's emphasis on education, for example, left the public schools untouched. The problem may be solving itself: Boarding-school enrollment has slumped while day-school popularity has climbed. Changing lifestyles have convinced many British parents that sending their children away is cruel and unloving.

schools. This did not solve the twin problems of educational quality and equality. Now better-off children go to boarding schools, middle-class children go to private day schools, while working class children go to mediocre state-funded comprehensive and technical schools, from which many drop out. Until after World War II, there was no free high-school system in Britain. Only 65 percent of British seventeen-year-olds are still in school (including technical training), the lowest level of any industrial land. (Comparative figures: Germany, 97 percent; United States, 88 percent; Japan, 83 percent.) In spite of the efforts of the Labour party since World War II, British education is weak and still divided by class.

Oxbridge Informal, Oxford and Cambridge universities.

Rhodes scholarship Founded by South African millionaire, sends top foreign students to Oxford.

class voting Tendency of classes to vote for parties that represent them.

■ "Oxbridge"

The real path to position and power in Britain is through the elite universities of Oxford or Cambridge. Nearly half of Conservative MPs are Oxford or Cambridge graduates (usually after attending a public school, such as Eton), while a quarter of Labour MPs are **Oxbridge** products. In the cabinet, these percentages are higher. And prime ministers are almost always graduates of either Oxford or Cambridge; Thatcher and Blair were Oxonians. In recent years, only Labour Prime Minister James Callaghan (1976–1979) and Conservative John Major (1990–1997) never went to college. In few other industrialized countries are the political elite drawn so heavily from just two universities.

British university education used to be elitist, enrolling the products of private schools. Since World War II, education opened to the working and lower-middle classes by direct-grant secondary schools and scholarships for deserving youths. Oxford and Cambridge became less class-biased in their admissions, and many lesser institutions were founded or expanded. (They are now called euphemistically "mainstream" universities.) The percentage of British secondary (high-school) graduates going to some type of higher education shot up from 14 in 1985 to nearly 40 today, approaching U.S. levels.

Only a small percentage of Oxbridge students go into politics, but those who do start with advantages. An Oxford or Cambridge degree—which takes three years to earn—commands respect. The Oxbridge experience hones political skills. One popular major for aspiring politicians is "PPE"—philosophy, politics, and economics—in effect, how to run a country. Debating in the Oxford or Cambridge Unions trains students to think on their feet and confound their opponents with rhetorical cleverness, a style that carries over into the House of Commons. Perhaps the main advantage of an Oxbridge education, however, is the "sense of effortless superiority" graduates carry all their lives. One U.S. president (Clinton), two Supreme Court justices, and several cabinet secretaries attended Oxford on **Rhodes scholarships**.

■ Class and Voting

Britain used to be a good example of **class voting**—a situation where most of the working class votes for the left party (in this case, Labour) while most of the middle class votes for the right (in this case, Conservative). Actually, class voting in Sweden is higher than in Britain, but nowhere is it 100 percent because some working-class people vote Conservative, and some middle-class people vote Labour. Class differences may be part of Britain's political culture, but they do not translate into class voting on a one-to-one basis.

deferential   Accepting leadership of social superiors.

the Establishment   Half in jest, supposed monopoly of clubby social elite in British politics.

civility   Good manners in politics.

What dilutes class voting? Some working-class people are simply convinced that Conservatives do a better job governing than Labourites. Some workers have a sentimental attachment to the country's oldest party. Some issues have little to do with class. The Tories win a large part of the working class on the issues of economic growth, keeping taxes down, and keeping out immigrants.

Going the other way, many middle-class and educated people are intellectually convinced that the Labour party is the answer to what they see as an establishment-ruled, snobbish class system. Such intellectuals provide important leadership in the Labour party. The leader of the Labour left for a long time was an aristocrat, Anthony Wedgewood Benn, or, as he liked to be known, Tony Benn. Furthermore, some middle-class people grew up in working-class families and vote like their parents.

Class voting changes over time. The British generation that came of age during and after World War II, especially the working class, was quite loyal to the Labour party, which it swept to power in 1945. Since then, class voting has declined in Britain and other advanced, industrialized democracies, including the United States. Class is not what it used to be in any country's voting patterns.

It is, however, still a factor. Typically, political scientists find voting behavior is influenced by social class plus one or more other factors, such as region, ethnic group, religion, and urban-rural differences. The 2005 British general election partially bears this out (see box on page 51). Tories were strongest in England, especially the south of England, and in small towns and rural areas. They were weaker in Scotland and Wales and in the big industrial cities, places with a long-term Labour identification and concern over unemployment. Class by itself explains only part of British voting patterns. Class plus region explains more.

The Deferential British?

One old image of the British was that they were **deferential**, that is, the average Briton deferred to the political judgment of the Oxbridge-educated **Establishment** and let it lead. The deferential model is now obsolete. Perhaps in earlier decades, when class differences were enormous, the working class deferred to its social betters, but they also built up resentment. As noted in Chapter 2, the labor movement came into British politics in the nineteenth century with a snarl. Some sectors of the British working class still show their resentment in the militant socialism within the Labour party and in indifferent work attitudes and a readiness to strike. The deferential model cannot explain such behavior.

The "working-class Tory" has been explained as a working-class person who defers to the Conservatives and votes for them. But such voting may have little to do with deference. Many such voters think the Conservatives have the right policies, the Labour party had swung too far left, and there are too many nonwhite immigrants. Furthermore, the 1997, 2001, and 2005 elections saw a return of the "middle-class Labour voter," a shift that has nothing to do with social deference.

British Civility

In Britain, **civility** is based on a sense of limits: Do not let anything go too far; do not let the system come unstuck. Thus, while Labourites and Conservatives have serious arguments, they keep them verbal. The British political game is not one of total annihilation, as it has sometimes been in France, Germany, and Russia. Accordingly, British politicians are fairly decent toward each other.

Geography

THE 2005 ELECTIONS: REGION AND CLASS

A country's electoral geography—rooted in the history, resentments, and culture of its regions—is long-lasting. Britain illustrates that how a region voted in the past likely predicts how it will vote next time. Labour won a third victory in 2005, but scored above its national average in Scotland, Wales, and the industrial areas of London, Liverpool, Yorkshire, and the Northeast, areas where it has long held sway. Social class is also a factor, as Labour scores well among people who feel disadvantaged: the Scots, the Welsh, and the working class. The areas where the Conservatives fare above average (the shaded portion) are mostly in England, especially in rural and suburban parts. In a nearly universal political pattern, large cities tend to vote left. Region plus class predicts the British vote.

Shaded: Where Tories Won above Average in 2005

heckling   Interrupting a speaker.

periphery   Nation's outlying regions.

center-periphery tension   Resentment of outlying areas at rule by nation's capital.

But British civility allows **heckling**. In Parliament a cabinet minister presenting a difficult case sometimes faces cries of "Shame!" or "Treason!" from the opposition benches. Margaret Thatcher faced Labourites chanting "Ditch the bitch." Insults and heckling are a normal part of British debates and are not viewed as out of bounds but rather as tests of a debater's poise and verbal skills.

Civility is usually the case in public also, but not always. Amateur orators at the famous Speakers' Corner of Hyde Park in London can have their say on any subject they like, although they too face heckling. British politics turned uncivil on the question of race, which we will discuss later, and there have been demonstrations and riots that led to deaths. Murder rather than civility became the norm for Northern Ireland. British civility has been overstated; Swedes are more civil.

Pragmatism

As noted in Chapter 1, *pragmatic* has the same root as *practical* and means using what works without paying much attention to theory or ideology. British political culture, like American or Swedish, is generally pragmatic. The Conservatives used to pride themselves on being the most pragmatic of all British parties. They were willing to adopt the policies of another party if they won votes. In the nineteenth century, Disraeli crowed he had "dished the Whigs" by stealing their drive to expand the voting franchise. In the 1950s, the returning Conservative government did not throw out Labour's welfare state; instead they boasted that Tories ran it more efficiently. This changed with the laissez-faire economic program of Prime Minister Thatcher in 1979. The fixity of her goals contributed to ideological debates within and between the two large and usually pragmatic parties. Pragmatism returned to the Tories after Thatcher.

The British Labour party historically offered little ideology beyond the hopeful image of a welfare state. With the Callaghan government in the 1970s, however, ideological controversy engulfed

Geography

CENTERS AND PERIPHERIES

A country's capital is often called its "center," even though it may not be in the precise center of the land. Closer to the boundaries of the state are the **peripheral** areas. Often these are more recent additions to the territory of the state. Some of them still speak a different language and resent rule by the capital. This **center-periphery tension** is nearly universal.

Over the centuries, England added Wales, Scotland, and Ireland. Resentment was so high in Ireland that Britain granted it independence in the last century. Now Britain retains only Northern Ireland, long a source of resentment and violence. Scotland and Wales also harbor grudges against rule by London and

demand more home rule. As we shall consider in Chapter 6, Tony Blair's Labour government tried to calm these feelings by granting Scotland and Wales their own legislatures.

The U.S. Civil War was an effort by the southern periphery to cast off rule by Washington. In terms of culture and economics, the North and South really were two different countries, a gap that has been partly closed since then. The center of U.S. population, politics, economics, communications, education, and culture long remained in the northeast. This still fosters slight center-periphery tension; some western politicians express irritation at rule by Washington.

Labour. Callaghan was a very moderate, pragmatic Labourite, hard to distinguish from moderate Conservatives. Many Labour personalities, including some union heads, resented Callaghan's centrism and rammed through a socialist party platform despite him. The moderate wing of the Labour party split off in 1981 to form a centrist party, the Social Democrats. As we shall consider in Chapter 5, a series of Labour party leaders pushed the party back to the nonideological center, leading to its 1997, 2001, and 2005 electoral victories.

hooliganism   Violent and destructive behavior.

There is and always has been a certain amount of ideology in British politics, but it has usually been balanced with a shrewd practical appreciation that ideology neither wins elections nor effectively governs a country. The ideological flare-up of the 1980s in Britain made it perhaps the most polarized land of West Europe. Ironically, at this same time, French parties, long said to be far more ideological than British parties, moved to the center, where British parties used to cluster.

One aspect of British pragmatism is their "muddling-through" style of problem solving. The British tend not to thoroughly analyze a problem and come up with detailed options or "game plans." They try to "muddle through somehow," improvising as they go. This often works with small problems, but with a big problem, such as the situation in Northern Ireland, it amounts to a nonsolution.

Traditions and Symbols

As noted earlier, British politics keeps traditions. Political usages often follow well-worn paths, observed even by left-wing Labourites, who, whether they recognize it or not, subscribe to Burke's idea of keeping the forms but changing the contents. As Burke saw, traditions and symbols contribute to society's stability and continuity; people feel disoriented without them.

The typical British man or woman likes traditions and symbols. Although some Britons wince at the tabloid lifestyle of the younger generation of "royals," only a minority would abolish the monarchy in favor of a republic with a president. Parades with golden coaches and horsemen in red tunics are not just for tourists—although they help Britain's economy—they also serve to deepen British feelings about the rightness of the system.

Traditions can also tame political radicals. Once they win seats in Commons, radicals find themselves playing according to established parliamentary usages. "Well, it simply is not done, old boy," is the standard lesson taught to newcomers in Parliament. They may still have radical views, but they voice them within traditional bounds.

Political Culture

FOOTBALL HOOLIGANISM

Underscoring the decline in British civility was the rise of football **hooliganism**, the gleeful rioting of some British soccer fans. Drunken fans sometimes charge onto the field in the middle of a game. In 1985, Liverpool fans killed thirty-eight Italian spectators by causing their bleachers to collapse. All over Europe, the English fanatics were feared and sometimes barred from games.

What causes the violence? Some blame unemployment; the games offer the jobless one of their few diversions. But most hooligans are employed and some earn good livings. Others see hooliganism as the erosion of civilization itself. "The truth is," said one self-confessed Manchester hooligan, "we just like scrappin'."

■ Legitimacy and Authority

Legitimacy is a feeling of rightness about the political system. As we noted in Chapter 1, it originally meant the right king was on the throne, not a usurper. As used by political scientists, it refers to public attitudes that the government's rule is rightful. Legitimacy is a feeling among the people; it is not the same as "legal." When a political system enjoys high legitimacy, people generally obey it. They will even do things they do not want to, such as paying their income taxes.

authority   Political leaders' ability to be obeyed.

Irish Republican Army   Anti-British terrorists who seek unification of all Ireland.

Malthusian   View that population growth outstrips food.

home rule   Giving region some autonomy to govern itself.

Eire   Republic of Ireland.

Orangemen   After King William of Orange (symbol of Netherlands royal house), Northern Irish Protestants.

Legitimacy is closely related to **authority**, obeying duly constituted officials. British legitimacy and authority were famous, but they were exaggerated and oversold. British policemen did not carry guns and had good relations with the people on their beat. Political scientists used to cite such points to illustrate Britain's nonviolent qualities. During the 1970s, however, Britain turned more violent. The **Irish Republican Army** (IRA) spread their murderous tactics from Ulster, planting bombs that killed dozens. In 1984, one bomb blew up near Prime Minister Thatcher. Criminals started using handguns. In Britain's inner cities, relations between police and youths, especially black youths, grew hateful and contributed to urban riots (which, nonetheless, cost very few lives). After the 2005 London subway bombings, police shot and killed an innocent passenger on the mistaken suspicion that he was a terrorist. Some critics decried the gunplay as the Americanization of their police. A few British policemen now carry guns and riot gear, a symbol of the erosion of legitimacy and authority in Britain.

■ The Ulster Ulcer

While we can say Britons on the whole still have attitudes of civility, pragmatism, legitimacy, respect for authority, and nonviolence, we must note that Northern Ireland (sometimes called Ulster) is a massive exception. Northern Ireland illustrates how a system that works amid widespread legitimacy fails when it is lacking. Unlike the rest of Britain, Ulster is a split society, more like those of Latin Europe—France, Spain, and Italy—where part of the population does not see the government as legitimate.

The Ulster problem has its roots in the eight centuries England ruled Ireland, at times treating the Irish as subhuman, seizing their land, deporting them, even outlawing the Catholic faith. In the 1846–1854 Potato Famine a million Irish starved to death while the English, with plentiful food stocks, watched. (An example of what happens when you make too many babies, admonished English **Malthusians**.) At that time about a million and a half Irish emigrated, most to the United States. The Irish problem was the great issue of nineteenth-century British politics, "the damnable question" of whether to keep it firmly under British control or grant it **home rule**.

In the spring of 1916, while the English were hard-pressed in World War I, the "Irish Volunteers" used guerrilla warfare in the Easter Rising in an attempt to win freedom for Ireland. (In 1919, they renamed themselves the IRA.) By 1922, after brutally crushing the rising, the British had enough; Ireland became a *free state* of the British Commonwealth. In 1949, the bulk of Ireland ended this free-state status and became sovereign **Eire**.

But this did not solve the Ulster problem; a majority of the 1.5 million people in these six northern counties are Protestant (descended from seventeenth-century Scottish immigrants) and are determined to remain part of Britain. Fiercely Protestant, for years these **Orangemen** treated Northern

Irish Catholics as a different race and feared they had "popish" plots to bring Northern Ireland into the Catholic-dominated Irish Republic to the south. In control of Ulster's local government, the Protestants shortchanged the Catholic minority in jobs, housing, and political power. For many years, most Catholics did not even have the right to vote for the Ulster legislature.

In 1968 Catholic protests started, modeled on U.S. civil-rights marches. But Catholic *nationalists* or *republicans*, who sought to join the Republic of Ireland, soon battled with Protestant *loyalists* or *unionists*, who insisted that

center-peaked   Distribution with most people in the middle, a bell-shaped curve.

center-seeking   Tendency of political parties toward moderate politics calculated to win the center.

Political Culture

THE SHAPE OF THE BRITISH ELECTORATE

Virtually all modern democracies show a strong clustering in the ideological center, with a tapering off toward the extremes: bell-shaped curves. Such a **center-peaked** distribution is probably necessary to sustain democracy, for it encourages **center-seeking** politics. A U-shaped distribution indicates extreme division, possibly heading toward civil war (example:

Spain, 1936). Pollsters and political consultants constantly remind their clients of the distribution of ideological opinion and warn them not to position themselves too far left or right. It took the Labour party several electoral defeats to get the message. Tony Blair finally pushed Labour into about the 5 position (exact center) with vague but upbeat party positions.

**The Self-Placement of British Voters
on a Left/Right Ideological Scale**

anglophile Someone who loves England and the English.

francophobe Someone who dislikes France and the French.

Northern Ireland stay a part of Britain. A *"provisional"* wing of the IRA enrolled Catholic gunmen, and Protestant counterparts reciprocated. Murder became nearly random. Over 3,600 were killed—including MPs, Earl Mountbatten, British soldiers, but mostly innocent civilians—and for some years the United Kingdom was the most violent nation in West Europe. Most Ulstermen welcomed a 1998 power-sharing agreement. Violence largely ended, but mistrust remains (see Chapter 6).

■ A Changing Political Culture

We are trying to put British political culture into perspective. Britons are neither angels nor devils. Political scientists used to present Britain as a model of stability, moderation, calm, justice, and niceness. In contrast, France was often presented as a model of instability and immoderate political attitudes. The contrast was overdrawn; neither the British nor the French are as good or as bad as sometimes portrayed.

Observations of a country's political culture can err in two ways. First, if you are favorably disposed toward a country—and Americans are great **anglophiles** (while many are **francophobes**)—you may overlook some of the nasty things lurking under the surface or dismiss them as aberrations. For years American textbooks on British politics ignored or played down the violence in Northern Ireland. Such "incivility" seemed too un-British to mention. Riots in impoverished parts of British inner cities caught many observers by surprise.

Second, studies of political culture are carried out during particular times, and things change. The data for Almond and Verba's *Civic Culture* (see box on page 8), were collected in 1959 and 1960. Their composite portrait of Britain as a "deferential civic culture" has not been valid for decades. Since World War II, Britain has undergone trying times, especially in the area of economics. This did not erase British culture wholesale; they simply made manifest what had been latent. Political attitudes change; they can get nastier or better.

Political Culture

THE IRA: BALLOTS AND BULLETS

The Irish Republican Army is illegal in both Eire and Northern Ireland, but its political arm, Sinn Fein (pronounced *shin fain,* "We Ourselves") is not. It still aims to get Britain out of Northern Ireland so it can unify with the Republic. Many Northern Irish Catholics vote for Sinn Fein candidates; in 2005 five were elected to Commons (where they do not vote). Sinn Fein leader Gerry Adams, an MP representing Belfast West, denies belonging to the IRA but never condemned its violence. Now voicing a moderate line, he urges peace and disarmament of all sides and only political means to unite Ireland. Ever disrespectful of the English Crown, he calls Queen Elizabeth "Mrs. Windsor."

In 1981 Ulster's Catholics elected Bobby Sands, an imprisoned IRA gunman, who starved himself to death in a hunger strike. The fact that so many men and women of Ulster are willing to vote for an extremist party indicates the depth of hatred and the difficulty of compromising on the basic question of which country to belong to, Britain or Ireland. There is really no middle ground here.

Key Terms

anglophile (p. 56)

authority (p. 54)

center-peaked (p. 55)

center-periphery tension (p. 52)

center-seeking (p. 55)

civility (p. 50)

class voting (p. 49)

deferential (p. 50)

Eire (p. 54)

Establishment (p. 50)

francophobe (p. 56)

heckling (p. 52)

home rule (p. 54)

hooliganism (p. 53)

Irish Republican Army (p. 54)

Malthusian (p. 54)

meritocracy (p. 48)

middle class (p. 48)

objective (p. 48)

old boy (p. 48)

Orangemen (p. 54)

Oxbridge (p. 49)

periphery (p. 52)

public school (p. 48)

Rhodes scholarship (p. 49)

social class (p. 48)

solidarity (p. 48)

subjective (p. 48)

working class (p. 48)

Further Reference

Adams, Ian. *Ideology and Politics in Britain Today*. New York: St. Martin's, 1998.

Adonis, Andrew, and Stephen Pollard. *A Class Act: The Myth of Britain's Classless Society*. London: Hamish Hamilton, 1997.

Curtice, John, Katarina Thomson, Lindsey Jarvis, Catharine Bromley, and Nina Stratford. *British Social Attitudes: Public Policy, Social Ties*. Thousand Oaks, CA: Sage, 2002.

Dahrendorf, Ralf. *On Britain*. Chicago, IL: University of Chicago Press, 1982.

Field, William H. *Regional Dynamics: The Basis of Electoral Support in Britain*. Portland, OR: F. Cass, 1997.

Madgwick, Peter, and Richard Rose, eds. *The Territorial Dimension in United Kingdom Politics*. Atlantic Highlands, NJ: Humanities Press, 1982.

McKittrick, David, and David McVea. *Making Sense of the Troubles: The Story of the Conflict In Northern Ireland*. Chicago, IL: New Amsterdam Books, 2002.

Miller, William, L., Annis May Timpson, and Michael Lessnoff. *Political Culture in Contemporary Britain: People and Politicians, Principles and Practice*. New York: Oxford University Press, 1996.

Mitchell, Paul, and Rick Wilford, eds. *Politics in Northern Ireland*. Boulder, CO: Westview, 1999.

Parry, Geraint, George Moyser, and Neil Day. *Political Participation and Democracy in Britain*. New York: Cambridge University Press, 1991.

Rose, Richard, and Ian McAllister. *The Loyalties of Voters: A Lifetime Learning Model*. Newbury Park, CA: Sage, 1990.

Ruane, Joseph, and Jennifer Todd. *The Dynamics of Conflict in Northern Ireland*. New York: Cambridge University Press, 1996.

Townshend, Charles. *Making the Peace: Public Order and Public Security*. New York: Oxford University Press, 1993.

Chapter 5

BRITAIN:
PATTERNS OF INTERACTION

In Britain, as in most democratic countries, the relationship between people and political parties is complex, a two-way street in which each influences the other. The parties project something called **party image**, what people think of the party's policies, leaders, and ideology. Most voters, on the other hand, carry in their heads a **party identification**, a long-term tendency to think of themselves as "Tory" or "Democrat" or whatever. The strategy of intelligent party leadership is to project a party image that wins the loyalty of large numbers of voters and gets them to identify permanently with that party. If they can do this, the party prospers and wins many elections.

Questions to Consider

1. What is party image? Party identification?
2. What is a "safe seat" and how do you get one?
3. Who picks British candidates?
4. What did Tony Blair call his party? What did it mean?
5. Why do the Liberal Democrats have such an uphill struggle?
6. How did Thatcher differ from a traditional Tory?
7. What is the big British labor confederation? How big?
8. Where and what is the Question Hour?
9. How democratic is Britain? As much as the United States?

Both party image and party identification are reasonably clear in Britain: Most Britons recognize what the main parties stand for in general terms, and most identify with a party. The situation is never static, however, for the parties constantly change the images they project, and some voters lose their party identification and shift their votes.

In every country, parents contribute heavily to their children's party identification. In Britain, if both parents are of the same party, most of their children first identify with that party, although this may later erode as young people develop their own perspectives. By the same token, party images are rather clear, and most Britons are able to see differences between their two largest parties: Labour aiming at helping people through social and educational reforms, and Conservatives aiming at economic growth through hard work with little state intervention.

For confirmed Labour or Conservative voters—those whose party identification closely matches the image of their preferred party—there is little doubt about whom to vote for. Until recently, most British voters were reliably Labour or Conservative. The **swing** vote are those who move their votes among parties, either because their party identification is not strong, or their perceptions of the parties' images shift, or both. A swing of a few percentage points can determine who will form the next government, for if each constituency shifts a little one way, say, toward Labour, the Labour candidate will win in many constituencies. Single-member districts often exaggerate percentage trends and turn them into large majorities of **seats**.

The game of British electoral politics consists of the parties trying to mobilize all of their party identifiers—that is, making sure their people bother to vote—plus winning over the uncommitted swing vote. In 1970 the Labour government of Harold Wilson suffered a surprise defeat by the Conservatives under Edward Heath. Labour identifiers had not suddenly switched parties; rather, some were unhappy with Wilson's policies and did not vote.

National and Local Party

Political scientists used to describe the British national party—Conservative or Labour—as nearly all-powerful, able to dictate to local party organizations whom to nominate for Parliament. As usual, though, when you look more closely you find that things are more complicated.

The name of the game for parliamentary candidates is the **safe seat** and getting adopted by the local **constituency** organization to run for it. Party leaders are normally assigned very safe seats, for it is highly embarrassing if one of them loses his or her seat in the Commons. Prime Minister Blair, for example, represents Sedgefield, a working-class constituency in the northeast of England. About 450 (of 646) seats are usually considered safe. There is a bargaining relationship between the parties' London headquarters and the local constituency party. The local party often requests lists of possible candidates from headquarters, settles on one, and then gets it approved by the central headquarters. Unlike the U.S. system, there is both national and local input into British candidate selection with a veto on both sides.

Some constituency organizations insist that a candidate actually live in the district. Americans expect all candidates to be from the district they represent; those who are not are called **carpetbaggers** and have an uphill battle. Most countries, however, including Britain, impose no such requirements, although being a local person can help. Some British constituencies like their people to establish a residence there once they have won. But many constituencies do not insist that their MP actually live there; after all, the MP's job is mainly in London, and periodic visits are sufficient for him or her to hear complaints and maintain ties with electors. Besides, in Britain, party is more important than personality. In any given House of Commons, probably a minority of MPs are natives of the constituency they represent.

What about the unsafe seats, those where the other party usually wins? These are the testing grounds for energetic newcomers to politics. The Conservative or Labour **central offices** in London may send a promising beginner to a constituency organization that knows it cannot win. Again, the local unit must approve the candidate. Even if the candidate loses, his or her energy and ability are carefully watched—by measuring how much better the candidate did than the previous one—and promising comers are marked. For the next election, the London headquarters may offer the candidate a safer constituency, one where he or she stands a better chance. Finally, the candidate either wins an election in a contested constituency, is adopted by a safe constituency, or bows out of politics. Many of Britain's top politicians, including several prime ministers (Blair among them), lost their first races and were transferred to other constituencies. There is no stigma attached; it is normal, part of the training and testing of a British politician.

party image   Electorate's perception of a given party. (See page 59.)

party identification   Psychological attachment of voter to political party. (See page 59.)

swing   Voters who change party from one election to next. (See page 59.)

seat   Membership in a legislature. (See page 59.)

safe seat   Constituency where voting has long favored a given party.

constituency   The district or population that elects a legislator.

carpetbagger   In U.S. usage, candidate from outside the constituency.

central office   London headquarters of British political party.

Politics within the Parties

British political parties, like British cabinets, are balancing acts. A party leader must neither pay too much attention to his or her party's factions nor totally ignore them. In constructing their policies, leaders usually try to give various factions a say but keep the whole thing under moderate control with an eye to winning the next election. The Labour party, portraying itself as more democratic, elects its leader at an annual party conference. Tories tried that for a time but in 2005 reverted to their old elite tradition of having only Conservative MPs elect their chief, not a party conference.

general election   British for nationwide vote for MPs.

Party leaders must balance between sometimes extremist party militants and a generally moderate voting public. If a party takes too firm an ideological stand—too left in the case of Labour or too right in the Conservative case—it costs the party votes. Thus party leaders tend to hedge and moderate their positions, trying to please both the true believers within their party and the general electorate. If they slip in this balancing act, they can lose either party members or voters or both. When Labour veered left in the 1980s and the Conservatives followed their hard-right Thatcher course, the centrist Liberal Democratic Alliance (later turned into a party) won a quarter of the 1983 vote, a warning to both major parties.

Although long described as ideologically moderate, both the British Labour and Conservative parties have important ideological viewpoints within their ranks. The Labour party is divided into "left" and "right" wings. The Labour left, springing from a tradition of militant trade unionism and intellectual radicalism, wants nationalization of industry, the dismantling of "public" schools, higher taxes

Democracy

2005: LABOUR SQUEAKS THROUGH

In the May 2005 **general election**, after eight years in office, Britain's Labour party won a third term, the first time Labour had done that. Its vote dropped from 41 percent in 2001 to 35 percent, but Labour still won a majority of Commons' 646 seats. Remember, Britain's electoral system overrepresents the winning party, just as in the United States. As usual for Britain, 2005 gave Labour only a plurality of the votes cast; since 1935 no British party has scored an actual majority. Turnout was a weak 61.3 percent (but higher than 59.4 percent in 2001).

The Conservatives gained a little in the popular vote and moved up from 25 percent of the seats to 30 percent. The Liberal Democrats gained too but were still underrepresented because their voters are territorially dispersed. The rest of the vote, 10.5 percent,

was scattered among small, mostly regional parties. Scottish, Welsh, and Northern Irish parties won a few seats each.

Labour won again because the British economy was excellent; its unemployment rate was the lowest in thirty years. Many Labour supporters, however, detested Blair ("Bush's poodle") for supporting President Bush in the Iraq War and voted Lib Dem. The Tories could not use this issue because they also supported U.S. policy on Iraq. The third Tory chief in four years, Michael Howard, made anti-immigration the Conservatives' big issue, but it never caught fire. The Tories became known as the "nasty party" with little positive to offer. Howard resigned after the 2005 elections, and the Conservatives were divided and unfocused.

	% Votes		Seats	
	2005	*2001*	*2005*	*2001*
Labour	35.2	40.7	356 (55%)	413 (63%)
Conservative	32.3	31.7	197 (30%)	166 (25%)
Liberal Democrat	22.0	18.3	62 (10%)	52 (8%)

Marxist Follower of socialist theories of Karl Marx.

Trotskyist Follower of Marxist but anti-Stalin theories of Leon Trotsky.

New Labour Tony Blair's name for his very moderate Labour party.

traditional Tory Moderate or centrist Conservative, not *Thatcherite*.

Thatcherite Free-market, anti-welfarist ideology of former British Prime Minister Margaret Thatcher.

neoliberalism Revival of free-market economics, exemplified by *Thatcherites*.

on the rich, leaving the European Union, and no nuclear weapons—British or U.S. Some **Marxists** and **Trotskyists** have won Labour offices. The Labour right, on the other hand, is moderate and centrist. It favors some of the welfarist approach of Continental social-democratic parties, such as the German SPD, but now wants no government takeovers of industry or higher taxes. It is pro-NATO, pro-Europe, and pro-American in foreign policy. The rightists in Labour argue that the left wing's ideas are extremist and cost the party votes. With Tony Blair, the Labour right won and told the left to shut up. For the 1997 election, Blair called his party **New Labour**, friendly to business, growth, and political reform.

As an amorphous party proud of its pragmatism, Conservatives were long thought immune to ideological controversy or factional viewpoints. This is not completely true, for the Tories comprise two broad streams of thought, which we might label as traditional and Thatcherite tendencies. The former is not a U.S.-style conservative, advocating a totally free economy with no government intervention. Instead, the **traditional Tory** wants a party that takes everybody's interests into account, plus traditional ways of doing things, and under the guidance of people born and bred to lead. This has been called a "one-nation" Tory.

The **Thatcherite** wing (which traces back to nineteenth-century liberalism and is called **neoliberalism** in Europe) is like American conservativism: They want to roll back government and free the economy. After World War II this view crept into the Conservative party and, with the 1975 elevation of Margaret Thatcher to party chief, moved to the forefront. Under Thatcher, the

Democracy

THE STRUGGLE OF THE LIBERAL DEMOCRATS

Public-opinion polls at times suggest that the Liberal Democratic party could become Britain's second-largest party. In some constituencies they already are. Widespread disillusionment with the two large parties gave the Liberal Democrats a boost in the 2005 elections, because they were the only ones opposed to the Iraq war. The Lib Dems, like the Liberals before them, used to be a center party between Labour and Tories, but now that Labour has taken over the center, the Lib Dems have taken up positions often to the left of the Labour party.

The Liberal Democrats were born of the 1988 merger of the old Liberal party and the small, new Social Democratic party that in 1981 had broken away from Labour. The two strands did not see eye-to-eye. On many questions—especially on the economy and defense matters—the Social Democrats were more conservative than the Liberals. The Liberals tended

to be ultra-liberal on questions of gay rights and open immigration. They wanted Britain out of NATO and free of nuclear weapons. True to their origins in the right wing of the Labour party, the Social Democrats were not unilateral disarmers and felt that lifestyle questions cost the party votes. The new party is a parallel to the many and incoherent viewpoints of the U.S. Democratic party.

The British electoral system—single-member districts with plurality win—is brutal on third parties (just as it is in the United States), especially those like the Liberal Democrats that are territorially dispersed. This discourages potential voters, who do not want to waste their votes on a party they fear will never be in power. The Liberal Democrats' great hope is to bring to Britain some elements of a proportional-representation election system.

traditional Tories were dubbed **wets**, the militant Thatcherites **dries**. (The terms were taken from boarding-school slang in which "wets" are frightened little boys who wet their pants, and "dries" are strong and brave lads who do not.)

The trouble here is that some old-style British Conservatives find total capitalism almost as threatening as socialism. As industries went bankrupt in record number, Thatcher faced a revolt of Tory "wets" against her "dry" policies. After Major took over, Thatcherite MPs sought to dump him. Attitudes toward European unity still split the Tories. Thatcher favored the Common Market but opposed turning it into a European Union that infringed on British sovereignty. She and followers were dubbed **Euroskeptics**. Major and his followers were enthusiastically pro-Europe—**Euroenthusiasts**—including the 1993 Maastricht Treaty, which took European unity a big step forward. Tory chief Michael Howard, a Euroskeptic, had trouble leading a party split between forward-looking "modernizers" and backward-looking "traditionalists" and resigned after losing the 2005 elections.

wets In Thatcher's usage, Tories too timid to apply her militant *neoliberalism*.

dries In Thatcher's usage, Tories who shared her *neoliberal* vision.

Euroskeptic Does not wish to strengthen EU at expense of national sovereignty.

Euroenthusiast Likes EU and wishes to strengthen it.

charisma (pronounced "kar-isma"; Greek for gift) political drawing power.

Democracy

SAVING LABOUR FROM THE UNIONS

From its 1983 electoral disaster, the Labour party struggled to recover. Part of its problem was a too-left party image. Another part was its doddering and ineffective leader, Michael Foot. At its annual conference that fall, the Labour party tried to repair both areas by overwhelmingly choosing as its new leader Neil Kinnock, a silver-tongued Welshman as charming as Margaret Thatcher was aloof. At forty-one, Kinnock, son of a coal miner, was the youngest Labour leader ever. Kinnock first had to curb Labour extremists; he got the Trotskyist Militant Tendency faction expelled (it formed a miniparty). Kinnock did well, lifting Labour from 27.6 percent of the popular vote in 1983 to 35.2 percent in 1992. But he came across as too slick and was still hurt by the Tory charge that Labour was dominated by the unions. Labour indeed was founded by and heavily based on trade unions, some led by militant socialists who would rather lose elections than lose their principles.

Following Labour's fourth defeat in a row in 1992, Kinnock resigned, making way for John Smith, a fifty-three-year-old Scottish lawyer even more pragmatic than Kinnock. Smith, a wooden speaker with little **charisma**, set out to reorient Labour more to the middle than the working class. Higher taxes and public ownership were out; discipline in education was in. But Smith had to break the union hold on the Labour party. Many union leaders resisted; they liked being able to control—through the proxy votes of millions of union members—90 percent of the vote at Labour's annual conferences. This union domination, often with a strong leftist slant, rendered Labour unacceptable to most British voters. In 1993, Smith got a change in Labour's rules to return the candidate selection process back to local party organizations; unions now control less than half the conference votes. In 1994 Smith died of a heart attack.

Tony Blair then took on the unions and got the party to drop its Clause Four, part of its constitution since 1918, that called for the "common ownership of the means of production," in other words, socialism. With Blair's very moderate 1996 manifesto, Labour—now called "New Labour"—started looking a lot like the U.S. Democrats. Although union and leftist militants dislike Blair, Labour's membership and electoral support climbed until it won three elections in a row, 1997, 2001, and 2005. It was not just Blair's doing, though; the process of pushing Labour back to the center had been underway since Kinnock began it in 1983.

As Labour had done earlier, the Tories tried to rebrand themselves by naming a fresh, young person as their leader in 2005: David Cameron (then thirty-nine). With Cameron—a product of Eton and Oxford, and a modernizer and moderate aiming to attract young Britons—Tory fortunes have climbed.

■ Parties and Interest Groups

What politicians say and what they deliver are two different things. Politicians speak to different audiences. To party rank and file they affirm party gospel (championing either the welfare state or free enterprise, as the case may be). To the electorate as a whole they usually tone down their ideological statements and offer vague slogans, such as "Stability and prosperity," or "Time for a change." But quietly, usually behind the scenes, politicians are also striking important deals with influential interest groups representing industry, commerce, professions, and labor. A large fraction of the British electorate belong to at least one interest group.

Trades Union Congress   TUC, British labor federation, equivalent to the U.S. AFL-CIO.

interested member   MP known to represent an interest group.

sleaze factor   Public perception of politicians on the take.

Confederation of British Industry Leading British business association, equivalent to U.S. National Association of Manufacturers.

Some 25 percent of the British work force is unionized, down from 55 percent when Thatcher took office but still a much higher percentage than in the United States or France (but only half that of Sweden). Labor unions are constituent members of the Labour party and, until 1993, controlled a majority of votes at Labour's annual conference, contributed the most to the party's budgets and campaign funds, and provided grass-roots manpower and organization. Especially important are the views of the head of the **Trades Union Congress** (TUC). No Labour party leader can totally ignore the wishes of Britain's union leaders.

This opened up Labour to charges that it is run by and for the unions, which earned a reputation as too far left, too powerful, and too ready to strike. To counteract this, both Labour party and union leaders deny union dominance. Indeed, one Labour party campaign tactic is to claim that only the Labour party can control the unions, rather than the other way around. Tony Blair forcefully pointed out to union chiefs the folly of losing one election after another. Ironically, Blair's Thatcherite economic policies pushed some British unions back into militancy. Blair partially broke the close association of labor federation to social-democratic party that had been the norm for the industrialized countries of Northern Europe, as we shall see when we study Germany.

Dozens of union members sit as Labour MPs in Parliament; dozens more MPs are beholden to local unions for their election. This union bloc inside the Labour party can force a Labour government to moderate measures that might harm unions. At times, however, Labour party chiefs have made union leaders back down, explaining to them that if the unions get too much, the Labour party will lose elections. To reiterate, to be a party leader means performing a balancing act among several forces.

MPs known to directly represent special interests—an **interested member**—are not limited to the Labour side. Numerous Tory MPs are interested members for various industries and do not try to hide it. When the connection is concealed or when money changes hands, an MP pushing for favors to a group becomes known as sleazy. The **sleaze factor** hurt the Tories under Major, but several Labourites under Blair got caught accepting money from questionable sources; some resigned. Politicians taking money on the side are found everywhere, in all parties.

The Conservative counterpart of the TUC is the influential **Confederation of British Industry** (CBI), formed by an amalgamation of three smaller groups in 1965. The CBI speaks for most British employers but has no formal links to the Conservative party, even though their views are often parallel. The CBI was delighted at Thatcher's antinationalization policies, although British industrialists gulped when they found this meant withdrawal of **subsidies** to their own industries. Thatcher could not totally ignore them, for CBI members and money support the Tories, and dozens of CBI-affiliated company directors occupy Conservative seats in Commons.

subsidy   Government financial help to individual or business.

Question Hour   Time reserved in Commons for MPs to query ministers.

The Parties Face Each Other

There are two ways of looking at British elections. The first is to see them as three- to four-week campaigns coming once every few years, each a model of brevity and efficiency, especially compared to the long, expensive U.S. campaigns. Another way, however, is to see them as nearly permanent campaigns that begin the day a new Parliament reconvenes after the latest balloting. The formal campaign may be only a few weeks, but long before then the opposition party is planning how to oust the current government.

The chief arena for this is the House of Commons. Unlike the U.S. Congress, British parliamentarians are seldom animated by a spirit of bipartisanship. The duty of the opposition is to oppose, and this they do by accusing the government of everything from incompetence and corruption to sexual scandal. The great weapon here is embarrassment, making a cabinet minister look like a fool. The time for this is the **Question Hour**, held Monday through Thursday when Commons opens. By tradition, this hour is reserved for MPs to aim written questions at cabinet ministers, who are on the front bench on a rotating basis. Most Wednesdays at noon, for example, Prime Minister Blair personally countered Tory criticism in Commons. Other cabinet ministers face questions on other days of the week. Each written question can be followed up by supplementary oral questions.

Political Culture

THE PROFUMO SCANDAL

In Commons' game of embarrassment, a classic play came with the 1963 Profumo affair. The Labour opposition got wind that Tory War Minister (at the departmental, not the cabinet, level) John Profumo was dating a party girl who at the same time was dating the Soviet naval attaché, a known spy. Questioned by Labour in the Commons, Profumo swore there had been no impropriety in his relationship with Christine Keeler and threatened to sue anyone who said otherwise. Being a gentleman of impeccable credentials—Harrow, Oxford, army brigadier—Profumo was believed by the Macmillan government. But the scandal refused to die down; it began to appear that security had been breached and that Profumo had been set up for blackmail.

Sensational news stories charged the Conservative government with laxity on national security, covering up for one of its "old boys," and debauchery at the highest levels of the Establishment. There was some truth to the charges, and Profumo resigned in shame. It was not, however, the shame of a married man, forty-eight, caught with a twenty-one-year-old call girl. That was forgivable. What was unforgivable in British political culture was that a gentleman had lied to Parliament. The Tory government mishandled the incident; Conservative MPs lost confidence in Prime Minister Macmillan, and voters lost confidence in the Conservative party, which was voted out the following year.

The opposition tries to push a minister into an awkward position where he or she has to tell a lie, fluff an answer, or break into anger. Then the opposition, in effect, smirks, "You see, they are not fit to govern."

■ The Cabinet and the Civil Servants

As we discussed earlier, British cabinet ministers are generalists, not specialists, and are chosen more for political reasons than for any special ability to run their departments. Who then does run them? The nominal head of each British department is the minister; he or she represents that ministry in cabinet discussions and defends it in Commons. But the minister does not run the department; civil servants do.

permanent secretary   Highest civil servant who runs a ministry, nominally under a minister.

knighthood   Lowest rank of nobility, carries title "Sir."

Treasury   British ministry that supervises economic policy and budgets of other ministries.

Ministers come and go every few years; the highest civil servants, known as **permanent secretaries** are there much longer. Permanent secretaries often have an edge on their ministers in social and economic terms as well. Most permanent secretaries are knighted later in life while few ministers are. Although **knighthood** is now purely honorific in Britain, it still conveys social superiority. Permanent secretaries earn more than ministers, in some cases nearly twice as much.

Ministers find it nearly impossible to fire or transfer permanent secretaries, who have a say in determining who will replace them when they retire or leave for well-paid positions in private industry; they tend to be a self-selecting elite. Permanent secretaries always play the role of humble, obedient servants, but some ministers come to wonder just who the boss really is.

The permanent secretary is assisted by several deputy secretaries who in turn are supported by undersecretaries and assistant secretaries. These names look like those of an American department, but there is a major catch: In most U.S. departments, all or most of these people are political appointees, serving at the pleasure of the president and resigning when a new president takes office. In Britain, only the ministers assisted by some junior ministers—about a hundred persons in all—change with a new government. What in America are temporary political appointees are permanent officials in Britain.

This gives them power. They are not amateurs but know their ministry—its personnel, problems, interests, and budget. Knowledge is power, and over time top civil servants come to quietly exercise a lot of it. While permanent secretaries or their assistants never—well, hardly ever—go public with their viewpoints, they reveal them through the kinds of ideas, programs, bills, and budgets they submit to the minister, their nominal boss. The minister theoretically commands them, but in practice he or she simply does not know enough about the workings of the ministry. Instead, the minister relies on them. Accordingly, while most bills and budget proposals pass through the cabinet, they do not originate there. The permanent civil servants do the jobs that are the stuff of governance.

The real power among the several British ministries is the **Treasury**. Sometimes called the "department of departments," Treasury not only supervises the main lines of economic policy but has the last word on who gets what among the ministries. Anyone with a bright idea in British government—a new minister or an innovative civil servant—soon comes up against the stone wall of Treasury, "the ministry that says no."

Britain's treasury minister goes by the old name of Chancellor of the Exchequer—originally the king's checker of taxes—and is now the second most powerful figure in the cabinet, the first being the prime minister. Some Chancellors of the Exchequer later become prime ministers, so the person in that office is watched close-ly. The popular and effective Chancellor Gordon Brown in the Blair cabinet was expected to succeed Blair.

> **rule of anticipated reactions** Friedrich's theory that politicians plan their moves so as not to anger the public.

Under the Chancellor are the usual secretaries and civil servants, but they are a breed unto themselves, smarter and more powerful than other bureaucrats. Operating on a team-spirit basis, Treasury chaps trust only other Treasury chaps, for only Treasury can see the whole picture of the British government and economy and how the many parts interrelate. The other departments see only their corner, hence they should not be heed-ed. This attitude gives Treasury and its people an image of cold, callous remoteness, "government by mandarins"—but no one has tried to replace them.

The Civil Service and Interest Groups

We mentioned earlier the relationship between interest groups and political parties. But this is only one way interest groups make their voices heard and is often not the most important way. Much interest-group impact is in their quiet, behind-the-scenes contact with the bureaucracy. In-deed, with Parliament's role curtailed as a result of powerful prime ministers and party discipline,

Democracy

HOW DEMOCRATIC IS BRITAIN?

The power of bureaucrats brings us to a fine irony. In centuries of British political evolution, we have seen how Britons marched toward democracy by first lim-iting the power of the monarch and then expanding participation. If we look closely, though, we notice that much important decision making is only partly democratically controlled. Civil servants make much policy with no democratic input.

Does this mean there is no real democracy in Britain? No, it means we must understand that no country exercises perfect control over its bureaucracy and that parties and elections are only attempts to do so.

Indeed, most of the interactions we have talked about are not under any form of popular control. Ideological infighting, the influence of interest groups on parties and the bureaucracy, the rela-tionship of top civil servants with ministers, the granting of titles—these and other interactions are removed from democratic control. The people do not even choose whom they get to vote for; that is a mat-ter for party influentials. All the people get to do is vote every few years, and the choice is limited.

Again, does this mean there is no democracy in Britain? No, not at all. Some people have an exag-gerated vision of democracy as a system in which everyone gets to decide on everything. Such a sys-tem never existed at the national level, nor could it. The most we can ask of a democracy is that the leading team—in Britain, the prime minister and cabinet—are held accountable periodically in elec-tions. This keeps them on their toes and anxious to pay attention to the public good, holds down special favors and corruption, and makes sure the bureaucracy functions. It is in the fear of electoral punishment that Britain, or any other country, qual-ifies as a democracy. What the great Carl J. Friedrich called the **rule of anticipated reactions** keeps the governors attentive. We will learn not to expect much more of political systems.

peerage   A Lord or Lady, higher than knighthood.

and cabinet ministers themselves dependent on permanent civil servants, many interest groups ask themselves, "Why bother with Parliament? Why not go straight to where the action is, the bureaucracy?"

This approach is especially true of business and industry; the major effort of the unions is still focused on the Labour party. The reason for this is partly in the nature of what trade unions want as opposed to what business groups want. Unions want general policies on employment, wages, welfare, and so on, that apply to tens of millions of people. Industry usually wants specific, narrow rulings on taxes, subsidies, regulations, and the like that apply to a few firms. Thus unions tend to battle in the more open environment of party policy while business groups often prefer to quietly take a government official to lunch.

In working closely with a branch of Britain's economic life, a given ministry comes to see itself not as an impartial administrator but as a concerned and attentive helper. After all, if that industry falters, it reflects on the government agency assigned to supervise it. In this manner civil servants come to see leaders of economic interest groups as their "clients" and to reflect their clients' views. When this happens—and it happens in every country—the industry is said to have "captured" or "colonized" the executive department.

Reinforcing this pattern is the interchange between civil service and private industry. A permanent secretary can make much more money in business than in Whitehall; every now and then one of them leaves government service for greener pastures. (We will also see this pattern in France and Japan.) By the same token, business executives are sometimes brought into high administrative positions on the dubious theory that if they can run a company well, they can do the same for government. The point is that cozy relationships develop between civil servants and private business.

Political Culture

THE UTILITY OF DIGNITY

Another quaint British holdover from the past is the monarch's bestowal of an honor such as knighthood. But more than quaint, it is a payoff system that serves a number of purposes. The granting of titles is a reward and an encouragement to retire, opening positions to fresh, energetic younger people. A person looking forward to a knighthood (Sir) or a **peerage** (Lord) is more likely to go quietly. These honors also civilize recipients; even militant union leaders and rapacious businessmen start talking philosophically about the common good once they have titles in front of their names.

The queen awards these and other distinctions only on the advice of the prime minister, who has a small staff that watches for meritorious civil servants, business people, unionists, soldiers, politicians, scholars, artists, and writers, and recommends who should get what. In addition to becoming knights and peers, distinguished Britons may be named to the Order of the British Empire, Order of the Garter, Order of Merit, Order of the Bath, the Royal Victorian Order, and many others. The granting of honors is a part of British political culture, a way of bolstering loyalty to and cooperation with the system.

Key Terms

carpetbagger (p. 60)
central office (p. 60)
charisma (p. 63)
Confederation of British Industry (p. 64)
constituency (p. 60)
dries (p. 63)
Euroenthusiast (p. 63)
Euroskeptic (p. 63)
general election (p. 61)
interested member (p. 64)
knighthood (p. 66)
Marxist (p. 62)
neoliberalism (p. 62)
New Labour (p. 62)
party identification (p. 60)
party image (p. 60)

peerage (p. 68)
permanent secretary (p. 66)
Question Hour (p. 65)
rule of anticipated reactions (p. 67)
safe seat (p. 60)
seat (p. 60)
sleaze factor (p. 64)
subsidy (p. 65)
swing (p. 60)
Thatcherite (p. 62)
Trades Union Congress (TUC) (p. 64)
traditional Tory (p. 62)
Treasury (p. 66)
Trotskyist (p. 62)
wets (p. 63)

Further Reference

Barberis, Peter. *The Elite of the Elite: Permanent Secretaries in the British Higher Civil Service*. Brook-field, VT: Ashgate, 1996.

Bartle, John, and Anthony King, eds. *Britain at the Polls, 2005*. Washington, D.C.: CQ Press, 2005.

Bevir, Mark, and R. A. W. Rhodes. *Interpreting British Governance*. New York Routledge, 2003.

Brivati, Brian, and Richard Heffernan, eds. *The Labour Party: A Centenary History*. New York: St. Martin's, 2000.

Dunleavy, Patrick, Andrew Gamble, Richard Heffernan, and Ian Holliday. *Developments in British Politics 6*. New York: Palgrave, 2002.

Geddes, Andrew, and Jonathan Tonge, eds. *Labour's Second Landslide: The British General Election 2001*. New York: Palgrave, 2002.

Hickson, Kevin, ed. *The Political Thought of the Conservative Party*. New York: Palgrave, 2005.

Kelly, Richard, ed. *Changing Party Policy in Britain: An Introduction*. Malden, MA: Blackwell, 1999.

King, Anthony, and Iain McLean, eds. *Rational Choice and British Politics: An Analysis of Rhetoric and Manipulation from Peel to Blair*. New York: Oxford, 2001.

McKinstry, Leo. *Fit to Govern*. London: Bantam Press, 1996.

McLean, Iain. *Rational Choice and British Politics: An Analysis of Rhetoric and Manipulation from Peel to Blair*. New York: Oxford, 2001.

Norris, Pippa, and Christopher Wlezien, eds. *Britain Votes 2005*. New York: Oxford University Press, 2005.

Seyd, Patrick, and Paul Whiteley. *New Labour's Grassroots: The Transformation of the Labour Party Membership*. New York: Palgrave, 2002.

Chapter 6

WHAT BRITONS QUARREL ABOUT

Britain was in economic decline for decades. At first it was only **relative decline** as the economies of West Europe and Japan grew more rapidly than the British economy. By the 1970s, however, Britain was in **absolute decline** that left people with lower living standards as inflation outstripped wage increases. The first industrial nation was embarrassed to see Italy overtake it in per capita GDP in the 1980s. Likewise, Britain's former colonies of Hong Kong and Singapore have higher per caps than does Britain. In Britain, **deindustrialization** seemed to be taking place; in some years the British GDP shrank. They called it the "British disease," and some Americans feared it was contagious.

Questions to Consider

1. What is the difference between relative and absolute decline?
2. What was the Thatcher cure for Britain's economy? Did it work?
3. What is the Beer thesis on Britain's decline?
4. What is productivity and why is it so important?
5. In what areas could Britain undergo constitutional reform?
6. Did Britain's National Health Service work? Compared to U.S.?
7. What is devolution? Does it indicate quasi-federalism?
8. Did Northern Ireland return to peace? Why or why not?
9. What is Britain's stance on the European Union? On the euro?

■ The "British Disease"

Why did Britain decline? There are two basic approaches to such a complex problem. One begins with what happens in people's attitudes—a psycho-cultural approach. The other begins with what happens in the physical world—a politico-economic approach. The two are not mutually exclusive but have a chicken-egg relationship to each other: One feeds into the other.

Some emphasize British nonwork attitudes as the root of the problem. The old aristocracy, which disdained work as tawdry moneymaking, was never thoroughly displaced in Britain. Rather, the rising entrepreneurs aped the old elite and became gentlemen of leisure and culture. In public schools and Oxbridge, young Britons learn to despise commercial and technical skills in favor of the humanities. The emphasis was on having wealth rather than creating it. Accordingly, Britain tended to lack daring and innovative capitalists. Many Britons prefer more leisure time to more money.

The British class system makes matters worse. British managers—mostly middle class—are snobbish toward workers; they do not mix with them and provide inadequate guidance and incentives. British workers react by showing solidarity with their "mates" and more loyalty to their union than to their company. If the psycho-cultural approach is correct, the only way to save Britain is to change British culture, but deep-seated attitudes resist change.

The other approach, the politico-economic, argues that the bad attitudes reflect faulty government policy. Change the policy to create a new context, and attitudes will change. Thatcherites propounded this view, blaming the growth of the welfare state that Labour introduced in 1945. This

relative decline   Failing to keep up economically with other nations. (See page 71.)

absolute decline   Growing weaker economically compared to one's own past. (See page 71.)

deindustrialization   Decline of heavy industry. (See page 71.)

consumption   Buying things.

production   Making things.

productivity   Efficiency with which things are made.

inflation   Increase in most prices.

monetarism   Friedman's theory that rate of growth of money supply governs much economic development.

pluralistic stagnation   Theory that out-of-control interest groups produce policy log jams.

counterculture   Rejection of conventional values, as in 1960s.

pluralism   Autonomous interaction of social groups on themselves and on government.

let many **consume** without **producing** and subsidized inefficient industries. Unions, given free rein by previous governments, raised wages and lowered **productivity**. The growing costs of the welfare state drained away funds that should have gone for investment. Insufficient investment meant insufficient production, which meant stagnating living standards. Cut both welfare benefits and industry subsidies and you will force—with some pain—a change in attitudes, argued Thatcherites.

◼ The Thatcher Cure

The Thatcher cure for Britain's economic problems is still debated in Britain. Thatcherites argue that her policies were not implemented thoroughly and long enough. Anti-Thatcherites in all the parties argue the policies had been brutal and ineffective. The way Thatcherites see it, the permissive policies of both Labour and previous Conservative governments had expanded welfare programs beyond the country's ability to pay for them. Unions won wage increases out of line with productivity. Nationalized and subsidized industries lost money. The result: **inflation** and falling productivity that were making Britain the sick man of Europe. The cure, in part, came from the **monetarist** theory of American economist (and Nobel Prize winner) Milton Friedman, which posits too-rapid growth of the money supply as the cause of inflation. Thatcher cut bureaucracy, the growth of welfare, and subsidies to industry in an effort to control Britain's money supply and restore economic health.

Key Concepts

"PLURALISTIC STAGNATION"

Harvard political scientist Samuel Beer advanced a provocative thesis on the cause of Britain's decline: too many interest groups making too many demands on parties who are too willing to promise everyone everything. The result was **pluralistic stagnation** as British groups scrambled for welfare benefits, pay hikes, and subsidies for industry. The two main parties bid against each other with promises of more benefits to more groups. In the late 1960s, a strong **counterculture** emerged in Britain, which repudiated traditional civility and deference and made groups' demands more strident. With every group demanding and getting more, no one saw any reason for self-restraint that would leave them behind. Government benefits fed union wage demands, which fed inflation, which fed government benefits . . .

The interesting point about the Beer thesis is that it blamed precisely what political scientists long celebrated as the foundation of freedom and democracy: **pluralism**. Beer demonstrated, though, that it can run amok; groups block each other and government, leading to what Beer called the "paralysis of public choice." Any comparison with your system?

Some Britons wondered if the cure was worse than the disease. Unemployment at one point reached 14 percent of the work force, thousands of firms went bankrupt, and Britain's GDP growth was still anemic. Even moderate Conservatives pleaded for her to relent, but Thatcher was not called the Iron Lady for nothing. "The lady's not for turning," she intoned. She saw the economic difficulties as a purge Britain needed to get well. One of her economists said: "I don't shed tears when I see inefficient factories shut down. I rejoice." Thatcher and her supporters repeated endlessly, "You cannot consume until you produce."

deregulation   Cutting governmental rules on industry.

privatization   Selling state-owned industry to private interests.

Gradually the argument began to take hold. Many Britons had to admit they had been consuming more than they were producing, that subsidized factories and mines were a drain on the economy, and that bitter medicine was necessary to correct matters. It was almost as if Britons had become guilty about their free rides and knew they now had to pay up. In the 1980s, more working-class Britons voted Tory than voted Labour.

But did Thatchernomics work? By the time the Tories left office in 1997 the picture was mixed but generally positive. Inflation was down and economic growth among the fastest in Europe. State-owned British Steel, British Leyland (motor vehicles), and other industries that had been nationalized since the war to prevent unemployment trimmed their bloated work forces and raised productivity. Many state-owned plants were sold off, a process called **privatization**. Competition was increased through **deregulation**. Renters of public housing got the chance to buy their homes at low cost, a move that made some of them Conservatives. Unions eased their wage and other demands, and union membership dropped sharply. Many weak firms went under, but thousands of new small and middle-sized firms sprang up. Capital and labor were channeled away from losing industries and into winners, exactly what a good economic system should do. A California-like computer industry produced a "silicon glen" in Scotland and a "software valley" around Cambridge University.

Part of the impact of Thatchernomics came from jolting workers out of their trade-union complacency ("I'm all right, Jack"). When the government's National Coal Board closed hundreds

Comparison

THE COST OF THE WELFARE STATE

The other side of the welfare state is how expensive it is. In 2004, all types of taxes at all levels of government took the percentages of GDP shown in the table on the right.

Almost all advanced industrialized countries have been cutting taxes. Most of the percentages shown in the table on the right are lower than a few years earlier, indicating growth in the overall economy and trims in welfare outlays.

Sweden	50
France	43
Italy	42
Euro area average	40
Britain	35
Germany	34
Canada	32
Australia	31
Japan	25
United States	25

Source: OECD.

entitlement Spending programs citizens are automatically entitled to, such as Social Security.

recession A shrinking economy, indicated by falling GDP.

of unprofitable pits and eliminated twenty thousand jobs, miners staged a long and bitter strike in 1984, which was supported by some other unionists. Thatcher would not back down; after a year, the miners did. (At about the same time, President Reagan faced down striking air-traffic controllers.) New legislation limited union chiefs' abilities to call strikes, and the number and length of strikes in Britain dropped drastically.

As in the United States in recent decades, income inequality grew in Britain. The number of Britons in families with less than half the average income increased under Thatcher and Major from 5 million in 1979 to 14 million in 1993. High youth unemployment led to urban riots. Major regional disparities appeared between a rich, resurgent South of England, with new high-tech industries, and a decaying, abandoned North, where unemployment hit hardest. Thatcher never did get a handle on government spending, much of which, like U.S. **entitlements**, must by law be paid. British welfare benefits actually climbed sharply during the Thatcher and Major years despite their best efforts to trim them. Cutting the welfare state is tempting but rarely successful; too many people have come to depend on its benefits. Furthermore, in the late 1980s, a credit and spending boom kicked inflation back up to over 10 percent, and the economy slumped into **recession**. Competitively, British productivity was low and its wages high, so Britain continued to lose manufacturing jobs to other countries.

Comparison

THE PRODUCTIVITY RACE

No production, no goodies. Production is what gets turned out. Productivity is how efficiently it gets turned out. You can have a lot of production with low productivity, the Soviet problem that brought down the Communist regime. Among the major economies, Britain's productivity was weak. In 2000, GDP per worker in the United States was 42 percent higher than in Britain, in France 13 percent higher, in Germany 7 percent higher, and in Japan 2 percent higher.

The growth of productivity—the additional amount a worker cranks out per hour from one year to the next—is the measure of future prosperity. Rapid growth in productivity means quickly rising standards of living; low growth means stagnation or even decline. The percent average annual growth in labor productivity from 1995 to 2004 is shown in the table on the right.

Ireland's rapid productivity growth was similar to Japan's in earlier decades. Newly industrializing countries, because they are starting from a low level, show the biggest percentage gains. After a while, all the easy gains have been made, and a country becomes

more "normal," like Japan. Earlier, U.S. productivity growth had been among the weakest of the industrialized countries. Its surge in the late 1990s reflected major investments in efficiency and information technology that made workers more productive.

Productivity does not tell the whole story of an economy, because it focuses on manufacturing. Advanced economies employ most people not in factories but in the service sector, where productivity gains are harder to make and to measure.

Ireland	5.1
United States	2.5
Japan	2.3
France	2.1
Britain	2.0
Germany	1.8
Canada	1.7
EU-15 average	1.5

Source: The Conference Board

Thatcher's main legacy is the changed terms of Britain's political debate. In 1945, Labour had shifted the debate to the welfare state, and Tories had to compete with them on their own terms, never seriously challenging the underlying premise that redistribution is good. Thatcher changed this all around and made the debate one about productivity and economic growth; now Labour had to compete on *her* terms. It was a historic shift, and one that influenced the political debate in other lands, including the United States. Labour Prime Minister Blair did not repudiate Thatcher's free-market economic policies; he stole them and possibly ran them better. In 2005 British unemployment was a low 4.7 percent while France's and Germany's were around 10 percent. And Britain had virtually no public debt or inflation. Britain had indeed turned around.

Democracy

WHICH BLAIR PROJECT?

Blair's chief project was not Britain's economy but its institutions. His bold constitutional reforms modernized Britain's political institutions, many of which had been little changed in centuries. Some of his projects were passed into law while others are still debated. Blair will go down as Britain's modernizer.

1. *A written constitution.* With no fixed limits, power can be abused in Britain. Written rules could make Britons freer, especially with the addition of . . .

2. *A bill of rights,* U.S.-style. Blair accomplished this by having Parliament adopt the European Convention on Human Rights as domestic law, bringing Britain into line with the rest of the EU, starting in 2000. For the first time Britons got legal guarantees of media freedom and protection from heavy-handed police methods.

3. *Judicial review.* Any bill Parliament passes is automatically constitutional in Britain. As in most of the world, British courts cannot check executive excesses. Many Britons admired the role of the U.S. Supreme Court, which, among other things, guarantees . . .

4. *Freedom of information.* Britain has an Official Secrets Act that comes close to censorship. All manner of government wrongdoing is concealed. Many Britons admired the U.S. Freedom of Information Act.

5. *A meaningful upper house.* As we discussed in Chapter 3, in 1999 Blair modernized Lords by kicking out most hereditary peers and leaving it largely in the hands of life peers. This still left it with little power. A next step would be to give it some powers to check Commons and the cabinet.

6. *Devolution,* which Blair carried out smartly in granting extensive home rule and elected assemblies to Northern Ireland, Scotland, and Wales. (See the subsequent discussions.)

7. *A new electoral system.* As we considered in Chapter 3, the traditional FPTP system overrewards the two big parties and penalizes third parties. Adding some PR ("topping off"), as is done in elections for the new Scottish and Welsh parliaments, would be much fairer, especially to the Lib Dems.

8. *Public services* are hurting in Britain. Education, railways, and the National Health Service lagged behind the rest of Europe. New management and money were needed to improve them, but would Britons be willing to pay higher taxes?

9. *Fox hunting* became an angry symbol of "a crisis in the countryside." Rural dwellers protest declining farm incomes, outsiders driving up home prices, and mishandling of a big hoof-and-mouth outbreak in 2001. Now they want to take away our old tradition and right of "riding to hounds," they complain. Their real message: more money to improve rural services.

A Privatization Too Far? Scotland's beautiful Isle of Skye used to be reached by a short ferry ride, but the new, private bridge costs $8 each way. Many Britons protest the new bridge as an example of privatization run amok, turning over a public service to private greed.

■ The Trouble with National Health

The centerpiece of Britain's extensive welfare state is the National Health Service (NHS), which went into operation in 1948 as part of Labour's longstanding commitment to helping working Britons. Before World War II, British medical care was spotty, and many Britons were too scrawny and unhealthy for military service during the war. Conservatives and the British Medical Association fought the NHS, but the tide was against them.

Did the NHS work? The answer is both yes and no. The British population is much healthier than it used to be. Infant mortality, one key measure of overall health standards, dropped from 64 out of 1,000 live births in 1931 to 5 now. The British working class has especially benefited. Britons spend only 9 percent of their GDP on health care but are more healthy than the Americans, who spend 15 percent.

But NHS has been unable to keep up with skyrocketing costs. Britons have become more elderly, and old people consume many times as much medical care as younger people. Technical advances in medicine are terribly expensive. The system requires many bureaucrats. With a staff of 1 million, the NHS is the largest employer in West Europe, but personnel and facilities have not kept pace with demand. The money simply is not there. If surgery is not for an emergency, patients may wait a year or more. The debate in Britain is over whether to keep funding the NHS by general tax revenues, which Labour favors, or to adopt European funding models, which include mandatory employee and employer contributions and a bigger role for private health care.

Is Northern Ireland Settled?

Alas, no. There is an unstable peace now in Ulster, but hatreds still run deep. Catholics and Protestants are more segregated than ever into two societies. There was hope for a settlement after thirty years of violence in Northern Ireland. In 1998, on Good Friday, the two sides reached a power-sharing agreement, but it soon failed as it did not settle the fundamental question: Should the North unify with the Republic of Ireland? What most Catholics want, Protestants angrily reject. The moderate parties on both sides shrank as the extremist parties grew. In 2005 the militant Democratic Unionists of Rev. Ian Paisley won nine of Ulster's eighteen seats. Gerry Adams, the Sinn Fein chief who once advocated violence, announced in 2005 that the IRA—which has lost support for its indiscriminate violence—would at last give up its arms and pursue its goals by political means, but Protestant militants did not believe it. Paisley calls Adams a terrorist, and indeed Adams is on the IRA's seven-member council.

Prime Minister Tony Blair took some of the credit for the **Good Friday agreement**; his Conservative predecessors would not negotiate with Sinn Fein. It looked good on paper. The agreement reopened the Northern Ireland Assembly at Stormont, which had been closed since 1974. Previously dominated by Protestants, it was one of the reasons for Catholic protest. It is now elected, using the type of proportional representation used in the Republic of Ireland. Ministries are awarded on a balanced basis; most of the parties in Stormont got at least one portfolio. First minister, for example, was leader of the (Protestant) Ulster Unionist party, but his deputy was leader of the (Catholic) Social Democratic and Labour party. Political scientists call such an arrangement **consociation**, sometimes useful to hold together fractured societies, but it could not achieve much in Northern Ireland.

Stormont's powers and budget could be substantial. It runs Northern Ireland's education, medical, social, housing, and agricultural services. In addition, a "north-south council" of officials from Northern Ireland and the Republic of Ireland supervises cross-border policies. The agreement was calculated to give peace a chance by involving both sides in governance, but they so mistrusted each other that London often has to suspend Stormont's powers and resume direct rule. The Good Friday agreement could not paper over Ulster's terrible division.

Good Friday agreement 1998 pact to share power in Northern Ireland.

consociation Sharing of political power at the executive level, giving all major parties cabinet positions.

subject Originally, a subject of the Crown; now means British citizen.

Commonwealth Organization of countries that were once British colonies.

Britain's Race Problem

British society, like U.S. society, is split along racial and religious lines. Whites have little to do with nonwhites and Muslims, and there is animosity between them. Starting in 1958, race riots flare in Britain every few years. Nonwhites, most born in Britain, are now about 7 percent (4 percent Asian, mostly Pakistanis, and 2 percent black) of Britain's population, many ghettoized in the declining industrial cities in the north of England.

The race/Muslim problem in Britain is a legacy of empire. Britain in 1948 legally made the natives of its many colonies British **subjects**, entitled to live and work in the United Kingdom. Although the colonies were granted independence from the late 1940s through the 1960s, as members of the British **Commonwealth** their people were still entitled to immigrate to Britain. In the 1950s, West Indians arrived from the Caribbean, then Indians and Pakistanis, taking lowly jobs that Britons did

regional nationalism Particularist and separatist movements in some peripheral areas.

not want, then sending for relatives. For years they labored in Britain's textile industry, but that has closed, leaving many Muslims unemployed. Britain now has more than 1.5 million Muslims, mostly Pakistanis. (France has far more Muslims.) Meanwhile, white resentment builds, especially among the working class in areas of industrial decline and high unemployment. Some Britons refer to "Londonistan" in a non-joking way. In 1967 an openly racist National Front formed, advocating the expulsion of all "coloureds" back to their native lands. Skinheads, supporting the Front or its successor British National party (BNP), like "Paki bashing." With slogans such as "Rights for Whites," the anti-immigrant vote grew but never won a seat in Parliament. The BNP was much weaker than its Continental counterparts such as the French National Front.

Geography

DEVOLUTION FOR SCOTLAND AND WALES

Britain, a highly centralized unitary state, has become a little less centralized. Northern Ireland, Scotland, and Wales show the center-periphery tensions that afflict many countries. In general, the farther from the nation's capital, the more regional resentment. Britain has the long Celtic memories of conquered Scots and Welsh. Wales has been a part of England since the Middle Ages; the thrones of England and Scotland were united in 1603, but only in 1707 did both countries agree to a single Parliament in London. The old resentments never died. Wales and Scotland were always poorer than England, leaving Welsh and Scots feel they were economically exploited.

In the twentieth century the political beneficiary of these feelings was the Labour party, which still holds sway in Wales and Scotland. Voting Labour in Scotland and Wales became a form of regional nationalism, a way of repudiating rule by England, which goes Conservative. Center-periphery tensions reveal themselves in voting patterns. In the 1960s the small Plaid Cymru (pronounced plyde kum-REE, meaning "Party of Wales") and the Scottish Nationalist party began to grow, and both win a few seats in Parliament.

Regional nationalism grew in many countries starting in the 1970s besides Wales and Scotland: Corsican and Breton in France, Quebecker in Canada, Basque and Catalan in Spain. In the 1990s, the Soviet Union and Yugoslavia fell apart. There are several causes of local separatism. Economics plays a role; local nationalists claim their regions are shortchanged by central governments. Nationalists emphasize their regions' distinct languages and cultures and demand that they be taught in schools. Some of the impulse behind local nationalism is the bigness and remoteness of the modern state, the feeling that important decisions are out of local control, made by distant bureaucrats. And often smoldering under the surface are historical resentments of a region that once was conquered, occupied, and deprived of its own identity. Whatever the mixture, local nationalism sometimes turns its adherents into fanatics willing to wreck the entire country to get their way. Happily, this did not happen in Britain. The Scots and Welsh never became as extreme as Basques in Spain or Corsicans in France.

In Scotland, the economic factor played a large part in its rising nationalism. When oil was discovered in the North Sea off Scotland in the 1960s, some Scots did not want to share the petroleum revenues with the United Kingdom as a whole: "It's Scotland's oil!" Oil offered Scotland the possibility of economic independence and self-government, of becoming something more than a poor, northerly part of Britain. (Alberta has much the same feeling about its oil.)

The leading issue for Welsh nationalists has been language, the ancient Celtic tongue of Cymric (pronounced *kim-rick*). Some 13 percent of Welsh speak

Two forces keep Muslims segregated: discrimination by whites and wanting to preserve their original faith and culture. Caught between two cultures, some unemployed and alienated Muslim youths fall under the sway of fanatic *Islamist* preachers (see page 550). In 2005 four Muslim youths (three of Pakistani origin but born in England, one born in Jamaica) set off three bombs on London's Underground and one on a bus that killed fifty-six and injured 700. Said one bitter young Muslim social worker, "When they bomb London, the bigger the better. I know it's going to happen because Sheikh bin Laden said so. Like Bali, like Turkey, like Madrid—I pray for it, I look forward to the day." A small but nontrivial minority of Britain's Muslims hate Britain. One possible side-effect came three weeks after the London bombings: The IRA ordered all its units to "dump arms" and use "exclusively political means." Muslim fanatics gave violence a bad name.

devolution Central government turns some powers over to regions.

referendum Vote on an issue rather than for an office.

quasi-federal Halfway federal.

Cymric, a number that has been growing as it is required in Welsh schools. Cymric is now officially co-equal with English within Wales, which has a Cymric TV channel.

The strategy of the Labour party has been to offer home rule or autonomy to Scotland and Wales. This was called **devolution**, the granting of certain governing powers by the center to the periphery. A 1977 devolution bill to set up Scottish and Welsh assemblies failed in **referendums**.

After the 1997 election, in which Scotland and Wales stayed overwhelmingly Labour, Tony Blair again offered Scotland and Wales their own parliaments, and this time the referendums passed. In 1999, at about the same time Ulster got home rule, Scots and Welsh elected regional parliaments with a new voting system that could eventually be adopted for Britain as a whole. The German-style system (see pages 191–194) gave each voter two votes, the first for FPTP single-member districts and the second for parties in multimember districts. The results of the second vote were used to "top off" the number of seats for each party until they were roughly proportional to its share of the votes. Labour took the most seats in both Scotland and Wales but not a majority, forcing them to form coalitions. This too could be a harbinger for things to come in Britain. The new assemblies have some powers in education, economic planning, and taxation. Some Scots dismiss their assembly as "a wee pretendy parliament."

How do you say "post office" in Gaelic? Although few Scots speak it, in the Highlands many public signs are now in Gaelic as well as English, an example of regional nationalism.

Britons do not use the word, but these moves amount to **quasi-federalism**. Will it solve Britain's problem or just whet appetites for more? The Scot Nats and about half the people of Scotland still say they want full independence. In addition, the Blair government set up eight Regional Development Agencies for England, whose task was economic growth. Some took these agencies as the beginnings of federalism within England. As we will see in France, regional planning councils can turn into political units. The shifts are examples of unitary systems loosening up into quasi-federalism or "regionalism."

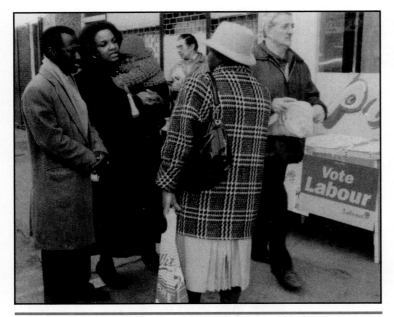

A black Labour candidate campaigns in London. Several black MPs have won Labour seats in Parliament.

Tories have long wooed voters with calls for a "clear end to immigration" before it "swamped" British culture, but both major parties have since 1962 tightened immigration to Britain until it is now very restrictive. Visibly angry, Prime Minister Blair denounced the 2005 London bombings and warned Muslim clerics who preach *jihad* to "share and support the values that sustain the British way of life. Those who break that duty and try to incite hatred or engage in violence against our country and its people have no place here." Blair's threat to deport preachers of violence made some worry about an erosion of civil rights in Britain.

It was an old problem: How does a tolerant society handle militant intolerance? Most Britons were prepared for a little less tolerance when it came to suicide bombers. Britain, like all Western countries, thus found itself debating where civil rights end and homeland security begins. No Western country tolerates **jihadis** on its soil. Notice how France (pages 154–157) and Germany (pages 234–236) face the identical problem. Compounding the problem is the fact that historically European lands have been countries of **emigration**, not countries of **immigration**. The United States handles immigration better because we are all immigrants or their descendants. Americans too, however, expect new arrivals to become patriotic Americans and get angry if they do not.

■ Britain and Europe

Until recent decades, Britons did not see themselves as Europeans; most looked down on anyone from across the English Channel. Rather than working toward a united Europe after World War II, as the Continental countries did, Britain emphasized its Commonwealth ties and its "special relationship" to the United States. As the rest of Europe kept distant from U.S. policy on Iraq, Tony Blair supported it with words and military forces.

jihadi   From *jihad* (holy war); Muslim holy warrior.

emigration   (one m) Moving out of your native country.

immigration   (two ms) Resettling into a new country.

Britain stayed out of the 1957 Treaty of Rome, which set up the European Community (EC, since 1993 the EU, for European Union), but in 1960 built a much looser grouping, the European Free Trade Association (EFTA). While the EC Six (France, West Germany, Italy, Belgium, the Netherlands, Luxembourg) economies surged ahead, the EFTA Outer Seven (Britain, Austria, Denmark, Finland, Iceland, Norway, Portugal, Sweden, and Switzerland) were slowly cut off from the main European market. In 1963, Britain applied to join the EC, but French President Charles de Gaulle vetoed British entry, charging that Britain was still too tied to the Commonwealth and the United States to be a good European. He was right.

By the time de Gaulle resigned in 1969, Britain was ready to join the EC, but not all Britons liked the idea. For traditional Tories, it meant giving up some British sovereignty to the EC headquarters in Brussels and even treating Europeans as equals. For everyone it meant higher food prices. For manufacturers it meant British products had to compete with often better and cheaper Continental imports that now come in tariff-free. For fishermen it meant British fishing areas were open to all EC fishermen. For workers it meant loss of some jobs. Many Britons want to stay firmly British.

The arguments in favor of the EU stress that Britain needs change and competition, the very forces that had invigorated European industries. Euroenthusiasts argue that geographically, strategically, economically, even spiritually, Britain really is part of Europe and should start acting like it. The Euro-debate cuts across party lines, sometimes producing a strange coalition of right-wing Tories and left-wing Labourites, each opposing Europe for their own reasons. In 1971, under a Tory government, the Commons voted 356 to 244 to join; 69 Labour MPs defied their party whip to vote in favor while 39 Conservatives, freed from party discipline, voted "no" along with Labour, demonstrating that British party discipline is not perfect. On January 1, 1973, Britain, along with Denmark and Ireland, made the Common Market Six, the Nine.

When Labour returned to power, Prime Minister Harold Wilson offered the British public a first—a referendum, something common in France. But Britain, with its tradition of parliamentary supremacy, had never held one before. The 1975 referendum found that most Britons wanted to stay in Europe, but one-third voted no. If put to another referendum, British voters would have rejected the new EU constitution, which French and Dutch voters did reject in 2005 (see pages 252–254).

Thatcher, a British nationalist and "Euroskeptic," took a tough line on the EU. A common market was fine, she argued, but not turning it into a supranational entity that would infringe on Britain's sovereignty. Many Britons rejected joining the European Monetary Union (EMU) or its new euro currency. Their slogan: "Europe yes, euro no." The EMU indeed takes away an important part

human capital Education, skills, and enthusiasm of nation's work force.
underclass Permanently disadvantaged people.

Comparison

HOW TO IMPROVE BRITISH EDUCATION

One limit to British economic growth has been poor educational levels. Britain's **human capital** does not compare favorably with other countries. Many leave school early with weak math and verbal skills, forming a U.S.-style **underclass**.

As in the United States, the British debate an old question: quality vs. equality in education. Many Tories opt for quality, returning to the old system of testing to send the best to elite high schools, some of them independent but with government subsidies.

Northern Ireland kept the selective system and shows better overall school performance. Labour, still seeking equality in education, generally prefers comprehensive schools but with improved funding, standards, and discipline.

By 2000, British 15-year-olds tested better than most of the Continent and much better than U.S. scores. Surprising: the drop in German scores to U.S. levels. Unsurprising: high Japanese math scores. The message: America, get serious about schooling.

unilinear   Progressing evenly and
always upward.

of sovereignty, the ability of each country to control its currency, and gives it to the European Central Bank in Frankfurt. Many Britons (and some other Europeans) feared that Europe's strongest economy—Germany—would dominate the EMU and that policy on money supply and interest rates would be set by the Bundesbank. Britain (along with Denmark and Sweden) stood aside as the euro was introduced. Blair, a cautious Euroenthusiast, waited to see how the euro worked. Euroskeptics lead the Tories, and Britain is still split over Europe. Some Britons would like to drop out of the EU. Perhaps Britain really is an Atlantic country and not a European one. Britain's natural community may be the English-speaking lands across the oceans.

Great Britain or Little England?

This sums up the dilemma of modern Britain: the problem of scaling down its vision of itself. Britain, in the course of a century, has clearly declined, both internationally and domestically. When Britain was a mighty empire and the most industrialized country in the world in the second half of the nineteenth century, it had power, wealth, and a sense of mission. This in turn fostered order, discipline, and deference among the British people. Losing its empire and slipping behind the economies of West Europe, decay, violence, and resentment appeared.

Britain's trajectory refutes the idea that progress is **unilinear**. In the case of Britain we see that what goes up can eventually come down. But this process is never static. Now that Britain is adjusting to its new reality—as one European country among many—regeneration has already begun. To see how another country has turned around, how a society and economy can change from static to dynamic, let us now consider France.

Key Terms

absolute decline (p. 72)

Commonwealth (p. 77)

consociation (p. 77)

consumption (p. 72)

counterculture (p. 72)

deindustrialization (p. 72)

deregulation (p. 73)

devolution (p. 79)

emigration (p. 80)

entitlement (p. 74)

Good Friday agreement (p. 77)

human capital (p. 81)

immigration (p. 80)

inflation (p. 72)

jihadi (p. 80)

monetarism (p. 72)

pluralism (p. 72)

pluralistic stagnation (p. 72)

privatization (p. 73)

production (p. 72)

productivity (p. 72)

quasi-federal (p. 79)

recession (p. 74)

referendum (p. 79)

regional nationalism (p. 78)

relative decline (p. 72)

subject (p. 77)

underclass (p. 81)

unilinear (p. 82)

Further Reference

De Bréadún, Deaglán. *The Far Side of Revenge: Making Peace in Northern Ireland*. Wilton, Ireland: Collins, 2001.

Denver, David. *Scotland Decides: The Devolution Issue and the 1997 Referendum*. Portland, OR: F. Cass, 2000.

Green, E. H. H. *Thatcher*. New York: Oxford University Press, 2006.

Hansen, Randall. *Citizenship and Immigration in Post-War Britain: The Institutional Origins of a Multicultural Nation*. New York: Oxford University Press, 2000.

Hearn, Jonathan. *Claiming Scotland: National Identity and Liberal Culture*. New York: Columbia University Press, 2001.

Mac Ginty, Roger, and John Darby. *Guns and Government: The Management of the Northern Ireland Peace Process*. New York: Palgrave, 2002.

Owen, Geoffrey. *From Empire to Europe*. New York: HarperCollins, 1999.

Paul, Kathleen. *Whitewashing Britain: Race and Citizenship in the Postwar Era*. Ithaca, NY: Cornell University Press, 1997.

Pierson, Paul. *Dismantling the Welfare State?: Reagan, Thatcher, and the Politics of Retrenchment*. New York: Cambridge University Press, 1994.

Robins, Lynton, and Bill Jones, eds. *Debates in British Politics Today*. New York: Palgrave, 2001.

Sawyer, Malcolm, ed. *The UK Economy*, 16th ed. New York: Oxford University Press, 2005.

Seldon, Anthony, ed. *The Blair Effect*. Boston, MA: Little, Brown, 2001.

Part II

FRANCE

Key Web Sites

Government of France
emulateme.com/france

Elections in France
lefigaro.scrutins.net/historique

French President's Office
elysee.fr/ang

French Newspapers
lemonde.fr
lefigaro.fr
libération.fr

UNITED
KINGDOM

NETHERLANDS

BELGIUM

GERMANY

LUXEMBOURG

ENGLISH CHANNEL

NORD

HAUTE-
NORMANDIE

PICARDIE

BASSE-
NORMANDIE

BRETAGNE

Paris

REGION DE
PARIS

CHAMPAGNE

LORRAINE

ALSACE

PAYS DE LA LOIRE

CENTRE

BOURGOGNE

FRANCHE-COMTE

BAY

OF

BISCAY

POITOU-
CHARENTES

FRANCE

SWITZERLAND

LIMOUSIN

AUVERGNE

RHONE-ALPES

ITALY

AQUITAINE

MIDI-PYRENEES

LANGUEDOC

PROVINCE
COTE D'AZUR

CORSICA

ANDORRA

SPAIN

MEDITERRANEAN

SEA

| 0 | 100 | 200 Miles |
| 0 | 100 | 200 Kilometers |

Chapter 7

FRANCE:
THE IMPACT OF THE PAST

"France has everything," many French rightly boast. Hexagon-shaped, with three sides on seas and three on land, France is simultaneously an Atlantic country, a Mediterranean country, and an Alpine country. It has lush farmland, navigable rivers, many minerals, and a moderate climate. It does not, however, have a moat like England; France is vulnerable to land attack from the north and the east. While England historically had a small army, France needed a large army, a point that helps explain the rise of French absolutism. French kings had troops to rely on.

Internally, France is divided into a North and a South. Culturally and temperamentally, the two regions differ and, until the late Middle Ages, even spoke different languages. The Germanic northerners spoke *langue d'oïl*, "the tongue of *oïl*," their word for yes, which grew into the modern French *oui*. The Mediterranean southerners spoke *langue d'oc*, after their word for yes, *oc*. It declined after the Paris kings conquered the South in the thirteenth century. To this day, southerners have a different accent and resent rule by Paris. The region is still called Languedoc.

Questions to Consider

1. Compare the Roman influence in France and Britain.
2. What is France's core area? How did it come to be?
3. Who epitomized French absolutism?
4. What was the theory of mercantilism?
5. What caused the French Revolution?
6. How did great French thinkers differ from the British?
7. What is Brinton's theory of revolution?
8. With what regime did France become a stable democracy?
9. What did the Dreyfus Affair show?
10. Who ran France during World War II?
11. How did de Gaulle come to power?

The Roman Influence

Like most peoples, the French are a mixture of ethnic stocks. In the centuries before Christ, tribes of Celts pushed into France and merged with the native Ligurians. The Romans conquered the area and called it *Gallia* (Gaul). Roman influence in France was longer and deeper than in England, which the Anglo-Saxons obliterated, but the Germanic tribes that moved into Gaul became Romanized themselves. Thus, English is a Germanic language and French a Romance language.

By the time the Roman Empire collapsed, one Germanic tribe, the Franks, had managed to take over most of present-day France. Their chief, Clovis—from whom came the name Louis—was baptized in 496, and France has been mostly Catholic ever since, the "eldest daughter of the Church." The Franks under Charles Martel turned back the invading Moors in 732, possibly saving Europe.

Charles Martel's grandson, Charlemagne, carved out a gigantic kingdom—the Holy Roman Empire—that encompassed what someday would amount to most of the six original EU countries. Although the empire soon disintegrated, Charlemagne had planted the idea of European unity.

■ The Rise of French Absolutism

In the confusion after Charlemagne, France was reduced to several petty kingdoms and dukedoms, as was Germany. While Germany stayed divided until the nineteenth century, French kings pursued unification and centralization of their power with single-minded determination. Pushing outward from the Paris area, the *Ile de France* (Island of France), French kings added territory while retaining control in Paris.

Estates-General   Old, unused French parliament.

Huguenots   French Protestants.

intendants   French provincial administrators, answerable only to Paris; early version of *prefects*.

Feudalism in France began to give way to absolutism with the crafty Louis (pronounced *Lwie*) XI, who ruled from 1461 to 1483 and doubled the size of France until it was nearly its present shape. He also weakened the power of the feudal nobles, ignored the **Estates-General**, and developed a royal bureaucracy to increase taxation. This pattern was strengthened for at least three centuries, leaving the France of today still highly centralized. Louis XI also cultivated relations with Rome. There was never an English-style break with the Vatican; instead, the Catholic church became a pillar of the French monarchy. The **Huguenots** were controlled, massacred, and driven into exile. In 1589, however, the royal line of succession fell to a Huguenot, Henry of Navarre. The Catholic church offered the throne to Henry only if he accepted Catholicism. Shrugged Henry: "Paris is well worth a Mass."

Under Louis XIII, Cardinal Richelieu became chief minister and virtual ruler from 1624 to 1642. Obsessed with French power and glory, Richelieu further weakened the nobles, recruited only middle-class bureaucrats, and sent out **intendants** to control the provinces for Paris. Richelieu was an organizational genius who put his bureaucratic stamp on France for all time.

Geography

RIVERS

Navigable rivers are economic arteries, tying a country together and sometimes boosting international trade. England's Thames also gives it an inland outlet to the sea. France's Seine, Rhine, Rhone, and Loire give it trade routes and outlets to the sea in all four points of the compass. French kings supplemented the rivers with an ambitious system of canals, some of which are still in use. The Rhine has for centuries served as a West European highway, connecting Switzerland, France, Germany, and the Netherlands. The Danube stitched together the Austro-Hungarian Empire, but for centuries its outlet in the Black Sea was controlled by the hostile Turks. Russia's rivers flow the wrong way, either to the Arctic Ocean or to the Black Sea, where the Ottomans held the vital Turkish Straits. China's economic and political life grew up around the Yangzi River.

Geography

CORE AREAS

Most countries have an identifiable **core** area, a region where in most cases the state originated. Some countries contain more than one core area, and this may produce regional tension. Typically, the country's capital is in its core area. Farther out are the peripheral areas, often more recent additions where people may speak a different language and resent rule by the core area. At times the resentment can turn deadly, as when provinces such as Serbia's Kosovo, Turkey's Kurdish area, and China's Taiwan attempt to break away. Part of the tragedy of Kosovo is that it was the medieval Serbian core, but after Turkish conquest in 1389, Serbs were displaced northward, and Kosovo slowly became a majority Albanian. Looking to their history, Serbs refused to give up their ancient heartland.

France is an almost perfect example of a core area, centered on Paris, spreading its rule, language, and culture with an eye toward perfecting national integration. This has been a slow process and one still not complete. In the nineteenth century, regions of France spoke strange dialects. By deliberate educational policy, corps of schoolteachers directed by Paris spread across France to turn "peasants into Frenchmen," in the words of historian Eugen Weber. Some peripheral areas still harbor resentments against Paris. Brittany, Corsica, and Languedoc try to keep alive local dialects and regional culture. Extremists in Corsica practice occasional violence.

England is the core area of the United Kingdom, and the Valley of Mexico is Mexico's core, established and reinforced by Toltecs, Aztecs, and Spaniards. A German core area is much less clear. The many German ministates of the Middle Ages kept their sovereignty and dialects for an unusually long time. Prussia led German unification in the nineteenth century, and Berlin indeed became the nation's capital. But many regions accorded Prussia little respect; Catholic lands such as Bavaria and the Rhineland disliked Prussia's authoritarianism and Protestantism. Germany remained riven by **particularism**, a factor that contributed to present-day federalism. Nazism was in part a contrived effort to bring all German regions under central control by means of lunatic nationalism. Nigeria, assembled by British imperialists, has no core, which is the root of its breakaway tribalism.

The Soviet Union represented a huge gap between its Slavic core area and its non-Slavic peripheral areas. Russia's numerous nationalities are still distinct and discontent. Lacking the kind of cohesion of other nation-states, the Soviet Union was a type of colonial empire. The Slavic core of Russia, Belarus, and Ukraine gradually beat back Tatars, Turks, and Swedes until it straddled the vast belt where Europe meets Asia. Then the tsars sent expeditions eastward to claim Siberia to the Pacific. In the mid-nineteenth century Russia acquired most of the Muslim-Turkic peoples of Central Asia. **Russification** proved impossible and fostered nationalist hatred against Moscow. The breakaway of republics from the Soviet Union may be seen as decolonization. The remaining Russian Federation still contains lands like Chechnya that would like to break away.

China's core area was the Yangzi Valley, but before the time of Christ, China had consolidated a major empire. So numerous and united—despite occasional civil wars—were the **Han** Chinese that the addition to the kingdom of a few outer barbarians (Mongols, Tibetans, Turkic Muslims, and others) bothered the Han little. Recently, however, Central Asian dissidents have set off bombs to protest rule by Beijing.

Japan, with Tokyo-Yokohama as its core area, has some center-periphery tension between East and West Japan and from agricultural and fishing prefectures. Iran has non-Persian-speaking peripheral areas that resent rule by Tehran. The U.S. core area began with the thirteen colonies along the Atlantic seaboard, especially the northern ones, which are still somewhat resented by the rest of the union.

core   Region where the state originated. (See page 89.)

particularism   Region's sense of its difference. (See page 89.)

Russification   Making non-Russian nationalities learn Russian. (See page 89.)

Han   Original and main people of China. (See page 89.)

aristocrat   Person of inherited noble rank.

autonomy   Partial independence.

Versailles   Palaces and park on outskirts of Paris begun by Louis XIV.

courtier   Person who hangs around a royal court.

mercantilism   Theory that nation's wealth is its gold and silver, to be amassed by government controls on economy.

bound   To name bordering countries.

French nobles fought centralization but lost. In 1648 and again in 1650 some French **aristocrats** staged an uncoordinated revolt called the *Fronde*. Recall that at this time English nobles and their commoner allies beheaded a king who tried to act like an absolute monarch. In France, the nobles were quickly broken and lost the **autonomy** enjoyed by English lords.

■ Louis XIV: The High Point of Absolutism

"*L'état, c'est moi*" ("The state—that's me"), Louis XIV is often quoted as saying. By the time Louis XIV became king in 1661, French absolutism was already well developed; he brought it to a high point. Louis's emblem was the sun, around which all things revolved. The Sun King further increased centralization and bureaucratization, all aimed at augmenting his own and France's power. Louis used his large army in almost continual warfare. He acted as his own prime minister and handled much administration personally. He never bothered convening the Estates-General. He constructed **Versailles** and made thousands of nobles live there, diverting them from power seeking to game playing—games of intrigue, love, and flattery. While English lords ruled as small kings on their estates, French nobles were reduced to **courtiers**.

Louis's policies of "war and magnificence" were financial drains. To harness the French economy to serve the state, Louis's minister, Colbert, practiced **mercantilism**, the theory that a nation

Geography

BOUND FRANCE

An old technique for teaching geography has been forgotten; we are going to revive it. It requires the student to cite, from forced recall, the boundaries of a given country in the following form:

Bound France

France is bounded on the north by Belgium and Luxembourg;

on the east by Germany, Switzerland, and Italy;

on the south by the Mediterranean Sea and Spain;

and on the west by the Atlantic Ocean.

The four directions need be only approximate. Germany is also on France's northern border but is mainly to the east of France. Bounding is a more effective learning tool than labeling a blank map, as a map gives several clues. **Bounding** forces students to reconstruct the map in their minds without clues. To reinforce your knowledge, from the map on page 85, sketch out and label France and its neighbors. Next do it again from memory. Once you can bound each of our nine countries, you will be able to label much of all the continents except Africa, which is extremely fragmented and complex. To fill in the blank spots, we also include other countries in our bounding exercises. Bounding has only limited utility for Britain, as the United Kingdom has only one land boundary. What is it?

was as wealthy as the amount of gold it possessed and that the way to amass gold was for the government to supervise the economy with plans, subsidies, monopolies, and tariffs. This set a pattern found in most European countries and in Japan: Instead of a totally free market, the government supervises the economy.

Personalities

THREE FRENCH GENIUSES: VOLTAIRE, MONTESQUIEU, ROUSSEAU

Voltaire

Montesquieu

Rousseau

Each in his own way, these three eighteenth-century thinkers helped persuade many French—especially middle-class intellectuals—that the *ancien régime* was rotten and that it was possible to construct a better system. Their weapon was reason—abstract, **Cartesian**, logical—in contrast to English thinkers, who relied more on empirical reality. The French dislike reality for failing to live up to their logical constructs, an approach that lends itself to radicalism.

Voltaire (1694–1778) was the epitome of the **Enlightenment**, doubting and ridiculing everything stupid he saw around him. His chief target: the Catholic church, which he saw as intolerant, irrational, and hypocritical. Voltaire's phrase, *"Ecrasez l'infáme"* ("crush the infamous thing," meaning the Catholic church), became the founding cry of anticlericalism and spread through most Catholic countries. (But not Ireland or Poland. Any idea why?)

The Baron de Montesquieu (1689–1755) traveled all over Europe to gather material for one of the first books of comparative politics, *The Spirit of the Laws.* Montesquieu was especially impressed with English liberties, which he thought resulted from the "checks and balances" of the different parts of their government. Montesquieu wrote about an idealized model of an English system that had already passed into history, but the American Founding Fathers read him literally. Montesquieu suggested that countries could more or less rationally choose their governmental institutions. The French have been choosing and discarding them ever since.

Jean-Jacques Rousseau (1712–1778), who was born in Geneva but lived in France, was the most complex and most dangerous of these thinkers. Rousseau hypothesized man in the state of nature as free,

happy, and morally good. Society ruined humans, corrupting them with private property, which leads to inequality and jealousy. Rousseau, in a famous phrase at the beginning of his book *The Social Contract,* wrote: "Man is born free but everywhere is in chains." How can humans be saved? Rousseau further hypothesized that beneath all the individual, petty viewpoints in society there is a **general will** for the common good. This could be discovered and implemented even though some people might object; they would be "forced to be free." Critics of Rousseau charge that he laid the intellectual basis for both nazism and communism because his theory lets dictators crush dissent and claim they "really know" what the people want and need.

The French political thinkers tended to call for major, sweeping change; English thinkers, for slow, cautious change that preserved the overall system. The French thinkers fundamentally hated their government; the English did not.

Cartesian   After French philosopher
René Descartes, philosophical analysis
based on pure reason without
empirical reference. (See page 91.)

Enlightenment   Eighteenth-century
philosophical movement advocating
reason and tolerance. (See page 91.)

general will   Rousseau's theory of
what whole community wants. (See
page 91.)

ancien régime   French for old regime,
monarchy that preceded Revolution.

Third Estate   Largest chamber of
Estates-General, representing
commoners.

Louis XIV was an able monarch who impressed all of Europe; other kings tried to imitate him. French cuisine, architecture, dress, and language dominated the Continent. From the outside, the France of Louis XIV looked more impressive than England. Without "checks and balances" to get in the way, the centralized monarchy of France accomplished great things. But the English, by developing political participation, devised a more stable system.

Why the French Revolution?

For all its external splendor, France in the eighteenth century was in difficulty. Its treasury was often near bankruptcy. Especially costly was French support for the American colonists against Britain; the French did it more for revenge than for love of liberty. The bureaucracy was corrupt and inefficient. Recognizing too late that mercantilism was bad economics, the regime tried to move to a free market, but by then French industry and agriculture were used to state protection and wanted to keep it. Also important was the spread of new ideas on "liberty," "consent of the governed," and "the general will." Ideas can be dynamite and undermined the **ancien régime**.

As Alexis de Tocqueville pointed out, revolutions seldom start when things are bad but, rather, when they are getting better. The French people enjoyed improving economic conditions for most of the eighteenth century, but that increased expectations and awakened jealousies toward people who were getting richer faster. As we shall see in Iran under the Shah, economic growth can be highly destabilizing. Furthermore, Louis XVI had decided to reform the political system and provide for some kind of representation. But as we shall see in Russia and Iran, the reforming of an unjust and unpopular system is extraordinarily difficult, often leading to revolution.

In the spring of 1789, Louis XVI convened the Estates-General for the first time since 1614. Its three estates—the clergy, the nobility, and the commoners—were elected by nearly universal male suffrage. The **Third Estate**, the commoners, demanded that all three houses meet together,

Democracy

LEFT, RIGHT, AND CENTER

The way delegates were seated in the National Assembly during and after the French Revolution gives us our terms for radical, conservative, and moderate. In a half-circle chamber, the most radical delegates, those representing the common people, were seated to the left of the speaker's rostrum, the most conservative, those representing the aristocracy, to the right. This allowed like-minded legislators to caucus and separated delegates who might start fist fights.

The precise meanings of left, right, and center have varied through the ages and from country to country. In general, however, the left favors greater equality of incomes, welfare measures, and government intervention in the economy. The right, now that it has shed its aristocratic origins, favors individual achievement and private industry. The center tries to synthesize the moderate elements in both viewpoints. Those just a little to one side or the other are called center-left or center-right.

meaning that the more numerous Third Estate could override the conservative First and Second Estates. The Third Estate argued that it represented the popular will, but Louis resisted. By the time he gave in, many parliamentarians were angry and radicalized and voted themselves into a **National Assembly**, its name today.

Shortly afterward, the common people of Paris, furious over rising bread prices, stormed the **Bastille** on July 14, 1789. Bastille Day became the French national day. Upon hearing of the Bastille incident the king exclaimed, *"C'est une révolte,"* meaning something that could be put down. A duke corrected him: *"Non, Sire, c'est une révolution."* It was the first modern usage of the word **revolution**.

One reason Louis XVI was unpopular was his frivolous and extravagant Austrian-born queen, Marie Antoinette. She was said to have once inquired why there had been riots and was told it was because the people had no bread. "No bread?" she tittered. "Then let them eat cake." The masses hated her. She was guillotined in 1793 a few months after Louis XVI.

National Assembly France's parliament.

Bastille Old and nearly unused Paris jail, the storming of which heralded French Revolution in 1789.

revolution Sudden and complete overthrow of regime.

alienated Psychologically distant and hostile.

Thermidor Month when Robespierre fell, a calming down after a revolutionary high.

Key Concepts

BRINTON'S THEORY OF REVOLUTION

The great Harvard historian Crane Brinton in his 1938 *The Anatomy of Revolution* argued that all revolutions pass through similar stages. He compared several revolutions, but his main model was the French. Brinton's stages are as follows:

- The old regime loses its governing effectiveness and legitimacy. It becomes inept and indecisive. Intellectuals especially become **alienated** from it. An improving economy provokes discontent and jealousy.

- The first stage of revolution comes with the growth of antiregime groups. Triggering the revolution is a political problem—such as whether the three estates should meet separately or together—that the old regime cannot solve. Rioting breaks out, but troops sent to crush it desert to the rioters. The antiregime people easily take over power amidst popular rejoicing.

- Moderates initially seize power. They opposed the old regime, but as critics rather than as revolutionaries. They want major reform rather than total revolution. Extremists accuse them of being weak and cowardly, and

true enough, they are not ruthless enough to crush the extremists.

- Extremists take over because they are more ruthless, purposeful, and organized than the moderates. In what Brinton likened to a high fever during an illness, the extremists whip up a revolutionary frenzy, throwing out everything old, forcing people to be good, and punishing real or imagined enemies in a reign of terror. In France, this stage came with Robespierre; in Iran, with Khomeini.

- A **Thermidor**, or calming-down period, ends the reign of terror. Every revolution has a Thermidor, which Brinton likened to a convalescence after a fever, because human nature cannot take the extremists and their revolutionary purity for too long. Power may then fall into the hands of a dictator who restores order but not liberty—a Napoleon or a Stalin.

Brinton's theory became a classic and has largely stood the test of time. Revolutions do seem to pass through stages, although their timing cannot be predicted with accuracy. Russia and Iran, as we shall see, followed the Brinton pattern.

From Freedom to Tyranny

In 1791 the National Assembly constructed a **constitutional monarchy**, and if it had stopped there the **French Revolution** might have resembled the English Revolution of a century earlier. But the French constitutional monarchy was undermined from two sides: from the king and some aristocrats who wanted to restore absolute power, and from a militant faction called the Jacobins, who wanted a radical revolution. Their cry: *"Liberté, Egalité, Fraternité!"* The king was caught conspiring with foreign princes to invade France and restore him to power. The attempted invasion of 1792 helped the Jacobins take over. With a makeshift but enthusiastic citizen army— "the nation in arms"—they repelled the invaders at Valmy.

constitutional monarchy   King with limited powers.

French Revolution   1789 popular ouster of monarch.

Reign of Terror   Robespierre's 1793–1794 rule by guillotine.

coup d'état   Military takeover of government.

tyrannical   Coercive rule, usually by one person.

plebiscite   Referendum, mass vote for issue rather than for candidates.

chauvinism   After Napoleonic soldier named Chauvin; fervent, prideful nationalism.

Bourbon   French dynasty before the Revolution.

Power fell into the hands of the misnamed Committee of Public Safety under Maximilien Robespierre, a provincial lawyer and fanatic follower of Rousseau who was determined to "force men to be free." Instituting the **Reign of Terror**, Robespierre and his followers guillotined more than twenty thousand people, starting with the king, queen, and nobles but soon spreading to anyone who doubted Robespierre. Finally, in 1794, during the revolutionary calendar's month of Thermidor, Robespierre's comrades, afraid they might be next, guillotined *him*, and the Terror ended.

During all this turmoil, the army became the only coherent institution, especially one young artillery officer, the Corsican Napoleon Bonaparte, who had won fame leading French armies in Italy and Egypt. In 1799 a **coup d'état** overthrew the weak civilian Directory and set up a Consulate with Bonaparte as First Consul. Brilliant in both battle and civil reform, Napoleon crowned himself emperor in 1804.

Above all, Napoleon loved war. As Henry Kissinger pointed out, a revolutionary power, like France in the midst of hostile conservative monarchies, can feel secure only by conquering all potential threats. Napoleon made France master of all Europe, using dashing tactics and a large, enthusiastic army to crush one foe after another until at last they went too far. Facing a British-led coalition, harassed by guerrilla warfare in Spain, and frozen in the Russian winter, Napoleon was defeated and exiled to the Mediterranean island of Elba in 1814. The next year he tried a comeback and thousands of his old soldiers rallied around him to fight at Waterloo and lose.

Napoleon left an ambiguous legacy. He claimed to be consolidating the Revolution but actually set up a **tyrannical** police state. Trying to embody Rousseau's elusive general will, Napoleon held several **plebiscites**, which he always won. He unleashed **chauvinism** by proclaiming France to be Europe's liberator. Napoleon was not just a historic accident, though, for we shall see similar figures emerge in French politics. When a society is badly split, as France was over the Revolution, power tends to gravitate into the hands of a savior, and democracy does not have a chance.

The Bourbon Restoration

Europe breathed a sigh of relief once Napoleon was packed off to a remote island in the South Atlantic and the brother of Louis XVI was restored to the French throne as Louis XVIII. In the **Bourbon** Restoration, exiles from all over Europe returned to France to claim their old rights. Many French disliked the returning Bourbons and sighed, "They learned nothing and they forgot nothing."

France was badly split. Most aristocrats hated the Revolution, while most commoners supported at least a version of it. The Catholic Church was reactionary, for the Revolution had confiscated church lands and ended its tax privileges. French Catholics for generations opposed the anticlericalist republicans, who in turn mistrusted the

Paris Commune Takeover of Paris government by citizens during German siege of 1870–1871.

church. Residuals of the clerical-anticlerical split persist in France. But France had also changed in the quarter-century since the Revolution. Parliaments now counted for something; kings could no longer rule without them. The civil reforms of Napoleon were preserved. People insisted on equality before the law.

At first the French, tired from upheaval and warfare, accepted the Bourbons. But by 1830 they proved to be as pig-headed as ever, and rioting broke out. In a semilegal switch, the liberal Duc d'Orleans, Louis-Phillipe, replaced the last Bourbon, Charles X. He too proved inept, and a small uprising in that revolutionary year of 1848 brought the Second Republic. This did not last long either.

The French have historically turned from tumultuous democracy to authoritarian rule. In 1848 they overwhelmingly elected Napoleon's self-proclaimed nephew, Louis Napoleon, as president. Using plebiscites, in 1852 he turned the Second Republic into the Second Empire with himself as Emperor Napoleon III. This brought two decades of peace and progress until Louis Napoleon, in 1870, allowed himself to be goaded into war with Prussia. Bursting with overconfidence, the French were quickly trounced. The Germans surrounded Paris and shelled it daily, but there was no French government left to surrender. In Paris itself, a revolutionary takeover by common citizens brought the short-lived **Paris Commune**, which conservative French troops crushed, killing some twenty thousand Parisians. Karl Marx mistakenly saw the Commune as the first proletarian uprising, and among leftists the Commune grew into a legend of worker power.

Geography

A TALE OF TWO FLAGS

The Bourbon flag had been blue and white with fleur-de-lis (iris). The Revolution introduced the tricolor of red, white, and blue. The post-Napoleon restoration brought back the old flag, for the tricolor symbolized everything the Bourbons hated. In 1830, the Orleanist monarchy, to mollify revolutionary sentiment, brought back the tricolor, France's flag ever since.

Blue

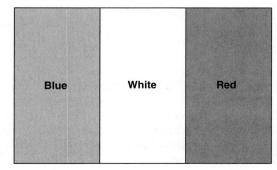

Blue · White · Red

■ The Third Republic

Amidst near anarchy, the **Third Republic**, France's first stable democracy, was born. Its first task was a humiliating peace with Germany that cost France the province of Alsace (which has many German-speaking people) plus a billion dollars in gold. The enraged French ached for revenge and transferred their traditional hatred of Britain to Germany.

Third Republic France's democratic regime from 1871 to 1940.

bourgeois Middle-class.

reactionary Seeking to go back to old ways, extremely conservative.

Maginot Line Supposedly unbreachable French defenses facing Germany before World War II.

belle époque "Beautiful epoch," France around 1900.

Zionism Jewish nationalist movement, founded Israel.

The accidental Third Republic turned out to be the longest-lasting French regime since the ancien régime. The Third Republic was basically fairly conservative and **bourgeois**. France was not healed during its long tenure; indeed, social tensions mounted. A **reactionary** Catholic right dreamed of an authoritarian system, while the left organized Socialist and later Communist parties. Economic and population growth was slow, and France slipped further behind the rapidly growing Germany. Still, the Third Republic staggered through the ordeal of World War I. At first the French were delighted with a chance for revenge against Germany, but soon the appalling losses—a million and a half French lives—turned France bitter and defeatist even though it was on the winning side. France regained Alsace but had no stomach to fight again.

French defeatism played into the hands of Nazi Germany, which swept easily through France in May–June 1940. Only one French unit fought well, a tank column commanded by an obscure colonel named de Gaulle, who had been warning for years of the need to develop better French armored forces. The French thought they could prevent a repetition of the World War I bloodshed by hiding behind the **Maginot Line**, but fixed defenses cannot move; the Germans simply went around them on the north.

Political Culture

THE DREYFUS AFFAIR

Nothing better reveals the deep division of French society in the late nineteenth century than the trial of Captain Alfred Dreyfus, an officer on the French general staff. In 1894, Dreyfus was accused of selling secrets to the Germans; he was given a rigged military trial with fake evidence and sent to Devil's Island for life. It soon became clear that Dreyfus was not the culprit and had been convicted by bigoted officers simply because he was a Jew, a handy scapegoat.

France split in two. Those defending Dreyfus—the *Dreyfusards*—supported the republican traditions of equality. These tended to be people on the left. Novelist Emile Zola published his famous letter *J'accuse!*

(I accuse!), charging the government with covering up for the military. The *Anti-Dreyfusards*—reactionary aristocrats, army officers, fanatic Catholics, and anti-Semites—were equally passionate in defense of prerevolutionary values. Most French took one side or the other; there was even street fighting.

Dreyfus was exonerated in 1906, but his trial left scars. It showed how the beautiful, civilized veneer of **belle époque** France concealed reaction and anti-Semitism. A Viennese journalist covering the trial, Theodore Herzl, was so shocked by the anti-Semitism unleashed by the trial that he immediately organized a world **Zionist** movement to save Jews from what he (correctly) feared would be worse outbursts.

■ Vichy: France Splits Again

The Germans largely let the French run occupied France. Named after the town of Vichy in central France where it was set up, the **Vichy** government was staffed by the same sort of reactionaries who earlier had reviled Dreyfus, people who hated democracy and admired the authoritarian Germans. The aged Marshal Pétain, hero of World War I, became chief of state, and an opportunistic politician, Pierre Laval, became premier without elections. Some French thought Vichy was an improvement over the Third Republic, which had voted the **Popular Front** into power in 1936. "Better the Nazis than the Communists," muttered Vichy supporters. French SS units fought in Russia. French police rounded up Jews for deportation to death camps. French workers volunteered to work in Germany. Although most French hated to admit it, many collaborated with the Germans and even liked them.

Other French, however, hated the Germans and Vichy. Some joined the **Résistance**, an underground network that sabotaged and spied on the Germans, rescued British and American airmen, and occasionally killed collaborators. Again, France split. The Vichy period was, in the words of Stanley Hoffmann, "a Franco-French war." The Resistance attracted French people of

Vichy   Nazi puppet regime that ran France during World War II.

Popular Front   Coalition government of all leftist and liberal parties in France and Spain in the 1930s.

Résistance   World War II underground French anti-German movement.

Political Culture

FRANCE'S POLITICAL ERAS

The political history of France is rich and complex. Notice how conservative and radical eras approximately alternate. It is more difficult to construct such a table for British political development because it has had no drastic regime changes since the Commonwealth in the seventeenth century.

Name	Years	Remembered for
Old Regime	−1789	Absolutist monarchy; centralized administration; supervised economy.
Revolution	1789–1799	Tumultuous; repel invaders; Reign of Terror; Thermidor.
Napoleon	1799–1814	Redoes civil code; conquers most of Europe; crowns self emperor.
Bourbon Restoration	1815–1830	Try to restore monarchy in badly split France.
Orleanist	1830–1848	Liberal monarchy.
Second Republic	1848–1852	Attempted liberal republic.
Second Empire	1852–1870	Louis Napoleon's conservative stability.
Third Republic	1871–1940	Bourgeois liberal democracy.
Vichy	1940–1944	German puppet government.
Provisional Government	1944–1946	De Gaulle-led coalition.
Fourth Republic	1946–1958	Unstable, fractious, immobilized; Indochina and Algeria.
Fifth Republic	1958–	De Gaulle strong president; state-led modernization.

Free French   De Gaulle's World War II government in exile.

Allies   World War II anti-Axis military coalition.

Fourth Republic   1946–1958 French regime.

immobilisme   Government inability to solve big problems.

decolonization   Granting of independence to colonies.

Indochina War   First Vietnam war, 1946–1954, between French and Communist Viet Minh.

many political persuasions, but the left predominated. The Communists, who refused to attack Germans until the 1941 invasion of Russia, became the most effective underground fighters and emerged from the war with prestige and a good organization.

The rallying point of the Resistance was Charles de Gaulle (promoted to general in the last days of the Third Republic), who broadcast from London: "France has lost a battle, but France has not lost the war!" Organizing French-speaking people around the world— France had sizable colonies and thousands of able-bodied men who fled from France—de Gaulle declared a provisional government comprised of **Free French** expatriates. Participating in military actions in North Africa, the Normandy landings, and the liberation of Paris in 1944, the Free French Army was of considerable help to the **Allies**. During the war de Gaulle came to think of himself as the savior of France, a modern Joan of Arc.

The Fourth Republic

From 1944 to early 1946, de Gaulle headed a provisional government. A newly elected constituent assembly, dominated by parties of the left, drafted a constitution for the **Fourth Republic** that gave great power to the legislative branch. De Gaulle opposed the new constitution and resigned with the warning that the Fourth Republic would have the same institutional weaknesses as the Third. He retired to the small town of Colombey-les-Deux-Eglises, not to return to power until the people called him back to save France again twelve years later.

He was right about the Fourth Republic resembling the Third: From its inception the Fourth was plagued by a weak executive, a National Assembly paralyzed by small, squabbling parties, and frequent changes of cabinet. The result was, as before, **immobilisme**. Politicians played games with each other; they were good at wrecking but not at building.

Still, like the Third Republic, the Fourth might have endured if not for the terrible problems of **decolonization**, problems the fractious parliamentarians could not solve. The first problem was Indochina, a French colony since the 1880s, occupied by the Japanese in World War II and then reclaimed by France. The **Indochina War** broke out in 1946 and dragged on until the fall of the French fortress of Dienbienphu in 1954. (The United States came close to jumping into the Vietnam conflict that year but backed off.)

Algeria was even worse. The French had been there since 1830, at first to suppress piracy but later to settle. Close to a million Europeans dominated Algerian economic, social, and political life; Algeria was even declared part of France. Algerian nationalists started their revolt in 1954 with urban terrorism. This time the French army, determined to win, hunted down nationalists and tortured them. When civilian politicians in Paris opposed the Algerian War, the French army in Algeria began a coup d'état in 1958. Paratroopers were ready to drop on their own country; France tottered on the brink of civil war. At the last minute both sides agreed to call back General de Gaulle. The army assumed he would keep Algeria French (he did not). De Gaulle, acting as if he had known all along that history would recall him to lead France, demanded as his price a totally new constitution, one that would cure the ills of the Fourth Republic. He got it. In the next chapter, we explore the institutions of the Fifth Republic.

Key Terms

alienated (p. 93)
Allies (p. 98)
ancien régime (p. 92)
aristocrat (p. 90)
autonomy (p. 90)
Bastille (p. 93)
belle époque (p. 96)
bound (p. 90)
Bourbon (p. 94)
bourgeois (p. 96)
Cartesian (p. 92)
chauvinism (p. 94)
constitutional monarchy (p. 94)
core (p. 90)
coup d'état (p. 94)
courtier (p. 90)
decolonization (p. 98)
Enlightenment (p. 92)
Estates-General (p. 88)
Fourth Republic (p. 98)
Free French (p. 98)
French Revolution (p. 94)
general will (p. 92)
Han (p. 90)

Huguenots (p. 88)
immobilisme (p. 98)
Indochina War (p. 98)
intendants (p. 88)
Maginot Line (p. 96)
mercantilism (p. 90)
National Assembly (p. 93)
Paris Commune (p. 95)
particularism (p. 90)
plebiscite (p. 94)
Popular Front (p. 97)
reactionary (p. 96)
Reign of Terror (p. 94)
Résistance (p. 97)
revolution (p. 93)
Russification (p. 90)
Thermidor (p. 93)
Third Estate (p. 92)
Third Republic (p. 96)
tyrannical (p. 94)
Versailles (p. 90)
Vichy (p. 97)
Zionism (p. 96)

Further Reference

Bernier, Olivier. *Louis XIV: A Royal Life*. New York: Doubleday, 1987.
Blanning, Timothy C. W. *The Culture of Power and the Power of Culture: Old Regime Europe, 1660–1789*. New York: Oxford University Press, 2002.
Gildea, Robert. *Marianne in Chains: Daily Life in the Heart of France During the German Occupation*. New York: Metropolitan Books, 2003.
Hazareesingh, Sudhir. *Political Traditions in France*. New York: Oxford University Press, 1994.
Jackson, Julian. *France: The Dark Years, 1940–1944*. New York: Oxford University Press, 2001.
Johnson, Paul. *Napoleon*. New York: Viking, 2002.
Kedward, Rod. *La Vie en Bleu: France and the French since 1900*. New York: Overlook, 2006.
Nossiter, Adam. *The Algeria Hotel: France, Memory, and the Second World War*. Boston, MA: Houghton Mifflin, 2001.
Schama, Simon. *Citizens: A Chronicle of the French Revolution*. New York: Knopf, 1989.
Weber, Eugen. *The Hollow Years: France in the 1930s*. New York: W. W. Norton, 1994.
Williams, Charles. *The Last Great Frenchman: A Life of General De Gaulle*. New York: Wiley, 1995.

Chapter 8

FRANCE:
THE KEY INSTITUTIONS

The British constitution grew piecemeal and has not yet been formalized into one document. French constitutions—fifteen of them since the Revolution—are all written but often altered in practice. Americans regard their Constitution with religious awe, but the French and most other Europeans have seen constitutions come and go and are not averse to rewriting them every few decades.

By 1958, many French agreed that the Fourth Republic was inherently flawed and unable to settle the ghastly Algerian War. The chief problem, as defined by de Gaulle, lay in the weakness of the executive, the **premier**. The **president** was simply a figurehead, typical of European republics. The premier depended on unstable **coalitions**. Faced with controversial issues, one or more coalition parties would often drop out, vote against the government in a **vote of no-confidence**, and thereby bring it down. In all, there were twenty cabinets ("governments") in less than twelve years. Politicians sometimes voted against effective premiers out of personal resentment. Pierre Mendès-France, for example, settled the Indochina War in 1954, but that made him too popular and effective, so the National Assembly voted him out.

The Fourth Republic embodied all the weaknesses of a multiparty parliamentary system that still plague Israel. Such a system can work well and with stability, as in Sweden, but it depends on the party system and the national political style. Given French parties and political style, a pure parliamentary system may never work well.

Questions to Consider

1. What are the weaknesses of multiparty parliamentary systems?
2. How has the French *semipresidential* system evolved?
3. What problem did *cohabitation* solve?
4. How does the French electoral system work?
5. What is a *technocrat?* Does the United States have any?
6. How has the French parliament been weakened?
7. What good is the French Senate? How does it compare with the U.S. Senate?
8. Why are the French and British party systems different?
9. Is France still a highly centralized unitary system?

■ A Semipresidential System

De Gaulle hated the executive weakness of the Fourth Republic, but neither did he like the American-style presidential system with its checks and balances that might hamper his style. So he devised a **semipresidential** system, a hybrid with both an executive president and a premier (see box on page 103). For over a quarter-century, however, instead of some kind of balance between the powers of the president and those of the premier, the president held sway by virtue of

premier   French for prime minister.
(See page 101.)

president   Elected head of state, not
necessarily powerful. (See page 101.)

coalition   Multiparty alliance to form
government. (See page 101.)

vote of no confidence   Parliamentary
vote to oust cabinet. (See page 101.)

semipresidential   System with
features of both presidential and
parliamentary systems. (See page 101.)

Fifth Republic   *Semipresidential*
regime devised by de Gaulle, 1958 to
present.

referendum   Mass vote on an issue
rather than on candidates, same as
plebiscite.

Elysée   Presidential palace in Paris,
equivalent to U.S. White House.

commanding the largest bloc of votes in the National Assembly. Thus, for the first twenty-eight years of the **Fifth Republic**, the system functioned as a presidential or even "superpresidential" system. Only with the parliamentary elections of 1986—which produced a conservative National Assembly while a Socialist president was still in office—did we finally see semipresidentialism in action.

Let us first examine the original setup of the Fifth Republic, the one de Gaulle devised and commanded from 1958 to 1969. The general structure of it continues, but the powers of the president have weakened. The French president was originally elected for seven years and could be reelected without limit. Realizing that a seven-year term is too long, a 2000 **referendum** shortened it to five years. Originally, the president was selected by an electoral college of parliamentarians and local office holders. De Gaulle soon discovered he wanted nothing—certainly no politicians—to stand between him and the people, so he led a referendum in 1962 to provide for direct election of the president. It has been that way ever since.

The constitution specifies some powers for the president and some for the premier, but the practice was unclear. On paper, the president appoints a premier (but cannot fire him) who then selects his own cabinet. No parliamentary approval is required for this. Until 1986 the president was so assured of an obedient National Assembly that he handpicked both premier and cabinet ministers as mere helpers to carry out the president's program. The president presided at cabinet meetings. Virtually all foreign and defense affairs were in his hands (still mostly the case). The **Elysée** originated most legislation, often with the advice of ministers, and could even force the National Assembly to vote simply yes or no on executive proposals. The president, however, does not have the power to veto legislation. De Gaulle saw the role of president in almost mystical terms, as a "guide" and "arbiter" of the nation.

One important—and perhaps overused—power de Gaulle liked is the calling of referendums. Such mass votes on issues are alien to British tradition but very much a part of French usage, especially by leaders who believe they embody the general will and communicate directly with the people, bypassing the politicians. De Gaulle called five such plebiscites (see Chapter 10) and won each except the last. Feeling repudiated, he resigned, perhaps establishing another constitutional tradition.

Another potentially major power at the disposal of the French president is the ability to invoke *emergency powers* in time of danger to the nation. While many democracies have such an

WHO WAS WHEN: THE FIFTH REPUBLIC'S PRESIDENTS		
Charles de Gaulle		1959–1969 reelected in 1965, resigned in 1969
Georges Pompidou	Gaullist	1969–1974 died in office
Valéry Giscard d'Estaing	UDF	1974–1981 served one term
François Mitterrand	Socialist	1981–1995 reelected in 1988
Jacques Chirac	neo-Gaullist	1995–reelected in 2002

emergency provision, it can be abused, as Hitler used Article 48 of the Weimar constitution to snuff out freedom. Article 16 of the French constitution seems to place no limits on what a president can do during an emergency, a situation that is up to the president to define. During such an emergency the National Assembly must meet, but it has no power to block presidential decisions. The emergency clause has been invoked only once—in 1961, when the same generals who put de Gaulle into power tried to overthrow him for pulling out of Algeria—and many agreed it was a genuine emergency.

> **deadlock**   U.S. tendency for executive and legislature, especially when of opposing parties, to block each other.
>
> **censure**   Legislative condemnation of executive.

Key Concepts

THE FRENCH SEMIPRESIDENTIAL SYSTEM

Most European governments are parliamentary; that is, they depend on votes in parliament to put a cabinet into executive power and keep it there (see page 38). The cabinet, usually composed of members of parliament, is a sort of parliamentary steering committee that also guides the ministries or departments. If no party in parliament has a majority, a coalition of parties is necessary, and this may be unstable. In policy splits, a *vote of no-confidence* may oust the cabinet. Where a single party dominates the parliament—mostly the case in Britain—the system can be very stable.

In a presidential system (also on page 38), such as the United States and Mexico, the executive does not depend on parliamentary support, for here the chief executive is elected more or less directly for a fixed term. The parliament can do what it wants, but it cannot oust the president in a vote of no-confidence. (It may impeach the president.) The advantage of a presidential system is its stability and certainty: There will always be a president to lead. The disadvantage is that the president and the legislature may **deadlock**, producing something similar to the *immobilisme* that plagues parliamentary systems.

The French system is *semipresidential,* for the cabinet still has a certain parliamentary connection. The premier is named by the president but can be **censured** and forced to resign by the National Assembly. If that happens—and it has occurred only once, in 1962—the president can dissolve the legislature and hold new elections. Influenced by the French model, Russia and China also adopted semipresidential systems.

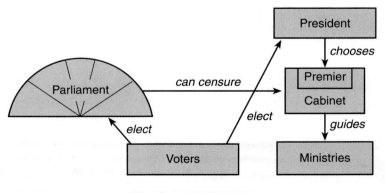

The French System

neo-Gaullist Chirac's revival of Gaullist party, now called Union for a Popular Movement (UMP).

cohabitation French president forced to name premier of opposing party.

turnout Percentage of those eligible who vote in a given election. (See page 105.)

The presidential paradise came to an end with the National Assembly elections of 1986, which produced, as expected, a legislature dominated by conservative parties. The problem was that President François Mitterrand, a Socialist, had two years remaining in his seven-year term. For the first time the Fifth Republic had a president who did not control the National Assembly. No one knew how to handle it; the constitution was unclear. Some feared a hostile deadlock and paralysis of government. Others thought Mitterrand would have to resign to make way for the election of a conservative president. Instead, Mitterrand played a waiting game that preserved him as president but reduced the powers of the presidency. Mitterrand thus clarified the French constitution and set a precedent when the same situation occurred in 1993 and 1997.

In 1986 Mitterrand called on the leader of the largest conservative party (sometimes called **neo-Gaullist**), Jacques Chirac, to become premier and went along with most of Chirac's cabinet choices. Mitterrand also did not block most of Chirac's legislative program, which rolled back many of Mitterrand's socialist experiments in the economy. The two struck an informal bargain—called **cohabitation**, living together but not married—in which Chirac concentrated on domestic affairs and Mitterrand on foreign and defense policy plus the symbolic functions of the presidency. In 1993, faced with another conservative victory in parliamentary elections, Mitterrand named another neo-Gaullist, Edouard Balladur, as his premier. In 1997, faced with a Socialist victory in the early parliamentary elections he had called, Chirac named Socialist chief Lionel Jospin as premier. As of this writing, France does not have cohabitation because both president and premier are of the same party. Should the split occur again, Paris knows how to handle it: cohabitation again. With cohabitation, French presidents are not as strong as de Gaulle was, and premiers are stronger than he intended. Institutions evolve.

If the French want to avoid cohabitation and restrengthen the presidency, they could cut the last link between legislative and executive branches (the "can-censure" arrow) and become a straight presidential system, U.S.-style. True, the U.S. system often deadlocks between the White House and Capitol Hill, but the president still has plenty of power to govern without permission from Congress.

Premier and Cabinet

Until cohabitation, French ministers, including the prime minister, served as little more than messenger boys for the president. The premier's main function was to push presidential measures through parliament. Under cohabitation, however, Premiers Chirac, Balladur, and Jospin gave much power to that office by pursuing their own legislative agendas. Even with no cohabitation since 1997–2002, the premiership did not return completely to the subservient model designed by de Gaulle. French presidents like to appear above ordinary politics, so they let their premiers do the heavy work, especially on the economy. The precise balance of powers between president and premier in France has not been settled and is likely to change with new personalities and situations.

Just after Chirac was humiliated by the French "no" vote on a new EU constitution in 2005 (see pages 252–254), he named Dominique de Villepin, a 51-year old career diplomat, as his new premier. As Chirac's foreign minister (2002–2004), de Villepin enraged the Bush administration with his strong and vocal opposition to the 2003 Iraq War, which he predicted would go badly.

Democracy

FRANCE'S PRESIDENTIAL ELECTION OF 2002

France shocked itself and the world in the first round of its 2002 presidential election. Instead of the expected runoff between France's top two political figures, neo-Gaullist President Chirac and Socialist Premier Lionel Jospin, extreme-rightist Jean-Marie Le Pen of the anti-immigrant National Front edged out Jospin to run against Chirac in the second round. France was ashamed: The land of liberty, equality, and fraternity had a racist as presidential contender.

Actually, Le Pen's win was more a fluke than an upsurge of French racism. Two factors made it happen: (1) an electoral system that runs the top two of the first round in a runoff two weeks later, and (2) too many leftist candidates dividing the total left vote, thereby narrowly pushing Jospin into third place on the first round. It was like the 2000 Green vote for Ralph Nader costing Gore the U.S. presidency.

French elections are held in two rounds. The first round on April 21 had sixteen candidates but drew only a 72 percent **turnout**, a record low for France. The results are shown in the table below.

Altogether, thirteen frivolous candidates took 47 percent of the first-round vote. Many French protest against the system by voting for no-chance parties on the first round, figuring that only the second round counts, and it will be between Chirac and Jospin. All the polls say so. This casual attitude siphoned off enough left votes to drop Jospin into third place and out of the contest. Jospin had been a dour but effective premier, especially on the economy; he immediately resigned from office and from politics. The moral: Be careful with your protest vote; you may get the opposite of what you want.

Horrified at what they had wrought, French voters, many reluctantly, rallied to Chirac—who was tarnished by scandal—in the second round on May 5. A pro-Chirac slogan: "Vote for the crook, not the fascist." An 80 percent turnout gave him the biggest victory in the Fifth Republic's history:

Chirac	82.2%
Le Pen	17.8

Legislative elections in June gave Chirac a solid majority of the National Assembly (see box on page 113), so he kept his like-minded Premier Raffarin and governed without cohabitation.

Jacques Chirac	Union for a Popular Movement	19.9%
Jean-Marie Le Pen	National Front	16.9
Lionel Jospin	Socialist	16.2
François Bayrou	Union for French Democracy	6.8
Arlette Laguiller	Workers Struggle	5.7
Jean-Pierre Chevènement	Republican	5.3
Noël Mamère	Greens	5.2
Olivier Besancenot	Communist Revolutionary	4.2
Jean Saint-Josse	Hunting, Fishing, Nature	4.2
Alain Madelin	Liberal Democracy	3.9
Robert Hue	Communist	3.4

Sorbonne Main branch of University of Paris.

Ecole Nationale d'Administration (ENA) France's school for top bureaucrats.

(De Gaulle warned Kennedy of the same in Vietnam.) De Villepin had also served as interior minister (2004–2005) but had little experience guiding an economy. The brainy de Villepin graduated from the elite National Administration School (ENA, see page 124) and writes books of poetry and history. He especially admires Napoleon and keeps a bust of him in his office. Some speculated that Chirac was lining up his protégé de Villepin for the 2007 presidential election,

Personalities

CHIRAC: BRAINY, WARM, CORRUPT

In many ways, French President Jacques Chirac was the opposite of his immediate predecessor, François Mitterrand. The two, although they governed together during the 1986–1988 cohabitation period, hated each other. Mitterrand, who died of cancer shortly after completing two full terms, was a left-leaning mystic. Chirac was right-leaning and governed by means of administrative and economic expertise. Mitterrand was a quiet and abstract intellectual and poet, a graduate of the **Sorbonne**. Chirac was an energized problem-solver, a graduate of the elite **Ecole Nationale d'Administration**. Mitterrand hated de Gaulle for his haughty ways during World War II; Chirac made his political career by worshipping de Gaulle. Mitterrand carried on the traditional French presidential style of aloofness and distance from the public; Chirac projected warmth and amiability and gave crowd-pleasing speeches.

But in some ways the two antagonists resembled each other. Both were extremely brainy, the norm for French leaders. Both created their respective political parties. Mitterrand, for years a leader of small centrist parties, took over the Socialists in 1971 when they were at a low ebb and remade them into a vote-getting center-left party, with which he rode into the presidency a decade later. Chirac took over and reorganized the moribund Gaullists in 1976, turning them into the biggest right-wing party, now the Union for a Popular Movement (UMP), often known as "neo-Gaullist." (De Gaulle left office in 1969 never having bothered to build a strong Gaullist party.)

For years Chirac, even as a leading member of the National Assembly, was also the elected mayor of

Jacques Chirac.

Paris, something perfectly legal and normal in France. More than half the National Assembly's deputies and most ministers are also mayors; it firms up their power base and shows they have local roots.

Chirac served as premier under center-rightist Valéry Giscard d'Estaing from 1974 to 1976, but the two parted in jealous anger over who was to be the leading figure on the French right. Chirac then served as premier under Mitterrand from 1986 to 1988, time enough for Mitterrand to get Chirac to catch the blame for economic problems and enable Mitterrand to win reelection in 1988. Another point in common: Both Mitterrand and Chirac knew how to wait, and both won the presidency on their third try.

As in much of Europe, scandal is semipermanent in France, and it touched Chirac. Accused of overseeing kickbacks on public-works projects (frequent in France) and using secret funds for luxury personal travel, Chirac let presidential immunity block investigation. Many French voters were angry at him in 2002 but voted for him anyhow to reject Le Pen (see box on page 105).

but the aristocratic de Villepin had never run for office before. A more likely and popular candidate: Nicolas Sarkozy, son of a Hungarian refugee, who served Chirac as finance and interior minister and headed his UMP party. Chirac and Sarkozy did not like each other.

Premiers name ministers, who do not have to be approved by the National Assembly but usually are. A cabinet not to the liking of parliament could be censured and ousted. Accordingly, Socialist Mitterrand felt he had to name neo-Gaullists Chirac and Balladur, because they had majority support in parliament. This is the general basis for selecting prime ministers throughout Europe (compare with Britain, page 34, and Germany, pages 183–184).

The president cannot directly fire a premier, but, if they are of the same party, the president may persuade the premier to resign. In 2002 Chirac named as premier Jean-Pierre Raffarin, a rumpled provincial senator, but got him to resign in 2005 after the EU constitution fiasco. Socialist President Mitterrand had earlier named and dropped several Socialist premiers; two of them served less than a year. Cohabitation actually improves a premier's tenure in office, because the president cannot use party pressure to get premiers to resign. During the first two cohabitation periods, Mitterrand had no party leverage over his neo-Gaullist premiers, Chirac and Balladur, who lasted two years until new elections. Curiously, Socialist Lionel Jospin, in cohabitation with Gaullist Chirac, was one of France's longest-serving premiers (1997–2002). Divided government may be good for France.

Another difference from parliamentary systems is that a French **deputy** chosen to be a minister must resign his or her seat. (A replacement is elected along with each deputy, so there is no need for by-elections, as in Britain.) In parliamentary systems, such as Britain, ministers keep their seats in parliament. De Gaulle wanted to make sure ministers could not run back to parliament to protest his policies. By the same token, unlike Britain, French ministers do not have to be members of parliament; many are experienced administrators and nonparty **technocrats** who have never been elected to anything. De Gaulle picked as one of his premiers Georges Pompidou, who had never run in an election (but who went on to become an effective president in his own right).

Like most European cabinets, the French cabinet can be easily remade to suit the premier. Ministries are not quite the same as U.S. departments, which are firmly fixed by statute and change

deputy Member of French and many other parliaments.

technocrat Official, usually unelected, who governs by virtue of economic skills.

interior ministry In Europe, department in charge of homeland security and national police.

Comparison

WASHINGTON GETS AN INTERIOR MINISTRY

In 2002, the United States finally got something like a European **interior ministry**, the Department of Homeland Security. America, fearing centralized police powers, had never accepted the European view that national government exists to supervise the nation. The terror attacks of 9/11 made Americans a little more European. By combining and centralizing portions of existing departments to safeguard Americans in their own country, the new DHS does many of the same things as a European interior ministry, although there is still no national U.S. police. The new U.S. department also demonstrated that from time to time governments must reshuffle departments to meet new situations. European governments do this frequently, whenever the prime minister wishes. The American process requires elaborate Congressional approval.

only after great deliberation. Paris ministries, often renamed, are almost ad hoc combinations of existing French agencies and bureaus and change according to the policy goals of the executive. In 2005 Premier de Villepin named a government of sixteen ministers (two of them women) for these ministries:

Foreign Affairs
Defense
Economy, Finance, and Industry
Interior
Justice
Employment, Social Cohesion, and Housing
Education
Transportation and Tourism
Ecology
Small and Medium Enterprises
Health and Solidarity
Agriculture
Culture and Communication
Civil Service
Overseas Departments
Youth and Sports

An additional fifteen *ministers delegate* filled more specialized offices within the ministries and were also considered part of the government. In general, left-wing governments have larger cabinets since they propose major changes under state supervision. Conservative governments, on the other hand, usually like smaller cabinets, as they do not plan to remake society. Repeated changes in ministries sounds chaotic to Americans, but the same career civil servants still run the various bureaus; the changes are only at the top, at the ministerial level. In France we see bureaucrats actually running the country, a pattern developed even more fully in Japan.

■ The National Assembly

During the Third and Fourth Republics the National Assembly was dominant. Making and unmaking cabinets, the parliament controlled the executive. Some say this sort of parliamentary system has a weak executive and strong legislature, but that is not quite accurate. In this case the legislature was not strong either. Divided into several quarrelsome parties that were unable to form stable coalitions, the French National Assembly was no more able to govern than were the cabinets. The government "fell" every few months on average.

This is not quite so chaotic as it sounds. When a government in a parliamentary system "falls," it does not mean the entire structure of government collapses; indeed, little changes. It just means there has been a policy quarrel among the parties so that the cabinet coalition no longer commands a majority in parliament. The cabinet then either resigns, is ousted in a vote of no-confidence, or limps along as a minority government. After several days or weeks of negotiations, another cabinet is put together that wins majority approval. Often this cabinet is composed of the same ministers in the same jobs as the previous cabinet. Instead of too much change, parliamentary systems often suffer from too little. As the French have said for decades: *"Plus ça change, plus c'est la même chose."* (The more it changes, the more it stays the same.) Some premiers have their hands so full just keeping the coalition together that they are often unwilling to risk doing anything that might make it come apart. The result is *immobilisme*.

Palais Bourbon Paris house of French National Assembly.

Meeting in the windowless **Palais Bourbon**, deputies prior to 1958 tended to play politics with each other and ignore what was happening outside. In a massive avoidance of responsibility, deputies concentrated on either getting into the cabinet or bringing it down. Things changed with the Fifth Republic; the legislators' paradise came to an abrupt end.

The National Assembly no longer makes cabinets; today that power belongs to the premier, in consultation with the president. Indeed, the relationship between the cabinet and the legislature has been deliberately weakened; as noted earlier, a deputy named to the cabinet must resign his or her seat. One link does remain: The National Assembly can censure a cabinet, indicating its extreme displeasure. The president on the other hand, can dissolve the National Assembly for new elections before the end of its normal five-year term, which is what Chirac did in 1997. The president is limited to one dissolution per year.

The premier and the president, not the legislature, now hold key powers of legislation. Most bills originate with the government. The government sets the agenda. If the government specifies, its proposals must be considered without amendments on a take-it-or-leave-it basis called a *blocked vote*. That is to prevent parliamentary dilution of legislation. The National Assembly no longer has the time or structure to consider legislation closely: Its sessions are limited to five and a half months a year; it has only six committees; and a bill cannot be bottled up in committee but must be reported out.

Comparison

ISRAEL'S EXPERIMENT

Israel to some extent followed in France's footsteps. Both had a weak executive dependent on a shaky coalition of parties elected by proportional representation. Both modified their systems. De Gaulle ended the Fourth Republic's parliamentary system and founded the Fifth's semipresidential one. Israel stayed parliamentary until it tried to strengthen the executive.

Israel's single house, the 120-member Knesset, is elected by proportional representation and permits any party that wins at least 1.5 percent of the national vote to have at least a few seats in parliament. (It used to be only 1 percent.) Israel has a dozen or more parties—some based on a single personality—none of them having a majority in parliament. Thus every Israeli government has been a coalition and prone to breakup when the parties in it quarreled. Israel too suffered immobilism in the face of major problems.

Taking a turn to semipresidentialism, Israel tried directly and separately electing its prime minister in 1996 by popular vote. Each Israeli voter had two votes, one for a party in the Knesset, the other for prime minister. Designed to bring greater stability to Israel's chief executive, the experiment failed, because the prime minister could still be ousted on a vote of no-confidence and coalition cabinets were as hard to form as ever. Israeli voters, figuring they had selected a strong prime minister, then scattered their votes among a dozen small parties, fractionating the Knesset even more. After two elections under the unique, hybrid system, Israel repealed it in 2001 and went back to the regular parliamentary system. The moral: Be careful when mixing components of different systems (presidential and parliamentary).

The government is able to pass many laws by simple decree, provided the premier and the president agree (and sometimes they do not). The 1958 constitution specifies the types of laws that must go through parliament; all others presumably do not need to. While most decrees concern details, the power of government decree also extends to the budget. Here, the legislature has lost its original, most fundamental, power—the power of the purse. Any parliamentary motion to either decrease revenues (a tax cut) or increase spending (a new program) are automatically out of order. And if the parliament cannot settle on the budget within seventy days, the government may make it law by simple decree.

A Senate That Fights Back

Most parliaments are composed of two chambers, and most do not know what to do with the upper chamber. Sweden simply abolished its upper house. The greatest value of an upper house is in representing territorial subunits, as the U.S. Senate represents the states. Where the system is unitary (Britain, France, China) rather than federal (the United States, Germany, Russia, Mexico, Nigeria) an upper chamber does not have much use.

unitary   System that centralizes power in capital with little autonomy for component areas. (See page 111.)

first-order civil division   Main territorial units within countries, such as departments in France. (See page 111.)

prefect   (French *préfet*) Administrator of department. (See page 111.)

Midi   (French for "noon") The South of France. (See page 111.)

département   (Department) French first-order civil division, equivalent to British county. (See page 111.)

France's main legislative body, comparable to the British House of Commons, is also the lower house, the 577-member National Assembly elected every five years (or sooner if the president wishes it). The upper house, the *Sénat*, has 316 members elected for nine years each—with elections for about a third every three years—by a gigantic electoral college made up of National Assembly deputies plus more than 100,000 regional and municipal councilors. De Gaulle thought that these councilors, because they would overrepresent rural and small-town France, would produce a conservative Senate amenable to his direction.

Rural France is not necessarily conservative; it looks out for farming. Above all, the Sénat represents farmers' viewpoints; indeed, 8.5 percent of senators are farmers. The French Senate criticizes and amends numerous government bills. Sénateurs are not under pressure like lower-house assembly members to pass what the government wants. The French Senate—sometimes called the "agricultural chamber"—is listened to by the government on farm matters, for angry French farmers can create havoc. Still, when the government wants a measure passed, it can override Senate objections by a simple majority in the National Assembly.

The French Senate, although not equal in power to the National Assembly, cannot be dissolved by the government. De Gaulle came to regret the Senate's autonomy and in 1969 tried to dilute its power by a plebiscite. The French people, annoyed by de Gaulle, supported their Senate, the last arena of French parliamentary freedom, and rejected the referendum. Chirac's UMP held a comfortable majority in the National Assembly but lost its majority in the Senate in 2004.

The French Multiparty System

Parties can make or break a political system. Britain's stability and efficiency would diminish if instead of one party with a solid majority in Commons there were half a dozen parties of about equal size. Much of what was wrong with the Third and Fourth Republics was not government institutions but the parties that tried to operate them.

Geography

DECENTRALIZING UNITARY SYSTEMS

The way a state is organized territorially—its "civil divisions" and their relationship to the capital—can heighten or dampen center-periphery tensions, although no sure-fire formula has been found. There are two approaches, **unitary** and federal. More than Britain, France is a unitary system, a carry-over from monarchical times, whereby the **first-order civil divisions**—counties in Britain, departments in France, prefectures in Japan—have little autonomy and serve mostly as administrative conveniences for the national capital.

These units can be changed and their boundaries redrawn with little ado. The leading executives in these civil divisions are appointed and supervised by the national government. France's **prefects** are perhaps the best examples of how the unitary state rules. There are, to be sure, elected county, departmental, and municipal councils, but their powers to tax and spend are limited. Any major project must be cleared with and usually funded by the national authorities. Most countries in the world are unitary systems. (U.S. states, although they look like federal systems, are actually unitary.)

The advantage of a unitary system is that it gives greater control to the center for rational administration and modernization. Standards can be enforced nationally. Central administration can knead disparate groups into a single nationality, as France has done over the centuries. The unitary system best suits a country like Japan that is not too large or does not contain different cultures and languages.

There are several difficulties with unitary systems. One is that they may ignore the wishes of local people, especially those at the periphery. Crushing the **Midi** caused centuries of resentment. Many of today's *méridionaux* (southerners) see themselves as a race separate from the northerners. Thus a unitary system may foster center-periphery tensions (see page 52). Corsican and Breton violence shows the incomplete integration of France's regional subcultures into a French whole.

Further, a unitary system, because it is so uniform, can be overly rigid and make big, nationwide mistakes that in a federal system would be implemented and corrected piecemeal, as the components tried various policies. Often there is too much national control over purely local issues. Even trivial matters such as a new traffic light might have to be approved by Paris or Tokyo.

Britain, France, and Spain in recent years loosened their unitary systems by instituting regional autonomy. Britain devolved some home rule to Scotland, Wales, and Northern Ireland. France's twenty-two regions and Spain's seventeen *autonomías* now have elected councils with considerable decision-making powers on economic growth, education, housing, and other regional concerns. Although not nearly federalism, these unitary systems have moved in a quasi-federal direction.

The change in France under Mitterrand is particularly striking, for it rolled back a tradition that started with Louis XI. French monarchs tried to erase regional differences but sometimes only worsened local resentments. Napoleon perfected this centralizing and homogenizing pattern. He abolished the historic provinces and replaced them with smaller, artificial units called **départements** named after rivers. The departments were administrative conveniences to facilitate control by Paris.

Each department—there are now ninety-six (plus four for overseas territories)—is administered by a prefect, a lineal descendant of Richelieu's old *intendant,* now an official of the Interior Ministry. Prefects, very bright and highly trained (often at the ENA—see page 124) monitored laws, funds, and mayors with Olympian detachment.

In 1982, Mitterrand got a law that reduced the domain of prefects and increased local autonomy. Elected councils in the departments and regions got policy-setting and taxation powers in education, urban and regional planning and development, job training, and housing. Soon French local and regional government became more important, and elections to their councils were hotly contested. Competition set in as cities, departments, and regions sought to attract new industries. Local taxes increased, but the ways of assessing them became widely divergent and innovative.

The subnational units of French government started acting somewhat like American states, developing their own strategies for prosperity. France in no sense became a federal system—indeed, its decentralization did not go as far as Spain's during this same period—but it was Mitterrand's most important and lasting contribution to the French political system.

National Front   French
anti-immigrant party.

We must avoid evaluating all two-party systems as good and all multiparty systems as bad. Americans especially disdain multiparty systems and often cite Italy and the Fourth Republic as examples of the ills they create. But several multiparty parliamentary democracies are stable and effective, for example, Sweden, Switzerland, Holland, and Belgium. At least as much depends on the way the parties behave as on how many parties there are.

By the same token, the Fifth French Republic would not have worked the way it did had not the Gaullist party ballooned into the largest party. Indeed, if the Fourth Republic had been preserved but with Gaullists occupying the largest slice of the National Assembly, the most troublesome problem of that system—immobilisme—would have disappeared, for de Gaulle would have had a stable majority at his disposal.

France has at present three large parties and three small ones, plus a sprinkling of minor parties. Two parties often ally—the center-right Union for French Democracy (UDF) and the larger and farther-right neo-Gaullists (UMP)—to win a majority of parliament and the presidency. The Socialist party (PS) occupies the center-left. Flanking these large parties are the Communists on the left and the racist **National Front** on the right. Fitting in somewhere on the left, the Greens finally got into the National Assembly in 1997. (For more on French parties, see Chapter 10.)

■ France's Electoral System

French presidential and legislative elections normally come every five years. The two were originally intended to be out of kilter, but starting in 2002 presidential elections come shortly before legislative elections. The pattern actually started under President Mitterrand, who followed his elections in both 1981 and 1988 by immediately dissolving the National Assembly so that his Socialists could increase their number of seats. That still left him with two cohabitation periods of two years each, as he had two years left in both his terms when conservative parliaments were voted in. The five-year presidential term that started in 2002 was in part to end the need for presidents to either cohabit or to dissolve the National Assembly for new elections.

The traditional electoral system of the Fifth Republic—single-member districts with runoff—is actually taken from the Third Republic. Like Britain and America, France uses single-member districts but instead of a simple plurality to win (FPTP) requires a majority (more than 50 percent). If the candidate does not get it on the first ballot—and that is usually the case—the contest goes to a runoff a week later, this time with either the top two candidates or those with at least 12.5 percent of the eligible voters of that district. Now only a simple plurality is needed to win. The second round, then, is the decisive one; the first round is a bit like U.S. primaries.

Presidential elections run under similar rules. All but the top two candidates for president are eliminated in the first round; a second round two weeks later decides between the top two. In 2002, the unexpected first-round win of the National Front's Le Pen humiliated France (see box on page 105). To prevent a recurrence, France might consider dropping the two-round system and go to simple plurality win (FPTP) in one round. That would force small parties to coalesce into larger parties before the election. No electoral system works perfectly, as Americans learned in 2000, when Gore outpolled Bush by half a million votes but still lost in the electoral college.

The French system permits or encourages several parties to exist but not necessarily to win; the Anglo-American systems discourage third parties. Proportional-representation systems, on the other hand, permit small parties to exist and even win. In Germany, for example, a Green vote of over 5 percent wins them dozens of seats. But the French party system is rooted in French society, and this is a more complex and fragmented society than the British or American. In any case, the French party system seems to be coalescing into two large blocs, one left and one right. Over the decades, there have been fewer and fewer relevant parties in France.

Democracy

FRANCE'S PARLIAMENTARY ELECTIONS OF 2002

France's parliamentary elections followed the victory of President Jacques Chirac and gave 357 of the National Assembly's 577 seats to a center-right coalition, the Union for the Presidential Majority (UMP) that he had just formed. (It was then turned into a new party, the Union for a Popular Movement, with the same initials, UMP.) As he had done in his first presidential win in 1995, Chirac promised more—tax cuts and job subsidies—than the economy can deliver, which soon angered voters. French voters are always angry.

The Socialists, still smarting from Jospin's ouster on the first round of the presidential contest (see box on page 105), also declined in the legislature. Because the legislative elections came just a month after presidential elections, the French voted four times (because each election has two rounds) in a month, one reason for weak turnouts (64 percent in the first round, 60 percent in the second). The June 9 first-round voting results:

Union for the Presidential Majority (UMP)	34%
Union for French Democracy (UDF)	5
Socialists (and allies)	24
National Front	11
Communists	5
Greens	5

There were several smaller parties and some independents. A few candidates won actual majorities in their districts, and they were declared winners immediately. In most districts, however, voters had to go to a runoff a week later. Candidates who had polled less than one eligible voter in eight in the first round were dropped. In most districts weaker candidates also withdrew and endorsed the candidate who most matched their preferences. For example, by prearrangement among the two large conservative parties, an UDF candidate who scored lower would withdraw and urge his supporters in the first round to vote for the better-scoring UMP candidate in the second round. The decisive second round yielded these votes and legislative seats.

Union for the Presidential Majority	47%	357 seats
Union for French Democracy (UDF)	4	29
Socialists (and allies)	34	140
National Front	2	0
Communists	3	21
Greens	3	3

With related small parties and independents, Chirac commanded some 400 seats and had no further need for cohabitation. The racist National Front got no seats, and the Communists continued their long decline (they won 38 seats in 1997). The real losers of the 2002 elections were the Socialists, who declined from 241 seats in 1997. Under Premier Jospin they had done a good job on the economy but did not have attractive leaders or a vision of the future. Learn from Blair.

■ The Constitutional Council

In the 1980s, a little-noticed branch of the French government started drawing attention: the Constitutional Council. Although it was part of the 1958 constitution, it came into its own as a buffer between Mitterrand and the conservative-dominated parliament during his two cohabitation periods. Some started comparing it to the U.S. Supreme Court. The comparison is shaky.

- Both have nine members, but the French serve for nine years, not for life. Three members of the French court are appointed each by the president, the speaker of the National Assembly, and the speaker of the Senate.
- The French Council members are rarely lawyers and see their role as political rather than legal. The U.S. Supreme Court sees its role the other way around.
- The scope of the French Council is much more limited. It can review the constitutionality of laws only after they are passed by parliament but before they have been signed by the president. It considers cases not from lower courts but on demand by the executive or any sixty members of either chamber of parliament.
- Rather than establishing legal precedents as the U.S. Supreme Court does, the French Constitutional Council has acted as a brake against hasty and ill-considered legislation. As such, the ruling parties in France tend to dislike its decisions while the opposition parties often like them.
- In 1999 the head of the Constitutional Court had to step down over allegations that he had siphoned off vast sums from a giant state-owned oil company he had earlier headed. This did the Court's reputation no good.

The role and powers of the U.S. Supreme Court are unique. Some French thinkers would like to see their council become more like the U.S. Supreme Court. The German Federal Constitutional Court is one of the few that approach the Supreme Court in importance.

Key Terms

censure (p. 103)
coalition (p. 102)
cohabitation (p. 104)
deadlock (p. 103)
département (p. 110)
deputy (p. 107)
Ecole Nationale d'Administration (p. 106)
Elysée (p. 102)
Fifth Republic (p. 102)
first-order civil division (p. 110)
interior ministry (p. 107)
Midi (p. 110)
National Front (p. 112)

neo-Gaullist (p. 104)
Palais Bourbon (p. 109)
prefect (p. 110)
premier (p. 102)
president (p. 102)
referendum (p. 102)
semipresidential (p. 102)
Sorbonne (p. 106)
technocrat (p. 107)
turnout (p. 104)
unitary system (p. 110)
vote of no-confidence (p. 102)

Further Reference

Bell, David S. *Presidential Power in Fifth Republic France*. New York: Berg, 2001.

———. *François Mitterrand: A Political Biography*. Cambridge, UK: Polity Press, 2005.

Cole, Alistair, and Peter Campbell. *French Electoral Systems*, 3rd ed. Brookfield, VT: Gower, 1989.

Elgie, Robert, ed. *The Changing French Political System*. Portland, OR: F. Cass, 2000.

Gaffney, John, and Lorna Milne, eds. *French Presidentialism and the Election of 1995*. Brookfield, VT: Ashgate, 1997.

Lewis-Beck, Michael, ed. *How France Votes*. New York: Chatham House, 2000.

Loughlin, John, and Sonia Mazeyln, eds. *The End of the French Unitary State? Ten Years of Regionalization in France 1982–1992*. Portland, OR: Frank Cass, 1995.

Raymond, Gino G., ed. *Structures of Power in Modern France*. New York: St. Martin's, 2000.

Safran, William. *The French Polity*, 6th ed. White Plains, NY: Longman, 2002.

Schmidt, Vivien A. *Democratizing France: The Political and Administrative History of Decentralization*. New York: Cambridge University Press, 1991.

Stone, Alec. *The Birth of Judicial Review in France: The Constitutional Council in Comparative Perspective*. New York: Oxford University Press, 1992.

Thody, Philip. *The Fifth French Republic: Presidents, Politics and Personalities*. New York: Routledge, 1998.

Chapter 9

FRENCH
POLITICAL CULTURE

Two Parisian families I knew during the Bicentennial of the French Revolution in 1989 illustrate the deeply divided nature of French society. One couple, although not university-educated, were bright and hard-working and had turned their small suburban house into a tidy and pleasant home. They read the conservative daily *Le Figaro* and a Catholic weekly and did not like the Socialist government. When they entered a church, they crossed themselves. They showed little interest in celebrating the Bicentennial July 14 and cautioned me about the crowds in Paris. They suggested a picnic in the countryside instead.

Questions to Consider

1. Describe the split nature of French political culture.
2. What is statism? Is it still found in Europe?
3. What was the slogan of the French Revolution?
4. What is anticlericalism? Where else is it found?
5. What is the typical education path into the French elite?
6. What is the ENA and why is it important?
7. How do presidential press conferences show differences of political culture?
8. What happened to Marxism in France?

The other family were typical Parisian intellectuals, both university-educated, inhabiting a charming, book-strewn older apartment not far from one of Paris's great boulevards. They read the leftish *Le Monde* and were irreligious. They liked the current Socialist government. They urged me to join the street festivities the night before July 14 and then catch the spectacular parade. They thought the French Revolution was really worth celebrating.

There, in miniature, was conservative France and radical France, the former Catholic and indifferent or even a little hostile to the French Revolution, the latter secular and enthusiastically in favor of it. The split created by the French Revolution continues to this day, although in subdued form. Conservative France no longer battles radical France; rather, the two preserve a chilly distance.

Both families deeply love France, but they love different facets of France. France has a mystique, a drawing power that can equally attract conservatives such as de Gaulle and Socialists such as Mitterrand. The conservatives are drawn to French civilization, its Catholic roots, and its *grandeur* (greatness). Liberals and leftists, on the other hand, are drawn to the ideals of the French Revolution—liberty, equality, fraternity—and see France as guarding these ideals. Some French envision their land as a person, a princess, or even a Madonna. They have a reverence for their country that few Americans or Britons can match. The dramatic and stirring "**La Marseillaise**" (see box on page 120) shows the depth of French patriotism.

French patriotism in the abstract, however, does not carry over into the real, grubby, daily life of French politics. The French are more cynical about politics than Britons or Americans. The French may be the world's greatest complainers: Nothing works right; all governments are crooked. France in the abstract is glorious; France in the here and now is shabby. De Gaulle said France

La Marseillaise   French national anthem. (See page 117.)

omnipotent   All-powerful.

statism   Idea that a strong government should run things, especially major industries.

bureaucratized   Heavily controlled by civil servants.

needs national greatness, for only with such a vision can the French rise above the sordid reality and pursue the mythical ideal.

Mitterrand was elected in 1981 in part because of his ability to project an idealistic vision of France with a leftist twist. "It is natural for a great nation to have great ambitions," he proclaimed. "In today's world, can there be a loftier duty for our country than to achieve a new alliance between socialism and liberty?" The French liked the sentiment, but once Mitterrand was in power they grew quickly disillusioned with the reality.

■ Historical Roots of French Attitudes

Where did this French political schizophrenia come from? Part of the problem is historical, traceable to the centralization of French kings, who implanted an **omnipotent** state, a state that tried to supervise everything. In theory, a centralized system should plan and build rationally; in practice, it often fails. The French, educated to expect a powerful government to help them (the ideal), are always disappointed when it does not (the real). This is reinforced by the promise of every new French government to cut France's high unemployment rate. They fail, leaving French citizens bitter. The solution: Either stop promising or dismantle the impediments to a free economy that would hire more people. Few French politicians are willing to do either.

French **statism** also stunted the development of a voluntary, do-it-ourselves attitude, something taken for granted in the United States. France simply has no tradition of voluntary groups of neighbors undertaking local governance. When local groups take responsibility and something goes wrong, you can only blame yourselves. In France, with all responsibility, until recently, in the hands of the central government, people blame Paris.

Centuries of **bureaucratized** administration also left the French used to living by uniform, impersonal rules—and lots of them. This creates hatred, the hatred of the little citizen on one side of the counter facing the cold, indifferent bureaucrat on the other. Centralization and bureaucratization are the products of the "order and reason" approach to governance that has been practiced in France for centuries. Order and reason, unfortunately, are mere ideals. Since they are always deficient in practice, the French become unhappy with a reality that always falls short of ideals.

Geography

SAILING THE MEDITERRANEAN

On your luxury yacht, you are sailing in a great, clockwise circle around the Mediterranean Sea, always keeping the shore a few kilometers to port (left, for you landlubbers). You enter through the Strait of Gibraltar. Which countries do you pass one after another on your left?

Spain, France, Italy, Slovenia, Croatia, Bosnia (minute shoreline), Croatia again, Montenegro (federated with Serbia until 2006), Albania, Greece, Turkey, Syria, Lebanon, Israel, Egypt, Libya, Tunisia, Algeria, and Morocco.

A Climate of Mistrust

In personal relations, the French are sometimes distant and mistrustful to people outside their family. Indeed, attitudes of mistrust are widespread throughout Latin Europe—they are extremely pronounced in Italy—while trustful attitudes are more common in North Europe. American scholar Laurence Wylie found villagers in the Vaucluse, in the south of France, constantly suspicious of *les autres*, "the others," those outsiders who talk behind your back, blacken your name, and meddle in your affairs. The best way to live, people there agreed, was not to get involved with other people and to maintain only correct but distant relations with neighbors. With modernization, such extreme mistrust has receded.

culmination   Logical outcome or end.

French philosopher and playwright Jean-Paul Sartre voiced a very French feeling about interpersonal relationships when he wrote, "*L'enfer, c'est les autres*" (Hell is other people). He meant, in his play *No Exit*, that having to get along with other people was his idea of hell.

Foreigners notice how shut off the French family is. Typical French houses are surrounded by high walls often topped by broken glass set in concrete. Shutters are not just for decoration; they bang shut as if to tell the world to mind its own business. Traditionally, French people rarely entertained at home—they would go to a restaurant instead; inviting outsiders to your table was an invasion of family privacy. This has changed, however; I have been invited into several French homes for superb meals.

Special mistrust is reserved for the government. In Wylie's village it was taken for granted that all government is bad, a necessary evil at best. The duties of a good citizen, which schoolchildren

Political Culture

HOW TO CELEBRATE A 200-YEAR-OLD REVOLUTION

The French Revolution was still a divisive political issue in 1989. Even choosing the official historian for the Bicentennial was a political problem. Conservative historians called the Revolution a giant mistake, the root of France's subsequent troubles. Such views anger the left and were hardly a way to celebrate the Bicentennial. Radical or leftist historians, on the other hand, read into the Revolution the harbinger of all things good and of the Bolshevik Revolution in Russia. This was hardly acceptable to conservative France.

In François Furet the Mitterrand government found their historian: a former Marxist who had turned away from radicalism to produce a moderate and sober synthesis with something for everyone. Furet found nothing wrong with the revolutionary ideals of *liberté, egalité, fraternité,* but he argued that with the collapse of the monarchy and takeover of the revolution by extremists, the revolution had to "skid out of control" (*dérapage*). It was not just evil or foolish people that caused the revolution to skid out of control, Furet argued, but the logic of revolutions themselves. Furet's thinking parallels that of Crane Brinton, discussed in Chapter 7.

A change in the political context enabled Furet and other French intellectuals to accept this troubling analysis of the French Revolution. For decades, many French intellectuals naively celebrated the 1917 Russian Revolution as a continuation of the French Revolution. With the erosion of French leftism and decay of Soviet communism, French intellectuals saw that the Bolshevik Revolution had been a mistake. But if 1917 was the **culmination** of 1789, then logically the French Revolution itself must have been badly flawed. The new attitude about communism forced the French to reevaluate their own revolution.

patrie   French for fatherland.

memorize in their civics course, are mere ideals, but in the real world, government is corrupt, intrusive, and ineffective. French children learn to love **la patrie** in the abstract but to disdain politics in the here and now. Politics are also best kept private and personal; discussing politics with others only leads to arguments. Besides, it is none of their business.

The Nasty Split

Catholic countries have a serious problem that Protestant (and Eastern Orthodox) countries do not have to worry about: the role of the Church. When Britain and Sweden broke with Rome and established national churches, they also subordinated churchmen to the state. The Anglican church in Britain and the Lutheran church in Sweden depended strictly on London and Stockholm, respectively, for support; they could not turn to Rome. As a result, in these societies the Church no longer played an independent political role.

In Latin European countries—France, Italy, Spain—the Roman Catholic faith retained its political power, supporting conservative regimes and retaining special privileges, such as control of education, tax exemption for church lands, and a considerable say in government policy. Because of this temporal power, many people in Latin Europe developed anticlerical attitudes. Their most brilliant spokesman was Voltaire (see page 91). Anticlericalism was not necessarily antireligion; it rather sought to get the church out of government, what Americans call the separation of church and state.

Anticlericalism spread in Latin Europe, especially among intellectuals. After the French Revolution and Italian unification (in mid-nineteenth century), many people wanted a purely secular state, that is, one with no church influence in government. That was easy to do in America, where there was no single established church, but it was hard in France, Italy, and Spain, where church

Political Culture

"LA MARSEILLAISE"

Possibly the world's greatest national anthem is the French "Marseillaise." Dashed off in a single night in 1792 by a 32-year-old army officer, Rouget de Lisle, to accompany volunteers from Marseille headed north to defend the Revolution, the "Marseillaise" soon became the Revolution's, and then France's, anthem.

Extremely stirring and bloodthirsty, it is the perfect song for fighting for a nation. The refrain:

Aux armes, citoyens, formez vos bataillons!
Marchons! Marchons!
Qu'un sang impur abreuve nos sillons!

(To arms, citizens, form your battalions!
We march! We march!
Until [the enemy's] impure blood overflows
our furrows!)

If you have never heard it sung, catch the movie *Casablanca* on late-night television. Like the French flag, the "Marseillaise" became a controversial political symbol. Part of the Revolution, it was banned by Napoleon and the Bourbons, accepted by the liberal Orleans monarch in 1830, banned again by Napoleon III, and made permanently the national anthem in 1879. In a split society, nothing is simple.

and state were intertwined. To separate them required drastic surgery: sale of church lands, banning of some Catholic orders (such as the Jesuits), and state rather than church control of schools. The reaction to this was predictable. Just as the Republic was anticlerical, the church turned anti-Republic. Church sentiment went from conservative to reactionary, and the Roman Catholic faith became a pillar of monarchical restoration because that meant a return of church privileges.

In this way conservative France retained its Catholic viewpoint, while revolutionary France became strongly anticlerical. The battle raged for more than a century. At one point the Vatican instructed faithful Catholics to steer clear of any political involvement with the "Jacobin" Republic. During the Dreyfus affair, French clericalists and anticlericalists took opposing sides. Finally, in 1905, the National Assembly completed the separation of church and state; France no longer had an established church. Until the twentieth century, to be in favor of the Republic meant to be anticlerical. France's great premier of World War I, Georges Clemenceau—*le tigre*—was a passionate republican and supporter of Dreyfus. He recalled how his father used to tell him, "There's only one thing worse than a bad priest—and that's a good one."

The parties of the French left—Socialist and Communist—still draw their supporters most heavily from the anticlerical tradition. The parties of the right—Gaullist and UDF—attract mostly people from the pro-church tradition. Indeed, in all of Latin Europe—Italy, Spain, and Portugal as well as France—if you know how often a person goes to Mass you can usually predict his or her vote; strongly Catholic almost automatically means politically conservative.

Most French babies are baptized into the Catholic faith, but only 13 percent of French Catholics attend Mass weekly. (Europeans in general are much less religious than Americans.) Although the great battles between clericalists and anticlericalists have subsided, some issues reawaken the old quarrel. The abortion controversy and question of state control of Church schools can still bring protest demonstrations in the streets of Paris. Once established, social and political cleavages have tremendous staying power.

Political Culture

FRANCE'S RELIGIOUS SPLIT

The first ballot of the 1981 French presidential election illustrates how religion is still part of politics in France. The two leading candidates were Socialist François Mitterrand on the left and Republican Valéry Giscard d'Estaing on the right. A poll showed the more religious were also the more conservative, a permanent feature of French voting.

Attend Mass	Mitterrand	Giscard d'Estaing
Weekly	8	48
2 or 3 times a month	17	34
Less often	20	27
Never	24	16

Source: IFOP survey reproduced in Howard R. Penniman, ed., *France at the Polls, 1981 and 1986: Three National Elections.* Durham, NC: AEI/Duke University Press, 1988, p. 161.

◼ School for Grinds

Schooling also contributes to French political culture. The curriculum was set generations ago and is changed only slowly and reluctantly. Heavy on memorization, French education tends to produce diligent grinds rather than lively intellects. Even small children lug home briefcases bulging with books. A "good" child is one who puts in long homework hours.

Until recently, everywhere in the country French children learned the same thing, as established by the Ministry of Education in Paris, with no local input. Generations ago an education minister looked at his watch and told an interviewer what Latin verb was being conjugated all over France. (Starting in the late nineteenth century, Paris used uniform education to replace local dialects and subcultures with common Frenchness.) Since then, French school curricula have become less centralized and less classical.

privatistic   Tending to purely private and family concerns.

The curious thing about the standardized, memorized French education, however, is its deeply humanistic and individualistic content. Outwardly, French schoolchildren appear to be mechanically digesting an inflexible, unimaginative curriculum; inwardly, they are exposed to ideas that would be banned in American schools (such as the novel *The Immoralist*). This tension between outward conformity and inward freedom gives rise to **privatistic** attitudes and occasional eruptions of rebellion. It encourages young French people to keep their thoughts to themselves. In this way, a set, rigid educational pattern may actually contribute to French individualism.

Comparison

THE INSTABILITY OF SPLIT SOCIETIES

Unlike the stable and settled countries of North Europe, such as Britain and Sweden, the countries of Latin Europe continued to experience political upheavals well into the twentieth century. In France, Italy, and Spain, regimes have tended to be personal creations (for example, those of de Gaulle, Mussolini, and Franco) that end or change with the demise of their creator.

The underlying factor in this instability seems to be the split quality of French, Italian, and Spanish political culture that is rooted in their histories. Roughly half the population of each country is Catholic and conservative and favors strong executive leadership; the other half is anticlerical and liberal or radical and favors a strong parliament. The center is small; people in Latin Europe historically tended to identify with either the left or right camp, each severely mistrusting the other.

When the right was in power—historically, most of the time—the left denounced the government with shrill Marxist rhetoric as the tool of capitalists. When the left was in power, the right denounced them as dangerous incompetents, possibly serving Moscow's interests. At any given time, roughly half the country regarded the government as illegitimate, and this stunted feelings of legitimacy about government in general. In Latin Europe, few take pride in their nation's governmental institutions.

In the absence of shared values and underlying consensus, political difficulties can lead to violence, coups, and even civil war, which in turn lead to authoritarian rule. In the 1930s, Spain split into left and right camps and exploded into a vicious civil war won by the Catholic and conservative forces of General Franco. Disgruntled rightists in the Spanish military attempted a coup as recently as 1981. Portugal had a coup in 1974. In 1958 France nearly had a military coup. In opposition, François Mitterrand referred to the Gaullist constitution as a "permanent coup." (In office, he found that the powers it gave him as president really were not so bad.)

The French pride themselves on the equality of educational opportunity that their system offers. France has few English-style boarding schools for the rich, but opportunities, as everywhere, are still skewed. While the French school system is open to all, the lofty content of French education is tilted toward the children of middle- and upper-class homes. Working-class and peasant children, not exposed at home to correct speech—and the French are maniacs about their language—or abstract, intellectual thoughts, begin school at a disadvantage and have lesser chances at higher education. (Is educational stratification in the United States the same?)

> **lycée**   French academic high school.
>
> **baccalauréat**   French high-school exam and diploma.
>
> **grande école**   French for "great school," an elite, specialized college.

The great gateway to social, economic, and political power in France is the **lycée**. Napoleon developed them to train army officers. Most lycées are state-run. Admission is competitive, and the curriculum is demanding. Not all communities have lycées, which are concentrated in cities. Students complete the lycée with an examination at age 18 and get a **baccalauréat**, which entitles them to university admission. Now, as the result of government policy to upgrade French educational levels, most French young people earn the "*bac*," but they still tend to be from middle-class families.

The "Great Schools"

Just as Oxford and Cambridge tower over other English universities, the **grandes écoles** dominate French higher education. French universities, which stress the "impractical" liberal arts, have long been regarded as unimportant. To get into a French university is not hard; indeed, so many have flooded the lecture halls that standards have dropped and graduates have trouble getting jobs. Altogether, some 45 percent of French twenty- to twenty-four-year-olds are in full-time education, the highest percentage in Europe and comparable to the United States.

Few, however, make it to one of the "Great Schools." Skimming off the brightest and most motivated few by means of rigorous entrance exams, the schools train (rather than "educate") French youths in the practical matters of running a country and then place them in top civil-service and managerial positions. The Great Schools form the people who run France. No other country has

Comparison

FRENCH AND AMERICAN PARTY IDENTIFICATION

Years ago, Philip E. Converse and Georges Dupeux compared French and American party identification. What they found was startling and still valid. Most Americans were able to quickly identify which party they preferred; most French people could not. Where did this difference come from? Converse and Dupeux also found that 76 percent of Americans could name their father's party while only 25 percent of the French could even specify their father's general political tendency (left or right). Many French respondents reported that their fathers had never talked about politics.

The Converse-Dupeux study illustrated that in French families, politics was not a fit topic for conversation. This lack of political guidance from the old generation to the young contributed to political confusion in France; for example, the rapid shift in votes between parties and the quick rise and fall of protest parties. People who have not been socialized by their family toward one party lack the *party identification* we saw in Britain (page 59) and easily change parties.

anything quite like them. It would be as if West Point produced not army officers but leading administrators. Some denounce the *grandes écoles* as elitist and undemocratic, but few suggest abolishing them. Indeed, their stranglehold on French leadership seems to grow stronger.

Although there are several Great Schools, three are politically the most important. The *Ecole Polytechnique* was used by Napoleon to train military engineers. Called X for short, *xiens* have their pick of technology and management jobs when they graduate. The *Ecole Normale Supérieure*, founded by Napoleon to create loyal lycée instructors, still produces many of France's leading intellectuals—among its graduates have been Jean-Paul Sartre, Raymond Aron, and President Georges Pompidou. The newest Great School, founded by de Gaulle in 1945, is the *Ecole Nationale d'Administration* (ENA), which quickly became the most important. Many of the country's top civil servants are "enarchs," as they call themselves.

Like all Great Schools, the ENA is extremely selective. Many of its students are already graduates of the *Institut d'Etudes Politiques* in Paris, itself a *grande école* (and still known as "Sciences-Po," a birthplace of modern political science). Getting into the ENA is even harder; typically, fewer than one in ten pass the legendary written and oral exams to join the entering class of 100 or so. ENA students get monthly stipends and spend half of their twenty-seven months interning in government ministries. Most ENA graduates get high positions in government. About one-third of France's prefects and ambassadors are ENA graduates. All cabinets are dominated by enarchs. President Chirac ('59) and Premier de Villepin ('80, along with his sister, Véronique) graduated ENA, as did Socialist leader François Hollande (also '80). Extensive privatization, however, has shrunk the number of positions running state-owned industries, and many bright young people now prefer MBAs and private industry.

Training in a Great School epitomizes the best and worst of French education. You have to be very smart and hard-working. But you also have to be cold, logical, and removed from ordinary people. Products of the *grandes écoles* may be brilliant, but they often lack common sense and humanity. Some critics call them, pejoratively, *technocrats* (see page 107), people who rule by technical criteria. In line with their training by the state, they also tend to propose the same old statist solutions. The perfect (negative) example is Alain Juppé, a brilliant ENA graduate ('72) and Chirac's first premier, whose cold, technocratic leadership made him the most unpopular premier of the Fifth Republic and the biggest single cause of his party's setback in the 1997 parliamentary elections.

Political Culture

How Would You Do on the "Bac"?

In about twelve hours of nationwide essay exams spread over a week, France's seventeen- or eighteen-year old lycéens face questions like the following, taken from the philosophy section of a recent baccalauréat exam. How would you do? Choose one. Spend no more than two hours.

- Why defend the weak?
- Comment on Rousseau's declaration that "one must have societies where inequality is not too great, where the tyranny of opinion is moderated and where voluptuousness reigns more than vanity."
- What is it to judge?
- Is it reasonable to love?

French students now get their choice of bac exams. Some are scientific or technical; the most prestigious is math (because you cannot bluff). The French government is trying to move students from the humanities to technology.

■ The Fear of "Face to Face"

Whatever the educational institution—lycée, university, or Great School—the teaching style is similar: cold, distant, uninvolved. Class discussion is rare. Questions are from the instructor, not the students. When I taught long ago at the University of Toulouse, I was deter-

hegemony	Being top or commanding power.

mined to break this pattern; I urged and demanded student participation. The result was stony silence; my request was outside their experience.

By the time they are teenagers, French adolescents have picked up one of the basic characteristics of French culture, what sociologist Michel Crozier called *"l'horreur du face-à-face."* Aside from family and intimate friends, French people feel uncomfortable with warm, cozy, face-to-face relationships. Some tourists find the French unfriendly. They really are not; they are simply reserved and formal to everyone, including other French people. The French style is opposite that of the American, which emphasizes informality and friendliness. In the United States everyone is supposed to be outgoing, use first names, smile, and say, "Have a nice day." Such behavior—much of it shallow—boggles the French mind.

To avoid face-to-face relationships, the French prefer a structured system with clear but limited areas of competence and set, impersonal rules. That way people know where they stand and nobody butts into another's private domain. British-style pragmatism and "muddling through" are not the French style.

Political Culture

THE FRENCH–U.S. LOVE-HATE RELATIONSHIP

The French have contradictory attitudes toward America. At times, anti-Americanism seems to be part of French political culture. Many French, especially intellectual and political elites, dislike the United States, its compassionless capitalism, its lack of culture, and its global **hegemony**, all symbolized by McDonald's. The United States has become a *"hyperpuissance"* (hyperpower) that tries to remake the world in its own image. But France, they say, will go its own way, based on its own traditions and culture. Millions of ordinary French people, however, like America and flock to U.S.-made movies and eat "McDos." McDonald's has grown rapidly to close to a thousand restaurants in France, all French-owned and French-run.

What is eating the French elites? First, they look back to the time when French power, language, and culture (and cuisine) dominated Europe and much of the world. They resent being replaced by U.S. power and English. De Gaulle, angered at not being treated as an equal by Roosevelt and Churchill during the war,

led France on nationalistic and anti-U.S. paths. France, not the United States, was to lead Europe. Many French, especially in the Foreign Ministry, still follow this design.

French elites do all they can to hold back the tide of Americanization. They outlaw English words (*"franglais"*). They limit the number of U.S. movies and TV shows. They reject a totally free market and cling to state ownership and supervision.

The French try to retain their Frenchness, much as the Japanese try to retain their Japaneseness. Neither are completely successful. Little by little, French ways resemble American ways, *"le business à l'améri-caine"* (an example of franglais). The international economy requires it; much business is now global and conducted in English. French firms buy American firms and vice-versa. Some French Great Schools now offer English-language MBAs. Some French think they are fighting American cultural domination, but they are really fighting modernization.

■ Freedom or Authority?

The points discussed so far—the lack of trust, fear of face-to-face relationships, rigid and rote education—all contribute to a French political personality that cannot quite make up its mind whether it wants freedom or authority. Actually, it wants both, the abstract *liberté* extolled by philosophers and the controlled hierarchies built for centuries by French bureaucrats. What happens is **compartmentalization**: The private French person loves freedom, while the public French person—in school, on the job, facing the bureaucracy—knows he or she needs reason, order, and formal, impersonal rules. A typical French person has been described as an anarchist who secretly admires the police but could equally be a policeman who secretly admires the anarchists.

compartmentalization Mentally separating and isolating problems.

The result of this mental split is a continual longing for freedom and a perfect society but an equal tendency to surrender to authority and a highly imperfect society. The balance is unstable; from time to time the quest for liberty bursts out, as in 1789, 1830, 1848, the Paris Commune of 1871,

Geography

THE PERSISTENCE OF REGION

In 1936 the leftist Popular Front won in the shaded départements (map left). In 1981, Socialist François Mitterrand won the presidency with a very similar pattern (map right). Region, as well as social class and religion, often produces distinct and durable voting patterns.

1936: Popular Front Vote

1981: Mitterand Vote

the Events of May of 1968, and the riots of youths in 2005 and 2006. We will explore this pattern more fully in the next chapter, but it is interesting to note that most of these outbursts ended with a surrender to authority. French political culture has been described as limited authoritarianism accompanied by potential insurrection. When they vote, some French say half in jest, "The heart is on the left, but the billfold is on the right."

Legitimacy in France is weaker than in Britain. Rather than a strong feeling of the rightness of institutions and authority, some French accord their system only half-hearted support. A few, on the extreme left and right, hate it.

■ Social Class

As is Britain, France is a class society. The gap between French working and middle class is one of the biggest in Europe and—with the educational system slanted in favor of middle-class children— social mobility is not what it could be. In France, as in Britain, few born working class or Muslim climb the income ladder. Distribution of income in France is more unequal than in Britain or even Spain. The rich live superbly in France; the poor scrape by.

Comparison

FRENCH AND AMERICAN PRESS CONFERENCES

A French presidential press conference offers a quick insight into French political style. A rare event— maybe once or twice a year—the press conference takes place in an imposing salon of the Elysée Palace, the French White House. The president is seated. On the wall behind him is either a brocade or tapestry. In keeping with the elegant setting, the president is attired in a conservative suit and plain tie.

The journalists sit quietly taking notes. The president expounds abstractly on progress, national greatness, reason, and order, like a professor giving a lecture. He speaks beautiful French, slowly and clearly, with utter confidence and literate, witty phrases, for he is the product of an elite education. Then, if there is time, the president takes a few questions from the reporters. The questions are polite, even timid, for no one dares to trip up or embarrass the president. The president in return treats the journalists like small children who do not understand the logic and clarity of his policies. The president is, in keeping with French political style, magisterial and rational.

The American presidential press conference takes place against a plain blue backdrop. The president stands at a lectern. He is wearing an indifferent suit and striped tie. The president is nervous and ill-at-ease, for he knows that the newspeople are out to get him, just as they have been out to get every president. As they see it, that is their job. He offers a few opening remarks in an almost defensive tone to explain his recent actions. Then, with a forced smile, he throws the conference open to questions from the floor. The journalists descend like a wolf pack, clawing at the air with their upraised hands, each one demanding attention.

The newsperson called upon—often by name, as the president wants to show he cares about them personally—gives a little lecture setting the background for his or her question. The question itself— implying a scandal or how the president's policies contradict themselves—is hostile, trying to catch the president in an uncomfortable situation. The president replies in stammering, ungrammatical English, for he is the product of an American college. The president, in keeping with the democratic American style, tries to treat the journalists as friends and equals, but his smile and handshakes as he leaves can scarcely conceal his adversarial relationship with the media.

Left Voter	Right Voter
Working class	Middle class
Anticlerical	Pro-church
Urban	Rural or small town

ideal-typical Distilling social
characteristics into one example.

Class differences tend to reinforce other cleavages in French society—clerical-anticlerical, urban-rural, radical-conservative, even to a certain extent North-South. That is, these factors tend to line up on one side—never perfectly, of course—but enough to produce a left-right split in French voting. Very broadly, the **ideal-typical** French voters of the left and the right are depicted in the table above.

The Great Calming Down

French intellectuals, some of them from the same *grandes écoles* as the governing elite, were for a long generation attracted to Marxism. Observing the huge gap between the ideal of equality and the reality of gross inequality, many educated and middle-class French turned to Marxist explanations and sometimes to membership in the Communist party. Philosopher Jean-Paul Sartre backed every leftist cause and urged other intellectuals to become likewise *engagé*. Another *normalien*, his conservative adversary Raymond Aron, disparaged Marxism as "the opium of the intellectuals," a play on Marx's famous statement that "religion is the opium of the masses."

Geography

"EVERY COUNTRY HAS A SOUTH"

Much truth is contained in this old saw. Except for very small countries, the south of most lands in the northern hemisphere is poorer and less developed than the north. Industry has tended to cluster in the north of France, Germany, Italy, Spain, and the United States. People in the south of these countries are often described as fun-loving but slow and lazy. The northern people are often described as efficient and hard-working. The south usually votes differently from the north. People of the *Midi* describe themselves as a different, Mediterranean race that does not like the cold, germanic northern French.

The picture breaks down when you go too far north; development in the Scandinavian countries and Russia generally centers on the temperate areas and avoids the frozen north. And in the southern hemisphere, nearly the reverse is true, for there the southerly areas are more temperate. Centuries ago, Montesquieu held that climate produces culture. Why should political and economic growth be more closely associated with temperate or even slightly chilly zones?

Under Mitterrand, if not before, this changed. French intellectuals became disillusioned with Marxism, communism, and traditional leftist positions. The French Communist party declined to irrelevance. There seem to be several reasons for this major shift, which has long-term implications for French political life. In the 1970s, a new generation of French intellectuals criticized the

Democracy

THE CENTRIST FRENCH

The real winner of recent French elections has been neither the left nor the right but the center. Observers referred to the "normalization" of French political life and a healing of the great split in French society. Politicians of the left and right tended to move to the center. Gone are the old ideological visions; moderation and pragmatism are now fashionable. Underscoring this was a 1992 poll that asked Frenchmen to place themselves on a nine-point ideological scale, ranging from extreme left to extreme right. The results are not too different from Britain (page 55) and Germany (page 212): Most people are centrist. French politicians are thus on notice: Any party or candidate perceived as too far left or right will lose. This helps explain the decline of the Communists. Once this lesson sinks in, France may turn into a "two-plus"-party system, like many other industrialized democracies.

The Self-Placement of French Voters
on a Left/Right Ideological Scale

Soviet Union and communism. In the early 1980s, many West German intellectuals turned anti-American over how to deal with the Soviets and especially over new U.S. missiles on German soil. There is no love lost between French and German intellectuals, and the French were happy to repudiate what they regarded as naive German pacifism. The Soviet-approved coup in Poland by a Polish general in late 1981 reminded many French of Marshal Pétain in the service of Germany during World War II.

But most important, with the election of a Socialist government in 1981, the left was in power. It was one thing to criticize a conservative government but quite another to run a government yourself. French intellectuals and leftists saw how difficult it was to improve the economy, assume a role in world affairs, and transform French society. Clever slogans do not translate into effective policy, and many French intellectuals became moderates. Some celebrated free-market capitalism, a strange position for French intellectuals. The Mitterrand presidency contributed a lot by freeing French society from the allure of leftist ideology and guiding it to a middle-of-the-road pragmatism, one that most governments continued. French politics became centrist, like politics in most of Europe. (Curiously, at this same time, U.S. politics polarized, and the middle ground shrank. Any idea why?) With the onset of the Bicentennial, much of the passion that earlier surrounded the French Revolution went out of it. French politics entered into what might be termed "the great calming down" of de-ideologized pragmatism. As François Furet put it, "The Revolution is over." Most French agreed.

Key Terms

baccalauréat (p. 123)
bureaucratized (p. 118)
compartmentalization (p. 126)
culmination (p. 119)
grande école (p. 123)
hegemony (p. 125)
ideal-typical (p. 128)

"La Marseillaise" (p. 118)
lycée (p. 123)
omnipotent (p. 118)
patrie (p. 120)
privatistic (p. 122)
statism (p. 118)

Further Reference

Bernstein, Richard. *Fragile Glory: A Portrait of France and the French*. New York: Alfred A. Knopf, 1990.
Ehrmann, Henry W., and Martin Schain. *Politics in France*, 5th ed. New York: HarperCollins, 1997.
Godin, Emmanuel, and Tony Chafer, eds. *The French Exception*. New York: Berghan, 2005.
Judt, Tony. *Past Imperfect: French Intellectuals, 1944–56*. Berkeley, CA: University of California Press, 1993.
Khilnani, Sunil. *Arguing Revolution: The Intellectual Left in Post-War France*. New Haven, CT: Yale University Press, 1994.
Mahoney, Daniel J. *De Gaulle: Statesmanship, Grandeur, and Modern Democracy*. Westport, CT: Praeger, 1996.

Reader, Keith A. *Intellectuals and the Left in France since 1968*. New York: St. Martin's, 1986.

Roger, Philippe. *The American Enemy: The History of French Anti-Americanism*. Chicago, IL: University of Chicago Press, 2005.

Sa'adah, Anne. *Contemporary France: A Democratic Education*. Lanham, MD: Rowman & Littlefield, 2003.

Scriven, Michael. *Jean-Paul Sartre: Politics and Culture in Postwar France*. New York: St. Martin's, 1999.

Singer, Daniel. *Is Socialism Doomed? The Meaning of Mitterrand*. New York: Oxford University Press, 1988.

Weber, Eugen. *My France: Politics, Culture, Myth*. Cambridge, MA: Harvard University Press, 1991.

Chapter 10

France:
Patterns of Interaction

Party image and voter identification with parties are less developed in France than in Britain. Many French voters do not have long-term party preferences, and French parties tend to come and go and change their names, blurring their images. One result is that many voters are not attached to one party and shift their votes as a form of protest. In 2002, this inadvertently led to a top contender, Socialist Premier Jospin, getting knocked out of the presidential race by a right-wing extremist (see page 105). In most of West Europe, elections show only small swings of a few points from the previous contest, but not in France, where new parties can rise and fall within a few years. French parties may gain or lose ten to twenty percentage points from their previous showing. French voting can be **volatile**.

(see page 105)

Questions to Consider

1. What does *volatility* do to French voting?
2. Why is the French party system more complex than Britain's?
3. How does the French electoral system force parties together?
4. What is *Gaullism?* Is it an ideology or a mood?
5. Why is the French right split into three?
6. Could something like the *Events of May* happen again?
7. How can referendums be misused?
8. How do French labor unions differ from British and U.S. labor unions?
9. How do statism, *dirigisme,* and *tutelle* relate to each other?

Few French parties have not changed their names at one time or another. The Gaullists especially change their name. From 1947 to 1952 they called themselves the Rally of the French People (RPF). With de Gaulle's coming to power in 1958, it became the Union for the New Republic (UNR), then in 1967 the Democratic Union for the Fifth Republic (UDVe), in 1968 the Union for the Defense of the Republic (UDR), in 1971 the Union of Democrats for the Republic (with the same initials, UDR), in 1976 the Rally for the Republic (RPR), and in 2002 the Union for a Presidential Majority (UMP), quickly renamed the Union for a Popular Movement (still UMP). An American would exclaim: "But how can you build up name recognition with so many changes?" The Gaullists saw themselves less as a structured political party than as a mass rally of patriotism. What makes sense in one political culture does not in another. The name changes showed the Gaullists were always starting fresh. Neo-Gaullist Jacques Chirac was elected president in 1995 and reelected in 2002.

The Socialists, founded in 1905, originally called themselves the French Section of the Workers International, or SFIO. In 1969, merging with some smaller left groups, they changed the name to the *Parti Socialiste* (PS). In 1981, the PS under Mitterrand won both the presidency and the National Assembly. It again became the largest party in parliament in 1997 but shrank to second-largest in the 2002 election.

The French center is unusually messy, possibly because many figures strive for prominence and do not like to merge into one party. The Union for French Democracy (*Union pour la Démocratie*

volatile   Rises and falls quickly. (See page 133.)
bloc   Grouping or alliance of parties.

Française, UDF), now one of the three largest parties, began as a parliamentary grouping in 1962 and first ran in elections in 1966 as the Republicans. In 1974 its leader, Valéry Giscard d'Estaing, was elected president and later merged several small centrist parties with the Republicans to form the UDF, a loose federation of five center-right parties. In 1998, the Republicans, now renamed Liberal Democracy, split from the UDF.

One French party does not play around with name changes, the Communists (PCF), although they too have trouble with their party's image. The Communists plunged from 25 percent of the parliamentary French vote in 1972 to only 6 percent in 2002. On the other side of the spectrum, the National Front emerged in 1986 as the anti-immigrant party. To make things even more confusing, left parties often run jointly as the Union of the Left or Common Program (Socialist and Communist), and right parties as the Majority or Alliance (Gaullists and UDF).

■ The Emerging Party System

The French party system is not as complex as it used to be; it is down from ten parties in 1958 to four or five relevant ones today. France's parties have been consolidating and forming into two **blocs**—one left and one right—possibly headed for a "two-plus" party system. Much depends on whether the Union for a Popular Movement (UMP) can unite the French right. Schematically it looks like this:

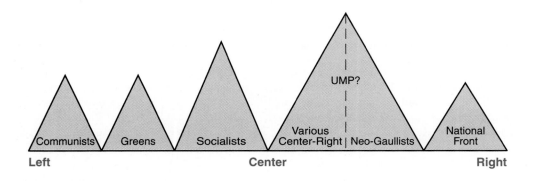

The two blocs are divided internally. As we shall see, the Communists and other far-left parties are always feuding with the Socialists, and the Republicans or UDF constantly striving for predominance with the Gaullists. If they can help it, none of the other parties wants anything to do with the racist National Front. In terms of voter appeal, however, the two blocs fit into two great French tendencies of which we spoke earlier. The left favors ways to make people more equal, by taxing the rich, controlling the economy, and providing more welfare benefits. The right also favors change, but more cautiously, based on economic growth and modest reforms. Both are statist and do not seek free-market solutions. France has never had a Margaret Thatcher and is not likely to. The National Front wants expulsion of most immigrants and France out of the EU.

■ The Demise of the French Communists

In most countries, Socialist and Communist parties were natural enemies ever since the Communists followed Lenin's command and broke from the Socialists shortly after World War I. Typically, where one was strong the other was weak. Britain, Sweden, Germany, and Spain all had large socialist-type parties and small Communist parties. In Italy, on the other hand, a large Communist party—now renamed the Democratic Party of the Left—overshadowed the Socialists. In France it used to be that way, but during the 1970s and 1980s the Socialists grew and the Communists shrank, so that now the PS is the largest left party in France.

Eurocommunism   1970s move by Italian Communists away from Stalinism and toward democracy.

Stalinist   Brutal central control over Communist parties.

protest vote   Ballot cast against existing regime.

The two parties have common roots. The PCF is a 1920 offshoot of the Socialists. In a battle that raged over the twentieth century, the Communists claimed that the Socialists were not militant enough, that they abandoned revolutionary Marxism for gradual, pragmatic reformism. The PCF echoed the Soviet line. As was the case worldwide, the Communists did not join in the Resistance until Germany attacked the Soviet Union in 1941. Since Stalin's time, however, the PCF gradually became more moderate. It denounced the 1968 Soviet invasion of Czechoslovakia and claimed to favor **Eurocommunism**. French voters cannot trust the Communists, though, for old **Stalinist** tendencies reappear—as when the party expels a dissenting intellectual, lays down a dogmatic line, or stabs fellow leftists in the back.

The result was an unstable alliance of Socialists and Communists. The two parties hated each other but knew they needed each other. The second round, or runoff, of a French election places a great premium on combining parties, for in the French runoff a simple plurality wins. If the Communists and Socialists ran separately on the second ballot they would always lose to the combined Gaullists and Republicans. Accordingly, the left parties—the PS, PCF, and now many small leftist parties—generally support the strongest left candidate, regardless of party, on the second ballot. It is the French electoral system that drives rivals on the French left together.

When François Mitterrand took over the shrunken and demoralized Socialist party in 1971, it was overshadowed on the French left by the Communists, who regularly won a fifth of the vote. Given France's peculiar electoral system—single-member districts with runoff—Mitterrand knew the PS could not grow on its own. He also knew that a good third of the Communist vote was not from committed Communists; it was a **protest vote** that could be won over by an attractive Socialist party. He cleverly embraced the Communists, used them, won away their lukewarm supporters, and then discarded the PCF. In 1984 a shrunken, demoralized PCF left the cabinet and has done worse and worse in elections ever since.

The decline of the French Communist party, however, did not solve the problem of the fragmented French left. It may have made it worse, as it spawned several far-left parties trying to grab its militant tradition and worker and intellectual electorate. In the 2002 presidential election, at least four far-leftist candidates fragmented the left vote and ruined Jospin. Two Trotskyist parties (Workers Struggle and Revolutionary Communists) together took 10 percent of the first-round vote. In France, as in most of Europe, at least a third of the electorate vote for one leftist party or another—ranging from the Socialists at center-left to the Communists at medium-left to far-left Trotskyists—because the issues that inspire the left are still there: poverty, inequality, unemployment, and U.S. hegemony. The demise of the French Communists meant the rise of other left parties.

◼ The Fractured Right

As the French left is fragmented, so is the right. Most countries have one large party on the right; France has at least three. Some trace the division of the French right back to the Revolution, which produced (1) an ultraconservative monarchist right, (2) a moderate Orleanist right, and (3) a populist Napoleonic right. Today, these three strands are represented by the (1) National Front (FN), (2) UDF, and (3) neo-Gaullists.

The neo-Gaullists, UDF, and newly independent Liberal Democracy, which peeled away from the UDF in 1997 in a Thatcherite direction, sometimes join forces. The UDF itself is a loose coalition of five smaller parties. Further right, outside of the Alliance, the National Front and other small groups spit venom at immigrants and the European Union.

For the right, ideology and doctrine are less important than personality. Gaullists traditionally have been skeptical of European unity and the free market, while most UDF parties have been for them. But in speaking to the same middle-class electorate, the UDF and Gaullists often cooperate so closely they agree on a single parliamentary candidate on the first ballot. In 2002 the neo-Gaullists attempted a grand merger of parties into the Union for a Popular Movement (UMP) that was based on the RPR but drew in Liberal Democrats and the UDF. A merger is difficult because on the right— and this is true of many countries—personality becomes the dominant issue.

Here, the shadow of de Gaulle still looms. The French right is torn between those who want to keep his image alive and those who favor more traditional center-right politics. De Gaulle, a Napoleonic figure above parties, never aimed at founding a political party. Like Franco, Mussolini, and Latin American military dictators, de Gaulle hated parties, blaming their incessant squabbles for all the troubles of the Third and Fourth Republics. De Gaulle did not even much care for the Gaullist party; he never formally headed or endorsed it. His attitude seemed to be: "Alright, if you must, go ahead and worship me." During his long reign (1958–1969), the Gaullist party was simply a tool for his control of the National Assembly. In the legislative elections of 1968, the Gaullists won 46 percent of the popular vote and an outright majority of National Assembly seats.

Comparison

BLAIR AND JOSPIN

As we saw in Britain, the Labour party moved toward the center, abandoning its socialist tenets. The French Socialists were a bit different. They, too, moved toward the center in practice but they denied it in words. They also fragmented into hard and soft factions; British Labourites held together much better.

Socialist Premier Lionel Jospin (1997–2002) privatized more than any of his predecessors but kept talking a big-government, help-the-workers line. Why? Partly political culture. The British pride themselves on pragmatism, the French on principle. Jospin simply could not tell his party that free-market capitalism really is best; Blair could.

Their different party systems also kept Jospin talking more left than Blair. Jospin faced several small parties to his left, various Communists and Trotskyists, who accused him of selling out socialist principles. Jospin, in trying to win over their voters, could never admit that. Blair faced no important parties on his left; he could tell far-left voters: "I don't need you. In fact, I do better by denouncing you and winning the centrist vote." Jospin could never say that.

Both Jospin and Blair were rational in their way. Both tried to position themselves to best advantage within different political cultures and structures. The problem is not so much personalities as different political systems. In France, everything is complicated.

A single charismatic figure leading a national movement is a tough act to follow. Such a leader does not tolerate other important personalities around him; he prefers obedient servants and yes-men. As a result, when de Gaulle departed in 1969, he left a vacuum that no one in the Gaullist party could fill. His former premier, Georges Pompidou, won the presidency that year, but by the time Pompidou died in 1974, the Republican candidate, Valéry Giscard d'Estaing (who later formed the UDF), was more attractive than the Gaullist candidate. Because de Gaulle disdained parties, he never bothered institutionalizing his movement into a durable party. The real genius in politics is the one who builds lastingly; de Gaulle did not.

passé Outmoded, receded into the past.

stalemate Politically stuck among competing groups.

Trying to fill the vacuum, Jacques Chirac in 1976 reorganized the moribund Gaullists into the Rally for the Republic, commonly called "neo-Gaullist." A slick performer who alienated many French people by his high-handedness, Chirac alternately quarreled and made up with the UDF. Pushed into a less-active role when he was forced to cohabit with a Socialist cabinet after the 1997 election, Chirac gave up party leadership. Chirac and his party were saved by the 2002 election debacle, which reelected him by default. The problem for the Gaullists parallels that of the Socialists: What do we stand for now? Most French now consider Gaullism **passé**, a vaguely conservative mood rather than a party.

The Neo-Gaullists show that there are several types of conservatism. The current party chief and Interior Minister Nicolas Sarkozy faces a tough rival in Premier Dominique de Villepin. Both are UMP and both are conservatives, but Sarkozy is more pro-market and pro-United States, while de Villepin wants to preserve the French welfare state and opposes U.S. power. Sarkozy is a modern, Thatcher-type conservative, de Villepin a traditional French big-government conservative. Conservatism means different things in different countries.

The relationships among the French right parties are similar to those among the French left parties: The electoral system has them compete with each other on the first round but ally on the second round. The difference on the right is that the hatred is largely personal, a struggle between bright, ambitious party leaders who want to be president. If parties merge, it means the leaders of one party become second fiddle, something most politicians dislike. Before you condemn French politicians as unusually petty and jealous, ask yourself if American politicians are much different.

Some observers fear that if the center and right parties do not merge into the UMP and come up with an attractive, modern program, the National Front will grow into the largest party on the right. The 2002 presidential election pointed to that possibility. The FN itself split over personal rivalry. The Front's leader Le Pen in 1998 expelled brainy Bruno Mégret (who has a master's degree from Berkeley), who took some of the FN with him. In France, everything fragments. One way to cure electoral fragmentation: Drop the first round of elections and go to straight FPTP, U.S.- and British-style, which would force like-minded parties together.

The Stalemate Cycle

French politics seems to run in a roughly cyclical pattern. "Normal" politics in France usually leads to a **stalemate** in which political groups, constantly feuding among themselves, block major change. This produces crises the stuck system cannot handle, which in turn lead to an explosion every generation or two. To get out of the stalemate, the French have repeatedly turned to a hero, a charismatic figure who has not been sullied by "status quo" politics. French politics seems to require a Napoleon from time to time.

After a dozen years of revolutionary turmoil, France welcomed the first Napoleon as a hero to end the chaos. Half a century later, they turned to Louis Napoleon for the same reason. In 1940 the French parliament actually voted dictatorial powers for the aged Marshal Pétain. Pierre Mendès-France was the thinking-person's hero in 1954 when he got France out of Indochina, but he lacked the charisma of the outsider who is above ordinary politics. That figure arrived in 1958 with de Gaulle, who saved France from civil war over Algeria.

De Gaulle believed he had ended France's recurrent stalemates by constructing a Fifth Republic with a strong president. But did the Fifth Republic really transcend French history? At first it appeared to. France withdrew from the Algerian tragedy, streamlined its party system, and surged ahead economically. In 1968, however, all hell broke loose (see box on page 139), and people began to wonder if the Fifth Republic was suffering from some of the same ills that had plagued predecessors.

Mitterrand also found that the transformation of French politics was not as complete as de Gaulle believed. De Gaulle's personal popularity ensured not only his election as president but a large Gaullist party in the National Assembly. This made it easy to govern; any law or budget de Gaulle wanted was rubberstamped in the Palais Bourbon. The Fifth Republic did not depend on the unstable coalitions of the Third and Fourth in order to govern. But how much did it depend on the same party maintaining control of both the executive and legislative branches?

France found out in 1986. With the election of a National Assembly dominated by the Republicans and Gaullists, Mitterrand named a conservative as premier but stayed on as president. Cohabitation (see Chapter 8) kept the government functioning, but only because Mitterrand consented to letting Premier Chirac pretty much have his way in naming ministers and pursuing conservative policies. Mitterrand played a waiting game, letting Chirac take the blame for unpopular

Comparison

THE RISE OF EUROPE'S ANGRY RIGHT

For some years most European lands have seen the growth of angry rightist parties led by charismatic speakers, such as Le Pen's National Front in France, Jörg Haider's Freedom party in Austria, Pim Fortuyn (assassinated in 2002) in the Netherlands, Germany's National Republicans and Law and Order Offensive, the Flemish Bloc in Belgium, the Danish People's party, and Italy's Northern League and National Alliance. While they differ in many respects, all are anti-immigrant, anti-crime, and anti-EU and can draw one voter in five. Even Japan has an angry, anti-immigrant nationalist as Tokyo's governor.

Some call them fascist, but they deny it and are probably not. Rather, they voice voter concerns that conventional politicians ignored for years. Many Europeans really do not like Muslim immigrants and crime. Nobody ever asked them if they wanted their neighborhoods taken over by foreign cultures. Mainstream politicians have been too politically correct

to talk about this. Likewise, European elites have almost reflexively favored the EU even though many ordinary citizens fear the loss of their countries' sovereignty, culture, and jobs in a united Europe (see Chapter 17). Anti-immigrant politicians simply filled the gap left by the conventional politicians. This is also happening inside the U.S. Republican party.

Is this a threat to European democracy, or is it democracy in action? If one party does not give voters what they want, another party will. In any country a certain percentage of disgruntled citizens is receptive to the simplified arguments of populist demagogues. America has its George Wallaces and Ross Perots but also has some advantages: (1) Americans are used to immigrants from all continents; and (2) many of the alienated Americans do not vote. (Perhaps we should be grateful for our low electoral turnout.)

policies. After some time, when Mitterrand's popularity eclipsed Chirac's, Mitterrand began to oppose some of Chirac's policies. A U.S.-style deadlock emerged as neither the president nor the premier could get his way. Chirac controlled parliament, but Mitterrand could denounce his legislative program and criticize him personally. The second cohabitation period was somewhat more relaxed as Mitter-

Events of May Euphemism for riots and upheaval of May 1968.

CRS Republican Security Companies, French paramilitary police.

rand, probably aware he was dying, attempted little. In the third cohabitation period, 1997–2002, Chirac named Jospin premier. It worked fairly well, but underneath was a smoldering discontent that gave Le Pen the edge on Jospin in the first round of the 2002 presidential election.

■ Referendum Madness

French presidents often use plebiscites or referendums to pose major questions directly to the people without going through elected representatives in parliament. The referendum, almost unknown in Britain, has been used twenty times since 1793 in France. It fits neatly into a very French tradition: Rousseau's idea of the general will. On the surface, nothing could be more democratic than consulting the people directly on their wishes.

In reality, plebiscites can be very tricky, an authoritarian tool that manipulates the citizenry. The key power in a referendum belongs to the one who writes the question. The question can be posed in such a simplified way that one almost has to vote yes. Furthermore, a referendum often comes after the decision has already been made and the leader just wants popular endorsement.

Political Culture

THE EVENTS OF MAY 1968

Just ten years after the near civil war over Algeria that brought de Gaulle to power, his regime suffered another explosion, the **Events of May**. A month of student and worker strikes and battles with police revealed that under the law-and-order surface of Gaullist France throbbed the old revolutionary tradition. The great split that had plagued France for generations had not completely healed; the cleavage still ran through French society like a California earthquake fault line, ready to crack open without warning.

Trouble began at the University of Nanterre in a suburb of Paris. Students—fed up with bad facilities and curricula—staged a strike that quickly spread to most universities and many factories. France split again, this time largely on age lines; the young were tired of obeying the old. The **CRS** (*Compagnies Républicains de Sécurité*) waded into protesters with tear gas and truncheons. De Gaulle placed troops and tanks around Paris.

But then the revolution—if that is what it was—burned out, like many previous uprisings in French history. De Gaulle promised more participation and held parliamentary elections in which a majority supported conservative candidates; Gaullists won an actual majority of seats in the National Assembly. "When the French are fearful," noted one French political scientist, "they swing to the right."

Some see the 2005 nationwide riots of North and West African youth and the 2006 student protests as resurgences of French revolutionary feeling. But 2005 was confined to young Muslim males alienated from French society who had no goals or purposes; some called it simple vandalism. The 2006 protests were focused against one new law that the students hated. The commonality of 1968, 2005, and 2006: angry young people marginalized by the system.

De Gaulle played the plebiscite game to the hilt. For him, a referendum was not merely to gain mass approval for a given policy but to reinforce his personal rule. After every plebiscite he could turn to his old enemies, the traditional politicians, and say, "You see, the people understand and support me. Who needs you?" In French political theory, again derived from Rousseau, a nation run by a leader who communicates directly with the people—without parties, parliaments, politicians, or interest groups getting in the way—is the ideal democracy. Some, however, see in this model the seeds of dictatorship.

De Gaulle attached his personal prestige to each referendum. "If the nation rejects the measure," he in effect told France, "it also rejects me, and I shall resign." This blunt approach worked every time until the last. In 1958 people were glad to get a new constitution. In 1961 and 1962 they were delighted to see Algeria become independent and French troops come home. But de Gaulle's second referendum of 1962 raised some questions. De Gaulle had made a mistake in the 1958 constitution in having the president chosen by a gigantic electoral college composed of local office holders, whom he assumed would be conservative and pro-de Gaulle; they were not. So in October 1962, by-passing the National Assembly, he asked the voters to amend the constitution to allow direct election of the president. The referendum passed with a 62 percent yes vote, but this represented only 46 percent of the total electorate, far less than de Gaulle expected.

The hint was clear—the French people were happy to get out of Algeria but not so happy about tinkering with the constitution—but de Gaulle ignored it. In 1969, after riding out the 1968 Events of May with resounding electoral success, de Gaulle once again sought to demonstrate that the people were behind him. He picked a rather technical issue that did not require a plebiscite: the reform (that is, weakening) of the Senate and the setting up of regional subunits. The French people said no, and true to his word, de Gaulle resigned. He went back to Colombey-les-Deux-Eglises, where he died the following year.

Since then, there have been five referendums. In 1972 Pompidou proposed enlarging the Common Market to include Britain, Ireland, and Denmark. Mitterrand's 1988 referendum on granting the Pacific territory of New Caledonia greater independence passed but with only a 37 percent turnout. In 1992, Mitterrand brought the Europe-unifying Maastricht Treaty before the French electorate, which narrowly endorsed it. The 2000 referendum to cut the presidential term to five years had only a 31 percent turnout. The 2005 French referendum to ratify a new EU constitution failed (see Chapter 17), humiliating Chirac. In none of these cases were referendums needed to solve a constitutional problem. Rather, presidents tried to use a referendum to bolster mass support and deflect attention away from more serious matters. Voter apathy and negativity suggest that the French have tired of referendums. (Have Californians?)

THE FIVE PLEBISCITES OF DE GAULLE		
Year	Question	"Yes"
1958	New constitution for Fifth Republic	79%
1961	Self-determination for Algeria	75
1962	Approve Algerian independence	91
1962	Direct election of president	62
1969	Reform of Senate and regions	47

Fragmented Labor Unions

In Britain we saw how interest groups were well-organized and powerful, especially big labor and big business. This pattern is true of North Europe in general, as we shall see in Germany. In France, and in Latin

Medef   French business association

Europe in general, there are plenty of interest groups, but they are usually splintered along party lines.

In Britain (and Germany and Sweden), for example, there is one big labor federation. In France (and Italy and Spain) there are several labor unions—Communist, Socialist, Catholic, and independent unions—competing against each other. The Communist-led CGT (Confédération Generale du Travail) is considered powerful in France, but on a comparative basis it is weak. Indeed, only 9 percent of the French workforce, heavily in the public sector, is organized into unions; even U.S. unions are proportionally bigger (about 13 percent of the workforce).

French unions also quarrel among themselves. The CGT has collided angrily with the smaller, Socialist-oriented CFDT (Confédération Française Démocratique du Travail) and nonparty Force Ouvrière. Labor's voice in France is weak and divided. Accordingly, French unions are strong neither in bargaining with management nor in making an impact on government. There are many strikes in France, but they tend to be short because unions lack strike funds.

Part of the problem with French unions is their political slant. Since the largest union, the CGT, is led by Communists, the other parties, especially those who control the government, ignore their demands. French unions engage in political strikes, actions aimed at government policy rather than bread-and-butter demands. In the 1980s and 1990s French unions often protested closures or layoffs at state-owned industries, much as in Thatcher's Britain. Few French unions take the American view that a union is a device to negotiate better terms with management, not a political tool.

The relative weakness of French unions has an important side effect: It makes them more, rather than less, militant and ideological. Feeling that the government has turned its back on them, French workers are more bitter than the workers of Germany and Sweden, where strong unions have an important voice in government. In those two countries, large and well-organized unions have become moderate and pragmatic.

Business and the Bureaucracy

French business is perhaps no more influential than labor. The French Enterprise Movement (*Mouvement des Enterprises de France*, **Medef**) seeks reforms to cut taxes, privatize pensions, and free up labor laws. Only business creates jobs, it argues, not government. This Thatcherite view

LATIN EUROPE'S DIVIDED UNIONS			
	France	Italy	Spain
Communist	CGT	CGIL	CO
Socialist	CFDT	—	UGT
Catholic	—	CISL	—
Other	FO (centrist)	UIL (soc. dem.)	CNT (anarchist)

structured access   Permanent openness of bureaucracy to interest-group demands.

wins little support in France, and Medef has little direct political access. Unlike Americans, most French people see business as callous, exploitive, and inhumane. No French politicians are openly pro-business the way American politicians are. It would be bad politics in France. Mitterrand ignored business interests to pursue a leftist economic program. This worried businesses; they cut investment in France and increased it in the United States. Mitterrand backed off and tried to make peace with French business. Premier and later President Chirac privatized large sections of France's nationalized industries, including a state-owned television network, but never endorsed a free-market society. Socialist Jospin continued privatization but talked about worker rights.

Medef is not as influential as the CBI in Britain because of the French tendency of individualism. A French firm may belong to Medef but rely only on its own resources for discreet contacts with the bureaucracy. The big advantage business has over labor is that the French business executive and civil servant are the same kind of people, often graduates of the same *grande école*, who move back and forth between top jobs in government and industry. Such connections give France's major firms **structured access** to the machinery of administration, something small-business people,

Democracy

THE BOREDOM PROBLEM

One reason for Le Pen's good showing in 2002 was the fact that the mainstream candidates, Chirac and Jospin, advocated essentially the same policies. Indeed, in most of the advanced democracies the major parties and candidates converge toward the center. Gone are the great ideological fights of the twentieth century. Conservatives are no longer reactionary rightists, and socialists are no longer radical leftists. They have become, at most, center-right and center-left, often hard to tell apart. The former accept the welfare state, the latter market economics. British Prime Minister Blair, who turned Labour into a centrist party, is an example of this transition. Even French President Chirac shared many socialist values.

But this leads to boredom. If the main parties have nearly the same centrist policies, who can get excited about politics or elections? This is why there has been—with the United States in the lead—a falloff in voting turnout in almost all of the advanced democracies. It also explains in part why characters like Pim Fortuyn in the Netherlands can suddenly attract a fifth of the vote: They are not boring.

Age contributes to the boredom problem. Few of France's major political figures have changed in three decades. The major contenders of the 1970s were still the major contenders at the turn of the century, most

in their sixties or even seventies. Current President Chirac has run for the presidency since 1981; he won reelection in 2002 at age 69. The thought of a 46-year-old like Bill Clinton becoming president is mind-boggling to the French. Said one French politician, "The French like to have a father figure for their president." Both de Gaulle and Mitterrand served until 78; age was never held against them. Even "young" Nicolas Sarkozy will be 51 for the 2007 French presidential election.

A political system that offers few new faces or ideas in several decades gets boring. Voters, especially young ones, turn off politics and away from the major parties. They feel no one speaks to their needs. Their discontent sometimes builds until they vote for a new, angry party. Unlike the American system, where state governorship may open the way to the presidency (Carter, Reagan, Clinton, Bush), in France, as in most of Europe, candidates must slowly work their way up through party ranks. You cannot "come from out of nowhere" as in America. In Germany, Joschka Fischer and Gregor Gysi won votes for their (respectively) small Green and Left parties because they were younger, unpredictable, and funny, in a word, non-boring. The boredom problem is not trivial in European politics.

farmers, and labor unionists do not enjoy. This builds up bitterness and frustration in the latter groups that explode from time to time in flash parties such as the National Front, in produce dumping by farmers, and in wildcat strikes. The political-bureaucratic systems of North Europe, by providing access for all major groups, generally avoid such outbursts.

dirigiste   Bureaucrats directing industry, closely connected to French statism.

Grands Corps   Top bureaucrats of France.

But neither do French businesspeople dominate government decision making. French political tradition is stacked against it. In the Anglo-American tradition, pluralism—the open interplay of interest groups with government—is respected, sometimes even celebrated. Lobbying by farmers, businesspeople, trade unionists, and ethnic groups in Washington is perfectly normal. In Britain's Commons, "interested members" make no secret that they represent certain industries. French political theory, however, still devoted to Rousseau's notion that interest groups are immoral—because they represent partial wills rather than the general will—tends to view such groups as illegitimate. The French tradition is **dirigiste**, from the top down, ignoring interest-group demands, and doing what civil servants deem best for French power and prestige. This gives great power to bureaucrats.

▉ The Eternal Bureaucracy

France has been developing its bureaucracy for five centuries. Almost every change of regime has led to growth in the number and functions of French bureaucrats. During the revolving-door cabinets of the Fourth Republic, people used to say that the fall of governments did not really matter that much because the bureaucracy ran the country anyway.

In France, civil servants oversee a great deal more than do their U.S. counterparts. The closest parallel to French bureaucrats are Japanese bureaucrats, who have similar powers and frames of mind. France has several nationalized industries—aircraft, automobiles, coal mines, banks, steel, gas, and electricity—in addition to the areas that are state-run throughout Europe, such as the "PTT" (post, telephone, and telegraph) and the railroads. Workers in these industries are not considered civil servants, but top management people are. Every French teacher, from kindergarten to university, is a civil servant.

The civil servants we are concerned with, however, are the several thousand who staff the Paris ministries, the **Grands Corps**, most of whom are graduates of one of the Great Schools. Even more powerful than their British counterparts, French civil servants of the administrative class (about the top 20 percent) run France. If anything, bureaucratic power grew with the coming of the Fifth Republic, for de Gaulle so hamstrung the National Assembly that it could no longer provide a policy counterweight to, or check on, the actions of the top civil servants. Furthermore, by long French tradition, many top politicians were themselves civil servants, now often graduates of the ENA or of another *grande école*. Typically, three-fourths of ministers and two-fifths of National Assembly deputies are civil servants. Premier de Villepin is a prime example. This close connection leads to government of the bureaucrats, by the bureaucrats, and for the bureaucrats.

This is not to say that French bureaucrats run things badly; often they do their jobs very well. It is the bureaucratic attitude that alienates their countrymen: aloof, arrogant, cold, logical, and rigid. It is not that they do not meet and interact with other Frenchmen; civil servants sit on some fifteen thousand committees and councils all over the country with representatives of business, labor, and farming. The highest of these is the national Social and Economic Council, but even it has a purely advisory capacity, and often advice is ignored as "unobjective." The composition of many of tutelle French for tutelage; bureaucratic guidance.

Inspection Short for General Finance Inspection, very top of French bureaucracy, with powers to investigate all branches.

these consultative bodies is increasingly bureaucratic; some 30 percent of the Social and Economic Council is named by the government, for example. The French bureaucratic approach is expressed in their term **tutelle**, for they act more as tutors than as servants of the public.

Many say the real elite running France is the *Inspection Générale de Finance*. Selected from among the top ten ENA graduates (see page 124) each year, the superbright *inspecteurs de finances* snoop all around France to see how public funds are spent. All levels of French government are afraid of them. Few countries have the precise equivalent of the **Inspection**. It would be as if the U.S. Government Accountability Office (formerly the General Accounting Office), a branch of Congress, had the enforcement powers of the FBI. *Inspecteurs* (among them: Giscard d'Estaing and Juppé) of all ranks and ages agree to always see each other. Inspectors who "put on the slippers" (see box below) still have clout, as they offer each other the best public and private jobs. And if they tire of these, they can return to the IGF at a top salary.

■ Government by Bureaucracy

More than in Britain, the civil service in France constitutes a powerful governing body uncontrolled by elected officials, who sometimes denounce the bureaucracy as an "administrative labyrinth" or even as "administrative totalitarianism." But they can do little about it.

We should not think France is unique in this regard, for no country has devised a way to keep its bureaucracy under control. France, with a longer history of bureaucratization and the Great Schools' monopoly over the top civil service, merely reveals the pattern more fully. In Japan, it reaches a high point. In trying to reform, trim, or democratize a bureaucracy we run into a problem: Almost any solution we can think of requires adding more bureaucrats. In France, for example, Mitterrand once tried a ministry for the reform of administration—still more bureaucracy.

We can see here why the French people, faced with an unresponsive, undemocratic bureaucratic maze, turn frustrated and bitter. Where bureaucracy thrives, democracy shrivels. In trying to fix this, France's top politicians step into a contradiction. Statism needs lots of bureaucracy—to run

Comparison

"PUTTING ON THE SLIPPERS"

The movement of top French civil servants to the executive suites of industries is called *pantouflage,* or "putting on the slippers." Japan has the exact same pattern, called "descent from heaven." In France, a graduate of the *Ecole Polytechnique* or the ENA, after a few years in a Paris ministry, can slip into a cushy, high-paying management job, often in a firm he or she used to deal with as an official. Over half the chief executives of France's largest firms are former high civil servants, and two-thirds are graduates of the ENA or X. *Pantouflage* is an important connecting link between French business and bureaucracy. It also invites corruption, which seems endemic in France. One top French administrator after another gets caught using business connections to supplement their income.

welfare programs, supervise industry, and plan the economy. But privatization means loosening bureaucratic controls and letting market forces guide society. Most mainstream French politicians oppose this, for that would mean turning away from what they regard as the humane French model of the welfare state and to a savage "Anglo-Saxon" market system (exception: Sarkozy). Again, France is stuck.

Key Terms

bloc (p. 134)
CRS (p. 139)
dirigiste (p. 143)
Eurocommunism (p. 135)
Events of May (p. 139)
Grands Corps (p. 143)
Inspection (p. 144)
Medef (p. 141)

passé (p. 137)
protest vote (p. 135)
stalemate (p. 137)
Stalinist (p. 135)
structured access (p. 142)
tutelle (p. 144)
volatile (p. 134)

Further Reference

Bell, David S. *French Politics Today*. Manchester, UK: Manchester University Press, 2002.

Converse, Philip E., and Roy Pierce. *Political Representation in France*. Cambridge, MA: Harvard University Press, 1986.

DeClair, Edward G. *Politics on the Fringe: The People, Policies, and Organization of the French National Front*. Durham, NC: Duke University Press, 1999.

Frears, John. *Parties and Voters in France*. New York: St. Martin's, 1991.

Friend, Julius W. *The Long Presidency: France in the Mitterrand Years*. Boulder, CO: Westview, 1998.

Hewlett, Nick. *Modern French Politics: Analysing Conflict and Consensus since 1945*. Malden, MA: Blackwell, 1998.

Levy, Jonah D. *Tocqueville's Revenge: State, Society, and Economy in Contemporary France*. Cambridge, MA: Harvard University Press, 1999.

Marcus, Jonathan. *The National Front and French Politics: The Resistible Rise of Jean-Marie Le Pen*. New York: New York University Press, 1996.

Morris, Peter. *French Politics Today*. New York: St. Martin's, 1994.

Pierce, Roy. *Choosing the Chief: Presidential Elections in France and the United States*. Ann Arbor, MI: University of Michigan Press, 1995.

Suleiman, Ezra N. *Elites in French Society: The Politics of Survival*. Princeton, NJ: Princeton University Press, 1978.

Tiersky, Ronald. *France in the New Europe: Changing Yet Steadfast*. Belmont, CA: Wadsworth, 1995.

Wilson, Frank L. *Interest-Group Politics in France*. New York: Cambridge University Press, 1988.

Chapter 11

WHAT THE FRENCH QUARREL ABOUT

The French economy was almost the opposite of the British, which declined after World War II, dropping Britain back among the industrialized countries. The French economy, which had grown only slowly in the nineteenth and early twentieth centuries, awoke as if from a slumber after World War II with growth rates reaching 6 percent a year. French still remember the period of 1945 to 1975 as *les trentes glorieuses* (the thirty glorious years). After that, however, French growth slowed and unemployment climbed. The growth policies of one epoch often fail in the next, and politicians are reluctant to inflict the pain of change on voters.

Questions to Consider

1. Why did the French economy improve after World War II?
2. Why are too many small farmers and shopkeepers a problem?
3. Why is the state sector of the French economy still large?
4. How does French conservatism differ from the U.S. variety?
5. Why is European unemployment so high?
6. Compare U.S. and European views on welfare.
7. How does France's racial problem resemble America's?
8. Can sports ease racial tensions?
9. How do France's education problems differ from ours?

What invigorated France after World War II? The typical French business firm prior to the war was a small family affair. Growth was not emphasized; keeping it in the family and earning enough for a good living was all that mattered. This meant lots of little companies and stores rather than a few big ones. Rather than compete by lower prices or better goods, the French, with a **petit bourgeois** mentality, sought to hide behind a protective government that would set prices and keep out foreign competition by high tariffs. It was a cozy arrangement for French business families, but it held France's economy back.

World War II jolted the French elite, which, smarting from German conquest and eager to restore France to world leadership, planned a growth economy. A Planning Commission set "indicative plans" to encourage—but not force—French businesses to expand in certain sectors and regions. Quite distinct from Communist-style centralized planning, **indicative planning** in effect said, "Look, everything is favorable for a new widget factory in the southwest. If you build one you will make a lot of money." With the warm connections between top French bureaucrats and businesspeople soon got the hint. The French Planning Commission provided economic research and incentives to nudge businesses along designated paths. (Japan's MITI did this even more; see Chapter 27.)

Foreign competition was another jolt. First, the European Coal and Steel Community (ECSC) in 1952, then the Common Market in 1957, dismantled France's **protective tariffs** (see Chapter 17). At first French businesspeople were terrified, sure that more aggressive German industry would swamp them. But gradually they learned that French firms could compete and gain major sales in the Common Market. French business firms changed, becoming bigger, more modern, and expansion-oriented. But success brought its own problems.

■ Big Guys versus Little Guys

petit bourgeois   Small shopkeeper. (See page 147.)

indicative planning   Government suggestions to industry to expand in certain areas. (See page 147.)

protective tariff   Tax on imported goods to prevent them from undercutting domestic products. (See page 147.)

hypermarché   French for "hypermarket," huge store that sells everything.

On a street where I lived in Toulouse, in the space of a few blocks, there were not only pharmacies, bakeries, butchers, cafés, and houseware, furniture, vegetable, and tobacco shops, but at least three of each type of store. Perhaps two miles distant, in a suburb, a one-stop **hypermarché** (fittingly named Mammouth) under one roof combined supermarket (offering perhaps a hundred different cheeses), discount house (everything from clothes to auto parts), and cafeteria. Selection and prices were better at Mammouth than among the myriad neighborhood stores. Such developments have been going on throughout France for years. Some call it the Americanization of France, but it is really just the modernization of an old-fashioned economy. The impact on the small shopkeepers is predictable: They are squeezed out, screaming all the way. What they regarded as their birthright—the small, family-owned, uncompetitive shops—are closing. As Marx put it: "One capitalist kills many."

Comparison

NUCLEAR POWER À LA FRANÇAISE

The French complain and quarrel about many things, but nuclear energy is not one of them. Most French accept nuclear energy, and none of the major parties is against it. The anti-atom Greens won a few seats in the 1997 legislative elections but fared poorly in 2002. The French, short of other energy sources, have gone all-out for nuclear-generated electricity and have made a success of it. France has sixty nuclear power stations that produce 77 percent of its electricity, compared to 34 percent in Japan, 31 percent in Germany, 23 percent in Britain, and only 20 percent in the United States, where big cost overruns have ended new nuclear-plant construction. Some U.S. plants have been scrapped before they were finished. French nuclear-generated electricity costs less than half of America's. New Hampshire's problem-plagued Seabrook reactor could have been built by the French for one-sixth its actual cost.

How do the French do what Americans cannot? Here we see some of the occasional advantages of centralized, technocratic rule. The state-owned utility, Electricité de France, developed a single type of reactor and stuck with it. Competing U.S. manufacturers proffered a variety of designs, some not well-tested. When Paris gives the word to build a reactor, the political, financial, regulatory, and managerial sectors mesh under central direction, and the project gets done on time. In the United States, those sectors quarrel and have no central guidance, and the project takes years longer than it should. Environmentalist groups in France—not very big or powerful groups anyway—have no legal power to block or delay projects. The centralized French system is also better able to train personnel; there have been no Three Mile Islands in France. Nuclear power plants are an important part of France's export trade. The very strengths of the American system—decentralization, competition, light regulation, and pluralist interplay—have tripped up the U.S. nuclear industry.

A parallel problem hits French farmers. There are too many small farms; half are run part-time. France remained a nation of peasants an unusually long time. A third of the French workforce was still on the land at the end of World War II. With postwar industrialization this changed so that now less than 3 percent of the labor force works in agriculture. Since 1950, three-fourths of France's farms, mostly small, have disappeared. Still, French agriculture, like its U.S. counterpart, overproduces, and French farmers often dump produce on highways to protest what they regard as inadequate prices. France is the world's second largest food exporter (first place: the United States) and the EU's largest food producer. One French idea: Instead of subsidizing farmers to produce more than is needed, pay them to look after the environment.

flash party   One that quickly rises and falls.

entrepreneurial   Starting your own business.

The small shopkeepers and farmers who are squeezed out contribute to France's electoral volatility. They shift allegiances rapidly, to whoever promises their survival. The Gaullists have been a major beneficiary, but the frightened shopkeepers have also contributed to extremist parties. There is no nice solution to the problem of too many small shops and farms; they must go, and it hurts. Attempts to retain them are hopeless and reactionary, the stuff demagoguery is made of. (Think this is a French problem? How do U.S. communities react to a proposed Wal-Mart?)

In 1953, for example, Pierre Poujade founded the Union for the Defense of Shopkeepers and Artisans (UDCA) to protect small-business people from the bigger, more efficient department stores and supermarkets that were driving many of them out of business. Tinged with reaction and anti-Semitism, Poujadism caught fire, and in the parliamentary elections of 1956 won 12 percent of the popular vote; some thought it was the coming party. It turned out to be a **flash party**, however; Poujadism disappeared in 1958 when de Gaulle took over the French right. Le Pen was a Poujadist and, some say, continues its views in his National Front.

Comparison

WHO HAS THE MOST RED TAPE?

Enterprise and **entrepreneurial** are French words but not French practice. French laws and regulations make France one of the hardest places to start your own business. The OECD rates government burdens and regulations on entrepreneurship, with 6 as the most restrictive. Figures for 1999:

France	2.75
Italy	2.75
Japan	2.30
Germany	2.10
Sweden	1.80
Netherlands	1.40
United States	1.25
Britain	0.50

Starting a business is easier in Britain than in the United States and much easier than in France. French presidents sometimes say that they will trim regulations, but that goes against France's statist tradition.

■ The Privatization Question

conservatism   Desire to preserve or return to old ways.

protectionism   Keeping out imports by tariffs and regulations so as to aid domestic producers.

For much of the postwar period, one-fourth of French business and industry was state-owned, more than any other West European country. Now, after major privatization programs, one-quarter of the French work force (including police, military, and school teachers) is still in the public sector, among the highest in Europe. In addition, the French government has majority ownership of some 1,500 private-sector businesses. Some industries such as telecoms and railways were state-owned in Europe from the start. Some, such as cars and steel, were taken over because without government subsidies they would close, creating unemployment. High-tech areas such as aircraft, nuclear power, and computers are state-owned prestige industries that boost France's world standing.

The French left traditionally demanded more nationalization, including all big banks and industries. They argued that under state control big industries would pay workers fairly, hire more people, and produce what French people really need rather than capitalist luxuries only a few can afford. Traditionally, much of the French right also liked state-owned industries, believing that they contributed to national power and greatness and were best run by brilliant *xiens* and *énarques* (see page 124). De Gaulle, for example, supported a major state sector in heavy and high-tech industry. Remember, **conservatism** in Europe is not the same as conservatism in America. In the 2002 elections, only the tiny Liberal Democracy party of Alain Madelin ran as free-marketeers.

Waves of privatization and deregulation by both left and right governments roll in about every two decades but then roll back, leaving France still with a great deal of state ownership, controls, and rules that always need to be pruned. Most French leaders flinch at thorough privatization because they fear making unemployment, already high, any worse. French public-sector unions demonstrate against privatization, which would end their high pay and early retirements.

Political Culture

THE FRENCH AND STATISM

Starting far back in the Old Regime, *étatisme* (statism) became part of French political culture. Also early, some French thinkers recognized that it was bad economics. France coined the term *laissez-faire* ("leave us be"). The French Physiocrats in the eighteenth century invented the free-market argument and profoundly influenced Adam Smith. In the mid-nineteenth century, French economist Frédéric Bastiat ridiculed trade **protectionism** by suggesting Paris protect French candlemakers from "the ruinous competition of a foreign rival"—the sun.

For many French, state ownership and protectionism just seem right, and it is not only a question of culture. Many employees owe their jobs and retirement at age 55 to state supervision of the economy. The political elite is trained in the statist mold of the ENA. Nearly all French politicians oppose full capitalism. Gaullist President Chirac swore "France will never let Europe become a mere free-trade area." His premier, de Villepin, called protectionism "economic patriotism." Earlier Socialist Premier Jospin (1997–2002) said firms should not be free to let workers go. In France, welfare, statism, and protectionism are entwined in French identity and worked to defeat the new European constitution in 2005 (see Chapter 17).

The center-right UDF under Giscard had perhaps the strongest commitment to privatization, but the pain of change led to the Socialist victory of 1981. Good economics is sometimes bad politics. But, as Mitterrand discovered, good politics is sometimes bad economics. Generous policies on welfare, wages, and benefits brought inflation, stagnation, and higher unemployment. The Socialists nationalized several large firms and banks and then discovered that they were money-losers. In 1983, Mitterrand reversed course in favor of private business and a market economy. "You do not want more state?" asked Mitterrand. "Me neither." (Compare with Clinton: "The era of big government is over.") Believers in socialism had received a real slap in the face and some abandoned their leftism for neoliberalism. Chirac, first as premier and later as president, reoriented the Gaullists toward privatization of state-owned industry. Much was sold, but unemployment was so huge it led to the Socialists' 1997 parliamentary election victory. The Gaullists no longer mention privatization. Jospin promised to slow or reverse privatization, but in practice he sold more French state-owned enterprises than all five of his immediate predecessors put together. He never, however, used the word "privatization," for that would be following an Anglo-Saxon policy.

Comparison

THE CONCORDE: TECHNOLOGICAL NATIONALISM

The United States has private firms such as Boeing to build jetliners. Europe uses state-owned firms. The Concorde supersonic aircraft illustrates what goes wrong with nationalized industries: They can build the wrong product for the wrong reason and cost taxpayers a fortune. The Concorde's development began in 1962 as a joint Anglo-French enterprise to give their lagging aircraft industries a technological jump on the Americans. They thought it would be purchased by airlines all over the world.

But huge overruns boosted development costs to $4.28 billion and the price per plane to $92 million, close to ten times what had been estimated. The Concorde consumed three times the fuel per passenger mile of a Boeing 747. Only British and French airlines purchased Concordes and then only because their nationalized air carriers were required to by law. Because they seldom filled their one hundred seats, the airlines lost money on Concorde runs. Only fourteen Concordes were ever finished before production shut down in 1978.

Why did Britain and France do it? A nationalized industry often has different priorities than a normal commercial venture. In this case "technological nationalism" was a factor; that is, they felt they had to boost their high-tech industries or lose to U.S. dominance. Employment was another factor; Britain and France created thousands of jobs with the Concorde. Once the project was underway and the cost overruns mounting, neither country wanted to admit it had made a mistake. Because the Concorde's makers had access to their national treasuries, they did not have to undergo the discipline of raising capital in the marketplace.

This is not to say that nationalized industries always do things wrong. Aerospatiale of France finally dropped Concorde to form a European consortium that produces the more conventional Airbus, which has pulled ahead of Boeing in world-market share and is used by some U.S. airlines. In 2004 Airbus flew its A380 super-jumbo, a challenge to the Boeing 747. Airbus, however, is still subsidized. Nationalized industries tend to inefficiency because they get government subsidies. Boeing charged this was unfair, but Airbus points out that Boeing was also subsidized through defense contracts to develop bombers, then used the technology for passenger planes. (Boeing's 707 jetliner was a lot like its B-52 bomber; prototypes of both first flew in 1954.)

■ Unemployment: The Giant Problem

"Unemployment is the true French disease," said French Premier de Villepin. U.S. unemployment is generally much lower than in West Europe, sometimes only half as much. And Europe's high unemployment has occurred when, for the most part, its economies were growing. Many believe the key problem is European **labor-force rigidities**. These are related to West Europe's generous welfare and unemployment benefits, which discourage many unemployed Europeans from seeking new jobs. Wages and **social costs** are so high that European firms are reluctant to hire new workers. A French employer pays almost half as much in taxes as in wages, a German employer even more. And there are some two-dozen taxes that must be enumerated on pay stubs, drastically increasing paperwork. Laws in most of Europe prevent easy layoffs; when a firm lets a worker go it must give hefty severance pay.

labor-force rigidities   Unwillingness of workers to take or change jobs.

social costs   Taxes for medical, unemployment, and pension benefits.

informal economy   Under-the-table transactions to avoid taxes and regulations.

Hence, the reluctance of French (and German) firms to hire: It is too expensive, involves much red tape, and you may not be able to let workers go in a downturn. The solution for business people: Either (1) do not hire anyone, or (2) hire on the **informal economy**, or (3) set up shop in another country. French businesses do all three. Europe's high off-the-books workforce indicates an economy choked with taxes and controls. In France, as in all of Europe, the working class generally votes left to protect jobs and wages—never mind if protection creates inefficiencies and unemployment—while managers press to roll back restrictions and free up the labor market. The U.S. labor force is much more flexible; wages and social costs are low; and hiring and layoffs are easy. Result: The U.S. economy creates far more new jobs a year, something West Europeans envy.

High French unemployment also puts a brake on further privatization. As we noted, one-fourth of French workers are employed in the public sector, compared to one-seventh in the United States

Comparison

EUROPEAN AND U.S. ATTITUDES TOWARD WELFARE

France, like most of Europe, approves of a more extensive—and expensive—welfare state than Americans do. The French constitution, for example, promises a "decent means of existence." French welfare recipients get about 50 percent more than their U.S. counterparts. Most Americans are delighted to cut welfare benefits and drop recipients off welfare rolls.

There is clearly a major cultural difference here. Many European politicians, especially but not exclusively leftists, attack the "savage" unrestrained capitalism of America and point to its large underclass.

"We will not become like the cruel U.S. economy," they say (not noticing France's large Muslim underclass). Not many Americans see their economy as savage or cruel; most see it as flexible and competitive with opportunities for all. Making something of that opportunity is up to individuals. Sociologist Seymour Martin Lipset defined the American ethos as "competitive individualism." Europeans tend to solidarity, to the view that society as a whole should look out for its weakest members. Like any element of culture, this view does not change easily.

and Britain, and one-sixth in Germany. Those figures are not just "bureaucrats" but anyone who works for any form or level of government,
including military personnel, police, and schoolteachers. French public-
sector workers enjoy job security plus good pay, benefits, and retirement
plans. Their unions stage strikes over any efforts to trim these bounties,
and Paris usually backs down, a pattern shared by other statist systems.

austerity Drastically holding down government expenses.

Another contributor to high unemployment: the euro. In order to join Europe's single-cur-
rency club, Chirac had to bring France's budget deficit down to 3 percent of GDP and maintain
a *franc fort* (strong franc). Britain said to hell with the euro and dropped out of the European
Monetary Union, but Chirac was determined, partly for reasons of prestige, to stay in, whatever
the domestic economic costs. Many considered Chirac's **austerity** policy foolishly rigid and the
chief cause of high unemployment and his loss in the snap parliamentary elections of 1997. In the
2000s, both France and Germany—each suffering around 10 percent unemployment—routinely
exceeded the 3 percent deficit limit.

How to cure unemployment? All incoming French governments swear it is their top priori-
ty, but most are voted out in part because they fail to make a dent in the problem. The Jospin government's bright idea came from Germany: France cut its work week from 39 to 35 hours without
cuts in pay on the theory that this would force firms to hire more workers. Results were mixed but
not all bad, because it forces firms to become more efficient, so labor productivity increased to
among the world's highest. Managers sought to make the 35-hour work week more flexible, most
workers did not, and unemployment stayed high.

In 1997 Jospin said that he would create 350,000 jobs, mostly for young people, in health services, schools, welfare, transportation, and construction. Almost reflexively, Paris turns to statist

Key Concepts

EUROPE AND U.S.-STYLE CONSERVATISM

One of the hardest points for American students of
Europe to understand is that conservatism in Europe
is not the same as in the United States. For Europeans,
U.S.-style conservatism is not conservatism at all; it
is the classic liberalism of Adam Smith: little government and a free market. (They're right.) European conservatism hearkens back to a time when monarchs and
aristocrats ruled and a strong state supervised the
economy for the sake of national power. In the twentieth century, European conservatives transferred their
loyalties to strong leaders and saw nothing wrong with
statism and the welfare state. Prime example: de
Gaulle and the Gaullists.

Gradually, however, U.S.-style conservatism took
hold in European conservative parties, spurred on by
intellectuals who saw that defending old class privileges and uncompetitive, state-owned industries retards growth and job creation. They called the
movement "neo-liberalism," a revival and updating of
Adam Smith. Prime example: Margaret Thatcher and
the Tory "dries." The movement appeared in France
with Premier Raymond Barre's efforts in the late 1970s
to liberalize the French economy. Even the Socialists
realized in the early 1980s that state ownership of
industry was a problem. First Mitterrand and then
Chirac privatized much French industry. But neither
would go all the way to a U.S.-style free market, precisely because it is American, and the French have a
cultural block against what they call "savage liberalism." Americans call it freedom.

Muslim Follower of Islam, also adjective of *Islam*.

value-added tax Large, hidden national sales taxes used throughout Europe.

remedies. Recipients got five-year contracts at minimum wage ($1,100 a month), most of it from government. Little came of the program. Hiring for public projects at taxpayers' expense seldom yields long-term solutions. For that, France will have to end laws that keep firms from easily hiring and firing. France made a step in that direction with a 2006 law allowing workers under age 26 to be fired with no delay or reason within their first two years on a job. Most French opposed the move to a freer labor market, and the government dropped the plan. The French, like many Europeans, have difficulty understanding that making it hard to let workers go means firms hire few new workers even in good times; they fear getting stuck with them in slack times. America's easy-hire, easy-fire policy contributes to labor-force flexibility and low U.S. unemployment rates. No one has come up with a legislative cure for unemployment.

France's Racial Problem

France has a worse problem with immigrants than Britain and Germany (and the United States). There are some 9 million foreigners living in France (if one counts naturalized citizens and the second generation), about 16 percent of the French population. France has long assimilated European immigrants. From 1880 to 1960 some 7 million Italians, Spaniards, Portuguese, Poles, and Russians were integrated into French society.

But starting in the 1960s, many **Muslims** arrived and fueled major racial tensions. Now numbering between 5 and 6 million, perhaps 9 percent of France's population, most are from former

Comparison

IS THERE A **VAT** IN OUR FUTURE?

Throughout Europe, governments raise close to 30 percent of their revenues through hefty (10 to 20 percent) **value-added taxes** (VAT). In contrast, U.S. sales taxes, mostly at the state level, average around 6 percent and altogether make up only 15 percent of all U.S. taxes (federal, state, and local). But European VATs are invisible; they are calculated at every stage that value is added to a product (for example, after pieces of cloth are sewn together to make a shirt), not added to the purchase price at the cash register, as in America. Accordingly, European governments reason that it is not so painful as other kinds of taxes.

Under the Bush 43 administration, Republicans, having run up massive budget deficits, floated the idea of a "consumption tax" or "national sales tax," in effect a VAT. They had cut income taxes and swore they would never raise them again. A tax on consumption would encourage Americans to save more and make more money available for loans to expand the economy. Because people would be less eager to spend, a VAT slows inflationary tendencies. A VAT, however, is a regressive tax, hitting the poor, working class, and retirees harder than the rich. Few gave an American VAT much chance of becoming law.

French colonies in West and North Africa—such as Algeria, Morocco, Tunisia, Senegal, and Mali. They flee misery and unemployment to take the hardest, dirtiest, lowest-paid work in France, but many are still unemployed, especially young people. They live in shabby high-rise public housing. When I stayed in the suburb of Aulnay-sous-Bois northeast of Paris in 1989, I reckoned that one-third of my fellow rail commuters were African or Arab. One French homeowner there ruefully wisecracked that it had become "Aulnay-sous-Cameroun." (In 2005, rioting hit Aulnay.)

Most French say there are too many Muslims in France, and some want them sent home, which the National Front advocates. All of France's main parties are against any more newcomers, so that now (legal) immigration is as tight as in Britain, and France turns away hundreds of thousands of desperate refugees each year. Said Interior Minister Nicolas Sarkozy (whose father fled Hungary): "France needs immigrants, but France cannot and should not welcome *all* immigrants."

The French republican ideal posits a single French identity without subgroups. France has no affirmative action and does not even collect official data on racial, religious, and ethnic groups, the way the U.S. Census does. Increasingly, critics say such statistics are needed to overcome the very obvious racial gaps. Sometimes equality demands paying attention to the problems of minorities. France now has millions of citizens of color who are treated as permanent foreigners. Said one West African who was educated in France: "The French don't think I'm French."

France now has angry Muslim youths who look a lot like the black underclass of U.S. ghettoes. Although most were born in France, they are still called "immigrants" and are largely outside French society. Often from broken homes, they slide into gangs, drugs, and petty crime and copy black American styles, such as rap music and hooded sweatshirts. A few are drawn to Islamic

Geography

THE GEOGRAPHY OF MIGRATION

Everywhere the Third World is trying to sneak into the First. The reason: economic opportunities. Pakistanis in Britain, Algerians in France, Turks in Germany, and Mexicans in the United States are all expressions of the same problem: not enough jobs in the home country. Japan tries to block foreign job-seekers, but even there one finds Filipino, Thai, Sri Lankan, and other workers. There is one place on earth where you can walk from the Third World into the First: the Mexico-U.S. border. In a kind of osmosis, migrants are drawn through a membrane (border) by the pressure of unemployment and low living standards.

But is this a problem? From a purely economic standpoint, no. The immigrants take jobs local people shun in favor of welfare. And, as we shall consider in Chapter 16, the rich countries have few babies and rapidly growing numbers of retirees. Without immigrants, there would be too few workers to pay for the oldsters' pensions. The problem comes when immigrants insist on preserving their old cultures in the new country. In France, discrimination and limited schooling mean immigrants and their children do not master French, gain no job skills, and become ghettoized into crime, drugs, and even extremist Muslim organizations. This in turn fuels resentment against immigrants and has led to the British and French National Fronts and the German National Democrats. Notice how the same causes and same feelings are found to a lesser degree in the United States.

extremism. The police harass them, and they hate the police. "No one will give you a job," said one youth. "How long can we stand here before we blow a fuse?" In 2005, the fuse blew as young males, mostly Muslim, rioted for three weeks across France and burned more than 8,000 cars. Tough police methods and a curfew finally quelled the riots. Sarkozy, the head of France's police, called the rioters "scum" and vowed to "clean out" their neighborhoods. Most French agreed, but few said so openly.

A running issue was *l'affaire du foulard* ("the question of the headscarf"), Muslim girls wearing the traditional *hijab*, required by their religion, in school. France, intent of keeping religion out of schools, outlawed it in 2004. Thundered one *imam* (Muslim cleric): "Allah's law takes precedence over French law." The French deported him, as they do any Muslin preacher who

Comparison

MEDICAL CARE AND COSTS

France delivers some of the world's best medical care at moderate cost, the World Health Organization has concluded. Medical care is tricky to measure, and the 2000 WHO study, the first to compare medical delivery worldwide, is controversial. Japanese are the healthiest people in the world (probably related to diet) and spend less, but those are indications of health, not of medical care. The two are not the same. Health is what God gives you, plus diet and exercise. Medical care is what doctors and hospitals give you. Spending more on the latter does little to improve the former. Some figures are shown in the table below.

Worldwide, medical costs are increasing, from 3 percent of gross world product in 1948 to 7.9 percent

half a century later. Americans spend by far the most on medical care but are less healthy than many who spend less (again, diet). The U.S. government does little to hold down costs, so insurance (some Medicare, mostly private) struggles to keep up with high-tech care and new, costlier drugs. Some 45 million uninsured Americans hope they do not get sick. Most of Europe has nationwide insurance (some public, some private) that covers everyone and caps costs. But Europeans pay in other ways, by long waits and not-so-high-tech treatment: de facto rationing. Will the United States have to do something similar to hold down its soaring medical costs?

	WHO Ranking	Medical Costs per Person/Yr.	Percent of GDP
France	1	$2,736	9.7
Japan	10	2,133	7.9
Britain	18	2,160	7.7
Germany	25	2,817	10.9
United States	37	5,274	14.6
Mexico	61	550	6.1
Iran	93	432	6.0
Russia	130	535	6.2
China	144	261	5.8
Nigeria	187	43	4.7

Source: World Health Organization

advocates *jihad*. A 1996 French law lets judges detain people for "association with wrongdoers involved in a terrorist enterprise." Faced with terrorism, the French are not as fastidious on human rights as the British or Germans. After 9/11 and the London bombings, the United States and Britain both moved closer to the French zero-tolerance position.

> **social mobility** Movement of individuals from one class to another, usually upward.

Most French politicians agree that the immigrants should be better integrated into French economic and cultural life, but they disagree on how. Improving the immigrants' housing, schooling, and jobs all cost money. The tax burden falls most heavily on the municipalities where there are the most immigrants, one reason the National Front vote is the strongest where there are more Muslims. The parties on the left, Socialist and Communist, are more willing to spend additional funds. Trying to curb radical tendencies and encourage dialogue, Paris in 2003 created the French Council of the Muslim Faith. In 2005, some 5,000 French Muslim delegates elected a moderate Council board.

Racial amity got a brief boost when the French soccer team won the 1998 World Cup: Eight of the twenty-two-man team were black or brown. France erupted with pride. The winning goal was made by Zinedine Zidane, born in Marseilles of Algerian parents. Sports may be more important than government programs in fostering racial integration. (Is that true in the United States?)

France's Education Problems

France has expanded educational opportunity in order to improve **social mobility** and integrate all, even immigrants, into French society. This effort is praiseworthy, reminiscent of U.S. efforts to solve social problems by increased school integration. But, as in the United States, it leads to new problems.

Paris decided that a much larger portion of French young people should achieve the "bac," discussed in Chapter 9. The Socialist government in 1985 began an ambitious plan to send 80 percent of all young people to *lycées* by 2000, a goal largely achieved. The bac has been expanded to include technical and vocational options in order to form the literate and qualified labor force needed by a modern economy. But even with a major upsurge in education spending, the public *lycée* system became severely overburdened, as evidenced by dilapidated buildings, crowded classrooms (some with over 40 students per teacher), and crime in the hallways and restrooms. (Sound familiar?) Middle-class French parents, afraid of school decay, increasingly send their children to private *lycées*. French student street protests from time to time shake the Paris government, reminders of the 1968 Events of May.

France and Europe

Unlike Britain, France did not hang back in building a united Europe. Indeed, the idea originated with two French officials, Jean Monnet and Robert Schuman, after World War II (see Chapter 17). France was one of the original six of the ECSC and then of the Common Market. Members

Common Agricultural Program EU
farm subsidies, biggest part of EU
budget.

cut tariffs with each other and let in workers from member countries. The invigorating effects of this boosted French economic
growth. The EU's **Common Agricultural Program** (CAP) eats half
the EU budget, and French farmers are the biggest beneficiaries.
French farmers like this; German and Dutch taxpayers do not.

French voters rejected a new EU constitution 55–45 percent in 2005. Most still favor the EU
in general but used the referendum to show their displeasure with the elites who run France and
the EU. Most French leaders also favor European unification, partly because they see France leading a united Europe, but they disagree on what kind of a Europe they want. Not all want a full federation, for that would blot out French sovereignty. Charles de Gaulle voiced this in the 1960s
when he spoke of a *Europe des patries* ("Europe of fatherlands," later the view of Britain's Margaret
Thatcher). This is especially true if newly unified Germany is Europe's leader, not France. And
how big should the EU be? Should it include Turkey? The further eastward the EU expands, the
more it makes Germany its natural hub. Many French oppose that privately but rarely say so publicly. Since German unification in 1871—after it beat France in a war—France has always worried about its large, powerful neighbor to the east, to which we now turn.

Key Terms

austerity (p. 153)

Common Agricultural Program (p. 158)

conservatism (p. 150)

entrepreneurial (p. 149)

flash party (p. 149)

hypermarché (p. 148)

indicative planning (p. 148)

informal economy (p. 152)

labor-force rigidities (p. 152)

Muslim (p. 154)

petit bourgeois (p. 148)

protectionism (p. 150)

protective tariff (p. 148)

social costs (p. 152)

social mobility (p. 157)

value-added tax (p. 154)

Further Reference

Chafer, Tony, and Brian Jenkins, eds. *France: From the Cold War to the New World Order.* New York:
     St. Martin's, 1996

Estrin, Saul, and Peter Holmes. *French Planning in Theory and Practice.* Winchester, MA: Allen &
     Unwin, 1983.

Favell, Adrian. *Philosophies of Integration: Immigration and the Idea of Citizenship in France and Britain.*
     New York: St. Martin's, 1998.

Fenby, Jonathan. *France on the Brink.* New York: Arcade, 1999.

Flynn, Gregory, ed. *Remaking the Hexagon: The New France in the New Europe.* Boulder, CO: West-
     view, 1995.

Fysh, Peter, and Jim Wolfreys. *The Politics of Racism in France.* New York: St. Martin's, 1998.

Gildea, Robert. *France since 1945.* New York: Oxford University Press, 1996.

Keeler, John T. S., and Martin A. Schain, eds. *Chirac's Challenge: Liberalization, Europeanization, and Malaise in France*. New York: St. Martin's, 1996.

Schmidt, Vivien A. *From State to Market? The Transformation of French Business and Government*. New York: Cambridge University Press, 1996.

Simmons, Harvey G. *The French National Front: The Extremist Challenge to Democracy*. Boulder, CO: Westview, 1996.

Smith, Timothy B. *France in Crisis: Welfare, Inequality, and Globalization since 1980*. New York: Cambridge University Press, 2005.

Smith, W. Rand. *The Left's Dirty Job: The Politics of Industrial Restructuring in France and Spain*. Pittsburgh, PA: University of Pittsburgh Press, 1998.

Part III

GERMANY

Chapter 12

GERMANY:
THE IMPACT OF THE PAST

Britain has natural borders. France claims to have natural borders, but one of its six sides (the northeast) has been disputed. Germany, however, has natural borders only on its north and south (the Baltic Sea and Alps), and this fact has contributed to its tumultuous history. Germany has expanded and contracted over the centuries, at times stretching from Alsace (now French) to East Prussia (now Polish and Russian). After World War II its eastern wing was chopped off, and the country was divided into eastern and western occupation zones, which in 1949 became East and West Germany. The Federal Republic of Germany that reunified in 1990 is considerably smaller than the mighty Second Reich at the turn of the century.

Questions to Consider

1. What are Germany's geographic problems?
2. How was Germany the opposite of French centralization?
3. What did *cuius regio* attempt to solve? How?
4. What did Prussia contribute to Germany?
5. How did nationalism combine with racism in Germany?
6. What were the First, Second, and Third Reichs?
7. How did Bismarck retard Germany's democratic development?
8. Why was the Weimar Republic doomed?
9. What were the main elements of Nazism?

Germany's location in the center of Europe and the flat, defenseless North European Plain imposed two unhappy options on the nation. When Germany was divided and militarily weak—its condition throughout most of history—it was Europe's battleground. On the other hand, when Germany united and became militarily strong enough to deter any combination of potential attackers, it was also strong enough to beat all its neighbors one at a time. When Germany unified in the nineteenth century, it automatically became a threat to the rest of Europe; it was big, populous, and strategically located. Some Europeans still fear a united Germany. Geography, in making a united Germany a threat, has been unkind to Germany.

Who Are the Germans?

Contrary to Nazi race theory, the Germans are as much an ethnic mixture as any people in Europe, maybe more. The original Germans identified by the Romans were a collection of several barbarian tribes, some of which became Romanized. The invasion of the Huns in the fourth century set off gigantic migrations throughout Europe as everyone fled from their advance. Many Germans sought refuge in Roman territory, and Rome hired some as mercenaries. Soon Germanic tribes were roaming through and destroying the Roman Empire and settling in various parts of it.

Since that time Germans have presented one face to the West and another to the East. To the West—to France and Italy—the heirs of Rome, they were respectful of their older high culture,

The Changing Shape of Germany

800: Charlemagne's Holy Roman Empire

1648: After Westphalia

1815: The German Confederation

1871: The Second Reich

1919: The Weimar Republic

1939: Hitler's Third Reich

1945: Occupied Germany (Four Zones)

1949: Two Germanies

1990: Reunited Germany

which they tried to copy. To the East, however, they saw barbarians—first Huns, then Slavs—whom they either Germanized, exterminated, or pushed back. Whole Slavic- or Baltic-speaking areas were Germanized, and many of today's Germans are of East European descent. The Nazis hated to admit it, but Germans are a combination of Celts, Romans, Jews, several Germanic tribes, Slavs, and Balts. When the Nazis introduced their model of the perfect Nordic specimen, some Germans quietly chuckled, for practically none of the Nazi leaders matched the tall, athletic, blond, blue-eyed image.

The Fragmented Nation

The Germanic tribes were so impressed by Rome—whose empire they were destroying—that they pretended to continue the empire. When in 800 the Frankish king Charlemagne (German: Karl der Grosse) was crowned in Rome, he called his gigantic realm the Holy Roman Empire (which, Voltaire later quipped, was "neither holy, nor Roman, nor an empire"). Although it soon fell apart, the German wing continued calling itself that until Napoleon ended the farce in 1806.

In England, as we saw, power between king and nobles was kept in balance, resulting in a constitutional monarchy that moved in spurts toward civil liberty, limited government, and rule by Parliament. In France, absolutism upset the balance as the French kings amassed more and more power leading to a centralized, bureaucratic state. Germany went the other way: The nobles gained more and more power until, by the thirteenth century, the emperor was a mere figurehead while princes and leading churchmen ran ministates as they saw fit. Germany was not one country but a crazy quilt of hundreds of independent principalities and cities.

Geography

BOUNDARIES: LINES ON A MAP

Precisely where one state leaves off and another begins is often unsettled. Looking at maps, you might think that boundary lines are real, perhaps decreed by nature, or at least hallowed by time to demarcate each people's allotted territory. Would that it were so. In point of fact, there are practically no natural boundaries in the world. Almost all boundaries are artificial, some more artificial than others.

Germany's boundaries, for example, consolidated, expanded, and contracted with great fluidity. Consider the maps of Germany (on pages 164–165) over the centuries. Germany's boundaries were drawn widest under Bismarck in 1871 and under Hitler before and during World War II. The Second Reich included much of present-day Poland and a large sweep of Prussia to the east. With defeat in World War I, Germany lost part of Prussia and Pomerania to make a "Polish corridor" to the Baltic. Alsace returned to France. Hitler expanded the map of Germany by adding Austria, Bohemia (now the Czech Republic), Alsace, and parts of Poland. These lands were immediately stripped away with Germany's defeat in World War II. Germany was also broken into two countries from 1949 to 1990.

Which are the "correct" boundaries for Germany? It is impossible to apply historical, moral, or even demographic standards to determine with certainty Germany's boundaries. One might attempt, as Hitler did, to draw Germany's borders so as to include all Germans. But the peoples of Europe—as in most of the world—are not neatly arrayed in demographic ranks, with, say, Germans on one side of a river and Poles on the other. Instead, they are often "interdigitized," with some German villages in Polish territory and Poles living in some German cities. Whatever border you draw will leave some Germans in Poland and some Poles in Germany.

Poland's boundaries are a perplexing example of border questions. As the empires that had partitioned Poland since the 1790s—German, Austrian, and Russian—collapsed in World War I, Polish patriots under Pilsudski reestablished Poland, but it included many Lithuanians, Belorussians, and Ukrainians. Stalin never liked that boundary and during World War II pushed Soviet borders westward. In compensation, Poland got former German territories, so that now its western border is formed by the Oder and Neisse Rivers. Millions of Germans were expelled. In effect, Poland was picked up and moved over 100 miles westward! After much hesitation (because of German interest groups from the Oder-Neisse territories), Germany confirmed the new boundary.

Only boundaries that have been set up and observed over the centuries are without controversy. To be legal, a border must be agreed upon in a boundary treaty and demarcated with physical indicators, such as concrete pylons. Few borders in the world are like that.

Control of borders is a chief attribute of sovereignty, and nations go to great lengths to demonstrate that they alone are in charge of who and what goes in and goes out across their borders. One of the first points of violence in Lithuania and Slovenia were their passport and customs houses. In forcibly taking over these border checkpoints, Soviet and Yugoslav federal forces respectively attempted to show that they, rather than the breakaway republics, were in charge of the entire national territory. They did not succeed, and their countries fragmented.

Boundary questions abound, such as India's border with Pakistan (especially over Kashmir), China's borders with India and with Russia, Venezuela with Guyana, Argentina with Chile (over Tierra del Fuego) and with Britain (over the Falklands), Syria with Lebanon (over the Bekaa Valley), Morocco with Algeria (over the former Spanish Sahara), and Iraq with Iran (over the Shatt al-Arab waterway). Such questions cause wars.

The split between Roman Catholics and Protestants accentu-ated Germany's fragmentation. Protestant reformer Martin Luther in the early sixteenth century reflected the feeling of much of northern Germany that the Roman church was corrupt and un-godly. The North German princes especially did not like paying taxes to Rome and found Lutheranism a good excuse to stop. South Germany and the Rhineland stayed mostly Catholic, the north and east predominantly Protestant, a pattern that still character-izes modern Germany.

> **Habsburg** Leading Catholic dynasty that once held Austria-Hungary, Spain, Latin America, and the Netherlands.
>
> **Thirty Years War** 1618–1648 Habsburg attempt to conquer and Catholicize Europe.
>
> **Westphalia** Treaty ending Thirty Years War.

Two wars resulted from the religious question. In the first, the Schmalkaldic War (named after the town of Schmalkalden where Protestant princes formed a coali-tion) of 1545–1555, the **Habsburg** Emperor Charles V nearly succeeded in crushing Lutheranism. The Protestants, however, allied with Catholic France to beat Charles. Trying to decide which parts of Germany should be Catholic and which Protestant, the Religious Peace of Augsburg in 1555 came up with the formula *cuius regio eius religio*—"whoever reigns, his religion." Thus the religion of the local prince decided an area's religion, a point that deepened the disunity of Germany and the power of local princes.

The peace proved shaky, though, and in 1618, as the Habsburgs again tried to consolidate their power, a much worse war broke out, the **Thirty Years War**. Again, at first the Catholic Habsburgs won. By 1631, help from other countries arrived. Cardinal Richelieu feared Habsburg power would encircle France, so he aided the Protestants. In international relations, power and national interests are more important than religious or ideological affinity. A strong Swedish army under Gustavus Adolphus battled in Germany for the Protestants. Germany suffered terribly, losing perhaps 30 per-cent of its population, most by starvation. Until World War I, the Thirty Years War was the worst in human history. The Treaty of **Westphalia** in 1648 confirmed *cuius regio* and left Germany atom-ized into 360 separate political entities.

Consider the political impact of religion on the three countries we have studied so far. England broke with Rome; the return of Catholic kings merely confirmed the power of Parliament. In France, the Catholic Church and *ancien régime* stayed loyal to one another while many French turned an-ticlerical, leading to a division of French society into conservative Catholics and anticlerical radi-cals. Germany did not split into clerical and anticlerical but into Catholic and Protestant. The result was ghastly: a long and ruinous war, further breakup of an already fragmented country, and centuries of ill will between Germans of different faiths.

Geography

MOUNTAINS

Mountains can serve as defensive barriers, making a country hard to invade. The Alps help guard Ger-many's southern flank; the Pyrenees do the same for France. Russia, with no mountains until the Urals rise up to form Europe's border with Asia, lay nearly de-fenseless before the horsemen of the east (who passed south of the Urals), the Swedes of the north, and the Germans of the west. Mountains can also slow political and economic development. Very mountainous countries, such as Spain and Mexico, may be harder to unify, as the nation's capital can-not easily penetrate regions shielded by mountains. As the West Virginia motto says, *Montani Semper Liberi* (Mountaineers are always free). Because much of Japan is too mountainous for farms or factories, most Japanese are forced to live in narrow and crowded coastal strips.

The Rise of Prussia

One German state eventually came to dominate the others. Brandenburg, later known as **Prussia**, expanded greatly during the eighteenth century, taking over the eastern German conquests of the Middle Ages along the Baltic and adding Silesia and parts of the Rhineland. In the eastern Baltic regions, a type of nobility had developed, descended from the old Teutonic knights, that had a major impact on German history. The **Junkers** held great estates worked by obedient serfs. Unlike the English lords, however, they did not retain their independence and act as a counterweight to the king but became a state nobility, dependent on the government and controlling all the higher civil-service and military positions. Famous for their discipline and attention to detail, the Junkers contributed to modern Germany a passion for excellence in both military and civil administration.

Prussia   Powerful North German state; capital Berlin.

Junker   (from *junge Herren,* young gentlemen; pronounced YOON care) Prussian nobility.

Prussian kings, with potential enemies on all sides, became obsessed with military power, leading to Voltaire's wisecrack that "Prussia is not a country with an army but an army with a country." In the early eighteenth century, King Frederick William acted as drillmaster to his entire people, demanding military obedience and Prussian efficiency, not only on the parade ground—where he personally marched his handpicked corps of oversize soldiers—but in civilian life as well. Especially in Prussia, obedience to authority became a German character trait.

His son, Frederick the Great, who ruled from 1740 to 1786, perfected what he inherited, as did France's Louis XIV. Frederick inherited the Prussian army, which he kept in such a high state of readiness that it frightened the monarchs of larger states. Administering his kingdom personally, Frederick became known as the "enlightened despot" who brought art and culture (Voltaire stayed at his court for a while), as well as military triumphs and territorial expansion, to Prussia. A brilliant commander and daring strategist, Frederick served as a model for expansion-minded German nationalists. Trying to identify himself with Frederick the Great, Adolf Hitler in 1933 announced the founding of the Third Reich from Frederick's tomb in Berlin.

German Nationalism

At the time of the French Revolution, there were still over three hundred German states. Prussia and Austria were the strongest of them, but they too were pushovers for Napoleon's legions. German liberals, fed up with the backwardness and fragmentation of their country, at first welcomed the

Geography

BOUND GERMANY

Germany is bounded on the north by the Atlantic, Denmark, and the Baltic Sea;

on the east by Poland and the Czech Republic;

on the south by Austria and Switzerland;

and on the west by France, Luxembourg, Belgium, and the Netherlands.

To reinforce your knowledge, sketch out and label Germany and its neighbors. Note also the old border between East and West Germany that disappeared with unification in 1990.

French as liberators and modernizers. Napoleon consolidated the many German ministates—but not Prussia or Austria—into about thirty, calling them the Confederation of the Rhine, and introduced new laws to free the economy and society from archaic laws.

Geography

BOUND POLAND

Poland is bounded on the north by the Baltic Sea, Russia (Kaliningrad Oblast), and Lithuania;

on the east by Belarus and Ukraine;

on the south by the Czech Republic and Slovakia;

and on the west by Germany.

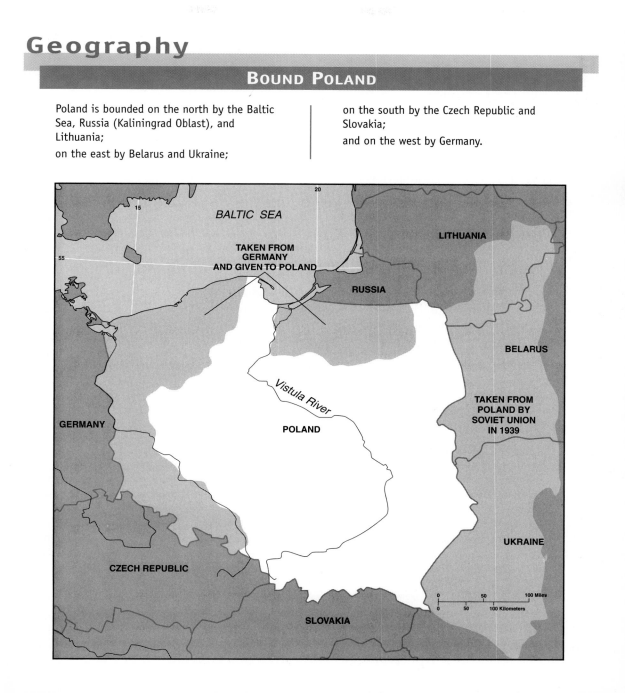

nationalism   Belief in greatness and unity of one's country and hatred of rule by foreigners.

Volksgeist   German for "spirit of the people"; has racist connotations. (Note: All German nouns are capitalized.)

Lebensraum   German for "living space" for an entire nation.

Metternichian system   Contrived conservative system that tried to restore pre-Napoleon European monarchy and stability.

The French brought with them more than liberalism, however; everywhere they went they infected conquered lands with the new idea of **nationalism**, the most contagious *-ism* of all; when one country catches it, so do neighboring lands. Soon Germans, Russians, and Spaniards were fired with anti-French nationalism. Napoleon, without realizing it, had let an imp out of the bottle; the push he gave to German nationalism indirectly led to three German invasions of France. Great historical events have unpredictable long-term consequences.

As we saw in the case of France's borrowing English and American notions of freedom, ideas conceived in one country often become warped, exaggerated, or distorted when applied to another. This happened with German nationalism, which became romantic, angry, and racist and hearkened back to a mythical past. German nationalist intellectuals of the nineteenth century spoke of a **Volksgeist**, a combination of *Volk* (people) and *Geist* (spirit), that implied a Germanic tribal spirit that was superior to other peoples. German geographers coined the term **Lebensraum** and argued that Germany was entitled to more territory. (Japanese militarists argued precisely the same.) Long before Hitler, many Germans favored expansionist nationalism.

Germany looked to Prussia for leadership in throwing off the French yoke, and Prussian troops did contribute to Napoleon's downfall. Like France, Germany after Napoleon was not the same. Caught up in nationalism and liberalism—more of the former than the latter—German thinkers wanted a unified and modernized nation. The ultraconservative Austrian Prince Metternich, who hated both nationalism and liberalism, helped create a German Confederation of thirty-nine states, which he thought would contribute to European stability after Napoleon.

In 1848 revolution broke out all over Europe as discontented liberals and nationalists sought to overthrow the **Metternichian system**. In the midst of urban uprisings, German liberals met in Frankfurt to set up a unified, democratic Germany. They sent a delegation to Berlin to offer the king of Prussia leadership of a German constitutional monarchy, but he contemptuously refused it with the remark that he "would not accept a crown from the gutter." The army cleared out the National Assembly in Frankfurt, and German liberals either converted to pure nationalism or emigrated to the United States.

■ The Second Reich

In contrast to the attempts of liberal nationalists in 1848, German unification came not from the people but from above, from the growth of Prussia. Neither was it the work of liberals but rather of a staunch conservative, Otto von Bismarck, who had seen the liberals in action in 1848 and thought they were fools. Bismarck, who became Prussia's prime minister in 1862, was not really a German nationalist; he was first and foremost a loyal Prussian servant of his king who saw German unification under Prussian leadership as the only way to preserve and defend Prussia. As such, Bismarck's goals were quite limited; he had no intention of turning a united Germany into a military, expansionist state.

For Bismarck, armies and warfare were just tools. In 1862, when the Prussian parliament was deadlocked over the military budget, Bismarck simply decreed new taxes and spent the money without parliamentary approval, declaring, "Not by speeches and majority decisions will the great questions of the time be decided—that was the fault of 1848 and 1849—but by iron and blood."

Bismarck used his military tools to solve the great question of his day: Who was to lead a unified Germany, Prussia or Austria? In a series of three limited wars—in 1864 against Denmark, in 1866 against Austria, and in 1870 against France—Bismarck first consolidated the many German states behind Prussia, then got rid of Austria, then firmed up German unity. The new Second **Reich** (Charlemagne's was the first) was actually proclaimed in France, at Versailles Palace, in 1871.

The Second Reich, lasting from 1871 to 1918, was not a democracy. The legislature, the **Reichstag**, had only limited power, namely, to approve or reject the budget. The chancellor (prime minister) was not "responsible" to the parliament—that is, he could not be voted

Reich   German for empire.

Reichstag   Pre-Hitler German parliament; its building now houses *Bundestag.*

Kulturkampf   Culture struggle, specifically Bismarck's with the Catholic Church.

Machtpolitik   Power politics (cognate to "might").

Realpolitik   Politics of realism.

Personalities

BISMARCK'S DUBIOUS LEGACY

Otto von Bismarck, Germany's chancellor from 1871 to 1890, was a Prussian Junker to the bone, and the stamp he put on a unified Germany retarded its democratic development for decades. Bismarck and Disraeli knew and liked each other, and many compared them as dynamic conservatives. English and German conservatism, however, are two different things. Disraeli's Tories widened the electorate and welcomed a fair fight in Parliament. Bismarck hated parties, parliaments, and anyone who opposed him. Bismarck left Germany an authoritarian and one-man style of governance that was overcome only by Allied occupation following World War II. Bismarck's **Kulturkampf** with the Catholic Church, which he wished to subordinate to the German state, sharpened Catholic resentment against the Protestant north, a feeling that lingers.

Bismarck's most dangerous legacy to Germany was in his foreign policy. He practiced both **Machtpolitik** and **Realpolitik** to manipulate first his own Prussia and then the rest of Europe to produce a unified Germany. War for Bismarck was just a tool. Cynical amorality was another pattern Bismarck bequeathed to Germany.

Germany's real problem was that Bismarck was a tough act to follow. Bismarck used power politics for a limited end, the unification of Germany. His successors picked up his amoral *Machtpolitik* but forgot about the limits, the *Realpolitik*. Bismarck, for example, could

Otto von Bismarck

have easily conquered all of Denmark, Austria, and France, but he did not because he knew that would bring dangerous consequences. Bismarck used war in a controlled way, to unify Germany rather than to conquer Europe. Once he got his Second Reich, Bismarck concentrated on making sure potential enemies would not form coalitions against it.

Bismarck cautioned that an alliance with Austria, supporting Austrian ambitions in the Balkans, could eventually lead to war. "The entire Balkans," he said, were "not worth the bones of one Pomeranian grenadier." His fear came true, for that was precisely the way World War I came about. Bismarck's successors, men of far less ability and great ambition, let Austria pull them into war over the Balkans. The tragedy of Bismarck is that he constructed a delicate balance of European power that could not be maintained without himself as the master juggler.

Kaiser   German for Caesar; emperor.

SPD   German Social Democratic party.

revisionism   Rethinking an ideology
or reinterpreting history.

out—and handpicked his own ministers. The German **Kaiser** was not a figurehead but actually set policy. The individual states that had been enrolled into a united Germany retained their autonomy, a forerunner of the present federal system.

Germany, which had been industrially backward, surged ahead, especially in iron and steel. The once-pastoral Ruhr region became a smoky workshop. With the growth of industry came a militant and well-organized German labor movement. In 1863 Ferdinand Lassalle formed the General German Workers' Association, partly a union and partly a party. In 1875 the group became the Sozialdemokratische Partei Deutschlands (**SPD**), now the oldest and one of the most successful social-democratic parties in the world.

Bismarck hated the SPD and suppressed it in 1878. He tried to take the wind out of the Socialists' sails by promoting numerous welfare measures himself in the Reichstag. In the 1880s Germany became the first country with medical and accident insurance, a pension plan, and state employment offices. Germany has been a welfare state ever since.

■ The Catastrophe: World War I

The Second Reich might have evolved into a democracy. Political parties became more important. After Bismarck was fired in 1890, the SPD came into the open to become, before World War I, Germany's largest party, with almost one-third of the Reichstag's seats. Gaining responsibility in elected offices, the German Socialists grew moderate, turning away from their Marxist roots and toward **revisionism**, the idea that socialism can grow gradually through democratic means rather than by radical revolution. So domesticated had the SPD become that in 1914, when the emergency war budget was placed before the Reichstag, SPD deputies forgot about the "international solidarity of all workers" and voted like good Germans—for it.

After Bismarck, Germany's foreign policy turned expansionist. Kaiser Wilhelm II saw Germany as a great imperial power, dominant in Europe and competing with Britain overseas. A program of naval armament, begun by Germany in 1889, touched off a race with Britain to build more battleships. Wilhelm supported the Boers against the British in South Africa and the Austrians who were coming into conflict with the Russians over the Balkans. By the time the shots were fired in Sarajevo in 1914, Germany had managed to surround itself with enemies, exactly what Bismarck had worked to prevent.

The Germans, with their quick victory of 1870 in mind, marched joyously off to war. In early August of 1914 the Kaiser told his troops: "You will be home before the leaves have fallen from the trees." All of Europe thought the war would be short, but it took four years and ten million lives until Germany surrendered.

Geography

BOUND HUNGARY

Hungary is bounded on the north by Slovakia, on the east by Ukraine and Romania,

on the south by Serbia and Croatia, and on the west by Slovenia and Austria.

Many Germans could not believe they had lost militarily. Right-wing Germans swallowed the **Dolchstoss** myth that Germany had been betrayed on the home front by democrats, socialists, Bolsheviks, and Jews. Fed nothing but war propaganda, Germans did not understand that the army and the economy could give no more. The war ended before there was any fighting on German soil, so Germans did not see their troops beaten. Worse was the **Versailles Treaty**, which blamed the war on Germany and demanded an impossible $33 billion in reparations. Germany was stripped of its few colonies (in Africa and the South Pacific) and lost Alsace and the Polish corridor. Many Germans wanted revenge. If a treaty is judged on what it produces, then Versailles was a catastrophe, for it led straight to Hitler and World War II.

Dolchstoss   German for "stab in the back."

Versailles Treaty   1919 treaty ending World War I.

Weimar Republic   1919–1933 democratic German republic.

hyperinflation   Very rapid inflation, more than 50 percent a month.

■ Republic without Democrats

Looking back, we can see how the **Weimar Republic**—which got its name from the town of Weimar, where its federal constitution was drawn up—started with three strikes against it. First, Germans had no experience with a republic or a democracy, yet suddenly Germany became a democratic republic when the Kaiser fled to Holland at the war's end. Second, for many Germans, the Weimar Republic lacked legitimacy; it had been forced upon Germany by the victorious allies and "back stabbers" who had betrayed the Reich. Third, the Versailles Treaty was so punitive and its demands for payment so high that Germany was humiliated and economically hobbled.

It has been estimated that only about one German in four was a wholehearted democrat. Another quarter hated democracy. The rest went along with the new republic until the economy collapsed and then shifted their sympathies to authoritarian movements of the left or right. Weimar Germany, it has been said, was a republic without republicans and a democracy without democrats.

The German government, in a crisis with France over reparations, printed money without limit, bringing a **hyperinflation** so insane that by 1923 it took a wheelbarrowful of marks to buy a loaf of bread. Especially hard hit were middle-class families whose businesses and savings were wiped out; many of them became eager recruits for the Nazis. The period left an indelible mark on Germans, and to this day the German government places great emphasis on preventing inflation.

By the mid-1920s the economy stabilized and things looked better. Cabinets changed frequently: twenty-six in fourteen years. The Social Democrat, Catholic Center, and Conservative parties were the largest; the Nazis were tiny and considered something of a joke. Hitler did resemble Charlie Chaplin. Then the world Depression started in 1929, and German democracy went down the drain. Moderate parties declined, and extremist parties—the Nazis and the Communists—grew (see box on page 174). Unemployment was the key: The more people out of work, the higher the Nazi vote.

One combination might have blocked the Nazis' rise to power. If the Social Democrats and Communists had formed a united front, the Weimar system might have been saved. But the German Communists, who split off from the SPD after World War I, reviled the Social Democrats as "social fascists." Under Stalin's orders, the German Communists rejected a joint program with the Socialists on the theory that Hitler would soon pass and, when Germany collapsed, the Communists would take over. This was one of Stalin's greatest blunders, and Communists and Socialists alike paid for it with their lives.

By late 1932, the Nazis had won a third of the German vote, and the aged President Hindenburg, a conservative general, named Hitler as chancellor in January 1933. The Weimar Republic, Germany's first try at democracy, died after a short, unstable life of fourteen years.

■ The Third Reich

Nazi was the German nickname for the National Socialist German Workers party. Nazism, like other forms of fascism, had a fake socialist component that promised jobs and welfare. The Nazis did not put industries under state ownership like the Communists in the Soviet Union; instead they practiced

Key Concepts

THE HORRORS OF POLARIZED PLURALISM

Columbia University political scientist Giovanni Sartori described what happens when a multiparty democracy such as Weimar's or Spain's in the 1930s gets terribly sick. The leading parties in the center face nasty opposition on both their right and left. In competing for votes in a highly ideological atmosphere, parties engage in a "politics of outbidding" by offering more radical solutions. Voters flee from the center to the extremes, to parties dedicated to overthrowing democracy. Sartori called this syndrome **polarized pluralism**, and the last years of Weimar are a good example of it.

Compare the percentage of votes parties got in 1928 with what they got in 1933, and the "center-fleeing" tendency is clear.

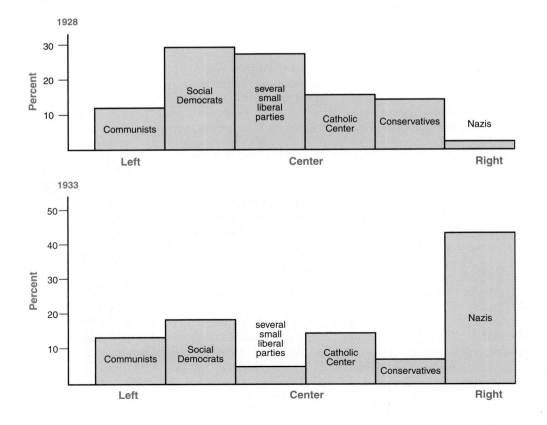

Gleichschaltung (coordination) of the economy under party supervision. Many Germans were delighted to get work on government projects, such as building the new **Autobahn**. Although the Nazis never won a majority in a fair election, by the late 1930s it is certain that a majority of Germans supported Hitler, whom they saw as restoring prosperity.

Since most Germans had not been enthusiastic about democracy, not many protested the growth of tyranny. Some Communists and Socialists went underground, to prison, or into exile, and some old-style conservatives disliked Hitler, who, in their eyes, was nothing but an Austrian guttersnipe. But most Germans got along by going along. Centuries of being taught to obey authority led them to accept Nazi rule.

For some, membership in the Nazi party offered better jobs and sometimes snappy uniforms. Many ex-Nazis claimed they joined only to further their careers, and most were probably telling the truth. You do not need true believers to staff a tyranny; **opportunists** will do just as well. The frightening thing about Nazi Germany was how it could turn normal humans into coldblooded mass murderers.

Among the first and worst to suffer were the Jews, who formed less than half a percent of the German population. Exploiting widely held racist feelings, Hitler depicted the Jews as a poisonous, foreign element who aimed to enslave Germany in the service of international capitalism, international communism, or both. Logical consistency was never the Nazis' strong point. Jews were deprived, one step at a time, of their civil rights, their jobs, their property, their citizenship, and finally their lives.

polarized pluralism   A sick multiparty system that produces two extremist blocs with little in the center. (See page 174.)

Gleichschaltung   Nazi control of Germany's economy.

Autobahn   Express highway, like U.S. interstate.

opportunist   Unprincipled person out for self.

The main extermination camp of the Nazi regime was at Auschwitz-Birkenau in the south of Poland. Here millions of Jews and inconvenient Christians were gassed and incinerated.

Final Solution   Nazi program to exterminate Jews.

genocide   Murder of an entire people.

nonaggression pact   Treaty to not attack each other, specifically the 1939 treaty between Hitler and Stalin.

Few Germans were aware of it, but Hitler ached for war. At first he seemed to be merely consolidating Germany's boundaries, absorbing the Saar in 1935, Austria and the Sudetenland in 1938, and Czech lands in 1939. And it was so easy! Germany's enemies from World War I, still war weary, did nothing to stop the growth of German power and territory. Hitler's generals, it is now known, were ready to overthrow him if the British had said no to his demands at Munich in 1938. It looked as though Hitler could amass victories without even fighting, and the German generals suppressed their doubts. Finally, when Hitler invaded Poland in September 1939, Britain and France declared war. France was overrun, Britain contained beyond the Channel, and by the summer of 1940 Germany or its allies ruled virtually all of Europe.

In 1941 Hitler ordered his **Final Solution** to the Jewish question to begin. Death camps killed some six million Jews and a similar number of inconvenient Christians (Poles, gypsies, and others). A new word was added to mankind's vocabulary: **genocide**. The Nazis kept their death camps secret, and many Germans claimed they did not know what was going on.

Hitler—just a week before he attacked Poland in 1939—had completed a **nonaggression pact** with Stalin. In the summer of 1941, however, Hitler assembled the biggest army in history and gave the order for "Barbarossa," the conquest and enslavement of the Soviet Union. Here, at last, Hitler's dream departed from reality. The Russian winter and surprising resistance of the Red Army devoured whole German divisions. From late 1942 on it was all downhill for Germany.

■ The Occupation

This time there could be no Dolchstoss myth; Germans watched Russians, Americans, British, and French fight their way through Germany. German government ceased to exist, and the country was run by foreign occupiers. At Yalta in February 1945, the Allied leaders agreed to divide Germany into four zones for temporary occupation; Berlin, deep inside the Soviet zone, was similarly divided.

Democracy

THE PLOT TO KILL HITLER

On July 20, 1944, a group of high-ranking German officers tried to kill Hitler. Had he not stepped away from the map table, the briefcase-bomb under it might have succeeded. More than two hundred anti-Nazi Germans were cruelly executed for their part in the plot. They came from all walks of life: generals, diplomats, Weimar politicians, trade unionists, scholars, both Catholic and Protestant theologians, and students. They were united in their opposition to totalitarianism, mass murder, and the war, which they would have ended immediately. Although they failed, they left a valuable legacy: the symbol that Germans fought Hitler, a moral statement for present-day German democracy.

The **Cold War** grew in large part out of the way the Soviets handled Germany. The Soviets, having lost some twenty-seven million people in the war, were intent on looting the conquered nation. They dismantled whole factories, shipped them home, and flooded the country with inflated military currency. The British and Americans, on the other hand, distressed at the brutal Soviet takeover of East Europe, decided to revive German economic and political life in their zones. The U.S. **Marshall Plan** and other aid programs pumped billions of dollars into German recovery. In 1948 the British and Americans introduced a currency reform with a new **deutsche Mark** (DM), which effectively ended Soviet looting of the western zones. In retaliation, the Russians blockaded Berlin, which was supplied for nearly a year by an incredible British-American **Berlin airlift**. The Cold War was on, centered in Germany.

Cold War Period of armed tension and competition between United States and Soviet Union, approximately 1947–1989.

Marshall Plan Massive U.S. financial aid for European recovery.

deutsche Mark German currency 1948–2002.

Berlin airlift U.S.-British supply of West Berlin by air in 1948–1949.

In 1949, the Western allies gave governing power back to West Germans in order to ensure their cooperation against Soviet power. A few months later, the Soviets set up East Germany. Both German regimes were children of the Cold War, with the Americans and the Soviets as the parents. When the Cold War ended—often dated to the fall of the Berlin Wall in late 1989—prosperous and democratic West Germany swallowed weak and dependent East Germany. To examine how West Germany succeeded, let us turn to Germany's institutions.

Geography

ANOTHER TALE OF TWO FLAGS

Like France, Germany's divided loyalties have been symbolized by its flags' colors. The German nationalist movement flag was black, red, and gold, colors of a Prussian regiment that fought Napoleon. By 1848 it symbolized a democratic, united Germany. Bismarck rejected it and for the Second Reich's flag chose Prussia's black and white, plus the white and red of the medieval Hansa commercial league.

The Reich's collapse in 1918 and the founding of the Weimar Republic brought back the democratic black, red, and gold German flag. Hitler, a fanatic for symbols, insisted on authoritarian black, red, and white colors. The Bonn republic designed the present German flag with the original democratic colors.

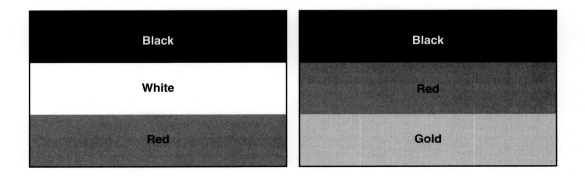

Political Culture

GERMANY'S POLITICAL ERAS

Name	Years	Remembered for
Holy Roman Empire	800–1806	Charlemagne, fragmentation, religious wars.
Nineteenth century	1806–1871	Consolidation, modernization stir.
Second Reich	1871–1918	Bismarck unites Germany; industry and war.
Weimar Republic	1919–1933	Weak democracy; culture flourishes.
Nazis	1933–1945	Brutal dictatorship; war; mass murder.
Occupation	1945–1949	Allies divide and run Germany.
Federal Republic	1949–	Democracy; economic miracle; unification; from Bonn to Berlin.

Key Terms

Autobahn (p. 175)

Berlin airlift (p. 177)

Cold War (p. 177)

deutsche Mark (p. 177)

Dolchstoss (p. 173)

Final Solution (p. 176)

genocide (p. 176)

Gleichschaltung (p. 175)

Habsburg (p. 167)

hyperinflation (p. 173)

Junker (p. 168)

Kaiser (p. 172)

Kulturkampf (p. 171)

Lebensraum (p. 170)

Machtpolitik (p. 171)

Marshall Plan (p. 177)

Metternichian system (p. 170)

nationalism (p. 170)

nonaggression pact (p. 176)

opportunist (p. 175)

polarized pluralism (p. 175)

Prussia (p. 168)

Realpolitik (p. 171)

Reich (p. 171)

Reichstag (p. 171)

revisionism (p. 172)

SPD (p. 172)

Thirty Years War (p. 167)

Versailles Treaty (p. 173)

Volksgeist (p. 170)

Weimar Republic (p. 173)

Westphalia (p. 167)

Further Reference

Berghahn, Volker R. *Imperial Germany, 1871–1914: Economy, Society, Culture, and Politics*. Providence, RI: Berghahn Books, 1994.

Carr, William. *A History of Germany, 1815–1990*, 4th ed. New York: Oxford University Press, 1995.

Craig, Gordon A. *Germany, 1866–1945*. New York: Oxford University Press, 1978.

Evans, Richard J. *The Coming of the Third Reich*. New York: Penguin, 2004.

———. *The Third Reich in Power, 1933–1939*. New York: Penguin, 2005.

Feldman, Gerald D. *The Great Disorder: Politics, Economics, and Society in the German Inflation, 1914–1924*. New York: Oxford University Press, 1993.

Kershaw, Ian. *Hitler, 1936–1945: Nemesis*. New York: Norton, 2000.

Kreuzer, Marcus. *Institutions and Innovation: Voters, Parties, and Interest Groups in the Consolidation of Democracy—France and Germany, 1870–1939*. Ann Arbor, MI: University of Michigan Press, 2001.

Merkl, Peter H. *The Origin of the West German Republic*. New York: Oxford University Press, 1963.

Peukert, Detlev J. K. *The Weimar Republic: The Crisis of Classical Modernity*. New York: Hill & Wang, 1992.

Pulzer, Peter. *Germany, 1870–1945: Politics, State Formation, and War*. New York: Oxford University Press, 1997.

Stern, Fritz. *Dreams and Delusions: The Drama of German History*. New York: Alfred A. Knopf, 1987.

Chapter 13

GERMANY:
THE KEY INSTITUTIONS

In 1949, the founders of the **Federal Republic of Germany** were hopeful that the east and west sections of their country would be reunified. Accordingly, in drafting their founding document—based in part on the 1848–1849 Frankfurt and 1919 Weimar constitutions—they called it the **Grundgesetz** (Basic Law) rather than *Verfassung* (constitution), which was to come only when Germany reunified. They meant to indicate that the Federal Republic was temporary and operating under temporary rules. More than half a century later, the question is a legal quibble; the Basic Law continues as unified Germany's constitution, and an excellent one at that.

Questions to Consider

1. How was the debate over Berlin as Germany's capital a question of core areas?
2. Is federalism the best route for Germany? Why?
3. How do the French and German presidencies differ?
4. How do the British and German prime ministries differ?
5. How does Germany's constitutional court differ from the U.S. Supreme Court?
6. What is the German lower house? How does it differ from the upper?
7. What are Germany's main parties?
8. How does the German electoral system work?

After World War II, West Germany revived an old pattern in German history, **federalism**. Germany's **Länder** have at least as much power as American states, maybe more. Education, medical care, police, and many other functions are the province of the Land government. Part of the reason for this strong federalism was to repudiate the centralization of the Nazi period and to make sure that such power could never again become so concentrated.

Berlin was a strange situation. Located 110 miles (180 kilometers) inside East Germany, Berlin was nominally governed by the four occupying powers. Soviets, however, in 1949 turned East Berlin into the capital of East Germany, and the American, British, and French sectors became, to all intents and purposes, a part of West Germany. Bonn counted West Berlin as its eleventh Land, but the wartime Allies did not recognize it as such. So officially West Berlin was not part of the Federal Republic, but in practice it was. West German currency, laws, and passports applied in West Berlin, but the city sent only nonvoting representatives to the Bonn parliament. The anomaly was solved in 1990 with the unification of the two Germanys. With the Berlin Wall down, Greater Berlin became a Land and in 1999 the official capital of united Germany, although six ministries (including defense) remained in Bonn.

East Germany, set up by the Communists in 1949, continued the Nazi pattern of centralized rule with fourteen administrative districts, each named after its leading city, without autonomy. Unification in 1990 brought back to life East Germany's five Länder, so now the Federal Republic has sixteen Länder, ten from West Germany, five from East Germany, plus Greater Berlin.

◼ The President

Germany's federal president (*Bundespräsident*) is the classic European president, a figurehead with few political but many symbolic duties. Like the monarchs of Britain and Scandinavia, the German president is an official greeter and ambassador of good will rather than working executive. The French president of the Third and Fourth Republics and today's Israeli president are other examples of forgettable presidencies. De Gaulle, of course, greatly strengthened the French presidency.

The president is the "head of state" rather than "chief of government" (for the distinction, see pages 31–32), and as such receives new foreign ambassadors who present their credentials to him rather than to the people they will actually be working with, the chancellor and foreign minister. The president proclaims laws (after they have been passed by parliament), dissolves the **Bundestag** (upon the chancellor's request), and appoints and dismisses the chancellor (after the leading party has told him to). In short, the German president is, to use Bagehot's terms, a "dignified" rather than "efficient" part of government.

The president is elected by a special Federal Assembly composed of all Bundestag members plus an equal number from the state legislatures. The president serves five years and may be reelected once. A sort of semi-retirement job, it is usually given as a reward to distinguished

Federal Republic of Germany   West Germany, now all of Germany. (See page 181.)

Grundgesetz   Basic Law, Germany's constitution. (See page 181.)

federalism   System in which component areas have considerable autonomy. (See page 181.)

Land   (plural *Länder*) Germany's first-order civil division, equivalent to U.S. state. (See page 181.)

Bundestag   Lower house of German parliament.

Mitteleuropa   Central Europe.

Geography

FROM BONN TO BERLIN

The 1991 debate that led to restoring Berlin as the capital of united Germany was essentially a conflict over core areas. Bonn, a small town in the Catholic Rhine area well to the west, had served as West Germany's capital since 1949. It shifted Germans' attention westward in values, economics, and alliances. Berlin, a major city near the eastern border of Germany, had earlier been the capital of Protestant Prussia but served as Germany's capital from 1871 to 1945. Moving back to Berlin shifted Germans' attention to the problems of the poorer, former-Communist, eastern part of their country. Some critics feared that in the long run it would turn Germany from the West and toward the old concept of a German-dominated **Mitteleuropa.**

Berlin clearly aims to become a world-class city and underwent massive reconstruction of ministries, parliamentary offices, embassies, museums, hotels, and office buildings. Berlin is the world's most wide-open city for innovative architecture; curving and

The Reichstag Dome, the work of British architect Lord Norman Foster, has become Berlin's top tourist attraction. Inside the redone building below the dome, the Bundestag meets.

soaring metal and glass structures predominate. Even the old Reichstag building was redone with a new glass dome visitors can climb via spiral ramps. By virtue of location, vitality, and architecture, Berlin already is the de facto capital of Central Europe.

senior politicians. In 2005, economist Horst Köhler, former head of the International Monetary Fund, was elected president with the support of the CDU and FDP. Urging the parties to stop feuding and pass reforms needed to cut Germany's high unemployment, he quickly became the most popular political figure in the country. Unfortunately, the president is not in charge of economic policy or much else.

chancellor German prime minister.

center In federal systems, the powers of the nation's capital.

The Chancellor

Germany has a weak president but a strong **chancellor**. Unlike the changing chancellors of the Weimar Republic, the FRG chancellorship has been a stable and durable office. Part of the reason for this is that the Basic Law requires the Bundestag to simultaneously vote in a new chancellor if

Geography

FEDERATIONS

Diversity is the advantage of federalism, a system that yields major autonomy to the components, be they U.S., Mexican, or Nigerian states, German Länder, or Canadian provinces. The components cannot be legally erased or split or have their boundaries easily changed; such matters are grave constitutional questions. Typically, certain powers are reserved for the federal government (defense, money supply, interstate commerce, and so on) while other powers are reserved for the components (education, police, highways, and so on). Large countries or those with particularistic languages or traditions lend themselves to federalism.

The advantages of a federal system are its flexibility and accommodation to particularism. Texans feel Texas is different and special; Bavarians feel Bavaria is different and special; Québécois feel Quebec is different and special; and so on. If one state or province wishes to try a new formula for funding health care, it may do so without upsetting the state-federal balance. If the new way works, it may be gradually copied. If it fails, little harm is done before it is phased out. U.S. states in this regard have been called "laboratories of democracy": You can try something in one state without committing the entire nation to it. Governments at the Land or state level also serve as training grounds for politicians before they try the national level. Examples: Texas Governor George Bush, Lower Saxony Premier Gerhard Schröder, and Guanajuato (Mexico) Governor Vicente Fox.

The disadvantage is inconsistent and sometimes sloppy administration among components. Many federal systems cannot achieve nationwide standards in education, environment, welfare, or health care. One state wants something and can afford it; another state cannot. One state says certain types of persons are eligible for a program; another says they are not. Federal systems are less coherent than unitary systems. To correct such problems, many federal systems have granted more power to the **center** at the expense of the states. The United States is a prime example of this; compare the relative powers of the states and of Washington over the course of a century.

One might say that in unitary systems there is a tugging in the direction of federalism, whereas in federal systems there is a tugging in the direction of unitary systems. This does not necessarily mean that the two will eventually meet in some middle ground; it merely means that neither unitary nor federal systems are finished products and that both are still evolving.

A federal system may also achieve a stable balance between local and national loyalties, leading gradually to a psychologically integrated country, like the United States, Germany, and Switzerland. This does not always work, though. Soviet, Yugoslav, and Czechoslovak federalism actually fostered resentments of the republics against the center. When their Communist parties weakened, local nationalists took over and declared independence.

constructive no-confidence
Parliament must vote in new cabinet when it ousts current one.

it wants to vote out the present one. This reform ended one of the worst problems of parliamentary (as opposed to presidential) governments, namely, their dependence on an often-fickle legislative majority.

The German reform is called **constructive no-confidence** because Bundestag has to offer something constructive—a new cabinet—rather than a mere negative majority to get rid of the old one. This has happened only once, in 1982, when the small Free Democratic party abandoned its coalition with the Social Democrats in midterm and voted in a new Christian Democratic chancellor. Constructive no-confidence makes ousting a chancellor between elections a rarity.

Another reason the chancellor is strong stems from the first occupant of that office: Konrad Adenauer, a tough, shrewd politician who helped found the Federal Republic and served as chancellor during its first fourteen years. First occupants, such as Washington in the American presidency, can put a stamp on the position, defining its powers and setting its style for generations. Adenauer—who was seventy-three when he first became chancellor—showed strong leadership and made numerous decisions without bothering parliament or his cabinet too much. A Catholic Rhinelander, he formed the CDU, set up a "two-plus" party system, pointed Germany decisively westward into NATO and the EU, and established a special relationship with France. Chancellors ever since Adenauer have been measured against him. His successor, for example, the amiable and intelligent Ludwig Erhard, was found wanting because he could not exercise firm leadership.

Partly thanks to the style Adenauer set, the German chancellor is approximately as powerful as the British prime minister, which is to say quite powerful. The chancellor picks his or her own cabinet—with political considerations in mind—like the British PM. He or she is responsible for the main lines of government policy and has to defend them before the Bundestag and the public. As such, he or she is implicitly held responsible for what ministers say and do.

Democracy

PREFIX TO DEMOCRACY

In Germany today almost everything associated with the federal government bears the prefix *Bundes-*, meaning "federal." Thus:

- *Bundesrepublik Deutschland* is the Federal Republic of German, FRG.
- *Bundestag* is the lower house of the federal parliament.
- *Bundesrat* is the upper house.
- *Bundeskanzler* is the federal chancellor (prime minister).

- *Bundeswehr* is the army.
- *Bundesministerium* is a federal ministry.
- *Bundesregierung* is the federal government.

The prefix *Bundes-* is relatively new, stemming only from the founding of West Germany in 1949, and as such it has a modern, democratic ring to it. The old prefix of many of the same words, *Reichs-* (imperial), has a slightly sinister, discarded connotation. In Germany, "federal" has become synonymous with "democratic."

WHO WAS WHEN: GERMANY'S CHANCELLORS		
Konrad Adenauer	CDU	1949–1963
Ludwig Erhard	CDU	1963–1966
Kurt Georg Kiesinger	CDU	1966–1969
Willy Brandt	SPD	1969–1974
Helmut Schmidt	SPD	1974–1982
Helmut Kohl	CDU	1982–1998
Gerhard Schröder	SPD	1998–2005
Angela Merkel	CDU	2005–

■ The Cabinet

The typical German cabinet is usually smaller than its French or British counterpart and is now even smaller than the fifteen-department U.S. cabinet. In 2005, Chancellor Merkel, after extensive negotiations between the two coalition parties, named a cabinet with fourteen ministries, eight headed by Social Democrats and six by Christian Democrats:

Foreign Affairs
Interior
Justice
Finance
Economy and Technology
Defense
Agriculture
Health
Families
Labor
Education
Development (foreign aid)
Environment
Transport

As usual in Europe, ministries are added, deleted, combined, split, and reshuffled from one cabinet to another. For example, Schröder combined the economy and labor ministries into a "super-ministry" to fight unemployment (it didn't work). Merkel's cabinet separated them again. Redefinitions of ministries are no big deal in Europe; what prime ministers want, they get. The chief job of the interior ministry is protection of the constitution (*Verfassungsschutz*), which includes monitoring extremist parties and movements. Unlike the French unitary system, though, the only police they have at their disposal are the Federal Border Police; all other police are at the *Land* or municipal level.

As in Britain (but not in France), practically all German cabinet ministers are also working politicians with seats in the Bundestag. Like their British counterparts, they are rarely specialists in their assigned portfolio. Most are trained as lawyers and have served in a variety of party and legislative positions. The job of parliamentary state secretary serves as a training ground for potential cabinet ministers. Below cabinet rank, a parliamentary state secretary is assigned to each minister to assist in relations with the Bundestag, in effect a bridge between executive and legislative branches, as in Britain.

Personalities

ANGELA MERKEL: A GERMAN THATCHER?

Some observers believe Angela Merkel, who became chancellor in 2005 at age fifty-one, wished to be a German Margaret Thatcher and give a free-market jolt to the German economy. But the 2005 election that brought Merkel to office produced a *grand coalition* (see page 189) that diluted Merkel's ability to push through needed reforms. The difference is in the two lands' electoral systems. The British FPTP system gave Thatcher and the Tories unfettered power to govern; the German *MMP system* (see page 192) fettered Merkel and her Christian Democratic Union.

Merkel is unusual in several ways. She is Germany's first woman chancellor and the first from East Germany. Her English is nearly perfect. A Protestant, she heads a heavily Catholic party. She is now in her second marriage and has no children. Merkel was born in West Germany but went as a baby to East Germany, where her pastor father was assigned a church. She grew up entirely in East Germany but kept her critical views of the Communist regime to herself. Instead of the usual law studies, she took a doctorate in physics at Leipzig University and did research in quantum chemistry. (Thatcher also began in science; she graduated Oxford in chemistry.)

When the Berlin Wall fell in late 1989, Merkel helped organize a conservative party that merged with Christian Democratic Union. Elected to the Bundestag, she still represents a constituency in the northern *Land* of Mecklenburg-Pomerania. Chancellor Helmut Kohl appointed Merkel to his cabinet, first as minister of women and youth and then environment. After Kohl's defeat in 1998, Merkel became CDU chair in

Chancellor Angela Merkel.

2000. After the CSU's Edmund Stoiber lost to SPD Chancellor Gerhard Schröder in 2002, Merkel became the leading opposition figure.

By this time, Chancellor Schröder was stalled and losing popularity. He proposed reforming Germany's slow-growth and high-unemployment economy but got little support from his own SPD, which fights any reforms that cut welfare benefits. Unable to govern, a frustrated Schröder arranged a Bundestag defeat to call elections a year early. Schröder, an outgoing personality and good speaker, was more popular than his party. "Angie," as her supporters call her, was a bland and poor speaker, less popular than her party. Personality matters in German politics, and the CDU saw its early 20-point lead over the SPD narrow to a maddening tie (see box on page 189). After two months of negotiations, the CDU and SPD agreed to a grand coalition with Merkel as chancellor. Merkel wants go farther with reforms to free the economy and trim the welfare state, but the SPD half of her cabinet confines her to what she calls "small steps," leaving her unlikely to become a German Thatcher.

The Bundestag

Konrad Adenauer, the authoritarian democrat, did not place great faith in the Bundestag. Germany never had a strong parliamentary tradition. Bismarck all but ignored the Reichstag (whose building the Bundestag now occupies). During the Weimar Republic, the Reichstag, unprepared for the governing responsibilities thrust upon it, could not exercise power. Then in 1949 came Adenauer who, like most Germans, had never seen an efficient, stable, responsible parliament, and so tended to disdain the new one. Since Adenauer's time, the Bundestag has been trying to establish itself as a pillar of democracy and as an important branch of government. Success has been gradual and incomplete. Many Germans still do not respect the Bundestag very much.

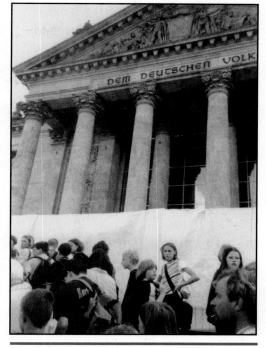

The Bundestag has at least 598 members but gets additional deputies and now totals 614. Deputies are elected for four years, but elections can be called early, as they were in 2005. Under a parliamentary (as opposed to presidential) system, the legislature can never be a severe critic of the administration in the manner of the U.S. Congress. After all, the Bundestag's majority parties produce the government; they cannot very well criticize it too harshly. Neither is the Bundestag the tumultuous assembly of the French Third and Fourth Republics; the FRG legislature can unmake a government only when it makes a new one. Nor is the Bundestag the docile rubber stamp that de Gaulle made of the French National Assembly. Still less is it the colorful debating chamber of the House of Commons, where brilliant orators try to sway the public for the next election. On balance, the Bundestag has less independent power than the U.S. Congress but more than the French National Assembly and possibly even the British House of Commons.

"For the German People," the original dedication on the Reichstag, now graces the Bundestag, which in 1999 met for the first time in its new Berlin home. The building is still called the Reichstag but is now modernized and topped by a glass dome. The Reichstag met there from 1894 to 1933.

One interesting point about the Bundestag is its many women members, close to a third, typical of North European systems that use proportional representation, which allows parties to place women candidates on party lists. Over 40 percent of Sweden's Riksdag are women. The number of women in most parliaments has grown in recent years: 18 percent of British, 16 percent of Mexican, 14 percent of U.S., and 11 percent of French national legislators. These lower numbers are partly the result of single-member electoral districts. PR is fairer to women. Japan has only 7 percent female legislators.

The Bundestag's strong point is its committee work. Here, behind closed doors (most sessions are secret), Bundestag deputies, including opposition members, can make their voices heard. German legislative committees are more important and more specialized than their British counterparts. German party discipline is not as tight as the British so that deputies from the ruling party can criticize a government bill while opposition deputies sometimes agree with it. In the give and take of committee work, the opposition is often able to get changes made in legislation. Once back on the Bundestag floor—and all bills must be reported out; they cannot be killed in committee—voting is on party lines with occasional defections on matters of conscience.

A symbol of reunified Germany is the refurbished Brandenburg Gate at the heart of Berlin near the Federal parliament, the Bundestag.

The Bundestag standing committees generally correspond to the cabinet ministries listed earlier in this chapter. The system is designed that way: Each cabinet minister can deal directly with a parallel, relevant Bundestag committee. The ministers, themselves Bundestag members, sometimes come over from their executive offices to explain to committee sessions a proposed piece of legislation.

In a parallel with French deputies, Bundestag membership is heavy with civil servants. German law permits bureaucrats to take leaves of absence to run for and serve in the Bundestag. Another important category is people from interest groups: business associations and labor unions. Together, these two groups usually form a majority of the Bundestag membership, contributing to a public feeling that parliament is dominated by powerful interests. Making this worse, a series of scandals revealed that many Bundestag members get "secret money" from private firms for no work, a parallel with British MPs' "sleaze factor."

■ The Constitutional Court

Very few countries have a judiciary equal in power to the legislative or executive branches. The United States and Germany are two; both allow the highest court in the land to review the constitutionality of laws. The **Federal Constitutional Court** (*Bundesverfassungsgericht*, BVerfG), located in Karlsruhe, was set up in 1951 partly on American insistence. The American occupiers reasoned that something like the Supreme Court would help prevent another Hitler, and many Germans agreed with what was for Germany (and indeed all of Europe) a new concept.

Federal Constitutional Court
Germany's top court, equivalent to U.S. Supreme Court.

The Karlsruhe court is composed of sixteen judges, eight elected by each house of parliament, who serve for nonrenewable, twelve-year terms. The BVerfG operates as two courts, or "senates," of eight judges each to speed up the work. Completely independent of other branches of German government, the court decides cases between Länder, protects civil liberties, outlaws dangerous political parties, and otherwise makes sure that statutes conform to the Basic Law.

The Constitutional Court's decisions have been important. It has declared illegal some right and left extremist parties on the grounds that they sought to overthrow the constitutional order. It found that abortion bills collided with the strong right-to-life provisions of the Basic Law and thus ruled them unconstitutional. (In 1993, however, it decided not to prosecute women who had first-trimester abortions.) In 1979 it ruled that "worker codetermination" in the running of factories was constitutional. In 1983 and 2005 it found that chancellors had acted within the constitution when they arranged to lose a Bundestag vote of confidence in order to hold elections early. In 1994 it ruled Germany can send troops overseas for peacekeeping operations. In 1995 it overrode a Bavarian law requiring a crucifix in every classroom. Judicial review has worked well in Germany, although the Constitutional Court, because it operates in the context of the more rigid code law, does not have the impact of the U.S. Supreme Court, whose decisions serve as precedents within the U.S. Common Law system.

extreme multipartism   Too many parties in parliament.

"two-plus" party system   Two big parties and several small ones.

monocolor   In parliamentary systems, cabinet composed of just one party.

grand coalition   A government composed of the largest parties, leaving only minor parties in opposition.

■ From "Two-Plus" to Multiparty System?

Much of the reason the FRG government worked rather well is the party system that evolved since 1949, but that may have ended in 2005. The Weimar Reichstag suffered from **extreme multipartism**; a dozen parties, some of them extremist, made it impossible to form stable coalitions. The Federal Republic seemed to have fixed that, and Germany turned into a **"two-plus" party system**, because German governments almost always consisted of one large party in coalition with one small party. Britain, with its majoritarian system, almost always gives one party a majority in parliament. Germany, with its proportional system, seldom produces **monocolor** governments. A two-plus party system is somewhere between a two-party system and a multiparty system. Recent elections, alas, turned Germany back into a multiparty system, with all the threats to stability that implies. (For a discussion of coalition formation in Germany, see page 213).

For most of the FRG's history the largest party has been the Christian Democratic Union (*Christlich Demokratische Union*, CDU), chaired by Angela Merkel, who became chancellor in 2005,

Key Concepts

GRAND COALITION

In 2005 Germany revived the **grand coalition** of Christian Democrats and Social Democrats that had governed from 1966 to 1969. It had functioned moderately well but hurt German democracy because it left only small parties to oppose and criticize. The advantage of a grand coalition: It has such an overwhelming majority in parliament that it cannot be ousted and can pass any laws it likes. The 2005 grand coalition had to happen because no other combination of parties was able to form a coalition (see page 213), but its two parties, the CDU and SPD, were at odds on economic reform and likely to stalemate.

The 1966–1969 grand coalition made citizens feel that no one could seriously criticize the government, that politics was a game rigged by the powerful, and that democracy was a sham. In the late 1960s a leftist "extraparliamentary opposition" grew and criticized the government in radical terms. Some of West Germany's terrorists first became active in disgust at the wall-to-wall grand coalition, which is probably useful only for emergencies; if it stays in office too long it starts undermining faith in democracy. A good democracy requires a lively interaction between "ins" and "outs" rather than collusion between the two.

Greens   Environmentalist parties.

regierungsfähig   Literally, "able to form a government," party that has matured and able to rule.

with its Bavarian affiliate, the Christian Social Union (CSU), chaired by Edmund Stoiber, Bavaria's governor and 2002 chancellor candidate. Together, the two are designated CDU/CSU. The original core of the CDU was the old Catholic Center party, one of the few parties that held its own against the growth of Nazism in the early 1930s. After World War II, Center politicians like Adenauer decided to go for a broader-based center-right party, one in which Protestants would feel welcome. Like most European conservative parties, the CDU never embraced totally free-market capitalism; instead it went for a "social market" economy (see Chapter 16). The CDU/CSU has been the largest party in every election except 1972 and 1998, when the SPD pulled ahead. In 2002 it tied the SPD with 38.5 percent of the national vote and in 2005 edged it out with 35.2 percent.

The Social Democratic party (*Sozialdemokratische Partei Deutschlands*, SPD) is the grand old party of European socialism and the only German party that antedates the founding of the Federal Republic. Originally Marxist, the SPD gradually revised its positions until, in 1959, it dropped Marxism altogether. It was then that its electoral fortunes grew as it expanded beyond its traditional working-class base and into the middle class, especially intellectuals. Now a center-left party, the SPD's socialism amounts basically to support for the welfare state. The SPD's lingering problem: Its leadership is generally centrist, but it still contains many firm leftists who try to gain control of the party. From 1998 to 2005 the SPD governed in coalition with the Greens. In 2005 it won 34.2 percent of the vote, just behind the CDU/CSU, which it joined in a grand coalition. That same year the SPD elected an East German, Matthias Platzeck, as party chief. The CDU and SPD are now led by East German scientists who got into politics only when the Communists fell.

The small Free Democratic party (*Freie Demokratische Partei*, FDP) is a classic liberal party seeking a free society, free market, more individual responsibility, and less government. It used to be placed in the center of the political spectrum between the CDU and SPD but now is often placed to the right of the CDU, rather like U.S. Libertarians. (Note again that liberalism in Europe means about the opposite of U.S. liberalism.) The FDP had trouble defining itself and dropped to 7.4 percent of the vote in 2002 but rebounded to 9.8 percent in 2005. The FDP, now Germany's third-largest party, is an alternative for voters mistrustful of the two big parties.

In 1983, a new ecology-pacifist party, the **Greens**, made it into the Bundestag. In 2005 it won 8.1 percent and shrank from third-largest to fifth-largest party. In the 1998–2005 coalition with the SPD, the leader of the Greens, Joseph (better known as Joschka, "Little Joe") Fischer, was foreign minister, the usual portfolio for the head of the second party in a coalition. The Greens, once radical, turned pragmatic and **regierungsfähig** during the 1990s. They want to phase out Germany's nuclear power plants and to put hefty "eco-taxes" on gasoline. Fischer, a slightly impish speaker and Germany's most popular politician, stepped down as Green leader in 2005.

As soon as the Wall came down in 1989, West Germany's parties simply moved in and took over East Germany. The small, new East German parties that had spearheaded the ouster of the Communists were elbowed aside by the CDU and SPD, who had the money and organization. One regional East German party survived, the Party of Democratic Socialism (PDS), composed of ex-Communists and those who feel ignored by the new system. In 2002 it fell below 5 percent but still won two districts (in East Berlin) outright, and it was entitled to keep those two seats in the Bundestag. With East Germany still poor, the PDS scored well there in Land elections. In 2005 the PDS joined with disgruntled SPD leftists to form a new Left party (*Linkspartei*), which ran well in the east and gained 8.7 percent of votes overall, making it the Bundestag's fourth-largest party. None of the other parties, however, considered it a fit coalition partner. Some small rightist parties, including neo-Nazis, win seats in local and Land elections but have never won seats in the Bundestag.

The Bundesrat

Neither Britain nor France really needs an upper house because they are unitary systems. The German federal system has a useful upper house, the **Bundesrat**. Not as powerful as the U.S. Senate—an upper house that powerful is a world rarity—the Bundesrat represents the sixteen Länder and has equal power with the Bundestag on most legislation, including finances and anything that effects the federal-state balance. On some types of laws, the Bundesrat (like the U.S. Senate) can block a bill, but the Bundestag can override it. On more serious bills, the matter goes to a mediation committee with sixteen members from each house, but compromise often eludes them. An SPD-dominated Bundesrat blocked the reform measures of CDU Chancellor Kohl in the 1990s. With things reversed in the early 2000s, a CDU-dominated Bundesrat blocked the reform measures of SPD Chancellor Schröder. When the Bundesrat is in the hands of the opposition party, Germany has the divided legislature found in the United States when one party controls the House and another the Senate.

Bundesrat Literally, federal council; upper chamber of German parliament, represents states.

Landtag German state legislature.

party list Party's ranking of its candidates in PR elections; voters pick one list as their ballot.

The Bundesrat has sixty-eight members. Every German Land, no matter how small, gets at least three. More populous Länder get four; the most populous get six. Each Land appoints its delegates and usually sends the top officials elected to the **Landtag**, who are also cabinet members in the Land government. They may be from different parties (if the Land government is a coalition), but each Bundesrat delegation must vote as a bloc, not as individuals or as parties. The theory here is that they represent states, not parties or themselves.

A Split Electoral System

Both Britain and the United States use single-member districts with plurality win (FPTP) in their parliamentary elections. The advantage with this system is that it anchors a deputy to a district, giving representatives an abiding interest in their constituents. The disadvantage is that the system does not accurately reflect votes for parties nationwide; seats are not proportional to votes. (It also gives U.S. Representatives too much interest in looking after the folks back home and too little interest in the good of the country as a whole.)

The alternative, proportional representation (PR), makes the party's percentage of seats nearly proportional to its votes. Weimar Germany had a PR system, which was part of its undoing. PR systems are theoretically the fairest but in practice often lead to difficulties. They permit many small parties in parliament, including antidemocratic extremist parties. They make coalitions hard to form and unstable because usually several parties must combine. Israel, with over a dozen parties in parliament, suffers these consequences of pure proportional representation.

The German system combines both approaches, single-member districts and proportional representation. The voter has two votes, one for a single representative in one of 299 districts, the other for a party. The party vote is the crucial one because it determines the total number of seats a party gets in a given Land. Some of these seats are occupied by the party's district winners; additional seats are taken from the party's *Landesliste* to reach the percentage won on the second ballot. This Landesliste (the right-hand column on the sample ballot on page 193) is a list of persons whom the party proposes as deputies, starting with the names at the top of the list. The **party list** is the standard technique for a PR system. Leading party figures are assigned high

threshold clause Minimum percent party must win to get any seats.

mixed-member Electoral system that combines single-member districts with proportional representation.

positions on the list to ensure that they get elected; people at the bottom of the party list do not have a chance.

The German system works like proportional representation—percentage of votes (nearly) equals percentage of Bundestag seats—but with the advantage of single-member districts. It is technically known as *mixed-member proportional* (MMP), as it preserves overall proportionality. (The systems discussed in the box below are just *mixed-member*, as their parliaments do not have overall proportionality of parties.) As in Britain and the United States, German voters get a district representative. More than in straight PR systems, personality counts in German elections; a politician cannot be just a good party worker but has to go out and talk with voters to earn their confidence on a personal basis. It is a matter of considerable pride among FRG politicians to be elected from a single-member district with a higher percentage of votes than their party won on the second ballot. It may mean that voters split their tickets because they liked the candidate better than his or her party.

For most of the postwar years, the partially single-member German system worked to slowly cut down the number of parties compared to Weimar days until it was a two-plus system (a big CDU and SPD, plus a small FDP). One reason: A party must win at least 5 percent nationwide to get its PR share of Bundestag seats. The **threshold clause** was designed to keep out splinter and extremist parties. More recently, however, some new small parties have made it into parliament, the Greens, the PDS, and now the Left party. Even if below 5 percent, a party gets whatever single-member constituency

Comparison

GERMANY'S ELECTORAL SYSTEM: AN EXPORT PRODUCT

Germany's hybrid **mixed-member** (MM) electoral system was much talked about for decades. In the early 1990s, several countries paid Germany the highest compliment by adopting mixed-member systems, with national variations. The aim in all cases was to combine the simplicity of single-member districts with some of the theoretical fairness of PR. Some of the German-inspired hybrids:

- Russian elections from 1993 to 2003 filled half of the 450-seat lower house by single-member districts and half by PR with a 5 percent threshold. Putin returned to straight PR in 2005.
- In 1993, Italy dropped its traditional PR system for one in which 75 percent of the seats of both chambers are filled from single-member districts and 25 percent by PR.
- In 1994, Japan turned from its unique electoral system of multimember districts with

plurality victors to an MM system in which more than half the members of each house are elected from single-member districts and the remainder by PR in eleven regions (see page 357).

- New Zealand in 1993 turned from straight Anglo-American single-member districts to an MM system for its unicameral legislature of sixty such districts plus sixty elected by PR at the national level with a 5 percent threshold.
- The 1999 elections for Scottish and Welsh parliaments had single-member FPTP districts but "topped off" the parties' seats by PR so that they are roughly proportional to their vote share.
- Mexico in 1986 adopted an MM system in which most lower and upper house seats are filled from single-member districts and the rest by PR (see page 495).

"You Have Two Votes": A German Ballot

seats it wins, the reason the PDS got two seats in the 2002 Bundestag. Variations on the German hybrid electoral system were adopted by several countries (see box on page 192).

German parties get government help for campaign funds, but after the election. Every party that makes it into the Bundestag gets several euros for each citizen's vote. Furthermore, parties' contributions and membership fees are matched 50 percent by federal funds. Typically, every German national election costs taxpayers $150 million or more (cheap by U.S. standards).

Democracy

2005: A SPLIT ELECTORAL SYSTEM IN ACTION

Chancellor Gerhard Schröder's SPD-led government found itself blocked in 2005. It proposed reforms to trim the welfare state and reinvigorate Germany's economy. Many SPD voters protested any cuts in their benefits. Even when Schröder got a bill through the Bundestag, the CDU-controlled Bundesrat would veto it. In May of 2005 the SPD lost elections in the large, industrialized Land of North Rhine-Westphalia, where it had held sway for 29 years. Schröder felt trapped in a declining situation, so he arranged to lose a Bundestag vote, allowing him to dissolve the Bundestag and hold elections a year early.

The SPD was supposed to lose big in the September 2005 elections. For weeks polls favored the CDU/CSU, sometimes by as much as 20 percentage points. But personality counts in German elections. Schröder was an outgoing personality who kept his points general while CDU leader Angela Merkel was stiff and detail-oriented. The SPD warned that the CDU/CSU would dismantle the welfare state many Germans had come to depend on. Schröder also influenced undecided voters with criticism of President Bush's Iraq policy. Schröder steadily narrowed the gap with Merkel. Election posters featured portraits of Schröder and Merkel, almost as if it were a presidential election.

A turnout of 78 percent barely made the CDU/CSU the largest party in the Bundestag, with 226 seats against the SPD's 222. But neither had a majority of seats and, after two weeks of negotiations, formed a grand coalition (see box on page 189) with each other. Germany's MMP electoral system (see box on page 192) is based on PR, but about half the seats are filled from single-member districts with plurality win (as in Britain). First, notice the percent of vote (on the right-hand, PR ballot) is close to the percent of Bundestag seats.

	% of Vote	Seats
CDU/CSU	35.2	226 (36.8%)
Social Democrats	34.2	222 (36.2%)
Free Democrats	9.8	61 (9.9%)
Left	8.7	54 (8.8%)
Greens	8.1	51 (8.3%)

But notice also that the parties got more seats than their percentage of the votes. This is partly because some small parties (the neo-Nazi National Democrats, for example) won less than 5 percent and got no seats. Further, ticket-splitting—voting, as many did in 2005, for the individual CDU candidate on the left-hand half of the ballot but for the FDP on the PR right-hand side—won the CDU more seats than did the percentage of their party votes. The Greens and FDP win seats almost entirely on the second ballot, the party list; they are rarely big enough to win a single-member district.

Those who win a single-member constituency (the left half of the ballot) keep the seat even if it exceeds the percentage their party is entitled to from the PR (right half of the ballot) vote. These "bonus seats" (in 2005 most of them went to the CDU) make the Bundestag larger than its nominal size of 598 seats; it now has 614 members. Is the German electoral system now clear to you? Not to worry. Many Germans do not fully understand it. Basically, just remember that it is a split system: roughly half single-member districts and half PR, but PR sets the overall share of seats. It is proportional but not perfectly proportional.

Key Terms

Bundesrat (p. 191)

Bundestag (p. 182)

center (p. 183)

chancellor (p. 183)

constructive no-confidence (p. 184)

extreme multipartism (p. 189)

Federal Constitutional Court (p. 188)

Federal Republic of Germany (p. 182)

federalism (p. 182)

grand coalition (p. 189)

Greens (p. 190)

Grundgesetz (p. 182)

Land (p. 182)

Landtag (p. 191)

Mitteleuropa (p. 182)

mixed-member (p. 192)

monocolor (p. 189)

party list (p. 191)

regierungsfähig (p. 190)

threshold clause (p. 192)

"two-plus" party system (p. 189)

Further Reference

Beyme, Klaus von. *The Legislator: German Parliament as a Centre of Political Decision-Making*. Brookfield, VT: Ashgate, 1998.

Conradt, David, Gerald R. Kleinfled, George K. Romoser, and Christain Soe. *Power Shift in Germany: The 1998 Election and the End of the Kohl Era*. Providence, RI: Berghan, 1999.

Eberle, Edward J. *Dignity and Liberty: Constitutional Visions in Germany and the United States*. Westport, CT: Praeger, 2002.

Glaessner, Gert-Joachim. *German Democracy: From Post-World War II to the Present Day*. New York: Berg, 2005.

Green, Simon, and William E. Paterson, eds. *Governance in Contemporary Germany: The Semisovereign State Revisited*. New York: Cambridge University Press, 2005.

Helms, Ludger, ed. *Institutions and Institutional Change in the Federal Republic of Germany*. New York: St. Martin's, 2000.

Jacoby, Wade. *Imitation and Politics: Redesigning Modern Germany*. Ithaca, NY: Cornell University Press, 2000.

Klein, Hans, ed. *The German Chancellors*. Carol Stream, IL: Edition Q, 1996.

Moeller, Robert G., ed. *West Germany under Construction: Politics, Society, and Culture in the Adenauer Era*. Ann Arbor, MI: University of Michigan Press, 1997.

Nicholls, A. J. *The Bonn Republic: West German Democracy, 1945–1990*. New York: Longman, 1997.

Quint, Peter E. *The Imperfect Union: Constitutional Structures of German Unification*. Princeton, NJ: Princeton University Press, 1997.

Schweitzer, Carl-Christoph, et al., eds. *Politics and Government in the Federal Republic of Germany, 1944–1994—Basic Documents*, 2nd rev. ed. Providence, RI: Berghahn Books, 1996.

Thaysen, Uwe, Roger H. Davidson, and Robert Gerald Livingston, eds. *The U.S. Congress and the West German Bundestag: Comparisons of Democratic Processes*. Boulder, CO: Westview, 1990.

Chapter 14

GERMAN
POLITICAL CULTURE

A German woman once recounted to me how the Americans, in the last days of World War II, had bombed her hometown, a charming North Bavarian place with a splendid church and no military value. The town was a mess: Bodies lay unburied, water and electricity were out, food supplies were unmoved. What did the people of the town do to meet this emergency? "Oh, nothing," she shrugged. "We waited for the Americans to come and tell us what to do."

Such were the beginnings of democracy in West Germany: A foreign implant grafted onto a people who were used to being told what to do. Can democracy be transplanted? (Even in Iraq?) Has it in fact taken root in Germany? This is the bothersome question. Germany's institutions are fine; in several ways the Federal Republic's Basic Law is a model constitution. But, as we saw with Weimar, good institutions are not worth much if people do not support them. Are democratic values sufficiently strong and deep in Germany to withstand economic and political hard times?

Historically, there has long been a liberal tradition in Germany, an outgrowth of the Enlightenment, as in France. In Britain, democracy gradually triumphed. In France, democracy and reaction seesawed back and forth, finally reaching an uneasy balance. In Germany, on the other hand, democracy was overwhelmed by authoritarian forces. In 1849 the German liberals were driven out of the Frankfurt cathedral. In Bismarck's Second Reich they were treated with contempt. In the Weimar Republic they were a minority, a pushover for authoritarians. Until the Bonn Republic, the democratic strand in German politics was a losing tradition.

East Germany attempted to develop "people's democracy" (communism) rather than **liberal democracy** in the Western sense. Although communism and fascism are supposed to be opposites, both aimed to make individuals obedient and powerless. This left many East Germans confused and skeptical at the onrush of democracy from West Germany in 1990; they had known nothing but authoritarian rule since 1933. It is taking some time and education for East German democratic attitudes to reach the levels of West Germany.

Questions to Consider

1. What is *liberal democracy?* Why was it weak in Germany?
2. How have Germans handled the Nazi period and the Holocaust?
3. How are German and American multiculturalism alike?
4. What is *postmaterialism?* Is it nearly everywhere?
5. What are Germany's *political generations?*
6. Why do Wessis and Ossis resent each other?
7. Is German democracy as solid as any? How can you tell?
8. How did Willy Brandt represent a turning point?

◼ The Moral Vacuum

In addition to a weak democratic tradition, Germany faced a more subtle problem after World War II. A liberal democracy requires certain moral foundations. If you are entrusting ultimate authority to the people through their representatives, you have to believe that they are generally moral, perhaps even a bit idealistic. When this belief vanishes, a democracy loses some of its legitimacy. People may go along with it but without deep faith. Such was the Weimar period.

liberal democracy Combines tolerance and freedoms (liberalism) with mass participation (democracy). (See page 197.)

denazification Purging Nazi officials from public life.

The Nazi period left a moral vacuum in Germany, and filling it has been a long, slow process, one still not complete. One problem that hindered German democracy was the persistence of ex-Nazis in high places. Every time one was discovered, it undermined the moral authority of the regime. People, especially young people, thought, "Why should we respect democracy if there are still the same old Nazis running it?"

Immediately after the war, the Allied occupiers tried to "denazify" their zones. Party members, especially officials and the Gestapo (secret police), lost their jobs and sometimes went to prison. Henry Kissinger, then a U.S. Army sergeant, rounded up Gestapo agents in the town he was running by advertising in the newspaper for experienced policemen; when they showed up he jailed them. Still, aside from the 177 war criminals tried at Nuremberg (twenty-five sentenced to death), **denazification** was spotty, and many Nazis got away, to Latin America or to new lives within Germany. Many made themselves useful to the occupation authorities and worked their way into business, politics, the civil service, and even the judicial system.

It was the judicial system that kept mass murderers from coming to trial. There are German laws against such people, but Nazi criminals were rarely brought to trial until the 1960s. By then younger people had worked their way up the judicial ladder and were willing to prosecute cases their elders let pass. This helps explain why Nazi criminals were still being tried in the 1990s.

The Cold War also delayed a thorough look at the Nazi past. By 1947 the Western Allies decided they needed Germany to block the spread of Soviet power, so they stopped rubbing Germans' noses in the past. Tough questions about the wartime behavior of German civilian and military officials were not asked; now they were on our side. (The same shift happened at the same time and for the same reason in Japan.) With the founding of the Federal Republic in 1949, such matters were placed in the hands of West German authorities, and many preferred not to "open old wounds."

Two presidents of the Federal Republic, Walter Scheel of the FDP and Karl Carstens of the CDU, and one chancellor, Kurt Kiesinger of the CDU, had once been Nazi party members. All asserted they were nominal rather than active members, "just opportunists" out to further their careers during a time when the Nazis controlled many paths to success. While none were charged with any crime, what kind of moral authority did "just an opportunist" lend to the highest offices of a country trying to become a democracy?

◼ The Remembrance of Things Past

Can a society experience collective guilt? Was it realistic to expect Germans as a whole to feel remorse for what the Nazis did? The West German response was initially to flush the Nazi era down the memory hole, to say in effect, "Past, go away!" German fathers were reluctant to say much about what they had done. For some decades, German history textbooks stopped at 1933 and picked up

Busy Berlin square features the reminder, "Places of Horror That We Must Never Forget," a list of World War II concentration camps. At the top: Auschwitz.

again in 1945. The result was ignorance among young Germans in the 1950s and 1960s about the Nazis and the **Holocaust**. Then, in 1979, the American-made TV miniseries "Holocaust" riveted Germans' attention and triggered German books, movies, documentaries, and discussion. In the 1980s, curricula and textbooks changed to treat the Nazi period more fully. This belated Holocaust flood, however, made some Germans feel resentful and picked-upon.

Holocaust   Nazi genocide of Europe's Jews during World War II.

Can a society simply forget its past, blot it out? West Germans tried. Climbing out of the ruins of World War II, they threw themselves with single-minded devotion into work, making money, and spending it conspicuously. The results were spectacular; the economy soared, and many Germans became affluent. The West German archetype became the *Wunderkind* (wonder child), the businessman who rose from rubble to riches in the postwar boom with a fat body, a fat cigar, and a fat Mercedes. But material prosperity could not fill the moral and historical void. Many young Germans in the 1960s were profoundly dissatisfied with the emphasis on materialism that seemed to be a cover-up for a lack of deeper values. Some of them turned to far-left and later "green" politics.

This factor contributed to the radical and sometimes violent politics among young Germans in the 1970s and 1980s. Certainly it was not because they were poor; their society was prosperous, and often they were from wealthy families. Prosperity and materialism, in fact, rubbed them the wrong way. Said one rich girl: "I'm sick of all this caviar gobbling." Then she joined the terrorists and helped murder an old family friend, a banker. (She and other gang members were arrested in 1990 in East Germany, where the secret police, the Stasi, had protected them.) The Baader-Meinhof gang committed murder and bank robbery in the name of revolution, and some young Germans sympathized with them. The terrorists, in their warped, sick way, put their finger

Vergangenheitsbewältigung
Literally, "mastery of the past," coming to grips with Germany's Nazi past.

multiculturalism Preservation of diverse languages and traditions within one country; in German *Multikulti*.

reparations Paying back for war damages.

on the German malaise: German society, avoiding its past, had developed a moral void with nothing to believe in but "caviar gobbling." The past, it seems, does not stay buried; it comes back to haunt the society trying to forget it. As American writer William Faulkner said: "The past is still with us; it isn't even past."

German Catholic writer Heinrich Böll in the 1950s coined the term **Vergangenheitsbewältigung** to direct Germans' attention to the moral vacuum. He meant that Germans must face the past squarely and admit a certain degree of collective guilt. Many German intellectuals take this as the necessary foundation of German democracy. If Germans cannot come to grips with their own past, if they try to cover it up, German democracy could again be taken over by mindless nationalists, cautioned former President Richard von Weizsäcker and leftist writer Günter Grass.

Under Communist rule, the East Germans used a different approach to avoid coming to grips with the past: deny it was their past. "We were not Nazis," taught the Communist regime, "We fought the Nazis. So we have nothing to be ashamed of or to regret. The Nazis are over there in West Germany." East Germany avoided moral responsibility by trying to portray the Nazis as a foreign power, like Austria has done. In this area, as in many others, East German attitudes lagged behind West German attitudes.

Political Culture

HOW TO HANDLE THE HOLOCAUST

Keep it front and center, or retire it as an overworked issue from a bygone era? This was the dilemma Germany faced as it restored Berlin as the nation's capital in the 1990s. The problem was more subtle than nazism and anti-Semitism, which are not serious threats. Some Germans felt that leftists had turned guilt for the Holocaust into an all-purpose tool to promote **multiculturalism** and political correctness. Many tired of hearing about the Holocaust, which only the oldest Germans have personally lived through.

Germany has paid some $60 billion in **reparations** for the Holocaust, and many Germans felt this was enough. A more recent question was whether and what kind of Holocaust memorial should be built in the heart of Berlin. CDU Chancellor Kohl had urged it; SPD Chancellor Schröder and his party had some doubts. Some argued that there were already enough such memorials. A new Jewish Museum opened in Berlin in early 1999 (designed and directed by Americans). Some argued that no memorial could possibly do justice to the magnitude of the horror. Some suggested

that a death camp was the proper site. Some wanted a big memorial, others small. Some wanted a traditional memorial, others abstract. In 1999, the Bundestag finally authorized a large memorial by a U.S. architect in the heart of Berlin; it opened in 2005.

German businesses had a rough time with the Holocaust issue as well. Under the Nazis, they had benefited from the money and property seized from Jews and from Jewish (and other) slave labor. For decades, German businesses, banks, and insurance companies rejected survivors' demands for compensation with the claim that private firms, like everyone else, had to follow Nazi orders. They belatedly made efforts to settle when faced with U.S. lawsuits. In 1999, Chancellor Schröder, backed by twelve major German firms, set up a $5 billion compensation fund "to counter lawsuits, particularly class-action suits, and to remove the basis of the campaign being led against German industry and our country." The controversy reminded some of the old Nazi line that an international Jewish conspiracy was keeping Germany down.

The Generation Gap

As a guest in a German home long ago, I saw how the family reacted when one of the daughters found, in the back of a china closet, an old poem, *"Die Hitlerblume"* (the Hitler flower), comparing the *Führer* to a lovely blossom. The three college-age children howled with laughter and derision. "Daddy, how could you go along with this garbage?" they asked. The father, an old-fashioned authoritarian type, grew red in the face and stammered, "You don't know what it was like. They had everybody whipped up. The times were different." He was quite embarrassed.

output affect Attachment to a system based on its providing material abundance.

system affect Attachment to a system for its own sake.

The incident underscores the rapid generational changes in German political attitudes; simply put, the younger the generation, the more open, free-spirited, democratic, and European it is. Most younger Germans give unqualified allegiance to democracy and European unity. Only a handful of personality problems hanker for an authoritarian system. Feeling no personal responsibility for what the Nazis did, they are also less inclined to ponder Germany's past.

The younger generation has also freed up German society a great deal. No longer are German women confined to *Kinder, Küche, Kirche* (children, kitchen, and church); most now work outside the home and participate in politics. German youngsters are not as obedient as they once were, and German fathers no longer beat them as in the old days. If democracy starts in the home, Germany now has a much better foundation for democracy.

The typical German of today is far more democratic in attitudes than the typical German of 1949, when the Federal Republic was founded. Those who would support another Hitler, trade civil rights for "security," or think a one-party system is best have steadily dwindled, while those who think democracy and civil rights are worthwhile values in their own right have steadily increased. West German attitudes are now at least as democratic as any of their European neighbors, and the East Germans are likely to become so.

Is the change permanent? Political scientist Sidney Verba drew a distinction between **output affect** and **system affect** in his discussion of German political culture. The former means liking the system for what it produces (jobs, security, and material goods), the latter, liking the system because it is perceived as good. Verba thought Germans showed more of the first than the second; that is, they liked the system while the going was good—they were "fair-weather democrats"— but had not yet become "rain-or-shine democrats" the way Britons or Americans are. Verba's point was made in the early 1960s. Since then, system affect among Germans has increased as the younger generation has come of age. Some East Germans, however, are still caught up in the output affect, judging democracy by the cars and jobs it provides them.

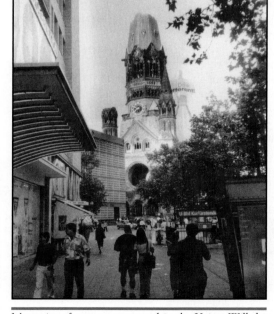

Memories of war are preserved in the Kaiser Wilhelm Church, which was deliberately left half-ruined in Berlin.

■ A Normal Germany?

Many Germans now argue that Germany has become a "normal" country and no longer bears any special guilt about the past. Most Germans were born after the Nazis, they note, and German democracy is as solid as any, with the same problems and hopes as its European neighbors. As good Europeans, Germans should help prevent massacres in Bosnia and Kosovo, a majority of Germans felt, thus breaking the FRG taboo against using German forces outside of Germany. Until recently, most Germans hid their nationalism, but now many politicians say they are patriotic and proud to be German.

Is Germany now strictly a normal country? The question flared in 2002 when the deputy leader of the small Free Democratic party, Jürgen Möllemann, sharply criticized Israel and sided with the Palestinians, as many Europeans do. In Germany, however, this is awkward; some say it is neo-Nazi. Others argue that in a "normal" country criticism of Israel is no longer taboo. Foreign Minister Fischer noted: "Whenever Israel is discussed in Germany, the fundamental debate about German identity is never far behind. Can we criticize Israel? The very question raises suspicion." Germany may never be a completely normal country.

The younger generation of Germans brings with them new concerns about jobs and the environment that the older generation did not worry about. A distance developed between many young Germans and the mainstream political parties. In the German party system, newcomers must slowly work their way up the ranks of the major parties, starting at the local and state levels, before they can have a say at the national level. By the time they can, few are young. (One interesting exception: In 1998, a twenty-two-year-old SPD candidate from East Germany won a seat in the Bundestag, the youngest German deputy ever.) In the meantime, they are expected to obey party dictates and not have much input. Some youth organizations of both the Social Democrats and Free Democrats became so rambunctious that they had to be disowned by their parent parties. For many young Germans, both the Christian Democrats and Social Democrats, who alternated in power, looked staid and elderly, and neither was responsive to young people.

Belatedly, some German politicians recognized the problem. Former President Richard von Weizsäcker worried about "the failure of my generation to bring younger people into politics." Young Germans, he noted, "do not admire the moral substance of the older generation. Our economic achievement went along with a very materialistic and very selfish view of all problems."

Young Germans also turned away from the United States. In the 1950s and early 1960s, young Germans nearly worshiped the United States; it was their model in politics, lifestyles, and values. Events over forty years reversed this. The assassination of President Kennedy—who had recently proclaimed *Ich bin ein Berliner* at the Berlin Wall—horrified Germans and made them wonder

Geography

SAILING THE BALTIC

Back on your luxury yacht, you are sailing in a great, clockwise circle around the Baltic Sea, always staying with land a few kilometers to port (left). Upon entering the Skagerrak, which countries do you pass on your left?

Norway, Sweden, Finland, Russia, Estonia, Latvia, Lithuania, Russia again (Kaliningrad Oblast), Poland, Germany, and Denmark.

about the United States. The Vietnam War was worse; some young Germans compared it with Hitler's war of aggression. Rising tensions between East and West and the warlike posture of President Reagan convinced many young Germans that the United States was willing to incinerate Germany. With the 2003 Iraq war most Germans saw Americans as violent and arrogant. It was ironic that the United States—which had tutored Germans to repudiate militarism—became the object of German antiwar feeling.

> **Ostpolitik** Literally "east policy"; Brandt's building relations with East Europe, including East Germany.

Personalities

WILLY BRANDT AS TURNING POINT

One of the signs that democracy had taken root in Germany was the 1969 election that made Willy Brandt chancellor. It would not have been possible even a few years earlier, for Brandt represented a repudiation of German history and society that few Germans could have tolerated earlier. First, Brandt was an illegitimate child, a black mark that Adenauer used in election campaigns. Second, Brandt was a Socialist, and in his youth in the North German seaport of Lübeck had been pretty far left (although never Communist). No Socialist had been in power in Germany for decades; the CDU kept smearing the SPD as a dangerous party, and many Germans believed it. Third, and most damaging, was that Brandt had fled to Norway in 1933, became a Norwegian citizen, and had not reclaimed his German nationality until 1947. Some even falsely accused him of fighting Germans as a Norwegian soldier.

With a record like that, it seemed Brandt was starting into German politics with three strikes against him. But many Germans, especially younger ones, admired Brandt. He was "Mr. Clean," a German who had battled the Nazis—literally, in Lübeck street fights—and who had never been "just an opportunist" who survived by going along. Brandt seemed to represent a newer, better Germany as opposed to the conservative, traditional values of Adenauer and the CDU.

As mayor of West Berlin from 1957 to 1966, Brandt showed how tough and anti-Communist he was by standing up to Soviet and East German efforts at encroachment. A leading figure in the SPD, Brandt supported its 1959 move away from Marxism. In 1964 he

Willy Brandt, FRG Chancellor 1969–1974.

became the SPD's chairman, and this boosted the party's electoral fortunes.

In 1966 the SPD joined the cabinet in a grand coalition with the CDU. As is usual in coalitions, the head of the second largest party is foreign minister. Here, Brandt showed himself to be a forceful and innovative statesman with his **Ostpolitik**. By 1969 the SPD had enough Bundestag seats to form a small coalition with the FDP, and Brandt became the FRG's first Socialist chancellor. The event was a symbolic breakthrough: Germany looked more democratic under an anti-Nazi than an ex-Nazi (Brandt's predecessor, Kiesinger).

The story, however, did not end happily. In 1974 it was discovered that a Brandt assistant was an East German spy. (West Germany was riddled with East German spies.) Brandt, regretting his security slip, resigned the chancellorship to become the grand old man of not only German but also West European social democracy. By the time he died in 1992 he could see the fruits of his Ostpolitik.

Wessi Informal name for West German.

Ossi Informal name for East German.

postmaterialism Theory that modern culture has moved beyond getting and spending.

affluence Having plenty of money.

The preceding attitudes fed the Green and later the Left parties. In elections, these two parties do best among young voters. Their attitudes also contribute to a new German nationalism that no longer follows in America's footsteps. Instead of automatically looking west, some young Germans look to a reunified Germany taking its rightful place as the natural leader of Central Europe. Some turned anti-United States and anti-NATO. The entirely new situation created by German unification, the end of the Cold War, fighting in Bosnia and Kosovo, and the 2003 Iraq War changed German attitudes, especially those of young people. Schröder boosted the 2002 SPD vote by criticizing U.S. policy on Iraq. Germans no longer look to the United States for guidance or solidarity.

■ The Disorienting Unification

There is still a big cultural gap between East and West Germans. When the Wall came down in late 1989, there was much celebration and good will. **Wessis** were generous to the **Ossis**, but soon the relationship soured. The Ossis kept demanding the bounties of the prosperous West as a right; after all, they were all Germans, and the Wessis had so much. The Wessis did not see things that way. "We've worked hard for more than forty years for this," they argued, "Now you Ossis must do the same." With newly acquired D-Marks, courtesy of West German taxpayers, Ossis snatched up modern products while their own economy collapsed. West Germans quickly developed negative stereotypes of East Germans living well at Wessi expense—like poor relatives who had come to sponge off them.

As the costs of bringing East Germany up to West German levels started to sink in, some Germans grew angry. The East German economy was found to be in far worse shape than foreseen and

Key Concepts

THE RISE OF "POSTMATERIALISM"

One of the trends among rich nations—especially pronounced in West Germany—is the feeling of some young people that modern society is too focused on material goods. Starting in the late 1960s, "countercultures" sprang up in every advanced country. Young people rejected the work-and-buy ethic of their parents and turned instead to beards, blue jeans, and "quality of life" questions. This caught on strongly in the Federal Republic as young Germans sought to repudiate the hypermaterialism of their parents.

Postmaterialism is found throughout the advanced industrialized world. Raised in conditions of **affluence** with no depression or war, young Britons, French, Germans, Japanese, and Americans tend to

ignore their parents' values and embrace few causes. The postmaterial generation is tolerant, introspective, fun-loving, and not drawn to conventional political parties or religions or marriage and family. Said young German writer Judith Hermann: "The older generation has been more interested in the past, the war, politics. My generation looks at itself."

Postmaterialism underlies the Federal Republic's leftist, antinuclear, ecology, and pacifist movements, much of which came together in the Greens. Postmaterialism also plugged into German romanticism and nationalism. Will postmaterialism last or decline? If it has created a vacuum of values, what might eventually fill the vacuum?

needed huge bailouts. Much industry simply had to be closed; unemployment shot up. West German business executives talk down to their East German counterparts. Wessis think Ossis have been trained into inefficiency by the Communists. Ossis feel belittled by and alienated from the West German system that was quickly imposed on them. This has led to an increase in East German consciousness, which is now greater than before unification. There is nothing like togetherness to separate people.

political generation Theory that age groups are marked by the great events of their young adulthood.

Politically, Ossis have weak party identification (see pages 59–133) and easily shift their votes from one election to the next, first to the CDU, then to the SPD, and recently to the Left party, the party of East German resentment and nostalgia (*Ostalgie*). The Left is supported by ex-Communists, people worried about their pensions, and Ossis who feel the other parties ignore them. The collapse of East Germany left citizens disoriented and lacking something to believe in. "Freedom" is not clear enough; some are still ideologically socialist and crave order and a system that guarantees their livelihood. One of the lessons of Germany's unification: You have to pay as much attention to psychological and social transitions as to economic ones.

The economy too was a problem. Since unification, German economic growth has been slow, making many Germans frightened of unemployment (more than twice as high in East Germany than in West) and resentful at the massive transfer of funds to the east. Some Germans wonder if unification has been worthwhile. Some are disoriented and ask which is the right way for unified Germany in a vastly different Europe. Some left-wing intellectuals warn of the return of a racist Germany. Neo-Nazi and skinhead youths (found throughout Europe) lent weight to the warnings: Over a decade more than a hundred Africans and Turks were killed and Jewish sites desecrated. Predicting a stable future for a united Germany is more difficult than was predicting it for West Germany alone.

Key Concepts

POLITICAL GENERATIONS IN GERMANY

German sociologist Karl Mannheim coined the term **political generations** to describe how great events put a lasting stamp on young people. We can see this in Germany. Today's young Germans were formed by the fall of the Berlin Wall in 1989. Sometimes called "89ers," they stand in marked contrast with previous German generations: the 45ers, who climbed out of the rubble and rebuilt a new Germany, and the 68ers, who rebelled against complacent materialism.

Many 68ers changed over time. Chancellor Schröder had been a Marxist Juso who turned quite centrist. Green leader Joschka Fischer dropped out of high school and fought police in the streets but became a popular and effective foreign minister. Otto Schily had been a far-left lawyer who defended terrorists but joined the SPD and became interior minister, which includes internal security. Most Germans were unbothered by their pasts.

The 89ers are relatively few in number (because of the strong trend to one-child couples) and worry about unemployment, destruction of the environment, and having to pay off the staggering burden of German unification and the lavish pensions of older Germans. Generally liberal and tolerant, *postmodern* Germans are also fun-loving, individualistic, irreligious, and apolitical; they do not much care for hard work, marriage, having children, or politics. Many do not vote, and few like the main political parties, but some are open to the Greens or Left. Few join formal groups or associations. Their chief concern is music; many would just like to rave to a techno beat. Many young people around the world are like this. (Are young Americans?)

■ The End of Shell Shock

Many Germans, especially the older generation who had gone along with the Nazis, felt so damaged by political involvement that they swore never to take an active part in politics again. To appreciate how an older German might feel shell-shocked and cautious about politics, imagine a German born in 1900 who was raised under a conservative monarchy and taught to obey authority. All of a sudden a republic comes that expects its citizens to be good democrats (they were not). Then comes a dictatorship that demands the enthusiastic, unquestioning complicity of all Germans. That collapses amid death, destruction, and the arrival of some 12 million Germans expelled from East Europe. In that confused postwar situation Allied occupiers tell Germans that they have been very wicked and must now become democratic. No wonder that in the first decades of the Federal Republic many Germans said *ohne mich* (without me) to politics. Some East Germans still feel this way.

bounce-back effect   Tendency of trends and values to reverse.

skinheads   Racist youth, begun in England, with shaved heads and quasi-military attire.

In their famous *Civic Culture* study, Almond and Verba described the German attitude of 1959 as one of detachment. Germans were often well informed about politics but did not want to participate in much more than voting. They were pragmatic and sometimes cynical about politics. If the system worked it was okay, but there was no point in getting personally involved. Germans showed low levels of social trust or willingness to discuss politics with others. In the decades since, however, this attitude receded, making West Germans among the most democratic and participatory in the world. Every decade there are fewer and fewer of the skeptical generation and more and more of the postwar generation. But now Germany, with unification, has entered the post-Cold War period, and it is a time of testing.

Democracy

A BOUNCE-BACK EFFECT?

Germans, especially young Germans, are looser, freer, and more open than ever. Some observers think this is the way things are going all over the world, the generational shift to *postmodernism* (see box on page 205). Historically, however, there have been **bounce-back effects** that have abruptly reversed values. American journalist William Shirer recalled how young Germans in the 1920s pursued fun and freedom, but this reversed under the Nazis. Young Germans in the 1950s and early 1960s were hard-working, moderate, and pro-American; by the late 1960s many were dropout anti-American multicultural radicals. In 2005, a nontrivial fraction of Germans voted left, green, and pacifist.

Many young Germans now face long-term unemployment. Some resent foreigners who, they think, take their jobs. German **skinheads** rob and beat foreigners. Some young Germans reject *Multikulti* and Holocaust guilt. They did not do it, so why should it concern them? Young Germans will likely continue to seek fun and freedom, but that can sometimes turn destructive. What comes is highly unpredictable, but it will probably be to a rock beat.

■ The German Political Elite

German elite recruitment is quite mixed, more like that of the United States than Britain or France. There is no German equivalent of Oxbridge or the Great Schools. The three German political collapses of this century left a relatively clean slate for bright talent to achieve political office. Some (such as Brandt) were not even university graduates, although most politicians now are (recent exception: Joschka Fischer).

As in America, the typical German politician has studied law, although in Germany this is done at the undergraduate rather than the postgraduate level. German (and other European) legal systems produce different attitudes than the Anglo-American Common Law system. Continental law developed from Roman law—usually in the updated form of the Napoleonic Code—and it emphasizes fixed rules. The Common Law, on the other hand, is judge-made law that focuses on precedent and persuasion; it is flexible. The former system produces lawyers who go by the book, the latter lawyers who negotiate and make deals. Consequently, German politicians with their legal background are heavily law-oriented rather than people-oriented.

Much of the work of the Bundestag, for example, is devoted to the precise wording of bills, making that house a rather dull, inward-looking chamber that has failed to win admiration from the German public. Likewise, cabinet ministers conceive of their role heavily in terms of carrying out laws. Every cabinet has many lawyers; often the chancellor is one (for example, Schröder).

Besides lawyers, a smaller group has had a disproportionate role in German politics: economists. In few other countries have professional economists achieved the stature they have in the FRG. One German chancellor had a Ph.D. in economics: Ludwig Erhard. Under Adenauer, the rotund, jolly Economics Minister Erhard charted Germany's rise to prosperity; later he became chancellor. Helmut Schmidt, an economics graduate, succeeded Brandt as SPD chancellor and managed to keep both inflation and unemployment low in Germany while much of the world went through a major recession. In Germany, economists are not just advisers but often become important politicians themselves.

Key Concepts

LEGITIMACY, AUTHORITY, SOVEREIGNTY

These three terms overlap, and weakness in one usually spreads to the others. Communist East Germany illustrates this overlap. The GDR had weak legitimacy (see page 9), especially as East Germans compared their lot with free and prosperous West Germans. In the absence of legitimacy, the Communist regime needed a massive police apparatus and, in 1961, the Berlin Wall to keep its citizens from leaving. This undermined the authority (see page 54) of GDR rulers.

As soon as they could disobey them, East Germans did, leading to the fall of the Wall in 1989. Then, without a leg to stand on, East German sovereignty (see page 1) evaporated and the GDR fell into the FRG's hands. Like falling dominoes, weak legitimacy toppled into authority that then collapsed sovereignty. (For more on the fall of East Germany, see pages 230–231.)

■ The German Split Personality

The French, as we discussed, often seem split between demanding impersonal authority and re-belling against it. The Germans have a sort of split personality, too, but it is between **romanticism** and realism.

Most of the time Germans are pragmatic realists: hard working, thrifty, clean, orderly, coop-erative, family-oriented. But a persistent romantic streak runs through German history that comes out every now and then: the nineteenth-century intellectuals (such as composer Richard Wagner) who reveled in the *Volksgeist*, the Nazi youth who really believed they were building a "thousand-year Reich," and in the 1970s, far-left terrorists who thought they could bring utopia by assassination. The latest German romantics are the Greens, who long for an imaginary pastoral idyll free of industry and pollution. German romanti-cism also manifests itself in the striving for perfection, which may lead Germans to undertake vast projects they may not have the resources for. Hitler's plan to conquer all of Europe, including Rus-sia, is an infamous example.

romanticism   Hearkening to an ideal world or mythical past.

Germans set high store by achievement. To work harder, produce more, and proudly let oth-ers know about it seems to be an ingrained cultural trait (although fading among young Germans). This helps explain Germany's rise after the war to Europe's number-one economic power. Both East Germany's leader Walter Ulbricht and West Germany's Helmut Schmidt toured their respective camps giving unsolicited advice on how other countries should copy the German economic mir-acle. East Germany's, although not as spectacular as the Federal Republic's, nonetheless made it the economic leader of the East bloc. Back when the Wall stood, I told an anti-Communist West Berliner that East Berlin also looked prosperous. He nodded and said, "Of course. They're Ger-mans too."

Perhaps the archetypal German figure is Goethe's Faust, the driven person who can never rest or be content with what is already his. This quality can produce both great good and evil. Former Chancellor Helmut Schmidt, himself a stereotype of the German realist strain, once said, "Ger-mans have an enormous capacity for idealism and the perversion of it."

Key Terms

affluence (p. 204)

bounce-back effect (p. 206)

denazification (p. 198)

Holocaust (p. 199)

liberal democracy (p. 198)

multiculturalism (p. 200)

Ossi (p. 204)

Ostpolitik (p. 203)

output affect (p. 201)

political generation (p. 205)

postmaterialism (p. 204)

reparations (p. 200)

romanticism (p. 208)

skinheads (p. 206)

system affect (p. 201)

Vergangenheitsbewältigung (p. 200)

Wessi (p. 204)

Further Reference

Barnouw, Dagmar. *The War in the Empty Air: Victims, Perpetrators, and Postwar Germans.* Bloomington, IN: Indiana University Press, 2005.

Berman, Paul. *Power and the Idealists: Or, The Passion of Joschka Fischer and Its Aftermath.* New York: Soft Skull Press, 2005.

Brinks, J. H. *Children of a New Fatherland: Germany's Post-War Right-Wing Politics.* London: I. B. Tauris, 2000.

Frei, Norbert. *Adenauer's Germany and the Nazi Past.* New York: Columbia University Press, 2002.

Kramer, Jane. *The Politics of Memory: Looking for Germany in the New Germany.* New York: Random House, 1996.

Markovits, Andrei S., and Philip S. Gorski. *The German Left: Red, Green and Beyond.* New York: Oxford University Press, 1993.

McAdams, A. James. *Judging the Past in Unified Germany.* New York: Cambridge University Press, 2001.

Mushaben, Joyce Marie. *From Post-War to Post-Wall Generations: Changing Attitudes Towards the National Question and NATO in the Federal Republic of Germany.* Boulder, CO: Westview, 1998.

Olivo, Christiane. *Creating a Democratic Civil Society in Eastern Germany: The Case of the Citizen Movements and Alliance 90.* New York: Palgrave, 2001.

Rohrschneider, Robert. *Learning Democracy: Democratic and Economic Values in Unified Germany.* New York: Oxford University Press, 1999.

Sa'adah, Anne. *Germany's Second Chance: Trust, Justice, and Democratization.* Cambridge, MA: Harvard University Press, 1998.

Williams, Howard, Colin Wight, and Norbert Kapfere, eds. *Political Thought and German Reunification: The New German Ideology?* New York: St. Martin's, 2000.

Yoder, Jennifer A. *From East Germans to Germans? The New Postcommunist Elites.* Durham, NC: Duke University Press, 1999.

Chapter 15

GERMANY:
PATTERNS OF INTERACTION

We saw how the Weimar Republic collapsed with the shrinking of the moderate parties and growth of extremist parties—"polarized pluralism." Could this happen in the Federal Republic? For most of the history of West Germany, the answer was "no." With only two-plus parties, they, for good political reasons, stuck close to the center of the political spectrum. Political competition in West Germany tended to be **center-seeking**. Voters had their choice of three moderate parties (there were several tiny parties on the ballot, but they were largely ignored), and these three parties could combine in only three different coalitions (CDU and FDP, CDU and SPD, SPD and FDP). This made West German politics stable compared to more tumultuous multiparty systems.

Questions to Consider

1. Why has German coalition formation become more difficult?
2. Why is a unimodal distribution of opinion necessary for democracy?
3. How does the German distribution of opinion resemble the British and French?
4. What is the difference between *Weltanschauung* and catchall parties?
5. How have German elections come to resemble presidential ones?
6. Are fund-raising scandals part of democracy?
7. Describe the union-party linkup in North European countries.
8. In what ways does voting follow geography?

With unification—and even a little before—German politics became less stable and more complex. The party system is no longer "two-plus," but with the arrival of the Greens and Left is now more accurately described as multiparty. The two large parties lost some of their votes to smaller parties. This made coalition formation more difficult, for now a German coalition may require three partners instead of the previous two. Now there are nine possible coalition combinations (see box on page 213). This in turn makes German government less stable and predictable.

Parties and the Electorate

Social scientists repeatedly find that political opinion in most modern democracies resembles a bell-shaped curve: A lot of people are in the center, with fewer and fewer as one moves to the left or right. If you want to sound more scientific you call this a **unimodal** distribution of opinion. (A **bimodal** distribution indicates extreme division, what happened during Weimar.) Routinely, Europeans are asked to place themselves on a one-to-nine ideological scale, one for the most left and nine for the most right. Germany comes out, like most West European countries, as a bell-shaped curve (see graph at the top of page 212).

**The Shape of the German Electorate:
The Self-Placement of German Voters
on a Left/Right Ideological Scale**

How does this affect political parties? When party leaders come to understand the shape of the electorate, either through modern polling techniques or by losing elections, they usually try to modify their party image so that it appeals to the middle of the opinion spectrum. If the Social Democrats position themselves too far left—say, at two on the nine-point scale—by advocating nationalizing private industry and dropping out of NATO, they may please left-wing ideologues in the party but do poorly in elections. Few Germans place themselves at the two position on the left. So the Social Democrats tone down their socialism and emphasize their commitment to democracy plus welfare measures, moving to perhaps the four position.

Now they do much better in elections, but the left wing of the SPD is unhappy with the dilution of socialist gospel. Finally, sniffing the possibility of becoming Germany's governing party, the SPD throws out socialism and tells the electorate that they will do a better job running the capitalist, market economy. At this point they are in roughly the five position. The party's left wingers are angry, accusing the SPD leadership of selling out to capitalism; some left-wing socialists even quit the SPD. But the SPD is doing well in elections. By emphasizing democracy and minimizing socialism, they win the votes of many centrist Germans. But now there is some vacant ideological space on the left, which the Greens and Left party fill.

The preceding, in a nutshell, was the history of the SPD to their electoral high point of 45.8 percent in 1972. A century ago the Social Democrats started to shed their Marxism, in practice if not yet in theory. In the 1950s, seeing the CDU triumphantly win the center, they decided to break out of their left-wing stronghold. Meeting in Bad Godesberg (just outside Bonn) in 1959, they drew up a Basic Program so moderate one can hardly find any socialism in it. Marxism was *kaputt*; the SPD proclaimed itself "rooted in Christian ethics, humanism and classical philosophy."

Now, while the Social Democrats moved rightward, the Christian Democrats had already taken a broad swath of the ideological spectrum, claiming to stand for everything, a party of all Germans, just as the British Conservatives used to claim to represent all Britons. The CDU downplayed its conservatism, for it too understood that if the party image were too rightist it would lose the big prize in the center. The result is two large parties that generally try to be centrist but in so doing rubbed their respective left and right wings the wrong way (see boxes on pages 214 and 215). They also make politics boring.

The game is never finished, though. While they had transformed themselves into a center-left party, the SPD allowed the area on their left to be taken over by newer, more radical parties, the Greens and

center-seeking   Parties trying to win big centrist vote by moderate programs. (See page 211.)

unimodal   Single-peaked distribution. (See page 211.)

bimodal   Two-peaked distribution. (See page 211.)

Left. (In one study Green voters placed themselves at 3.4 on the scale.) Partly to try to win over these leftist voters, partly in response to Juso (see box on page 214) influence within the SPD, and partly out of irritation at the hawkishness of the Reagan administration, the SPD moved leftwards in the late 1980s, much like the British Labour party had done earlier. The SPD came out against both U.S. nuclear missiles in Germany and nuclear power plants, two key Green demands. But the shift hurt the SPD in elections; they dropped from 42.9 percent of the vote in 1980 to 33.5 in 1990, their poorest showing since 1957.

Key Concepts

GERMANY'S COALITIONS

Two-party coalitions have been the norm for Germany, usually consisting of one large and one small party. When either of the two large parties (CDU or SPD) gets around 40 percent of the vote (and of Bundestag seats), formerly the case, it forms a coalition with a small party that won around 10 percent and thus controls a (bare) majority of the Bundestag. This relatively happy situation gives rise to possibilities 1 through 4, which have governed the FRG thus far:

1. Christian-Liberal Coalition: The CDU/CSU wins about 40 percent of Bundestag seats and the FDP wins about 10 percent, allowing for the same coalition that had sustained Kohl and earlier cabinets in power.
2. Social-Liberal Coalition: The SPD edges out the CDU with about 40 percent of Bundestag seats and turns to the FDP with, say, 10 percent to rebuild the coalition that had supported Brandt and Schmidt in the 1970s.
3. Grand Coalition: If the two big parties, the CDU and SPD, shrink to around 35 percent, and the small parties get about 10 percent each, then points 1 and 2 are impossible. The two big parties could make a coalition with each other; they did in the late 1960s and again in 2005 (see page 189).
4. Red-Green Coalition: If the SPD (red) gets 40 percent and the Greens get 10 percent, they build a social-ecological coalition, which Schröder did from 1998 to 2005.

Five other coalitions are possible but difficult:

5. "Traffic Light" (Ampel) Coalition: Red, green, and yellow (for the FDP). If the SPD won under 40 percent, it might need two small coalition partners, each with 6 to 10 percent of Bundestag seats, to build a majority. The Greens and Liberals, however, are ideologically incompatible.
6. "Jamaica" Coalition (after the colors of the Jamaican flag): This would be the rightwing counterpart of the above Ampel—black (CDU), yellow (FPD), and green, but again the FPD and Greens oppose each other.
7. An SPD-Left coalition. The new Left party is too far left for most other parties but in a pinch the SPD could turn to it. A complicating factor: Left leader Oskar Lafontaine had earlier led the SPD but split angrily with centrist Schröder; they still hate each other.
8. An all-left coalition. If the SPD gets about 40 percent and the Greens and Left get 5 percent, all three could form a leftist coalition.
9. A "government of national unity" of all parties. These can be useful for emergency situations such as war, but not for much else. According to the theory of coalitions, you stop adding partners once you have topped 50 percent; there is no point to adding more. And an all-party coalition would not stay together for long.

The fragmentation of the German party system into five parties makes one long for the old and relatively simple "two-plus" system in which the only alternatives were, with two exceptions, points 1 and 2.

The SPD is still pulled in two directions. Tugging leftward is the traditional socialist wing once headed by former party chairman and finance minister Oskar Lafontaine. This wing, based heavily on workers and older people, wants to help those in need and to preserve the welfare state. Tugging rightward is the Blairite wing of Chancellor Schröder, which wants reforms to cut taxes, pensions, subsidies, bureaucracy, unemployment, and regulations that slow economic growth. The two men had such serious differences that Lafontaine resigned from the cabinet and as party chair in 1999 and in 2005 joined the new Left party. His departure drew sighs of relief from the business community. But Schröder could not turn the SPD into a genuine New Middle on the model of Blair's New Labour. By his second term, many Germans were fed up with Schröder's incoherence and indecisiveness.

■ The Chancellor and the Electorate

Two factors especially hurt the SPD in the 1990s. The CDU's embrace of rapid unification made the SPD look narrow and carping in its warnings about the expense and economic impact of quick merger. Go slow and think it through, was the SPD message, not a popular one in 1990, although their "I told you so" won them some votes in 1994. SPD chancellor-candidate Oskar Lafontaine in 1990 was also part of the problem. He was too clever and radical for many German voters. The SPD's next candidate, the bearded young intellectual Rudolf Scharping came across in 1994 much the same way. In 1998, the SPD took a leaf from Tony Blair's 1997 success in Britain: Assume vague, centrist positions; emphasize that the conservatives have been in office too long; and offer a younger, outgoing personality for prime minister. The SPD, in effect, learned the unimodal shape of the German electorate in the 1950s and 1960s, forgot it in the 1980s, and remembered it in the late 1990s.

Political Culture

UNHAPPY ON THE LEFT: THE JUSOS

In his youth, Gerhard Schröder was a Juso hothead, but he calmed as he aged. The youth branch of the SPD—the *Jungsozialisten,* or Jusos for short—has been a continual thorn in the left side of the party. Limited to people under thirty-five, the Jusos attract (and create) young radicals and Marxists. Impatient and idealistic, many Jusos find the mainstream SPD too moderate and gradualist. One favorite Juso target is now, ironically, Schröder, their leader long ago.

Periodically, the SPD has to disown its offspring. If it does not, it costs the party votes. Some Jusos cannot understand that Germans as a whole are moderate in their political views, and there is little support for pulling out of NATO, nationalization of industry, "cultural revolution," and massive taxes on the rich. When the Jusos helped move the SPD toward such positions in the early 1980s, the party lost four national elections in a row, just like the British Labour party. Some Jusos defected to the Greens or Left. The SPD faces the question of whether to try to retain young radicals by moving leftward.

Chancellor Schröder cleverly positioned himself slightly leftwards in the 2002 election. By criticizing Washington's plans to attack Iraq and distancing Germany from any part in the effort, Schröder won over some leftists who might otherwise have voted PDS (explaining why it slumped below the 5 percent threshold) and some pacifists who might not have voted at all. It angered President Bush but narrowly won the election for Schröder. Typically, that is all politicians care about.

Weltanschauung Literally "world view"; parties offering firm, narrow ideologies.
catchall Nonideological parties that welcome all.

In Germany, as in most advanced countries, personality has become more important than ideology in the mind of many voters. With the decline of **Weltanschauung** parties (see box on page 216) and the move of most large parties to the center of the political spectrum, the personality of candidates is often what persuades voters. This has long been the case in the United States and is now becoming the European norm as well. Some call it the Americanization of European politics, but it is less a matter of copying than it is of reflecting the rise of **catchall** parties. Throughout Europe, election posters now feature the face of the top party leader, the person who would become prime minister. Although voting may be by party list, citizens know that in choosing a party they are actually electing a prime minister. In 2005 Schröder was more popular than the SPD while Angela Merkel was less popular than the CDU.

German (and British) campaigns are conducted almost as if they were for the direct election of a president—as in the United States and France. Officially there is no "candidate for chancellor," but in practice the leading figures of the two big parties are clearly identified as such—in the media, on billboards, and in the public mind—so that much of the campaign revolves around the personalities of the two leading candidates.

A German candidate for chancellor must project strength and levelheadedness. In a country that still fears inflation, the candidate's economic background plays a bigger role than in most nations. Two of Germany's postwar chancellors have been economists. The candidate's adherence to democratic rules also plays a role, and Franz Josef Strauss's authoritarian streak contributed to his defeat in the 1980 race.

Political Culture

THUNDER ON THE RIGHT: CSU

Bavaria is the Texas of Germany, a land with its own raucous brand of politics. On principle, the Christian Social Union (CSU) never let itself be absorbed into the CDU; instead it calls itself an allied party and sometimes threatens to burst out of Bavaria—where it sometimes wins a majority of the vote—and set itself up in nationwide competition with the CDU.

Current CSU chief and Bavarian state premier Edmund Stoiber makes no secret of wanting to become chancellor. The CSU is to the right of the CDU, demanding a tougher anti-immigrant stance, a firmer crackdown on radicals, and a rollback of welfare. The CSU's kingpin was the late Franz Josef Strauss, Germany's right-wing tough guy who minimized the Nazi past and used to say, "I do not care who is chancellor under me." Stoiber, the 2002 chancellor candidate, hurt the CDU in the 2005 election when he called East Germans welfare-dependent.

dealignment   Voters losing
identification with any party.

Personality contributed to the results of the 1990s elections, too. The CDU/CSU had the steady, optimistic image of Helmut Kohl. SPD candidates of the 1990s came across as radical intellectuals until Gerhard Schröder ran in 1998. By that point, many Germans were tired of Kohl, who had been in office sixteen years and was showing his age. Much of postwar German politics can be described as parties groping for the right leader to bring them to power in the Bundestag and chancellor's office. When they find the right ones—such as Adenauer and Kohl of the CDU—they stick with them for a long time.

■ German Dealignment?

For many years political scientists have worried that American voters were showing an increasing **dealignment** with the main parties. That is, some decades ago, U.S. parties used to present a fairly clear "party image" and most voters carried around in their heads a fairly clear "party ID." Where the two connected (for example, U.S. Democrats and blue-collar workers), you had reliable party-voter "alignments." These could change every few decades in what were called "realignments," new matches of voters to parties. But some think U.S. voters are dealigning: Their preferences, often unfocused, connect with no party on a long-term basis. Their votes easily shift from one party to another in response to candidate personality and clever advertising.

Key Concepts

THE "CATCHALL" PARTY

In prewar Europe, many political parties used to imbue their supporters with a "view of the world" (*Weltanschauung*) corresponding to the party's ideology and philosophy. This was especially true of parties on the left, and it came to a high point in Weimar Germany. After World War II most Weltanschauung parties disappeared as they broadened their appeal or merged into bigger parties.

Noting their demise, German political scientist Otto Kirchheimer coined the term "catchall party" to describe what was taking their place: big, loose, pluralist parties that have diluted their ideologies so they can accommodate many diverse groups of supporters. His model of a catchall party was the CDU, a political vacuum cleaner that draws in all manner of groups:

farmers, businesspeople, labor, women, Catholics, Protestants, white-collar workers, blue collar, you name it.

For a while, under crusty Kurt Schumacher, the SPD tried to stay a Weltanschauung party, defining itself in rigid and ideological terms that turned away many middle-of-the-road voters. Since 1959, the SPD too has become a catchall party, appealing to Germans of all classes and backgrounds. Indeed, by now the catchall party is the norm in modern democracies. Almost axiomatically, any large party is bound to be a catchall party, for example, the French neo-Gaullists, Canadian Liberals, British Conservatives, Japanese Liberal Democrats, and, of course, both major U.S. parties.

Is electoral dealignment spreading to West Europe? There is evidence of it in Britain, France, and Germany. Increasingly, Germans dislike both major parties and doubt that either does any better in office than the other. German turnout in elections, as in most of Europe, is falling, from a high of 91 percent in 1972 to a low of 78 percent in 2005. More citizens now scatter their votes among a variety of small parties all over the political spectrum, from left to right. One center-right group that enjoyed brief notice called itself the *Statt* (instead of) party.

> **transparency**   Making public political and economic information.

Where does dealignment come from? It is not a sinister plot (although it can have some negative repercussions), but the normal and natural maturation process that many advanced democracies go through. One step in this process is the catchall party (see box on page 216). If two catchall parties face each other, as in the United States and Germany, their positions become so moderate and similar that they become boring. Neither offers much in the way of exciting new choices, programs, or personalities. Joschka Fischer was popular because he was not boring. (After his fourth divorce he got a younger girlfriend. Imagine that in U.S. politics.)

Meanwhile, the society is being hit by problems scarcely anyone could imagine a generation ago: immigration, environmental degradation, the movement of jobs to low-wage countries, and crushing tax and debt burdens. None of the catchall parties has any convincing solution; all waffle in some middle ground. Also, suddenly gone is the cement that helped hold the system together: the Soviet threat and the Cold War. It is a disorienting time, and none of the great catchall parties provides much in the way of guidance. (To what extent is this true of U.S. politics?) The public response is lower voter turnouts and small and less-stable shares of the vote for the catchall parties; in a word, dealignment.

Democracy

GERMANY'S FUND-RAISING SCANDALS

At the start of the new millennium, former Chancellor Helmut Kohl almost single-handedly wrecked his CDU party. As chancellor during the 1990s, Kohl got millions in secret donations for the CDU. Ironically, Kohl himself had demanded a new strict **transparency** law, which requires declaring the source and amounts of big contributions. Then Kohl's successor, Wolfgang Schäuble, admitted to illegal contributions. The CDU declined against the SPD in polls.

The trouble is, soon Land SPD branches stood accused of corruption along with their CDU and CSU counterparts. Bribes, tax evasions, false invoices, and kickbacks on waste-disposal and construction contracts are rife in Germany, involving both major parties. The SPD defense minister was fired for taking money on the side, and the PDS party chief and several other Bundestag members were ousted for personal use of government frequent-flier miles. Peter Eigen, founder of Transparency International in Berlin (see page 537), said Germany "is much more corrupt than previously thought."

Notice how all advanced democracies—the United States, Britain, France, Germany, and Japan—have party fund-raising scandals. They seem to come with democracy. Parties need big money to conduct elections, and economic interests always need friends in high places. The good news is that all over the world citizens are getting fed up with "money politics" and demanding reforms. For more on these scandals, see Chapter 26 on Japan, where they are especially pronounced.

■ The Bundestag and the Citizen

One reason German elections have turned into almost presidential elections for chancellor is the murky status of the Bundestag in the mind of many voters. They know what the chancellor does but are not too clear on what the Bundestag does. Part of the blame for this rests on the concept Bundestag deputies have of their role. The **Rechtsstaat** tradition is focused on laws. The Bundestag, now housed in the old Reichstag building in Berlin, is staffed heavily by lawyers and civil servants and has become a law factory.

Rechtsstaat   Literally, state of laws; government based on written rules and rights.

But is it not a legislature's purpose to legislate? Well, not entirely. By confining their activities to law books and committee meetings, the Bundestag deputies have failed to grasp the less obvious functions of a legislature. Actually, the most important role of a legislature is probably in overseeing the activities of the national government, catching corruption and inefficiency, uncovering scandals, threatening budget cuts, and, in general, keeping the bureaucrats on their toes.

The harsh glare of publicity is the best medicine for governmental wrongdoing. Too-cozy relationships between ministers and business thrive in the dark. It is in this area that the Bundestag has been weak. Although there are commissions of inquiry and a question hour, the former are not pursued as thoroughly as on Washington's Capitol Hill—where televised committee hearings are a major preoccupation—and the latter is not carried out with as much polish as in the House of Commons. (Bundestag deputies can be quite insulting, but it comes across as crude rather than clever.) In functioning as little but lawmakers, German legislators have contributed to the boredom problem.

One function the Bundestag has failed to develop is that of education. The way a legislature operates, the arguments that are presented, the manner in which members of parliament conduct themselves, these are great teachers of democracy. Instead, Bundestag activity seems calculated to make a weak impression. The Bundestag does not generate good press because it is a dull story. U.S. senators and representatives get more attention because they do interesting and often unpredictable things, like disobeying their own party, something that rarely happens in Germany.

Another function an effective parliament must perform is to represent people. Voters must feel that someone speaking for them really understands their point of view. In this the Bundestag suffers from a problem common to all elected legislatures: It is not representative of the voters. The average Bundestag deputy is close to fifty years old, male, trained as a lawyer, and employed as a civil servant, party leader, or interest-group official.

The strong German party system means that people must slowly work their way up in party ranks before they will be put on a ballot. Accordingly, candidates tend to be older, seasoned, party loyalists rather than bright, fresh, new faces. Unlike the American system, a German candidate cannot "come from out of nowhere" and win an election on his or her own. You are either a piece of the party machine, or you are nothing. The result is unrepresentative representatives. Said one German newspaper: "This gap between electorate and elected has become too wide." Many Germans do not feel represented; they feel that the Bundestag is the arena where the powerful interests of society work out deals with little reference to the common citizen, the little guy. Such feelings contributed to the Green and Left vote.

UNION-PARTY LINKS IN FOUR COUNTRIES		
Country	Union	Party Linkage
Britain	TUC	Labour
Sweden	LO	Social Democrat
Germany	DGB	SPD
United States	AFL-CIO	Democrat

■ The Union-Party Linkup

Unions in Germany are still strong but not what they used to be, another sign of the fraying of Germany's "consensus model" (discussed in the next chapter). One historical characteristic of North European political systems—and here we include Britain and Sweden along with Germany—has been the close relationship between labor unions and social-democratic parties. In these countries unions were large and cohesive; blue-collar workers were heavily organized, and their unions formed a single, large labor federation. Such federations supported the social-democratic parties with money, manpower, and votes. Often union leaders actually ran for office on the party ticket.

Compare this pattern with the Latin European systems. Labor was weakly organized and fragmented into several federations—Communist, Socialist, Christian, and other. The fragmentation reduced the effectiveness of a working-class voice. American unions are also fragmented into several federations and historically did not tie themselves to one party. U.S. labor no longer has the same kind of political input as North European labor. In North Europe, labor unions founded the welfare state.

In Britain, TUC unions are actual constituent members of the Labour Party. In Sweden, the gigantic LO is so close to the Social Democrats that some of their top personnel are the same. The German Basic Law forbids a formal union-party tie, but here too, everyone knows that labor support is an important pillar of SPD strength.

In the United States only 13 percent of the labor force is unionized; in Germany 20 percent is (in Sweden, some 50 percent). Eleven German industrial unions—the largest being the metalworkers (*IG Metall,* with 2.4 million members)—are federated into an umbrella organization, the *Deutscher Gewerkschaftsbund* (DGB) with 6.8 million members, down from 11.8 million in 1990. (Notice how U.S., British, French, and German unions have all declined. Is this permanent or reversible?) The DGB's voice is still heeded by the Social Democrats; its leaders are regularly consulted by SPD chiefs and get some of what they want: an elaborate welfare system, a short work week, and even directors' seats on the boards of large companies (more on this in the next chapter). Many of the SPD's Bundestag deputies have union ties. The labor minister in Schröder's cabinet was deputy chairman of IG Metall.

A new force on the labor front: In 2001 five service unions formed the 3-million-member Verdi (*Vereinte Dienstleistungsgewerkschaft*) to orchestrate everything from clerks to nurses to civil

"Friendly to the environment" is the German phrase for using bikes and recycling glass (three, in the center) and paper. The ecology movement is big in Germany.

servants. Service unions like Verdi have different demands than those of the industrial unions in the DGB. As the industrial sector shrinks in favor of services, unions shift too. In modern societies, unions grow mostly among government employees and teachers.

The catchall nature of the SPD prevents any one group dominating it. The more the SPD seeks votes in the center of the political spectrum, the more it has to turn away from one-on-one cooperation with unions. (The British Labourites faced the same problem with the TUC; when they let the unions dominate, they lost.) Starting in the 1970s, the SPD and unions diverged. Helmut Schmidt, representing the SPD right, was a better democrat and economist than he was a socialist. Union relations with the SPD grew cool. Still, most German unions are locked into supporting the Social Democrats for the simple reason that no other party will treat them as well. The Schröder government had to tell unions that raising wages and benefits works against adding new jobs. Instead, it had to tell them that cutting benefits and flexible work rules were necessary. The unions did not want to hear it and grew angry at Schröder.

On the management side, there is a similar pattern. The powerful *Bundesverband der Deutschen Industrie* (Federation of German Industries, BDI) has warm connections with the CDU, but not as close as those of unions with the SPD. The BDI wants flexible labor contracts and tax cuts, points the CDU also likes. One point of conflict: German business wants select immigration (such as computer specialists) to fill high-tech vacancies, but the CDU/CSU says no to all immigration. When the Social Democrats are in power, the BDI finds it can get along with them quite well too. As in Britain and France, big business does not need to get closely involved with one party; it is to their advantage to be able to work with all parties. The major focus of business is the bureaucracy, not the parties. Providing information to the relevant ministry, explaining to civil servants why regulations should be modified, going along with government economic plans—in these and other ways business quietly cements ties with government.

■ The Länder and Berlin

Britain and France are unitary systems that have moved, respectively, to devolution and decentralization. Germany is a federal system that some would like to make a little more centralized. The interesting thing here is that in both unitary and federal systems there are pressures to move toward a middle ground. Centralization in France was rigid, inefficient, and ignored local wishes and regional pride. Federalism in Germany is often uncoordinated, powerless, and deadlocked and encourages federal-state squabbles. In some ways the distinctions between unitary and federal systems are overdrawn; some see the emergence of a new "regional" pattern midway between the unitary and federal.

West Germany was founded as a federal republic for at least two reasons: (1) Germany has a long history of particularism and regionalism and (2) the occupying powers, fearful of a resurgence of German might in a centralized state, wanted it that way. The French in particular would have been delighted to see Germany broken up into several independent states that could never again threaten France. Postwar German politicians themselves, aware of the abuses of power of Hitler's centralized Reich and proud of their regional origins, were committed to a federal structure.

Germany is probably more federal than the United States; that is, its Länder run more of their own affairs and get a bigger portion of taxes than do American states. For example, individual and corporate income taxes are split between Berlin and the Länder with equal 42.5-percent shares; local governments get 15 percent. The Länder also get 45.9 percent of the value-added tax, the large but hidden sales tax used throughout Europe (see page 154). Poorer Länder—the new eastern ones—get additional funds. German Länder, in addition to raising some of their own taxes, are directly plugged into the federal tax system, an idea Americans might consider.

Germany's federalism has some drawbacks. For example, there is really not much of a nationwide police force, so law enforcement is a Land affair. Terrorists who committed their crimes in one Land could flee to another, counting on communication and coordination foul-ups to delay police. The cleaning of the seriously polluted Rhine River still lacks a central authority because such matters are controlled by the states, and each state sees its environmental responsibilities differently. Only in 1986 did the Bundestag set up a federal environment ministry, but it could not override Land environment ministries. The decentralized nature of education has made it impossible for federal authorities to insist on the nationwide study of the Nazis and their crimes in schools.

Many Germans would like Berlin to have a little more control over things. But the German Länder, like American states, stoutly resist moves that would erode the powers of Land officials, and they have the perfect means to do so: the Bundesrat. Not directly elected, Bundesrat delegations are designated by Land governments, which usually means the state's political chiefs. The Bundesrat must concur on any move that would alter the balance of powers between federation and state. Under Kohl, the Bundesrat was dominated by Social Democrats (because they won the most Land governments), but after Schröder's election the SPD lost control of several states and with it control of the Bundesrat. The Bundesrat, like the U.S. Senate, acts as a check on both the cabinet and the lower house.

As to the question of unitary versus federal systems, there is no simple answer. If you have one system, you usually want a little of the other. On balance, the German federation works pretty well. Further, in founding a new democracy it was probably wise to give people a smaller unit to focus on, to serve as a building block for developing nationwide democratic loyalties.

■ German Voting Patterns

In Britain, as we saw, the vote is structured at least in part along lines of social class and region. That is, Labour usually wins much of the working class, plus Scotland, Wales, and large industrial cities. French voting is similar, with the added factor of religious attitude, clerical or anticlerical. West

Geography

Virtually all elections when charted on maps show geographical voting patterns. There are almost always regional variations in party strength. The map of Britain showing where parties scored above average seldom needs to be changed; major parties tend to preserve their regional strength. Once rooted, regional voting patterns can persist for decades. Here are some of the patterns.

1. *Cities vote liberal.* Urban areas are almost always to the left of rural areas. Cities are places of education, intellectuals, and critical thinking calling for change and reform. Workers tend to be urban, and they are often discontent over wages and benefits. The countryside tends to be calmer, more accepting of the status quo, and often still controlled by political bosses or old traditions. Rural and farming people often resent urban intellectuals for having more experimental notions than common sense. Accordingly, in most countries, big cities vote liberal or left while the countryside and small towns vote conservative or right.

England outside of the big cities votes Conservative; central London votes Labour. Catholic Bavaria votes Christian Social, but Munich votes Social Democrat. Paris needs some qualification, for in Paris the better-off people live in the city while the working class lives in the suburbs. This tends to give Paris a conservative core but a "red belt" around the city, now eroding as the old working-class suburbs gentrify. In Russian elections the big cities, led by Moscow and St. Petersburg, more strongly support relatively liberal parties than the countryside, which is still partially under the thumb of Communist party bosses and feared economic disruption. Iranian city dwellers are more moderate or liberal, rural people more religious and traditional. U.S. elections show strong urban-rural splits.

2. *Every country has regional voting.* Regions vote their resentments. Typically, the periphery votes against the core area. If the core votes for party X, the periphery votes for party Y. Much depends on how the core area acquired the peripheral region. If by conquest, the periphery long remembers this fact, as has the U.S. South. Scotland and Wales show their resentments at England by voting Labour, but England stays Tory. France south of the Loire River and Spain south of the Tagus River tend to go Socialist, acting out their resentments of, respectively, Paris and Madrid. The south of Italy, on the other hand, was long a bastion of conservatism. More recently, the north of Italy spawned a breakaway movement over resentment at paying for the impoverished south. As the Soviet Union's republics held free and fair elections, many strongly nationalistic republic governments took office and proclaimed their independence. The hatred of Lithuanians and Georgians against Moscow led them to support nationalistic parties.

3. *Voting follows religion.* Religious attitudes tend to be distributed regionally. Indeed, the religion factor is one explanation for points 1 and 2 that were just discussed. Big cities tend to be less religious than small towns, inclining the cities to vote liberal or left. Some regions have different religions than the core area. Scottish Presbyterians show their difference from the Anglicans by not voting Tory. German Protestants are still a bit inclined to see the Christian Democratic Union as a Catholic party and therefore to vote against it, a tendency muddied by other factors. Immediately after unification, largely Protestant East Germany went CDU but has since swung to leftist parties, the SPD and Left. Religion helped to pull the Soviet Union apart, as Muslim republics installed Islamic administrations that are implicitly anti-Christian. In the Caucasus and Central Asia, persons of Christian origin, even if irreligious, feel threatened. Surrounded by hostile Islamic peoples, they elect implicitly anti-Muslim Christian governments, as in Armenia and Georgia.

Compare Percent of Catholics per Land (top) to Percent of CDU/CSU Vote per Land (bottom)

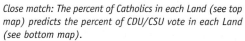

Close match: The percent of Catholics in each Land (see top map) predicts the percent of CDU/CSU vote in each Land (see bottom map).

223

German voting patterns also tended to follow class, region, and religion, but the addition of East Germany in 1990 muddied some of these generalizations. The general dealignment of the period muddied them further.

In Germany religion means Catholic or Protestant. German Catholics are more likely to vote CDU, so heavily Catholic Länder such as Baden-Wurttemberg generally go CDU. The CSU has long had Catholic Bavaria sewn up. Further north, in the largely Protestant Länder, the SPD tends to do better, as they do in large cities. In Germany the rural and small-town vote tends to the CDU. German workers, especially those belonging to a labor union, are generally more loyal to the SPD than British workers are to the Labour party. Thus, an *ideal-typical* (see page 128) SPD voter in Germany is a Protestant worker in a large northern city. His CDU counterpart is a middle-class Catholic in a small southern town. The Free Democrats appeal to some of the Protestant middle class, the Greens attract the young, and the Left attracts East Germans who feel left out of prosperity.

East Germany, although almost completely Protestant and with a pre-1933 SPD voting tradition, went heavily Christian Democrat in 1990. As the costs and disappointments of unification sank in, some East Germans moved to the SPD, confirming the SPD as a party more attractive to Protestants and to urban workers. But a good number of Ossis lent their votes to the Greens (who had merged with the East German Alternative/90 in early 1993), then to the ex-Communist Party of Democratic Socialism, and in 2005 to the Left party. German voting, like the German party system, has become more complex and less predictable.

Key Terms

bimodal (p. 212)

catchall (p. 215)

center-seeking (p. 212)

dealignment (p. 216)

Rechtsstaat (p. 218)

transparency (p. 217)

unimodal (p. 212)

Weltanschauung (p. 215)

Further Reference

Alan, Christopher S., ed. *Transformation of the German Political Party System: Institutional Crisis or Democratic Renewal?* Providence, RI: Berghahn, 1999.

Braunthal, Gerard. *Parties and Politics in Modern Germany.* Boulder, CO: Westview Press, 1996.

Dalton, Russell J., ed. *The New Germany Votes: Reunification and the Creation of a German Party System.* Providence, RI: Berg, 1993.

Glees, Anthony. *Reinventing Germany: German Political Development since 1945.* Providence, RI: Berg, 1996.

Hancock, M. Donald, and Henry Krisch. *Germany.* Boulder, CO: Westview, 1998.

Huelshoff, Michael G., Andrei Markovits, and Simon Reich, eds. *From Bundesrepublic to Deutschland: German Politics after Unification.* Ann Arbor, MI: University of Michigan Press, 1993.

Lafontaine, Oskar. *The Heart Beats on the Left.* Malden, MA: Blackwell, 2000.

Mayer, Margit, and John Ely, eds. *The German Greens: Paradox between Movement and Party.* Philadelphia, PA: Temple University Press, 1998.

Padgett, Stephen, ed. *Parties and Party Systems in the New Germany.* Brookfield, VT: Dartmouth, 1993.

Pulzer, Peter. *German Politics, 1945–1995.* New York: Oxford University Press, 1996.

Chapter 16

WHAT GERMANS
QUARREL ABOUT

The great quarrel in Germany—indeed, in most of Europe—is over the overly generous welfare state and its onerous taxes and rules that keep unemployment high and economic growth low. Keep them or cut them? Once a welfare state has been built, it is terribly difficult to cut, because people expect the state to provide job and income security and fear the uncertainties of a free economy. (Notice how U.S. politicians of both parties do not cut Social Security or Medicare.) German welfare benefits grew during the **Wirtschaftswunder** of the postwar years, when it seemed like the economy could afford almost anything. But now the miracle is over. Business leaders warn that Germany is no longer competitive, but many Germans are so comfortable with the welfare state that they resist any trims in it.

Questions to Consider

1. What made the German *Wirtschaftswunder?* Can there be a second one?
2. What did the German Model consist of? Is it over?
3. Which country has the highest labor costs? What are its effects?
4. How were the major "left" governments of West Europe different? Who did the best job?
5. Could East and West Germany have merged gradually?
6. Why are immigrants necessary for a country like Germany?
7. How does the new Berlin Republic differ from the Bonn Republic?
8. What difficulties came with the euro?

Nothing produces economic miracles, it has been said, like losing a war. This is surely the case in West Germany and Japan following World War II. There was simply nothing to do but work. Some German factories were destroyed by Allied bombing. Many machine tools were ripped out and shipped back to the Soviet Union by the vengeful Red Army. The British and Americans patched up their old industries, but the Germans were forced to rebuild theirs with new and more efficient equipment.

The aftermath of war had some psychological benefits. Almost everybody was poor; food and fuel were barely sufficient for survival. This produced greater material equality among Germans; income distribution was more equitable in Germany (and Japan) than in the victorious countries. Consequently, the bitter class antagonisms found in Britain and France did not develop in Germany. Everyone started from a similar low level, and most West Germans felt that everyone got a share of economic growth. Furthermore, defeat in the war and empty stomachs following it left Germans with more modest expectations than Britons or Americans, who expected some kind of postwar paradise. For West Germans after Hitler, hard work to foster economic growth was their only outlet for national pride.

Under the leadership of the CDU and Economics Minister (later Chancellor) Ludwig Erhard, Bonn pursued a largely laissez-faire policy. While Britain turned to Labour's welfare state and France

Wirtschaftswunder   German for "economic miracle." (See page 227.)

Sozialmarkt   "Social market," Germany's postwar capitalism aimed at reconstruction and welfare.

Modell Deutschland   German economic model.

consensus   Agreement among all constituent groups.

Mitbestimmung   "Codetermination," unions participating in company decisions.

wage restraint   Unions holding back on compensation demands.

to *planification* after World War II, West Germany relied mainly on market forces. During the 1950s, the West German economy recovered almost miraculously. It was built on the **Sozialmarkt** of Ludwig Erhard, which was basically a free market but aimed by bank loans to socially needed ends, such as rebuilding Germany's bombed-out cities. It continued and expanded the welfare state begun by Bismarck. Some called it "capitalism with a conscience."

During the 1970s the **Modell Deutschland** that stressed **consensus** among all social groups was successful and admired. In it, no one's views were ignored. Workers, for example, have **Mitbestimmung**, which gives unions a role in overall company policy. Each large firm has a supervisory board with half its directors chosen by labor and half by top management and big shareholders. For example, in 1999, when BMW ousted its top management, the ten worker representatives on the board vetoed a proposed chief executive they did not like and got one they did. Codetermination is one reason Germany has had very few strikes; workers feel they are part of the system. With slow economic growth and massive unemployment, however, critics now blame codetermination for stifling economic innovation and expansion.

The End of the Miracle

By the time of unification in 1990, however, the miracle had worn off. German wages and welfare benefits had climbed during the 1970s and 1980s, making Germany less of an economic dynamo. Basically, rapid economic growth comes from wages that lag behind productivity. That is, where you have skilled workers efficiently producing desired goods at prices that beat others, you will gain a large piece of the world market. Germany (and Japan, with a few years' lag time) fit this pattern. After the war, German workers' skills were still high, and much of Germany's infrastructure was intact. German labor unions practiced **wage restraint**; they did not demand every DM they could get but let capital grow until it provided jobs and good wages for all. This period—from the 1950s through the 1970s—was the time of Germany's rapid growth. In contrast, British and U.S. productivity lagged behind wage increases, meaning they sold less and less to the world.

By the 1980s, however, German wages surpassed U.S. wages, German social taxes were much higher, and German productivity was no longer growing quickly. In the meantime, America was getting more and more competitive; wages had been essentially stagnant (by the time you account for inflation) since the early 1970s, but productivity grew. The U.S. welfare floor, always much lower than the German, was less of a tax burden. By 1997, with U.S. labor averaging $18 an hour (including benefits and taxes) while German labor cost $28, and with U.S. productivity some 20 percent higher than in Germany, it cost two-thirds as much to make something in the United States as in the other major industrial countries (see box on page 232). Until recently, individual and corporate taxes were more steeply progressive in Germany than in America, and Germany still has far more regulations. Under such economic pressures, German capital flees abroad. German investment in the United States, for example, has created some two-thirds of a million jobs for Americans while job growth in Germany stagnates.

By the 1990s, Germans enjoyed short work weeks (thirty-five hours), long vacations (six to eight weeks!), the world's highest pay, lush unemployment benefits, male retirement at sixty-three (women at sixty) with fat pensions, and almost no strikes. With these *labor-force rigidities* (see page 152), however, firms hired few new workers. In 2005 German unemployment hit a postwar record of 12.6 percent overall (twice as high in the east as in the west) even as the German economy grew smartly and again became the world's biggest exporter (in dollar amounts), ahead of the United States or China. GDP growth does not guarantee low unemployment. Can Germany's consensus model still work in a very different world from the 1950s when it was created? Some urged abandoning the cozy consensus model for a more competitive "Anglo-Saxon" model, which the German left (like the French) denounced as savage "neo-liberalism." Many Germans did not understand that competitive capitalism is precisely what made Germany prosperous.

blocked society One in which interest groups prevent major, necessary change.

In a 1996 austerity package, the Bundestag cut Germans' health, unemployment, and welfare benefits and gradually raised the retirement age to sixty-five for men and sixty-three for women (now being slowly raised to sixty-seven, already the U.S. norm). Kohl's CDU government defended the cuts as moderate, necessary, and supported by most Germans, who were fed up with high taxes. Opponents of the cuts, including the SPD, called them "socially obscene" and the "destruction of the welfare state." The cuts helped the SPD win the 1998 elections, but Schröder had to deliver similar austerity budgets, tightening of welfare benefits, and greater work and wage flexibility. The left wing of his SPD howled—some deserted to the new Left party—but the economy allowed him no choice. Merkel campaigned on going further than Schröder. She pledged to stand up to Germany's powerful unions, drop job-protection laws, and cut the very high payroll taxes that fund the welfare state. The SPD did not like this Thatcher-type program, and they were half of her coalition. Germany could be stuck over this vital question.

And here we see the trouble with the consensus model. With all major groups having a say, any one group can veto change. Try telling unions they will have to accept lower pay and work longer hours. Try telling factories and farmers they must lose their subsidies. Try telling the jobless that their unemployment benefits must be cut. Try telling retirees that their pensions must be trimmed. All fight like hell to keep their cushy deals. Earlier, France had been called a **blocked society**; now the title may be passing to Germany. (Does the United States exhibit some of these problems?)

Comparison

EUROPE'S DIFFERENT "LEFTS"

Most of West Europe has recently had center-left governments, but notice—comparing Blair, Jospin (France's premier 1997–2002), and Schröder (Germany's chancellor 1998–2005)—how they were quite different. Blair accepted the Thatcherite notion that business, not government, creates jobs. Instead of trying to undo her promarket reforms, he tackled important noneconomic issues—Northern Ireland, devolution, education—that the Tories had neglected. In Blair's "Third Way," there was little left left.

Jospin, on the other hand, proclaimed "democratic socialism" and was a still-traditional *dirigiste* who never publicly accepted the primacy of markets (few French do); he still saw a major role for the French state. For example, to cut unemployment he proposed publicly funded jobs and training. In France, the left was still left.

Schröder's "New Center" accepted the free market but turned almost reflexively to Germany's consensus model—his Alliance for Jobs, an attempt to bring down unemployment that did not work. In a parallel to Jospin's plan, Schröder aimed to place 100,000 German youths in jobs or training programs. In each country "left" meant something different, something rooted in each land's political culture.

Schröder promoted an "Alliance for Jobs"—labor, capital, and government together coming up with ideas to create jobs. It was an attempt to refurbish the old consensus model when there was no more consensus. It produced few jobs. Schröder then had to carry out—with much anger inside his own SPD—what he called Agenda 2010, conservative-type reforms in taxation, welfare, and workforce flexibility. Schröder's policies were not much different from Kohl's. The need for economic reforms also leaves Angela Merkel little choice.

Geography

COULD GERMANY HAVE UNIFIED GRADUALLY?

Probably not. The real problem behind the difficulties and costs of merging the two Germanys is the speed with which it occurred. Some Social Democrats and economists urged a gradual unification over several years. But that really could not happen, for once the ball started rolling, it could not be slowed. Events took on a fast-paced life of their own.

1. The hardline Honecker regime in East Berlin refuses all thought of reform for most of 1989. But East Germans, seeing reforms taking place elsewhere in the Soviet bloc, become more restless.

2. Hungary lets East Germans exit into Austria. The Communist regime in Budapest had pledged not to let East German tourists flee to the West, but in the summer of 1989 they stop enforcing this pledge. Why? My hunch is that debt-burdened Hungary, by then under reform-minded Communists, got some nice financing from Bonn. Economic carrots had long been part of West German policy in East Europe. At an accelerating rate, thousands of East Germans "vacation" in Hungary but proceed to West Germany. East Berlin screams in protest, and Budapest shrugs. By September, more than 18,000 East Germans flee via Hungary, another 17,000 via Czechoslovakia. East Germany closes its border with Czechoslovakia to staunch the flow.

3. Massive demonstrations break out in East Germany in September, centered in Leipzig. In October Gorbachev visits to urge reform and warn Honecker, "Life punishes those who delay." Clearly, Gorbachev wishes to be rid of the problems and expenses of maintaining a Soviet empire in East Europe. By now some 100,000 protesters march in Leipzig chanting "Gorby! Gorby!"

4. Honecker orders a "Chinese solution" like the massacre at Tiananmen Square that June (see page 460) and tells police to get ready to fire on the Leipzig demonstrators. But security chief Egon Krenz fears catastrophe and countermands the order. On October 18, Honecker is out and Krenz becomes party chief and president. By now a million East Germans, led by intellectuals in the New Forum movement, protest for democracy.

5. On November 9, 1989, Krenz orders the Berlin Wall opened to gain some good will and time for reform. The Wall has kept East Germans locked in since 1961, and now tens of thousands pour into the West with no intention of returning. At this point, the days of a separate East Germany are numbered. Krenz resigns; much has happened because he countermanded the order to fire on protesters. Liberal and reform-minded Communists take over the party and government and pledge free elections.

6. Too many East Germans pour into the West because they are not sure that their own system is going to change. They want the good life of West Germany. Some half a million come across in the four months after the Wall opens, overburdening West Germany's job and apartment market, financial resources, and patience. Stay home, Chancellor Kohl urges; we will merge and rescue you soon enough.

7. Free East German elections in March 1990 put Christian Democrats in power. They see things Kohl's way and want speedy unification; this is why East Germans voted for them. Impatiently, East Germans want West Germany's economic prosperity.

8. Bonn gives East Germans a favorable exchange rate. East German marks are not worth much, but East

How to Merge Two Economies

The sudden merging of two very different systems added to Germany's economic difficulties. Over forty-five years, the largely free-market West German economy had become a world giant, in some years exporting more (in dollar value) than the United States. The centrally controlled and planned East German economy, although it was the envy of the East bloc, had a per capita GDP half that of West Germany. Wessis were roughly twice as rich as Ossis. West German products were desired

Germans argue that they have worked for and saved Ostmarks for decades. They demand a one-to-one exchange. Bonn argues that Ostmarks are essentially funny money and should be exchanged at a much lower rate. They compromise on one-to-one for each Ossi's first 2,000 marks (about $1,000) and one Westmark for two East above 2,000. It is a generous deal for East Germans, but if Bonn had not agreed to it, Ossis would have continued to pour into West Germany. In a sense, the one-to-one rate is a bribe to get them to stay put. On July 2, 1990, the Westmark becomes the official currency for both Germanys.

9. East Germans buy everything Western, nothing Eastern. With Westmarks in their pockets and Western products on store shelves, they turn their backs on their own products, now seen as junk. Suddenly, competing in a free market with the West, the East German economy collapses; it never had a chance to adjust.

Could anything have been done to prevent or slow the preceding sequence? We would have to go back to step one and get the Honecker regime committed to reforms that would gradually turn the East German economy into a market system that could compete with Western products. Then the two economies could merge without one of them collapsing. But Honecker was a devoted Communist to whom marketization meant abandoning communism, something he would not budge on. And once East Germans started pouring across, what could Bonn do? Rebuild the border fence between the two Germanys to make East Germans wait at home? The critics of too-rapid unification are right: It would have been better if it had been slower. But that was not in the cards.

Top: Brandenburg Gate in East Berlin behind the Wall. Bottom: Party time as the Wall comes down in November 1989.

unit labor costs What it costs to manufacture the same item in different countries.

throughout the world; East German products were sold mostly to the Soviet bloc plus some Third World lands too poor to afford better. Two very different German economies existed side-by-side but with little trade between them, so they did not directly compete.

In 1990, the physical and political barriers between the two Germanys suddenly disappeared. West German currency and products flooded into East Germany, and the East German economy collapsed with a speed and thoroughness no one had foreseen. It was thought to have been a working economy that just needed modernization. Many supposed that West German firms would bring their capital and know-how into East German enterprises and quickly lift them up to West German levels. This scenario was much too rosy. East Germans simply ceased buying East German products as soon as they could buy nicer West German goods. As gigantic state subsidies ended, East German factory and farm production plummeted. East German unemployment shot from essentially zero into the millions, and both East and West Germans turned angry. Few East German enterprises survived the transition to a market economy.

Saving the East German economy required tons of money, far more than anticipated—€ 1.3 trillion (about $1.5 trillion) so far—from the federal government. Ultimately, of course, it comes from West German taxpayers. Some 4 percent of Germany's GDP flows to the east every year as subsidies. Thus, the first great quarrel of united Germany grew out of how to merge the two economies and who was going to pay for it. Chancellor Kohl said the bailout of the East German economy could be done without higher taxes. The opposition Social Democrats scoffed—their chief, Oskar Lafontaine, chided, "read my lips" (in English) in the 1990 election—and sure enough, the Kohl government next year put on a 7.5 percent "solidarity surcharge" on income taxes. Nobody liked the tax, which lasted for years, but Germany needed it to try to get its budget deficit below 3 percent of GDP, as required for the new European currency. (Both France and Germany now continually run deficits higher than 3 percent, and the *European Central Bank* does not know what to do about it.)

Comparison

WHO WINS THE MANUFACTURING RACE?

Not necessarily those with the lowest wages. What you need to win in the global manufacturing race is lower wages combined with higher productivity. Here is how the situation looked among our five industrialized democracies in the late 1990s:

	Total Hourly Labor Costs	Unit Labor Costs
Britain	$16	106
Japan	19	103
France	18	100
Germany	28	100
United States	18	67

Source: Swedish Employers' Federation, OECD

Total hourly labor costs, here for 1997, include bonuses, benefits, and social security and other taxes (such as health insurance), which in Germany add 80 percent to regular wages. These "social taxes" are low in the United States and Japan. **Unit labor costs** combine total labor costs with productivity. The clear winner: the United States. Productivity figures, though, change constantly. The German figures here are already an improvement; a few years earlier German labor costs were $32 and its unit labor costs were 140. China surely beats them all but is not a member of the OECD, and its productivity gains are hard to measure.

East Germany before and after the arrival of West German money: a Street in Stalsund (Stralsund) in 1990 (top) and in 1995 (bottom).

Can West Germany's earlier economic miracle apply to the East German economy? The desperate postwar feelings that made West Germans work so hard are not found in post-Wall East Germany. Under the Communists' centrally planned economic system, East Germans did not develop attitudes of hard work and entrepreneurial risk-taking. They got used to a vast welfare system that offered security for all but few incentives for individual exertion. Ossis say, "It's not our fault that the Communists saddled us with an inferior economic system. Besides, you Wessis got billions of dollars in U.S. Marshall Plan aid; we got ripped off by the Soviets. So it's only fair that you boost us up to your standard of living, and quickly."

Many West Germans are appalled at such attitudes, which seem like excuses to avoid work. Why set up factories in East Germany when you can get good productivity out of Poles and Czechs, whose labor costs are a fraction of German levels? Resentment flared in each half of Germany against the other half. From this resentment, especially in the East, grew some of the extremist groups that targeted foreign workers.

How Much Welfare?

As we considered with Britain, European countries are welfare states, and all are under pressure to cut welfare. One-third of Germany's GDP goes for social spending, a heavy tax burden on Germany's manufacturing competitiveness. Germany's welfare system is Europe's oldest, tracing back to Bismarck's innovations in the late nineteenth century. Since then, it has grown and become accepted by just about everyone, even conservatives. The CDU, for example, has a tradition of Catholic trade-unionism.

But now one of the great questions of European politics has become, "How much welfare can we afford?" Even previously committed social democrats worry that their generous welfare provisions are pricing them out of the market. Both CDU and SPD governments had to cut unemployment and welfare benefits.

Gastarbeiter   "Guest workers," temporary labor allowed into Germany.

fertility rate   How many children an average woman bears.

demography   Study of population growth.

German pensions are also generous, but to pay for them German workers must contribute 20 percent of their wages, and this will soon rise to an impossible 30 percent if present trends continue. Without further drastic reforms, the German welfare system will impose an impossible burden on the younger generation (see box below).

■ The Flood of Foreigners

Like Britain and France, Germany gets immigrants from poor countries seeking jobs while citizen resentment of them builds. There are 7.4 million foreigners in Germany (some 9 percent of Germany's population), mostly from Mediterranean nations (Turkey, ex-Yugoslavia, Greece, Italy, and Spain). Over 2 million are workers; the rest are spouses and children.

The trend started in 1955 when the economic miracle had absorbed all working Germans and was still short of labor. Italian and later Spanish **Gastarbeiter** were invited to West Germany and they came, eager for the plentiful jobs. Soon Germans began abandoning dirty, dangerous, and unskilled work for better positions, leaving their old jobs to foreigners. At first the impact seemed temporary: The migrant workers were supposed to stay three years and rotate back home. But the "guest workers," faced with unemployment at home, often remained and sent for their families. Large numbers began arriving from Turkey, where unemployment is especially high. There are

Geography

THE GEOGRAPHY OF DEMOGRAPHY

Almost all industrialized countries produce few babies. In Germany, for example, despite hefty children's allowances, an average German woman bears only 1.3 children, one of the world's lowest **fertility rates** (which is not the same as the "birth rate," a different measure). France has the same rate. In comparison, an average American woman bears 2.1 children, a British 1.7, a Japanese 1.3, and a Russian 1.2. Poor countries generally have higher rates: Nigeria at 5.8, Mexico at 2.8, Iran at 2.6, but China at only 1.8.

Replacement fertility rate is 2.1—one for each parent and a little to spare—the level at which a population will hold steady, and it is found in few advanced industrialized countries. Large families are not prized, and women now have increased educational and career options. These rates take no account of immigration and are one reason why all of these countries need

immigrants to do the work that supports the increasing portion of the population that is retired.

By 2025, an estimated 24 percent of Germans and Japanese will be sixty-five or over; some 20 percent of Britons, French, and Americans will be in that age bracket. By 2050, Germany's population is projected to drop to 60 million from 83 million, with one German in three over 65. All of West Europe faces the problem of soon having too few people in the work force supporting too many people in retirement. Germany already has the heaviest burden, with two working persons supporting one retiree, one reason German taxes are high. By 2035, the ratio could become an impossible 1:1. The solution: either more babies, more immigrants, or (what is already happening) later retirements. **Demography** leads to tough political choices.

Turkish women in the Kreuzberg district of Berlin, a center for Turkish immigrants, of whom there are 2.3 million in Germany.

now some 2.3 million Turks in the FRG; whole neighborhoods have turned Turkish, and the Turkish *döner* (lamb slices and salad in a pita) has become Germany's fast food (highly recommended). The "guests" had come to stay.

By the 1980s, poor people worldwide had discovered Germany's very liberal asylum law. Simply upon arriving in Germany, foreigners had only to claim they were politically persecuted back home. Although motivation was usually economic, legal tangles let asylum-seekers stay in Germany for years, all the while on welfare. The FRG, along with Austria, strengthened border controls and expelled many undocumented visitors. Amid great political controversy (with the SPD fighting it), the asylum law was

tightened to exclude most claimants. Britain, which also had a liberal asylum policy, had to do the same.

As in Britain and France, antiforeign feeling grew; many Germans believe foreigners bring crime and terrorism. Two-thirds of Germans oppose more immigration. A new racism appeared in Germany, exaggerated by FRG law: A person of German descent arriving from Russia or Romania, whose ancestors had left Germany centuries ago, gets instant FRG citizenship; a Turk born and raised in Germany could not, until recently, become a German citizen. Turks and Africans who had been working in Germany for many years were murdered. In some cases, police and

Although media attention focused on the crimes of a few against foreign workers in Germany, large crowds, such as this one at Cologne's Opera Square, turned out to protest antiforeigner sentiments as a type of racism.

xenophobia Fear and hatred of foreigners.

jus sanguinis Latin for "right of blood," citizenship based on descent.

jus soli Latin for "right of soil," citizenship given to those born in the country.

neighbors did nothing to stop the violence. On the other side, hundreds of thousands of Germans attended rallies and protests against **xenophobia** and violence.

Immigration has become a major issue, with the CDU/CSU strongly against. In 2005 Foreign Minister Joschka Fisher was humiliated by accusations of—wittingly or not—letting German consulates in Ukraine issue thousands of visas to human traffickers. Immigration to Germany, as in all of Europe, is now controlled. Germany issues limited numbers of "green cards" (they borrow the U.S. word for work visas) to skilled immigrants, such as 20,000 computer specialists from India. Conservative politicians huffed: *"Kinder statt Inder"* (Children instead of Indians), but the German fertility rate would have to shoot up to an impossible 3.8 (from the current 1.3) to fill the need. As more Germans retire, Germany will need some quarter of a million new workers a year. How can there be both 4 million unemployed and a need for new workers? Few of the unemployed have the skills for the job openings, and many will not take minimum-wage work.

Like the British and French National Front parties, small anti-immigrant parties sprang up in Germany that would expel foreigners and get tough on crime, issues the CDU/CSU used to its advantage. As in the United States, *multiculturalism* (see page 200) came under criticism. "Multiculturalism has failed, big time," said CDU leader Angela Merkel, who became chancellor in 2005. Actually, many immigrants are integrating into German society, much like the U.S. melting pot. There are SPD and Green Bundestag members of Turkish origin.

■ Is Berlin Weimar?

By most measures the Federal Republic of Germany is an unqualified success story. Its constitution, leading parties, and economy deserve to be studied by other countries. But some observers have wondered if, under the glittering surface, democracy has taken firm root. How will German institutions function with a multiparty system instead of a two-plus party system? Could the present democracy go the way of Weimar's?

Geography

CITIZENSHIP: BLOOD OR SOIL?

Europe traditionally used **jus sanguinis** to determine citizenship: If your parents were German, you are German. The United States from its beginning used **jus soli**: If you were born here, you are an American. Other countries of immigration, such as Australia and Brazil, also use *jus soli*. Slowly and grudgingly, Germany is introducing *jus soli*. Under SPD sponsorship, a 2000 law allows German citizenship for those who have resided eight years (down from fifteen) in the FRG and makes it automatic for children born in Germany, provided one parent lived there eight years. This is a major switch in Germany's definition of who is a German, and it provoked conservative opposition. Elections went against the SPD over the citizenship issue. (Notice the parallel with U.S. Democrats and Republicans on rights for immigrants.)

All survey data have said no. Germans have grown more democratic in their values. By now they are at least as committed to a pluralist, free, democratic society as the British and French. They weathered terrorism and economic downturns as well as any of their democratic neighbors. Now, with much pain and complaint, East Germans are slowly turning into free-market democrats.

Things have changed in both the domestic and international contexts of German democracy, however. Germany's consensus and welfare state has become rigid and costly. Like most of West Europe, Germany's wages, taxes, welfare benefits, and overregulation have led to high and seemingly incurable unemployment. Competition from low-wage, low-tax countries is fierce, and many German firms have moved production to Poland, the Czech Republic, or Slovakia. Berlin hotels send their laundry to Poland.

Both Germanys were children of the Cold War. At times, a third of a million U.S. soldiers were camped in West Germany, over half a million Soviet soldiers in East Germany. This situation was tense but stable. The FRG was firmly anchored to NATO and the European Union, the GDR to the **Warsaw Pact** and **Comecon**. Suddenly the international context changed. The Cold War is over and

Warsaw Pact   Soviet-led alliance of Communist countries, defunct.

Comecon   Trading organization of Communist countries, defunct.

European Central Bank   Supervises interest rates, money supply, and inflation in the euro area, like U.S. Fed.

Geography

EURO OR DM?

Germans were among the most enthusiastic supporters of European union, but many did not like the euro replacing the DM, symbol of a solid and hard-working German economy since it was introduced in 1948. If it had been brought to a vote, it would have failed in Germany. The euro debuted in 1999 with electronic transactions (such as credit-card purchases). Price tags gave the price in both euros and marks. In the beginning of 2002, however, the euro replaced paper money and coins in all twelve of its member countries (Britain not among them). No more DM, francs, or lire.

The euro brought some terrific advantages. No more changing money (with a fee of several percent) at borders. Trade and transactions could move even more freely across West Europe. American tourists were delighted with the simplicity of a uniform currency that was close to $1. Psychologically, the euro was meant to make Europeans feel equal to Americans and no longer dependent on the dollar.

But many Germans saw disadvantages. Merchants used the switch to boost prices. German currency was no longer under German control. Did the euro mean inflation? The Bundesbank, remembering the worthless Weimar and Nazi currencies, had been tough on

inflation. At German insistence, euro members had to limit their budget deficits to 3 percent to block inflation. The **European Central Bank** located in Frankfurt would supervise and fine any government that went over. But Germany was one of several countries that topped the limit in order to fund generous welfare benefits while cutting taxes. The ECB did not punish limit-breakers, and its credibility took a beating. If Germany and France cheat, why not everyone? That could bring inflation.

Some economists had warned of difficulties from locking West Europe into one currency and predicted that euroland could break up. Some countries need to expand money in circulation to promote growth; others need to freeze it to halt inflation. Ireland, on an economic roll, expanded currency over the limit and did not apologize. Some countries may cheat and print more euros than they are entitled to. (Each member country prints its own, with a standard pattern on one side and a national one on the other, all equally good.) If Europe's largest economy ever abandons or alters the terms of the euro, the EU would be drastically set back. In monetary policy, one size does not fit all.

Bonn Republic   West Germany, 1949–1990, with capital in Bonn.

Berlin Republic   Reunified Germany, since 1990, with capital in Berlin.

Germany is unified. The Soviet troops left and only a few U.S. troops remain. The **Bonn Republic** was anchored to the West. Will the new **Berlin Republic** stay cemented to Western ideals and institutions, or could it someday go off on its own, with a nationalistic and expansionist foreign policy?

Unlikely. German democracy is solid. The new institutions of a uniting Europe are making Germans good Europeans, and most major politicians are committed to Europe. The German army is small (250,000) and has no ABC (atomic, biological, or chemical) weapons. Three of Germany's European neighbors have nuclear weapons, which by itself means that Germany will never go on the warpath. Germans have no taste for militarism, for they have seen what it leads to. Germany has accomplished so much more by peaceful economic means than it could ever obtain by warlike means. The Weimar analogy is misplaced on present-day Germany. For a gigantic country that has trouble establishing democracy, let us next turn to Russia (starting with Chapter 18).

Key Terms

Berlin Republic (p. 238)

blocked society (p. 229)

Bonn Republic (p. 238)

Comecon (p. 237)

consensus (p. 228)

demography (p. 234)

European Central Bank (p. 237)

fertility rate (p. 234)

Gastarbeiter (p. 234)

jus sanguinis (p. 236)

jus soli (p. 236)

Mitbestimmung (p. 228)

Modell Deutschland (p. 228)

Sozialmarkt (p. 228)

unit labor costs (p. 232)

wage restraint (p. 228)

Warsaw Pact (p. 237)

Wirtschaftswunder (p. 228)

xenophobia (p. 236)

Further Reference

Brady, John S., Beverly Crawford, and Sarah Elise Wiliarty, eds. *The Postwar Transformation of Germany: Democracy, Prosperity, and Nationhood.* Ann Arbor, MI: University of Michigan Press, 2000.

Dettke, Dieter, ed. *The Spirit of the Berlin Republic.* New York: Berghahn, 2003.

Edinger, Lewis, and Brigitte Nacos. *From Bonn to Berlin.* New York: Columbia University Press, 1998.

Garton Ash, Timothy. *In Europe's Name: Germany and the Divided Continent.* New York: Random House, 1993.

Hampton, Mary, and Christian Soe, eds. *Between Bonn and Berlin: German Politics Adrift?* Lanham, MD: Rowman & Littlefield, 1998.

Heneghan, Tom. *Unchained Eagle: Germany After the Wall.* London: Pearson, 2000.

Larres, Klaus, ed. *Germany since Unification: The Development of the Berlin Republic*. New York: Palgrave, 2001.

Markovits, Andrei S., and Simon Reich. *The German Predicament: Memory and Power in the New Europe*. Ithaca, NY: Cornell University Press, 1997.

Mattox, Gale A., Geoffrey D. Oliver, and Jonathan B. Tucker, eds. *Germany in Transition: A Unified Nation's Search for Identity*. Boulder, CO: Westview, 1999.

Merkl, Peter H., ed. *The Federal Republic of Germany at Forty-Five: Union Without Unity*. New York: New York University Press, 1995.

Starkman, Ruth A., ed. *Transformations of the New Germany*. New York: Palgrave Macmillan, 2006.

Turner, Lowell. *Fighting for Partnership: Labor and Politics in Unified Germany*. Ithaca, NY: Cornell University Press, 1998.

Wolfgramm, Doris G. *The Kohl Government and German Reunification: Crisis and Foreign Policy*. Lewiston, NY: E. Mellen, 1997.

Chapter 17

THE EUROPEAN UNION

What is the European Union? A big nation? No, not nearly. A trade bloc? More than that. A confederation? Stronger than that. A federation? Well, trying to become one. There is no good name for this emerging entity. Instead of "nation-state," some suggest "market-state." At what point should we treat the EU as sovereign? Perhaps when it demonstrates that the powers of the EU headquarters in Brussels override the sovereignty of member states. In the United States, this began only after the Civil War.

Europe has a long way to go to reach the U.S. level of federation but with the debut of the **euro** currency took a big step in that direction. Some observers of the European scene argue that it makes less sense to consider the nations of West Europe separately, because increasingly it is the **European Union** that determines Europe's laws and economy. They have a point. A third to a half of Europe's new legislation comes out of EU headquarters in Brussels, not from national capitals. In standardizing currency, taxes, and regulations, increasingly the EU calls the tune.

Questions to Consider

1. How does the EU compare to the United States under the Articles of Confederation?
2. What would make the EU institutional structure effective?
3. What is a "qualified majority vote"? How might the problem be handled more simply?
4. Will the many nationalities of Europe ever think of themselves as "Europeans"?
5. What is the quarrel between "liberal" and "social" Europe?
6. Should the EU attempt to be a counterweight to U.S. power?
7. Why did ratification of the EU constitution fail?
8. Should the EU go "wider" or "deeper"? Or neither?
9. Does complexity limit popular acceptance of laws and constitutions?

But the EU is not yet a union in the way the United States is. EU members may opt out of some provisions they dislike. Of the EU's twenty-five members, only twelve currently use the euro (but most are likely to adopt it eventually). Sovereignty still resides in London, Paris, Berlin, and other national capitals rather than in Brussels. Institutionally, the EU structure is still undemocratic. A new constitution drafted in 2004 that reformed and consolidated the EU's several institutions failed to win ratification in 2005. The EU's inability to do anything about Bosnia in the 1990s illustrates the EU's lack of concerted foreign and security policies, something they are trying to overcome. European unity is building, but it will be some time before it blots out the distinctive politics of its member countries.

For the sake of consistency, we will examine the EU with the same five-part approach we use with our nine regular countries. We will, of course, try to avoid reification (see page 2), of pretending that the EU is already a sort of superstate. At a certain point, it may become a United States of Europe when it takes over sovereignty from its member countries; that is, when the important laws and policies are determined at the EU headquarters and not in Lisbon, Vienna, or Riga. The ultimate test of this will be when the EU can declare and wage war as a sovereign entity. Some Euroenthusiasts would like it to develop this ability soon.

IMPACT OF THE PAST

◼ A History of Wishful Thinking

Rome may have planted the seed of European unification with an empire that at its height in the first century A.D. covered most of West Europe, including the western portion of what is now Germany. Weakened from overextension and overrun by barbarians, the western half of the Empire finally collapsed in A.D. 476 (The eastern half lingered but slowly declined until the Ottoman Turks conquered its last remnant, the once-great capital of Constantinople, in 1453.) The Roman idea of a great empire, however, lived on.

euro (symbol: €) Currency for most of West Europe since 2002; value recently around $1.30. (See page 241.)

European Union (EU) Quasi-federation of most European states; began in 1957 as Common Market. (See page 241.)

When Charlemagne—himself of Frankish, that is to say barbarian, descent—formed his giant realm in 800 he called it the Holy Roman Empire. Charlemagne, the grandson of Charles Martel who beat back the invading Moors in 732, thought he could unite much of Western Christendom. His empire included all of what later became France (except Brittany), Belgium, and the Netherlands, most of Germany, and the northern half of Italy. These are precisely the same six countries that founded the Common Market in 1957, the core of the present European Union. Charlemagne is the father of European union, although his own empire was short-lived.

The Holy Roman Empire splintered among Charlemagne's grandsons, but the Roman Catholic Church kept alive a dream of European unity under the banner of "Christendom," led by Rome. Kings were supposed to be crowned by the pope or his representative to emphasize that they owed their first allegiance to Rome. Europe's kings, however, usually intent on expanding their kingdoms by war, often disobeyed the pope. The notion of Christendom perhaps reached a high point with a papal call

Geography

WHO'S IN THE EU?

Grouping EU members into six groups of three plus one group of five and one group of two will help you remember them. (And yes, they will be on the examination.)

The Big Three: Britain, France, Germany

The "Benelux" Countries: Belgium, Netherlands, Luxembourg

Latin Europe: Portugal, Spain, Italy

The Nordics: Denmark, Sweden, Finland

The Periphery: Ireland, Austria, Greece

Ten joined in 2004:

The Baltics: Lithuania, Latvia, Estonia (former Soviet republics)

The Central Europeans: Czech Republic, Hungary, Poland, Slovakia, Slovenia (first four were Soviet satellites, Slovenia was part of Yugoslavia)

The Mediterraneans: Cyprus (just the Greek part) and Malta

Notice that Norway and Switzerland are not members. Bulgaria and Romania are slated to join soon. Discussions have begun for eventual Turkish membership.

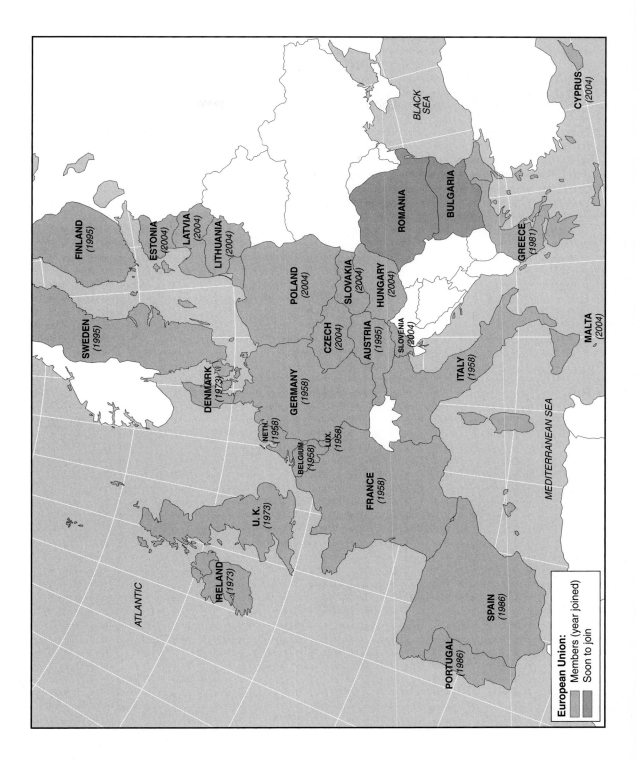

BLACK
SEA

CYPRUS
(2004)

FINLAND
(1995)

ESTONIA
(2004)

LATVIA
(2004)

LITHUANIA
(2004)

ROMANIA

BULGARIA

GREECE
(1981)

SWEDEN
(1995)

POLAND
(2004)

SLOVAKIA
(2004)

HUNGARY
(2004)

CZECH
(2004)

AUSTRIA
(1995)

SLOVENIA
(2004)

MALTA
(2004)

DENMARK
(1973)

GERMANY
(1958)

ITALY
(1958)

NETH.
(1958)

LUX.
(1958)

BELGIUM
(1958)

FRANCE
(1958)

MEDITERRANEAN SEA

U. K.
(1973)

IRELAND
(1973)

ATLANTIC

SPAIN
(1986)

PORTUGAL
(1986)

European Union:
Members (year joined)
Soon to join

Geography

There are no binding definitions of Europe's regions, but the end of the Cold War made the old division into eastern and western obsolete. There is still, to be sure, a West Europe, which may be defined as those states that touch the Atlantic, plus Italy and Switzerland. The ex-Communist countries in what used to be called East Europe, though, should be separated into Central Europe (a pre–World War II term now revived) and the Balkans.

Central Europe is the region between West Europe and Russia that used to be, in whole or in part, the Habsburgs' Austro-Hungarian Empire. It includes Austria, Hungary, the Czech Republic, Slovakia, Slovenia (do not confuse the two), Croatia, and Poland (southern Poland was Austrian-ruled before World War I, as was part of northern Italy). These countries are predominantly Catholic and (with the exception of Austria, which was never Communist) poorer than West Europe. Freed from Communist rule, most turned quickly to democracy and market economies.

The Balkans (Turkish for mountain), for centuries part of the Ottoman Turkish Empire, are largely Eastern Orthodox and a more backward area that includes Romania, Bulgaria, Albania, Greece (which was never Communist), and half of Yugoslavia. These countries lag behind Central Europe in setting up democracies and market economies. Yugoslavia was a special problem, because half of it (Slovenia and Croatia) was under the Habsburgs while the other half (Serbia, Bosnia, and Macedonia) was under the Turks. And it is precisely on this fault line that Yugoslavia violently split apart in the early 1990s, with half Central European in character and the other half Balkan. Russia, because it reaches clear to the Pacific is, along with other ex-Soviet republics, sometimes called "Eurasia."

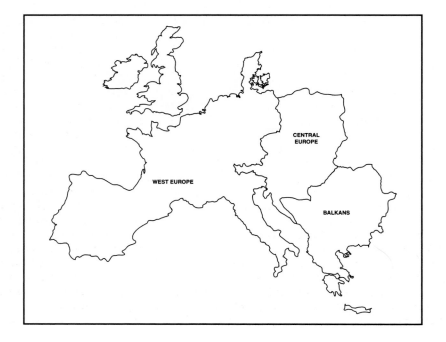

for the First Crusade (1096–1099), which knights from much of Europe joined to battle Islam for control of the Holy Land. Meanwhile, a loose grouping of princely states called the "Holy Roman Empire" lingered for centuries, mostly in Germany. French writer Voltaire wisecracked that it was "neither holy, nor Roman, nor an empire."

The Habsburg Empire reached its height of power and wealth in the sixteenth and seventeenth centuries when it attempted to unite Europe by the sword and return Protestant lands to the Catholic Church. With gold and silver freshly looted from Latin America and large armies from Spain and Central Europe, the Habsburgs might have done it, but Protestant countries and France fought them to a draw, formalized in the 1648 Treaty of Westphalia.

The **Enlightenment** revived the dream of a united Europe. Prussian philosopher Immanuel Kant suggested a "League for Perpetual Peace" in which Europe's monarchs would conciliate their differences. Napoleon briefly united most of Europe by conquering it, but his dreams died in the snows of Russia in 1812. Actually, occupation by

Enlightenment Eighteenth-century philosophical movement advocating reason and tolerance.

supranational Organizations that group together several countries, literally "above national."

Maastricht 1992 treaty setting up EU.

Schengen 1990 treaty ending passport controls in most of West Europe.

NAFTA 1994 North American Free Trade Agreement among the United States, Canada, and Mexico.

Mercosur "Southern market"; free-trade area covering southern part of South America.

Geography

BEYOND THE NATION-STATE?

Many thinkers suggest that the nation-state has outlived its usefulness. By jealously guarding its sovereignty, the modern state whips up destructive nationalism, spends too much on arms, engages in unnecessary wars, impedes the free flow of trade and travel, and is unable to tackle global problems such as hunger, overpopulation, and environmental degradation. The fact that the modern state is only about five centuries old suggests that it is not the last or highest form of human organization. Humanity may be headed toward **supranational** forms of organization.

At **Maastricht** in the Netherlands, in 1992 EC members concluded the Single European Act that turned the EC into the present European Union, its name since 1993. (The British Parliament debated long and hard before ratifying it.) Since 1994 the **Schengen** agreement has lifted passport controls among most EU members (but not Britain). Once you have gone through customs at the Paris airport, for example, you do not have to show your passport to enter Germany or Italy. (Britain stayed out of "Schengenland," but aloof Switzerland joined it.)

With such measures, the EU is our best example of a supranational political entity. It uses economic means to a political end: European integration. Is this a glimpse of the future? The EU's parallel—not a close one—is **NAFTA**, which links Canada, the United States, and Mexico in a common market that may expand southwards, eventually combining with **Mercosur**. NAFTA, however, has no supranational aims or structures; it is just a trade area with no intention of unifying the Americas into one political entity.

Supranationalism has some good and some bad points. The economic growth is good, but if the blocs erect trade barriers to keep out the products of other blocs, world trade will shrink and international tensions will climb. Already the EU is locked in chronic feuds with the United States on trade in everything from beef to jetliners. One of the great international questions today is whether to build regional trade blocs or skip the blocs and work on opening the entire world to unrestricted trade.

Napoleon's arrogant legions created Spanish, German, Russian, and other brands of nationalism, making Europe harder to unify than ever. After Napoleon, Europe's leading monarchs set up a vague "Concert of Europe" to suppress liberalism and nationalism. In 1849, a time of revolutionary hopes throughout Europe, French writer Victor Hugo appealed for a unified Europe that even included Russia. The point is that until recently a unified Europe had either been a cover for conquest or wishful thinking.

■ "Ever Closer Union"

Hitler too dreamed of a unified Europe, unified under Germany, that is. The horrors of World War II convinced many Europeans that nationalism must never be permitted to run amok again, that Europe had to move beyond the sovereignty of individual states and create a supranational entity. The path to unity, charted by two French officials, Jean Monnet and Robert Schuman (see box below), was to use economics to pull Europe together and gradually add political institutions.

Personalities

MONNET AND SCHUMAN

Jean Monnet   *Robert Schuman*

The Common Market was invented by two Frenchmen, a high civil servant, Jean Monnet, and a politician, Robert Schuman. Their ultimate aim: to prevent further war. Said Schuman, "Because Europe was not united, we have had war." They used economic means for a political end, and it worked, eventually becoming today's European Union.

Monnet (1888–1979) was a brilliant young French economist who very early realized that purely national economies were outmoded and ineffectual. During World War I he worked on meshing the Allies' economies and then worked as an economist at the Versailles Peace Conference, which set up the League of Nations. Monnet was the League's deputy secretary general from 1919 to 1923. In 1925 a New York investment bank made him its Paris partner. With the start of World War II in 1939, he was named chair of the Franco-British Economic Coordination Committee and urged a Franco-British economic union.

After the fall of France in 1940, Monnet worked in Washington as part of the British Supply Council. There he concluded that one of the keys to American prosperity was its continent-sized market wherein goods and labor moved without barriers. In 1943

Monnet went to newly liberated Algeria to become a top economic administrator of de Gaulle's Free French government. With France liberated, Monnet headed a committee to plan France's economic recovery, the 1947 Monnet Plan. De Gaulle appreciated Monnet's talents but never shared his interest in what de Gaulle called "supranational monstrosities."

Schuman (1886–1963), first elected to the French National Assembly in 1919, was arrested by the Gestapo after the Germans occupied France in 1940. He escaped and worked underground in the Resistance until Liberation in 1944 and then helped found the centrist Popular Republican Movement party. Schuman served as France's premier (1947–1948) and foreign minister (1948–1952), in which capacity he pushed for the European Coal and Steel Community, the first step toward today's EU.

It started with the six-nation European Coal and Steel Community in 1952 but really got serious with the 1957 Treaty of Rome, which set up what was colloquially known as the "Common Market." (The official name was the European Economic Community, EEC.) By cutting 10 percent off their tariffs with each other every year, after a decade goods, capital, and labor flowed freely from one member country to another. It was never intended to be just a trade bloc but was to move to "ever closer union," in the famous words of the 1957 treaty. With the Treaty of Maastricht coming into effect at the beginning of 1993, the EU took its present name and became one economy, which means that it was also becoming one political entity.

By the early 1960s the Common Market was such a resounding economic success that many other European countries decided they had to join. Free trade and the movement of workers among countries invigorated the economies of all six members. Nonmembers, who in 1960 organized the loose and ineffective European Free Trade Area (EFTA, dubbed the *Outer Seven*), fell behind. By the early 1960s, even Britain, which had originally rejected the Common Market, saw its economic advantage was in membership and applied. President de Gaulle of France, however, convinced that Britons were not wholehearted Europeans (he was correct), in 1963 vetoed British entry with his famous *Non!* Britain reapplied later and with Denmark and Ireland joined the EEC in 1973, making the Six into the Nine. (Ireland was the first non-NATO member to join the EEC, but several other non-NATO countries have since done the same.) Norway considered joining the EEC in 1973, but Norwegians rejected membership in a referendum.

The Nine became the Ten with Greece's entry in 1981, and then the Twelve with Spain and Portugal in 1986. Finland, Sweden, and Austria (nonmembers of NATO) made it the Fifteen when they joined in 1995. (Norwegians voted to stay out for the second time; they think they can go it alone with their oil.) The eastern part of Germany automatically became a member when it unified with West Germany in 1990. Freed from communism, Poland, Hungary, Czech Republic, Slovakia, Slovenia, Lithuania, Latvia, and Estonia immediately applied and, after six years of complex negotiations, joined in 2004, along with the Mediterranean islands of Malta and Cyprus. West Europe is their natural market, source of investment capital, and outlet for surplus labor. To stand outside the EU is to risk economic stagnation. Now even some Swiss would like to bring their aloof country into the EU.

The EU now has twenty-five member nations with a combined population of 456 million and a combined $12.3 trillion GDP. The United States has nearly the same GDP but a population of only 296 million; both the U.S. economy and population grow faster than the EU's.

The growth of the EU, both in members and economic integration, led to the gradual and cautious transfer of certain aspects of sovereignty from national capitals to Brussels, home of the EU Commission. With this developed some supranational political power. The EU introduced a common currency, the euro, in 2002, and as it forges a combined foreign policy, it will become more than a trade bloc and start taking on the characteristics of a nation, except that it will be composed of many states that will never fully surrender their sovereignty. It will be a new entity, one for which we do not yet have a good name.

THE KEY INSTITUTIONS

The EU's governing institutions are not those of an ordinary country. Most were initially set up by treaties in the 1950s when the Common Market had only six members and did not undertake nearly as many responsibilities. It was more like a meeting of ambassadors. Laws and regulations were

subsidiarity   Letting smaller
government units decide most
questions (equivalent to U.S. Tenth
Amendment, "reserved to the states").

supposed to be based on the principle of **subsidiarity**, of not concentrating power in Brussels. Now, with twenty-five members and Brussels handling major laws and responsibilities, the structure is odd, maybe unworkable. The 2004 constitution would have modernized and streamlined it but was voted down in France and the Netherlands (see below). The EU's main bodies are as follows:

The European Commission is a sort of twenty-five member collective presidency. Located in Brussels, which is in effect the EU's capital, the powerful but unelected Commission both initiates and executes laws and policies. The EU member states designate a Commission President with a five-year term. This president then, in consultation with member states, names one commissioner from each country, but they are supposed to represent the EU as a whole, not their countries. The Commission president, currently José Manuel Barroso of Portugal, does not have nearly the powers of the U.S. presidency. The Commission also oversees some 24,000 EU civil servants, most of them selected by competitive examinations.

The Council of the European Union (formerly Council of Ministers) is a sort of upper house of twenty-five ministers but in a unique way. Ministers are sent from their home-country cabinets to Brussels to represent their country. Which minister attends depends on the subject area under consideration. Each country's foreign minister, for example, participates when the Council discusses external relations. When the Council takes up farm issues (a very big and expensive item), twenty-five agricultural ministers attend.

The Council has a six-month rotating presidency, really little more than a temporary chairperson who also changes along with subject areas. The first half of 2006 was Austria's turn, the second half Finland's, so meetings on the environment in the fall of 2006 were chaired by Finland's environment minister. The Council, often jointly with the European Parliament, decides on Commission initiatives and budgets and can veto them.

Voting in the Council is weighted according to population, but with much compression. The four biggest members—Britain, France, Germany, and Italy—get twenty-nine votes each. Little Malta gets three votes; total is 321. Until 1987 unanimity was required, which meant even one small country could veto something. Now most issues require a *qualified majority* to pass. First, a majority of the twenty-five member countries (in some cases, two-thirds) must approve. Second, 232 out of the 321 total votes must be for it. Third, if a member state requests, states representing 62 percent of the EU population must be for it. Some sensitive areas, such as taxes and immigration policy, still require unanimity. This complicated system (everything about the EU is complicated) is designed to prevent either the big countries deciding everything or little countries blocking everything. (Notice how the U.S. bicameral system is designed to do the same.)

The European Parliament, which has offices in both Brussels and Strasbourg, France (near the German border), is a bit like a lower house. It can censure the Commission and ask it to resign, but this has never happened. The 732 Members of the European Parliament (MEPs) are elected directly in their home countries for five years. Like the Council, with whom it shares legislative and budgetary powers, seats are somewhat proportional to population, ranging from ninety-nine for Germany to five for Malta. MEPs are organized along EU-wide party lines, ranging from Socialists through Christian Democrats. The 2004 EU constitution would have made the European Parliament more important and helped solve the EU's "democratic deficit."

The European Court of Justice, located in Luxembourg, is a sort of EU supreme court. Its twenty-five judges adjudicate the growing body of EU law, including claims by and against the Commission and disputes among member states.

Democratic Deficit

The student of comparative politics notices at least two things about EU institutions: (1) They lack a clear locus of power, and (2) they are not very democratic. The EU structure has no strong executive like the presidents or prime ministers we have studied. This is understandable, as the EU is not a sovereign entity and was not set up as one. The EU executive is the twenty-five member Commission. The Council and Parliament have only weak checks on the Commission. Only the Parliament is democratically elected, but turnouts for MEP elections are weaker than for national elections, as Europeans recognize that the Europarliament is far less important than their own parliaments.

The EU draft constitution of 2004 was meant to remedy some of these defects, but it failed to win ratification. The Common Market, later the EU, has never had a constitution. It was started and built in a series of treaties between member countries. Its structure, at first very loose, was better suited to just the original six members. By the time it got to fifteen, it was clumsy. Even before it reached the current twenty-five in 2004, many realized that EU institutions had to be codified and streamlined.

Drafting a constitution began in 2003 with 105 delegates from all member countries under the chairmanship of former French President Valéry Giscard d'Estaing (1974–1981). Self-consciously modeling themselves on the United States in the late 1780s, they called the meeting their "Convention," capitalized Constitution, and likened pro-ratification arguments to the *Federalist Papers*. It was a poor analogy, as twenty-five European countries with diverse languages and histories are a lot harder to unite than thirteen colonies that were culturally very close and had not (yet) warred among themselves.

Comparison

U.S. FOUNDING DRAMAS

It was relatively easy for the United States to form a distinctly American consciousness. A nation of immigrants crossing the seas to enter a new land where all started equal and fresh—and had to learn English—was quite different from the centuries of historical, linguistic, and religious baggage the Europeans still carry. The founding American dramas—the Revolutionary War with England and the framing of the Constitution—stirred mass enthusiasm. Washington was a genuinely charismatic figure. Americans eagerly read and discussed the eighty-five *Federalist* essays by Alexander Hamilton, James Madison, and John Jay and after two years of debate made an informed decision to adopt the Constitution. All this planted a political culture taught and accepted by generations of Americans.

Europe was quite different. It had no distinct founding drama, just a sense of weariness and futility following World War II, in which the enemy had been fellow Europeans. During the long Cold War, America in large measure took over the defense of Europe as the leading power in NATO. There were no great historical incidents or charismatic figures that caused Europeans to rally together. Instead of dramas that stirred the heart, Europe was founded and is still constructed by bureaucrats who produce thousands of pages of mind-numbing rules no one can love or even understand. A constitution is more than a big law; to be effective, it must have an emotional or psychological component.

The EU constitution that was completed in 2004 was not a total redo of current usages but more of a consolidation that included the following:

- A Council president who could be elected for up to five years instead of the rotating six-month presidencies staffed by member-country top leaders. This would have strengthened the Council presidency.
- A new European foreign minister who would try to get the EU to speak with one voice on the world scene, implicitly to stand up to the United States. Many Europeans liked this idea but did not like giving up their countries' ability to stake out individual national positions on foreign policy.
- Qualified majority voting in the European Parliament that would have required approval by fifteen of the twenty-five member states representing at least 65 percent of the EU's total population.

The proposed constitution contained only modest changes from the existing setup, but it was entirely elitist, far too long and detailed, and written in legal jargon. When subject to referendums in France and the Netherlands, ordinary citizens found fault with it for those very reasons. (See below for why it was rejected.)

THE POLITICAL CULTURE OF THE EU

One of Italy's nineteenth century unifiers famously proclaimed, "Having made Italy, we must now make Italians." He meant that his countrymen continued to think of themselves as Tuscans, Sicilians, Venetians, and so on, not as Italians. The same problem now applies to citizens of the EU: Few think of themselves as Europeans, and most still think of themselves as French, German, Italian, and so on. Making them psychologically European will take a long effort.

European enthusiasm comes in spurts or waves. A few years of enthusiasm and adding new members is typically followed by a decade or two of indifference as the EU adjusts to its enlarged size. In the early 1960s, not long after the Common Market began its tariff cutting, Europeans were proud of what they were building. Some put EEC flag decals (a circle of gold stars on a blue field) on their cars. By the late 1960s, however, the enthusiasm had largely faded. New members in the 1970s and 1980s brought other spurts of Euroenthusiasm. The massive addition of ten new members in 2004, most of them in the east, brought doubts that the EU was trying to swallow too many poor countries at once. It will likely take some years for another wave of enthusiasm.

utilitarian Promotes material payoffs, "useful."

A basic problem is that the EU was founded on an economic or **utilitarian** basis: "Sure the Common Market is good. It makes my country more prosperous." This approach to building Europe was perfectly rational, even a necessity. Millions of Europeans understand that integration into a Continent-size market has enhanced their prosperity and security. Missing, however, is a sense of European patriotism, a love of country, and the sense that it is good and legitimate. Political scientist (and Carter advisor) Zbigniew Brzezinski claimed that "no 'European' is willing to die for 'Europe.'" (Actually, dozens of West European soldiers—with Spain in the lead—died in Bosnia for Europe.)

PATTERNS OF INTERACTION

■ An Elite Thing

Some European nationalities, such as the Italians, are Euroenthusiastic; others, such as the British, are Euroskeptical. But no European nationality identifies more with Europe than with their own country. (Virtually all Americans identify with their country more than with their state.) If European integration had to rely on mass support, it would have made little headway. Instead, European integration is very much an elite thing. Its founders, Monnet and Schuman, were high French officials, who were trained to "guide" their society from an elite perspective. Indeed, most of Europe (and Japan) has a bureaucratic governing mentality, the English-speaking lands less so. The absence of mass participation and discussion throughout the history of the EU led to public distrust. Said the Dutch economy minister, as his countrymen voted down the new EU constitution in 2005: "The nondebate of the past twenty years cannot be overcome in three weeks."

The march to European unification is a great success, no matter how much EU citizens grumble. It lifted the confidence and economies of its members, made war unthinkable, and, among its new members, implanted democracy. Actually, new members are admitted only after they demonstrate they are democracies, but the inducement of EU membership persuaded several East European lands to get democratic faster. Now Turkey, hoping to join the EU, emphasizes human rights and moderate politics like never before. No democracy, no membership.

Political Culture

ANTI-AMERICANISM

Europeans have little that positively unites them but have one major negative point that many agree on: their growing dislike of the United States. Actually, European attitudes are more complex than simple dislike. After World War II America, which had just liberated West Europe and then stabilized it against Stalin's designs, was greatly admired. Some leftists criticized the United States for alleged brutal capitalism, exaggerated material consumption, racism, and militarism. Some elites criticized America for lack of a refined and classic culture. (They likely resented the attractiveness of U.S. popular culture to young Europeans, who love rock and rap.)

As Europe gained strength and the threat of Soviet invasion receded, Europeans picked up different perspectives. The Vietnam War was a watershed. Washington asked for European help or at least political support, but no European government contributed, and many Europeans thought the U.S. war was foolish and mistaken. De Gaulle publicly warned against war in Vietnam, where France had been beaten in 1954. West Europe did support the United States in the 1991 Gulf War and contributed small military units. Support for the 2003 Iraq War was much weaker—only Britain sent major forces—and some 80 percent of Europeans opposed the war. Dislike of President Bush 43 was especially strong.

One of the selling points for the 2004 EU constitution, especially pushed by French President Chirac, was that only a united Europe could stand up to the United States and form a counterweight to excessive U.S. power. Few Europeans really cared. Europeans admire what America has accomplished in building a free and prosperous continental democracy but fear giving up any more national sovereignty to Brussels.

Helsinki Final Act 1975 agreement to make Europe's borders permanent.

The big question facing the EU now is whether it attempted to grow too big too quickly. The EU has a built-in and very positive impulse to include all or most of Europe. The payoffs are peace and prosperity. The new members in Central Europe are growing much faster than the earlier members. Much of this is the result of the statistical quirk that poorer countries, starting with a smaller denominator, register bigger percentage gains than richer countries. (If you give $1 to a man with $10, he enjoys a 10 percent gain. If you give it to a man with $100, he gets only a 1 percent gain.) Technology does not need to be developed; it is simply transferred eastward. Much lower wages and taxes in Central Europe pull West European investments eastward. Central Europe and the Baltics are now cemented into the EU and NATO with little to fear from Russia. All of Europe relaxes.

But there are losers in this process: West European workers fear for their jobs. Notice how this parallels American workers who worry about their manufacturing jobs going to China. Such fears underlay the failure of the proposed EU constitution.

■ Attack of the Polish Plumbers

As France and the Netherlands rejected the new EU constitution there was much talk of soon having to compete with low-wage "Polish plumbers." The term caught on, half in jest, as a threat to West Europe's jobs in general. EU membership includes the free movement of labor, although

Geography

PERMANENT BORDERS FOR EUROPE

In Helsinki in 1975, thirty-five nations agreed to the Final Act of the Conference on Security and Cooperation in Europe (CSCE). Among its provisions to calm and stabilize Europe was Principle III of Basket I: "The participating States regard as inviolable all one another's frontiers as well as the frontiers of all States in Europe." Europe's boundaries can be changed only by peaceful means. Europe's boundary problems are over, especially the very touchy German-Polish border.

But other problems loom. First, the **Helsinki Final Act** is not a treaty, although it is treated virtually like one. It lacks the legally binding quality of treaties. Second, some of the CSCE's other provisions conflict with Principle III. For example, Principle VIII guarantees "self-determination of peoples," which was used to justify German unification and the dissolution of the Soviet Union,

which left behind several potential boundary conflicts. Third, Serbia attempted to enlarge its boundaries by taking portions of Croatia and Bosnia, with great bloodshed and "ethnic cleansing" that tore a great hole in the CSCE agreement. Serbs were eventually pushed back but still hold part of Bosnia. Later, Albanians in Kosovo broke away from Serbia. Which governs: permanent borders or self-determination?

Still, the CSCE Final Act was a praiseworthy attempt to settle Europe's boundaries, especially the German-Polish border. Conflicts may arise, as between Albania and Greece, Hungary and Romania, and Romania and Russia (over the Romanian-speaking republic of Moldova, annexed by Stalin in 1940). But the conflicts are likely to be peripheral and containable. Now called the OSCE (for Organization), the body shows a Europe trying to overcome centuries of warfare, much of it concerning boundaries.

there was a delay of several years before workers from the new member states in the east could move freely into West Europe. Such movement is natural but angers those who feel their livelihoods are threatened. (In 1989 in Paris I met a Portuguese plumber who had immigrated to France, which has a shortage of plumbers.)

In mid-2005 the French voted *non* and Dutch voted *nee* to the new EU constitution, which was actually in the form of a 2004 treaty among EU member states. Indeed, European unification is nothing but a series of treaties, which has always been one of its problems. Treaties seldom grab public enthusiasm. Polls had predicted both rejections, but they still shocked the Eurocratic elite who drafted the constitution and thought they did a great job.

Each EU member country ratifies treaties its own way. Most simply have their parliaments approve a treaty, like the U.S. Senate does. Several EU countries earlier had their parliaments ratify the new constitution without much fuss: Lithuania, Hungary, Slovenia, Italy, Greece, Slovakia, Germany, and Austria. But eleven EU states decided to refer the question to the entire electorate. Spain did this, and it passed. France especially has a long tradition of *referendums*, a mass vote on an issue rather than for candidates (see pages 139–140). This tradition, a dubious one, doomed the EU constitution in 2005. The French voted it down 55–45 percent with a hefty 69 percent turnout. Then the Dutch, who have no tradition of referendums, voted it down 62–38 percent with a 63 percent turnout. Since the constitution had to be approved by all twenty-five members to take effect, it died. Further ratifications were symbolic and superfluous.

France and the Netherlands, both founding members of the original Common Market, were actually expressing negative opinions found throughout West Europe. (East Europeans are still Euroenthusiastic.) If they had a chance, many EU electorates would have voted against the constitution on a variety of grounds:

- Increasing power in Brussels infringes on national sovereignty (true, precisely the point of the EU).
- The constitution promotes competition in a free-market economy. (True, but this is what made Europe prosperous.)
- We were not consulted on the EU suddenly adding ten new, poor members to the east in 2004 (true). Now we're saying what we think about that.
- Unemployment here is terrible, around 10 percent (true) and made worse by shipping our jobs to the new, low-wage members in the east (likely untrue). Even worse, "Polish plumbers" will come here and take our jobs. We'll lose our 35-hour workweek.
- The new constitution is too long, detailed, and complex to understand. (This is absolutely correct.)
- No one consulted us on Turkey joining the EU, and by voting "no" we reject it.
- The new constitution will let in even more non-European immigrants, who bring crime, unemployment, and Islam with them. (This is not part of the constitution but is happening anyway.)
- The introduction of the euro currency in early 2002 did not bring the promised economic growth, just inflation (true, but we cannot be sure the euro caused it).
- A narrow political elite, out of touch with ordinary citizens, has been telling us what to do and think for too long, and now we repudiate them (valid).
- For the French: Chirac is a crook and mismanaged the economy; we do not trust him. For the Dutch: Prime Minister Jan Peter Balkenende is ineffective. (Who elected them?)

direct democracy   One in which citizens vote on many issues, bypassing elected representatives.

representative democracy   One in which citizens do not rule directly but through elected and accountable representatives.

aggregate   Items or persons taken together.

Note that several of the items have little or nothing to do with the new constitution; they were a way of showing mass resentments on a variety of issues, blowing off steam. And this is why it is often a mistake to submit complex issues to the electorate: They may vote against the question for unrelated reasons. Almost by definition, any government-sponsored referendum that fails was a mistake. The French and Dutch governments misunderstood mass opinion. **Direct democracy** can be dangerous; all modern countries are **representative democracies**, which calm and guide mass passions.

The most valid complaint about the mammoth new constitution, 448 articles in 450 pages, is that no one could understand it. Millions of copies were distributed, but few bothered to read or discuss it. A sample, Article III-139, shows why:

> This subsection shall not apply, so far as any member state is concerned, to activities which in that state are connected, even occasionally, with the exercise of public authority. European laws or framework laws may exclude certain activities from application of this subsection.

Protocol 9, Article 61, limits outsiders who might buy vacation homes on Malta. Constitutions should be clear, brief, and general, outlining the parts of government and civil rights, nothing more. Details should come later, in statutes. This EU constitution seemed calculated to either make people laugh or turn them off.

Key Concepts

THE LIMITS OF COMPLEXITY

One reason the EU constitution failed in 2005 was that it was just too long and complicated to understand, a problem not limited to Europe. President Clinton's health plan and Bush's Social Security changes and Medicare drug benefits earned public opposition because few could make sense of them. Americans hate the Internal Revenue Service in part because of its 10,000 pages of rules. Only specialists understand portions of it, and that is because the clauses benefit their interest groups.

Why do legislators add complexity without limit? They do not mean to; they mean to add only small items that benefit the groups they represent or receive money from. They argue that their minor insertions are rational and fair. In the example mentioned, Maltese claim that foreigners would soon buy up much of their island. Accordingly, the EU convention inserted the comically specialized protocol to keep Malta for the Maltese. But when every group inserts its special demands, the document becomes incoherent. What is individually rational, in the **aggregate** can be insane.

Another factor contributes to the complexity problem: These documents are drafted by lawyers and other specialists. They are trained to and enjoy delving into every possibility and detail. Their general argument: "Look, we live in a complex society and economy, so you cannot expect simple solutions." That may be true, but the payback they get from the public is often anger, rejection, and indifference. The complexity factor may set limits to the amount and level of legislation that citizens in a democracy can support. Both European and American drafters of laws should remember the acronym KISS (Keep It Simple, Stupid).

WHAT EUROPEANS QUARREL ABOUT

■ Liberal Europe versus Social Europe

As you noticed in our discussions of Britain, France, and Germany, all West European countries are welfare states with elaborate and expensive subsidies to protect citizens from the ups and downs of market forces. This has produced, as we discussed, *labor-force rigidities* and high unemployment. Some European thinkers—and not all of them conservatives—recognize that persistent joblessness of around 10 percent and anemic economic growth will slowly degrade European living standards and bankrupt several governments. There is simply not enough tax revenue coming in to cover government spending, especially as Europeans rapidly age into retirement. (Notice how America has the same problem but not as urgent.) And Europe's taxes are about 40 percent of GDP compared to America's 25 percent (see page 73).

liberal European and Latin American for unrestrained capitalism (Note: approximately opposite of U.S meaning).

social European for welfare state ("liberal" in U.S. terms).

Some Europeans, probably a minority, recognize the looming economic dangers and urge reforms to cut welfare outlays, taxes, and labor-force rigidities. They would like to move Europe in a more U.S. economic direction. Europeans call such measures "**liberal**" or even "ultra-liberal." A majority want to stick with what they call "**social**" protections of welfare and jobs. For them, "Anglo-Saxon" (that is, British and American) economic competition is "savage" and "heartless."

Thus one of the great EU questions is whether Europe should move away from the social model and in a liberal (in the European sense) direction. Many French and Dutch voted against the EU constitution in 2005 out of fear that it was too liberal, that is, that it stripped away welfare and job protections. Once used to such programs, citizens fight any trims in them. Americans too oppose even small cuts in Social Security or Medicare, which, compared to Europe, are modest programs.

■ Europe's Budget Battles

The EU as a whole has a GDP of $12.3 trillion, slightly larger than that of the United States, $11.8 trillion. The EU population of 456 million, however, means that its per capita GDP is $26,875, considerably lower than the U.S. per cap, $40,100. (These figures can change quickly, as the euro constantly fluctuates in value against the dollar.)

Like a regular country, the EU battles over who gets what. Compared to member states' budgets, the EU's is small, only about 1 percent of combined GDPs, but that is still over $120 billion a year. Europe's big problem is that 40 percent of that goes to the Common Agricultural Program (CAP). French farmers are the biggest recipients, and German and Dutch taxpayers are the biggest payers. Roughly half of West European farmers' incomes are from subsidies (compared to two-thirds for Japanese and one-third for American farmers). Rich farmers get the most. An average European cow gets $2.20 a day in subsidies.

European "liberals" (see above) see these subsidies as madness, producing "mountains of butter and lakes of wine" that cannot be sold. They sit in warehouses at taxpayer expense. Accordingly, European liberals would like to cut the CAP and shrink both farm surpluses and the number of farmers. "Social" Europeans, with French farmers in the lead, say, "Don't you dare. The subsidies preserve both our traditions and Europe's food independence from the dreadful U.S. agribusiness and its genetically modified crops."

The British handle the CAP another way. Prime Minister Margaret Thatcher, a Euroskeptic, thundered against the CAP because Britain has relatively few farmers and would pay far more than it received. In 1984 Thatcher got her way, and Brussels now rebates several billion a year back

Geography

WHERE DOES EUROPE END AND ASIA BEGIN?

This seemingly theoretical question turned real with the collapse of the Communist regimes of East Europe in 1989 and of the Soviet Union itself in late 1991. How far east does Europe extend? Which countries would be eligible to join the European Union? Central Europe was clearly eligible and indeed joined (along with the Baltic states) in 2004. The Balkans were always marginal to Europe, but Greece was already a member, and Romania and Bulgaria are soon likely to be. But what about Turkey, Russia, and the other ex-Soviet republics?

De Gaulle once spoke of Europe "from the Atlantic to the Urals," using the common standard for defining Europe. There is no natural border between Europe and Asia. The Urals are not much of a barrier and do not extend across Central Asia. The Mongols went south of the Urals to conquer Russia in the thirteenth century. On a globe, Europe is just a small peninsula of Asia.

Most geographers accept an arbitrary line that runs down the Ural Mountains, then follows the Ural River south into the Caspian Sea to Baku, then eastward along the Caucasus Mountains, across the Black Sea, and through the Turkish Straits. By this definition, most of Russia, Turkey, Georgia, Armenia, Azerbaijan, and Central Asia are not in Europe. There is nothing legally binding about this line. Cyprus, which falls well outside of this line, is the easternmost EU member.

Some urge a cultural definition, namely, that Europe consists of historically Christian lands. Where Christianity ends, they argue, so does Europe. This would shift the boundary to the south of the Caucasus ridge line to include Georgia and Armenia but not

Azerbaijan. Many Europeans feel this criterion should be applied to exclude Turkey from EU membership.

At present, Russia has no interest in joining the EU, but Ukraine does. Moscow will not subordinate its sovereignty to Brussels. A proud and nationalistic Russia sees the EU as a rival and possible threat and is interested in nothing more than commercial ties with the EU. Russia sells Europe much of its oil and natural gas. Ukraine, on the other hand, sees EU membership as its path to prosperity and independence from Russia and will likely apply.

Most of Turkey's elites—especially its military—insist that Turkey is in Europe and belongs in the EU, although few Europeans like the idea. Given a chance to vote on Turkey joining the EU, Europeans would overwhelmingly reject it. They fear people of a very different culture and religion swarming into West Europe. Some note that centuries ago Europe pushed back two Muslim invasions, the Moors in Spain and the Ottomans in the Balkans. Every West European country has an anti-immigrant party, all implicitly or explicitly anti-Muslim.

The Muslim ex-Soviet republics—Azerbaijan in the Caucasus and Kazakhstan, Turkmenistan, Uzbekistan, Kyrgyzstan, and Tajikistan in Central Asia—are culturally even less European than Turkey. They are more Middle Eastern as they are mostly Muslim, speak Turkic languages, and for centuries were parts of the Persian empire. The Caucasian lands of Georgia and Armenia, however, are mostly Christian and are likelier candidates for the EU. But if Europe eventually admits them, could it exclude Azerbaijan? Where to draw Europe's boundary became a major EU political question.

to London. (In 2005 Britain contributed some $18 billion to the EU budget but got $6.18 billion back as a rebate.) Some other EU members see this as unfair and wish to cut or end the rebate for Britain. The real problem is the CAP itself, but so far, no one has been able to cap the CAP.

A related problem is how the EU helps poorer members with its *solidarity funds*, EU aid to lift up poor regions. Ireland, Spain, Portugal, and Greece got substantial EU aid and are now no longer poor. (Irish on average are now a bit richer than Britons.) The EU is reluctant to accept very poor countries as new members because they will cost too much, one argument against admitting Turkey. Actually, most EU member countries now fall within a modest 1:2 range in per capita GDPs. Aside from superrich Luxembourg (per cap around $60,000), the EU's largest countries—Britain, France, Germany, and Italy—are all around $28,000 per cap, only about twice as much as the new members from Central Europe. (Poorest: Latvia at $11,500 per cap, but rising fast.) The EU solidarity fund is a fine, idealistic policy, but it leaves many West European taxpayers resentful that both their euros and their jobs are going to the new, poorer members.

What Next?

The failure to ratify the 2004 EU constitution did not mean a crisis or collapse. The EU simply rumbled on as it had for years, operating under the rules that had been added over the years in a series of treaties. The EU structure was clumsy, undemocratic, and slow, in urgent need of reform. Several pro-Europe observers actually hoped the 2004 constitution would be rejected. It was too long and complex and still left the EU undemocratic. Taking it back to the drawing board and consulting with ordinary Europeans, they could come up with a considerably better constitution.

Who will likely join the EU in the future? Some approximations:

Romania and Bulgaria in 2007 or 2008. This looked like a sure thing, but rejection of the EU constitution made everyone pause.

The Western Balkans—Croatia, Bosnia, Albania, Macedonia, Serbia, Montenegro, and Kosovo, should it separate from Serbia—could follow in several years. One limiting factor: Croatia, Bosnia, and Serbia must first surrender those among them accused of war crimes to the Hague tribunal for trial.

Ukraine and Belarus, former Soviet republics, could follow a few years after that. Ukraine is making good strides toward democracy; its 2004 Orange Revolution seemed to show that democracy could take root in the ex-Soviet Union. Belarus is Europe's last dictatorship and closely tied to Russia.

Turkey will likely not join the EU anytime soon. Although accession talks between the EU and Turkey began in 2005, the rejection of the EU constitution warned politicians to not let Turkey in. The Turkish issue was put back on permanent hold, where it had been for many years.

Some suggest putting "ever closer union" on indefinite hold and returning to the original concept of Europe as a free-trade area with some added features (such as movement of labor), like the original Common Market. Such a looser arrangement would give little power to Brussels and keep members sovereign. Britain has always favored a looser EU. One of Europe's debates has been "wider or deeper?" Those favoring "wider" wanted the EU to enroll most of Europe but stay structurally loose. Those favoring "deeper" wanted it to become a genuinely federal system. Some critics say the EU was looking for trouble when it tried to do both simultaneously: ten new members and a new constitution in 2004. Those who wish to unify Europe should be warned of seeking too much at once.

Key Terms

aggregate (p. 254)

direct democracy (p. 254)

Enlightenment (p. 245)

euro (p. 242)

European Union (p. 242)

Helsinki Final Act (p. 252)

liberal (p. 255)

Maastricht (p. 245)

Mercosur (p. 245)

NAFTA (p. 245)

representative democracy (p. 254)

Schengen (p. 245)

social (p. 255)

subsidiarity (p. 248)

supranational (p. 245)

utilitarian (p. 250)

Further Reference

Bartolini, Stefano. *Restructuring Europe: Centre Formation, System Building, and Political Structuring between the Nation State and the European Union*. New York: Oxford University Press, 2005.

Beach, Derek. *The Dynamics of European Integration: Why and When EU Institutions Matter*. New York: Palgrave, 2005.

Dell'Olio, Fiorella. *The Europeanization of Citizenship: Between the Ideology of Nationality, Immigration and European Identity*. Burlington, VT: Ashgate, 2005.

Dinan, Desmond. *Ever Closer Union: An Introduction to European Integration*, 3rd ed. Boulder, CO: L. Rienner, 2005.

Hosli, Madeleine O. *The Euro: A Concise Introduction to Europe's Single Currency*. Boulder, CO: L. Rienner, 2005.

Leonard, Mark. *Why Europe Will Run the 21st Century*. London: Fourth Estate, 2005.

Martin, Andrew, and George Ross, eds. *Euros and Europeans: Monetary Integration and the European Model of Society*. New York: Cambridge University Press, 2004.

McCormick, John. *The European Union: Politics and Promises*, 3rd ed. Boulder, CO: L. Rienner, 2004.

Morgan, Glyn. *The Idea of a European Superstate: Public Justification and European Integration*. Princeton, NJ: Princeton University Press, 2005.

Nelsen, Brent F., and Alexander Stubb, eds. *The European Union: Reading on the Theory and Practice of European Integration*. Boulder, CO: L. Rienner, 2003.

Norman, Peter. *The Accidental Constitution: The Story of the European Convention*, rev. ed. Brussels: EuroComment, 2005.

Reid, T. R. *The United States of Europe: The New Superpower and the End of American Supremacy*. New York: Penguin, 2004.

Rifkin, Jeremy. *The European Dream*. New York: Penguin, 2005.

Van Oudenaren, John. *Uniting Europe: An Introduction to the European Union*, 2nd ed. Lanham, MD: Rowman & Littlefield, 2004.

Part IV

RUSSIA

Key Web Sites

Country Study
lcweb21.loc.gov/frd/cs/rutoc.html

Historical and Ethnic Photos
loc.gov/exhibits/empire

Scholarly Reviews
www2.h-net.msu.edu/~russia

Russian Embassy in Washington
russianembassy.org

Institute for the Economy in Transition
iet.ru/index_e.htm

Democracy in Russia (Yabloko Party)
eng.yabloko.ru

Radio Free Europe/Radio Liberty
rferl.org

News Sources
europeaninternet.com/russia
russiatoday.com
moscowtimes.ru
russiajournal.com
valley.net/~transnat
wps.ru:8101/chitlaks/politruk/en

Chapter 18

Russia:
The Impact of the Past

Russia is immense, stretching eleven time zones across the northern half of Asia to the Pacific. Looking at a map of Russia, you notice that only a small part of it is in Europe. (Look at a globe and you notice that Europe itself is only a small peninsula of Asia.) Perhaps a country as big and ethnically diverse as the Soviet Union was not meant to be. Just holding it together required strong central control backed by force. The very size of Russia may incline it to **tyranny**.

With few natural boundaries, Russia is easy to invade from east or west, although its very size and harsh winters doomed the invasions of Charles XII of Sweden, Napoleon, and Hitler. Winters give Russia a short growing season, making agriculture a chancy business, with crops failing on an average of one year in three. Geography is not as kind to Russia as it is to the United States. The vast territory that **Siberia** adds to Russia's size is problematic; its weather is hostile to settlement, and its mineral and forest wealth is hard to extract. Most of the Russian population continues to live in the "European" part, that is, west of the Ural Mountains. Plans to settle in and develop Siberia, some of them going back to tsarist days, fall short of expectations.

Another geographic problem is the difficulty of reaching the open sea. The first Russian states were totally landlocked; only under Peter the Great at the beginning of the eighteenth century did Russians overcome the Swedes to reach the Baltic and the Turks to reach the Black Sea. The North Russian ports ice over in winter, and the Black Sea is controlled by the Turkish Straits, still leaving European Russia without year-round, secure ports. One of the great dreams of tsarists and Communists alike was for warm-water ports under exclusive Russian control.

Questions to Consider

1. Does Russia's size make it inherently difficult to govern?
2. What geographic disadvantages has Russia faced over its history?
3. Why does Russia always seem to require modernization from above? Why can it not come from below?
4. How much practice has Russia had with democracy?
5. How does the clash of Westernizers and Slavophiles echo to this day?
6. Why did Marxism catch on in Russia, where it was not supposed to?
7. How did Lenin alter Marxism?
8. Could the Provisional Government have stayed in power? How?
9. Was Stalin an accident?

The Slavic People

Occupying most of East Europe, the Slavic peoples are the most numerous in Europe. Russians, Ukrainians, Poles, Czechs, Slovaks, Serbs, Croats, Bulgarians, and others speak languages closer to each other than are the Romance languages (Italian, Spanish, French) of West Europe. A Slovak peasant can converse with any other Slavic peasant—so similar are their vocabularies and syntax.

tyranny Coercive rule, usually by one person. (See page 263.)

Siberia From Russian for "north"; that part of Russia east of the Ural Mountains. (See page 263.)

Constantinople Capital of Byzantium, conquered by Turks in 1453.

Cyrillic Greek-based alphabet of Eastern Slavic languages.

Tatar Mongol-origin tribes who ruled Russia for centuries. (*Not* Tartar.)

The way the Slavic languages are written, though, differentiates them. The Western Slavs (Poles, Czechs, Croats, and others) were Christianized from Rome; hence their alphabet is Latin. The Eastern Slavs (Russians, Ukrainians, Serbs, and others) were converted by Eastern Orthodox monks from **Constantinople**, and their languages are written in a variation of the Greek alphabet called **Cyrillic**, after St. Cyril, one of the monks who first converted Slavs.

Their Orthodox Christianity (as opposed to Roman Catholicism) and Cyrillic writing contributed to the Russians' isolation from the rest of Europe. In addition to being at the geographical fringe of Europe, Russia was beyond its cultural fringe for centuries. The important ideas that helped modernize Catholic and Protestant Europe penetrated Russia only much later. Rome was a lively fountainhead of thought in West Europe, but the headquarters of the Orthodox faith, Constantinople, under the Turks ceased to provide intellectual guidance for its followers. At the same time West Europe was experiencing the invigoration of the Renaissance, which rippled outward from Catholic Italy, Russia stayed isolated and asleep. It missed most of the Enlightenment.

A more important factor explaining Russia's isolation and backwardness was its conquest in the thirteenth century by the Mongols, later known as the **Tatars**. The Mongols crushed the first Russian state, centered at Kiev in present-day Ukraine, and enslaved much of the population. For two

Political Culture

"MOSCOW IS THE THIRD ROME"

The monk Philotheus of Pskov uttered these words after Constantinople fell to the Turks in 1453, indicating that Russia was the last and only center of true Christianity. Rome and Constantinople had failed; now Moscow would guard the faith. Over the centuries, many Russians repeated Philotheus's dictum: "Moscow is the third Rome; a fourth is not to be." After the Bolshevik Revolution, Russia's new rulers felt the same way about world communism, namely, Moscow was its capital and there could be no other. Even today, some Russians still feel that Russia has a holy mission.

St. Basil's cathedral recalls Moscow's former role as a center of Christianity. Russia's tsars were not merely heads of state but also heads of the Russian Orthodox Church.

centuries, while West Europe moved ahead, Russian culture under the barbaric Mongols declined. Some historians believe even after the Tatar yoke was lifted, it still took five centuries for Russia to catch up with the West.

> **tsar** From "caesar"; Russia's emperor. Sometimes spelled old Polish style, *czar*.
>
> **autocracy** Absolute rule of one person in centralized state.
>
> **exclave** Part of country separated from main territory.

Russian Autocracy

Under the Tatars, the duchy of Moscow became the most powerful Russian state, first as a tax collector for the Tatars, then as their triumphant enemy. Moscovy's Ivan the Terrible (1530–1584) had himself crowned **tsar**. Under Ivan, Russian territory expanded greatly, down the Volga to the Caspian Sea and into Siberia. Ivan was both murderous and successful; his brutal use of force set a standard for later rulers. To this day, many Russians think only a strong and ruthless leader can achieve national greatness.

When the Russian nobles (*boyars*) came into conflict with Ivan, his secret police, the *Oprichnina*, exiled or executed them. Since that time, the Russian nobility never played an autonomous role in political life. It was as if the absolutism of France was applied early and completely to a culturally backward country. The result was **autocracy** under the tsar. Unlike the countries of West Europe, Russia never experienced the mixed monarchy of autonomous nobles, church, commoners, and king. Accordingly, Russians had no experience with limited government, checks and balances, or pluralism. As Ivan grew older he became madder. Able to trust no one, he murdered those around him—even his own son—at the least suspicion. By the time he died he had carved out the modern Russian state.

Absolutism or Anarchy?

One of the reasons Russians put up with autocracy—and sometimes admired it—was because they felt that without a firm hand at the top the system would degenerate into anarchy. This happened in the early seventeenth century, the "Time of Troubles." Lacking a strong tsar, unrest, banditry, civil war, and a Polish invasion plagued the land. Russians also accepted the idea that they had to serve a powerful state. The Russian Orthodox church, which the tsar also headed, became a pillar

Geography

BOUND RUSSIA

Russia is bounded on the north by the Arctic Ocean; on the east by the Bering Sea and Sea of Okhotsk; on the south by North Korea (tiny), China, Mongolia, Kazakhstan, Azerbaijan, Georgia, and the Black Sea; and on the west by Ukraine, Belarus, Lithuania, Latvia, Estonia, Finland, and Norway.

The Russian **exclave** of Kaliningrad Oblast (region), formerly Koenigsberg of old East Prussia, is wedged between Poland and Lithuania.

caesaropapism   Combining top civil ruler (caesar) with top spiritual ruler (pope), as in Russia's tsars.

Ukraine   From Slavic for "borderland"; region south of Russia, now independent.

of autocracy, teaching the faithful to worship the tsar as the "little father" who protected all Russians. The tsar integrated the offices of head of state and head of church, a pattern called **caesaropapism**. Russia has been called a "service state" in which all walks of life, from nobles to peasants to priests, served the autocrat. Western concepts such as liberty and individual rights were absent.

During the fifteenth and sixteenth centuries, Russia actually moved backwards in one crucial area. Previously free peasants became serfs, tied to the land to labor for aristocrats as almost subhuman beasts. While West Europe ended serfdom centuries earlier, Russia found itself with the vast majority of its population poor and ignorant farm laborers.

From time to time these wretched people revolted. Some ran off and joined the Cossacks, bands of mounted freebooters in the border regions between the tsarist and Turkish empires. One Cossack leader, Stenka Razin, immortalized in ballad, led a peasant revolt that seized much of **Ukraine**. In time, the Cossacks turned into semimilitary federations, which the tsars enrolled as effective and ruthless cavalry.

Forced Modernization

By the time Peter I became tsar in 1682, Russia lagged behind the rest of Europe. Peter, who stood six feet nine inches (206 cm.), forced Russia to modernize and become a major power. Peter personally handled Russia's legislation, diplomacy, war, and technical innovation and was the first tsar to travel in West Europe. Admiring its industries, he ordered them duplicated in Russia. Nearly continually at war, Peter pushed the Swedes back to give Russia an outlet on the Baltic. There he ordered built a magnificent new capital, St. Petersburg (later Leningrad), modeled after Amsterdam, to serve as Russia's window to the West.

Copying the tight Swedish administrative system, Peter divided Russia into provinces, counties, and districts, each supervised by bureaucrats drawn from the nobility. All male nobles had to serve the tsar from age fifteen until death, either as bureaucrats or military officers. Even the bureaucrats were organized on military lines, complete with ranks and uniforms. With Peter, the Russian government apparatus penetrated deep into society. A census determined the number of males available for military conscription, and each community had a quota. Draftees served for life. Taxation squeezed everybody as Peter ordered his officials to "collect money, as much as possible, for money is the artery of war."

When Peter died in 1725, Russia was more modern and Westernized but still behind West Europe. Peter the Great contributed a pattern of forced modernization from the top, pushing a poor, gigantic country forward despite itself. Russia paid dearly. The mass of peasants, heavily taxed, were worse off than ever. The Westernized nobility—forced, for instance, to shave for the first time—was cut off from the hopes and feelings of the peasantry. The pattern continued for a long time.

Westernizers and Slavophiles

Napoleon's invasion of Russia and capture of Moscow in 1812 made Russian intellectuals painfully aware of the backwardness of their land. Many sought to bring in Western politics and institutions, including a constitutional monarchy that would limit the autocratic powers of the tsar. These were called

Westernizers. Others disliked the West; they saw it as spiritually shallow and materialistic. The answer to Russia's problems, they argued, was to cultivate their own Slavic roots and develop institutions and styles different from and superior to the West's. "Russia will teach the world," was their view. These **Slavophiles** (literally, "lovers of the Slavs"), who stressed the spiritual depth and warm humanity of Russian peasants, were romantic nationalists who disdained West European culture. In our day this pattern continues in parts of the Third World that reject Western materialism in favor of traditional spiritual values. And in Russia today the old debate still echoes: Liberal reformers are still pro-West while conservative authoritarians are anti-West nationalists.

Westernizers Nineteenth-century Russians who wished to copy the West.

Slavophiles Nineteenth-century Russians who wished to develop Russia along native, non-Western lines. Also known as "Russophiles."

zemstvo Local parliaments in old Russia.

Narodniki From Russian for "people," *narod;* radical populist agitators of late nineteenth-century Russia.

anarchism Radical ideology seeking to overthrow all conventional forms of government.

proletariat According to Marx, class of industrial workers.

From Frustration to Revolution

Despite calls for far-reaching changes in Russia, reform during the nineteenth century made little progress. All tsars rejected becoming a *constitutional monarchy*. Even Alexander II, the "tsar-liberator," carried out only limited reforms. In 1861 he issued his famous Edict of Emancipation, freeing serfs from legal bondage. Most of them remained in economic bondage, however. He set up district and provincial assemblies called **zemstvos** but gave them only marginal local power.

The reforms were meant both to modernize Russia and to improve the living conditions of the masses. Under certain conditions, however, reforms may actually make *revolution* more likely rather than less. Alexander's reforms, which he saw as extensive and generous, were regarded by an increasingly critical *intelligentsia* (the educated class) as not nearly enough. Whatever he granted, they wanted more. The reforms merely whetted the critics' appetites. Many intellectuals became bitter and frustrated.

Some tried action at the grass-roots level. In the 1870s thousands of idealistic students put on peasant clothes and tried "going to the people" in the villages to incite radical action. These **Narodniki** made absolutely no progress; the suspicious peasants either ignored them or turned them over to the police. Others turned to **anarchism** and violence, believing that killing the right official constituted "propaganda of the deed," a way to arouse the inert masses. One group of revolutionaries, *Narodnaya Volya* (People's Will), after seven attempts killed the tsar with a bomb thrown into his carriage in 1881.

Actually, Russia made considerable progress in the nineteenth century. Archaic usages were swept away, industry started (with an infusion of British, French, and German capital), railroads were built, and intellectual life flourished. But in the crucial area of political reform—parliaments, parties, elections, and the sharing of power—Russia essentially stood still. Political reforms do not make themselves, and in many ways they are more basic to the peaceful evolution of society than social, cultural, or economic reforms. A ruler who modernizes his economy but not his political system is asking for trouble.

Marxism Comes to Russia

According to Marx's theory, backward Russia was far from ready for proletarian revolution. There simply was not much of a **proletariat** in the still overwhelmingly agricultural land, where industrialization was just beginning in the late nineteenth century. Marx believed revolution would come

Personalities

LENIN, THE GREAT REVOLUTIONARY

Some claim that Lenin was out for revenge against the tsarist system for hanging his older brother, Alexander, in 1887 for his part in a bomb plot against the tsar. That cannot be proved, but it is clear Lenin was dominated by a cold, contained fury aimed at one goal: revolutionary socialism in Russia.

Born in 1870 as Vladimir Ilyich Ulyanov, son of a provincial education official, Lenin was from the intellectual middle class rather than the proletariat in whose name he struggled—a pattern typical of revolutionary socialist leaders. Quickly expelled from university for alleged subversive activity, Lenin was sent into rural exile. With incredible self-discipline, Lenin taught himself and breezed through law exams with top marks.

In the early 1890s Lenin, like many Russian intellectuals, discovered Marx and wrote Marxist analyses of the rapidly growing Russian economy. Recognized as a leading Marxist thinker, Lenin quickly rose to prominence in underground revolutionary circles.

In December 1895, while editing an illegal socialist newspaper, Lenin was arrested and sent to prison for a year followed by three years' exile on the Lena River in Siberia. There he took the name Lenin, the man from the Lena. The solitary hours gave him time to read, learn foreign languages, and write. Released in 1900, Lenin fled to Zurich, Switzerland, where he spent most of the next seventeen years. Until taking power in Russia in 1917, Lenin never held a job.

In Swiss exile Lenin at times worried there would never be a revolution in Russia. The working class was concentrating on higher wages rather than revolution. The Russian Social Democratic Labor party was small, with only a few thousand members in Russia and in exile. Lenin was determined to transform this small party into an effective underground force. Size was not important; organization was everything. His 1902 pamphlet *What Is to Be Done?* demanded a tightly disciplined party of professional revolutionaries, not a conventional social-democratic party open to everybody. Under Lenin the early Communists forged the "organizational weapon": the Party.

Vladimir Lenin

But how could a proletarian revolution happen in preindustrial Russia? In solving this problem, Lenin greatly changed Marxism. Marx theorized that revolution will come in the most advanced countries, where the proletariat was biggest. Lenin said not necessarily: Revolution could come where capitalism is weakest, where it is just starting. **Imperialism** had changed capitalism, Lenin argued, giving it a new lease on life. By exploiting weaker countries, the big imperialist powers were able to bribe their own working class with higher wages and thus keep them quiet. Where capitalism was beginning—as in Russia with heavy foreign investment—was where it could be overthrown. The newly developing countries, such as Russia and Spain, were "capitalism's weakest link," said Lenin.

Lenin also disagreed with Marx's insistence that peasants could never be revolutionary. Marx dismissed country life as "rural idiocy," but Lenin believed that, under certain conditions and leadership, peasants could turn revolutionary and, throwing their weight in with the small working class, provide a massive revolutionary army. (Three decades later, Mao Zedong elaborated on these themes to argue that China, a victim of imperialism, could have a socialist revolution based entirely on the peasantry. Mao completed the train of thought that Lenin started.)

Lenin was not a great theoretician but a brilliant opportunist, switching doctrine to take advantage of situations, like all successful revolutionaries. He was less concerned with pure Marxism than with using it to overthrow the system he hated. Once in power, he practiced the same bloody ruthlessness later associated with Stalin. It is not clear that had Lenin lived he would have been any better than Stalin.

first in the most industrially advanced countries, such as Britain and Germany. Marxism, though, caught on more strongly in Russia than anywhere else. Marx's works were eagerly seized upon by frustrated Russian intellectuals who badly wanted change but did not have a theoretical framework for it. Here at last, they believed, they had found a reason and a means to carry out a revolution.

> **imperialism** Powerful countries turning other lands into colonies. (See page 268.)
>
> **communism** Economic theories of Marx combined with organization of Lenin.
>
> **Bolshevik** "Majority" in Russian; early name for Soviet Communist party.

There were several schools of Marxism in Russia. The "Legal Marxists," noting Russia's economic underdevelopment, thought the country would first have to go through capitalism before it could start on socialism. Marx had a very deterministic view of history and saw it developing in economic stages, first capitalism, then socialism. Loyal to Marx's historical analysis, the Legal Marxists believed they would have a long wait for revolution and must first work to promote capitalism.

Another school of Russian Marxism was called "Economism." Stressing better wages and working conditions through labor unions, the Economists thought the immediate economic improvement of the working class was the essence of Marxism. In this they resembled West European social democrats, whose Marxism mellowed into welfarism.

Opposing these two gradualist schools were impassioned intellectuals who wanted first and foremost to make a revolution. They argued they could "give history a shove" by starting a revolution with only a small proletariat, gaining power, and then using the state to move directly into socialism. Lenin made some theoretical changes in Marxism so it fit Russian conditions (see box on page 268). Since then, the doctrine of Russian **communism** has been known as Marxism-Leninism.

In 1898, after several small groups had discussed Marxist approaches to Russia, the Russian Social Democratic Labor party was formed. Immediately penetrated and harassed by the *Okhrana*, the tsarist secret police, many of its leaders went into exile in West Europe. Its newspaper, *Iskra* (the Spark), was published in Zurich and smuggled into Russia. One of its editors was Lenin.

In 1903 the small party split over a crucial question: organization. Some of its leaders wanted a normal party along the lines of the German Social Democrats, with open but committed membership that tried to enroll the Russian working class. Lenin scoffed at this kind of organization, arguing tsarist secret police would make mincemeat out of an open party. Instead, he urged a small, tightly knit underground party of professional revolutionaries, more a conspiracy than a conventional party.

Lenin got his way. At the 1903 party congress in Brussels, Belgium (it could not be held in Russia), he controlled thirty-three of the fifty-one votes. Although probably unrepresentative of total party membership, Lenin proclaimed his faction **Bolshevik** (majority), and the name stuck. The *menshevik* (minority) faction at the congress continued to exist, advocating a more moderate line.

■ Curtain Raiser: The 1905 Revolution

At the beginning of the twentieth century two expanding powers, Russia and Japan, collided. The Russians were pushing eastward, consolidating their position on the Pacific by building the Trans-Siberian Railway, the last leg of which ran through Manchuria. Japan was meanwhile pushing up from Korea to Manchuria, which was nominally a part of China. The tsar's cabinet, certain they could defeat any Asian army and hoping to deflect domestic unrest, thought war with Japan might be a good idea. Said the interior minister: "We need a little victorious war to stem the tide of revolution." Instead, the Japanese fleet launched a surprise attack against the Russians at Port Arthur, then beat the Russians on both land and sea.

The Russo-Japanese War revealed the tsarist military as unprepared, inept, and stupid. Weak regimes should not count on a "little victorious war" to paper over domestic unrest; wars make troubles worse. In Russia, rioting and then revolution broke out. Some naval units mutinied. (See Eisenstein's film classic *Battleship Potemkin*.) Workers briefly seized factories in St. Petersburg. It looked like revolution was breaking out.

Tsar Nicholas II gave way and decreed potentially important reforms: freedom of speech, press, and assembly and the democratic election of a **Duma**. Briefly, his 1905 October Manifesto looked as if it would turn autocracy into constitutional monarchy. The tsar and his reactionary advisors backed down on their promises, however. Nicholas, none too bright, refused to yield any of his autocratic powers. Four Dumas were subsequently elected; each was dissolved when it grew too critical. Finally the Duma was turned into an undemocratic debating society without power. The Duma was Russia's last hope for a peaceful transition to democracy. People in modern times need to feel they participate at least in a small way in the affairs of government. Parties, elections, and parliaments may be imperfect means of participation, but they are better than violent revolution. Since the failed Decembrist revolt of 1825, Russian intellectuals had been trying to tell this to the tsar, but he refused to listen.

World War I and Collapse

Communists liked to speak of the Russian Revolution as inevitable, the playing out of historical forces that had to lead to the collapse of imperialism and capitalism. There was nothing inevitable about the October Revolution. Indeed, without World War I, there would have been no revolution in Russia at all, let alone a Bolshevik revolution. Lenin himself, in early 1917, doubted he would live to see a revolution in Russia.

Things were not so terrible in Russia before the war. The Duma struggled to erode tsarist autocracy and in time might have succeeded. Industry grew rapidly. Peasants, freed from old restrictions on land ownership, turned into prosperous and productive small farmers. The war changed everything. Repeating their overconfidence of 1904, the tsarist military marched happily to war against Germany in 1914 with a large but badly equipped and poorly led army. Major offensives ground to a halt before the more effective German forces. The Russian economy fell apart. Troop morale disintegrated, and many deserted. Peasants seized their landlord's estates. The government was paralyzed, but the tsar refused to change anything.

By 1917 the situation was desperate. In March of that year a group of democratic moderates seized power and deposed the tsar. Resembling Western liberals, the people of the Provisional Government hoped to modernize and democratize Russia. The Western powers, including the United States, welcomed them, thinking they would rally Russians to continue the war. The Provisional Government, which by July was headed by Alexander Kerensky, tried to stay in the war, and that was its undoing. If Kerensky had betrayed the Western Allies and made a separate peace with Germany, the moderates might have been able to retain power.

Meanwhile, the German General Staff, looking for a way to knock Russia out of the war, thought it would be clever to send the agitator Lenin into Russia to create havoc. In April 1917 Lenin and his colleagues traveled in a famous "sealed train"—so the Bolshevik bacillus would not infect Germany, where revolutionary discontent was also growing—across Germany, Sweden, and Finland to Petrograd, the World War I name for St. Petersburg (which sounded too German). Without German help and funds, Lenin might never have made it back to Russia.

At Petrograd's Finland Station, Lenin issued his stirring slogan, "Bread, Land, Peace," speaking respectively to workers, peasants, and soldiers. Lenin immediately saw that a "dual authority" was trying to rule Russia. The Provisional Government controlled the army and foreign policy. But in the most important city, Petrograd, a council (*soviet* in Russian) of workers, soldiers, sailors, and revolutionaries ran things. Soon these councils appeared in many Russian cities. The composition of these soviets was mixed, with the Bolsheviks a small minority. Lenin pursued a double strategy: Make the soviets the only effective governing power and make the Bolsheviks the dominant power in the soviets. Lenin's slogan for this: "All Power to the Soviets."

◼ The Revolution and Civil War

The actual seizure of power in October (see box on page 272) was amazingly easy. In a scene exaggerated by Soviet historians, soldiers and sailors loyal to the Petrograd soviet charged across a big square into the Winter Palace to oust the Provisional Government. But control of Petrograd and Moscow was one thing, control of all gigantic Russia was something else.

The tight organization and discipline of Lenin's Bolsheviks paid off. In a situation of almost total chaos, the best organized win. By a series of shrewd moves, the Bolsheviks were able to dominate the soviets and win many converts from deserting soldiers and sailors. Lenin headed the new government and immediately took Russia out of the war, accepting a punitive peace treaty from the Germans at Brest-Litovsk in March 1918. It was a dictated treaty (*Diktat* in German) that enabled the Germans to seize large areas of Russia and redeploy nearly a million troops to the western front.

Personalities

KERENSKY: NICE GUYS LOSE

In the late 1950s at UCLA I had an eerie experience: seeing and hearing Alexander Kerensky speak. History lives. Still fit and articulate in his seventies, Kerensky recalled his brief stint (July to November 1917) as head of Russia's Provisional Government. One man in the audience, a Russian emigré, asked angrily why Kerensky did not use his power to have Lenin killed. Kerensky reflected a moment and said, "Sometimes when you have power it's hard to use it."

That was Kerensky's problem. A decent man, he would not have a political opponent murdered. The Western Allies begged him to keep Russia in the war, and he did not have the heart to betray them. What Kerensky lacked in political ruthlessness he may have gained in longevity. Living in New York City, he

Alexander Kerensky

spent his years justifying his brief rule and denouncing both the Bolsheviks and Russian rightists who tried to bring him down. He died in 1970 at age eighty-nine.

war communism Temporary strict socialism in Russia, 1918–1921.

NEP Lenin's New Economic Policy that allowed private activity, 1921–1928.

Feeling betrayed and concerned that allied military supplies would fall into German hands, the Western Allies sent small expeditionary forces into Russia. American troops actually fought the Bolsheviks in North Russia and Siberia in 1918–1919. This started the Soviet propaganda line that the capitalist powers tried to strangle the infant Bolshevik regime in its cradle.

From 1918 to 1920 civil war raged. The White Army, led by reactionary Russian generals and admirals and supplied by the Western Allies, tried to crush the Communists' Red Army. Both sides were ruthless in a life-or-death struggle. Millions of Russians perished from starvation. Expecting their revolution to spread, the Red Army invaded Poland in 1920, hoping to trigger a Europe-wide socialist upheaval. Instead, the Poles threw back the Red Army and seized parts of Ukraine and Belarus. Lenin and his colleagues saw there would be no world revolution and settled for building the world's first socialist country.

■ War Communism and NEP

During the civil war, the Bolsheviks tried to plunge directly into their utopian system by running the ruined economy by executive fiat. This **war communism**, as it was euphemistically called, was due as much to the demands of a desperate civil war as to visionary schemes. To motivate workers, Lenin ordered: "He who does not work, neither shall he eat" (from 2 Thessalonians 3:10). War communism led immediately to starvation, and only the charity of American grain shipments (supervised by Herbert Hoover) held deaths to a few million.

Lenin saw that Russia was far from ready for pure socialism, so he conducted a planned retreat of state control to the "commanding heights" of heavy industry and let most of the rest of the economy revert to private hands. This period of Lenin's **New Economic Policy (NEP)** brought relative prosperity; farmers worked their own land, "nepmen" behaved like small private entrepreneurs, and life in general relaxed. There was one catch: The NEP was not moving the Soviet Union, as it was now called, any closer to socialism, and industry grew only slowly. It is likely that Lenin meant the NEP only as a temporary rest before moving on toward socialist construction.

Geography

WHY THE OCTOBER REVOLUTION WAS IN NOVEMBER

Every November 7, Russia used to celebrate the anniversary of the Great October Revolution. If this sounds curious, it is because Russia, following its Orthodox church, in 1917 was still using the ancient Julian calendar, which (because it counted too many leap years) ran thirteen days behind the more-accurate Gregorian calendar, in use in Catholic countries since 1582. Protestant countries, fearing a popish plot, also delayed adopting the Gregorian calendar. The Bolsheviks finally switched Russia to the Gregorian calendar but then had to recalculate the October Revolution into November.

That changed when Stalin took full power in the late 1920s. In 1928 he began the first of the government-enforced **Five-Year Plans** that accelerated collectivization and industrialization (see box on pages 274–275). Peasants resisted giving up their fields, farm production dropped, and millions (especially Ukrainians) were deliberately starved to death. In new factories, workers toiled with primitive tools to boost production of **capital goods**. Setting a pattern for all Communist countries, **consumer goods** were deliberately neglected, and the standard of living declined. While many admit the forced industrialization of the 1930s was brutal, some argue it gave the Soviet Union the industrial base to arm against the German invasion in 1941.

As it was, the German invasion caused some twenty-seven million Soviet deaths. The Nazis cared nothing for Slavic lives; starvation was their standard treatment for Russian prisoners of war. Faced with extinction, the Soviet Union pulled together. Stalin, like Lenin, recognized the force of Russian nationalism beneath the Communist surface. Reviewing troops marching from Moscow to the front,

Five-Year Plans   Stalin's forced industrialization of Soviet Union starting in 1928.

capital goods   Implements used to make other things.

consumer goods   Things people use, such as food, clothing, and housing.

gensek   Russian abbreviation for "general secretary," powerful CPSU chief. (See page 274.)

CPSU   Communist Party of the Soviet Union. (See page 274.)

paranoia   Unreasonable suspicion of others. (See page 274.)

purge   Stalin's "cleansing" of suspicious elements by firing squad. (See page 274.)

Geography

ANOTHER TALE OF TWO FLAGS

At the end of 1991 the familiar Communist red flag (with the gold hammer and sickle) came down as the Soviet Union dissolved. Red had been the color of socialist movements (taken from the red shirts of Italian unifier Garibaldi) ever since the nineteenth century, and the Bolsheviks used it in the national flag in late 1917. The old tsarist flag was developed by Peter the Great, who brought the Netherlands tri-color back with him from his stay in Dutch shipyards in 1699, but changed the stripes from the original Dutch (from the top: red-white-blue) to white-blue-red, sometimes with an imperial double-headed eagle (from Byzantium) on it. The Provisional Government removed the eagle in 1917; this is what the Russian Federation revived as its flag in 1991.

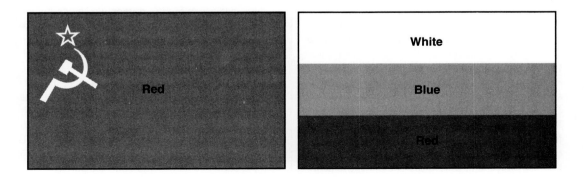

Personalities

STALIN: "ONE DEATH IS A TRAGEDY; A MILLION IS A STATISTIC"

The Soviet system was not so much Lenin's as Stalin's. Lenin was fifty-four when he died in 1924, before giving definitive form to the system. Exactly who is to blame for the horrors that developed—Lenin or Stalin—is controversial both within and outside Russia. Some still argue that if Lenin had lived, his intelligence and sophistication would have set Russia on the path to "true socialism." Others say the structure Lenin created—concentrating power first in the party, then in the Central Committee, and finally in his own person—made the abuse of power inevitable.

Stalin aptly illustrates Acton's dictum, "power corrupts." Stalin lived to amass political power and was very good at it. Born Yosif Vissarionovich Djugashvili in 1879, son of a poor shoemaker, Stalin lacked Lenin's intellectual family background and education. Some of Stalin's behavior can be traced to his homeland of Georgia, part of the Caucasus, a mountainous land with a warm climate and fiery people given to personal hatred and blood-feuds. In Georgia, "Soso" (his Georgian nickname) is still praised as a local boy who made good.

The young Djugashvili started to study for the Orthodox priesthood but soon turned to revolution. Expelled from the seminary, he joined the Georgian Marxist underground as an agitator and strike organizer. Repeatedly arrested, jailed, and exiled to Siberia, he always managed to escape. (There is some evidence that he was a double agent for the tsarist police.) Going underground, he took the name Stalin, Russian for "man of steel."

Never a great theoretician, Stalin attracted Lenin's attention as a non-Russian who could write the Bolsheviks' position on the nationalities question. Playing only a moderate role in the October Revolution, Stalin was named commissar for nationalities in 1918 and then, in Lenin's worst mistake, chosen as the party's first general secretary in 1922. People thought the new office would be a clerical job with little power. Lenin and Stalin were never close—although Stalin's historians tried to make it look that way—and toward the end of his life Lenin had an inkling of what Stalin was like. In one of his last messages Lenin urged the party to reject Stalin as "too rude."

It was too late. Using his position as **gensek**, Stalin organized the **CPSU** to his advantage by promoting to key posts only those personally loyal to him. It was this organizational spadework that gave Stalin the edge over his rival, Leon Trotsky, organizer of the Red Army and a far more intelligent Marxist. Stalin beat him in party infighting and had him expelled from Russia in 1929 and murdered in Mexico in 1940. Reviled as a deviationist traitor, Trotsky did try to organize an anti-Stalin opposition within the CPSU, a point that fed Stalin's natural **paranoia** and contributed to his ruthlessness in exterminating officials on the slightest suspicion of disloyalty.

Stalin, an uncanny manipulator, played one faction against another until, by the late 1920s, he was the Kremlin's undisputed master. Like Peter the Great, Stalin was determined to modernize regardless of human cost. In 1928 he instituted the first Five-Year Plan, beginning the forced industrialization of Russia. Farmers, very much against their will, were herded into collectives and forced to produce for the state, sometimes at gunpoint. Better-off farmers, the so-called *kulaks*, were "liquidated as a class," a euphemism for killed. Economic development was defined as heavy industry, and steel production became the chief goal of the man of steel.

In 1934, during the second Five-Year Plan, Stalin became obsessed with "Trotskyite" disloyalty in party ranks. Thus began Stalin's **purges**: up to one million party comrades killed, some after they confessed to being British spies or Trotskyite "wreckers." People in positions of prominence trembled that they would be next—and many were. Stalin ordered all managers to train two replacements. Stalin even had all his generals shot, a blunder that hurt the Soviet Union in the 1941 German attack. Perhaps another ten million ordinary citizens, arrested on fake charges, also perished, many in Siberian forced-labor camps. In total, Stalin's orders led to the death of over fifteen million people during collectivization and the purges.

Was Stalin mad? There was some Trotskyite opposition to him, but he exaggerated it. It was Plato who first observed that any tyrant, even one who starts sane, must lose his mind in office because he can trust nobody. More than a question of personality, Stalin shows what happens when one person assumes total power. The Communists did not like to admit it, but it was their *system* that was at fault more than any particular individual.

During his lifetime Stalin was deified as history's greatest linguist, art critic, Marxist theoretician, engineer, agronomist, you name it. His communization of East Europe led to the **Cold War**. By the time he died in 1953—while preparing yet another purge—Stalin had turned the Soviet Union into *his* system,

Joseph Stalin

and, in basic outlines, it never did change much. When Mikhail Gorbachev attempted to seriously reform it, the system collapsed. Today, Stalin is being quietly restored as a symbol of Russian power.

These three St. Petersburg graves of victims of Stalin's Great Purge convey some of the horror of Stalin's "cleansing" of people he supposed were unreliable. The family of the victim on the right, by erecting a life-size statue of a man in Bolshevik Young Guard uniform, meant to show that he was a faithful Communist all along.

Cold War Period of armed tension and competition between the United States and the Soviet Union, approximately 1947–1989. (See page 275.)

Stalin mused: "They aren't fighting for communism or for Stalin; they're fighting for Mother Russia." In Russia today, World War II is known as the Great Patriotic War. By the time he died in 1953, Stalin had transformed a backward country into a gigantic empire and major industrial power. He also founded a system that in the long run proved to be inefficient and unreformable and finally collapsed in 1991.

Key Terms

anarchism (p. 267)

autocracy (p. 265)

Bolshevik (p. 269)

caesaropapism (p. 266)

capital goods (p. 273)

Cold War (p. 276)

communism (p. 269)

Constantinople (p. 264)

consumer goods (p. 273)

CPSU (p. 273)

Cyrillic (p. 264)

Duma (p. 270)

exclave (p. 265)

Five-Year Plans (p. 273)

gensek (p. 273)

imperialism (p. 269)

Narodniki (p. 267)

New Economic Policy (NEP) (p. 272)

paranoia (p. 273)

proletariat (p. 267)

purge (p. 273)

Siberia (p. 264)

Slavophiles (p. 267)

Tatar (p. 264)

tsar (p. 265)

tyranny (p. 264)

Ukraine (p. 266)

war communism (p. 272)

Westernizers (p. 267)

zemstvo (p. 267)

Further Reference

Figes, Orlando. *Natasha's Dance: A Cultural History of Russia.* New York: Metropolitan Books, 2002.

Fitzpatrick, Sheila. *Everyday Stalinism: Ordinary Life in Extraordinary Times.* New York: Oxford University Press, 1999.

Gilbert, Martin. *The Routledge Atlas of Russian History: From 800 B.C. to the Present Day,* 3rd ed. New York: Routledge, 2002.

Gooding, John. *Socialism in Russia: Lenin and His Legacy, 1890–1991.* New York: Palgrave, 2002.

Hosking, Geoffrey. *Russia and the Russians.* Cambridge, MA: Harvard University Press, 2001.

Kort, Michael. *The Soviet Colossus: History and Aftermath,* 6th ed. Armonk, NY: M. E. Sharpe, 2006.

Lewin, Moshe. *The Soviet Century.* London: Verso, 2005.

Lieven, Dominic. *Empire: The Russian Empire and Its Rivals.* New Haven, CT: Yale University Press, 2001.

Madariaga, Isabel de. *Ivan the Terrible*. New Haven, CT: Yale University Press, 2005.

Montefiore, Simon Sebag. *Stalin: The Court of the Red Tsar*. New York: Knopf, 2004.

Read, Christopher. *The Making and Breaking of the Soviet System: An Interpretation*. New York: Palgrave, 2001.

Riasanovsky, Nicholas V., and Mark D. Steinberg. *A History of Russia*, 7th ed. New York: Oxford University Press, 2005.

Service, Robert. *Lenin: A Biography*. Cambridge, MA: Harvard University Press, 2001.

———. *Stalin: A Biography*. Cambridge, MA: Harvard University Press, 2005.

Ulam, Adam B. *The Bolsheviks: The Intellectual and Political History of the Triumph of Communism in Russia*. Cambridge, MA: Harvard University Press, 1998.

Chapter 19

RUSSIA:
THE KEY INSTITUTIONS

Russia now exemplifies the **weak state**, one that cannot effectively collect taxes, pass laws, administer justice, and help its citizens. One characteristic of the weak state, typical of Latin America, is the penetration of crime into government. Corruption, lawlessness, and insecurity are the norm. In such a climate, citizens flock to a leader who rules with a strong hand: Putin.

Russia has slid part way back to its authoritarian past, and democracy is unlikely in the near term. Accordingly, we must consider two models, the old Soviet system formed under Stalin and a post-Communist system that tried to break with the past but did not succeed. The dramatic end of the Soviet Union in late 1991 and the birth of a new Russia, we now realize, was less than a **system change**. The new Russian government was not a new broom, and it did not sweep clean. Virtually all of the current leadership has roots deep in the old Soviet system; Russia's constitution overconcentrates power in the presidency, and President Putin has concentrated it more. Much of the old Communist system underlies today's Russia, so we must consider it. As Faulkner said, "The past is not dead. In fact, it's not even past."

Questions to Consider

1. What were the main points of the Stalin system?
2. Why did all three Communist federal systems fail?
3. Is socialism possible without a large bureaucracy?
4. What is the CIS?
5. How do the Russian and French executives compare?
6. In what ways did Yeltsin resemble Gorbachev?
7. How has Putin changed the Russian electoral system? What is it now?
8. Describe the Russian party system. Does it resemble any of the ones we have studied previously?

The Stalin System

The Soviet system started by Lenin and perfected by Stalin lasted into Gorbachev's tenure. The system changed over time, but not much. Its main structural features were as follows.

The Communist Party in Command

Said Lenin: "The Communist party is not a party like other parties." Lenin meant that the Bolsheviks would not play the normal political games of democratic parties, contesting elections and leaving office when voted out. The CPSU was going to run Russia without opposition, and it did, for seven decades.

The CPSU was constitutionally defined as "the leading and guiding force of Soviet society." No other parties were permitted, and no factions were allowed inside the Party. The Party did not run things directly but was a central brain and nervous system that transmitted policy lines, oversaw

weak state   One unable to govern effectively; corrupt and crime-ridden. (See page 279.)

system change   Displacement of one set of political institutions by another. (See page 279.)

Central Committee   Large, next-to-top governing body of most Communist parties.

apparatchik   "Man of the apparatus," full-time CPSU functionary.

the economy, reported discontent, and selected, promoted, and supervised the system's personnel. There was much overlap between Party and state system, so that at the top, most government ministers were also on the Party's **Central Committee**.

Party membership was tightly controlled. Less than seven percent of the Soviet population (at one point, about nineteen million out of 285 million) were Party members, selected on the basis of good records as workers, students, or youth leaders. The CPSU aimed to skim off the best of Soviet society. The Party was organized like a giant pyramid, with primary party organizations at the bottom; district, province, and republic party conferences in between; and an all-union party conference at the top. Presiding over each conference was a committee. Each level "elected" delegates to the next highest level (actually, they were handpicked from above) in what was called "democratic centralism." Party administrators, **apparatchiki**, held the *apparat* together.

Key Concepts

SECURITY POLICE

Security police—sometimes called "secret police," after the Nazi Gestapo—are what make dictatorships work and last. In 1991, defeat of the Iraqi army mattered little; Saddam Hussein could not be toppled because he still had his security police, the guardians of his system. Unlike regular police, security police are highly political and focus on preventing any criticism, dissent, or movements that might harm the regime. They often use terror, "the linchpin of the Soviet system," the key element that held it together.

During Stalin's time there was much truth to this, but after Stalin, terror—the fear of being arbitrarily arrested, imprisoned, sent to Siberia, or shot—receded as a means of political control. The security police, later called the KGB (Committee on State Security) were active until the end (and still are), but their methods were more refined and subtle than the Cheka of Lenin's tenure or the NKVD of Stalin's.

Some three-quarters of a million KGB agents were everywhere: guarding the borders, in factories, hotels, and universities; informing on anyone who contacted foreign tourists, handled classified materials, or dissented against the Soviet system. Millions of Soviet citizens had KGB dossiers, and some found out that the KGB was able to recite even trivial incidents from years earlier. Part-time informers, *stukachi* (squealers), were everywhere.

While the KGB could not actually try most cases—which went to a regular court—they rigged evidence. As the KGB used to say, "Give us the man and we will find you the crime." Dissidents could lose jobs, get sent to psychiatric hospitals, be denied university entrance, have their rooms bugged, lose the right to live in a city, and generally be made uncomfortable by a word from the KGB.

Although the KGB was formally dissolved with the Soviet Union, its chief component reappeared as the Federal Security Service (FSB in Russian), which is staffed by old KGB hands and carries on with the same tasks: supporting the authorities and eliminating any threats to their power. President Putin handpicked his security police heads and is personally friendly with them. The FSB has strong powers to investigate and arrest, even based on anonymous accusations. Murder and corruption run rampant, but the FSB arrests few. The implication: They are in on the crooked deals and are gathering *kompromat* (compromising materials) with which to blackmail anyone influential.

Three of Yeltsin's prime ministers in a row were high up in the old KGB and then in the FSB. President Putin was a KGB officer and then head of the FSB, and many of his top appointees—known as *siloviki*, the powerful men—are drawn from the two organizations. The more it changes, the more it stays the same.

WHO WAS WHEN: SOVIET PARTY CHIEFS		
Party Chief	Ruled	Main Accomplishments
Vladimir I. Lenin	1917–1924	Led Revolution; instituted War Communism, then NEP.
Josef Stalin	1927–1953	Five-Year Plans of forced collectivization and industrialization; purges; waged World War II; self-deification.
Nikita Khrushchev	1955–1964	Destalinized; experimented with economic and cultural reform; promised utopia soon; ousted.
Leonid Brezhnev	1964–1982	Partially restalinized; refrained from shaking up system; let corruption grow and economy slow.
Yuri Andropov	1982–1984	Cracked down on corruption and alcoholism; suggested major reforms but soon died.
Konstantin Chernenko	1984–1985	*Nichevo.*
Mikhail Gorbachev	1985–1991	Initiated sweeping change, unwittingly collapsed Soviet system.

The All-Union Party Congress of some five thousand delegates would meet for a few days every few years, ostensibly to elect the Central Committee of about 300 full and 150 candidate members. The Central Committee would meet twice a year, usually just before the meeting of its government counterpart, the Supreme Soviet, since the membership of the two bodies overlapped.

Politburo "Political bureau," small, top governing body of most Communist parties.

Above the Central Committee and really running things was the **Politburo**, a full-time decision-making body with about a dozen full members and six candidate members. Politburo decisions were automatically approved by the Central Committee, whose decisions were approved by the Party Congress, and so on down the line. Running the Politburo was a general secretary (*gensek*), called in the West the "party chief." This person in practice usually became supreme boss of both Party and state and assumed dictatorial powers. In most Communist systems, the party chief is the most powerful figure, for he controls the apparat and selects *apparatchiki* who are personally loyal to him.

A Less-Important State Structure

Outside observers agreed that the gigantic Supreme Soviet, with 1,500 members, was not a real parliament. It met only a few days a year to rubber-stamp laws drafted by the top echelons of the Party. Nominally bicameral, the Supreme Soviet "elected" a governing Presidium of twenty members that overlapped with the Politburo. The Presidium simply decreed whatever laws it wished. The Presidium also served as a collective presidency, and its chairman was often called the "president" of the Soviet Union. Since Brezhnev, the Party general secretary was also named president, so as to make clear he headed both state and Party.

The Supreme Soviet also chose a sort of cabinet, the mammoth Council of Ministers, with some eighty-five highly specialized ministries, mostly concentrated on branches of the economy (for example, Ministry of Machine Building for Animal Husbandry and Fodder Production). The Council of Ministers rarely met for collective deliberation. Only Politburo members served as prime minister, or minister of state security (KGB), interior, defense, and foreign affairs, the "power ministries."

■ A Centralized Federal System

The Soviet Union was a federation—like the United States, Canada, and Germany—but one long dominated by the center. What the Politburo in Moscow laid down was implemented throughout the country by the Party. The Soviet Union had some two dozen major nationalities and many more minor ones—104 in all. The fifteen largest got their own Soviet Socialist **Republic** (for example, the Uzbek SSR), which together made the USSR (Union of Soviet Socialist Republics). The nationalities, however, are somewhat dispersed; there are ethnic Russians in every newly independent republic—one-third of the populations of Latvia and Kazakhstan are Russian—and this has sharpened a dangerous nationalities question.

republic   First-order civil division of Communist federal systems, equivalent to U.S. states.

The Russian Federative Republic was by far the biggest and is still today a federation of numerous autonomous regions for the bewildering variety of ethnic groups within it. The chief purpose of Soviet federalism was preservation of language rights. Stalin, who developed Soviet nationality policy, recognized that language and culture are potential political dynamite, so it was best to let each nationality feel culturally autonomous while in fact they were politically subordinate. Stalin's formula was: "National in form, socialist in content." This deception turned out to be unstable. All three of the world's Communist federal systems failed—messy in the Soviet Union, bloody in Yugoslavia, but peaceful in Czechoslovakia—and today the huge Russian Federation still has problems with unity.

The tsarist system imposed a unitary pattern on the empire that was so hated that old Russia was called "the prison of nations." With the Bolshevik Revolution, Finland and the Baltic states of Lithuania, Latvia, and Estonia happily escaped to independence. (In 1940, Stalin swallowed the Baltics and treated their citizens cruelly.) Stalin thought he could retain the tsarist empire in a Soviet Union that, on paper, granted each republic great autonomy.

With Gorbachev's *glasnost* (openness) policy of relative freedom of speech and press, out came the nationalities question with a vengeance. Amid economic uncertainty, many republics prohibited shipment or sale of scarce commodities to other republics, thus nullifying the main point of a federation: economic integration of a large area. In 1991, all fifteen republics departed from the union and legally dissolved it.

Many ex-Soviet nationalities fear, hate, or resent other nationalities. Attitudes border on racism. Particularly delicate is the question of the 25 million Russians who now live outside of Russia. The Russian army has made clear that it will use force to protect them and has already done so in Moldova, where several hundred Romanian-speakers were gunned down. The newly independent republics fear antagonizing Russia.

Why did Soviet federalism fail to integrate its peoples? There are many factors. First, there are so many national groups that not all could have their own territories. Second, the nationalities are dispersed; in Uzbekistan, for example, there are Tajiks, Russians, Jews, Tatars, Koreans, and many others in addition to Uzbeks. It would not be possible to draw a clean line separating nationalities.

Third, the Soviet federal system was devised by Stalin, who drew the borders deliberately to make sure there would be ethnic tension. This gave Stalin the ability to arbitrate disputes and thus increase his own power, the old "divide and rule" technique. Every republic would depend on Stalin. Fourth, the center held too much power, chiefly through the Communist party and KGB, so the federalism was less than genuine.

The Soviet Union paid the price for Stalin's fake federal system. Can a Russian federalism now be devised that will hold the Russian Federation with its eighty-nine component parts together by bonds of trade, laws, and mutual respect? Some fear the Islamist terrorism in the North Caucasus shows how fragile the Russian federal system is.

A Gigantic Bureaucracy

Karl Marx argued that after socialism eliminated class differences, the state would "wither away." German sociologist Max Weber countered that socialism required much more state power and a much larger bureaucracy. Marx was wrong; Weber was right. The Soviet bureaucracy became monstrous, with some eighteen million persons administering every facet of Soviet life. **Bureaucratization** spelled the ruination of the Soviet Union, whose civil servants were slow, marginally competent, inflexible, indifferent to efficiency, corrupt, and immune to criticism except from high Party officials. This bureaucracy, carried over largely intact from Soviet days, still delays and blocks important reforms. Getting bureaucrats to change is one of Putin's hardest tasks.

The Party, in fact, interpenetrated and guided the bureaucracy, what the Party called its *kontrol* function. The Party appointed and supervised all important officials, and this kept them on their toes. If they fouled up or were egregiously crooked, they could get demoted or transferred to a remote area. This tended to make officials extremely cautious and to go strictly by the book. On the other hand, if officials were effective and successful, the Party could recommend them for higher positions. The key tool in this was the **nomenklatura**, a list of some 600,000 important positions and another list of reliable people eligible to fill them, nearly all of them Party members who generally stayed on the list until retirement.

Central Economic Planning

The State Planning Committee, **Gosplan**, was the nerve center of the Soviet economic system, attempting to establish how much of what was produced each year and setting longer-term targets for some 350,000 enterprises. Central planning produced both impressive growth and massive dislocations. Under Stalin, it enabled the Soviet Union to industrialize quickly, albeit at terrible human cost. But it also meant chronic shortages of items the Gosplan ignored. One year no toothbrushes were produced in the entire Soviet Union, a Gosplan oversight.

bureaucratization Heavily controlled by civil servants.

nomenklatura Lists of sensitive positions and people eligible to fill them, the Soviet elite.

Gosplan Soviet central economic planning agency.

Geography

GOVERNMENT IN A FORTRESS

Many great cities were founded as fortresses, but few still have their walls. The Kremlin (from the Russian *kreml*, "fortress") is a walled city dating back centuries. (The present walls were built in 1492.) Triangular in shape and a mile and a half around, the ancient Kremlin houses both government buildings and cathedrals (now public museums). Right next to the Kremlin wall is Lenin's tomb, once used as a reviewing stand by the Politburo for parades in Red Square on May 1 (International Workers' Day) and November 7 (anniversary of the revolution). Also facing Red Square: the colorful onion-shaped domes of St. Basil's Cathedral.

junta Pronounced Spanish-style, "khun-ta"; group that pulls military coup.

Soviet leaders claimed that a planned and centrally directed economy was more rational than a Western market economy. Actual results refuted that, but Soviet bureaucrats were reluctant to surrender central planning, an article of faith of "scientific socialism." In Gosplan the hopes, aims, fears, and sometimes caprices of the Soviet system converged and struggled. Gosplan, itself quite sensitive to the wishes of the Politburo, determined who got what in the Soviet Union, whether steel grew at x percent this year and plastics at y percent next. Heavily computerized, Gosplan was the steering wheel of the Soviet economy.

Democracy

1991: THE COUP THAT FAILED

In August 1991, as Gorbachev was on vacation in the Crimea, most of his cabinet tried to overthrow him. An eight-man **junta** (Russians used the Spanish loan word) of conservatives, calling themselves the "Emergency Committee," said Gorbachev had taken ill and declared his vice-president acting president.

Some Western experts had been predicting a coup for three years. Gorbachev's reforms, cautious as they were, threatened the Soviet system and the jobs and comforts of the Soviet ruling elite. Gorbachev had been warned repeatedly of their anger. In December 1990 Foreign Minister Eduard Shevardnadze resigned in public protest at what he said was a coming dictatorship.

Gorbachev zig-zagged between promising major reforms and reassuring Party conservatives that he would not reform too much. In 1991 Gorbachev again favored reform and with the leaders of nine of the Soviet republics drafted a new union treaty that would give the republics great autonomy within a market economy. This was the last straw for the conservatives. The day before the treaty was to be signed they staged their coup.

For three days the world held its breath. Would the coup by not-very-bright Kremlin apparatchiks succeed? They seemed to hold the upper hand. Among them were the head of the military, the KGB, and the interior ministry. The following are some of the reasons the coup failed:

- Few supported the coup. Tens of thousands of citizens favoring democracy publicly opposed

the coup. Gorbachev was not very popular, but the junta was much worse.

- Boris Yeltsin stood firm. About a mile and a half from the Kremlin is the parliament of the Russian Republic, then presided over by reformist Yeltsin. Yeltsin and his helpers holed up in the building and declared the junta's decrees illegal. A tank column that was sent to take the building instead sided with Yeltsin and defended it. Thousands of Muscovites came to stand guard and to protest the coup. Yeltsin's toughness galvanized opposition.

- The Soviet armed forces started to split. Many commanders either stood on the sidelines or opposed the junta. Facing a bloody civil war, the junta lost its nerve.

- International pressure opposed the coup. All of the major countries made it clear that the Soviet economy, desperate for foreign help, would get no outside investments if the coup succeeded. Foreign broadcasts (heard by Gorbachev himself) heartened the anti-junta forces.

A haggard Gorbachev returned to Moscow vowing further reform. The junta was arrested (one committed suicide). The coup attempt actually hastened the end of the Soviet Union. After it, Gorbachev was revealed as an indecisive failure. Yeltsin bumped him out of power and proclaimed an independent Russia. Democracy got a chance.

The New System

In the months after the failed coup of August 1991, the old Soviet system collapsed, and from the rubble emerged a new system that looks democratic on paper but under Putin is not.

Central Asia Lands between Caspian Sea and China, formerly part of Russia and Soviet Union.

No More Soviet Union

All of the fifteen Soviet republics took advantage of the turmoil of late 1991 to declare their independence. The Baltic republics especially—Lithuania, Latvia, and Estonia—led the way to full, immediate independence. They expelled Soviet police, issued their own passports and visas, and took control of their borders. The other republics soon followed and now all are independent, some more than others. Although Ukraine had been part of tsarist Russia for centuries and was the breadbasket of the Soviet Union, many Ukrainians resented being ruled by Moscow, especially after they read about what Stalin's farm collectivization had done to them—deliberately starved six million people to death. They voted independence and, in 2004, for a pro-Western democracy.

Belarus (formerly Belarussia, the area between Russia and Poland), which had never been an independent country or harbored much separatist feeling, voted for independence, too. But Belarus still uses the Russian ruble as currency and gets sweetheart trade deals with Russia. Its army is closely linked to the Russian army. Belarus in reality never cut its Russian ties and is ruled by Europe's last dictator.

The scariest problem was the ethnic tension that came out in the republics. Minorities who had lived in peace for generations (probably because the KGB was watching) became the target of

Geography

THE FIFTEEN EX-SOVIET REPUBLICS

We should learn the names and approximate location of each of the fifteen former Soviet republics; they are now independent countries, but many are under Russian influence. (See the map at the beginning of Chapter 18). To help you remember the republics, note that there are three groups of three, plus a **Central Asia** group of five (the five -stans), plus one oddball.

Slavic	Baltic	Caucasian	Central Asian	Romanian-Speaking
Russia	Lithuania[†]	Georgia	Turkmenistan*	Moldova (formerly Moldavia)
Ukraine	Latvia[†]	Armenia	Kazakhstan*	
Belarus	Estonia[†]	Azerbaijan*	Kyrgyzstan*	
			Uzbekistan*	
			Tajikistan*	

[†]not in CIS.
*predominantly Muslim.

nationalist resentment. In the Caucasus, blood flowed. Many politicians at the republic level played the nationalist card, and this easily turned into violence. Their messages were simple and effective: Georgia for the Georgians, Uzbekistan for the Uzbeks, Armenia for the Armenians, even Russia for the Russians.

All of the Central Asian republics plus Azerbaijan have a Muslim majority and speak a Turkic language, except the Tajiks who speak a type of Persian (like Iran). There has been Muslim-Christian violence between Azeris and Armenians and in Georgia. Inside the Russian Federation, Muslim Chechnya, brutally crushed by the Russian army, produces murderous terrorists. All together, however, more were killed in ex-Yugoslavia. A big question: In which direction will the ex-Soviet Muslim republics go—toward the modern and secular example of Turkey, to Islamic fundamentalism, or back to an economically and militarily dominant Russia?

A Commonwealth of Independent States

Is anything left of the old Soviet federal system? As it officially ceased to exist at the end of 1991, most of its component republics agreed to form a "Commonwealth of Independent States" (CIS), with headquarters in Minsk, Belarus. Conspicuously missing were the three Baltic republics and

Democracy

RUSSIA'S 2004 PRESIDENTIAL ELECTIONS

Russian presidential elections, held every four years, are modeled on the French two-round system. The 2004 results resembled those of 2000 except Putin won a bigger majority on the first round of 2004, so in neither case was there a second round. In 2004 Putin had less opposition—few dared run against him—and won with more than 70 percent. Russians liked the stability and economic growth Putin had brought.

Turnout was an unenthusiastic 64.4 percent, as many Russians knew Putin would easily win. Three and a half percent voted for "none of the above," allowed on the Russian ballot. The 2004 results are shown in the table on the right.

If no one had won a majority, a runoff would have been held two weeks later between the top two, as was done in 1996. Between the two rounds in 1996, deal-making rounded up majority support for incumbent President Boris Yeltsin. In both 1996

and 2000, most of the Russian mass media, owned by newly rich *oligarchs,* supported the incumbents, and voting irregularities were reported. By 2004, almost all of the media was back in state hands and fawned on Putin. The 2004 election was not democratic. There was nominal competition, but several competing candidates endorsed Putin. And competition is the crux of democracy. Putin, who could have won a fair election, likes to control everything.

Candidate	Party	Percent
Vladimir Putin	United Russia	71.3
Nikolai Kharitonov	Communist	13.7
Sergei Glazev	Motherland	4.1
Against all candidates		3.5

Personalities

PUTIN: THE KGB PRESIDENT

Russian President Vladimir Putin is hard to read and likes it that way; he keeps his emotions and upcoming moves to himself. At first, many dismissed him as a mediocre mid-level KGB bureaucrat (which he was) without the color, intellect, or vision to lead Russia. But he soon emerged as a cold, secretive authoritarian, who stabilized Russia and took near-total power. Unlike his predecessor Yeltsin, Putin is rational, sober, and healthy.

In four months, Putin (pronounced POOH-tin) rose from obscurity to powerful president of the Russian Federation, first as acting president and then elected on his own in 2000. In August 1999, Yeltsin named Putin, then forty-six years old, as his fifth prime minister in seventeen months. Many thought that Putin was another temp, but Yeltsin soon designated him as successor. Yeltsin, extremely unpopular by that point, resigned at the end of 1999, and Putin constitutionally became acting president.

Putin's KGB connections had brought him one good job after another, and his taking of power represents a quiet KGB coup. Nothing else explains how he could rise so fast from obscurity. Putin graduated law school in 1975 and went right into the KGB, where he became a lieutenant colonel in spy operations in East Germany. As the Soviet Union collapsed, Putin worked in St. Petersburg's municipal government, where he became vice mayor in 1994. In 1996, Yeltsin brought him to the Kremlin to supervise relations among Russia's regions and in 1998 made him head of the FSB. In 1999 Putin was named secretary of the powerful Security Council and then premier, his first substantial exposure to the public. His election to president in 2000 (on the first round) was his first run for any office.

Putin is reasonably bright, but his great strength is his background and sponsors in the KGB (now FSB), who have *kompromat* on Russia's most powerful people. They know exactly who is corrupt and

Vladimir Putin

who stashes money overseas, including politicians and oligarchs.

Many call Putin authoritarian, but Russians have always rallied to a strong ruler in times of danger and decay, precisely what the Yeltsin years brought. No pure democrat could survive and govern Russia at this stage of its development. By new laws, threats, demotions, or criminal trials, Putin controlled the bureaucracy, media, Duma, regional governors, oligarchs, and private groups and now, unlike Yeltsin, is fully in charge.

Putin created mass support by renewing the war in Chechnya (see page 329). Chechen bombs in several Russian cities blew up apartment houses and schools and killed hundreds. The Russian people and army wanted revenge. Putin's orders to crush Chechen rebels drew nearly complete support and let him easily win the presidency in 2000 and re-election in 2004. He is limited to two terms.

Putin allowed President Bush to portray him as a warm friend, especially after 9/11, but by 2003 turned hostile over the Iraq war and alleged U.S. meddling in Russian and Ukrainian politics. Putin's economic views are vague. He passed some long-overdue legal and commercial reforms but brought Russia's oil and gas—its major exports—back under Kremlin control. Putin's goals are those of a KGB officer: restore Russia's power and old borders. Democracy got in the way and was repealed.

Georgia. Georgia was later forced, in the middle of a civil war abetted by Moscow, to sign the CIS treaty. No one quite knows what the powers of the CIS are, but most now think it is a Moscow plan to regain control over the ex-Soviet republics, in effect, to rebuild the Russia of Peter the Great.

There are reasons for some republics retaining ties with giant Russia. First, eight of the twelve CIS member republics are landlocked and need Russia for access to the outside world. Industrially, all are tied to the Russian economy for manufactured goods and energy. Financially, over the decades many of these republics benefited from major Soviet aid.

New Constitution

Along with voting for a new parliament, in late 1993 Russians also approved a new and completely different constitution, one modeled on de Gaulle's 1958 French constitution.

A Strong President   Many observers now say that the presidency, borrowed from French *semipresidentialism*, started too strong, got stronger, and is being misused. The Russian president—elected for a maximum of two four-year terms—sets basic policy, names the prime minister and other top officials, and can veto bills and dissolve parliament. In many areas the president can simply rule by decree. The president can give himself strong emergency powers. The president's power could theoretically be offset by opposition parties in the Duma, but President Putin owns the Duma. There is no vice-president; if the president dies or is incapacitated, the prime minister serves as acting president until elections are held within three months. This happened when Yeltsin suddenly resigned at the end of 1999.

A Prime Minister   Again on the French model, Russia has a prime minister who serves as the president's chief administrator. The president can name and fire prime ministers at will, but they must be confirmed by the Duma, and Yeltsin had some trouble doing this. Putin has no such trouble; the

Geography

RUSSIA'S COMPLEX FEDERALISM

Unlike U.S. states or German *Länder,* Russia's subdivisions are not the same or equal. Instead, there are a confusing five levels:

- seven huge regions set up by Putin in 2000, overseen by his hand-picked "super-governors."
- twenty-one republics, homelands of the major non-Russian nationalities. For example, the

Tatars have Tatarstan, and the Buryats have Buryatia.

- fifty-two *oblasts* (provinces), mostly populated by Russians.
- six *krais* (territories).
- ten autonomous *okrugs* (districts), ethnic portions of oblasts or krais that claim special status.

Duma simply obeys. If the Duma rejects the president's nominee for prime minister three times, the president can dissolve the Duma and hold new parliamentary elections. In 2004, President Putin named an experienced administrator, Mikhail Fradkov, as his prime minister with solid Duma approval. Fradkov speaks English and Spanish.

A Federal System The federal system is carried over from the old Soviet structure. The country's official name is the Russian Federation; it consists of eighty-nine regions—most of them *republics*—twenty-one of which are predominantly non-Russian. Each region is supposed to be bound by treaty to the Federation, but not all have signed, and they do not all like Moscow's rule.

Democracy

1993: THE SECOND COUP THAT FAILED

The 1991 coup attempt was carried out by members of Gorbachev's own executive branch and was stopped by members of the Russian (not Soviet) parliament in its White House some distance from the Kremlin. The October 1993 coup attempt was by a paralyzed parliament that occupied the White House and was crushed by armed forces under President Yeltsin, who was now in the Kremlin.

The trigger of the 1993 attempt was Yeltsin's order to dissolve the Russian parliament and hold new elections. (The old Supreme Soviet disappeared with the USSR at the end of 1991.) The Russian parliament had been elected in 1989 under the old regime, when the CPSU still held sway; accordingly, it was incoherent and incapable of passing a new constitution. Yeltsin could no longer govern with this parliament, and, indeed, it was high time for free and fair parliamentary elections.

But the old parliament did not like being put out of business and called Yeltsin dictatorial. A majority of deputies declared the dissolution illegal and holed up in the White House, hoping that the country and especially the army would side with it. They did not; instead, tanks shelled the White House until it caught fire.

Yeltsin won but he lost. New elections were held in December 1993, but by then so many Russians were

Russian Parliament, the "White House" some distance from the Kremlin, was the scene of two dramatic showdowns. In 1991 Boris Yeltsin stood here and faced down the junta that attempted to oust Gorbachev, but in 1993 it was Yeltsin who ordered the building shelled to break a coup attempt by parliamentarians. The White House was quickly restored and now houses Russia's State Duma.

disillusioned with reforms that brought crime, inflation, and unemployment that they voted in a parliament, now called the State Duma, that was heavily antireformist and anti-Yeltsin. Yeltsin had to dump many reformist ministers.

de facto   In fact even if not formally admitted.

State Duma   Lower house of Russia's parliament.

One Caucasian Muslim republic, Chechnya, which had resisted Russian rule since its original tsarist conquest, won temporary **de facto** autonomy but was then shelled into ruin.

During the 1990s, local strongmen—"elected," but not democratically—turned republics into corrupt personal fiefdoms. Putin ended that by giving himself the power to appoint republic governors. He further recentralized power in Moscow by creating seven new large regions and personally appointing their governors from FSB ranks. Current Russian federalism is no more genuine than was Soviet federalism: Both give the most power to the center. Given the size and unruly nature of many areas and nationalities, Russia needs considerable centralization of power if it is to hold together. Under Yeltsin, Russia was falling apart, so Putin did what he had to do.

A Bicameral Parliament   The bicameral parliament resembles the U.S. Congress but no longer has any power to contradict the Russian presidency. The lower house, the **State Duma**

Democracy

RUSSIA'S 2003 OBEDIENT PARLIAMENTARY ELECTIONS

Russia's 2003 Duma elections were far less competitive than the previous ones in 1999. Basically, Putin's United Russia party took over the Duma, turning Russia from a fragmented party system into a dominant-party system. Two small liberal parties were wiped out. Fewer Russians bothered voting; turnout was only 56 percent. International observers called the elections flawed because of the state-controlled media and ballot-box stuffing.

In 1999, of the twenty-six parties that ran for the State Duma, six cleared the 5-percent threshold to win some of the 450 seats. In 2003, only four parties cleared the 5-percent threshold.

Total seats were not proportional to party vote because half of the seats were filled in 225 single-member districts. In 2004 fifteen independent deputies were elected on that basis, but that will not happen again as Putin eliminated the single-member constituencies. Several seats were unfilled, either because of voting irregularities or the war in Chechnya. The next parliamentary election will be under the straight PR system that Putin preferred.

Party	Orientation	Percent PR Vote	Total Seats
United Russia	pro-Putin	38	306
Communists	socialist	13	52
Liberal Democrats	right nationalist	11	36
Motherland	left nationalist	9	38
Yabloko	democratic	4	0
Union of Right-Wing Forces	reformist	4	0

(reviving the old tsarist name), consists of 450 deputies elected for up to four years (but not in sync with presidential elections). The Duma passes bills, approves the budget, and confirms the president's nominees for top jobs. It can vote no confidence in a cabinet and, along with the upper house, can theoretically override a presidential veto with a two-thirds majority. That is unlikely to happen under Putin.

The upper house, the Federation Council, consists of two members named by each of the eighty-nine regional governments of the Russian Federation. Since Putin names the regional governors, he indirectly also picks the regions' deputies for the Federation Council. The Council's duties differ somewhat from the Duma's. Only the Federation Council can change internal boundaries and ratify the use of armed forces abroad. It appoints top judges and prosecutors and can remove them. Putin controls both houses of parliament, and they pass any law he wants, including laws that give him more power.

A Proportional Electoral System   In 2005 Putin told the Duma to institute straight *proportional representation* (see page 191) with voting by party list and not for individuals. The Duma obeyed. This replaced the system Yeltsin had instituted, a *mixed-member* system inspired by Germany, with half of the Duma's 450 seats elected by proportional representation (with a 5-percent threshold), and half by single-member districts with plurality win. Under Putin's new PR system, there are no longer any independent candidates because there are no more single-member districts.

A Constitutional Court   The constitutional court is borrowed chiefly from the United States but with some French and German features. The Russian Constitutional Court has nineteen judges appointed by the president and confirmed by the upper house. These judges are supposed to be independent and cannot be fired. They may act both on citizens' complaints and on cases submitted by government agencies. The court is supposed to make sure all laws and decrees conform to the constitution. Putin however, put it back under political control so that it does little to promote the rule of law in Russia.

■ A Party System under Construction

From a one-party system under the Soviets, Russia went to a fragmented system of many weak parties to what is now effectively a dominant-party system (see page 358). Several of Russia's political parties sprang up quickly but were weak, divided, constantly changing, and *personalistic*, like Latin American parties (see page 499). Russia's top parties aimed chiefly at getting their leaders elected. In the 1999 Duma elections, five parties had present or former prime ministers as leaders. Putin invented the United Russia party, his vehicle to win the presidency twice and dominate the Duma. And not all Russian parties are democratic; some preach chauvinism or a return to communism.

The party system is perhaps the foundation of political stability in the modern world. Britain is basically a "two-plus" party system, France is a multiparty system, and Germany has recently turned from a "two-plus" to a multiparty system. A system with too many parties, some of them extremist, poses a serious threat to democracy. Some thought that Russia was headed that way, but the 2003 Duma elections show Russia going the other way, to a dominant-party system (see the chapter on Mexico) with no democratic checks or balances on an all-powerful president. Yes, Russians could theoretically elect a Duma to offset the president, but with the Russian preference for a strong hand at the top and the media back in government hands, this will not soon happen.

Key Terms

apparatchik (p. 280)
bureaucratization (p. 283)
Central Asia (p. 285)
Central Committee (p. 280)
de facto (p. 290)
Gosplan (p. 283)
junta (p. 284)

nomenklatura (p. 283)
Politburo (p. 281)
republic (p. 282)
State Duma (p. 290)
system change (p. 280)
weak state (p. 280)

Further Reference

Andrews, Josephine T. *When Majorities Fail: The Russian Parliament, 1990–1993.* New York: Cambridge University Press, 2002.

Baker, Peter, and Susan Glasser. *Kremlin Rising: Vladimir Putin's Russia and the End of Revolution.* New York: Scribner, 2005.

Brown, Archie, ed. *Contemporary Russian Politics: A Reader.* New York: Oxford University Press, 2001.

Knight, Amy. *Spies without Cloaks: The KGB's Successors.* Princeton, NJ: Princeton University Press, 1996.

Marsh, Christopher. *Russia at the Polls: Voters, Elections, and Democratization.* Washington, D.C.: CQ Press, 2002.

Medish, Vadim. *The Rise and Fall of the Soviet Union,* 5th ed. Upper Saddle River, NJ: Prentice Hall, 2002.

Nichols, Thomas M. *The Russian Presidency: Society and Politics in the Second Russian Republic.* New York: Palgrave, 2001.

Pravda, Alex, ed. *Leading Russia: Putin in Perspective.* New York: Oxford University Press, 2005.

Remington, Thomas F. *The Russian Parliament: Institutional Evolution in a Transitional Regime, 1989–1999.* New Haven, CT: Yale University Press, 2001.

―――. *Politics in Russia,* 4th ed. New York: Longman, 2006.

Rubenstein, Joshua, and Alexander Gribanov, eds. *The KGB File of Andrei Sakharov.* New Haven, CT: Yale University Press, 2005.

Walker, Edward W. *Dissolution: Sovereignty and the Breakup of the Soviet Union.* Lanham, MD: Rowman & Littlefield, 2003.

White, Stephen. *Russian Politics.* New York: Oxford University Press, 2006.

Chapter 20

Russian
Political Culture

As the Soviet regime declined and collapsed in the late 1980s and early 1990s, the word "democracy" had a positive ring among Russians. It stood for a new beginning, for justice and prosperity, and for joining the Western world. The leading political party was *Demrossiya*, Democratic Russia. Now, after living through several years of economic decline, lawlessness, and national weakness, few Russians care about democracy. They want food on the table, order, and stability, and most think the authoritarian Putin has given it to them. Polls find that only a minority of Russians think democracy is always best, and many say they would vote for Stalin. The school system never educated Russians on the crimes of Stalin, so many think he was just a strong leader. Under orders, Russian schools dropped an honest textbook on Stalin. Germans imperfectly faced their past, Japanese less so, but Russians hardly at all.

Ignoring the crucial factor of political culture, we naively assumed the collapse of the Communist regime would unleash liberal democracy and free-market prosperity. Instead it brought monumental lawlessness and poverty. A handful of **oligarchs** got very rich buying state business (especially oil) at giveaway prices. Mafia gangs were into everything, including the government. Some called the system, half in jest, a **kleptocracy**. The breakdown demonstrated what some scholars long suspected, that under the law-and-order surface of Soviet rule, Russian society was very weak—indeed, it had been made deliberately weak—and could not sustain a free democracy, at least not for some time.

Questions to Consider

1. How can democracy grow in a country where "democracy" brought decay and poverty?
2. Why is democracy harder in Russia than in ex-Communist Central Europe?
3. Was Solzhenitsyn right about American culture? Why then has it spread worldwide, especially among young people?
4. How can you tell if a system is based on ideology? Was the Soviet system? What empirical indicators could you look for?
5. What is *civil society* and how do you get it? Is it the same as *pluralism?*
6. Has Russia now stabilized, or is it still "Weimar Russia"?
7. What is the difference between immoral business behavior in America and Russia?
8. Why did we think Russia after communism would quickly become like us?

The Russian Difference

Central Europe discarded its Communist regimes in 1989, and within five years Poland, the Czech Republic, and Hungary were functioning democracies with growing, mostly private, market economies. During this period, the Soviet Union, trying to make the same transition, collapsed

oligarchy   Rule by a few. (See page 295.)

kleptocracy   Rule by thieves. (See page 295.)

indigenous   Home-grown, rooted in the local soil.

glasnost   Gorbachev's policy of media openness.

rump state   Leftover portions of a country after dismemberment. (See page 297.)

both economically and politically. Why the difference between Central Europe and Russia?

First, there are cultural differences between the mostly Roman Catholic countries of Central Europe and Eastern Orthodox Russia (see box on page 298). Second, the Communists succeeded in capturing Russian *nationalism,* so that a Russian could take a certain pride in communism. For Central Europeans, communism was put and kept in place by Soviet bayonets and was profoundly at odds with **indigenous** nationalism.

Perhaps more basically, communism had been implanted in Central Europe much later (after World War II) than in the Soviet Union (during World War I); it did not have as much time to take hold. Russians had nearly three-quarters of a century of Communist rule (1917–1991), enough for three generations to know only one system. Furthermore, the previous tsarist system had not been democratic either and was just in the early stages of capitalist economic development.

The system Russians were used to provided them with jobs (constitutionally guaranteed) and a low but generally predictable standard of living. An apartment, once you got one, was tacky by Western standards but cost only a few dollars a month. Few Russians worked hard; there was little point to it. Now, suddenly Russians were told their jobs are not guaranteed and that reward is linked to individual achievement.

The result was psychological disorientation and fear. The economy declined, inflation grew, unemployment increased, and parents worried over how to feed their children. The old legitimacy of Party and leadership collapsed, and nothing took its place. First Gorbachev and then Yeltsin lost their early credibility; they had indecisively zigged and zagged so long on the economy that few saw them as leaders.

In the vacuum of belief, cynicism and despair reign. Some Russians rediscovered their Orthodox church, which grew after the Communist collapse but has not kept growing. Few attend Orthodox services (but Catholicism and Protestantism are expanding in Russia). Many Russians believe in nothing and say everything is going wrong. Most are politically numb and care nothing for democracy. But people have to believe in something; cynicism cannot sustain a society. Western values of a free society, of morality rooted in religion, of civil rights, and of individual achievement in a market economy are talked about by some intellectuals but not widely held. Seven decades of Communist rule stomped them out; they are being painfully relearned.

■ The Mask of Legitimacy

For decades, the CPSU tried to pound into Soviet skulls the feeling that the regime was legitimate—that is, it had the right to rule—and was leading the country through the difficulties of "building socialism" to the working utopia of communism. It is impossible to say how many really believed this. At various times, many did. Foreigners were treated to performances of marchers, youth delegations, and seemingly frank conversations with officials that were designed to show that Soviets believed in the system. In private, Western journalists were sometimes able to establish contacts who told them otherwise: dissident intellectuals, bitter workers, and even Party members who had come to doubt the worth of the system.

When Gorbachev permitted increased freedom of expression in the late 1980s, **glasnost**, torrents of criticism poured out. Freed from fear of the police, the media bitterly criticized the

Geography

Serbia is bounded on the north by Hungary;
on the east by Romania and Bulgaria;
on the south by Macedonia, Albania, and Montenegro;
and on the west by the Adriatic, Bosnia, and Croatia.

In 2003 Yugoslavia, a **rump state**, changed its name to Serbia and Montenegro. The old Yugoslavia of 1918–1941 and 1945–1991 included Slovenia, Croatia, Bosnia, and Macedonia, all of which are now independent. Why not just call it Serbia? Its government wished to preserve the boundary agreements that used the name Yugoslavia. In 2006, Montenegro (Black Mountain) voted in a referendum to depart from the federation. Serbia lost its outlet to the sea and returned to what it was called before World War I. In 1999, Serbia lost control of Kosovo and its largely Albanian population. With the bounding exercises you have now done, you should be able to locate most countries of Europe. Which European lands have not been named in our bounding exercises?

bureaucracy, the Party, and the corruption of both. The mask of Soviet legitimacy slipped away to reveal a system that satisfied few. The trouble was that there was no consensus on what should replace it. The broad masses (Russian: *narod*) generally wanted a cleaned-up socialism that guaranteed everyone a good standard of living. They showed little understanding of democracy or a market system. Many of the better-educated, on the other hand, understood that socialism was defective and should be scrapped in favor of free politics and free economics. Those whose jobs depended on the old system saw change as a threat. And many Russians simply did not know what to think. They had never before been asked for their opinions.

Many Russians have turned to Russian nationalism, a powerful impulse long manipulated by the Communists, and to newly freed Russian Orthodox Christianity, which enjoyed an upsurge for a few years. Russian nationalism and the Orthodox faith, however, cannot cement Russia together: Twenty-one ethnic republics are non-Russian, mostly Tatar and Muslim (over 10 percent of Russia's population), which harbor their own nationalism and separatism. No symbols unite all Russians. Some like the new tricolor flag (based on a tsarist design); others want to bring back the red flag with hammer and sickle. National day is no longer November 11 to celebrate the revolution (although thousands, out of nostalgia, still parade) but June 12 to celebrate Russia's declaration of independence in 1990 (for which few parade). Many Russians deplore the breakup of the Soviet Union.

Geography

HUNTINGTON'S "CIVILIZATIONAL" DIVIDE IN EUROPE

In an influential but controversial 1993 article in *Foreign Affairs,* Harvard political scientist Samuel P. Huntington argued that with the Cold War over, profound differences of culture were dividing the world into several "civilizations" that have trouble understanding each other. What Huntington called "civilizations" mostly follow religious lines: the West European (with a North American branch), the Slavic/Orthodox, Muslim, Hindu, Confucian, Japanese, and Latin American.

In Europe, said Huntington, the key geographic line is still where Eastern Orthodoxy meets the two branches of Western Christianity, Catholicism and Protestantism, a line running south from the Baltic republics (Lithuania is mostly Catholic, Latvia and Estonia Protestant) and along the eastern borders of Poland, Slovakia, Hungary, and Croatia. West European civilization, initially in Protestant countries, led the way to democracy and capitalism. Catholic Europe followed more recently. Poland, the Czech Republic, and Hungary turned quickly to market systems and democracy after ousting their Communist regimes in 1989.

But notice the difficulty experienced by Slavic/Orthodox countries such as Russia, Ukraine, Serbia, and Romania in making this transition. Basic assumptions about individual freedom and choice, private property, personal rights, and the rule of law that are widespread in West Europe have not developed in the same way in Slavic/Orthodox Europe. One key point: Orthodox culture is much less individualistic, and this helps account for economic behavior.

Economic *shock therapy* (the sudden introduction of a free market) soon brought rapid growth to Poland. Applied in Russia, it simply collapsed the economy: "shock without therapy." Many observers suggest the differences between Poland and Russia are cultural, that Poland has always faced west and Russia not. Huntington's theory does not mean that other civilizations cannot become free-market democracies, just that it may take some time.

The Illusion of Ideology

Some studies of the Soviet Union paid great attention to Marxism-Leninism, the *ideology* of communism. In truth, for many years ideology had counted for little in the Soviet Union; with *glasnost* it disappeared from sight. Much of Soviet "ideology" was little more than Russian national pride masking feelings of inferiority.

Gulag The Soviet central prisons administration.

Political Culture

SOLZHENITSYN, A RUSSIAN MYSTIC

In 1963 a short, grim novel, *One Day in the Life of Ivan Denisovich,* burst on the Soviet literary scene. In detailing the horrors of Siberian forced labor, its author spoke from intimate experience: Alexander Solzhenitsyn had lived in such a camp from 1945 to 1953 and then in Siberian exile for another three years. His crime: As an artillery captain he criticized Stalin in a letter to a friend.

But the nightmare conditions did not break Solzhenitsyn; they made him stronger. Freed during Khrushchev's brief period of liberalization, Solzhenitsyn resolved to tell the whole story of Soviet repression through novels and nonfiction. But *One Day* was about as much of the truth as the regime allowed—and that was under the unusual circumstances of Khrushchev's destalinization drive—and Solzhenitsyn was soon expelled from the official writers' union and unable to publish.

Smuggled to the West, though, his works were celebrated. Solzhenitsyn has a boundless love for Russia and long believed communism was a temporary mistake—imported from the West—that could be cured. Like a nineteenth-century Slavophile, Solzhenitsyn wrote a long letter to the Kremlin's rulers urging them to abandon communism, world empire, heavy industry, and domination over non-Slavic nationalities and to return to the Orthodox faith, a simple agricultural life, and the spiritual roots of old Russia.

In 1973 his monumental *Gulag Archipelago* was released in Paris. A massive compilation of the reports of 227 other camp survivors, *Gulag* showed that capricious terror was built into the Soviet system, that by the 1940s there were from 12 to 15 million people in the **Gulag** at any one time, and that most had committed no crime. That angered the authorities, who bundled Solzhenitsyn onto a plane in 1974 and did not let him back.

Solzhenitsyn was not merely anti-Communist. He also hated anything Western: rationality, technology, materialism, legality, even personal freedom (which, he held, has degenerated into license). He was not particularly impressed by the United States and lived as a recluse on a Vermont estate. At the 1978 Harvard commencement, he thundered:

> Should someone ask me whether I would indicate the West such as it is today as a model to my country, frankly I would have to answer negatively. Through intense suffering our country [Russia] has now achieved a spiritual development of such intensity that the Western system in its present state of spiritual exhaustion does not look attractive. After the suffering of decades of violence and oppression, the human soul longs for things higher, warmer, and purer than those offered by today's mass living habits, introduced by the revolting invasion of publicity, by TV stupor, and by intolerable music.

Although Solzhenitsyn became a U.S. citizen, he never became culturally American. Instead, he returned to Russia in 1994 with his mystical Russian nationalism. There his TV show flopped, and few Russians cared to hear about Stalin's crimes. Young Russians want to make money; material longing trumped spiritual longing. The materialist West had won.

civil society Associations larger than the family but not part of government and the pluralistic values that come with them.

Marxism, by predicting the collapse of the capitalist West, tried to reassure Russians that they would eventually emerge superior. They were "building socialism," which at a certain point would surpass the United States and turn into a Communist utopia with no social or economic problems. In earlier decades some Soviets believed it, but many American academics went way overboard in supposing ideology was the basis of the Soviet system. The Soviet system turned people into opportunists. Young people joined the Party to get into universities, to win job promotions, to become military or civilian officials. Most were cynical and cared nothing for Marxism-Leninism. They were motivated by careers, not ideology.

Marxism is basically a method of analysis, one that stresses social classes and their conflicts. As such, it stayed far livelier in the West, where it faced constant argument and challenge. In the Soviet Union, it atrophied. Applying this tool of analysis to Soviet society was the last thing the *apparat* wanted, as it would have revealed a pampered Party elite lording it over a wretched proletariat. Soviet Marxists thus focused on the West and cranked out the standard clichés, such as the "sharpening of contradictions" and "increasing tempo and magnitude of crises." The West was supposed to collapse any minute. After some decades, few took it seriously. Soviet students took required classes on Marxism-Leninism with the enthusiasm of American students going to compulsory chapel.

The constant mouthing of a dead doctrine created a climate of cynicism, hypocrisy, and opportunism. With the collapse of the Soviet system, Marxism-Leninism collapsed like the house of cards it always was. Marxist ideology was always a defective foundation, but what kind of society can they build with no foundation?

■ The Rediscovery of Civil Society

Political scientists since Tocqueville (in his brilliant *Democracy in America* in the 1830s) have held that the crux of democracy is the autonomy of **civil society**. Independent enterprises, churches, associations, clubs, educational institutions, and the media interact with each other and with government to produce democracy. No pluralism, no democracy. The crux of the Soviet system, however, was the stomping out of civil society by the state. Nothing was to be autonomous; everything in society was to be under strict state supervision, in turn supervised by the Party. The Communists had deliberately crushed civil society, and the Soviet collapse left a vacuum where there should be one. Some happily anticipated that civil society would emerge in post-Communist Russia as it had in Central Europe.

Initially, civil society did emerge in Russia, and within a few years some 450,000 private groups and charities were voicing citizen concerns and demands. In 2005, however, an obedient Duma passed two Putin measures to bring civil society under government control. One new law requires all associations to register with the state, effectively banning independent political groups, especially foreign foundations that promote democracy and civil rights. Such groups encouraged Ukraine's 2005 Orange Revolution, and Putin did not want a replay of it in Russia. Another bill set up a "Public Chamber" of 126 distinguished citizens (one-third appointed by Putin), allegedly representatives of civil-society organizations, to monitor government and strengthen democracy. Few were fooled, and many called it a smokescreen to strengthen Putin's power. The crux of civil society is the autonomy of its many groups; place them under state control and they are no longer civil society.

The concept of civil society starts with the notion that state and society are two different things, although they clearly influence each other. Society over time evolves informal manners, usages, and customs that make living together possible. The "civil" (as in civilized) indicates a reasonable level of trust, politeness, public spirit, and willingness to compromise. A civil society through parents, churches, and schools **socializes** its members to right behavior and "rules of the game" that continue even when the state, through its police and bureaucrats, is not watching.

socialize To teach political culture, often informally.

The state, the formal institutional structures that wield power, cannot substitute or replace civil society, although the Communists tried. Attempting such a substitution creates a system where people lack basic civility and see no need to play by informal rules of the game. Businessmen cheat and mafia gangs muscle into all sectors of the economy. Politicians attack each other hysterically, immoderately, with no possibility of compromise; they have never learned restraint. Citizens feel little need to obey the law if they can get away with breaking it. Legitimacy is terribly weak.

The West had centuries to build up its civil societies. Philosophers such as Hobbes and Locke explained rationally why civil society is necessary. Churches, often with threats of eternal damnation, inculcated right behavior. The market system generated usages aimed at keeping dealings fair and predictable. Laws and courts enforced this with a system of contracts, both written and unwritten. All of this has been missing in Russia since the 1917 Revolution. Americans tended to take their civil society for granted until corporate misdeeds reminded them that businesses without ethics undermine the whole system. All civil societies need maintenance and reform from time to time when cheats take advantage of the trust that has been built up.

Political Culture

THE PHILOSOPHICAL GAP

One of the key differences between us and the Russians is philosophical; namely, we are the children of John Locke and they are not. Although few Americans study the philosopher who is at the root of much of our thinking, most have assimilated what the seventeenth-century English thinker had to say: People are rational and reasonable; they have a natural right to life, liberty, and property. Government is good if it preserves these rights and bad if it infringes on them. If this sounds like the Declaration of Independence, it is; Jefferson was an ardent Lockean, as were most of the Founding Fathers. Ever since, Americans have taken to Locke like a duck takes to water; we love his common-sense emphasis on small government and individuals working for the good of themselves and their families. To Russians, this is not common sense.

Russian thought comes out almost the opposite of Locke and traces back to the geographical dilemma of living on a defenseless plain: Either build a strong state or perish. Plugging into the Russian tradition of a strong state is Jean-Jacques Rousseau (see page 91), the radical eighteenth-century French thinker whose theory of the "general will" rejected Lockean individualism in favor of using state power to "force men to be free." With Locke, people form society, and then society sets up a state, all with an eye to preserving property. With Rousseau, the flow goes the other way: The state, guided by the general will, molds society and then redoes individuals. Marxists added a class-struggle gloss to this; Lenin bought the package and then sold it to the Russian people.

Many Americans thought that once communism was overthrown Russians would rapidly become like us: capitalist entrepreneurs and democrats. This neglected the centuries of philosophical underpinning that is utterly lacking in Russia. If there could be a Peace Corps in Russia, the teaching of the philosophical basis of markets, pluralism, and limited government might be one of its first and most urgent tasks. Without a new philosophical outlook, one taken mostly from the West, the Russians will likely stay trapped in their *statist* frame of mind. (For more on statism, see the Mexico chapter.)

In Russia, unscrupulous cheats are the norm, and Russian corporations do things far worse than Enron or Worldcom. When communism fell, we thought the sudden imposition of democratic institutions and a market economy in Russia would quickly bring a civil society. We now see that without the philosophical, moral, economic, and legal understandings of civil society, Russia turns back to authoritarianism.

Political Culture

THE MORAL GAP

America has its share of corporate crooks and cheats, but what would America be like if one could go back over three generations and systematically strip out most moral teachings? What if parents, churches, and schools did not attempt to inculcate a sense of innate right and wrong in young people? What if no one could trust anyone else? The result, I suspect, would be rather like Russia today. This is another area we overlooked in thinking that once communism ended, Russians would quickly become like us.

Russians had ethical training, but it was relativistic, superficial, and based on Marxist theories of social class. That which helps the working class is good, went the litany. The Communist party helps the working class, so it must be good. The Soviet state is totally devoted to the working class, so it must be very good. The Party and the state must therefore be obeyed, respected, and defended. Anyone who goes against them is insane, a wrecker, or a spy. Crime is something that happens only in capitalist countries, where the poor are forced to steal. Private property is inherently wicked, because it has been stolen from the workers who produced it. Under communism, there were no moral absolutes. The Russian Orthodox Church, tightly controlled by the government, confined itself to religious ritual and avoided moral instruction. By contrast, the Polish Catholic Church, for centuries the pillar of Polish civil society, stayed free of state control and critical of communism, always trying to face Poland westward. Religion matters.

Communist rhetoric aside, Soviet citizens soon learned to treat the system with cynicism. With the KGB and its informants everywhere, no one could trust anyone else, and they still do not. With no individual responsibility, stealing, especially from the state, was

okay. After all, it really belonged to no one. Under communism, monstrous rip-offs became standard: Everyone stole and bribed.

When the Soviet Union collapsed, things got worse. Knowing the Party and KGB were watching restrained some Soviets to small rip-offs. Once these external controls vanished, a spirit of "anything goes" was unleashed. Nothing happens without bribes. People who were smart, ruthless, or well-connected grabbed whole industries. Russia was robbed from within by its own bureaucrats. Since Soviets had always been taught that capitalists and *biznesmeny* (long a term of derision, now adopted as a loan word) were crooks and their gains were ill-gotten, many Russians went into business with that image as their norm. The crime rate shot up; only Colombians are more likely to be murdered than Russians. Massive protection rackets, enforced by professional *keelers* (another loan word), were all right because they were just stealing from capitalist thieves.

What escaped both Russians and Americans is that a modern capitalist culture has a considerable moral basis; people have to be able to trust each other. Such a system draws from religious and ethical teachings, legal enforcement, a spirit of trust, and the knowledge that cheating businesses get few repeat customers. It may take a long time to build up this moral consensus. We made the mistake of thinking it would automatically arrive with the free market, which we suppose to be generally self-policing. We have recently discovered that U.S. financial institutions are not self-policing but need some outside controls. For most Russians, a free market means legal cheating. (Some American CEOs think so too.) For capitalism to work right, both in Russia and America, the moral gap must be filled.

■ Natural Egalitarians?

Marxism-Leninism may have vanished in Russia, but many Russians display a tendency toward extreme equality, a natural socialism. Russians resent differences of wealth or income and enviously try to bring the better-off down to their level. Most Russians hated the new-rich oligarchs and were delighted to see Putin break and jail them. Some observers argue that the Russian peasantry, who for centuries tilled the soil in common and shared the harvest, developed highly egalitarian attitudes, which the Communists nourished. Perhaps so, but attitudes are not genetic; they are learned and can be unlearned, given the right conditions. Until new attitudes are learned, however, the old ones can trip up the best-laid plans of reformers.

Political Culture

THE ECONOMICS GAP

In addition to the philosophical and moral foundations of a civil society, another basic point has been overlooked in the eager assumption that Russians would quickly become like us: People have to learn capitalism. A market economy may be something that occurs naturally (whenever buyers and sellers meet), but it is not understood naturally. You have to take courses in market economics and read books and articles about it. Soviet courses covered "bourgeois economics" as part of the history of economic thought but gave it short shrift as a doomed system riven with contradictions, unfairness, and depressions. When their system collapsed, only a few Russian economists had a decent grasp of what makes market economies work.

Especially missing was any appreciation of how money plays an autonomous role in the economy. In Communist countries, there simply was no theory of money. For example, I have tried the following mental experiment on a seminar (at the U.S. Army War College) of U.S., Central European, and Russian colonels, all bright and well-educated. Imagine, I tell them, a miniature country with ten citizens, each of whom works in one hamburger shop. The ten workers make a total of ten hamburgers a day and each is paid $1 a day. Then each buys one hamburger a day with their $1. The government decides to raise the pay of each to $2 a day (by printing an extra ten $1-bills). The output of the workers is still

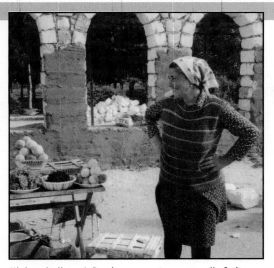

Mini-capitalism: A Russian peasant woman sells fruit near Moscow.

ten hamburgers a day. Within a day or two, what is the price of a hamburger?

The Americans respond fast and almost instinctively: $2! The East Europeans and Russians do not get it. "You haven't given us enough data," they say. Well, how would you explain it to them? It is not so simple. Phrases like "supply and demand" by themselves do not explain much. What we accept as basic and self-evident, Russians do not. (By the way, once you can explain the parable, you have a rudimentary theory of money.)

Americans also favor equality, but it is "equality of opportunity": Everyone has a chance; the results are up to you. An American who gets ahead is usually applauded for his or her ability and hard work. Most Russians do not understand this kind of equality; they expect "equality of result," with each person collecting the same rewards. Those who get ahead are presumed to have cheated, exploited, or bribed (actually, many have). "The rich are living on our poverty," said one elderly Russian lady. In polls, most Russians say the free market and small state are wrong for Russia; only a few favor them. American values of individual work and achievement lend themselves to capitalism; Russian values generally do not.

Russian Racism

With glasnost, hate-filled racist attitudes latent among Soviet nationalities came into the open. Under Soviet law, citizens had their nationality stamped in their internal passports, and, contrary to U.S. usage, nationality throughout East Europe and the ex-Soviet Union does not equal citizenship. For example, one can be a Russian citizen of the Komi nationality. This approach is asking for trouble, because it encourages people to demand an independent state. Educated Russians admire the U.S. approach, which prohibits the official identification of citizens by race or national origin.

Political Culture

THE LEGAL GAP

Much of Russia is lawless, one characteristic of the weak state. Russian police and courts are chaotic and easily bribed. Law is used selectively: Regime opponents get arrested and convicted, but major assassinations go unsolved, and corrupt officials are untouched. Said one Russian law expert ruefully, "The only lawyer around here is a Kalashnikov," a favorite weapon of *keelers*.

The Soviet legal structure broke down almost completely, and it was deficient to begin with. Soviet law paid minimal attention to property. Any big property (land, factories) automatically belonged to the state, and stealing state property could be harshly punished as a form of treason. The Lockean notion that property is a natural right and basis for human freedom was rejected out of hand. Russians, having been inculcated with the Marxist notion that "all property is theft," have trouble grasping the democratic and capitalist notion that "private property means personal freedom."

Weak or absent in the old Soviet socialist legal code, which Russia inherited, are such basics of the Common Law as ownership, contracts, torts, and bankruptcy. If you set up a business in the United States, Canada, or West Europe, you are reasonably confident your property and earnings will not be taken from you. In Russia, you have little confidence. Not only are business and property laws brand new, there is no legal culture built up over the years that regards these areas as important. One result is that foreigners and Russians alike are reluctant to invest in Russia; they may lose everything.

By way of contrast, Poland adopted its excellent Commercial Code in 1935, borrowed heavily from the Italian. The Polish Communist regime never repealed this code and after the Communists' ouster in 1989, Polish jurists simply dusted it off and put it into practice. Both Poles and foreigners who invest in Poland enjoy legal protections. Result: The Polish economy was for most of the 1990s the fastest growing in Europe. Russia finally passed commercial and criminal codes in 2002, based in part on Western legal concepts.

And Russians tend to pigeonhole everyone on the basis of their nationality. Some nationalities are acceptable, others despised. Russians, for example, respect the Baltic peoples as European, civilized, and "cultured." On the other hand, Russians speak scathingly of the Muslim peoples of the **Caucasus** and **Central Asia** as lawless and corrupt mafiosi who make too many babies. The theme of the differential birthrate comes up often. Most Russian families nowadays have one child (also the norm in much of West Europe). Muslim families have many children, sometimes eight or more. Some Russians fear that their stagnant numbers will be swamped by a tide of inferior peoples. When bombs blew up apartment houses in 1999, killing close to 300 people, the Russian government and the people eagerly blamed alleged Chechen terrorists and supported a new war to crush them. People from the Caucasus and Central Asia were often the victims of ethnic violence by Russians.

Caucasus Mountainous region between Black and Caspian Seas

Central Asia Region between Caspian Sea and China.

The non-Russian nationalities feel little affection or affinity for the Russians. In Central Asia, several republics have made their local language the only official language. Educated Uzbeks, for example, know Russian perfectly, but now they speak only Uzbek as a way of making local Russians feel unwelcome. Many Russians are getting the message and leaving Central Asia. Virtually none have fled from the Baltic republics, however, and some Russians there even support independence. They feel they would be treated fairly by the cultured Balts. They fear the Muslims of the Caucasus and Central Asia.

Antisemitism, deliberately cultivated in tsarist Russia, is back but unofficial and played down in public statements. Russian nationalists and Communists point to the handful of oligarchs of Jewish or partly Jewish origin and see a sinister international conspiracy called "Zionism." Small nationalist parties of skinheads urge violence against Jews, and tens of thousands of Russian Jews have moved to Israel. Most Russians, however, condemn antisemitism, and in 2002 President Putin got the Duma to pass a law against ethnic extremism.

A Culture of Insecurity

Average Russians are terribly insecure. Crime, corruption, and economic decay dominate their lives. Some compared the 1990s to the Time of Troubles in the early seventeenth century. Others used the phrase "Weimar Russia" to suggest a coming fascism. Before Putin took power, most Russians described the situation as "tense," "critical," or "explosive" and expected anarchy. Many feel Putin made things more secure; they liked his increased power and paid no attention to his undemocratic methods.

Ultimately, Russia can become as democratic as Germany or Spain, but not under conditions of chaos. Putin did restore some order and is much better than Communists, extreme nationalists, and gangsters, but he has no plans for full-fledged democracy.

We now realize that in the early 1990s, when Communist rule cracked and then collapsed, we were expecting too much. We paid insufficient attention to crucial factors of political culture and assumed that capitalism and democracy bring their own political culture with them. They do, but it takes a long time. Thrust onto an unprepared population in the midst of economic decline, democracy and capitalism have not yet taken root in Russia. Spain under Franco was a police state, but strong economic growth made a majority of Spaniards middle class, and in the late 1970s Spain moved easily to democracy. If Putin can do something similar for Russia, he may be remembered favorably.

◼ Russia: Paranoid or Normal?

"We could have been contenders," Russians seem to be saying. We once had a great empire that challenged the Americans; suddenly it vanished. Although support of client states around the globe was a net drain on the Soviet economy, many Russians were proud of their empire. Some analysts argue that the feeling of belonging to a mighty empire served to quiet discontent over shortages and poor living conditions. Every time a new client signed up—Cuba, Vietnam, Ethiopia, Angola—Russians could say, "See, we really are the wave of the future." The loss of empire was a psychological letdown for many Russians.

Russians used to feel they were the equals—maybe the superiors—of the Americans; now the arrogant Americans sneer at Russia. Indeed, it was they who craftily engineered the fall of the Soviet Empire and the collapse of the Soviet Union. Now they are moving in for the kill: the destruction of Russia. What else could the extension of NATO eastward—by adding first Central Europe and now the Baltic states—mean? See what they did to our little Slavic brother Serbia. The Americans gave Russia little money and a lot of bad economic advice, making sure our economy collapsed. Now that we are weak, they cut us off.

Remembering the definition of paranoia—unreasonable suspicion of others—observers were distressed at Russia's signs of paranoia. The images carried by many Russians are terribly untrue. The Soviet and later Russian systems collapsed from their own chiefly economic weaknesses; it was not a U.S. plot. Moscow rejected most Western economic urgings and then got angry when Western banks refrained from investing. Foreign support for building democracy in Russia is not a plot to take over Russia. Such a victim mentality contributed to the growth of nationalist authoritarianism.

The September 11, 2001, terrorist strikes on America produced a remarkable (but short-lived) shift in Kremlin policy. Putin declared solidarity and cooperation with America. Presidents Bush and Putin exchanged warm visits. Putin decided that Russia's modernization lay with the West, especially with America, and 9/11 gave him the opportunity to put it into practice. Hostility to America in

Democracy

FREE MEDIA

One of the basic components of democracy—in addition to competitive elections—is a free press. The easiest way to tell if a country is democratic is to see whether its mass media are controlled or muzzled. If television, radio, newspapers, and magazines routinely criticize the regime and remain open, you probably have a democracy. The government closing them down or taking them over is one of the first signs of authoritarianism. Freedom of information is indispensable to democracies but undermines dictatorships.

As Robert Mugabe consolidated his grip on Zimbabwe, critical newspapers were closed and critical journalists were jailed or expelled. Mugabe's definition of critical: anyone not supporting his regime and its policies. The struggle for democracy in Iran is inseparable from the struggle of independent publications to stay open. Conservatives close them every few months, but they reopen under new names. Russia has moved sharply in this direction, with most of the national media, especially television, taken over by government-linked corporations and the rest cowed into "self-censorship," afraid they will be next. The Kremlin, never stating its intentions, forced some "oligarchs" to relinquish their television networks and newspapers—which had supported first Yeltsin and then Putin in elections. Moscow also prosecutes Russian writers and journalists for critical views. Although not as bad as in Communist times, all of Russia's national media now praise President Putin.

the Russian Duma, media, and military declined—Putin ordered it so. Since the 2003 Iraq War, Russia again turned frosty to America. Paranoia can be turned up or down by government policy.

One of the leading studies of Nazi Germany blamed its rise on "the politics of cultural despair," a situation where everything seems to have failed, where the bonds of civil society have dissolved and nothing has taken their place. How far can despair go before something snaps? Under Yeltsin, Russia was headed for the abyss; Putin seems to have pulled it back just in time.

There are hopes for political stability—but not necessarily democracy—in Russia. Under Putin, the economy grew—based heavily on oil and natural gas exports—and few Russians worried about the choking off of pluralism and democracy. Eventually more Russians are likely to care about democracy. Russians are no more inherently ungovernable or authoritarian than Germans or Spaniards, both of whom grew to democracy after World War II. With some decades of stability and prosperity, Russians can do the same.

Key Terms

Caucasus (p. 305)

Central Asia (p. 305)

civil society (p. 300)

glasnost (p. 296)

Gulag (p. 299)

indigenous (p. 296)

kleptocracy (p. 296)

oligarchy (p. 296)

rump state (p. 296)

socialize (p. 301)

Further Reference

Alexander, James. *Political Culture in Post-Communist Russia: Formlessness and Recreation in a Traumatic Transition.* New York: St. Martin's, 2000.

Brudny, Yitzhak M. *Reinventing Russia: Russian Nationalism and the Soviet State, 1953–1991.* Cambridge, MA: Harvard University Press, 1999.

Bugajski, Janusz. *Cold Peace: Russia's New Imperialism.* Westport, CT: Praeger, 2004.

Chulos, Chris J., and Timo Piirainen, eds. *The Fall of an Empire, the Birth of a Nation: National Identities in Russia.* Brookfield, VT: Ashgate, 2000.

Colton, Timothy J. *Transitional Citizens: Voters and What Influences Them in the New Russia.* Cambridge, MA: Harvard University Press, 2000.

Lukin, Alexander. *The Political Culture of the Russian "Democrats."* New York: Oxford University Press, 2000.

Meier, Andrew. *Black Earth: A Journey Through Russia after the Fall.* New York: Norton, 2003.

Merridale, Catherine. *Night of Stone: Death and Memory in Russia.* London: Granta, 2000.

Pipes, Richard. *Property and Freedom.* New York: Knopf, 1999.

Schmemann, Serge. *Echoes of a Native Land: Two Centuries in a Russian Village.* New York: Knopf, 1997.

Shleifer, Andrei. *A Normal Country: Russia after Communism.* Cambridge, MA: Harvard University Press, 2005.

Smith, Kathleen E. *Mythmaking in the New Russia: Politics and Memory in the Yeltsin Era.* Ithaca, NY: Cornell University Press, 2002.

Chapter 21

RUSSIA:
PATTERNS OF INTERACTION

Going back two centuries, Russian politics has been a tug-of-war between reformist and conservative forces. Post-Communist Russian politics reflects, and to some extent continues, Soviet and even earlier Russian patterns. Since tsarist times Russia has been a system that cries out for reform but contains many conservative forces able and happy to block reform. A hundred years ago educated Russians could recognize the problem: How to reform the unreformable system? Many have tried, and ultimately all failed to both reform and preserve the system.

Questions to Consider

1. How are we watching an old problem in Russia?
2. What did Khrushchev attempt to do and why? Why did he fail?
3. What is the difference between totalitarian and authoritarian?
4. What did Gorbachev attempt to do and why? Why did he fail?
5. Explain *conservative* and *liberal* in the Russian context.
6. Who were Russia's *oligarchs* and what became of them?
7. Why did reforms work in Central Europe but not in Russia?
8. Is *semipresidentialism* inherently unstable? Why?
9. Is Putin building an authoritarian system?

Reformers versus Conservatives

The trouble with Russia is that there are few rules or institutions to regulate and moderate political clashes. Without experience in multiparty competition, a free press, voluntary associations, tolerance, and simple politeness, the new forces freed by the ending of Party control started to play a new game without rules. Their clashes were bound to be chaotic, and they were made worse by insiders who used the unregulated privatization to grab state enterprises cheap.

Earlier editions of this book argued that under the uniform surface of political life in the old Soviet Union existed a permanent struggle between liberals and conservatives, the former for major change toward Western models, the latter for standing pat with the essentially Stalinist system. It is here argued that this conflict continues in the post-Soviet era. In the 1990s, how to build democracy was discussed openly, but now discussions are more subdued, as Putin has deepened and extended his power.

Most of the reformers who rallied to Gorbachev and then to Yeltsin resigned or were dismissed from high office. In many respects they hearkened back to the Russian Westernizers of the nineteenth century who wanted to import Western ways nearly wholesale: a market economy, free democracy, and individualistic philosophy. This led the new reformists to attempt the economic **shock therapy** recommended by Columbia economist Jeffrey Sachs, which earlier worked in Bolivia and Poland. In Russia, such therapy was never fully and correctly applied, and the economy plunged downward (see next chapter).

shock therapy Sudden replacement of socialist by market economy. (See page 309.)

cult of personality Dictator who has himself worshiped. (See page 311.)

What we are calling here "conservatives" covers a broad swath from moderates to extremists. What they have in common is their opposition to the thorough restructuring of the Russian economy. Russia may need reforms, some concede, but they must be our reforms tailored to our conditions. Some old-line Party types would go back to a centralized command economy. Like the old Russophiles of the nineteenth century, they reject Western models and would turn inward, to Russia's roots; accordingly, they are nationalistic, some rabidly so.

These two general camps are halves of the Russian political spectrum that contains several gradations and combinations. Some worried that two extremes of the political spectrum could form a

Democracy

DEFINING DEMOCRACY

Democracy is not a simple thing or one that automatically grows after *authoritarian* or *totalitarian* regimes have fallen. We were naïve about stable democracy soon coming to Russia and Iraq. Democracy is a complex balancing act, requiring (as we explored in the last chapter) a political culture with the right philosophical, moral, economic, and legal underpinnings. Most definitions of democracy include the following:

Accountability. Elected officials must face a real possibility of losing reelection. This induces them to adopt Friedrich's *rule of anticipated reactions* (see page 67).

Equality. One person, one vote. No citizens can be excluded. All may run for office.

Competition. Several candidates and parties compete in free and fair elections. A one-party system cannot be democratic.

Alternation. Occasional turnovers in power replace the "in" party with the "out" party.

Representation. "The room will not hold all," so a few fairly represent the many. The electoral system does this, either by single-member districts (as in the United States and Britain) or proportional representation (as in Germany and Israel).

Free media. Only democracies permit the press to criticize the government. This is the quickest check for democracy.

Harvard political scientist Samuel P. Huntington suggested a "two-turnover test" for stable democracy. Two alternations of government—the "outs" replacing the "ins"—suggest a firmly rooted democracy. Since the Polish Communist regime fell in 1989, Poland has had several turnovers from left to right and back again, indicating stable democracy. Russia has not had a turnover since 1991 and is not soon likely to. Russia's democracy is dubious.

Freedom House in New York City uses a seven-point scale to annually rank countries on how much they accord citizens political rights and civil liberties. This is basically the same as democracy. FH calls 1 to 2.5 "free," 3 to 5 "partly free," and 5.5 to 7 "not free." Russia slid lower during the Putin years. Some of FH's 2006 findings:

United States	1.0	free
Canada	1.0	free
Britain	1.0	free
Japan	1.5	free
Mexico	2.0	free
Brazil	2.0	free
Turkey	3.0	partly free
Nigeria	4.0	partly free
Russia	5.5	not free
Iran	6.0	not free
China	6.5	not free
Saudi Arabia	6.5	not free

Personalities

FAILED REFORMERS: NIKITA KHRUSHCHEV

The Soviet Union had petrified under Stalin, and Nikita Khrushchev attempted to revitalize the system and get it moving toward communism again. He was only partly and briefly successful, for much of the Soviet party and bureaucracy resisted him. We now realize Khrushchev was far from the undisputed master of the Kremlin that Stalin was and had to overcome opposition. Like Gorbachev, he failed.

Born in 1894 of an ethnic Russian family in Ukraine, Khrushchev joined the Bolsheviks shortly after the revolution and worked his way up through party jobs. A protégé of Stalin, Khrushchev did some of the dictator's dirty work in the 1930s, which earned him a full Politburo membership in 1939. During the war he was a political general on the Ukrainian front. After the war he organized party work in Ukraine and then the Moscow region, and carefully packed the party leadership with his supporters, the key to success in Soviet politics.

Stalin's death in 1953 opened a period of jockeying for power. All the Politburo had feared Stalin and longed for stability and personal security. Accordingly, they immediately had the head of the secret police, Lavrenti Beria (like Stalin, a Georgian) shot, putting the KGB under Party control. The first post-Stalin premier was Georgi Malenkov, who advocated relaxing the Stalin system and producing more consumer goods. But Khrushchev was made party first secretary, a post that was always more powerful, and craftily built a coalition against Malenkov, who in 1955 was demoted to minister for power stations. The Soviet leadership abandoned violent death as a way to run a political system.

To consolidate his power and trounce his enemies within the Party, Khrushchev took a dramatic step: He denounced Stalin to a Party congress. A CPSU that was still Stalinist was immobile, incapable of reform or innovation and blocking the productive potential of the Soviet Union under a blanket of fear and routine. At the Twentieth Party Congress in February 1956, Khrushchev delivered a stinging, hours-long tirade against the "crimes of Stalin" who, he said, had murdered thousands of Party comrades and top military officers. Stalin had built a **cult of personality** that must never be allowed again.

Nikita Khrushchev

Communist parties the world over had based themselves on Stalin-worship, and when the speech leaked out, all hell broke loose. A Hungarian uprising was crushed by Soviet tanks; Poland nearly revolted. In the West, longtime Communists resigned from the party. In China, Mao Zedong was horrified at Khrushchev for undermining the Communist camp by denouncing its symbol. Thus began the Sino-Soviet split.

To revitalize the Soviet economy, Khrushchev proposed decentralization. Outvoted in the Politburo, he called a 1957 Central Committee meeting packed with his supporters and backed by the army, which forced his opponents, the "antiparty group," to resign. But CPSU leaders grew irritated at his "harebrained schemes" to boost production (especially of consumer goods), eliminate class differences (everyone would have to work before college, even the elites' children), and outfox Americans by placing missiles in Cuba. They considered him a reckless experimenter and liberalizer, and in October 1964 the Politburo *voted* him out of office, a rare thing in Communist systems. He retired and died in 1971.

The Khrushchev era brought major changes in domestic and foreign policy. A generation of young Party members, including Gorbachev, came of age wanting economic reform. These people, "Khrushchev's children," later staffed the Gorbachev reform effort. Khrushchev was a flamboyant, can-do character, who promised major change. He stressed consumer goods over heavy industry, and this infuriated managers and the military. He permitted publication of anti-Stalin works (such as Solzhenitsyn's *One Day*), then backed off when he saw things getting out of hand. Khrushchev was trying to reform against the interests of the Party *apparatchiki,* the same people who brought down Gorbachev.

red-brown A possible combination of Communists and Fascists, the brown standing for Hitler's brownshirts.

totalitarianism Attempts to totally control society, as under Stalin and Hitler.

authoritarianism Dictatorial rejection of democracy, as Spain under Franco and Chile under Pinochet.

perestroika Russian for "restructuring," Gorbachev's proposals to reform the Soviet economy. (See page 313.)

"**red-brown**" coalition of old Party supporters plus lunatic nationalists. (Moderate conservatives cluster in the Communist party.) Putin's takeover prevented that, so we should not be too critical of him.

Under the label "centrist," another group seeks a middle ground of moderate reforms cushioned by continued state subsidies and ownership. Unfortunately, under Yeltsin this approach led to incredible corruption. Thoroughgoing reformers and democrats, such as the small Yabloko party, are weak because few Russians share their Western-type thinking. One interesting possibility emerged with the 1999 Duma elections. Prime Minister and later President Putin, whose Unity (later United Russia) catchall spanned all political views, indicated he could work with the economic reformers of the Union of Right-Wing Forces. Putin, however, has been cautious about pursuing economic reforms. He prefers control.

■ President versus Parliament

Executive and legislative have been at serious odds in Russia recently, and their competing claims led to anger and violence. The initial problem, as noted earlier, was the carryover from Soviet times of a Russian parliament elected under the old rules and under the Communists in 1989. Most members of this parliament stood firm with Yeltsin during the abortive coup of 1991.

Key Concepts

TOTALITARIAN VERSUS AUTHORITARIAN

Since the 1930s, political science has debated the nature of modern dictatorships. Some political scientists developed theories and models of **totalitarianism** to explain Mussolini's Italy, Hitler's Germany, and Stalin's Soviet Union. Carl J. Friedrich and Zbigniew Brzezinski argued that totalitarian dictatorships have these six points in common:

1. An official ideology
2. A single, disciplined party
3. Terroristic police control
4. Party monopoly of the mass media
5. Party control of the armed forces
6. Central direction of the economy

Widely accepted for years, the totalitarian model gradually came under criticism as unrealistic and oversimplified. Far from total, the systems of Mussolini, Hitler, and Stalin were quite messy. Many citizens knew the regimes were frauds; plans were often just improvisations. The dictators like their systems to *look* total. Totalitarianism was an attempt at total control that always fell short.

The word "totalitarianism" fell into disfavor; instead **authoritarianism** was used to describe modern dictatorships. It can be quite brutal but does not aim for total control of society. Politics is in the hands of a dictator, such as Spain's Franco or Chile's Pinochet, but wide areas of the economy and cultural life are open. Most or all of the above six points are missing.

Political scientist Jeane J. Kirkpatrick in 1980 argued there are still useful distinctions between the two terms. Authoritarian regimes, more loose and open, can change and reform themselves into democracies. This happened throughout Latin America in the 1980s. Totalitarian systems, especially Communist ones, she argued, cannot reform; they are too rigid. In a way, Kirkpatrick was right. The Communist regimes of East Europe and the Soviet Union never did reform; they collapsed.

Personalities

FAILED REFORMERS: MIKHAIL GORBACHEV

Mikhail Gorbachev

"Life punishes those who delay," said the Soviet president in 1989 as he urged the East German Communist regime to reform before it was too late. The East Berlin regime ignored Gorbachev and collapsed. But Mikhail Sergeyevich Gorbachev did not grasp that he too was engaging in delayed and halfway reforms that collapsed the Soviet regime and his own tenure in power.

Amid great hopes Gorbachev assumed the top Soviet political position—Party general secretary—in 1985. The Soviet Union had gradually run down during Brezhnev's eighteen-year reign; growth slumped while cynicism, alcoholism, and corruption grew. Two elderly temporaries, Andropov and Chernenko, followed as the Soviet system atrophied. Gorbachev—age fifty-four, a mere kid in Politburo terms—announced wide-ranging reforms to shake up the Soviet system.

Born into a peasant family in the North Caucasus in 1931, Gorbachev graduated in law from Moscow University in 1955 and returned to his home area for Party work. As Party chief of Stavropol province in 1970, he impressed Brezhnev, who summoned him to Moscow in 1978 to oversee agriculture. (Gorbachev had taken another degree, in agronomy, by correspondence.) Gorbachev by now was under the wing of Andropov, head of the KGB, and Mikhail Suslov, a Politburo kingmaker from Stavropol. Gorbachev was elected to the Party's Central Committee in 1971, to candidate member of the Politburo in 1979, and to full member in 1980. When Andropov took over in 1982, Gorbachev assisted him closely and implemented his tough anticorruption policies.

In 1985 Gorbachev began his reforms as the hero who would turn the Soviet Union into a modern, possibly democratic, system. He announced "new thinking" in foreign policy that led to arms control agreements with the United States and to the freeing of East Europe from the Communist regimes imposed by Stalin after World War II. With these steps, the Cold War ended.

Gorbachev ordered *glasnost* in the Soviet media, which became more pluralist, honest, and critical. Corrupt big shots were fired. Gorbachev also urged *demokratizatzia;* competitive elections were introduced, and a partially elected parliament convened.

Gorbachev at first tried to fix the economic system with old remedies: verbal exhortations, anti-alcohol campaigns, "acceleration," and importing more foreign technology. Then, after having hesitated too long, he ordered **perestroika** that slowly and gingerly began to decentralize and liberalize the Soviet economy. Farms and factories made more of their own decisions and kept more of their own profits. Private businesses called "cooperatives" were permitted and grew. But it was too little, too late. By 1989 economic disaster loomed. Economic dislocations lowered Soviet living and dietary standards and angered everyone.

With a freer press, the many nationalities (including Russians) demanded greater autonomy or even independence. Violence between ethnic groups flared. The *apparat* and *nomenklatura* sabotaged economic reforms by hoarding food and raw materials. Some generals and the KGB indicated they would not stand for the growing chaos, which would have soon led to the dismemberment of the Soviet Union, so Gorbachev pulled back from reforms and tightened up in late 1990.

In early 1991 Gorbachev appeared to favor reform again. In opposition, conservative hardliners in his own cabinet—hand picked by Gorbachev—attempted a coup against him in August 1991 (see page 284). The coup failed due to splits in the Soviet armed forces and the stubbornness of Russian President Boris Yeltsin, who then pushed a weakened Gorbachev from office and broke up the Soviet Union by pulling the vast Russian federation out of it.

In part, Gorbachev had himself to blame for the Soviet collapse. He dawdled too long and changed course too many times. He sought to preserve the Party and "socialism" and never did adopt an economic reform plan. Life indeed punished him who delayed.

But then Yeltsin gathered more power into the office of the presidency. The Russian parliament reacted, claiming Yeltsin was becoming dictatorial. They also disliked seeing their own power and perquisites diminished. Some deputies who had earlier counted themselves as reformers began to discover the negative side of reforms and to slide into the conservative camp. To make clear who was in charge, in 1993 Yeltsin sponsored and won a referendum that endorsed both reform and the power of the presidency. Later that year, he pushed through a new constitution with Gaullist-type presidential powers. The last straw was Yeltsin's dissolution of parliament in order to hold new elections; that produced the parliamentary coup attempt of 1993.

Then parliamentary elections turned into slaps at Yeltsin. Some of the biggest votes were for the Communists and other antireform parties. Yeltsin backed down, jettisoned his main reformers, and made a string of cautious reformers his prime ministers but fired each after a few months.

But is this not just democracy in action? An executive starts showing dictatorial tendencies and implements policies that go farther and faster than citizens want, so the citizens, through their elected representatives in parliament, put on the brakes. That is the way the State Duma liked to see itself, but the problem in Russia is trickier. Without major economic reforms, democracy in Russia does not stand a chance. But such reforms are seldom initiated by purely democratic means because they inflict too much pain, at least temporarily. Major reforms need strong executive leadership; a fragmented parliament cannot do it. If the executive is blocked, the result will likely not be democracy but chaos, and out of chaos grows dictatorship.

■ The Taming of the Oligarchs

Moscow privatized ("piratized" might be more accurate) the Russian economy in such a way as to make a few people incredibly wealthy. Clever wheeler-dealers, some of them already in management—who understood the value of state-owned firms, chiefly in the oil and natural-gas industries—bought them at giveaway prices. Most of what they did was legal because there were few laws in these areas. Russia privatized badly.

Comparison

SEMIPRESIDENTIALISM IN RUSSIA

Borrowing the French model, which has both an executive president and a premier, Russia borrowed its problems as well. President Yeltsin, in eight years in office, had six prime ministers, some lasting just a few months. An erratic drunk, Yeltsin tried to deflect blame away from himself for Russia's economic collapse and to appease an opposition-dominated Duma. But there were other, deeper causes for the mess.

As we discussed in France, semipresidential systems may be inherently unstable. French semipresidentialism actually worked as written only when *cohabitation* forced the president to share powers with a prime minister. Most semipresidential systems tilt strongly to a powerful president. Yeltsin would stand for no cut in his presidential power. He really did have dictatorial tendencies. His throwaway prime ministers were a crude attempt at cohabitation that made no one happy and hurt Russia's chances for democracy. One solution: Get rid of this crazy semipresidential system. In effect—without rewriting the constitution—Putin has done this by assuming virtually all power. His premiers, like those of de Gaulle, are simply messenger boys.

These oligarchs, as they were soon called, either had or quickly developed ties to leading politicians. One of the best-known oligarchs was Boris Berezovsky, a former math professor turned used-car king and then media and oil magnate. Berezovsky's money, newspapers, and TV network helped first Yeltsin and then Putin win election. Putin then had Berezovsky prosecuted and shorn of most of his properties. Berezovsky now lives in exile.

Russia's oligarchs did not act like the old U.S. "robber barons," who invested and then reinvested to make the economy and jobs grow. Russian oligarchs simply stripped assets from their companies—for example, selling oil abroad—and did not reinvest the money but stashed it in foreign (Swiss, Cayman Islands, Cyprus) banks. They did not like paying taxes or competing in a free market. As they got rich, the Russian economy got poor.

Comparison

THE TIMING OF REFORMS

In addition to the cultural factors we have already discussed, the timing or *sequencing* of reforms can make a crucial difference to the successful founding of democracy. The differences in timing between what happened in Central Europe and what happened in Russia are instructive.

First, in Central Europe (Poland, Czechoslovakia, and Hungary) a broad anti-Communist movement formed while the Communists were still in power. By the time liberal Communists held free elections in 1989 or 1990, an aware electorate completely voted the Communists out of power. It was a new broom sweeping clean. The initial winner was the broad catchall of anti-Communist forces, the leader of which became either the president (Walesa of Poland and Havel of Czechoslovakia) or the prime minister (Antall of Hungary). Later, these catchalls fell apart, but they had done their job: Communism was out, and democracy and market economies were established. In a few years these countries joined NATO and the EU.

In Russia, there was no new broom and the old one did not sweep clean. There was no nationwide anti-Communist catchall movement like Solidarity or Civic Forum. The Communists never allowed that. Instead, the Communists held semifree elections but did not allow themselves to be voted out of power. Gorbachev, who was never elected anything, stayed in office believing he was supervising important reforms.

But Gorbachev still faced major conservative (that is, Party) forces and continually changed course in the face of them. Sensing his weakness, Party conservatives attempted to overthrow him. After their defeat, the Party was finally ousted from office (late 1991) but was still influential in parliament, industry, and the countryside. Yeltsin, with no mass movement behind him, attempted serious reform but was still blocked by conservative forces, some of them remnants of the Party.

If Russia had done it like Central Europe, there would have been multiparty elections in late 1991 instead of late 1993. At the earlier date, there might have been sufficient enthusiasm to elect a proreform majority; by the latter date, the declining economy had produced despair and a backlash. This happened in Central Europe as well; in both Poland and Hungary economic hardship gave electoral wins to their Socialist parties (ex-Communists). But by then both democracy and the market economy were established and could not be rolled back. The Socialists had no intention of dismantling a working market system; instead, they made minor adjustments in the "social safety net" of Poland and Hungary.

The desirable sequence, as illustrated by Central Europe: First, form a broad mass movement; second, thoroughly oust the Communists in elections; third, institute political and economic reforms. The Russians tried to do it backward.

---

runaway system Influential people use their resources to amass more resources.

How to fix? Stop subsidizing industries and let the money-losers go bankrupt. Institute a Polish-type commercial code to regulate banks and businesses. Force the oligarchs to behave like real capitalists. But the oligarchs were well-connected and had many politicians on their payroll. They ousted a reform-minded cabinet in just five months, as well as those who vowed to collect taxes. In the name of keeping a vital industry alive and of not increasing unemployment, the subsidies, sweetheart contracts, and tax breaks continued. Another name for this process is corruption. Western executives call Russia one of the most corrupt countries in the world. (To see a ranking of corrupt countries, go to page 537).

Russians, with their penchant for equality, hated the oligarchs and liked how President Putin cracked down on them. Most are in jail or in exile. His *siloviki* targeted some for tax evasion (in a system where everyone cheats on taxes) and forced them to turn over their companies—including, oil and gas industries, television networks, and newspapers—to government fronts. Under Putin, most of the big Russian media came under state control, and few dared criticize him. Several oligarchs, fearing prosecution, fled abroad. One, Mikhail Khodorkovsky, lost his huge (and well-run) Yukos oil firm, allegedly for fraud and not paying taxes but more likely for trying to bring in U.S. partners. He got a show trial and nine years in prison. Putin brought Yukos under state control. Like many Russians, he felt that something as important as oil should never have been privatized. Putin also wanted to stop Khodorkovsky from becoming a political rival. A few smaller oligarchs, who do things Putin's way and stay out of politics, survive. The oligarchs were egregious, greedy, and sometimes criminal, but their television stations and newspapers gave Russia a brief period of freedom of information.

Key Concepts

RUNAWAY SYSTEMS

We earlier (Chapter 19) referred to President Putin as authoritarian, a strong ruler who concentrated power in his own hands but preserved democratic forms. Is it likely that Russia and Putin will tend to greater authoritarianism? The process seems to be already underway.

Yale political scientist Robert Dahl noted that powerful people tend to use their resources (legal, political, economic) to gain more resources. If there are no counterbalancing institutions or strong laws to check them, some amass power without limit: Stalin. Engineers call this a **runaway system**, which keeps concentrating power until it breaks. (Example: The New York Yankees use their resources to buy more top ballplayers, who win more games, which nets the Yankees even more resources, which enable them to

buy . . .) More than unbalanced personalities, this is the product of lawless systems in which any loss of control leads to overthrow. The presidents of Syria or the Congo cannot be nice, easygoing guys. Leaders in such lands must be control freaks; relaxation soon ends in their deaths.

Putin is a test case for the runaway-systems theory. Gradually and skillfully—never revealing his ultimate intentions—he amasses power. Will he reach a point where he has "enough" power, or will he always seek more? One indicator to watch: Will Putin step down in 2008 after his two four-year terms, or will he have the Duma alter the constitution to keep him in power? One rumor: Putin will name and supervise a puppet replacement for one term, then return to office.

■ The Mafia

The **mafia** (Russians use the loan word *mafiya*) is an important interest group in Russia, for it stands for much more than the criminal underworld. In Russia, the word covers a multitude of meanings, ranging

mafia   A criminal conspiracy.

from local strongarm rackets (virtually all businesses pay protection money) to the sophisticated takeover of natural resources by daring and well-connected insiders. Anyone in their way gets murdered—bankers, journalists (including American Paul Klebnikov in 2004), old people (for their apartments), American businessmen, and Duma members. Most "banks" are simply money-laundering operations. And no one is brought to justice, indicating the police are either connected to crime or ordered to not interfere. The FSB could solve such crimes but does not. Putin controls the FSB.

Russian mafiosi flaunt their new wealth, flashy cars (any make you can name, often stolen), clothes, lady friends, and parties. The average Russian hates those who have rapidly enriched themselves as they have degraded Russia, and this hatred feeds support for politicians who vow to crack down on them. Thus, lawlessness helped President Putin consolidate his power. Russians have long argued that without strict supervision and draconic controls they are the most lawless of peoples. Americans, they say, have internal controls that Russians have not. Historically, freedom in Russia meant chaos and bloody anarchy, and many Russians have welcomed rule by a strong hand, however harsh.

■ The Army

When a country is in chaos, the army becomes a major player, sometimes injecting itself directly into the political system. The Soviet army played a role in the process of attempted reform; namely, some sectors of the Red Army saw the need for economic changes in order to boost military technology to catch up with the Americans. In 1983 the chief of the Soviet General Staff, Marshal Nikolai Ogarkov, told *New York Times* editor Leslie Gelb that the Soviet military was falling behind technologically. He was later pushed out of command for his outspokenness. "Modern military power is based upon technology," he told Gelb, "and technology

Veterans, like these in Moscow, wear war medals on their suits, a Soviet custom. Generally conservative, most veterans oppose reforms leading to capitalism.

is based upon computers," an area where the Americans were well ahead. His conclusion:

> We will never be able to catch up with you in modern arms until we have an economic revolution. And the question is whether we can have an economic revolution without a political revolution.

The price of military backwardness became clear with the quick U.S.-led victory over Soviet-equipped Iraq in early 1991. Late that year, portions of the Soviet army participated in a coup.

The new Russian armed forces are much smaller (nominally 1.2 million members) than the old Soviet armed forces (some 4 million) but still in a wretched condition. Many soldiers and officers

Personalities

FAILED REFORMERS: BORIS YELTSIN

Boris Yeltsin

Gorbachev was the first *prezident* (they use the loan word) of the Soviet Union. Boris Yeltsin was the first prezident of the Russian Federation. As with Gorbachev, both Russians and the world initially hailed Yeltsin as a great reformer who would make a prosperous and peaceful Russia. Both disappointed with halfway, half-hearted reforms that ruined the economy and their approval ratings. Neither were convinced democrats; by background and training both acted like Party big shots. Yeltsin, however, was a gutsy risk taker who put his career and even his life on the line.

Born in 1931 (as was Gorbachev) near Sverdlovsk (now Yekaterinburg) in the southern Urals of a poor peasant family, Yeltsin studied engineering and worked in the housing industry in his hometown. Joining the Party in 1961 at age thirty, Yeltsin was promoted to the Central Committee in 1976. He was noticed as an energetic manager and reformer, and Gorbachev elevated him to head the Moscow Party organization in 1985 and made him a candidate member of the Politburo. A natural populist, Yeltsin, unlike other Soviet leaders, mingled with the people and denounced the privileges of the *nomenklatura*. The common people rallied to him.

Then came a bizarre series of events that, if the Soviet system had not been collapsing, would have led to Yeltsin's permanent banishment if not imprisonment. In a 1987 speech to the Central Committee, Yeltsin attacked Party conservatives by name for dragging their feet on reform. For that, he was relieved of his Party posts and demoted.

But he bounced back. In the first partly competitive election in 1989, he ran on his populist credentials and easily won election to parliament, where he criticized Gorbachev for dawdling on reforms. Shifting his attention to the Russian (as opposed to the Soviet) government, Yeltsin won election to the Russian parliament in 1990. Yeltsin sensed that the Soviet Union was doomed,

but Russia would survive. In July 1990 Yeltsin resigned from the Party and was now free to be as critical as he wished. As a non-Communist, he won fair elections to become president of the Russian Federation in 1991. This gave him another edge on Gorbachev, who had never been popularly elected to anything.

In the attempted coup of 1991, Yeltsin became a hero, standing firm on a tank in front of the Russian parliament. Mocking Gorbachev as an indecisive weakling, Yeltsin pulled the Russian Federation out of the Soviet Union in late 1991, thus collapsing the entire structure. Conservatives think it was a terrible mistake to break up the Soviet Union.

As president, Yeltsin went from bad to worse. Frequently drunk or ill, Yeltsin and his ministers bungled privatization, the economy tanked, corruption soared, and Russians turned bitterly against him. Consulting with no one, Yeltsin ordered the crushing of breakaway Chechnya (see page 329). Although reelected in 1996 as the lesser of two evils, during his last years in office Yeltsin's public approval rating was under 5 percent. The Duma tried to impeach him but was too divided. One of Yeltsin's favorite stunts was, every few months, to blame his prime ministers for economic failures and replace them. One of the questions of today's Russia is whether a first president other than Yeltsin could have done things differently or better.

have to work off-base. (In comparison, U.S. armed forces total 1.4 million and are superbly fed and led.) Russian armed forces are absurdly top-heavy, with as many officers as enlisted soldiers (U.S. ratio: 1:6). Officers, fearful of losing their jobs and starved for decent housing, are angry. Soldiers go unpaid for months and have to grow much of their own food. Hundreds of conscripts, hazed and starved, commit suicide each year. Most young men ignore the twice-yearly draft calls.

Several leading generals either supported the 1991 coup or did not oppose it. Many Soviet higher officers were fired. One, Marshal Sergei Akhromeyev, committed suicide. The Soviet armed forces had been consuming a quarter of the country's gross domestic product, a figure that was cut drastically. The army is still one of the few semistable institutions in Russia and, if Russia's strong presidency ever weakens, could play a direct political role.

When a political system starts falling apart, whatever groups are best organized amid growing chaos are most likely to seize power. This usually means the army. (See the box entitled "Praetorianism," page 532.) In much of the Third World, military coup is the standard way to change governments. Some believe the Russian army could play such a role, although historically it never has. In 1991 and 1993 the military was divided and most of it hung back, afraid of being used by politicians and of starting a civil war among army units.

The army is surely an interest group within Kremlin politics, and it is an angry one, having suffered several humiliations. Gorbachev tried to limit its size. In 1988 he admitted that the Soviet invasion of Afghanistan had been a mistake and withdrew Soviet forces. In 1989 he gave up East Europe, which the Soviet military defined as a defensive shield. In 1994–1996 Chechen "bandits" beat them; in revenge in 1999 the army began the merciless demolition of Chechnya. Many high

Democracy

TRANSITIONS TO DEMOCRACY

The spread of democratic regimes in the late twentieth century—what Harvard's Samuel Huntington called democracy's "third wave"—provoked much theorizing and attempts to find common patterns. Some thinkers saw democracy arising after economic growth produced a large, educated middle class (see page 447). Some saw it as going through similar stages—opening, breakthrough, and consolidation—but others saw "multiple paths" to democracy. Several said it needed agreement among elites—a "pacted transition"—to work. Many found that early institutional choices produced "path-dependent development" that deepened democracy with each successful attempt.

By the early twenty-first century, however, doubts arose about "transitology," as it was derisively dubbed. Some theories of transition explained the coming of democracy in one cultural area (such as Latin America) but not others (such as East Asia). Even in the Communist lands of East Europe, the relatively smooth transition to democracy in Central Europe was not duplicated in the Balkans. One size did not fit all. None of the theories fit Russia.

The toughest criticism asked: "Do all transitions lead to democracy?" Transitologists tended to assume that they did, but this was not always the case. Some countries enjoyed only brief democratic interludes (Peru, Ecuador, Venezuela) but became unstable or quasi-authoritarian. Huntington noted long ago that after every wave of democracy washes in, a reverse wave washes out, as in the rise of the totalitarian dictatorships between the two world wars. Many countries, including Russia, stalled in authoritarianism with democratic trappings.

Theories in political science seldom last more than a generation. They can yield new insights, provided we do not reify them. Theories are only attempts to get a handle on reality; they are not reality itself. Take all theories with a grain of salt. (For more on the dangers of theorizing too much, see the next chapter, page 325.)

officers resent the retreat of Russian power and their shrinking defense budget and manpower. They are also highly nationalistic and see an American plot in the eastward expansion of NATO and U.S. presence in Central Asia. Putin's defense minister, former KGB colleague Sergei Ivanov, wants to reduce draft calls in favor of a professional and volunteer army like that of the United States.

■ Transition to What?

In the last quarter of the twentieth century, democracy spread, leaving about half the world's nations (close to a hundred) to some degree democratic. Starting in the mid-1970s, democracy replaced dictatorships in Portugal, Spain, and Greece, and then in Latin America, East Asia, and finally, in late 1989, in East Europe. Soon academics developed theories to explain the growth of democracy (see box on page 319). Some applied them to the collapse of the Soviet Union and to the new institutions of a democratic Russia. They did not fit.

The collapse of the Soviet system was unique, one of a kind. Much of the old system carried over into the new, stunting the growth of democracy. Culturally, only a minority understood or wished genuine democracy. Economically, Russia collapsed under Yeltsin; people feared chaos and breakup of the federation. Putin was the necessary if authoritarian corrective to this slide. As a friend and supporter of democracy, I am sad to admit this, but if it had not been Putin, it would have been someone worse.

Key Terms

authoritarianism (p. 312)

cult of personality (p. 310)

mafia (p. 317)

perestroika (p. 312)

red-brown (p. 312)

runaway system (p. 316)

shock therapy (p. 310)

totalitarianism (p. 312)

Further Reference

Beissinger, Mark R. *Nationalist Mobilization and the Collapse of the Soviet State.* New York: Cambridge University Press, 2002.

Breslauer, George W. *Gorbachev and Yeltsin as Leaders.* New York: Cambridge University Press, 2002.

Brown, Archie, and Lilia Shevtsova, eds. *Gorbachev, Yeltsin, and Putin: Political Leadership in Russia's Transition.* Washington, D.C.: Carnegie Endowment, 2001.

Golosov, Grigorii V. *Political Parties in the Regions of Russia: Democracy Unclaimed.* Boulder, CO: L. Rienner, 2004.

Hoffman, David. *The Oligarchs: Wealth and Power in the New Russia.* New York: PublicAffairs, 2003.

Lynch, Allen C. *How Russia Is Not Ruled: Reflections on Russian Political Development.* New York: Cambridge University Press, 2005.

McFaul, Michael, Nikolai Petrov, and Andrei Ryabov. *Between Dictatorship and Democracy: Russian Post-Communist Political Reform*. Washington, D.C.: Carnegie Endowment, 2004.

Ottaway, Marina. *Democracy Challenged: The Rise of Semi-Authoritarianism*. Washington, D.C.: Carnegie Endowment, 2003.

Ross, Cameron, ed. *Russian Politics under Putin*. New York: Palgrave, 2004.

Satter, David. *Darkness at Dawn: The Rise of the Russian Criminal State*. New Haven, CT: Yale University Press, 2003.

Shevtsova, Lilia. *Putin's Russia*, rev. ed. Washington, D.C.: Carnegie Endowment, 2005.

Taubman, William. *Khrushchev: The Man and His Era*. New York: Norton, 2003.

Wilson, Andrew. *Virtual Politics: Faking Democracy in the Post-Soviet World*. New Haven, CT: Yale University Press, 2005.

Chapter 22

WHAT RUSSIANS
QUARREL ABOUT

We are interested in why the Soviet Union collapsed not out of purely historical curiosity but to serve as a warning about what can go wrong again. Whatever happened to the Soviet Union can happen to Russia; the problems and resistance Khrushchev, Gorbachev, and Yeltsin faced, Putin still faces. The question is also part of current Russian politics.

Why the Soviet Union Collapsed

Many Russians, especially strong nationalists, refuse to believe that the Soviet Union collapsed largely because of the inherent economic inefficiency of socialism. They blame sinister forces, especially the Americans, the functional equivalent of the "stab in the back" myth that so harmed Weimar Germany.

The real explanation is that socialist economies—meaning state-owned and centrally planned, "Communist," if you prefer—work poorly. They do not collapse overnight but slowly run down over time. Under certain circumstances, to be sure, centrally planned economies can grow very fast, as did the Soviet Union under Stalin's Five-Year Plans in the 1930s. A backward country borrowed capitalist technology and threw all its resources, including labor, into giant projects, chiefly into making steel and then making things from steel. From the 1930s through the 1960s, many observers assumed that the Soviet Union would catch up with and eventually overtake the United States in terms of economic production.

But as the Soviet Union tried to catch up, its economy became more complex and harder to control. Gosplan's **input-output tables** required hundreds of mathematicians to make the thousands of calculations necessary to set the targets of the Soviet economy on a centralized basis. Product quality was poor, as only quantity was calculated and required. Designs, often copied from old Western products, were out of date. Efficiency counted for nothing; there was not even a Russian word for efficiency (the closest was "effective"). Many factories produced things nobody wanted.

The consumer sector, deliberately shortchanged, offered too few products to motivate Soviet workers, who had to wait years for an apartment or a car. Accordingly, workers did not exert

Questions to Consider

1. What is to blame for Russia's current troubles?
2. Why did political scientists fail to grasp the decay of the Soviet Union?
3. Is it fair to compare Poland's economic *shock therapy* with Russia's?
4. Does Russia now have capitalism? Why or why not?
5. What happened to Russia's economy in 1998? How does it compare to Mexico?
6. What happened in Chechnya? Could similar things occur?
7. What is the *near abroad* and why do Russians want it?
8. What are the difficulties of "middle ways"?

input-output table   Spreadsheet for economy of entire nation. (See page 323.)

themselves but chuckled: "They pretend to pay us, and we pretend to work." Many took afternoons off to shop for scarce goods; standing in lines took hours each week. These and other factors made Soviets angry with the system. By the early 1970s, the Soviet economy slowed, especially in comparison to the surging economies of West Europe and the Pacific Rim.

This by itself, however, was not enough to bring down the system, which could have lumbered on in shabby decay. The real killer was technological backwardness, especially as it impinged on the Soviet military. The computer age had arrived, and thinking machines were spreading fast into Western businesses, research labs, and military systems. The Soviets fell behind in computerization, and the Soviet military knew what that meant: getting beat. (See the words of Marshal Ogarkov on page 317). With U.S. President Ronald Reagan came an even worse technological menace: a "Star Wars" shield in space that would make America invulnerable. An important sector of the Soviet military thus turned to economic and technological reform out of the fear of falling behind.

Many thinking Soviet Party people, especially younger ones, knew by the 1980s that economic reforms were necessary and were eager for someone like Gorbachev to lead the way. But by themselves, they could not prevail against the conservative forces of managers and *apparatchiki*, many of whose jobs were at stake. It took, I believe, the high-tech sections of the armed forces to ally themselves with Gorbachev and give the green light to economic reforms in the expectation that these would lead to military technology to equal the Americans.

Oil plays a roller-coaster role in first keeping afloat and then sinking the Soviet/Russian economy. The rapid increase in oil prices in the 1970s meant that Soviet petroleum exports—at that time the USSR was the world's biggest oil producer and exporter—could for a few years pay for Soviet imports of food and technology. When oil prices fell, so did the Soviet Union. Now Russia is too dependent on oil exports. The 2004 and 2005 jump in world oil prices brought great earnings and taxes, but oil-price spikes never last, and neither will Russia's oil.

■ How to Reform?

At no time did Mikhail Gorbachev adopt a thoroughgoing plan of economic reform. His advisors presented him with several, each bolder than the previous, but he never implemented any. He never wanted capitalism; instead, he sought a middle path or "third way" between capitalism and socialism. Gorbachev hesitated and changed his mind more or less annually, one year for economic reform, the next year against. Later he admitted several mistakes. First, he now says, he should have liberalized agriculture, as the Chinese did under Deng (see page 428). Instead, Gorbachev tried a couple of timid steps he inherited from his mentor, the late Andropov: "intensification" and an anti-alcohol campaign. Both failed.

When it came to real reforms, Gorbachev choked, both out of fear for the consequences and in the face of massive resistance by conservative Soviet forces. Gorbachev finally freed most prices, but he did not privatize industry. The result was far too many rubles chasing too few goods: inflation. Everyone wanted dollars as the ruble dwindled in value. Worried citizens muttered that things could not go on like this. It was against this background that Gorbachev's own cabinet plotted a coup in 1991. Before the year ended, the Soviet Union was dissolved, Gorbachev was a private citizen, and Yeltsin was president of the Russian Federation. At last, reform started looking serious, but Yeltsin too faced opposition from conservative forces.

■ From the Rubble of the Ruble

The Russian economy is growing again. With the right policies, growth could have happened much sooner. Gorbachev never restructured the Soviet economy. Yeltsin did not fully restructure the Russian economy. Are we asking for the impossible? Poland initiated a *shock therapy* at the beginning of

Key Concepts

LACKING FACTS, THEY THEORIZED

The most stupendous change of the late twentieth century took political scientists by surprise. Why did we fail to anticipate—notice that I am not asking for prediction—the collapse of the Soviet Union? Only a handful of historians and economists sounded warnings. Curiously, it was a demographer who made the best prediction. Nicholas Eberstadt examined the statistical decline of Soviet health and saw doom years in advance. Political scientists tended to see more of the same, with some reforms.

Why did we miss it? I see several mental blocks we built for ourselves, mostly by reading each others' books and articles, what intelligence officers call *incestuous amplification*.

1. *Lousy Empirical Data:* Much of the Soviet system was secret; we had to piece together flimsy indicators and infer how things worked. We filled the informational vacuum with theory, much of it misleading. In Yugoslavia, by way of contrast, you could get accurate data and candid interviews. As early as the 1960s some saw cracks in the Yugoslav federation. Little theory came out of studies of Yugoslavia, as researchers did not need to theorize; they had facts. Lacking facts, Soviet specialists theorized. The moral: We are only as good as our data.

2. *Systems Theory:* Since the 1960s, political scientists had been trained to see all countries as *political systems* that have varying structures but perform the same functions. Whenever the system is thrown off balance, it always corrects itself, by new leaders, parties, or reforms. Systems were thus presumed to be highly durable, possibly immortal. Systems theorists could simply not envision system collapse.

3. *Anti-Anticommunism.* The anticommunist hysteria of the early Cold War years, especially McCarthyism, was so primitive that some thinkers gave Communist systems the benefit of the doubt. Specialists tended to accept Communist systems as givens (as did systems theorists) and to conduct detailed studies of how they worked. Anyone who suggested Communist systems were inherently flawed and doomed was read out of the profession as speculative, right wing, and unscholarly.

4. *Undervaluing Economics.* Many Soviet specialists paid little attention to economics; they assumed politics dominated economics. (Economists assume the opposite.) Few appreciated that a deteriorating economy eventually drags the entire country down with it. Some economists noted Soviet economic decline for years, but political scientists largely ignored them.

5. *System Reformability.* Political scientists supposed Soviet problems could be fixed with reforms. (This too derives from systems theory.) If the system has an economic or structural problem, it will correct it, was the bland assumption. Eventually, some thought, the Soviet system would reform itself into a social-democratic welfare state. The brittleness of the Soviet system occurred to few.

6. *Fixation on Personalities.* Because reforms are necessary, they will be carried out; they just need the right personality. Ah! Here comes Gorbachev, the man both we and Russian liberals have been waiting for. His reforms will produce a much nicer Soviet Union. In this way, we read into Gorbachev heroic and reformist qualities he never had. Clueless would be more like it.

asset-stripping   Selling off firm's property and raw materials for short-term profit.

public finances   What a government takes in, what it spends, and how it makes up the difference.

flight capital   Money that owner sends out of country for fear of losing it.

hard currency   Noninflating, recognized currencies used in international dealings, such as dollars and euros.

default   Not being able to pay back a loan.

1991 and within two years had gone through the worst of its inflation and industrial decline and for several years was the fastest growing economy of Europe.

Yeltsin's first prime minister (until late 1992) and later finance minister, the dynamic reformer Yegor Gaidar, tried to induce shock therapy as he privatized the large, obsolete industrial enterprises the Communists had built. Terribly inefficient and overstaffed and with no concern for consumer needs, many Soviet plants actually *subtracted* value from the raw materials they processed. But these industries were the wealth and power of the bureaucrats and *apparatchiks* who ran them and gave employment to those who listlessly worked in them. Accordingly, they were able to pressure Moscow to keep the subsidies flowing. In any rational system, they would have been declared bankrupt immediately. But you cannot throw millions of people out of work all at once, protested many Russians.

Privatization in Russia (and some other ex-Communist lands) was carried out badly. A handful of clever operators bought up factories and raw materials cheap and turned themselves into a new class of capitalists. Many of these industries still get government subsidies (such as cheap energy), which allows the new owners to reap enormous profits as they export oil, natural gas, and minerals. Much of the profit does not return to Russia, though; it goes into foreign banks, a pattern typical of South America. Because this capital was not recycled back into the Russian economy, the rest of the economy declined, making poor people poorer. Capitalism in Russia began as **asset-stripping**, which is no basis for long-term future. Only recently has it begun to work like capitalism elsewhere, with capitalists reinvesting their money inside Russia.

August 1998 showed what bad policies can bring. Some observers saw trouble coming well in advance, in the area of **public finances**. Russia was collecting less than half the taxes it was supposed to. Everyone cheated on taxes. As a result, the budget went dangerously into deficit, so the Yeltsin government simply printed more money. Banks—and anyone in Russia could open a bank—were unregulated and made unsecured loans to friends. Chief monetary instrument of Russian banks: U.S. $100 bills, some of them counterfeit. Knowing the perils of the Russian economy, Russian oligarchs stashed between $150 billion and $350 billion in **flight capital** offshore. Eventually, this system had to crash. When it did, in 1998, the ruble lost some three-quarters of its value in relation to **hard currencies**. Many banks closed, leaving depositors with nothing. Russia's fledgling stock markets dived. Some industries collapsed. Russia **defaulted** on its loans (biggest losers: German banks, with over $30 billion lent to Russia) and had to beg for new credit. Badly burned, foreign investors fled Russia.

Apartment houses in Russia are prefabricated and small. There is a terrible housing shortage, so flats like these in a Moscow suburb are eagerly sought.

Russians felt angry and betrayed. We had told them that the free market is the path to prosperity, but it brought them only misery. A third now fell below the official (very low) poverty line. Actually, Russia had never fully implemented a functioning market system. Much Western advice was ignored. Most of the $66 billion in Western aid disappeared. There were too many government subsidies and tax breaks and too few rules and regulations that keep a market economy steady. Money, always a weak point with Russians (see page 303), was just something you printed. In the words of one Russian reformer, it was "the most expensive economic education in history."

Before the 1998 collapse, some people got rich fast while many went hungry. Having long been taught by the Communists that material equality is good and just, Russians witnessed the explosive growth of inequality. (Income inequality in Russia is now greater than in the United States.) Some *biznesmeny* and mafiosi (the two words are linked in the Russian mind) enjoyed new wealth while most Russians lived worse than ever.

Good emerged from the rubble of the ruble. Fake businesses collapsed, and entrepreneurs started investing their profits in Russia. Russia's

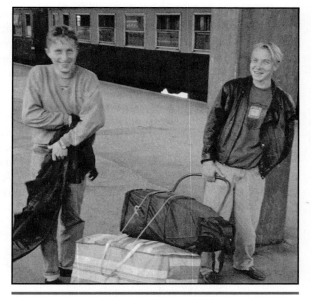

Traveling Salesmen: These young Russians make a niche in the economy by buying Russian medicines (in the big bags) and selling them in outdoor markets in Sofia, Bulgaria. After a few days at the market, they return home for more, bribing their way across borders. They showed me how to catch a train from Romania to Bulgaria without a ticket: "Just bribe the conductor," they shrugged, "It's a Russian train."

Key Concepts

THE TERMINOLOGY OF ECONOMIC REFORM

- *Liberalize:* Cutting prices free to find their own level. Instead of using centrally designated prices, factories charge whatever they can get on the free market (sometimes called *marketize*).

- *Privatize:* Putting state-owned enterprises and land into private hands by selling them to local investors, foreign investors, their own workers, or the citizenry at large through vouchers. In Russia, only a few benefited.

- *Shock Therapy:* Liberalizing and privatizing simultaneously and rapidly. This proved successful in Central Europe but not in the ex-Soviet Union.

- *Currency Convertibility:* The ending of fake, imposed exchange rates, brought about by

letting the local currency be exchanged for foreign currency at whatever rate the market sets. Convertibility makes it impossible to disguise inflation.

- *Stabilization:* Controlling the amount of currency in circulation, both by limiting the printing of money and by denying government loans to industry, so as to slow inflation and make currency worth predictable.

- *Tradeoff:* The choice between inflation and unemployment, allowing one to rise in order to keep the other low. Several ex-Soviet type economies elected to let inflation roar in order to hold down unemployment.

near abroad Non-Russian republics of old Soviet Union.

economy, helped by the runup in world oil prices and cheap currency, has recently grown by several percent a year. The federal budget is in balance, and inflation eased from 80 percent in 1998 to a few percent. Russia's trade balance, again thanks to oil, has been very positive (in contrast to big U.S. deficits). Putin's reforms of taxes, banks, and land sales, could promote growth. Said Putin in 2002: "Our economy must grow much faster." (Stalin said the same in 1931.) The big test: Will Russia's economy be honest enough to let it join the World Trade Organization, which it very much wants to do?

Two clouds of uncertainty hang over the Russian economy, and Russians live in fear of a major downturn. The first is oil prices, which reached $70 a barrel. But oil prices are volatile and cannot be counted on. The second is Putin's persecution of oligarchs such as Khodorkovsky (see previous chapter), which panicked foreign investors. Seeing Putin bring back industries (especially energy) under state control, foreign investment plunged, and it is an important component of economic growth. Russia's economy is not yet stable.

■ Recover the Lost Republics?

President Putin described the breakup of the Soviet Union as "the greatest geopolitical catastrophe of the century" and worried that the "epidemic of collapse has spilled over into Russia itself." Most Russians feel the same. The non-Russian republics that departed from the Soviet Union in 1991 are what Russians call the **near abroad**. Most of them had been incorporated into the tsarist empire, and many Russians still think of them as belonging to Russia. Some want to restore the Russian empire, especially the Russian army, which still has troops in most of the ex-Soviet republics. For U.S. policy, Moscow's influence in Central Asia was not all bad. Putin helped the U.S. military to use bases in Uzbekistan and Tajikistan to overthrow the Afghan Taliban after 9/11. Until landlocked Central Asia gains access to the outside world through Iran, Afghanistan, and Pakistan, it will remain dependent on Russia for trade and transportation.

Geography

WILL RUSSIA FALL APART?

Russia is an extreme case of center-periphery tensions, one that could have led to the breakup of the Russian Federation. As starvation loomed and Russia's eighty-nine republics and regions got no help from Moscow, many ignored the center and set up their own economic systems, with price controls, limits on "exports" to other parts of Russia, and barter systems. Some talked about introducing their own currency. Some ethnic groups claimed sovereignty; a few even declared independence. Many regions refused to pay taxes to Moscow. Many of the republics are authoritarian dictatorships where opposition candidates or media are not tolerated.

Trying to rein in unruly republics, Putin in 2000 created seven super-regions and named mostly KGB and FSB officials as super-governors. Since then, things have stabilized somewhat under Moscow's tighter control. This may be undemocratic, but what would the fragmentation of the giant Russian Federation lead to? As we mentioned in Chapter 18 (page 263), its very size means Russia must be ruled with a firm hand from the center.

In many ex-Soviet republics, the "new" leaders are old Party big shots, and a corrupt and authoritarian elite continues to rule. Not counting the Baltic republics, Russia had the most progressive and most reform-minded leadership. Other republics lagged behind. A

North Caucasus Mountainous region north of Georgia and Azerbaijan; includes Chechnya.

Geography

THE UNRAVELING OF THE NORTH CAUCASUS

Violence flares in Russia's **North Caucasus** despite— or maybe because of—Moscow's brutal efforts to tame it. Like all mountainous regions, it is hard to control and permits small ethnic and religious groups to develop distinct cultures that resist outside rule. The rugged region—home to more than 6 million people, mostly Muslim—is a crazy quilt of ethnic groups, most consolidated into their current borders by Stalin. From west to east they are Karachayevo-Cherkessia, Kabardino-Balkaria, North Ossetia, Ingushetia, Chechnya, and Dagestan. Islamist terrorism and urban shootouts between security forces and rebels are common.

The tsarist army finally subdued the region only in the early nineteenth century. Emblematic was the tsarist fortress built in 1784: Vladikavkaz (Master of the Caucasus), now the capital of North Ossetia. Few locals liked Russian rule, and Russians despised them as bandits. In 1944, Stalin accused several Caucasian nationalities, Chechens among them, of collaborating with the German invaders and brutally exiled them to Central Asia.

Decades later, a Chechen, Jokar Dudayev, became a general in the Soviet air force. Assigned to an Estonian airbase in the 1980s, Dudayev sympathized with the Estonians, who, like Chechens, hated Russian rule. Dudayev blocked the landing of Soviet troops in early 1991, helping Estonia win independence. He then retired, won an election in Chechnya, and proclaimed its independence as the Soviet Union broke up in late 1991. But Chechnya, unlike Estonia, had never been a "union republic"; it was part of the Russian Federation, and Moscow feared unrest spreading to all the North Caucasus, which is happening. Heavy-handed repression by Russian security forces persuaded many locals to join an Islamic revival.

Yeltsin, in late 1994—with no discussion among military professionals, parliamentary debate, or publicity—gave the order to quickly crush Chechen

independence. But the military campaign stalled; the Russian army was pathetic, and Chechens fought boldly and tenaciously. Some 80,000, mostly civilians, were killed, and the capital, Grozny, was shelled into ruin. Most Russians, even military officers, hated the war; partly because of it, Yeltsin's popularity plummeted. Ex-General Alexander Lebed worked out a shaky peace with Chechen fighters in 1996, leaving them an undefined autonomy.

In 1999, Chechen-led Muslim fundamentalists attempted to take over neighboring Dagestan. Moscow retaliated sharply, pursuing the guerrillas back into Chechnya. In Russian cities, several apartment houses were blown up, killing nearly 300. Some suspect it was a put-up job, but Moscow immediately blamed Chechen terrorists and launched a major invasion of Chechnya. This time the Russian army was in much better shape, and the Russian people were behind them. Putin's tough stance boosted his popularity. Putin declared victory in 2002, but guerrilla warfare, banditry, and terrorism continue and have spread through the North Caucasus. Theatergoers and schoolchildren have been victims. Such horrors allowed Putin to concentrate more power in his hands, and most Russians applauded.

Chechnya's two bloody wars could be just the beginning of the unraveling of the North Caucasus region. In the first war, 1994–1996, Chechen rebels pushed the Russian army out. In the second, 1999–2002, Russians bloodily occupied Chechnya, but Islamism quickly spread throughout the region. Now local Islamists talk of a North Caucasus *caliphate*. Foreign leaders condemn the violence, but no one offers a solution. Putin, angry at U.S. criticism, asked: Just what is the United States doing in Iraq? Putin vowed to wipe out terrorism. "We showed weakness," he said of the Chechen problem, "and the weak are trampled upon." Stalin could not have said it better.

particularly tragic example is Ukraine, potentially rich and European, whose ex-Communist leaders (now out of power) instituted no economic reform program. The result was a hyperinflation that made the Russian economy look good.

One crucial fact in Russian thinking concerns the 25 million ethnic Russians who live in the near abroad. (The term does not refer to the former East European satellites such as Poland and Hungary.) Some Russians in these republics feel threatened. Any outright violence against them, however, provokes the Russian army, which feels it has a right and duty to come to the rescue. This could someday be used as an excuse to seize all or part of the near abroad.

Recovery of the lost republics could come about by more subtle means as well: economics. As the economies of other republics plunged downward, some turned desperately to Moscow for help. Under the banner of the Commonwealth of Independent States, Moscow delivers some aid (for example, a good deal on oil and natural gas) but in return gets trade concessions and general obedience. Moscow successfully used this approach on Belarus—which now uses the Russian ruble as currency—and briefly cut natural gas to Ukraine to warn it to behave.

A tricky third way appeared in Georgia, which itself is home to many non-Georgian nationalities. The Muslim Abkhazians of western Georgia broke away by force of arms, many of those arms supplied quietly by the Russian army. Georgia had originally refused to join the CIS in 1991 but, faced with military defeat, did so in 1994. Then the Russians changed sides and

Geography

YUGOSLAVIA: A MINIATURE SOVIET UNION?

The former multiethnic Balkan federal system of Yugoslavia resembled the ex-Soviet Union. Both countries had a Slavic core nationality: Russians in the Soviet Union and Serbs in Yugoslavia. Serbs and Russians are both Eastern Orthodox Christians and use the Cyrillic alphabet. Both defined themselves as the founders and guarantors of their respective nations. They regarded breakaway republics as traitors to the nation.

The other nationalities resented this overbearing attitude. In each country an advanced northwest (the Baltic republics in the Soviet Union and Slovenia in Yugoslavia) grew tired of being held back by the less-developed core nationality, which economically drained the advanced area. Interestingly, the Baltics and Slovenia declared their independence first.

The second largest nationality in each country was also Slavic but with a distinctive culture and resentments against being bossed by the center; thus, Ukraine and Croatia quickly broke away. In the south, feisty Muslim nationalities demanded greater autonomy and

fought neighboring Christian nationalities (the Azeris against the Armenians and the Bosnian Muslims and Kosovar Albanians against the Serbs). In most of the newly independent republics in both the ex-Soviet Union and ex-Yugoslavia, the "new" leaders had been local Communist bosses prior to independence.

A final touch: Russians and Serbs, respectively, formed the bulk of the officer corps of the old Soviet and Yugoslav armies. The top officers were conservative and dedicated to keeping their countries intact. They were not adverse to using force to do so. In 1991, both armies started intervening directly in politics. The key difference is that conservative Communists took over in Belgrade and, with the army's general staff in agreement, attempted to hold Yugoslavia together by force. When that quickly failed, they turned to building a *Greater Serbia* by military conquest, coupled with *ethnic cleansing*. In the ex-Soviet Union, the death toll has not been as large, but it too experienced wars in the Caucasus region, which could get worse.

began supporting Georgia with arms and troops. They called it "peacekeeping," but it was more like a protection racket.

Should we as Americans criticize Russians for wishing to recover the near abroad? What did President Lincoln do when faced with the breakup of the Union? Americans should have a bias toward holding unions together. And has not West Europe turned itself into the EU? But Moscow used economic bribes and threats to recoup the near abroad. Gazprom, 51 percent owned by the government, sold natural gas cheap to those ex-Soviet states that stayed loyal. Those who turned westward paid more than twice as much. In early 2006 Russia demanded a huge price increase in natural gas sent by pipeline to Ukraine and briefly cut off supplies. Moscow said price was the issue, but it was really Ukraine's westward turn with its 2005 democratic revolution. The move underscored Putin's Soviet-era mentality and alarmed Europe, which gets much of its natural gas from Russia.

Comparison

SCANDINAVIAN-TYPE SOCIALISM FOR RUSSIA?

Confusion surrounds the term *socialism*. Many Russians and East Europeans now tell you they no longer know what the word means. Some call the welfare states of Scandinavia "socialist" because freely elected Social Democratic governments have gradually introduced elaborate medical, unemployment, educational, housing, and other programs to lift up the lower rungs of society: cradle-to-grave welfare. These Social Democratic parties started out Marxist but all of them shed it. They are all based on large labor-union federations. The aim of these parties is to wipe out poverty without resorting to coercion or state control.

And here's where Scandinavian *welfarism* differs sharply from Communist-style socialism. The Scandinavian lands have little nationalized industry, and what was nationalized was done so for nonideological reasons (for example, to hold down unemployment). The bulk of the economy is private and capitalist. Swedish managers especially developed a ferocious reputation for efficient, money-making plant operation. Taxes, to be sure, are high, but the economy is otherwise free.

In sum, Scandinavia is not socialist; it is a variation on capitalism called *welfarism*. If you wish to call it socialism, of course, you may. But please note that it was developed after and on top of Scandinavia's capitalist industrial base. First came capitalism, then came welfare. It is doubtful if the order can be reversed or if they can be built simultaneously.

No one has yet found a way to combine capitalism and socialism on a long-term, stable basis. For a while, such a combination sometimes seems to work. But soon the private sector starts bumping into the restricted, slow-moving state sector. The private sector needs raw materials, labor, infrastructure, and transportation on a flexible, ever-changing basis. The state sector, still run by a central plan, cannot possibly deliver and has no incentive to. If you allow state enterprises to enter the private-sector market, you are gradually desocializing the economy. It gets more efficient but less socialist. Eventually you come to a point where you must either bury the socialist sector as a bad experiment or curb and recontrol the private sector. The mix will not hold steady; you must go one way or the other. China, as we shall see, is caught up in this dilemma.

Many Russians, including Putin, still think they can find a middle way that is uniquely Russian. Experience suggests that if they try to build a middle way, it will lead to an unstable, declining system with high inflation.

■ A Middle Way for Socialism?

middle way   Supposed blend of capitalism and socialism; also called "third way."

infant mortality rate   Number of live newborns who die in their first year, per thousand; standard measure of nation's health.

Putin's ultimate problem—inherited from his predecessors—was that he thought there was a **middle way** between a centrally planned socialist economy and a free-market economy. Reforms, some argue, can blend a market economy with a socialist economy. They do it in Sweden, do they not? (No, they do not. See box on page 331.) Some Russians think that they can reserve the "commanding heights" of heavy industry for the state while permitting small enterprises to operate in a free market. This is what Lenin did under the NEP in the early 1920s, and the NEP was frequently mentioned as a model by Gorbachevites. But the NEP was inherently flawed and was running down in the late 1920s when Stalin dropped it in favor of forced industrialization.

■ Which Way Russia?

Observers of Russia divide into two camps: optimists and pessimists. Pessimists see a botched job. Capitalism has not taken root. At first the oligarchs looted state enterprises and stashed the money abroad; then Putin stole it back from them. The oil and gas industry has returned to state control, much of it owned by Gazprom, which says it's a company but acts like a ministry. Corruption and lawlessness link authorities (including the police) and mafias. Many Russians live worse than ever. No country can take the kind of chaos and decay the Yeltsin era brought. Either Russia was going

Geography

RUNNING OUT OF RUSSIANS

Almost all industrialized countries produce few babies, but Russia is in serious *demographic* decline. In 1989, before the Soviet collapse, an average Soviet woman (many non-Russian) bore 2.17 children. Now an average Russian woman bears only 1.2 children, among the world's lowest *fertility rates,* which is not the same as the *birth rate,* a different measure (for comparative rates, see page 234).

In Russia, declining health standards raised the **infant mortality rate**, but lately it has recovered to around 15 per thousand live births, still much worse than West or Central Europe. Expectant mothers are poorly nourished and so are their babies, many of whom suffer protein deficiency. There have been isolated reports of children starving to death. Most Russian families have only one child. Meanwhile, the

Russian death rate climbed; life expectancy of adult men dropped to fifty-eight years, lower than in much of the Third World. Result: Russia's population shrinks by nearly 700,000 a year.

One of the causes of death is prodigious alcohol consumption (some of it poisonous home-brew) leading to industrial accidents. Russian environmental poisoning, both chemical and nuclear, is among the world's worst, and environmentally caused diseases are common. (Russia's closest rivals: East Europe.) The air in Russia's industrial cities is dangerous. "To live longer," said one official, "we should breathe less." Many factories just dumped toxic and nuclear wastes into shallow landfills. Once-pristine Lake Baikal, long revered as a symbol of Mother Russia, is now polluted.

to collapse or be taken over by an authoritarian. Many expected that authoritarian to be an ex-general, but it was a policeman, Putin.

The optimists point to the fact that most of Russia's economy is private and, after the collapse of 1998, growing nicely. Inflation is dropping, and **current-account balances** are very positive, thanks to high oil prices. The remaining oligarchs have shifted from asset stripping to production and reinvestment, a healthy sign. Privatization was chaotic and crooked, but now owners have a stake in rule of law to keep their gains. Reasonably free elections have been held in which most Russians rejected both Communists and extreme nationalists. Putin is a control freak, but he is better than many alternatives one can imagine. A market is now being built in Russia, argue optimists, and in a few years it may lead to democracy. (We will hear similar rosy projections on China's evolution.)

Which way will Russia go? The stakes for us are enormous. We hoped to have a friendly, democratic Russia as a trading partner but now face growing Russian hostility. Many Russians blame America for their decline, and Putin accuses critics of working for foreign interests. True, American economists gave advice that overlooked the lack of cultural and institutional bases for capitalism in Russia. They casually assumed that Russia was a big Poland.

> **current-account balance**   A country's exports minus its imports.
>
> **geopolitics**   Influence of geography on politics and use of geography for strategic ends.

Geography

FEAR OF INVASION

Russians are unhappy and fearful that their former Central European satellites (Poland, the Czech Republic, Hungary) joined NATO in 1999 and the former Soviet republics of Lithuania, Latvia, and Estonia joined NATO in 2004, along with Bulgaria, Romania, Slovakia, and Slovenia. NATO, the enemy during the long Cold War, has taken over their former security belt. No Russian likes this, but Putin knows there is nothing he can do about it now.

Geopolitics has always been important to the Kremlin's rulers. Starting under the tsars but reemphasized by Stalin during and after World War II, it became an article of Kremlin faith that Russia needed East Europe—which Moscow organized as the *Warsaw Pact*—as a defensive shield against attack from the west. There have indeed been many such invasions; the Nazi invasion of 1941 was the most recent. Until Gorbachev, all Soviet civilian and military leaders accepted this argument. To prevent East Europe's departure from the Soviet orbit, Khrushchev crushed the 1956 Hungarian uprising and Brezhnev crushed the 1968 Prague Spring. Both nearly invaded Poland.

But East Europe was a major economic and military drain on the Soviet Union, and it blocked improved relations with the West. By 1989, Gorbachev had decided to no longer support the Communist regimes of East Europe, and the regimes fell. Central Europe quickly became democratic with free markets. Russia's strategic situation actually improved, for the end of the Cold War removed the military threat from the West. NATO, with declining defense budgets and small armies, poses no danger. Costs to Russia, in garrison troops and subsidized trade deals, have been drastically cut. Instead of selling Russian gas and oil at sweetheart prices to their satellites, Russia can get world-market prices for them, and in hard currency. Potentially, Russia is now open for trade with and investment from the West, the ticket to prosperity. Still, many Russian conservatives argue that Gorbachev gave away Russia's defensive shield; a few want it back. The very old fear of invasion from the West played into the hands of demagogic Russian politicians.

Russia is frosty to the West, but this will not be a new Cold War, because Russia is too poor and weak to stand up to the West. In the rigged 2004 Ukrainian elections Putin charged Western interference—he favored the pro-Russian authoritarian candidate—but Putin backed down, and new elections were held. Moscow has to take external pressures into account. To attract foreign investment, Russia needs rule of law. To get major loans it must adhere to major banks' austere limits on budget deficits. With NATO expanded eastward and Russia's military terribly weak, Moscow must be strategically cautious; few fear Russia any more.

Is Russia now a democracy? No. Freedom House (see page 310) demoted Russia from "partly free" to "not free," closer to dictatorship than to democracy. There is little competition, and state control of the mass media skews elections. Institutions are unbalanced, the presidency too powerful and the legislature too weak. Corruption dominates everything. A democratic sprit of tolerance and fair play is absent. Some scholars argue that Russia is comparable to several developing countries in this "in-between" stage. We do not expect instant democracy from them, and neither should we expect it from Russia.

Can Russians eventually govern themselves in a moderate, democratic fashion? I think they can, but it will take many years. There is nothing genetically authoritarian about Russians. In the twentieth century Germans and Spaniards were deemed unfit for responsible self-government, but now they are practicing democracy as well as any Europeans. I believe Russia will eventually turn democratic, in your lifetime if not in mine.

Key Terms

asset-stripping (p. 326)

current-account balance (p. 333)

default (p. 326)

flight capital (p. 326)

geopolitics (p. 333)

hard currency (p. 326)

infant mortality rate (p. 332)

input-output table (p. 324)

middle way (p. 332)

near abroad (p. 328)

North Caucasus (p. 329)

public finances (p. 326)

Further Reference

Åslund, Anders. *Building Capitalism: The Transformation of the Former Soviet Bloc*. New York: Cambridge University Press, 2001.

Birgerson, Susanne M. *After the Breakup of a Multi-Ethnic Empire: Russia, Successor States, and Eurasian Security*. Westport, CT: Praeger, 2002.

Breslauer, George W., and Victoria E. Bonnell, eds. *Russia in the New Century: Stability or Disorder?* Boulder, CO: Westview, 2001.

Cox, Michael, ed. *Rethinking the Soviet Collapse: Sovietology, the Death of Communism, and the New Russia*. New York: Pinter, 1998.

Goldman, Marshall I. *The Piratization of Russia: Russian Reform Goes Awry*. New York: Routledge, 2003.

Herspring, Dale R., ed. *Putin's Russia: Past Imperfect, Future Uncertain*, 2nd ed. Blue Ridge Summit, PA: Rowman & Littlefield, 2004.

Jack, Andrew. *Inside Putin's Russia: Can There Be Reform without Democracy?* New York: Oxford University Press, 2004.

Kempton, Daniel R., and Terry D. Clark. *Unity or Separation: Center-Periphery Relations in the Former Soviet Union.* Westport, CT: Praeger, 2001.

Kuchins, Andrew C., ed. *Russia after the Fall.* Washington, D.C.: Carnegie Endowment, 2002.

Meier, Andrew. *Chechnya: To the Heart of a Conflict.* New York: Norton, 2004.

Reddaway, Peter, and Dmitri Glinski. *The Tragedy of Russia's Reforms: Market Bolshevism against Democracy.* Herndon, VA: U.S. Institute of Peace, 2001.

Shlapentokh, Vladimir. *A Normal Totalitarian Society: How the Soviet Union Functioned and How It Collapsed.* Armonk, NY: M. E. Sharpe, 2001.

Trenin, Dmitiri, and Aleksei V. Malashenko. *Russia's Restless Frontier: The Chechnya Factor in Post-Soviet Russia.* Washington, D.C.: Carnegie Endowment, 2004.

Xenakis, Christopher I. *What Happened to the Soviet Union? How and Why American Sovietologists Were Caught by Surprise.* Westport, CT: Praeger, 2002.

Part V.

JAPAN

CHINA

RUSSIA

NORTH
KOREA

SOUTH
KOREA

SEA

OF

JAPAN

HOKKAIDO

HONSHU

JAPAN

Tokyo

Yokohama

Hiroshima

SHIKOKU

Nagasaki

KYUSHU

Korea Strait

PHILIPPINE

SEA

45°

40°

35°

30°

25°

130°   135°   140°

| 0 | 100 | 200 Miles |
| 0 | 100 | 200 Kilometers |

Chapter 23

JAPAN:
THE IMPACT OF THE PAST

As with other countries, geography helps explain Japanese history, politics, and culture. Japan was close enough to China to be heavily influenced by Chinese culture but far enough away to resist Chinese conquest. The rough mountainous terrain of most of Japan and division into four main islands and hundreds of small islands made Japan hard to unify. Japan has little **arable** land, much of it historically devoted to rice, a crop so important it took on religious significance over the centuries.

The Japanese like to see themselves as a pure-blooded single tribe, but they are the descendants of immigrants from various parts of the Pacific Rim, especially from the Korean peninsula. The Japanese language has the same grammatical patterns as Korean, and some scholars suggest that the imperial family is of Korean origin. This finding is hotly controversial, as Japanese look down on Koreans as racial inferiors. In truth, both Japan and Korea drew much of their culture from classic China, a civilization so magnificent that it held most of Asia in awe. One can see the clear Chinese influence today in the pictographic writing of Japan and Korea, the architecture, ancient weapons, and the philosophical influence of **Confucianism** (see page 414) and **Buddhism**.

The early Japanese gradually pushed back the original inhabitants of the islands, whom they called *Ainu*, until only a handful now remain on the northernmost island of Hokkaido. In doing this, Japanese developed a warrior ethos that lasted for millennia. The Japanese were undisturbed on their islands for many centuries, and this allowed their culture and social structure to evolve away from the Chinese model. What came in from China was often accepted, but bent and trimmed to suit Japanese needs. Buddhism and Confucianism arrived in Japan in the sixth century from China, along with Chinese writing, but all soon took on Japanese characteristics. This pattern of borrowing ideas and usages but changing them reappeared more recently in Japan's history.

The name Japanese gave to their land, *Nihon* ("sun origin") is from the national myth that all Japanese are descended from the Sun Goddess. An alternative and more elegant pronunciation of the characters "sun" and "origin" is *Nippon*, a name that was originally used in the West for Japan but has since died out. Marco Polo seems to have recorded the Mongol name *Zipangu*, which among Westerners turned into Japan.

Questions to Consider

1. Why have Britain and Japan, both island nations, developed so differently?
2. Was feudalism in Japan longer and deeper than in Europe?
3. Was the Tokugawa policy of keeping Japan isolated wise?
4. Were the Meiji reforms a logical outcome of Japan's opening by Perry?
5. What were the *zaibatsu* and how did they modernize Japan?
6. In conquering Asia, was Japan copying the West?
7. Could the Japanese style of modernization be copied elsewhere?
8. Was a U.S.-Japan war inevitable? What could have prevented it?

In 1274 and 1281, Japan trembled when the Mongol emperor of China, Kublai Khan, who controlled much of Asia, sent invasion fleets against Japan. Japanese warriors fought the Mongols to a standstill, and both times typhoons hit the invasion fleets, which were wrecked or withdrew. The Japanese thus claim that a "divine wind" (*kamikaze*), plus the fighting ability of their samurai, saved Japan. The Japanese nobility treasured and celebrated an image of themselves as a superior warrior race until 1945.

■ Japanese Feudalism

One of the strongest patterns of Japanese history is its long domination by clans and their leaders. According to Japanese tradition (still practiced in the **Shinto** faith), Jimmu, a descendant of the sun goddess, founded the Land of the Rising Sun in 660 B.C. Myth aside, a kingly court appeared in Yamato in the third century A.D. and by the seventh century had largely unified central Japan on the Chinese imperial model, bolstered by Confucianism and ruled by a *tenno* (emperor). The forms of Chinese centralized rule took hold, but not the substance. Under the surface, the clans exercised control. The emperors' powers were soon usurped by powerful clan chiefs, who could make or break figurehead emperors and hold them prisoner in the palace.

arable   Useable for agriculture. (See page 339.)

Confucianism   Chinese philosophy of social and political stability based on family, hierarchy, and manners. (See page 339.)

Buddhism   Asian religion that seeks enlightenment through meditation and cessation of desire. (See page 339.)

Shinto   Japan's original religion; the worship of nature, of one's ancestors, and of Japan.

As we discussed in connection with Britain, feudalism is a pattern that tends to develop spontaneously as central authority breaks down. This breakdown occurred in Japan from the ninth to the twelfth centuries and led to seven centuries of feudalism, ending only in the nineteenth century. China overcame feudalism early to become a bureaucratic empire. England overcame feudalism slowly and in a way that set up limited, constitutional government. France overcame feudalism by means of absolutism. Japan, it has been argued, was feudal so long and so deeply that feudal characteristics are still powerful in Japanese politics

Comparison

THE UNIQUENESS TRAP

The key question for Japan is whether it is a country like other countries or something unique. Many Japanese and some foreign observers claim the Japanese are a race and society like no other, sort of a tribe or large family. Indeed, during World War II, Japanese propagandists cultivated this image for domestic consumption. More recently, some have used this image to explain Japan's economic successes.

It is the view of this book—and indeed probably the basis of comparative politics—that descriptions of a country as totally unique are unwarranted.

Granted, Japanese political culture is plenty different from the European political cultures we have discussed so far. When you compare, though, you discover any country's political patterns can be understood. Much of Japan can be explained by prolonged feudalism. You find that people everywhere are quite human. For example, Japanese politicians take money from interest groups just like politicians everywhere. Avoid the uniqueness trap and the related Mystique Mistake, the overly romantic fascination with another country.

The essence of feudalism is power diffused and quarreled over among autonomous aristocratic lords, each supported by many warrior-helpers, who become the noble or knightly class. Typically, only these men are allowed to bear arms in normal times. They subscribe to a knightly code—in Japan, *bushido*, the way of the *bushi* (warriors)—that turns obedience and honor into religious virtues and places knights at a higher social level.

> **shogun** Feudal Japanese military chief who ruled in name of emperor.
>
> **daimyo** Feudal Japanese regional lords.
>
> **samurai** Literally, "those who serve"; Japanese knights.

The sure sign of feudalism is castles, as each lord needs a secure base from which to rule his lands and resist infringements from other lords and from the king or emperor. Japan has many lovely castles. To guard his autonomy, the lord had to be ready to fight at any time. War and feudalism tend to go together. Medieval Europe—with its trinity of king, lords, and knights—corresponds fairly closely to medieval Japan, where they respectively were the *tenno* (starting about 1600, eclipsed by the **shogun**), **daimyo**, and **samurai**. Japan was different from Europe, but not totally. Europe started growing out of feudalism in the fifteenth century or earlier, as modernizing monarchs crushed their aristocratic competitors to found the "strong state" of centralized power and sovereignty. Japan lagged far behind this pattern.

■ The European Jolt

The first Europeans to reach Japan were daring Portuguese navigators in their little caravels in 1543, followed by the Spanish in 1587 and Dutch in 1609. The Japanese could not keep them out, and soon Portuguese traders and Catholic missionaries made great inroads. St. Francis Xavier turned

Geography

JAPAN AND BRITAIN

There are interesting geographical similarities between Japan and Britain. Both are offshore islands that derived much of their culture from the nearby continent. Why then are Japan and Britain so different? England very early became a great industrial seapower, exploring, trading with, and colonizing much of the world. Aside from a short-lived invasion of Korea in the 1590s, Japan stayed home and did not develop industry beyond the craft level. There was some Japanese piracy off the China coast, but no fleets or explorations. England evolved from feudalism to democracy. Japan stayed feudal.

One clue to this puzzle is the power each faced on their respective nearby continents. Europe was fragmented into many competing states and was rarely a threat to England. Indeed, England played power-balancer on the Continent by injecting its armies at the right time and place into Europe's wars to make sure there was no unified Europe that might invade England.

Japan faced a unified China that was a nearly permanent threat. The Mongol invasion attempts of the thirteenth century reinforced this fear. Only Korea was a possible takeover target for Japan, but early on Japan decided isolation was its safest course. In the ninth century, Japan cut most of its contacts with and borrowings from China and turned inward. Unlike European monarchs, Asian monarchs did not engage in competitive expansion, so Japan had no incentive to discover new lands. (Imagine if Japan had crossed the Pacific about the same time England crossed the Atlantic.)

Tokugawa   Dynasty of *shoguns* who ruled Japan from 1603 to 1868; also known as the Edo Period.

shogunate   Political system headed by *shogun*.

gaijin   Literally, "outside person"; foreigner. (Japanese suffix "jin" means person, thus Nihonjin and Americajin.)

the Jesuits to converting Asia by learned argumentation and better knowledge of astronomy (to impress the imperial court). Dedicated Jesuit priests learned Japanese and made as many as 150,000 converts (2 percent of Japan's population) by 1582. Instinctively, though, Japan's rulers feared Christianity was the opening wedge of foreign takeover (which it was in much of the world) and banned it in 1597. Gradually, over the next few decades, missionaries were excluded and Japanese Catholics slaughtered. In 1635, Japanese were forbidden to travel abroad.

During this period, the **Tokugawa** clan managed to defeat the others and establish a powerful **shogunate** in 1603. (The 1978 TV miniseries *Shogun*, a fictionalized portrayal of this period, may be available on video cassette.) The Tokugawa shogunate was a combination of feudalism, military rule, and police state. Spies were everywhere, especially watching the *daimyo* to make sure none got any ideas about rising up against the shogun. As in France under Louis XIV, lords had to spend much time, or leave their family, at the palace. The long period of fifteen hereditary shoguns laid down early the tradition of the Japanese police state.

The Tokugawa era brought Japan two centuries of peace, prosperity, isolation, and stagnation. The shoguns moved the capital from Kyoto (now an important Buddhist cultural site) to Edo (modern Tokyo). Aside from one Dutch trading post allowed on an island in Nagasaki harbor, Japan effectively shut the door to foreign contact. (Unlike the Portuguese Catholics, the Dutch Protestants did no missionary work.) The Tokugawa shoguns feared **gaijin** ways and wares were threats to Japanese stability but kept informed of the outside world through Chinese couriers.

The Japanese people were kept ignorant of the outside world, which was portrayed as barbaric and menacing. Actually, considering what the Europeans, led by Britain, were doing in and to the rest of Asia, the picture was not totally wrong. The Europeans penetrated China by trade, military power, missionaries, and education, slowly deranging and collapsing a great civilization. The Japanese, by keeping the foreigners at bay, preserved their civilization and territorial integrity until they were ready to accept the West on Japanese terms in the mid-nineteenth century.

■ The Forced Entry

By the middle of the nineteenth century Japan was an unusual country. It had a distinctive and highly developed civilization with essentially no Western influence. It had enjoyed internal peace for two centuries. Although lacking industry and trade with the outside world, the Japanese were

Geography

SAILING THE EAST CHINA SEA

Now you are on an aircraft carrier entering the East China Sea from the south, the Taiwan Strait. Sailing clockwise in a great circle that includes the Yellow Sea to the north, which countries do you pass on your left?

China, North Korea (steer well away from here), South Korea, Japan (including its Ryukyu Islands), and Taiwan.

reasonably prosperous. A merchant middle class emerged, and with their wealth the arts flourished (the "floating world"). If it were up to the Japanese, they might have preferred to have been left alone forever. But the West would not leave Japan alone.

The United States did a great deal of business on the China coast, which, by the 1840s, was carved up into **spheres of influence**. The Americans, proud of not being colonialists, had no such sphere but tagged along after the British, concentrated in Shanghai. Shipwrecks in the East China Sea sometimes washed Western sailors onto Japanese shores. (Even then Japan controlled the Ryukyu Islands, chief of which is Okinawa, which rim this sea on the east.) These sailors could be gotten back only with difficulty, through the Dutch trading post. Furthermore, Japan looked like a tempting target for commercial expansion.

In 1846, two U.S. warships called at Yokohama (Tokyo's port) to request diplomatic relations; they were rebuffed. Then U.S. President Millard Fillmore ordered Commodore Matthew Perry to sail into the port and force the Japanese to have dealings with us. Perry arrived in 1853 with four ships that combined steam power with sails. The Japanese were frightened by these black, fire-belching sea monsters. Unprepared and confused, they begged Perry to return next year, when they would have an answer to his call for diplomatic relations.

How to best deal with the *gaijin* was a difficult and divisive issue for Edo. Ultimately, Japan's rulers decided they could keep the world out no longer, and when Perry returned in 1854, a large, splendidly attired Japanese imperial delegation met him and acceded to his demands for both diplomatic and trade relations. Soon Europeans followed in Perry's wake, and Japan quickly opened. But the Japanese managed to do it their way.

spheres of influence Understandings among imperial powers as to which held sway in given areas.

caste Hereditary social stratum or group.

Meiji Period starting in 1868 of Japan's rapid modernization.

■ The 1868 Meiji Restoration

The long Tokugawa period of internal peace had made the samurai **caste** unemployed and superfluous. With the challenge posed by the opening of Japan to the West, a group of these samurai found a new calling: to save Japan by modernizing it quickly and beating the West at its own game. Taking advantage of the accession of the new Emperor Mutsuhito, whose era took the name **Meiji**, these samurai had the emperor declare a restoration of his power and issue a series of "imperial rescripts" in 1868 that ordered the modernization of everything from education and military organization to industry and commerce. Although called a "restoration" of the emperor's power (from the hands of the shoguns), the emperor was largely a nationalistic symbol for rule by certain samurai clans.

Geography

CRUISING THE SEA OF JAPAN

Your carrier is now entering the Sea of Japan from the south, through the Korea Strait. Cruising in a clockwise direction, which countries do you pass to port (left)?

South Korea, North Korea, Russia, and Japan. (It looks like China has a tiny outlet to the sea here, but it does not.)

The traditional Japanese interiors are almost modern in their clean-lined simplicity. Shoes are removed to walk on rice mats. Diners sit or kneel on the floor in front of a low table. Futons are generally rolled aside every morning.

The slogan of the Meiji modernizers: "Rich nation, strong army!" Everything changed. Within a generation Japan went from the Middle Ages to the modern age. The Tokugawa were out. The *daimyo* lost their big hereditary estates (but got good deals in the new industries). Feudalism ended, and, on paper at least, all Japanese were legally equal. No more could a samurai legally kill someone who disrespected him. (Even today, those of samurai origin are proud of it, but it confers no special advantages.) It was a controlled revolution from above, the only kind of revolution Japan has known.

Various daimyo and samurai clans were given monopolies on branches of industry and ordered to develop them. These formed the basis of the industrial groupings known as **zaibatsu**. Japanese emissaries were sent out to study and bring back the best the West had to offer: British shipbuilding and naval warfare, French commercial law and civil organization, and German medical care, steelmaking, and army organization. All was faithfully copied and put into operation. For taxes, the Meiji modernizers unmercifully squeezed the peasants.

The Meiji elite wanted Western technology but few wished Western values and philosophies on democracy, equality, and individual rights. On questions of governance and social structure, Japanese values were deemed superior. Western ideas crept in anyway and, among many Japanese intellectuals, were highly influential. The Meiji modernizers copied the political system of newly unified Germany; they liked Bismarck's authoritarianism. The 1889 Japanese constitution included a monarch, an elected parliament, and political parties, but underneath, patterns of governance were thoroughly Japanese and largely brokered by traditional holders of power. It only looked democratic and modern.

zaibatsu Industrial conglomerates headed by samurai clans; formed under Meiji period and lasting through World War II.

Japan enjoyed rapid economic growth. In thirty-four years, from 1885 to 1919, Japan doubled its per capita GDP. Although puny by today's standards, this 2 percent annual growth rate was probably the world's fastest up to that point in time. Japanese products, starting with textiles and simple handicrafts, charged onto the world market using cheap labor to undercut Western producers. (Notice how China is now doing the same.) The purpose of Japanese economic growth, however, was less to make individual Japanese prosperous as proposed by Adam Smith than to make Japan powerful as a nation. Some argue that this impulse never ceased to dominate the thinking of the Japanese government.

■ The Path to War

As soon as Japan was sufficiently armed in the Western style, it picked a fight with and beat China in 1895, seizing Taiwan as its prize (and keeping it until 1945). Then it proceeded to gradually take over Korea—which was even more of a hermit kingdom than Japan had been—and finally made Korea a Japanese colony in 1910. If these moves sound wicked, we might pause and ask just what it was that the West had done in Asia over the previous couple of centuries. The West had taken Asia with the sword, so why should not Japan do the same?

state-led modernization
Government pushes change and growth.

In 1904, amid growing diplomatic tensions and military preparations, Japan attacked the Russian fleet at Port Arthur on the Manchurian coast. With a combination of disciplined and enthusiastic soldiers, bright and daring officers, and British naval and German army advisors, the Japanese devastated the incompetent Russians on both land and sea. U.S. public opinion favored the Japanese—Teddy Roosevelt called them "plucky little Nips"—partly because tsarist Russia had a terrible, repressive reputation in the United States. President Roosevelt personally mediated an end to the war in Portsmouth, New Hampshire, and won a Nobel Peace Prize for it.

Several *zaibatsu* grew into economic giants that bought control of political parties. Japanese politicians, like those of today, eagerly took money from private industry. In 1927, even before the Great Depression, the Japanese economy collapsed. The rich *zaibatsu* got richer as the middle class got poorer and peasants starved. Japanese army officers, whose families and soldiers were often just off the farm, bitterly resented the economic concentration and crooked politicians who made it happen. The officer corps, long a hotbed of fanatic right-wing nationalism and emperor-worship, turned its hatred against the democracy and capitalism that began to bloom in the 1920s and moved gradually to bend and subvert them.

The Japanese military had zero civilian control but ran itself as it saw fit, without even informing civilian authorities or diplomats. In the cabinet, the war minister was a general and the navy minister was an admiral; they got whatever budget they wanted. The Japanese armed forces were

Comparison

A JAPANESE MODEL OF INDUSTRIALIZATION?

A couple of points should be noted about Japan's impressive, rapid modernization, which is sometimes offered as an example for the Third World to follow. It was not carried out on the basis of purely free-market capitalism; it was **state-led modernization** with much government guidance and funding. Furthermore, it was not particularly nice or painless; some families, especially those of certain favored samurai, got rich, but many peasants were turned into a downtrodden proletariat.

Next, its centralization set up Japan for takeover by fascistic militarists and later, after World War II, by bureaucrats intent on making Japan a major industrial power no matter what the foreign or domestic costs. It bequeathed present-day Japan the problem of how to reform a government-led industrializing machine that lumbers on long after it has become a hindrance. We should think twice before prescribing the Japanese style of modernization for other countries. Besides, could it work in a country with a completely different culture?

Kempeitai   Japan's army-run security police before and during World War II.

Greater East Asia Coprosperity Sphere   Asia run by Japan, Tokyo's World War II propaganda line.

Manchuria   Northeasternmost area of China.

Manchukuo   Puppet state Japanese set up in Manchuria.

embargo   Not selling certain goods to disfavored country.

also split by rival cliques—feudalism again—who sometimes put each other down by gunfire. In a theme that we will explore more fully later, no one was in charge. Emperor Hirohito, although largely a figurehead, enthusiastically approved and supported plans to expand his empire.

Established in Korea and southern Manchuria, the Japanese army built a state within a state aimed at further conquests. Any civilian politicians in Tokyo who protested the army's expansionist program were assassinated. By the early 1930s, the army was in control of the Tokyo government, although for public purposes most of the official leaders were still civilians. Ordinary Japanese soon learned to say nothing critical, as the dread **Kempeitai** kept tabs on everyone; they were called the "thought police."

The ideology of the militarists—who supposed that the "Japanese spirit" was invincible—was quite similar to that of the Nazis, a combination of racism, extreme nationalism, militarism, and a bit of socialism. Both defined their peoples as a biologically superior, warrior race, destined to conquer their parts of the world and exterminate or dominate inferior neighboring peoples. Both were convinced that they needed new lands for their growing populations. Both built societies structured on military lines into tight, obedient hierarchies. Both offered the working class and farmers minimum economic standards. The difference is the Nazis did it through a party, the Japanese through the army; parties in Japan were unimportant. It was no great surprise when Imperial Japan linked up with Nazi Germany in the 1936 Anti-Comintern Pact and in 1940 joined the Axis. The two had little contact during the war and, fortunately for both Russians and Americans, did not coordinate their military campaigns.

The Japanese propaganda line was "Asia for the Asians." The evil European colonialists were to be kicked out and the nations of the region enrolled in the **Greater East Asia Coprosperity Sphere**, led, of course, by Japan, which would make all Asians prosperous. Some anticolonial Asians stepped forward to serve the Japanese (Ne Win of Burma, Sukarno of Indonesia, and Subhas Chandra Bose of India), although the Japanese were worse colonialists and racists than the Europeans had been. The Japanese governed with a bloody hand, mostly through the *Kempeitai*.

■ The Great Pacific War

In 1931, the Japanese army in **Manchuria** detonated a bomb on some railway tracks at Mukden (the Manchu name, now Shenyang) and claimed the Chinese Nationalist army had done it. Using this as a pretext, the Japanese army quickly conquered all of Manchuria and set up a puppet state they named **Manchukuo**. The civilian prime minister in Tokyo protested and was assassinated. The Tokyo government was simply not in charge; the army was operating on its own. The world did not know what to do. The League of Nations condemned Japan, so Japan simply walked out of the League. Britain and France, with extensive Asian colonies, did not want to antagonize Japan, so they kept silent. The United States, as an avowed "big brother" to China, protested with words but not with military power, which simply made the Japanese militarists more contemptuous of the Americans, who obviously were bluffing.

In 1937, the Japanese army began its ambitious conquest of all of China. Sharply opposed but wishing to avoid war, the United States increasingly applied economic **embargoes** on Japan. Starting in 1940, no U.S. scrap steel was shipped to Japan. The Japanese, with no iron ore of their own, had been major buyers on the world scrap metals markets; this was also one of the reasons they needed Manchuria. Later that year, the United States, then a major oil exporter, barred oil shipments to Japan.

Open Door U.S. policy of protecting China.

This convinced the Japanese militarists that they had to conquer the Dutch East Indies (now Indonesia) for their petroleum. Washington thought its moves were important restraints and warnings to the Japanese; Tokyo thought they were steps in an undeclared war the Americans were waging. Washington never fully comprehended that these steps were leading to war. The mercenary Flying Tigers, for example, were all U.S. soldiers on leave from their military branches, as if this fooled anyone.

The last straw for Tokyo came in 1941 when Washington froze Japanese assets in American banks, a serious and hostile move. One clique of the Japanese military—few in the Tokyo government even knew about it—immediately began planning Pearl Harbor, which, as far as they were concerned, was retaliation for U.S. economic warfare that had been going on against them for some years. The militarists never dreamed of physically conquering and occupying the United States. They hoped that by knocking out the U.S. Pacific Fleet they would persuade Washington to leave the Western Pacific to them. This ignored, however, the crucial if irrational factor of American rage, something the militarists could not comprehend across the cultural gap. They thought the Americans were cowardly bluffs. The Japanese people were informed of and consulted on nothing.

The war itself, probably because of cultural and racial differences, was unusually cruel, even by twentieth-century standards. It was, as one American historian put it, "war without mercy." Both Japanese and Americans killed many war prisoners and inflicted tremendous civilian damage. The Japanese fought like fanatics, partly because surrender meant shame and partly because they thought they would be killed if they were captured (many were). This fanatic quality persuaded President Truman—in order to avoid what all thought would be a costly invasion of Japan's main islands—to drop the newly developed atomic bomb on Hiroshima and Nagasaki. This finally brought Tokyo to surrender in August 1945.

Even then it was touch and go. Some of the militarists wanted to keep fighting to the last Japanese. They were even willing to disobey the emperor they professed to worship. With the atomic bombs, Emperor Hirohito turned against the war and decided to end it to prevent the complete

THE UNITED STATES AND JAPAN: COLLISION IN THE PACIFIC

The United States and Japan turned imperialistic at precisely the same time, in the late nineteenth century. Both were relative latecomers to the imperial game, and, with both expanding in the Pacific, it was only a matter of time before they collided. The United States constructed a modern fleet in the 1890s and was eager to use it against Spain in 1898. The cause was supposed to be Cuba, but Washington used the war as an excuse to seize the Philippines from Spain. At the same time, the United States took Hawaii, Midway, Wake, Guam, and Western Samoa. One of the unstated reasons for the U.S. expansion in the Pacific was the fear that if we did not take the islands the Japanese would.

Could America and Japan have lived side-by-side in the Asia/Pacific region? The problem was the U.S. commitment to protect China, a policy that began in 1900 with the **Open Door** notes. Originally designed to make sure that China trade was open to all, they soon turned into U.S. guarantees for the "territorial and administrative integrity" of China. As the Japanese military began conquering China, starting in Manchuria in 1931, they put themselves on a collision course with the United States.

destruction of Japan. If the war continued for another year, Japan would starve. He tilted the cabinet toward the peace party. The Japanese language is extremely subtle and usually avoids blunt or harsh statements. Thus in August 1945, Hirohito went on radio (for the first time ever) to explain to his ruined country and army why Japan would have to "endure the unendurable" and surrender: "Developments in the war have not necessarily gone as well as Japan might have wished." It was a classic Japanese understatement.

■ Up from the Ashes

Japanese cities were seas of grey rubble at the close of World War II. The old capital of Kyoto was spared upon the pleas of American scholars because it was a world cultural (chiefly Buddhist) treasure and of little military value. U.S. bombs burned much of Japan's crops in the field; starvation

Geography

ANOTHER TALE OF TWO FLAGS

In keeping with the myth that they are descended from the sun goddess, some ancient Japanese clans used a sun in their flags at least six centuries ago. With the Meiji modernization, Japanese ships needed a national flag to identify themselves. The present Japanese flag—*Hinomaru* or rising sun—suggested by the head of the powerful Satsuma clan in southern Japan, was first used in 1860 (by the first diplomatic delegation to visit the United States).

The sinister Japanese flag shows the sun's rays radiating out; it became a symbol of militaristic expansion. The army version had thicker red rays, the navy version thinner red rays. The U.S. occupation government abolished the sun-ray flag, but the Naval Self-Defense Force resumed using it in 1954.

The national anthem *Kimigayo* ("His Majesty's Reign") was also used by the militarists until 1945. Like the *Hinomaru*, it was never written into postwar law or required at ceremonies. Some nationalistic politicians wanted to do that in the late 1990s, but they were opposed by the leftist teachers, who feared a recrudescence of militarism. The Diet finally made both official and legal in 1999. Japanese students and teachers are now required to face the flag and sing the anthem.

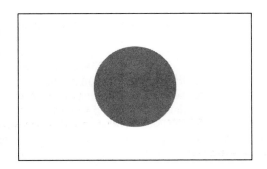

loomed. U.S. submarines sank a greater percentage of Japanese shipping than German U-boats sank of British shipping. In 1945, the
Japanese were desperate, even more desperate than the Germans were.

MacArthur Constitution   Japan's
U.S.-drafted postwar constitution.

keiretsu   Japan's postwar industrial
conglomerates.

Without the slightest resistance, General Douglas MacArthur
and his staff moved into one of the few buildings in Tokyo still standing, that of the Dai-Ichi Bank (later one of the world's largest banks).
Emperor Hirohito soon called on MacArthur to express his willingness to take the blame for everything Japan had done. MacArthur, speaking as one emperor to another, told him that would not be
necessary and that he could keep his throne, but as an ordinary mortal, not as a "living god." Most
Japanese already understood that the emperor was no living god, but some still revered him. To get
Japan on the U.S. side in the Cold War, in 1947 the U.S. occupation began covering up Hirohito's
support for the war and dumping blame on General Tojo, the wartime prime minister, who was
hanged. Critics claim that MacArthur's "reverse course" of 1947 let Japan avoid coming to grips
with what it had done during the war.

In 1946 MacArthur's staff wrote a new constitution in five days, somewhat modeled on the
British pattern. Why the hurry? The Americans wanted to block a Japanese attempt to just lightly
revise their prewar constitution. U.S. Colonel Charles Kades, a lawyer in civilian life, produced a
document to guarantee freedom, parliamentary democracy, and peace. Japanese elites did not like
the **MacArthur Constitution**—among other points, it made the emperor merely the symbol of
Japan—but grudgingly accepted it when the emperor endorsed it. Many educated Japanese were delighted to see Japan back on the path of democracy and equality and the old elite thrown out.

Although it has been Japan's constitution since 1947, it has not functioned precisely as written, as Japanese power does not flow in neat, Western-type channels. Industry was revived, much
of it under the supervision of the old militarists who had run it as part of the Japanese war machine.
The old *zaibatsu* conglomerates were broken up, but as the Cold War loomed MacArthur let banks
reassemble them under the new name of **keiretsu**, giant industrial-financial combinations with

Political Culture

JAPAN'S POLITICAL ERAS

Since the Tokugawa shogunate, Japan's political eras
are named for the reigns of each emperor. Indeed, for
domestic use only, years in Japan are those of the
emperor's reign. Thus 2000 is given as year 12 of the
reign of Akihito (add 1988 to this imperial year to
get the Western year). Wherever they can, the Japanese do it their way.

Name	Years	Remembered for
Edo Period	1603–1868	Tokugawa shogunate; military feudalism; isolated Japan.
Meiji	1868–1912	Rapid modernization under "restored" emperor; military expansionism begins.
Taisho	1912–1926	Normal but corrupt democracy.
Showa	1926–1989	Militarists take over, lead country to war; postwar economic boom.
Heisei	1989–	Economic slowdown; efforts at reform.

the same names as the old *zaibatsu*. For the same Cold War reason, MacArthur let many of the old elites return to political power. In Japan, as in France, the more it changes, the more it stays the same.

The Japanese economy revived, and spectacularly, as we shall see in Chapter 27. The economy did not function on a strictly *laissez-faire* basis, however; much economic growth was supervised and encouraged by government bureaucracies. Democracy also revived, but it did not function on a strictly Western basis either, as we shall explore in the next chapter.

Key Terms

arable (p. 340)

Buddhism (p. 340)

caste (p. 343)

Confucianism (p. 340)

daimyo (p. 341)

embargo (p. 346)

gaijin (p. 342)

Greater East Asia Coprosperity Sphere (p. 346)

keiretsu (p. 349)

Kempeitai (p. 346)

MacArthur Constitution (p. 349)

Manchukuo (p. 346)

Manchuria (p. 346)

Meiji (p. 343)

Open Door (p. 347)

samurai (p. 341)

Shinto (p. 340)

shogun (p. 341)

shogunate (p. 342)

spheres of influence (p. 343)

state-led modernization (p. 345)

Tokugawa (p. 342)

zaibatsu (p. 344)

Further Reference

Bix, Herbert P. *Hirohito and the Making of Modern Japan*. New York: HarperCollins, 2000.

Buruma, Ian. *Inventing Japan, 1853–1964*. New York: Modern Library, 2003.

Dower, John W. *War without Mercy: Race and Power in the Pacific War*. New York: Pantheon, 1986.

———. *Embracing Defeat: Japan in the Wake of World War II*. New York: Norton, 1999.

Gordon, Andrew. *A Modern History of Japan: From Tokugawa Times to the Present*. New York: Oxford University Press, 2003.

Hane, Mikiso. *Modern Japan: A Historical Survey*, 3rd ed. Boulder, CO: Westview, 2001.

Jansen, Marius B. *The Making of Modern Japan*. Camridge, MA: Harvard University Press, 2000.

Koseki, Sochi. *The Birth of Japan's Postwar Constitution*, ed. and tr. by Ray A. Moore. Boulder, CO: Westview, 1997.

McClain, James L. *Japan: A Modern History*. New York: Norton, 2001.

Moore, Ray A., and Donald L. Robinson. *Partners for Democracy: Crafting the New Japanese State Under MacArthur*. New York: Oxford University Press, 2004.

Seagrave, Sterling, and Peggy Seagrave. *The Yamato Dynasty: The Secret History of Japan's Imperial Family*. New York: Random House, 2000.

Sims, Richard. *Japanese Political History since the Meiji Renovation, 1868–2000*. New York: Palgrave, 2001.

Tipton, Elise K. *Modern Japan: A Social and Political History*. New York: Routledge, 2002.

Chapter 24

Japan:
The Key Institutions

If we were to go strictly by appearances and by what many Japanese want us to believe, we would portray Japanese political institutions as variations on the British pattern that was foisted on Japan by the Americans after the war. As is often the case with appearances in Japan, this would be deceptive. Several British-type institutions are present in Japan, but none of them function as they do in Britain.

The Monarchy

The Japanese monarchy, which was constitutionally divine until 1945, still claims it can trace its direct lineage back to 660 B.C. But for most of history, the monarch was a figurehead, a court prisoner of the real power. For some Japanese, especially elders and conservatives, the monarch is still divine, symbolizing the entire nation in a way that has long vanished in Europe. Right-wingers punish critics of the monarchy, sometimes by killing them. Few young Japanese pay the monarchy any attention. The two royal marriages since the war were both to commoners, and this has helped demystify the Imperial Household.

It is not clear if the emperor can influence Japanese politics. The constitution specifies he has no "powers related to government." A prisoner of ritual and ceremony, he goes along with what is expected of him. In 1945, Emperor Hirohito, who had earlier supported imperial expansion, did play a policy role in deciding for peace; with the cabinet deadlocked but many generals willing to keep on fighting, Hirohito threw his weight behind the peace party, and it tipped the balance. Let off the hook by MacArthur, Hirohito for the first time met his subjects face to face and became a symbol of poor little Japanese bravely making do under U.S. occupation.

In public speeches nowadays, Emperor Akihito, son of Hirohito, is generally vague and idealistic. Some observers believe, however, that the emperor gives a kind of tacit assent; that is, if things are not going horribly, he says nothing. This could continue for decades. If during a crisis an emperor should take a clear stand on an issue, however, it could make an impact. Crown Prince Naruhito will succeed Akihito, but Naruhito has only a daughter, and Japanese law reserves the throne for males. Changing the law to allow for an empress stalled in the Diet. Conservatives were horrified at the thought, but most Japanese approved. After all, they are descended from the sun goddess and have had eight empresses in their history, the most recent in the eighteenth century. (For the same reason, Spain's Cortes voted to allow a queen.)

Questions to Consider

1. Do Japanese institutions resemble British? Or just seem to?
2. Contrast the Japanese diet with the Japanese Diet.
3. How is Japan's prime minister different from other prime ministers?
4. Have the Liberal Democrats become a real political party?
5. What is wrong with a coalition of many parties?
6. Explain Japan's "dominant party system."
7. How was Koizumi an unusual Japanese prime minister?
8. How does the new Japanese electoral system work?

Comparison

Both the British and Japanese monarchs are respected figureheads, but the Japanese much more so. Neither has anything but symbolic duties. The British press sees little admirable in the younger generation of "royals." The media snoop on and photograph them and take particular delight in their marital troubles. The Japanese media would never snoop around the Imperial Household. The *Washington Post* first broke the story of the engagement of Crown Prince Naruhito in 1993, a story the Tokyo press would not touch until the official announcement. Once the *Post* pierced the "chrysanthemum curtain" around the imperial household, however, the Japanese media began to comment on their royalty, especially on the mood swings of the empress.

Another interesting point of difference: The prince picked a commoner (but of very good family), Masako Owada, to be the future empress, the second time this has happened in modern Japan. The prince's own mother, Empress Michiko, was herself a commoner (but of a rich family). So far, British royal marriages of those directly in line for the throne have all been with aristocrats. In Britain in 1936, Edward VIII abdicated after less than a year on the throne "to marry the woman I love," an American divorcée. The British press printed nothing on the drama until the formal announcement; Britons in 1936 could read of it only in the American and Continental press.

Japan's imperial family: From left, Emperor Akihito, Crown Prince Naruhito, Crown Princess Masako, Empress Michiko.

■ The Prime Minister

In contrast to most European systems, Japan's prime minister has not been the real seat of power. Prime Minister Junichiro Koizumi may have become a stronger prime minister, but we cannot be sure his powers have been *institutionalized* (see page 491) or are merely personal and short-lived. Will Japan's next prime minister be fairly powerful, or will the office slide back into its weakened condition?

Americans often mistake Japanese prime ministers for their British or German counterparts. In trade talks, for example, the Japanese prime minister would visit Washington and make some concessions to the U.S. side, but then nothing would change. The prime minister does not have nearly the power, in the face of major interest groups and their friends in government ministries, to change much. For most of its history, Japan's prime minister has not been the analog of a European or Canadian prime minister; he was more of a figurehead. There is no Japanese equivalent of a Thatcher or Adenauer, tough leaders who founded new systems or changed old ones.

Japanese prime ministers have averaged only about two years in office. By far the longest-serving prime minister was Eisaku Sato, who served from 1964 to 1972. Junichiro Koizumi did well with his five years, 2001–2006, a time limit that the LDP has put on its leader, not a government requirement. The LDP would have happily lifted the limit for Koizumi, but he retired in the fall of 2006. Ordinary cabinet ministers averaged about a year in office. The chief limits to their tenures are not votes of confidence or the splintering of coalition cabinets in the manner of the French Third or Fourth Republics. Until 1993, the Liberal Democrats had a comfortable majority in the House of Representatives and could easily brush off no-confidence motions.

Much of the problem has been the fragmented nature of the Liberal Democrats, in which the leaders of the several **factions** make and unmake prime ministers and ministers in behind-the-scenes deals. Many ministers are simply front-men for their factions. Some observers of Japanese politics alleged the LDP faction leaders were considerably more powerful than prime ministers.

faction   A party within a party.

shadow shogun   Unofficial term for top faction chief who names and controls Japan's prime minister.

There were instances when leading LDP politicians passed up a chance to become prime minister because faction chief was a more important job. Typically, the leader of the dominant LDP faction, called only half in jest the **shadow shogun**, arranged deals to set up the cabinet and the prime minister. If Koizumi has indeed been able to make the LDP a more coherent party, the role of factions and shadow shoguns may recede.

For ten months in 1993–1994 Japan had an eight-party coalition, possibly a world record. The parties were mostly splinters of the LDP, some of which subsequently returned to the LDP. Poland in 1991–1993 had five- and seven-party coalitions. Such governments are recipes for instability. Short-term Prime Minister Morihiro Hosokawa had his hands full as the many parties jockeyed for power within the coalition, just as the LDP factions had done. Indeed, many of the members of "new" parties had recently fled from the LDP as its electoral fortunes started to crumble. They brought with them the LDP traditions of infighting and power-brokering. Look for how long a Japanese prime minister stays in office and why he or she is replaced. The real weakness in the Japanese prime ministership is the parties, either fragmented, as in the case of the LDP, or splintered, as in the case of coalitions.

Personalities

JUNICHIRO KOIZUMI

Most Japanese political leaders are bland and color-less, but Prime Minister Junichiro Koizumi of the LDP won both the 2003 and 2005 elections chiefly on personality. (In Japanese, as in Chinese and Hungarian, family names are first, so we should say "Koizumi Junichiro.") In contrast to most Japanese politicians, Koizumi flaunted his long hair, colored shirts, spiffy suits, and outgoing personality. The Tokyo establishment at first thought Koizumi was strange and flamboyant, but he was popular and won elections. With Koizumi, Japan's parliamentary system (as have Britain's and Germany's) "presidential-ized" itself as voters are increasingly drawn to personalities more than to parties. Koizumi thus represents a modernizing step of the stuffy Japanese political system.

Koizumi was born into politics in Kanagawa Prefecture southwest of Tokyo in 1942. His father was high up in the wartime government as director of the war ministry and member of the Diet. Koizumi graduated Keio University in economics in 1967 and studied briefly in London. In 1970 he became an assistant to LDP faction chief Takeo Fukuda and worked his way up in the **Liberal Democrats**, serving as minister of health and welfare and of posts and telecoms before becoming both LDP chief and prime minister in 2001. First elected to the Diet from his home prefecture in 1972, Koizumi was been reelected there eleven times. He married in 1978 and had three sons but divorced in 1982, vowing never to remarry.

Koizumi was not a standard LDP deputy, one who simply obeyed his faction chief in order to bring pork projects back to his home district. Instead, he became convinced of the need for major Japanese political reform but decided to do it inside the LDP rather than against it. In 1994, when the LDP was briefly in opposition and undergoing much ferment and rethinking, Koizumi helped form a new LDP faction, Shinseiki, composed of younger, reformist deputies. He tried for the LDP presidency in 1995

Junichiro Koizumi

and 1999 and made it on his third attempt in 2001. Two days later he became prime minister by vote of the Diet's lower chamber. Remember, in parliamentary systems a new prime minister does not necessarily mean nationwide elections. For Koizumi, those came later, in 2003 and 2005.

Koizumi developed some reformist issues that increased his popularity. With the Japanese economy and government stuck in old patterns, he promised "structural reform without sanctuary." Young Japanese (especially girls) put up posters of him. But conservative factions of his own LDP blocked or diluted major reforms, and he accomplished little. But Koizumi did not give up, and the LDP had no one nearly as popular to replace him with.

Trouble inside the LDP came to a head in 2005 over Koizumi's demand to privatize the giant banking and insurance parts of Japan's postal system (for details, see Chapter 26). Prime Minister Koizumi got the measure through the lower house, but the upper house blocked it. Koizumi dissolved the lower house and held new elections two years early. He also kicked out thirty-seven LDP deputies who had not supported his postal reform. It was a bold and risky move, but Koizumi led the LDP to a landslide victory. Both Japanese and foreign observers hoped that Koizumi has broken the old pattern of weak and short-lived prime ministers

■ The Diet

The Japanese diet is optimal: light on fat, cholesterol, and calories. The Japanese Diet is marginal: heavy on payoffs, pork, and political squabbling. The 1947 constitution, in the best Lockean style, specifies the **Diet** (legislature) as the "highest organ" of Japanese government. Not strictly true in Europe, it is even less true in Japan. While the bicameral Diet selects the prime minister and can oust him on a vote of no-confidence, much of Japan's real decision-making power lies elsewhere, in the powerful ministries.

Japan's lower house, the House of Representatives, has 480 members, 300 elected from single-member districts and 180 on the basis of proportional representation by party lists in eleven regions, a *mixed-member* system (see page 192). The house's term is a maximum of four years. The new Japanese system, which began only with the elections of 1996, resembles the German hybrid system but does not use PR to set the overall number of seats per party (the German system, which does, is *mixed-member proportional*).

As is standard in parliamentary systems, the lower house can be dissolved early for new elections, which Prime Minister Koizumi did in 2005 (and won a resounding victory). The non-LDP coalition of 1993 rewrote some of the rules that were widely (if not necessarily accurately) blamed for Japan's endemic political corruption. (See the box on page 386 on reforming Japan's electoral system.)

Japan's lower house has more power than the upper, the House of Councilors. This is always the case with parliamentary systems. If the upper chamber rejects a bill from the lower chamber, the latter may override the objection with a two-thirds majority vote. After the 2005 elections, Koizumi had the support of two-thirds of the lower chamber, allowing him to shrug off any blocking moves in the upper chamber. The House of Councilors has 247 members elected for six-year terms; half are elected every three years. The upper house cannot be dissolved early for new elections.

With only one short break from 1955 to the present, the lower house of the Diet (and usually the upper house as well) has been in the hands of the Liberal Democrats. The Diet served as a sometimes raucous debating society in which the opposition parties, led by the doctrinaire Socialists, attacked the Liberal Democrats, and Liberal Democratic factions attacked each other, sometimes with fists as well as with words.

Behind the show of parties, elections, and debates, the larger question of any parliament is whether it actually controls government policy. The career professionals who staff the Tokyo ministries regard most members of the Diet as essentially clowns, who

Liberal Democrats   LDP, Japan's dominant party, a catchall. (See page 356.)

Diet   Name of some parliaments, such as Japan's and Finland's.

The Japanese Diet in Tokyo, a product of the 1920s, was completed in 1936. By then the military ran Japan.

COMPARISON OF PARTY SYSTEMS		
System	Example	Probable Causes
two-plus	Britain	Single-member plurality election districts; not-so-complex history.
multiparty	France	Historical complexity; runoff elections.
two-plus tending to multiparty	Germany	Hybrid single-member and PR elections.
dominant-party	Russia	Personality-based consolidation from fragmented system.
dominant-party	Japan	Postwar consolidation; weak opposition; obedient political culture.

pass around the **pork barrel** to get reelected but do not have the time, knowledge, or interest to run government. The Diet, like the British parliament, has a Question Time, but bureaucrats, the people who really know what is happening, answer most of the questions, not ministers. The attitude of Japan's bureaucrats: Let the parliamentarians play their little games, so long as they leave the running of Japan to us. Actually, this attitude of civil servants toward elected legislators is found in many governments; it is just stronger in Japan.

The Parties

Japan is an example of a **dominant-party system**, one with several parties but with one much stronger than any of the others. In such systems, the dominant party can theoretically be voted out but seldom is. Mexico and India for many decades had dominant-party systems but may have grown out of it. For most of the postwar period in Japan one party, the LDP, was so strong that some jested that the Japanese system was a "one-and-a-half party system." (The much-weaker Socialists were the "half" party.) In the 1990s, some thought the LDP was ready to crack apart into a multiparty system, but the LDP keeps on going as the dominant party.

The Liberal Democrats were actually an amalgamation of several existing centrist and conservative parties that had been ruling Japan since 1947. With the coming of the Cold War, the United States grew concerned that radical Japanese parties, the Communists and Socialists, might either come to power or make Japan ungovernable. The Americans therefore encouraged the mergers that created the LDP. Only one thing mattered: Do not let Japan go Communist or turn neutral between East and West.

The Liberal Democrats, although they enjoyed unbroken electoral success and controlled the government until 1993, barely cohered as a party; only the winning of elections and gaining of spoils kept the LDP from breaking up. Some saw it less as a party and more an **electoral alignment** of factions grouped around powerful chiefs,

pork barrel   Government projects that narrowly benefit legislators' constituencies.

dominant-party system   One party is much stronger than all others and stays in office many decades.

electoral alignment   Temporary coalition of parties in order to win elections.

much as samurai clans in olden times gathered around daimyo. Instead of swords, the faction chiefs used money. This feudal arrangement meant that no single faction or chief dominated for long, and no one was interested in or responsible for policy. The LDP is considered "conservative" not out of any ideological convictions but merely because it opposes change. There were no important ideological divisions within the party either, only loyalties to chiefs, some of whom were unsavory holdovers from the World War II militarist government. Asked his political views, one local LDP activist proudly proclaimed, "I am a soldier in the Tanaka faction."

Japan's party system is messy and constantly changing. In the early 1990s, the LDP fell into disarray. Dozens of leading LDP politicians stalked out of the LDP to form centrist-reformist parties—Japan Renewal, Japan New Party, and New Party Harbinger—that constantly reshuffled and renamed themselves into the Democratic, Liberal, and Conservative parties, some of which coalesced into the Democratic Party of Japan (DPJ), which has become the new "half party" of the system. The DPJ bills itself as free-market in economics but would withdraw Japanese forces from Iraq and improve relations with China and Korea. It is now the main opposition to the conservative LDP, but the DPJ is incoherent—a mixture of former Liberal Democrats and Socialists—rather like the U.S. Democrats. DPJ hopes were dashed by the 2005 elections; it shrank and the LDP boomed.

The old "half party," stuck in permanent minority status, was the Japan Socialist party (JSP), which was born with the warm approval of MacArthur's occupation government because it seemed

Comparison

THE LDP AND ITALY'S CHRISTIAN DEMOCRATS

There is an uncanny resemblance between the Japanese Liberal Democratic party and the (now renamed) Italian Christian Democratic party (DC). Both were founded after World War II, with U.S. blessings and CIA dollars, by combining preexisting political conservative-to-centrist groups to fight Communist or neutralist takeovers of Japan and Italy.

Both parties were successful and dominated their country's political life for most of the postwar decades. The LDP, with an outright majority of parliamentary seats, was mostly able to govern alone; the DC needed a multiparty coalition. Both parties oversaw major economic growth but neither were totally free-market, as both Japan and Italy had major state oversight of the economy (and, in the Italian case, major state-owned industries).

The negative side of the two parties was even more similar. Both were riven by at least half-a-dozen factions grouped around strong personalities who mostly hated each other. Corruption was rampant in both parties, and scandals were frequent. They stayed in power because not enough voters would switch to the radical parties, the Japanese Socialists or Italian Communists. The LDP and DC were the lesser of two evils in the minds of many voters.

With the Cold War over and the anti-Communist pressure removed, both parties declined in the early 1990s. In 1993 the DC changed its name to the Popular party. Voters, who could no longer stomach the crooked ruling parties, scattered their votes among several new, smaller parties. In the same year, both countries reformed electoral laws by shifting heavily to single-member districts, with an eye toward curbing corruption and party factions.

-to   Japanese suffix for party (Komei party is Komeito).

to repudiate the militarist regime. (Actually, some Japanese socialists had cooperated with the militarists.) The JSP hit an electoral high in 1958 with nearly one-third of the vote but declined because it was doctrinaire and rigid, caught up in the sort of Marxist slogans that Europe's postwar Socialist and Social-Democratic parties abandoned. The JSP, for example, urged neutralism for Japan and gave the Soviet Union and North Korea the benefit of the doubt while it strongly criticized the United States. Renamed the Social Democrat Party of Japan, it joined and ditched the shaky 1993–1994 coalition, then bizarrely joined with its LDP archenemies in a 1994–1996 coalition with Social Democratic leader Murayama as a weak figurehead prime minister. This sellout for the appearance of power alienated many Social Democratic voters, and the JSDP now has only seven of the 136 seats it had in 1990. Some of its voters went to the new DPJ.

Some less-privileged Japanese who were aware that the LDP was corrupt but were unattracted to socialism, turned to the strange Komei, or Clean Government, party. It too was stuck in minority status because it was a 1960s offshoot of the Soka Gakkai religious movement of evangelical-fundamentalist Buddhism, which many Japanese think is warped and fanatic. **Komeito's** program, aside from clean government, remained vaguely in favor of improved welfare benefits and quality of life. In coalition, the LDP and Komeito together now have two-thirds of the lower house's seats, enough to override the upper house.

A small Communist party, rooted in certain sectors of the working class and among radical intellectuals, consistently wins a few seats in the lower house. Torn between support for Beijing or for Moscow, the JCP was in a quandary when both headed for capitalism. Surveying Japan's messy and rapidly changing party system, we can say that no party is strong, not even the LDP, but the opposition parties were too fragmented to unseat the LDP. Half of Japanese say they support no political party.

Japan's Electoral System

Until 1993, at least part of the blame for the weakness of Japan's parties and party system was placed on its electoral system, which was like no other. Under that system, elections for the more-important lower chamber, the House of Representatives, were by 130 districts, 128 of which sent from two to five deputies to the Diet, supposedly based on district population. (One small district sent one deputy, and one very large district sent six.)

Instead of European-style proportional representation, though, Japanese voters marked their ballots for one candidate rather than for one party, and the winners were simply those with the most votes. If there were seven candidates in a four-person district, the four highest vote-getters were elected. Candidates of the same party actually competed directly against each other in the same constituency, a system that begged for factionalism within the parties and helped explain why the LDP became so terribly faction-ridden and corrupt. The need to spread around campaign money became desperate and with that the opportunity for corrupt political payoffs by private industry.

The new coalition put into office by the 1993 election blamed the Japanese electoral system for many of the political system's ills and immediately reformed it. First, they divided Japan into three hundred single-member districts with roughly the same number of people. This was to solve one problem that cried out for reform: unfairness in number of voters per elected representative. The 1947 constitution was devised at a time when Japan was still two-thirds rural and used the electoral districts of 1925. Since then, Japan has become over three-quarters urban, but the size of electoral districts changed only a little, some by legislation and some by court order. In 1980, it took up to five times as many urban votes as rural votes to elect someone to the Diet. In the 1993 election, after some reforms, it still took up to three times more urban votes than rural votes to elect one deputy. Even today, the gerrymandered districts still give some rural votes twice the weight of urban votes. The system greatly magnifies the voice of Japan's farmers and gives the LDP Japan's rural prefectures, since the LDP-dominated Diet keeps out imported food and lavishly subsidizes inefficient Japanese farmers. This gives Japanese consumers some of the highest food prices in the world and angers foreign food exporters, such as the United States.

Now, after the 1993 reforms, three hundred districts elect only one member each, and by simple plurality (not necessarily a majority) of the votes. This was aimed at two problems. It was supposed to cut the number of parties in the Diet, since such systems penalize small parties, as we discussed in connection with the British electoral system. This, however, is not absolutely the

Democracy

THE 2005 ELECTIONS: A HYBRID SYSTEM IN ACTION

In the 2005 legislative elections—which Prime Minister Koizumi called two years early—the Liberal Democrats scored a massive victory that gave them over 60 percent of the House of Representative's seats. The table below shows what the Diet's lower chamber looked like in 2005 (with a 67.5 percent turnout).

Is the new mixed-member electoral system accomplishing its goal? The lower house of the Diet is less fragmented than before, and the LDP bounced back from decline to become more dominant than ever. But we should give it more time. If the post-Koizumi LDP returns to its old fractious ways and is unable to reform Japan's economy, voters could turn to the Democrats, who could eventually challenge the LDP and give Japan a "two-plus" party system with alternation in power.

	Single-Member Seats	PR Popular Vote	PR Seats	Total Seats	Change from 2003
Liberal Democrat	219	38.0%	77	296	+54 seats
Democratic party	52	31.0	61	113	−64 seats
Komeito	8	13.0	23	31	−3 seats
Communists	0	7.0	9	9	no change
Social Democrats	1	5.5	6	7	+1 seat
Other parties	20	5.5	4	24	
Total	**300**		**180**	**480**	

METI   Japan's powerful Ministry of
Economy, Trade, and Industry (formerly
MITI).

case, as third and fourth parties that are territorially concentrated have good chances to win in at least a few districts. Next, by ending the old Japanese system of candidates from the same party competing against each other in multimember districts, the reform was supposed to overcome some of the dreadful factionalism within the LDP or any other large party.

The remaining 180 members of the lower house are now elected by proportional representation based on parties. This, too, was supposed to heal the factionalism that paralyzes the LDP. In such a system, candidates from the same party have to run as a team rather than as competitors. This was supposed to give Japan's parties greater ideological coherence. The reformers' end goal: a responsible two-party system with alternation in power, like a real democracy. Years later, Japan's electoral reforms have yet to accomplish this. Japan is still a dominant-party system, but now with a more coherent leading party. This could be a step toward a two-party system.

Election for the upper chamber, the House of Councilors, in which half the members are up for reelection every three years, are similar. Each prefecture has from two to eight councilors based on population, and here voters also have two ballots, German-style. One goes for an individual candidate, with the top vote-getter winning, as for the lower house. These account for 149 seats. Proportional representation at the national level fills another 98 seats. The electoral system for *both* Japan's upper and lower houses thus resembles the system for Germany's lower house. Because they use similar hybrid electoral systems, the two Japanese houses resemble each other in the distribution of seats. In the upper house, the LDP is the largest party (but short of a majority), Democrats second, Komeito third, and so on. One may wonder what is the point, especially in a unitary system that really does not need an upper house anyway, of an upper house elected on the same basis as the lower house.

■ The Ministries

Who, then, does have the power in Japan? First, there is no strongly focused center of power in Japan as in most other countries; power is diffused among several centers. Many observers argue that the 19,000 career bureaucrats who staff the executive levels of the ministries, particularly the Finance Ministry and Ministry of Economy, Trade, and Industry (**METI**)—formerly the famous MITI, the Ministry of International Trade and Industry—are the real seat of power in Japan. The Ministry of Land, Infrastructure, and Transport (formerly Ministry of Construction) has great clout too, as it distributes vast public-works projects to benefit the "road tribe," Japan's overlarge construction industry and its friends in the LDP. The four most important ministries—trade, finance, foreign affairs, and police—usually assign one of their top bureaucrats to serve as secretaries to the prime minister, a further bureaucratic hold on power, one not unknown in other countries.

The Japanese cabinet, like most European cabinets, can be easily changed from year to year, with ministries combined, renamed, or instituted. The cabinets of the 2000s had the following ministries:

Foreign Affairs
Justice
Finance
Education, Culture, Sports, Science, and Technology
Health, Labor, and Welfare
Agriculture, Forestry, and Fisheries

Economy, Trade and Industry (METI)
Land, Infrastructure, and Transport
Internal Affairs and Communications
Environment

vice-minister   Top bureaucrat in Japanese ministry.

In addition, the cabinet included several "ministers of state" for lesser-ranked specialized functions:

Disaster Management
Defense
Okinawa and Northern Territories
Financial Services
Economic and Fiscal Policy
Administrative and Regulatory Reform
Science and Technology Policy
Youth, Gender Equality, and Declining Birthrate

A minister may get more than one portfolio. For example, in Koizumi's 2005 cabinet the minister for internal affairs and communications was also in charge of "privatization of the postal services," a political controversy in Japan. The minister of state for youth affairs also handled gender equality and "measures for declining birthrate," which is not a trivial problem in Japan. Although not a minister, Japan's chief cabinet secretary is considered second in command after the prime minister and also serves as official spokesman for the government. Shinzo Abe, named to the position in 2005, could succeed Koizumi in 2006.

There are a few interesting points about Japan's cabinet. Notice that Defense is in the cabinet but does not rate the title of ministry. According to the constitution, Japan is not supposed to have armed forces. At least five ministries or agencies deal directly with economic development. The foreign minister usually doubles as deputy prime minister. In addition, a state minister serves as chief cabinet secretary under the prime minister.

At least half of the ministers must be members of the Diet, and most are members of the lower house. A few are members of the upper house, and occasionally respected specialists or academics not in the Diet are brought in. The ministers are not necessarily experts in their portfolios (ministerial assignments), which are based more on political criteria than on subject-matter competence. Bureaucrats run the ministries, not ministers.

As is the case in Europe, every party in a coalition has at least one top leader named to be a minister. The eight-party coalition of 1993, for example, had representatives of eight different parties in the cabinet. Even the small parties got a portfolio, but the coalition-member parties with the most seats got several. Such distributions of ministries are payoffs used to form and hold a cabinet together. After the 2005 elections, in which the LDP won a majority of seats, LDP Prime Minister Koizumi governed in coalition with the small Komeito, with most portfolios in LDP hands.

Below the minister, a civil-service **vice-minister** really runs the ministry. The Japanese vice-ministers, who correspond to the British *permanent secretaries*, are more powerful than their nominal bosses, also the case in most of Europe. Reportedly the vice-ministers meet twice weekly to draw up the agenda the cabinet follows the next day. The ministries' top appointed officials—and they are appointed internally on the basis of merit, as defined by the individual ministry, not on the basis of political connections—have years of experience and knowledge; the minister may last only a few months in office. This gives the top civil servants a great deal of power and the feeling that they alone should run Japan.

■ Japanese Territorial Organization

Japan is a unitary system that looks a bit like a federal system. It has forty-seven administrative divisions, forty-three of them **prefectures**, after the French *prefect*, the head of a *département*. The other four are special situations: Tokyo, Osaka, and Kyoto are run as large metropolitan districts, and the thinly populated northernmost island of Hokkaido is one big district.

---
prefecture   First-order Japanese civil division, like French department.

Each Japanese prefecture has an elected governor and unicameral assembly to decide local matters and raise local taxes. These taxes, though, cover only about 30 percent of prefectural needs, so the prefectural government is always asking Tokyo for additional revenues. Japanese call this "30 percent autonomy." The Ministry of Internal Affairs in Tokyo still oversees prefectural matters and can override the local governor. The Japanese situation resembles the modern French territorial structure: unitary, but with certain local-democracy features. Many Japanese, who are proud of their local communities, wish they had greater autonomy from Tokyo.

Key Terms

Diet (p. 357)
dominant-party system (p. 358)
electoral alignment (p. 358)
faction (p. 355)
Liberal Democrats (LDP) (p. 357)
METI (p. 362)

pork barrel (p. 358)
prefecture (p. 364)
shadow shogun (p. 355)
-to (p. 360)
vice-minister (p. 363)

Further Reference

Abe, Hitoshi, Muneyuki Shindo, and Sadafumi Kawato. *The Government and Politics of Japan*. Tokyo: University of Tokyo Press, 1994.

Dolan, Ronald E., and Robert L. Worden, eds. *Japan: A Country Study*. Washington, D.C.: U.S. Government Printing Office, 1992.

Hartcher, Peter. *The Ministry*. Boston, MA: Harvard Business School Press, 1998.

Hayes, Louis D. *Introduction to Japanese Politics*, 4th ed. Armonk, NY: M. E. Sharpe, 2004.

Jain, Purnendra, and Takashi Inoguchi, eds. *Japanese Politics Today: Beyond Karaoke Democracy?* New York: St. Martin's, 1997.

Kataoka, Tetsuya. *The Price of a Constitution: The Origin of Japan's Postwar Politics*. Bristol, PA: Taylor & Francis, 1991.

Kim, Paul S. *Japan's Civil Service System: Its Structure, Personnel, and Politics*. Westport, CT: Greenwood, 1988.

Kuroda, Yasumasa. *The Core of Japanese Democracy: Latent Interparty Politics*. New York: Palgrave, 2005.

Ruoff, Kenneth J. *The People's Emperor: Democracy and the Japanese Monarchy, 1945–1995.* Cambridge, MA: Harvard University Press, 2001.

Shibata, Tokue. *Japan's Public Sector: How the Government Is Financed.* Tokyo: University of Tokyo Press, 1992.

Stockwin, J. A. *Governing Japan: Divided Politics in a Major Economy,* 3d ed. Malden, MA: Blackwell, 1998.

Chapter 25

Japanese
Political Culture

Japan is one of the few non-European countries that modernized while retaining its own culture. Scholars ponder why Japan could do this while many other cultures cannot. One clue may be the *absence* of deep religious values in Japan. Japanese religion, light and flexible, never got in the way of modernization. Japan took on some appearances of Western culture but kept its inner core of Japaneseness (*Nihonjinron*). For this reason, Harvard political scientist Samuel Huntington (and many others) sees Japan as a unique civilization.

Germany and Japan both suffered defeat and occupation but came out quite differently after World War II. Missing from the U.S. occupation of Japan was the sort of denazification that was practiced, however imperfectly, in Germany. The Western Allies, by means of the Nuremberg War Crimes Tribunal and their control of the media and schools, were able to instruct many Germans on the horrors of the Nazis and on the merits of democracy. No such instruction took place in Japan, partly because there was no Nazi-type party to blame or put on trial (just army officers) and partly because MacArthur did not depose the emperor or dismantle the Japanese political structures but rather used them to run Japan. Japanese bureaucrats and politicians mostly carried over from wartime militarism and quietly resolved not to change Japan too much. Some Germans felt guilty about their Nazi past, but very few Japanese felt guilty over their brutal expansion. (For the difference between guilt and shame, see box on page 368.)

Many Japanese to this day refuse to believe that Japan did much evil during the war. The way they see it, the victors vindictively punished the Japanese losers by hanging some seven hundred officers who had done their patriotic best. Bayonet practice on Chinese babies? Never. Germ warfare experiments on American prisoners? No way. Korean "comfort ladies"? Not our doing. If you want to see war crimes, say some Japanese, look at Hiroshima and Nagasaki. The Japanese tend to see themselves as poor, downtrodden victims.

Only recently have some Japanese officials admitted war guilt—or is it shame?—for World War II. In 1991, Emperor Akihito apologized to Koreans for Japan's colonial occupation (1910–1945). In Beijing in 1992, he told Chinese officials that he "deeply deplored" Japan's long (1937–1945) war in China, which killed, by Beijing's estimate, 35 million Chinese. His father, Hirohito, had maintained a discreet silence about World War II. Reformist Prime Minister Morihiro Hosokawa began his brief term in office (eight months, 1993–1994) in a most unusual way, by describing the Pacific

Questions to Consider

1. How do postwar German and Japanese political cultures differ?
2. How can you tell if Japanese feel guilt or just shame?
3. Is there a distinct "Japaneseness"? Describe it.
4. Why does Christianity have an uphill struggle in Japan?
5. Are the United States and Japan destined to misunderstand each other?
6. How does a *sarariman* differ from his U.S. counterpart?
7. What is *wa*? How does it relate to *nemawashi*?
8. Will the *shin jinrui* transform Japanese culture?

guilt   Deeply internalized feeling of personal responsibility and moral failure.

shame   Feeling of incorrect behavior and violation of group norms.

War as Japanese aggression and apologizing for the "pain" Japan inflicted on other countries. Prime Minister Junichiro Koizumi in 2005 observed the sixtieth anniversary of the Japan's surrender with the words: "Our country has caused tremendous damage and pain to the peoples of many countries, especially Asian countries, through colonial rule and invasion. Humbly acknowledging such facts of history, I once again reflect most deeply and offer apologies from my heart."

Japan's apologetic signals are mixed, however. Many Japanese still do not admit the truth and few show remorse. They claim Japan was never aggressive or brutal and had fought only "for self-defense and the independence of Asian countries," the old Greater East Asia Coprosperity Sphere line. A 1995 Diet proposal for a resolution of apology was dropped in the face of a petition signed by five million Japanese and supported by most of the LDP. In 1994, a minister claimed the 1937 Japanese "rape of Nanking" was a fiction. He resigned in the uproar that followed. A book by a Chinese-American author with the same title could not find a Japanese publisher.

Hundreds of Japanese politicians—including prime ministers—annually visit Tokyo's controversial Yasukuni Shrine. They claim they are simply paying respect to Japan's 2.5 million war dead, but the Shinto shrine also honors Japan's militarist past and fourteen Class A war criminals—including wartime chief Tojo—hanged by the Americans. Its attached museum portrays the war as Japan's liberation of Asia from Western imperialists. Fascistic youths in World War II uniforms parade at Yasukuni. LDP chiefs cultivate the important Bereaved Families Association as well as

Political Culture

GUILT VERSUS SHAME

Some foreign observers of Japan have argued that Japanese, unlike Westerners, are not driven by a sense of **guilt** but by the more superficial feeling of **shame**, of not upholding group standards. Guilt is woven into the Judeo-Christian ethos, starting with the Fall and continuing through the Crucifixion. The idea that God gives you moral choices and judges you is an important component of Western civilization and, according to some, the basis of Western individualism.

Japanese religion—and the Japanese are among the least religious people in the world—has no such reference points. Shintoism, a form of animism in which one's ancestors play a major role, now means basically worshiping Japan. There is no God or code of morality besides serving and obeying. State Shinto was refined into an organized religion by the Meiji modernizers to ensure loyalty during times of tremendous change, and as such lent itself to nationalist militarism. Buddhism, which exists side-by-side with Shintoism, is vague on the existence of God; Lord

Buddha was merely enlightened, not divine. Either way, from Shinto or Buddha, few Japanese are on guilt trips.

Instead of guilt, according to this theory, Japanese are strongly motivated by shame. To let down the group is a terrible thing. In World War II, many Japanese preferred death to surrender, which meant shame. (Americans who surrendered were shameless cowards worthy only of harsh treatment.) One Japanese soldier who hid on Guam until 1972 said upon his heroic welcome back in Japan, "I have a gun from the emperor and I have brought it back." He also apologized: "I am ashamed that I have come home alive." There are few Japanese criminals, as trial and conviction brings devastating shame to the family. (The shame technique has been suggested for use on American criminals, but it does not work too well here.) The shame theory helps explain Japanese anti-individualism and the leitmotif of suicide that runs through the Japanese warrior code, politics, and even personal relationships.

political right-wingers and militarists who cluster in the Liberal Democratic party. Beijing claims such gestures are evidence of continuing Japanese militarism.

archipelago Chain of islands.

Japan's Education Ministry carefully screens textbooks to promote unity and patriotism. Doubts and war crimes get screened out. How history books handle World War II is a continuing touchy subject. One older Japanese textbook said mildly, "We must not forget that Japan caused inconvenience to neighboring Asian countries in the past." China and Korea protested this deceptive understatement, and the Education Ministry in 1992 ordered a tougher line substituted: "We must not forget that Japan caused unbearable suffering to neighboring nations in the past." Every year, however, new textbooks come out that revert to the blameless line. Japan only halfheartedly admits war guilt; Germany did a better job and did it decades earlier.

The view of themselves as the permanent disadvantaged underdogs colors many aspects of Japanese life. Japanese point out that they are confined to an **archipelago** about the size of California, most of it useless for crops, too mountainous to build on, and with zero mineral resources. We have to take special steps to ensure our survival, they argue; we cannot afford to be as free and open as big, rich countries. Furthermore, we have just been devastated in a terrible war.

In the immediate postwar years, there was clearly great validity in these attitudes. But after a quarter-century, by 1970, Japan was a sparkling, rich society with no need for special protection for any of its sectors. Psychologically, though, many Japanese, especially older people, act as if they are trapped in the worst years of wartime and postwar poverty and scarcity. Thus they "make do" with high tariffs, outrageous prices, cramped living quarters, and obedience and loyalty to company and bureaucratic authority.

Older Japanese especially display the psychological overshoot of insecure, worried people who have had to claw their way out of poverty. Such people work extremely hard and accomplish much, but they are often difficult to deal with, as it is impossible to calm their sense of deprivation. Mercifully, the younger generation, raised in postwar comfort, is repudiating the old attitudes, and we may expect policies to shift accordingly as more of this generation enters politics. This will take some time, however, as many of those ruling Japan were born before World War II and still remember the war and postwar period.

Ritual dance at the Shinto shrine on Miyajima, home of the famous "floating torii" (gate in the background), teaches Japanese school-children about their culture.

The Cult of the Group

Americans pride themselves on their individualism, Japanese on their groupness. We are trained from childhood to "be ourselves" and to attract attention: "Hey, look at me!" Japanese are trained to fit into the group and not attract attention: "It is the nail that sticks up that gets pounded down," goes a Japanese folk adage.

enryo Nonpresumptuousness, not asking for too much.

nihonjinron "Discourse on the Japanese," Japaneseness.

Almost like a big family, Japanese feel they can communicate with and understand only other Japanese. Foreigners, even if they live in Japan a long time and master the language, cannot do this, believe many Japanese, implying that Japanese have evolved to a higher human level. More plausibly, Japanese groupness is the result of centuries of isolation and feudalism, which taught that everyone has a place and must keep it.

Viewed in a less benign light, Japanese groupness is an expression of Japanese obedience. And Japanese are obedient. The crime rate is very low. There are fewer murders in all of Japan in one year than in Baltimore most weeks. (There are practically no private handguns in Japan.) Students hit the books with little complaint. Japanese bureaucrats instruct businesspersons on correct strategies, something no American businessman would tolerate for a moment.

Unlike Western (especially American) individualists, Japanese generally try not to make waves. One should not attract attention to oneself or make a fuss, an attitude called **enryo** (more or less opposite of *chutzpah*, widely practiced by Americans). One should be polite and smile at all times, even in adversarial situations. One should not take legal actions, certainly not take someone to

Political Culture

THE ROOTS OF NIHONJINRON

Japanese political culture is so distinctive that some Japanese claim their brains are physically different. During the war the militarists touted this racist explanation, but now only a few old people believe it. There are several theories of **nihonjinron**, and it is probably a combination of all.

- *Shintoism* taught that Japan and the Japanese are a wonderful, perfect society superior to others.
- *Buddhism* still teaches the renunciation of desire, enduring pain and difficulties, and being careful and mindful of all persons and things.
- *Confucianism* taught that one is born into a strict hierarchy and must obey authority and defer to superiors with great politeness.
- *Feudalism*, deep and prolonged in Japan, taught all to obey and honor superiors and keep their place but diffused power among several centers.
- *Dependency* is inculcated into young Japanese by their parents and teachers. Unlike young Americans, Japanese are not trained for independence but to remain dutiful and submissive to the authority of both the job and the government.

- *Rice-farming* requires sharing water and working in teams that go down the rows at the same speed. Some argue that this makes Japanese cooperative but unoriginal.
- *Crowded* into a small land, Japanese had to develop nice manners and cooperation to make daily life possible. (This would not explain New Yorkers.)

The simplest explanation of Nihonjinron may be the best: centuries of feudalism where even the hint of disobedience—such as not bowing low enough—to higher authority could be punished by beheading on the spot. Reinforcing this was the basic unit of the Japanese feudal system (borrowed from China through Confucianism), the *ie* (household), in which the patriarch had complete control over his wife and children.

To this day, one can distinguish the social ranking of Japanese by noticing who bows lower. An underling bows very low and from the waist; his superior returns it with a curt, slight bow of the head. The Japanese do not have some special group or obedience gene; they were simply late in getting out of feudalism.

court, but should settle disputes quietly. (Japan has fewer lawyers than U.S. law schools produce each year.) One should not go to the doctor too much; small maladies will go away by themselves. (Japanese medical costs are half of America's, and Japanese have lower infant mortality and live longer.) Wow, maybe we should try a little *enryo*.

There is a negative side to this group-minded obedience: Japanese are severely shortchanged in the civil-rights and legal areas Americans take for granted. Some American lawyer-haters celebrate the fact that the Japanese rarely sue; they settle quietly, allegedly for the sake of social harmony. But this almost always leads to settlement in favor of the stronger party, no matter how rightful is the claim of the aggrieved party. In Japan, the rich and powerful company or bureaucracy is always right; the individual is always wrong.

Crowded Japan: Because most of Japan's islands are mountainous, Japanese must live in narrow streets and tight houses. To minimize earthquake damage, two-story houses are preferred.

Traditional Japanese gardens feature the close control that is part of Japanese culture. Note the small trees in enclosed settings: nature tamed. Indeed, the famous miniature bonsai trees are deliberately stunted rather than encouraged to grow. Some say Japanese children are also raised that way.

■ Education for Grinds

The Japanese are strong on education, one of the keys to their success. The Japanese work force is considerably better educated than the American, especially in mathematics, the basis of all high-tech operations. On average, a Japanese high-school graduate knows more math than an American college graduate. Children do their homework—often supervised by "education mamas," mothers intent on their children's academic success—with a determination that leaves French grinds far behind. Of course, Japanese students who do poorly on exams may commit suicide out of shame.

Japanese youngsters run a demanding obstacle course to get into the right schools and universities. As an almost perfect **meritocracy**, all admissions are based on tests; athletic ability or family connections do not help. Cram courses may help, and many Japanese youngsters attend them after regular school hours. Getting into the right high school or university means "examination hell," a period of several days during which entrance exams are given.

meritocracy Advancement based only on intellectual ability.

Once into college, however, many Japanese students relax and do little work until their junior year, when they take exams that lead to jobs. Probably more important than what you learn in college is the fact that you got into a top college. If you have been admitted sararimen   Literally, "salary men," mid-level employees.

to the best, Tokyo University (*Todai*), you have a head start over those who have been admitted to lesser institutions. Every prefecture has a public university; the U.S. occupation installed the U.S. model of state universities. In addition, Japan has hundreds of private colleges and universities. Few Japanese students do graduate study, so few need a high grade-point average. Where you studied rather than grades matter for getting a job.

Most Japanese students care and know nothing about politics, something now found throughout most advanced industrial countries. (See the box on *postmaterialism* on page 204.) In some of the better universities, however, a few students under the influence of leftist professors learned to criticize the system that produced them. A few went into radical politics and protests, a handful into extremist terrorism. With graduation, though, almost all Japanese students get a haircut and new suit and dutifully become obedient **sararimen**. College in Japan is a brief respite of protest and freedom between the grind of grade school and the grind of work. Entrepreneurialism is rare; you either get a job with a big company or you are nothing. Only recently have some young Japanese begun starting their own companies, which is difficult in Japan.

The content of Japanese education is heavily slanted to rote learning and multiple-choice exams. Creativity and innovation are not highly prized; going along with the group is. Debate is normally taught only as part of English-language instruction, implying that only with foreigners does one have disagreements. One interesting contrast with U.S. classrooms: In Japan, the fast learners are assigned to help the slow. This is good for the education of both of them and builds groupness.

Political Culture

JAPAN'S CRITICAL CHRISTIANS

Religion everywhere has a major influence on political culture, and one clear difference between Japan and the West is the Japan's lack of Christianity. Christians of all denominations (mostly mainstream Protestant) form less than 1 percent of Japan's population and are not growing much. (The Jesuits in the sixteenth century did better, gaining 2 percent.) Although Christian-related schools and colleges (many with U.S. ties) are numerous and popular, few students are drawn to Christianity. Western-style weddings, complete with marriage chapels and white gowns, are popular but just for show.

Japan's Christians see themselves as an embattled, prophetic minority. They no longer face discrimination, just indifference. They deplore the lack of higher values among Japanese, whom they see caught up in "secular materialism"—the godless getting of money and things. They see Shinto and Buddhism as empty ritual, providing no moral grounding. The Japanese who drop in on a Buddhist service for a few minutes are simply doing a little relaxation therapy. Japanese Christians are among the few willing to face Japan's responsibility and guilt for World War II and to warn that Japan's new emphasis on "patriotism" could be misused.

Christianity always had an uphill struggle in Japan, where it was regarded as a foreign subversion of Japaneseness. There is much truth to this, as Christianity brings with it individualism, guilt, and equality (especially between the sexes). Christianity would have greatly changed Japan, but this is unlikely to happen. The Japanese are content in their irreligiosity. In contrast, some 30 percent of South Koreans are Christians. Koreans, under the long Japanese oppression, saw churches (many U.S.-sponsored) as a comfort and support for their Koreanness.

Americans and even some Japanese criticize the rote aspect of Japanese education, arguing that it hampers flexible, new thinking later in life. But problem-solving in mathematics does precisely that, and Japan's quick rise indicates that Japanese are plenty innovative. As U.S. classrooms have moved away from memorization, they have also lost the attentiveness that comes with it. We might actually wish to reintroduce a bit of memory work. Besides, Japanese schooling is changing, producing a more spontaneous, questioning sort of student. Japanese education is losing some of its rigidity.

---

nemawashi Literally, "root-binding," as in gardening; the formation of group consensus.

Death of a Sarariman

The typical Japanese *sarariman*—who wears a suit no matter what the weather—would probably like to spend his entire working life with the same company. (We say "he" because traditionally most Japanese women were content to be "office ladies" for a few years before marriage, but now many scorn marriage in favor of careers, leading to a plunging birth rate.) The company would like to reciprocate by offering "lifetime employment" to its people. At its peak, however, only about 30 percent of the Japanese work force was covered by lifetime commitment from employers, chiefly large

Comparison

DESTINED TO MISUNDERSTAND?

Viscount Eiichi Shibuzawa (1840–1931), one of the founders of modern Japanese business and an advocate of strong U.S.-Japanese ties, grew exasperated with the difficulties he encountered. Wrote Shibuzawa: "No other countries exist which are as different from each other as the United States and Japan. These two countries seem to have been destined to misunderstand one another."

This shows up frequently in the distinct U.S. and Japanese business cultures. For example, two business seminars are held in New York City, one for twenty-five Japanese executives in America, the other for twenty-five American executives working for Japanese firms in the United States. The Japanese, all males, arrive in dark suits and keep their coats on even though the room is hot. They take exactly the allotted ten minutes for a coffee break. They ask no questions until they get to know each other over lunch. They politely defer to the speakers.

The American group includes eight women. Many of the men immediately take off their coats in the hot room. Chatting during the coffee break lasts more than twenty minutes. The Americans ask many questions, and some dispute the speakers.

These are just a few of the cultural differences between Japanese and American managers. Americans view conflict within the firm as normal; Japanese practice **nemawashi**, patient discussion leading to a consensus that all then follow. American managers want quick profits; Japanese want bigger market share and greater efficiency, building for the long run. American firms hire people for specific skills, then downsize them when they are no longer needed. Japanese firms hire for what the person can learn and contribute to improved efficiency and try to not let the employee go. American managers respond to questions quickly and directly, for that indicates frankness. Japanese managers pause before answering and give discreet replies, for that indicates thoughtfulness. Sometimes one wonders if we are indeed destined to misunderstand each other.

karoshi   Death by overwork.

concerns, and this dwindled during Japan's long economic downturn. Smaller companies are forced to hire and lay off as economic conditions dictate, although for most of the postwar period, economic growth was so consistent that unemployment appeared only in the late 1990s.

Until recently, most Japanese employees felt duty-bound to stay with their firm. American-style job-hopping was frowned upon as opportunistic and disloyal. Decades ago, I assured a Japanese colleague from the Associated Press's Tokyo bureau it would be perfectly all right for him to leave AP for a much better-paying job. It just went against his grain to desert a company. He was finally persuaded, he told me, when he saw me leave AP in New York for a better job, an easy decision for an American. This has changed; along with Japan's corporate downsizing has come job-hopping.

Japanese work very hard, probably too hard. An eight-hour day is rare for a *sarariman*; twelve hours is common. Some Japanese literally die of overwork, an illness they call **karoshi** (not to be confused with bar-singing *karaoke*, which is how many *sararimen* relax). *Karoshi* victims typically work prodigious overtime or weeks without a day off. Recently, though, some bereaved families have sued the companies that worked the husband into an early grave. (One benefit offered by some large firms: burial in the corporate cemetery, so you can be with your group for eternity.) The new generation of Japanese does not like to work so hard (or be buried in the company plot). They prefer leisure time to overtime and ask, "Why kill yourself for the company?"

A great puzzle of postwar Japan is why its people work so hard and produce so much but ask for so little. *Sararimen* are willing to live in rabbit-hutch apartments and commute for hours standing up in a crowded rail car to their urban jobs. The cost of living is among the highest in the world, especially for housing. Europeans and Americans would long since have gone out on strike in such conditions. Japanese unions are weak, many are organized by and for companies, and, if they must strike, do so over lunch hour so as not to disrupt work.

Comparison

HOW WOULD YOU DO ON A JAPANESE EXAM?

This solid-geometry problem is from an entrance examination to Japan's elite Tokyo University. It is aimed at young Japanese in their last year of high school.

A regular pyramid with a height of V and a square base of width a rests on a sphere. The base of the pyramid passes through the center of the sphere, and all eight edges of the pyramid touch the surface of the sphere, as is shown in the illustration.

How do you calculate (1) the height of V and (2) the volume that the pyramid and sphere share in common?

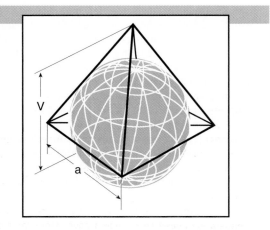

Well, you say, I'm not a math major and should not be expected to know such advanced stuff. But this question is from the exam for *humanities* applicants.

How can the Japanese put up with it? The explanation is that Japanese culture really is different—or at least has been different until now. Centuries of obedient, feudal relations have taught the Japanese

wa   Japanese for social harmony.

not to ask for much but to work hard for the lord (or company) and take pride in living modestly, even frugally. Japan never developed a social safety net or social-security system, so the Japanese learned to save for hard times and for their retirement. The Japanese are bigger savers than the Germans, and the money for investment this made available to banks and businesses explains much of Japan's magnificent postwar economic growth: plentiful capital.

■ Political Suicide

Now a minor part of Japanese culture is the willingness to commit suicide under certain circumstances. Originally a component of *bushido*, the nobles' code of honor, *seppuku* (vulgarly known as *hara-kiri*) showed that a samurai was willing to die to avoid shame on himself and his family. Although only a small fraction of the Japanese population is of knightly descent, a greater number pretend to be and admire and affect its styles. As U.S. forces took Saipan in 1944, some four thousand Japanese women and girls committed suicide by jumping off cliffs. Prince Konoe, prime minister just before the war and grandfather of Prime Minister Hosokawa, when ordered to turn himself in for trial as a war criminal by the U.S. occupation, committed suicide in 1945.

In addition to atoning for personal shame, suicide has another use: It induces a sense of shame in others. If I sincerely believe in a cause but am not getting my way, by committing suicide before those I am trying to convince I make them ashamed and thus pressure them to follow my way. By dying, I win. This is still understood if no longer widely followed. In 1993, for example, a right-wing politician went to Japan's leading newspaper, *Asahi*, to complain about its liberal slant. After rambling on before bored editors, he pulled out two guns and shot himself to death with both. In 1999 a Bridgestone manager disemboweled himself before the company president to protest downsizing.

Political Culture

WHY IS WA?

Some argue that the Japanese word **wa** is the key to Japanese culture. Japanese are trained to seek and cultivate harmonious relations with each other. Japanese love *beisabaru* but never argue with an umpire. *Wa* is what gives Japan its cooperative, group-mindedness where everyone looks out for everyone else. (Notice how the only way to play Pokémon is by cooperation.)

Critics argue, however, that the concept of *wa* is deliberately hyped to provide a cover story for promoting conformity and obedience. Under the doctrine of harmony, anyone questioning or criticizing the way things are run is disturbing the domestic peace and tranquility and is therefore a troublemaker. *Wa* can be a device for social control.

Wa can also lead to terrible financial losses when corporations and government bureaucrats cover up financial problems rather than face them early and honestly. Several giant Japanese corporations have lost fortunes in financial mistakes—all kept quiet until too late. Sumitomo Corporation revealed in 1996 that a single copper trader had compounded one mistake into another and lost the company $1.8 billion. And the company had known about it all along but did not want to disturb the harmony.

shin jinrui (Shin = new, jin = person, rui = class of) Japanese for new human race, the younger generation.

pietà Italian for "pity"; artistic representation of Mary cradling body of Jesus.

Japan's most famous postwar suicide was that of novelist Yukio Mishima in 1970. At age 45, Mishima was internationally acclaimed as Japan's greatest writer. He was also a tortured spirit and fanatic right-wing militarist who sponsored his own private army to inculcate young men with the old warrior spirit of Japan. Mishima specifically hated the clause of Japan's constitution that forbade it to have an army, even though it does have a hefty "self-defense force." Mishima tried to change this by seizing the old Imperial Army Headquarters in Tokyo with a small group. When the takeover failed, Mishima, in a military-type uniform, committed *seppuku* on a balcony at the Headquarters before hundreds of horrified officers. Mishima ritually disemboweled himself with a special knife; then a friend beheaded him with a sword. His aim was to convince the officers to shake off the lethargy of peace and return to the way of the warrior. Suicide, because it is so traditional, tends to be used by conservatives who hark back to old ways. As such, it occurs less and less frequently.

The "New Human Race"

As you have noticed, the generation gap is wide in Japan, perhaps the widest of all the countries we study in this book. Older Japanese are amazed and not completely happy at how much the younger Japanese have changed and call the youngsters the **shin jinrui** because they are so different.

Comparison

THE MINAMATA PIETÀ

An environmental catastrophe on Japan's Minamata Bay illustrates the different moral and legal attitudes between the United States and Japan. A chemical company had long dumped mercury waste into the bay. Children of those who ate mercury-contaminated fish from the bay were born deformed. Famed U.S. photographer W. Eugene Smith, a man of great humanistic conscience, felt he had to tell the story. Few Japanese photographers or news media were interested. One of Smith's moving photos, of a Minamata mother bathing her deformed child, won the accolade "Minamata **pietà**," as it reminded viewers of Renaissance paintings and sculptures.

Many Japanese were not moved by the moral or legal challenge of toxic-waste dumping. Chisso Chemical, the dumper, was a major employer, and government policy stressed the economy, not ecology. Chisso workers severely beat Smith for daring to impugn their company's honor. Smith had trouble getting his photos displayed until the manager of a big Tokyo department store decided to take the heat for the sake of artistic and ethical truth. He was criticized for disturbing the harmony of Japanese society. The victims finally sued Chisso, but the courts let the case drag on for a third of a century before making Chisso pay a paltry $60,000 each to the 3,000 worst-harmed victims and $22,000 each to thousands of others.

In the United States, the media and photographers, many with a strong environmentalist slant, would cover the situation fully. American lawyers would be eager to take the victims' case, which would be for millions, not thousands, of dollars. U.S. courts generally rule that companies face "strict liability" in such cases; if they caused the damage they must pay for it. Japanese courts make plaintiffs prove "negligence," that the company not only caused the damage but should have known it was doing so. In Japan, judges decide cases, not juries. Lawyers, courts, and lawsuits do have their uses; America may have too many, but Japan has too few. Indeed, Japanese universities are now expanding their law programs by adding U.S.-style three-year postgraduate law schools.

Physically, Japanese 20-year-old males are on average nearly 4 inches taller than those of the postwar generation, females 2.7 inches taller. Almost all of the Japanese gain has been in the legs and is believed to be related to a more Western-type diet that is richer in protein than the traditional Japanese rice-based diet. Indeed, rice has been declining in popularity while McDonald's and Kentucky Fried Chicken have become, respectively, Japan's first and second most popular restaurants. With the growth spurt, however, the higher-fat diet has brought some obesity, never before known among Japanese youngsters. Another factor: Japanese no longer kneel in the home and office but sit in chairs; this has eliminated the constant pressure on the knees that stunted the growth of Japanese legs. (Earlier, the children and grandchildren of Japanese immigrants to America showed precisely the same startling increases in size.)

on Duty or debt of honor.

But more importantly, Japanese attitudes are rapidly changing among young people. Working long hours for the sake of the company is no longer seen as normal and desirable. Desiring leisure time for family, hobbies, and travel makes younger Japanese similar to their European and American counterparts. Holding down consumption in order to save money is no longer the norm. Many younger Japanese have traveled or studied in the United States and have sampled the indulgent lifestyle of American youth. American fashions and lifestyles are popular. (One recent fad: Martha Stewart.) Young Japanese want the good life and want it now.

Some now turn their back on the standard path of work for males and marriage for females. Because jobs are now scarce and apartments terribly expensive, many Japanese in their twenties continue to live with their parents and work only as *freeters*, temporaries (probably from the German *freie Arbeiter*, free workers). They avoid marriage, have fun, and spend their money on clothes and colorful hairdos.

To a considerable extent, this is the continuation of the "new human race" that has made recent political changes possible. The older generation, schooled in discipline and deprivation, simply obeyed for most of the postwar period. What the company and government offered was good enough. Younger Japanese have lost some of these characteristics and are more likely to switch their jobs and their votes. Older Japanese could tolerate the corruption and factionalized leadership of the LDP; after all, the party had led Japan to prosperity. Younger Japanese are more likely to say the system needs a thorough housecleaning. Japanese political attitudes are not entirely different from the attitudes of other advanced industrial countries and with time are likely to increasingly resemble them.

Political Culture

THE HONOR OF ON

Another remnant of feudalism in Japan is **on**. It is social and symbolic rather than legal and monetary and underlies the Japanese sense of obligation. If someone has done you a small favor, he or she has incurred your *on*, and you are expected to remember it and return the courtesy someday. *On* lubricates much Japanese social life. If you visit Japan, bring small, inexpensive gifts for your hosts (one favorite: college-logo T-shirts).

For example, I repeatedly invited an American friend and his Japanese wife to visit my family for a weekend, but I was always politely turned down. My American friend explained why. My invitation had come without any basis in *on,* so his Japanese wife felt awkward in accepting. My friend had an idea to overcome the problem. He sent me two lovely books of photos as a gift, thereby incurring my *on*. At that point it was honorable for them to come and visit. The offering of gifts is also a normal and even required part of Japanese political life.

Comparison

CHANGING POLITICAL CULTURES IN GERMANY AND JAPAN

German political culture shared some characteristics with Japan. Both had a history of strong feudal hierarchies and stress on obedience. Both marched eagerly to war under dictators who knew how to manipulate traditional-looking symbols. Neither country took to democracy until it was imposed on them after World War II. The devastation of war and lean postwar years taught Germans and Japanese to work hard and ask for little. Reliable conservative parties, the CDU and LDP, delivered growing prosperity, and voters were not in the mood for experiments. Student radicals could fuss over the U.S. alliance and nuclear weapons, but solid citizens understood they were necessary. The difference is, Germany shed its postwar stability in about a generation; the Japanese are taking two or more generations.

Why is Japan slower? First, Japan's feudalism lasted longer and its obedience patterns were inculcated deeper than Germany's. Second, Japan was more isolated even after World War II and its people traveled less than West Germans. Third, Japan did not go through the reeducation that West Germany did after the war. Fourth, Japan was a poor country, poorer than most of West Europe, until it sprinted forward in the 1960s and 1970s. As Japan got richer and more open to the world, its political culture became less distinctive. Now young Japanese resemble young Germans: free, single, apolitical, and fun-loving.

Looked at over the span of a century and a half—since Perry—Japanese political culture appears as a continual rearguard action designed to preserve the core of *nihonjinron*. Gradually and grudgingly over time, Japan gives way to *gaijin* ways, accepting some superficially and altering others. The Meiji modernizers in effect said: "All right, we have to modernize to prevent the West from taking us over. But we will do it our way." After World War II, Japan in effect said: "All right, we have to become a capitalist democracy. But we will do it our way."

After many such changes, Japanese political culture does shift, but never in a rapid or revolutionary way. It is the nature of *systems* that you cannot change just one thing, for when you do everything else changes. For example, equality of women, although in the MacArthur Constitution, is just now slowly being implemented. Women are going to college in large numbers. Some even seek the executive track in corporations. They drive cars, marry later (if at all), and work after marriage. This slowly changes male attitudes (many do not like it), the birth rate, child-rearing patterns, household income, and eventually political attitudes. But they will always preserve that inner core of *nihonjinron*. Japan does change, but changes are usually incremental and nearly invisible, almost as if the elites of Japan meet quietly for a great *nemawashi* (see page 373) to construct a new consensus that will give in partway to the *gaijin*.

Key Terms

archipelago (p. 369)

enryo (p. 370)

guilt (p. 368)

karoshi (p. 374)

meritocracy (p. 371)

nemawashi (p. 373)

nihonjinron (p. 370)

on (p. 377)

pietà (p. 376)

sararimen (p. 372)

shame (p. 368)

shin jinrui (p. 376)

wa (p. 375)

Further Reference

Cutts, Robert L. *An Empire of Schools: Japan's Universities and the Molding of a National Power Elite*. Armonk, NY: M. E. Sharpe, 1997.

Garon, Sheldon. *Molding Japanese Minds: The State in Everyday Life*. Princeton, NJ: Princeton University Press, 1998.

Hendry, Joy. *Understanding Japanese Society*, 3rd ed. New York: Routledge, 2003.

Ikegami, Eiko. *Bonds of Civility: Aesthetic Networks and the Political Origins of Japanese Culture*. New York: Cambridge University Press, 2005.

Itoh, Mayumi. *Globalization of Japan: Japanese Sakoku Mentality and U.S. Efforts to Open Japan*. New York: St. Martin's, 2000.

Johnson, David T. *The Japanese Way of Justice: Prosecuting Crime in Japan*. New York: Oxford University Press, 2001.

Karan, Pradyumna P. *Japan in the Twenty-First Century: Environment, Economy, and Society*. Lexington, KY: University Press of Kentucky, 2005.

Kumagai, Fumie, and Donna J. Keyser. *Unmasking Japan Today: The Impact of Traditional Values on Modern Japanese Society*. Westport, CT: Praeger, 1996.

Leheny, David Richard. *The Rules of Play: National Identity and the Shaping of Japanese Leisure*. Ithaca, NY: Cornell University Press, 2003.

McVeigh, Brian J. *Nationalisms of Japan: Managing and Mystifying Identity*. Lanham, MD: Rowman & Littlefield, 2003.

Nathan, John. *Japan Unbound: A Volatile Nation's Quest for Pride and Purpose*. Boston, MA: Houghton Mifflin, 2004.

Sakai, Naoki, Brett de Bary, and Iyotani Toshio, eds. *Deconstructing Nationality*. Ithaca, NY: Cornell University Press, 2005.

Schwartz, Frank J., and Susan J. Pharr, eds. *The State of Civil Society in Japan*. New York: Cambridge University Press, 2003.

Chapter 26

JAPAN:
PATTERNS OF INTERACTION

Japanese political interactions are sometimes described as an **iron triangle** consisting of the Liberal Democratic party, economic interest groups, and the ministries. Since the 1993 electoral upheaval, with its promise of major change, all new prime ministers have vowed to break the iron triangle. At most, they have dented it, for such triangles represent powerful interests.

The classic Japanese iron triangle formed during the long reign of the LDP works as follows. Liberal Democratic politicians promise most of the country's economic interest groups—with agriculture and the construction industry prominent among them—to look out for their interests. In return, the interest groups deliver plentiful campaign funds, enabling the LDP to greatly outspend rival parties. (Some LDP politicians also put funds in their own pockets.)

The LDP, however, rarely translates interest-group demands directly into law and policy; instead, they let the ministries and agencies adjudicate the demands by means of contracts, loans, regulations, subsidies, and trade protection. The ministries have been there longer, know all the right people and how to deal with them, and can generally come up with workable compromises.

The ministries, the commanding corner of the triangle, have their own agenda, and it is not Adam Smith's vision of a free and open market in which competition delivers the best products and the lowest prices. Instead, the Tokyo ministries focus narrowly on their industries and sectors and seek to protect them by controlled markets in which domestic competition is limited lest it become cutthroat, and foreign competition is artfully excluded wherever possible. This setup makes the Japanese economy—which superficially looks like a free-market economy—one of the most regulated in the world. Although recently reformed a little, some ten thousand bureaucratic regulations govern every aspect and branch of the Japanese economy. The Japanese economy is not a good example of a free-market system.

The ministries do not serve the interest groups, the way it usually works in the United States or Europe. Rather, the interest groups get some of what they want from the ministries in return for overall obedience to the ministries' schemes to build regulated markets under the control of bureaucrats. The Japanese arrangement, reminiscent of the controlled mercantilist system of the French kings, suits Japanese interest groups. Japanese consumers, on the other hand, get robbed by outrageous prices.

Questions to Consider

1. Are most countries run by "iron triangles"?
2. Is Japan a good example of a free-market economy?
3. Which are more important in Japan, interest groups or the bureaucracy?
4. Compare and contrast top French and Japanese bureaucrats.
5. Could something like METI work in America?
6. Between interest groups and government, who bribes whom?
7. Can Japan's "money politics" be reformed?
8. Explain the "no one in charge" theory. Is it valid?
9. What are *shadow shoguns* and do they still run things?
10. Did the 2005 elections change Japanese politics?

■ Bureaucrats in Command

In emphasizing the political importance of top civil servants, we must understand where Japan's ministries came from. They are not the product of a free-market democracy but of a militaristic system planning for and conducting World War II. Munitions, heavy industry, the development of Manchuria, transportation and communications, and many other sectors of Japan's economy were under state control and supervision. Indeed, the very founding of the modern Japanese economy during the Meiji Restoration was ordered and controlled by the state. Japan has not really known a free-market economy.

iron triangle   Interlocking of politicians, bureaucrats, and business people to promote flow of funds among them. (See page 381.)

Democracy

JAPAN'S MAJOR INTEREST GROUPS

Japanese interest groups tend to follow the French model; that is, they are usually subordinate to bureaucratic authority, but even more than the French groups, the Japanese interest groups until recently have seldom disputed or ignored the ministry that supervises them. Japanese pluralism is not the same as American pluralism, where interests strive to capture the relevant agency or, failing that, fight it. The following are some top Japanese interest confederations:

- *Keidanren,* Federation of Economic Organizations, the most important business group, speaks for most large corporations and used to work closely with METI to promote exports. Now it is working around ministerial control in favor of deregulation and competition.
- *Shin Rengo,* Japanese Trade Union Confederation, formed from the 1989 merger of smaller union federations, speaks for eight million members in a moderate and nonideological voice, even though it still has some ties to the Social Democrats.
- *Nissho,* Japan Chamber of Commerce and Industry, with good ties to the LDP, seeks to curb competition, large stores, discounting, and foreign imports.
- *Nokyo,* Central Union of Agricultural Cooperatives, argues for self-sufficiency in food and

The leftist union of Japanese school teachers protests against Japanese rearmament, NATO, and the United States, and for socialism, in a peaceful demonstration across the street from the Diet.

the exclusion of farm imports to its close friend, the LDP.

- *Nikkyoso,* Japan Teachers Union, left-wing, pacifist, critical of government and powerful among schoolteachers; tied to the Social Democrats.
- *Jichiro,* the Prefectural and Local Public Employees Union, is Japan's largest single union and is quite influential. It is also leftist and tied to the Social Democrats.

After the war, precisely the same bureaucrats who ran Japan's war economy were given the job of economic recovery. This they proceeded to do—and do very well—in the same spirit they had displayed during the war: Economic development is too important to be left to capitalists. Japan is fighting for its economic life and does not have the luxury of slowly finding its way by means of the inefficient system of supply and demand, went the postwar argument. The attitude of Japan's top bureaucrats was that nothing but Japan's economic growth mattered, and we are the only folks who know how to make it happen.

guided capitalism   State supervision but not ownership of the economy.

public corporation   Special-purpose economic unit owned in whole or in part by government (U.S. example: TVA).

Todai   Short name for Tokyo University, Japan's best (China's equivalent: *Beida*).

This would not properly be called a "socialist" system, for it kept ownership private and did not attempt to redistribute wealth or income from the rich to the poor. It was not directly aimed at rapid improvement of individual living standards but at the growth of the Japanese economy as a whole. Some call such a system "statist," a system, as we have considered in France and will examine again in Mexico, where the state is the number-one capitalist and owns major industrial and financial institutions. This is not the case in Japan, where almost all industry is privately owned. Perhaps the best name we can come up with for Japan is **guided capitalism**.

The Japanese government does run numerous **public corporations** aimed at aiding various economic sectors and the development of several regions, especially poorer ones, such as its thinly populated northernmost island of Hokkaido. The Japanese bureaucratic method of control is to leave industry in private hands but to prod—often over dinner and drinks—the industry to go this way or that by rational persuasion and bank loans. The targets are the likely areas where Japanese

Comparison

BUREAUCRATIC ELITES IN FRANCE AND JAPAN

The concept of a strong bureaucracy operating on its own, with little guidance or input from elected officials, is nothing new. France had such a system for decades, and neither de Gaulle's Fifth Republic nor Mitterrand's reforms made French bureaucrats answerable to the electorate. The Japanese bureaucratic elite is a moderately close analog to the French *grand corps*. Both groups are very bright and highly educated and placed into the top executive positions with mandates to modernize and upgrade the economies of their respective countries. Both tend to think that they alone can save their countries and that elected politicians are a necessary evil who come and go and are not to be taken seriously.

The French are trained in a Great School, such as the National Administration School or Polytechnical, whereas the brainiest young Japanese gain admission to the prestigious Tokyo University, **Todai**, which is publicly funded. Upon graduation, both enter bureaucratic fast tracks for the executive level, and both may retire early into better-paying jobs in private industry. The French bureaucratic elite disdains the views of interest groups as un-French and unobjective. The Japanese bureaucrats generally listen earnestly to the views of the interests they are assigned to supervise, but then they gently persuade the interest group to change its views to match those of the ministry.

A big difference is that French bureaucratic elites mostly read from the same sheet of music and cooperate across ministries. The Japanese are soon immersed in their ministries' *sakoku* (closed environment) and pay little attention to other ministries or elected officials. There is no grand plan in the Japanese model, and sometimes ministries work at cross-purposes.

advantages allow them to undercut foreign producers and then secure an overwhelming world-market share. (The strategy with the Japanese camera industry against the German was one such success. See the box about this in the next chapter, on page 395.)

Those industries certified as growth leaders got long-term, low-interest loans from banks that were connected with the important ministries. Those industries not moving down the desired paths did not get big loans. This is a far more subtle way of steering an economy than the outright state control of Soviet-type socialism. (It also meant, by the 1990s, that many loans were mistakes that ruined Japanese banks. There is a down side to everything.) The Japanese approach was similar to the French *indicative planning* but stronger and more effective because it could make the cash flow, and it took place in the cooperative Japanese setting where business generally obeys government.

For the most part, the top bureaucrats of Finance and METI did a good job. Handpicked from the brightest graduates, they are promoted rapidly and given major responsibilities while young. Their salaries, however, are not high, and if they wish to move into lucrative positions in private industry in mid-career (what the Japanese call "descent from heaven" and the French call "putting on the slippers"), so much the better. That way the ministry broadens its ties with private industry (and, with it, the breeding grounds for corruption). Japan recovered quickly after World War II and went on to set economic growth records. As we shall explore in the next chapter, however, the bureaucratic guidance may have led to dangerous distortions in the Japanese economy that plunged it into difficulties later.

For some time, defenders of Japan claimed proponents of the overpowerful-bureaucracy theory were engaging in Japan-bashing. Then in 1993 the reformist Hosokawa government publicly agreed that the ministries were too powerful and needed to be curbed and coordinated. By the 1996 elections, virtually all parties agreed and made reforming the bureaucracies and regulations part of their campaign promises. Yesterday's Japan-bashing became today's conventional wisdom. Prime Minister Koizumi wished to further cut the role of the state in Japan's economy.

THE UNITED STATES AND JAPAN: AN AMERICAN DETI?

If Japan's Ministry of Economy, Trade, and Industry helped speed Japan to the upper ranks of the industrialized countries after World War II, could not a U.S. equivalent—a Department of Economy, Trade, and Industry (DETI)—do the same for the United States? Here, we see how hard it can be to transfer institutions from one country to another.

METI functioned well in a Japanese political culture of cooperation and obedience. METI bureaucrats, to be sure, did not order businessmen to do things. They persuaded them, often by lengthy wining and dining. Soon enough, businessmen could get the point that what was good for them was also good for Japan.

A DETI would have to operate in a far more individualistic American context, one where businessmen are taught to disdain government and go their own way. Washington has no national "industrial policy" and is unlikely to develop one any time soon. U.S. antitrust laws might make collaboration between firms illegal, not a problem in Japan. The U.S. government's ability to provide bank loans would mean a major redo of the U.S. banking system. Actually, the United States is trying government-led technological development. Sematech brought together five U.S. computer-chip manufacturers, exempt from antitrust laws, to share manufacturing technologies. The results of this small experiment have been positive.

It will not be easy; the bureaucrats are used to their power. Fumed one high official of the powerful and conservative **Okurasho** about some of the changes proposed by a reformist cabinet: "We won't accommodate them, I assure you. They will accommodate us." In 2002, the popular and outspoken woman foreign minister, Makiko Tanaka (daughter of a prime minister), was fired when the ministry's civil servants mutinied over her attempts to fight corruption by imposing accountability. Japanese bureaucrats do not like civilian control.

Okurasho   Japan's finance ministry.

scandal   Corrupt practice publicized by news media.

walking-around money   Politicians' relatively small payments to buy votes.

The economic downturn of the late 1990s showed the bureaucrats were unable to pull Japan out of its slump; the formulas of yesteryear no longer worked. Impatient, the top industrialists of Keidanren organized their own Competitiveness Committee and made some hard-hitting recommendations to the government, bypassing METI altogether. Keidanren's message to the cabinet and the Diet: Fix this creaky economic machine or we move our factories overseas (which is what they were doing anyway). The bureaucracy lost prestige too. Law students at the elite Todai, who used to compete to enter the civil service, now turn to private industry. Said one senior: "The bureaucrats have a bad image now—rigid, inflexible, annoying." If Japan cuts the power and status of its bureaucrats it will mark the evolution of Japan into a more normal country.

Corruption Scandals

Another leg of the "iron triangle," connecting the government to interest groups, is the fertile ground for corruption. Japan seems to have a new **scandal** every year, accompanied by officials' resignations and sometimes arrests. It used to be widely accepted, among both foreign and Japanese observers, that a little corruption was normal in Japan—an artifact of the electoral system—and that most Japanese did not especially mind it. **Walking-around money** is part of many political systems, and voters expect favors from politicians. But corruption in Japan goes deeper than elected politicians; many civil servants are caught up in it too.

Few books on Japanese politics mentioned corruption except in passing; it did not seem to be an important point. Japanese, according to many area experts, like other Asians, understand and tolerate graft up to a certain level and object only when takers get conspicuously greedy. Maybe this was once the case, but as the corruption scandals got bigger, the previously rather docile Japanese media started going after corrupt politicians, and the Japanese public was less and less tolerant of political corruption.

In 1974 Lockheed was found to be delivering major bribes to Japanese politicians to get them to purchase Lockheed jet fighters for the Japanese air force. Lockheed pleaded that it was just doing business like everyone else in Japan. Japanese politicians said they needed the money for party campaign expenses, but much of it stayed in private pockets. Energetic Prime Minister Kakuei ("the computerized bulldozer") Tanaka (1972–1974) was brought down by the scandal and arrested and jailed briefly in 1976.

In 1988 and 1989 the Recruit Corporation privately sold at bargain prices untraded shares of stock to many LDP and a few opposition politicians. Some made as much as $1 million overnight. The public was enraged, and Prime Minister Noboru Takeshita resigned in shame in 1989. A top aide committed suicide. Former Prime Minister Yasuhiro Nakasone, also implicated in the scandal, resigned from the LDP.

In 1992 Sagawa, a parcel express firm, was found to be paying off more than sixty politicians, with the top prize of $4.2 million going to LDP faction chief Shin Kanemaru of the old Tanaka

money politics   Lavish use of funds to win elections.

¥   Symbol for yen, Japan's currency, fluctuates around 110 to the dollar.

structure   Institutions of government such as constitution, laws, and branches.

soft money   In U.S. politics, funds given to parties and other groups rather than to candidates in order to skirt restrictions.

faction. During the war, right-winger Kanemaru was an Imperial official in Manchukuo and later became the LDP's main fund-raiser. Kanemaru's sources included organized crime. His office safe held $50 million in cash and gold bars, but Kanemaru was fined less than $2,000. Public outrage mounted and carried over into the following year's elections.

The signs that corruption is a serious problem in Japan had been evident for some time. Everyone knows that most public works such as dams, highways, and bridges are unneeded—little Japan reportedly uses more concrete a year than the United States—but they reward the construction industry, which kicks back a percentage into party or personal coffers. Komeito was founded in the 1950s as the "clean government party" to fight corruption.

Corruption is rooted in Japan's **money politics,** as the candidates (until the 1993 reforms) did not distinguish themselves by party platform or personality but by size of cash gifts. Under the old electoral system, LDP candidates often ran against other LDP candidates, a system that begged for factionalism and corruption. Prior to 1993, neither the government nor the party provided much funding for candidates or incumbents, who were left to raise funds for themselves.

And running for and holding office in Japan is not cheap. In addition to the usual local offices and constituent services, Japanese politicians by tradition must endear themselves to voters by attending weddings and funerals in their districts and giving nontrivial presents of cash to newlyweds and the bereaved. (It incurs their *on.*) A typical LDP incumbent spent an estimated ¥120 million (about $1 million) a year but got an allowance of only ¥20 million. The remaining ¥100 million had

Democracy

CAN "MONEY POLITICS" BE BROKEN?

One of the questions of interest to political scientists in the Japanese electoral and campaign-funding reforms of 1993 is whether money politics is so deeply rooted into Japanese political culture that no amount of legal tinkering can end it. It is an example of a classic question: Which is more important in political systems, **structure** or psychology? In 1993, the Diet changed the structure a bit. Did the psychology also change as a consequence?

Japan's money politics continued with subsequent elections, as electoral reforms do not necessarily work as hoped or planned. The United States has gone through several reforms of campaign financing only to find that both candidates and contributors come up with new ways to beat the system. (Now it is **soft money.**) The underlying problem is both the need for campaign funds (in America for televised spots and

in Japan for sound trucks and gifts) and the need to please blocs of voters.

The Japanese reformers argued that changing their electoral system would eliminate some of this desperate need for campaign money. So far, it has not worked. The United States, France, and Germany have very different electoral systems, but each have recurring scandals related to fund-raising. Why? Because in each system parties and candidates figure out ways to skirt the law. And in each system, some candidates use campaign contributions—both legal and illegal—for personal expenses, which often leads to additional scandals. Notice the underlying similarity: All politicians—American, Japanese, French, and German—are addicted to money. In the words of California political boss Jesse Unruh, "Money is the mother's milk of politics."

to be raised somewhere, by the donations of friends, supporters, businesses, and even the gangster underworld.

Although supposedly controlled by law in Japan, money politics leads to one scandal after another when the amounts are too big, the conflicts of interest too obvious, the methods of donation secretive, or the sources too dirty. The new electoral system was designed in part to break this pattern. To further break the money politics system, other new laws allowed corporate contributions only to parties, not to individuals, and offered public subsidies totaling some ¥30 billion (some $250 million) to parties for campaign expenses.

By the early 1990s, the entire LDP was looking dirty, and some LDP politicians, generally younger and with an eye to the future, began bailing out of the party before it also tarnished them and began forming new parties. In 1993, voters, many now openly fed up with corruption, deserted not only the LDP but the perennial second party, the Social Democrats, who were also tarred with scandal. The immediate reason was both parties' failure to devise and lead the reforms necessary to curb corruption, make voting fair, and break out of the rigid patterns of a state-led export economy that was in difficulty.

The increasing clamor over corruption shows the Japanese voting public is growing more mature and more democratic. What an older generation accepted as normal, a younger generation

Democracy

GOING POSTAL IN JAPAN

Koizumi's efforts to privatize parts of the Japanese postal system illustrate how interest groups and their bureaucratic allies can block reform. Founded in 1871, Japan Post not only delivers mail but also functions as a savings bank and insurance company. Meiji modernizers and militarists used it to amass capital to build the economy and the war machine. Japanese like the polite, helpful postmasters, sometimes one person in a small village. Japanese trust the system; 85 percent of households have postal savings accounts.

But by the late twentieth century, it had become bad economics. Japan Post, with ¥330 trillion (almost $3 trillion) in assets, was the world's largest financial institution. It controlled too much of Japan's capital, paid miserly interest, and stunted the private insurance business. LDP governments used it as its piggy—literally, pork—bank for road projects and low-interest loans to small businesses and other political supporters. The assets of Japan Post funded political patronage, corruption, and wasteful investments.

Koizumi, as postal minister in the early 1990s, understood the problem and got the idea to privatize the system. Conservative forces long aligned with the LDP—270,000 postal workers, the "road tribe" (highway builders), and rural politicians—worked to block reform. In 2005, Koizumi got the lower house to pass a bill to take insurance and banking away from Japan Post in 2007 and privatize them in 2017. It was not a sudden or dramatic reform; Japan changes slowly. The upper house, however, rejected it. An angry Koizumi kicked thirty-seven noncompliant LDP members out of the party and dissolved the lower house for new elections (he cannot dissolve the upper house).

Koizumi took a risk with early elections and won big. (At exactly the same time, German Chancellor Schröder also called elections early but lost.) Most Japanese admired Koizumi's guts and agreed that it was high time for such reforms. The DPJ, which criticized the reform bill, lost big. Now, with help from Komeito, the lower house can override the upper house. Some saw Japan Post as a breakthrough issue on the path to further reforms in the economy, government, and the LDP. But many other interests will try to block further reforms.

brands as dirty, dishonorable, and undemocratic. Notice how at this same time Italian and Brazilian politicians were also brought down by the sort of corruption that had been going on for decades. These scandals were good signs, for they showed that people worldwide really do understand that they are ill-served by corrupt governments. A Japanese party that lets itself be drawn into the old patterns now understands that it will suffer electoral punishment. Even the LDP pledged to reform itself and the system.

■ No One in Charge?

One of the most damning accusations made by the so-called "Japan-bashers"—chief among them Karel van Wolferen, a Dutch journalist with many years' experience in Japan—was that behind an impressive façade of powerful and orderly government, there was no real center of decision-making power in Japan, no one in charge. (As hurricane Katrina revealed, the United States is not immune to the accusation of "no one in charge.")

Prime ministers did not lead; they hung on to office for perhaps two years until the LDP faction chiefs dumped them. The faction chiefs did not lead; they simply amassed feudal power with which to battle each other. Parliamentarians did little but collect money from private interests to ensure their reelection. And even the mighty bureaucracies, such as the *Okurasho* and METI, led only in their narrow subject areas. They promoted their particular vision of the growth of Japanese industry and exports, nothing else. Japanese government, in this light, looked like a computerized, high-tech juggernaut: It rumbled on very efficiently, crushing anything in its path, but no one steered; it did not even have movable wheels and thus proceeded in a straight line.

The "no one in charge" theory—still controversial—helps explain the uncoordinated drift of Japan into World War II: The government in Tokyo said peace, but the army kept on conquering China. It helps explain the maddening difficulty in getting genuine trade commitments from Tokyo: The prime minister would promise to open up the Japanese market to American products, but Japanese bureaucrats would quietly veto the idea by failing to implement any policy changes that come from outside their ministry.

Each Tokyo ministry is like a feudal fiefdom, little answerable to outside authority. Neither do these government agencies have any common purpose or leadership. Each is dedicated to supervising its sector of the economy. The agencies and ministries do not so much respond to the calls of interest groups as direct the various interest groups to go along with bureaucratic plans, few of which are coordinated at the top.

If the "no one in charge" theory is approximately accurate, it means Japan suffers from serious institutional underdevelopment. A government

Japanese Communists politely try to interest passers by in Kyoto but get few takers. The JCP was always a small party.

that still operates under a basically feudal arrangement is not able to handle the economic problems of the twenty-first century, including economic distortions that produced a massive slump and monumental trade imbalances that put Japan on a collision course with many other countries. The big question for Japan now is whether Prime Minister Koizumi created a new and coherent LDP and curbed state supervision of the economy, as he vowed to do. Previous reforms have budged Japan only a little. We will have to wait and see if subsequent prime ministers can budge it more.

No Losers

Related to the "no one in charge" theory of Japanese politics is the understanding that no one gets injured by economic change. Although whale meat is now a trivial part of the Japanese diet, Tokyo still defends the right of Japanese whalers to slay the endangered animals. Why? To give into international pressures would put whalers out of business, and in this country no one gets hurt. A single farmer on three acres of eggplants blocks the badly needed expansion of Tokyo's overburdened Narita airport, which has only one runway. Why? To expand the airport would put him out of business, and in this country we do not do that.

The "no losers" impact on Japanese politics is to stifle change. In France (Chapter 11), we considered how economic modernization, such as hypermarkets, drives out small shops. In Japan, interest groups such as small retailers have been able to block and delay construction of big department

Democracy

WHO BRIBES WHOM?

There are two important flows of money in modern politics. The first is from interest group to political party, implicitly in return for favors. When narrow interests (for example, a certain corporation) seek specific favors (say, on accounting standards), such "money politics" looks dirty. Especially after Enron, U.S. critics portrayed these connections as a form of bribery. It is found everywhere, in Europe, America, Japan.

A much bigger flow of money, however, is from government to voting bloc, designed to win votes. It too is found everywhere and has grown, as all modern governments are committed to helping various groups with spending programs, construction projects, subsidies, trade protection, and so on. Here the bribery flows the other way and is probably a bigger motivator of politicians' choices. Fear of alienating a bloc of voters makes cowards out of politicians, who often compromise or abandon their positions. For example, who dares say no to farmers? Not the Tokyo government and not even the "conservative" Bush administration (and congressional Democrats), which lavishly increased farm payments. All of them need the farm vote. Mostly governments bribe groups rather than the other way around.

Typically, politicians strive for their immediate advantage (namely, getting reelected) and pay little or no attention to outcomes (such as war, budget deficits, or inflation). Politicians have to play short-term games and ignore long-term consequences, which are sometimes terrible. "I need votes, and I need them now!" think politicians. "What might happen five years from now does not help me win the next election." Those who do not play this game could be voted out. Much of modern democracy is a system to pay off key groups. Some fear it also undermines democracy, as few think of the long-term good of the whole country. Campaign-law reforms, either in Japan or in America, must pay attention to the two kinds of bribery. Fixing one—such as limiting "earmarks" (a polite term for *pork*)—does not fix the other.

unit veto   Ability of one component to block laws or changes.

alternation in power   The electoral overturn of one party by another.

stores and supermarkets. It took years to get permission for Toys "R" Us to open in Japan; small shopkeepers objected. (It is now Japan's biggest toy retailer.) Slowly and with a great lag time, Japan is modernizing its retail sector, and now most Japanese are happy to shop in large stores, such as the Daiei hypermarkets.

Japan has what political scientists call a **unit veto** system, one in which any component of the system, no matter how small, can veto an innovation desired by most. Farmers especially have benefited from this. Even within the Tokyo area—at 35 million people the world's largest metropolitan area—there are small patches of farmland that the owners will not sell to make way for badly needed apartment houses, and they are supported by laws and lavish subsidies. Actually, it is not quite right to say there are no losers in this arrangement. Japanese consumers lose through the high prices and cramped life they must endure.

Reform without Change

France and Germany have been described as "blocked societies," systems that need change and modernization but are prevented from reform by entrenched interests. Typically, such systems continue unchanged for decades until pressures for change become so great that old structures suddenly give way to new ones. Eventually, the balloon pops. Incremental change would be better but too many groups block it. De Gaulle's 1958 arrival in power exemplified how a blocked society dramatically unblocks. Japan has a similar but perhaps worse problem, for there is no one in charge and no single center of power that can bring about major change. Some observers see Japan as stuck in an institutional paralysis that caused its economy to slow and its status as regional leader to lapse.

Democracy

CAN JAPANESE POLITICS ALTERNATE?

Maybe eventually. One of the defining features of a democracy is **alternation in power**. If the same party stays in office seemingly forever, the system is probably not a democracy. The ruling party, of course, claims that it is the voters' choice, but its control over the media and ballot boxes makes sure it wins. Few observers counted Mexico, whose Institutional Revolutionary party (PRI) was in power for most of the twentieth century, as a true democracy. Vicente Fox's 2000 victory over the PRI candidate for Mexico's presidency may mark the beginning of alternation (see Chapter 33).

Does power alternate in Japan? It did very briefly, in 1993–1994, but that was an unstable eight-party coalition that fell apart after ten months. (Multiparty coalitions are always difficult to sustain.) Then the LDP, with Social Democrat Tomiichi Murayama as figurehead prime minister, took over again. Will the LDP ever be really ousted and spend a few years in opposition?

There are both structural and psychological reasons for the LDP's long tenure. The rural overrepresentation of Japan's electoral system and the unwillingness of Japanese to throw out the party that had brought prosperity explain much of the LDP's longevity. Money politics also favors the LDP. These factors, plus Koizumi's popularity, boosted the LDP in the 2005 election and gave it absolute control of the Diet.

The other part of the problem is that Japan does not have a good opposition party. The old rigid Socialists were too doctrinaire to become more the "half party" opposing the LDP. Now the incoherent Democrats are the lame half party that offers no clear alternative to the LDP. Until an opposition party can get its act together, Japan's dominant-party system seems destined to continue. Japan has always shown a strong persistence of pattern; nothing changes dramatically in Japan.

For years, Japanese prime ministers have pledged to deregulate the Japanese economy—now they call it *risutora*, "restructure"—but it has been mostly empty talk. Instead of major, sweeping reforms that would in effect reinvent the Japanese way, prime ministers offer minor, almost cosmetic reforms that change little. Many Japanese favor major reforms—Keidanren strongly backs them—hoping to kill as many as four birds with one stone. Namely, by deregulating the strongly regulated Japanese economy, including its barriers to foreign imports, reforms could fight recession, raise living standards, reduce trade surpluses, and curb the bureaucracy. In Japan, reform is always coming but never arrives.

Key Terms

alternation in power (p. 390)

guided capitalism (p. 383)

iron triangle (p. 382)

money politics (p. 386)

Okurasho (p. 385)

public corporation (p. 383)

scandal (p. 385)

soft money (p. 386)

structure (p. 386)

Todai (p. 383)

unit veto (p. 390)

walking-around money (p. 385)

¥ (p. 386)

Further Reference

Beason, Dick, and Dennis Patterson. *The Japan That Never Was: Explaining the Rise and Decline of a Misunderstood Country.* Albany, NY: SUNY Press, 2004.

Bouissou, Jean-Marie. *Japan: The Burden of Success.* Boulder, CO: L. Rienner, 2002.

Broadbent, Jeffrey. *Environmental Politics in Japan: Networks of Power and Protest.* New York: Cambridge University Press, 1998.

Colignon, Richard A., and Chikako Usui. *Amakaduri: The Hidden Fabric of Japan's Economy.* Ithaca, NY: Cornell University Press, 2003.

Curtis, Gerald L. *The Logic of Japanese Politics: Leaders, Institutions, and the Limits of Change.* New York: Columbia University Press, 1999.

Hrebenar, Ronald J. *Japan's New Party System.* Boulder, CO: Westview, 2000.

Nakano, Minoru. *The Policy-Making Process in Contemporary Japan.* New York: St. Martin's, 1997.

Otake, Hideo, ed. *Power Shuffles and Policy Processes: Coalition Government in Japan in the 1990s.* Tokyo: Japan Center for International Exchange, 2000.

Richardson, Bradley. *Japanese Democracy: Power, Coordination, and Performance.* New Haven, CT: Yale University Press, 1997.

Rothacher, Albrecht. *The Japanese Power Elite.* New York: St. Martin's, 1994.

Schlesinger, Jacob M. *Shadow Shoguns: The Rise and Fall of Japan's Postwar Political Machine.* New York: Simon & Schuster, 1997.

Schwartz, Frank J. *Advice and Consent: The Politics of Consultation in Japan.* New York: Cambridge University Press, 1998.

Wolferen, Karel van. *The Enigma of Japanese Power: People and Politics in a Stateless Nation.* New York: Vintage Books, 1990.

Woodall, Brian. *Japan under Construction: Corruption, Politics, and Public Works.* Berkeley, CA: University of California Press, 1996.

Chapter 27

WHAT JAPANESE QUARREL ABOUT

In a parallel to Germany, the Japanese economy soared after World War II but then leveled off and slumped. Over time, the postwar economic advantages enjoyed by the two countries faded. From 1990 to 2005 Japan's GDP grew little. There are now signs of revival, but nothing like the 1950s through the 1980s, when Japan's economy seemed to head upward forever. All "economic miracles" tend to undermine themselves. Remember this when we consider China's current incredible growth.

The Japanese Economic Miracle

Questions to Consider

1. What explains Japan's economic success?
2. What went wrong with the state supervision of Japan's economy?
3. Has Japan overcome its economic downturn?
4. How does Japan resemble Germany demographically?
5. Explain purchasing power parity.
6. What is *gaiatsu* and why does Japan resist it?
7. Does Japan practice a kind of mercantilism?
8. Is Japan's no-war clause now a dead letter?
9. Is a strong U.S.-Japan alliance a good idea?

For some years after the war, "made in Japan" suggested a product was junk, probably tin cans recycled from the ashes of Japan's cities. In some cases, the term was justified. All countries that are just starting their economic climb seem to produce cheap products of dubious quality. Many, however, soon climb out of the junk stage, as Japan did in the 1950s.

In 1960, Japan was the richest country in Asia but still had a per capita GDP of only $380 (around $2,000 in today's dollars), one-eighth the American. By 1990, Japan's per capita was nominally higher than America's. (This is tricky to measure. See the box on "Purchasing Power Parity" on page 399.) The catalyst was the Korean War that began in June 1950. U.S. forces in East Asia suddenly found themselves unequipped and gave contracts for clothing, footwear, and other items to low-bid Japanese producers. (South Korea's industrial takeoff followed precisely the same pattern in the late 1960s, only now the catalyst was the Vietnam War.) The quality of the Japanese goods was not bad. After the war, many U.S. manufacturers of civilian goods followed the U.S. military lead and gave Japanese similar contracts. The quality got better all the time, and the costs were a fraction of U.S. producer costs. In the 1960s, Japanese cars were looked down on as a joke, but by the 1970s they were respected for economy and workmanship. Now Toyota is the world's largest (and best-run) car company, worth more than the three big U.S. car makers put together. A continual pattern has been to underestimate the Japanese product—until it puts you out of business.

As in postwar West Germany, workers in postwar Japan did not ask for much; they were glad to have a job that put food on the family's table. In politics most were also cautious and gave their votes to the moderate conservative party with the misleading name Liberal Democrat. This party—

Four Tigers South Korea, Taiwan, Hong Kong, and Singapore.

more accurately, a collection of political factions—ruled Japan with only a brief pause from the time of its formation in 1955 until the present, and thus became an important institution and pillar of stability. For most Japanese, the LDP brought jobs and growth, and that was enough. They lived to work and, accustomed to modest living standards and obedience, did not vote for change.

In 1990, Japan's period of extraordinary economic growth finally ended with a major recession that brought unemployment for the first time in a generation. Japanese unemployment rose and once even surpassed the U.S. rate. And large Japanese firms are overstaffed ("in-house unemployment"); if they let excess employees go the Japanese rate would double. The collapse of Japan's stock-market and real-estate bubbles left corporations and banks looking poorer and foolish. The long-ruling LDP started looking incompetent. A younger generation of Japanese were well-educated and well-traveled and saw how people in other industrialized countries do not live in rabbit hutches and pay exorbitant prices. Many were no longer willing to support the status quo.

■ The Secret of Japan's Success

Since the 1960s, when the West realized how fast the Japanese economy was growing, observers have tried to explain the "Japanese model" as a new, different, and better system, combining elements such as Confucianism, education, savings, and state supervision. Many now suspect there was no magic formula.

Confucianism

As comparativists, we make comparisons to solve puzzles like Japan's rapid economic growth. First, do other countries show similar patterns of rapid growth? Yes, in fact many East Asian countries do. In addition to China (see Chapter 32), the **Four Tigers** have for the last couple of decades also shown remarkable growth. Culturally, all share a Confucian background because all were under the cultural sway of China. Confucianism stresses hard work, stability, and obedience. It frowns on high

Geography

LIVING WITHOUT LEBENSRAUM

Geography influences international relations, both because of its real, physical impact and because decision makers *think* that certain geographic features are important, even if they are not. As in many areas of human endeavor, the real feeds into the psychological, which in turn feeds back into the real.

German thinkers of the nineteenth century, for example, came up with overly deterministic theories

of *geopolitics*. The Nazis and Japanese militarists eagerly accepted theories such as *Lebensraum* (living space) as justification for their imperial expansion. After their defeat, Germans and Japanese learned that they have never lived so well as when confined to their present crowded countries. If you have the economy, you do not need much land. Prosperity depends not so much on territory as on smart, energetic people and sound economic policy.

personal consumption; people should save, not spend. Some have argued that a Confucian work ethic gave East Asia the functional equivalent of a Protestant work ethic, a religious or psychological motivation to work hard.

Productivity

Another factor for rapid growth is a level of productivity higher than the level of wages; that is, workers who produce a lot without getting paid a lot. (See the "Productivity" box on page 74.) In Britain, we saw how productivity increases were mediocre while wages and other costs climbed, gradually squeezing British products off the world market. In Germany, we saw how wage restraint coupled with increases in productivity gave German products a competitive edge and a major export market. More recently, however, German wages climbed out of line with productivity. The same happened in Japan. For some decades, Japanese productivity stayed ahead of wages, giving Japan an opening to produce much of the world's advanced consumer electronics. Japanese factories could simply put more high-quality labor into a product than other countries, but this is no longer the case.

Education

As we discussed in earlier chapters, productivity is partly the result of new, more efficient machines and partly of increasingly skilled workers and managers who know how to use them. Japan (and the Four Tigers) paid a lot of attention to education, especially at the primary and secondary levels (from

Comparison

JAPAN DESTROYS THE GERMAN PHOTO INDUSTRY

One of the first indicators of what the Japanese could do in terms of quality came in the photo-optical industry. Photojournalists covering the Korean War tried Japanese-made lenses from Nikon and Canon on their German cameras and found them excellent, sometimes better than German lenses. Soon they found the Japanese-made camera bodies were good too. The German photo industry should have started running scared, but, like most Westerners, scoffed at anything made in Japan.

In addition to lower wages, the Japanese photo industry constantly innovated. The Germans might bring out a new model every decade; the Japanese firms, desperately competing with one another, brought out new models every couple of years. In 1959, Nikon introduced the landmark Nikon F. Nikons, constantly modified and improved, became the professional workhorses for decades. Boasted Nikon ads: "Today, there's almost no other choice." During the 1960s, the Japanese photo industry captured most of the world market as the German photo industry shrank and disappeared. Change or die.

In this process we see some of the factors that contributed to Japanese manufacturing success in other areas. With low wages (now no longer the case), a skilled and dedicated work force, constantly innovative designs, government encouragement, and far-sighted bank loans, Japan went from cameras to consumer electronics, where it also became the world leader. Whether it can keep its lead is another question. With high labor costs, much of the Japanese photo and electronic industries have set up in other East Asian lands with cheap labor. My latest Canon was made in Malaysia.

elementary through high school). Such education is supervised at the national level and compulsory. This gave Japan a highly skilled labor force, one that can read, follow instructions, and do math computations. (Much of the U.S. labor force cannot.) Interestingly, Japan and its high-growth neighbors pay less attention to higher (college and university) education, finding that much of it contributes little to economic growth.

Savings

Japanese save a lot and consider debt shameful; Americans save little and are almost proud of their debts. Japanese use credit cards far less than Americans and pay off balances monthly. For Japanese, thrift is an old tradition, and Japanese pension plans and social security are weak for an advanced country. To have a comfortable old age, Japanese know they must put aside their own money. Some economists think that savings alone is the biggest element in explaining Japanese economic growth. More recently, however, some say Japanese save too much; their reluctance to spend kept Japan in recession.

The propensity to save, for most of the postwar period, made Japanese banks the world's biggest and made mountains of capital available for investment in growth industries. Unfortunately, Japan's banks encouraged businesses to expand until they overexpanded; then banks loaned ever more to these "zombie" companies, piling up mountains of bad loans. Under Koizumi, Japan's banks *wrote off* (see page 467) about half of the dud loans and put the banking system back on sounder footing.

State Supervision

This is where a discussion of Japanese economic growth gets controversial, although probably more Americans quarrel about it than Japanese. Is state supervision, going back to the Meiji modernizers and continuing with METI (formerly MITI) and the Finance Ministry, the key factor in Japan's rapid growth? Most of the other fast-growth East Asian economies have some degree of Japanese-style state supervision as well. (Hong Kong has none, and China's vigorous free-market sector, based heavily on foreign investment, is essentially unplanned; China's state-owned enterprises lose money.)

macroeconomy Big picture of a nation's economy, including GDP size and growth, productivity, interest rates, and inflation.

microeconomy Close-up picture of individual markets, including product design and pricing, efficiency, and costs.

What do we mean by "state supervised"? Some take it to mean simply getting the **macroeconomy**, "the fundamentals," in order—little public debt, plentiful savings (and hence investment capital), and low inflation—and then standing back and letting the market do its stuff (example: postwar Germany's *Sozialmarkt*). Others take it to mean government intervention in the **microeconomy** as well, with state technocrats choosing which industries to foster or phase out. This was the Japanese model, but even Japan has largely abandoned it and shrunk the importance of METI. The value of state planning has not been proved.

Some critical Western economists are skeptical about any "Japanese model" and say there is little evidence that state supervision boosted Japanese growth rates. Japan got its macroeconomy or "fundamentals" right, which was all that really mattered, and might have done just as well or even better without MITI. Some Japanese firms prospered with no help from a ministry, and some with plenty of help did poorly. (Sony founder Akio Morita publicly disdained government help and got none.) Which is right, the "Japanese model" or its doubters? The only way you could demonstrate that Japanese economic intervention worked is to have two very similar countries operate under different policies, say, one with a MITI and the other without, and see which grows faster. Such controlled experiments are hard to come by in the real world.

■ From Bubble to Burst

Japan's economy grew at an amazing average rate of 10 percent a year from 1955 to 1973. The world had never seen anything like it. From 1973 to 1991 it grew at an average of 4 percent a year, still good but hardly spectacular. But since then it grew at an average of only 1 percent a year and in some years actually declined. The years of fast growth were over; the best Japan can hope for now is the modest growth of a mature economy. No longer could Japan simply copy foreign products or quickly improve productivity. Japanese wages and other costs were high, and most Japanese investment flowed to countries with lower wages and fewer regulations.

Investment mistakes were made in Japan. Under MITI prodding and financing, Japanese electronics firms sunk and lost vast sums trying to develop the "fifth generation" of computers and high-definition television. Both projects bombed. MITI encouraged Japanese car makers to go for ever-larger world market shares—instead of the usual capitalist goal of profitability—so that for many years Japan's eleven (11!) car companies had major excess capacity and most lost money. MITI pushed car makers to expand until they overexpanded.

Government and banks had pushed the export sectors (cars, electronics) of Japanese industry into high levels of automation, productivity, and efficiency. Other sectors got left behind. Distribution was largely in the hands of neighborhood mom-and-pop stores that were convenient and friendly but not price-competitive. Until recently, U.S.-style discounting was hated, feared, and denounced in Japan as ruinous of family shops and family values. Gradually, though, as more Japanese traveled and found they could buy Panasonics and Canons cheaper in the United States, foreign retail chains started opening in Japan.

Agriculture got left behind. The typical small Japanese farm of a few acres was hopelessly inefficient, but the Agricultural Ministry protected Japanese farmers from cheaper imports. This cost Japanese consumers dearly and angered Japan's trading partners. Many Japanese farmers turned to part-time farming anyway, a pattern typical of industrializing countries. Young Japanese are not going into farming, and now many of Japan's farmers are elderly. In economic terms, they should sell their small holdings, either to larger and more efficient farmers or to developers to build badly

Geography

RUNNING OUT OF JAPANESE

In 1975, the number of births in Japan started to drop and kept declining for the rest of the century. In 2005 Japan's population began to shrink and could drop below 100 million by mid-century. Japan's colleges and universities worry that the number of eighteen-year-olds, which declined by half since 1974, will not be enough to fill classrooms. Industry worries about sufficient workers. (One suggested solution: Encourage more Japanese women to work; relatively few do.)

The biggest worry is how to support all the Japanese on retirement—and Japanese are the longest-lived folks in the world, seventy-eight years for men and eighty-five for women—with so few workers. Japan's pension system will soon be in the red. Can one Japanese worker support one retiree? Notice that Germany has exactly the same problem, but Japan admits very few foreign workers. Only 1 percent of Japan's population is foreign, and that includes descendants of Chinese and Koreans who have lived in Japan for generations. Japanese discriminate against immigrants—even against Japanese born in Brazil. Japan is a closed society that must learn to open up.

excess liquidity   Too much money floating around.

deflation   Decrease in prices, opposite of inflation.

deficit   Government spends more in a given year than it takes in.

debt   Sum total of government *deficits* over many years.

needed apartments. There is protected and tax-exempt farmland in and near major cities that really should be subject to market forces. Its sale would make some "farmers" rich while helping solve Japan's housing shortage.

Japanese were generally well satisfied with their economic growth since World War II. During the 1990s, however, they grew less satisfied. The shortcomings of their supervised market system became increasingly clear. Under bureaucratic guidance, the Japanese economy produced **excess liquidity**, which fueled stock-market and real-estate bubbles, which both burst in 1989. The Tokyo stock exchange lost three-quarters of its peak value and recovered only slowly and partially. Real-estate prices plunged as well, and many Japanese banks and corporations were insolvent or nearly so. Japan suffered from **deflation**, the great plague of the 1930s Depression. Deflation is worse than inflation, as it destroys the value of homes and businesses. Some Japanese who bought apartments around 1990 saw them lose half their worth but still have to pay off the huge mortgages.

To fight the slowdown of the 1990s, Tokyo threw money into the economy—around $1 trillion, mostly in public-works spending—giving Japan the world's biggest **deficits** and national **debt** but producing no economic growth. Tokyo was doing what it had always done—bail out any sector of the economy that is in trouble. But no government can bail out everything forever, and Koizumi trimmed this foolish public-works spending from 6 percent of GDP in 2001 to 4 percent in 2005. More cuts are due.

Bailing out firms merely disguises their illnesses and blocks the market's signals that this company must change or fold. Tokyo tried to keep Japan's large banks from collapsing, although based on their assets, several should have. Actually, all governments tend to react that way—they think of angry depositors and shareholders—but if they do it too much, they prop up industries that should be forced to change. (China's banks face a parallel problem.)

Increasingly, both Japanese and foreign analysts doubted that throwing money at problems works, and Koizumi accepted their analyses. Foolish investments to help weak banks and businesses and the "road tribe" mask the problems for a short time but do not solve them. With the reform of Japan Post (see page 387) as his opening wedge, Koizumi urged cutting back Japan's huge subsidies in favor of a free-market economy. He tried to become a Japanese Thatcher (see Chapter 6) but had to fight Japan's highly organized interest groups, and there is no guarantee that his *neoliberalism* will prevail.

If it does not, Japan is in trouble. The new age is one of lower-cost competitors and open markets. Other lands have taken over several areas that used to be Japanese: steelmaking, shipbuilding, and even consumer electronics. China is a growing economic giant that is taking over much of the world's manufacturing. Many Japanese know that their economic miracle of 10 percent annual growth is over. This is not necessarily a cause for despair; it just means Japan has become a mature economy with growth rates of around 3 percent. And Japan has an excellent foundation for long-term prosperity: a well-educated population, a magnificent high-tech sector, and vast investment capital.

■ Should Japanese Live Better?

Yes, it would be good for them and good for us, because they would buy more U.S. products, such as foodstuffs and building materials. They have earned it. They lifted their country from the rubble of World War II to heights few Japanese dreamed of. Holding down domestic consumption while accumulating vast capital resources was a great prescription for rapid economic growth. But pursued too long, it overshot the mark and produced serious imbalances. The yen, held too low for too long, suddenly shot from 330 to the dollar to 80 to the dollar at one point in 1995. (The value of the yen is expressed in how many yen per dollar, so when the yen goes "up" it is getting cheaper in relation to the dollar; when the yen goes "down" it is getting more expensive. With the euro, conversely, up means up.) A too-strong yen hurt many Japanese firms that lost foreign sales, for now their products were too costly.

trade surplus   Exporting more than you import.

purchasing power parity (PPP) Adjustment of GDP figures to take cost of living into account.

One of the problems with Japan's guided capitalism was the mammoth **trade surpluses** Japan accumulated, especially with the United States. They did no earthly good, but for decades MITI was obsessed by them, a sort of latter-day mercantilism. Japan produced goods that Americans eagerly bought, accepting dollars in payment. They accumulated a mountain of dollars but this forced the dollar to decline in relation to the yen. In effect, Japan sold its products too cheaply to Americans and got not enough in return. They only hurt themselves.

If the Japanese had simply consumed more—including more imported goods—at an earlier date, they might have avoided the excess liquidity that fueled the stock-market and real-estate bubbles. Too many yen chased investments to the sky; then the bubbles burst, doing great harm to Japan's growth and stability. Ironically, Japanese investors got terribly burned in buying U.S. firms. They overpaid, found many firms were not profitable, and often sold them at a loss. Americans for

Comparison

PURCHASING POWER PARITY

Per-capita GDP (GDPpc) figures can deceive because they do not take into account the cost of living in each country. Japanese on average make nearly as much a year as Americans but live more poorly. To correct this discrepancy, economists now calculate **purchasing power parity (PPP)** in addition to the usual per-capita GDP that is translated into dollars at the "market exchange rate." Notice in the table on the right how much the two differ in these figures from 2004.

On average, Americans still live better than Japanese because everything is expensive in Japan. Britons, French, and Germans also lived poorer in 2004 than their exchange rate indicated, again because of their higher living costs. Notice how the two measures seriously diverged in our five poorest countries, indicating their lower costs of living and suggesting that the country's currency was undervalued. For example, Chinese lived a lot better—although still only one-eighth the American level—than the exchange-rate

figure of $1,300 would indicate. Caution: These figures change rapidly, as the dollar rises and falls and windfall oil profits boost the economies of Russia and Iran.

	GDPpc at Exchange Rate	Purchasing Power Parity
United States	$38,600	40,100
Japan	36,100	29,400
Britain	36,000	29,600
France	33,400	28,700
Germany	32,700	28,700
Mexico	6,500	9,600
Russia	4,100	9,800
Iran	2,400	7,700
China	1,300	5,600
Nigeria	500	1,000

Sources: First column World Bank, second column CIA.

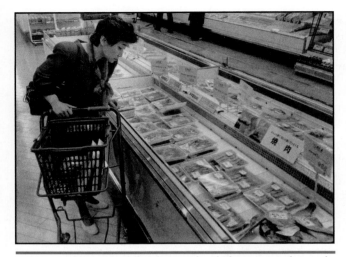

A Japanese shopper carefully selects steak, which costs several times the U.S. price. Modern hypermarkets, like this Daiei, have forced many small merchants to close.

a while were frightened of Japanese investments. They should not have been. The investments are all to our good. If rich people want to overpay for your property, do not discourage them.

But it was foolish for Japan. If more profits had been channeled into pay and dividends, the Japanese could have consumed more and lived better. But, curiously, some Japanese do not want to live better, at least not if that means harming the livelihood of other Japanese. For example, by keeping out foreign rice and subsidizing small, inefficient rice farms, Japanese are forced to pay five or six times the world price for rice. Many do not mind, for they understand they are keeping Japanese farmers employed. Thus, overpriced Japanese foodstuffs are a sort of indirect welfare transfer to help cousin Kenji on the farm. Japanese pay above world prices for just about everything, at an annual cost to them of many trillions of yen.

Increasingly, young Japanese think this is ridiculous. They notice that cousin Kenji works only part-time on his rice patch anyway because he cannot earn a living from it; most of the week Kenji works in town. Young Japanese are more likely to have traveled and been amazed at the cheap cost of living abroad. They find the taste of American rice acceptable—California growers now mostly plant short-grain oriental-style rice—and even bring back a bag as tourists. Many have developed a taste for beef and want it at $5 a pound, not $25. Younger Japanese are thus more likely to want a Japan open to two-way world trade than are their parents, who prefer the one-way model.

Comparison

THE JAPANESE NON-WELFARE STATE

Japan is almost the opposite of the West European welfare state: It provides almost no welfare. Instead, families are obliged to provide (an echo of the old *ie* system of household responsibility). Only those without families and physically unable to work may qualify for a dole under strict standards. Never mind if they cannot find a job. This harsh setup bothers few Japanese, who have almost no sense of American-style entitlement. Result: Only 0.7 percent of Japanese receive welfare benefits, compared to about 10 percent of the U.S. population. Another

result seen during the recent downturn: homeless Japanese men camping out in parks and public places.

This is not to say the Japanese have absolutely no welfare system. In a way, the whole Japanese economy has been rigged to make sure no one loses their jobs. Inefficient firms, farms, villages, and stores are kept in business by regulations, subsidies, and blocking imports, the costs of which are passed on to the Japanese consumer. One might call it welfare by indirect means.

Young Japanese also tend to dislike their cumbersome merchandising system—in which everything passes through costly layers of trading companies to small retail outlets, which carry few foreign goods. By law, it was very difficult for foreign firms to break into Japanese retail commerce.

gaiatsu   Foreign pressure.

Should Japan Re-Arm?

Since World War II, Japan has preached and practiced peace. In the aftermath of a devastating war, MacArthur's staff put a "no-war clause" (Article 9) into Japan's new constitution. It states that the Japanese people "forever renounce war as a sovereign right of the nation and the threat or use of force as a means of settling international disputes" and adds that "land, sea, and air forces, as well as other war potential will never be maintained." In 1947 this seemed like a fine idea, but with North Korea's attack on South Korea in 1950, some Americans and Japanese began to have second thoughts. Would Article 9 mean that Japan would stay defenseless in a rough neighborhood or depend forever on U.S. protection? The question went back on the front burner in the late 1990s as China staked out territorial claims far into the South and East China Seas. North Korea lobbed rockets over Japan as "tests" and built nuclear weapons. As a result, the United States and Japan dusted off their defensive alliance.

In the 1950s, Japan began building "Self-Defense Forces" but informally limited defense spending to 1 percent of GDP and has no draft. Nonetheless, given the size of Japan's GDP, its defense budget is now among the world's highest, even though its military manpower, at about 238,000, is low. Japan's Self-Defense Forces are small but well-funded and well-equipped.

Japanese leftists argue that their Self-Defense Forces are clearly at odds with both the letter and spirit of the constitution, and expanding them would compound the error. Most Japanese think their forces, which are not supposed to be used outside of Japan, are a prudent and necessary shield; some

THE UNITED STATES AND JAPAN: AMERICA-BASHING

Some Japanese leaders have turned nationalistic and anti-American. The underlying cause is the inner core of Japaneseness that does not easily give in to **gaiatsu**, but there were two specific causes. First, many Japanese grew tired of the United States hectoring them, especially about opening the Japanese market to U.S. products and ending bureaucratic supervision of Japan's economy. "Who are you to tell us how to run our economy?" they asked. "We do things the Japanese way, not to please you." The founder of Sony and a flamboyant politician coauthored a bestseller along these lines entitled *A Japan That Can Say No*. Actually, Japan's recent downturn demonstrated that much of the American criticism was accurate. Still, hectoring wins no friends.

A second area of Japanese complaint concerned security arrangements: Should Japan follow the U.S. lead in regional defense, and should U.S. bases stay on Japanese soil? That flamboyant politician, Shintaro Ishihara, was elected governor of Tokyo in 1999, partly on an America-bashing platform (see page 402). He demanded the closing of a U.S. air base in suburban Tokyo. Such bases—the biggest is on Okinawa—have long been irritants; they occupy scarce land, their jets make too much noise, and their personnel commit occasional crimes. Some Japanese would like to be rid of all U.S. bases. Tension with China and North Vietnam curbed some of this sentiment, but it shows a Japanese nationalism not far under the surface.

Hiroshima, Ground Zero: This municipal building partially withstood the first atomic bomb blast and now reminds Japanese of what war does.

Article 9   No-war clause in Japan's constitution.

would be willing to drop Article 9 and even acquire a few nuclear weapons to deter attack. The United States also thinks Japan should be able to defend itself and take a leadership role in regional security—as Japan did splendidly in Cambodian peacekeeping—and encourages Japan to do more. Japan also sent 550 troops to Iraq for noncombat duties. Many Japanese disliked having even unarmed troops in Iraq, but the Tokyo government thought it was a prudent investment to ensure U.S. protection against the growing power of China.

The great question: Should Japan expand its Self-Defense Forces to the point where they can defend Japan on their own and keep the peace regionally? For much of the postwar period, Japan's neighbors feared expansion of Japanese military power, but with the possibility that China will seize Taiwan and North Korea could again invade South Korea, many East Asian countries now see Japan as a strategic partner in a defensive situation. The question parallels the controversy Germany has gone through over military forces. Many Germans and their neighbors opposed them, but now most say it is time Germany became a normal country and participated in regional security, as in Kosovo. Many Japanese and their neighbors now think Japan too should become a normal country with a credible but not a threatening defense capability.

Japan's **Article 9** will probably not be directly repealed; that would be too controversial. One defense minister was forced to resign after he suggested such a constitutional revision. Instead, look for new laws or interpretations permitting the Japanese Self Defense Forces to participate more fully in UN and other multilateral peacekeeping efforts, as they have in Iraq. The move will be sold to the public as part of Japan's contribution to world and regional peace. Leftist intellectuals will oppose it

Comparison

A JAPANESE LE PEN?

Like France's clever demagogue Jean-Marie Le Pen (see pages 105 and 112), Tokyo governor Shintaro Ishihara delivers a populist and nationalist line that bashes China, America, and above all foreigners, who bring crime. Many Japanese agree. Some also agree with him that Japan should end its U.S. alliance, build a bigger navy, acquire nuclear weapons, and inculcate patriotism in schools. Once

a novelist and friend of militarist writer Mishima (see page 376), Ishihara served as a Liberal Democrat member of the Diet. The funny, energetic, and popular Ishihara is now an independent and bashes prime ministers for being too timid on reforms. Ishihara shows that under the bland and polite surface of Japan runs an undercurrent of Japanese nationalism and racism.

mightily. Japan will also likely reinforce its claim to the Senkaku Islands near Taiwan, bringing Japan into a tough showdown with China. For this reason, look for Japan to form **de facto** alliances with Taiwan and South Korea.

The really explosive question is whether Japan should acquire nuclear weapons. For most of the postwar period, the answer was a resounding "no." But with North Korea building nuclear bombs and missiles able to reach Japan, more Japanese have begun to think Japan should acquire a few nukes for deterrence. The United States has not encouraged the idea and has pledged its armed might to protect Japan from, say, a North Korean bomb. Like de Gaulle decades earlier, some Japanese have begun to wonder if this U.S. promise is reliable. As the Cold War ended, more and more Japanese do not like remaining dependent on U.S. protection, and many Americans dislike giving other lands free security at U.S. expense.

Even if North Korea ceases its nuclear program, Japan would still face two nuclear powers in Asia: China and Russia. If it faces them alone, it will increasingly debate the need for nuclear weapons. As history's only victims of nuclear war thus far, many Japanese adamantly oppose any nukes on Japanese soil, and even hints at a nuclear program could set off massive protests. Accordingly, the issue is likely to linger out of public debate for a long time, but it will always be there.

Before Japan can play a major role in East Asian security, it will have to reflect deeply on its World War II atrocities and put them in school textbooks, as Germany has done. This is hard to do in Japan. Many Japanese politicians, especially in the LDP, cannot or will not say they are sorry for Japan's World War II aggressions. Instead, they honor Japanese war dead. Tojo's grand-daughter still mourns him as a patriot. Some LDP politicians even let slip that Japanese occupation of Taiwan and Korea was good for those two lands. Amid howls of protest from Taipeh and Seoul, they usually resign.

de facto In practice although not officially stated.

strategic Important to nation's life.

national interest What is good for the country as a whole in international relations.

Geography

U.S. STRATEGIC INTERESTS IN EAST ASIA

Should the United States, probably allied with Japan, play the role of strategic balancer in East Asia? It is an important question that Americans must face. Much depends on the precise nature of China: Is it transitioning to a market democracy or stuck under a Party dictatorship that aims at expansion? (We will consider this in the China section.)

We have to be careful here, for once an area has been labeled **strategic** it becomes, in the mind of many, genuinely strategic, even if it is not. In the 1960s the United States defined South Vietnam as strategic. By the 1980s, hardly any Americans thought it had been strategic. In the heat of the moment, we may overuse the term. You can end up calling every point on the globe strategic. And if you call something strategic, your adversary will likely do it too. Are the Senkaku Islands, just north of Taiwan and claimed by both China and Japan, really part of the U.S. **national interest**?

Accordingly, we have to make some clear-headed judgments on America's interests in East Asia and whether they should be defended by force. As China and North Korea made threatening noises, the United States, Japan, South Korea, Taiwan, and other countries of the region were drawn together defensively. Remember, without fully understanding it, U.S. support for China in the 1930s drew us into a war with Japan. Could the reverse now happen?

In 1996, gangster-supported nationalistic Japanese groups reinforced Japan's claim to the small, uninhabitable Senkaku Islands near Taiwan. The Tokyo government gave quiet assent. China, Taiwan, and even Hong Kong joined in angry opposition, for China claims the islands as well. (The real reason: probable oil and natural gas under the seabed around the islands.) Germany has more or less mastered its past, and now Germany's small army is a necessary and welcome participant in Europe's security. Japan could play the same role in East Asia, but first it must face its past.

A New Japan?

Japan is undergoing considerable change, but it is slow. The certainties of most of the postwar period—Japanese politics are stable, corruption does not count, and the Japanese economy grows rapidly—have ended and are not likely to be restored, at least not in their old shape. But a new system has not yet fully emerged.

Will it come out where we want it to come out? Will we have a new, clean democratic partner across the Pacific ready to trade with us on a two-way basis? Or will we face an angry, protectionist Japan where some of the old nationalism links up with an enlarged military?

Neither the Japanese nor Americans fully understand the political implications of Japan's new economic situation. If, instead of being a growing economic giant with jobs for all, it undergoes years of slow or no growth, how will the Japanese people and political parties react? If Japan is at last becoming a "normal" country, one with approximately the same problems as other advanced, industrialized democracies, the changes are all to the good. If not, we may wish we had the old Japan of the LDP and cheap transistors back. How Japan fits into the modern world will determine a great deal for the peace of Asia. To see how another Asian land is handling the onslaught of modernization, let us now turn to China.

Key Terms

Article 9 (p. 402)
debt (p. 398)
de facto (p. 403)
deficit (p. 398)
deflation (p. 398)
excess liquidity (p. 398)
Four Tigers (p. 394)

gaiatsu (p. 401)
macroeconomy (p. 396)
microeconomy (p. 396)
national interest (p. 403)
purchasing power parity (PPP) (p. 399)
strategic (p. 403)
trade surplus (p. 399)

Further Reference

Alexander, Arthur J. *In the Shadow of the Miracle: The Japanese Economy since the End of High-Speed Growth.* Lexington, PA: Lexington Books, 2002.

Berger, Thomas U. *Cultures of Antimilitarism: National Security in Germany and Japan.* Baltimore, MD: Johns Hopkins University Press, 1998.

Flath, David. *The Japanese Economy,* 2nd ed. New York: Oxford University Press, 2005.

Katz, Richard. *Japan: The System That Soured: The Rise and Fall of the Japanese Economic Miracle*. Armonk, NY: M. E. Sharpe, 1998.

Kingston, Jeff. *Japan's Quiet Revolution: Politics, Economics, and Society*. New York: Routledge, 2004.

Maswood, S. Javed. *Japan in Crisis*. New York: Palgrave, 2002.

Matray, James I. *Japan's Emergence as a Global Power*. Westport, CT: Greenwood, 2001.

McCormack, Gavan. *The Emptiness of Japanese Affluence*. Armonk, NY: M. E. Sharpe, 1996.

Smith, Dennis B. *Japan since 1945: The Rise of an Economic Superpower*. New York: St. Martin's, 1995.

Suzuki, Takashi. *Japan's Budget Politics: Balancing Domestic and International Interests*. Boulder, CO: L. Rienner, 2000.

Tabb, William K. *The Postwar Japanese System: Cultural Economy and Economic Transformation*. New York: Oxford University Press, 1995.

Part VI

CHINA

Key Web Sites

Country Study
lcweb21.loc.gov/frd/cs/cntoc.html

Statements from U.S. State Department
state.gov/www/current/debate/china.html

News Sources
South China Morning Post
scmp.com

Hong Kong Standard (Business)
standard.com.hk

Far Eastern Economic Review
feer.com

People's Daily
english.people.com.cn

Chapter 28

China:
The Impact of the Past

China is immense—stretching in latitude both further north and further south than the United States (without Hawaii or Alaska)—but only one-third of China's territory is arable, rice in the well-watered south and wheat in the drier north. Lack of surplus grain to feed cattle or hogs made Chinese largely vegetarians. Traditional Chinese cooking uses only bits of meat for flavoring. China now has less than half an acre of farmland (and currently shrinking) for each Chinese, and this has long imposed limits on politics, economics, and social thought.

Rice cultivation, for example, uses much water and human labor to get major crops (two and even three times a year in South China) from small plots. This labor-intensive farming kept most Chinese tied to the land as peasants—even to this day—and encouraged strong family organization and obedient, cooperative behavior. It has also meant that a central authority was needed to control water canals and determine who got how much water. The need for irrigation helps explain why Mesopotamia, Egypt, and China produced history's first kingdoms and empires.

Questions to Consider

1. What is civilization? How is it related to cities?
2. Is Confucianism basically government by political culture?
3. Are *cycles* a general political phenomenon? Why?
4. Contrast the political development of China and Europe.
5. Why was it easy for Europeans to penetrate and derange China?
6. Did Japan handle the Europeans more cleverly than China?
7. Could the United States have uplifted old China?
8. Without the Japanese invasion, could the Nationalists have consolidated their rule?
9. How were the Chinese Nationalists and Communists similar?
10. How did Mao and the Communists beat the Nationalists?

According to the archeological record, **civilization** began in ancient Mesopotamia, followed closely by Egypt and then China. During the **Neolithic** age, humans began the several-thousand-year transition from hunter-gatherers to settled farmers around 10,000 years ago in Mesopotamia and 8,000 years ago in China. With the **Bronze Age** came the founding of cities around 5,500 years ago in Mesopotamia and 4,000 years ago in China. The shifts occurred first in Mesopotamia (present-day Iraq), scholars believe, because the Middle East was home to more plants and animals that could be domesticated—including wheat and sheep—than anywhere else on the planet. Both the Middle East and China, however, founded civilizations far earlier than Europe, which was just getting out of the ice age.

The Bureaucratic Empire

China, in sharp contrast to Europe, unified and ended feudalism very early. During the Bronze Age, small but rather advanced kingdoms—about as advanced as ancient Greece—appeared along the Yellow River—the Xia around 2000 B.C., the Shang around 1600 B.C., and the Zhou around 1045 B.C.

409

civilization   City-based culture with writing, social classes, and complex economic and political organization. (See page 409.)

Neolithic   New Stone Age, beginning of agriculture. (See page 409.)

Bronze Age   Beginning of metal-working and cities. (See page 409.)

Warring States   China's early period (475–221 B.C.), before unification.

Middle Kingdom   China's traditional name for itself, in the middle of the heavens.

Han   Early dynasty, 206 B.C. to A.D. 220, that solidified China's unity and culture.

Confucius was a public official and philosopher during the late Zhou period. After a period of **Warring States** from the fifth century B.C to 221 B.C., the short-lived Qin dynasty (earlier spelled Ch'in, origin of the name China) established the first unified empire, the **Middle Kingdom**. The next dynasty, the Han (206 B.C. to A.D. 220), developed Confucianism into a bureaucratic empire that replaced the old aristocratic families.

Europe too had a great empire, Rome, but it collapsed, leading to centuries of feudalism and warring states. During roughly this same time China was a prosperous, mostly unified, highly organized empire, complete with impartial civil-service exams to select the best talent. The resulting Mandarin class—schooled in the Confucian classics, which stressed obedience, authority, and hierarchy—was interested in perpetuating the system, not changing it. A gentry class of better-off people served as the literate intermediaries between the Mandarins and the 90 percent of the population that were peasants. The words of one peasant song:

When the sun rises, I toil;
When the sun sets, I rest;
I dig wells for water;
I till the fields for food;
What has the Emperor's power to do with me?

China and Rome invite comparison. Both arose about the same time; the Roman Republic in 509 B.C., the Qin dynasty in 221 B.C. Both achieved their greatest glory as empires, the Roman from 27 B.C. to A.D. 476, the **Han** from 206 B.C. to A.D. 220. At their peak they were about the same size; Rome covered the Mediterranean basin and much of West Europe, the Han most of present-day China. The two empires knew of each other and traded a little via the Silk Road through Central Asia. Both achieved a high degree of civilization in terms of art, architecture, administration, commerce, and writing.

There are many contrasts between ancient Rome and China. In the first century A.D. Buddhism arrived in China from India but never established itself as a state religion before it faded.

Geography

CITIES AND CIVILIZATIONS

The root of "civilization" is the Latin word *civitas,* city, and it is indeed the early cities that created high cultures of art, architecture, writing, money, social classes, and specialized economic functions. Cities arrived only after the domestication of plants and animals, which enabled humans to grow more food than their families needed. Growers traded their food surplus for utensils and clothing produced in towns. Food and other production were taxed to support rulers' courts and a professional officer class, who became nobles. Cities, civilization, and taxes were born triplets.

Rome eventually accepted Christianity, which became Europe's unifying culture. Rome kept expanding until it overexpanded. Its legions were superb but too few to hold off barbarians and put down revolts. China did take over the northern parts of Vietnam and Korea for a while but was

Geography

BOUND CHINA

China is bounded on the north by Russia, Mongolia, and Kazakhstan;

the east by Korea and the Yellow, East China, and South China Seas;

the south by Vietnam, Laos, Myanmar (formerly Burma), India, Bhutan, and Nepal;

and on the west by Pakistan, Afghanistan (minutely), Tajikistan, and Kyrgyzstan.

By knowing China's boundaries, you can label most of mainland Asia. Only Cambodia, Thailand, and Bangladesh do not border China.

The People's Republic of China. (The solid black line shows the approximate route of the 1934–1935 Long March.)

dynastic cycle Rise, maturity, and fall of an imperial family.

Pinyin Current system of transliterating Chinese into English.

not keen on expansion. Once it carved out its large Middle Kingdom (in the middle of heaven), it rested content. The Roman economy was based on slaves, China's on peasants, giving China more stability. The Han—who developed paper, silk, the compass, and the rudder—were ahead of Rome in technology.

The chief difference is what the two empires left behind. When the Western part of the Roman Empire fell to barbarians in A.D. 476, it fragmented into separate states and stayed that way. After the Han, China too suffered periods of disunity, but during their four centuries the Han implanted a culture so deep that later dynasties used it to put China back together. Chinese intellectuals always insisted that China was one country; China broken into separate kingdoms always seemed wrong. China, it has been said, is not a country but a civilization with 4,000 years of cultural continuity.

Dynasties came and went every few hundred years in what is called the **dynastic cycle**. As the old dynasty became increasingly incompetent, water systems were not repaired, famine broke out, wars and banditry appeared, and corruption and palace conspiracies grew. As more influential families got their lands exempted from taxation, peasants had to bear heavier and heavier tax burdens

Political Culture

CHINESE WORDS IN ROMAN LETTERS

In contrast to Western alphabetic writing systems, China, starting nearly 4,000 years ago, developed and perfected an ideographic system based on symbolic word-pictures, a system that was copied and modified by Korea, Vietnam, and Japan. Literacy involves memorizing thousands of pictographs, much harder than Western phonetic systems. The pictographs are useful, however, precisely because they do not represent specific sounds. People speaking very different languages—the Wu and Cantonese of South China or even Japanese—can read the same newspaper. This was a great help in unifying China, which is still a country of many different languages. An official did not need to speak the emperor's language in order to understand his written edicts. In the 1950s and 1960s Beijing simplified the pictographs, making them easier to learn and type electronically. Chinese send text messages in pictographs; the keys make different brush strokes.

Chinese is also tonal; it sounds like singing a song. Standard Chinese has four tones (in addition to no tone). Speak a syllable with the wrong tone and you have said a completely different word, sometimes to comic effect. Because it is both ideographic and tonal, Chinese is terribly difficult to transliterate into English. One system, the Wade-Giles, devised in the 1860s

by two Cambridge dons, was used for more than a century. Unfortunately, Wade-Giles did not sound much like the Chinese pronunciation.

In 1958, Peking—sorry, Beijing—introduced a new system, **Pinyin**, that is much closer to the correct pronunciation. In 1979 China made Pinyin the official standard, and most English-language publications went along with it. You may still see some Wade-Giles spellings in older books, for example:

Wade-Giles	Pinyin
Mao Tse-tung	Mao Zedong
Chou En-lai	Zhou Enlai
Kuomintang	Guomindang
Peking	Beijing
Nanking	Nanjing
Chungking	Chongqing
Shanghai	Shanghai (the same!)
Szechwan	Sichuan
Sinkiang	Xinjiang
Canton	Guangzhou
Ch'in	Qin (Q sounds "ch")

until they revolted. In the eyes of the people, it looked as if the emperor had lost the "Mandate of Heaven," that is, his legitimate right to rule. A conqueror, either Chinese or foreign (**Mongol** or **Manchu**), found it easy to take over a delegitimized empire. By the very fact of his victory, the new ruler seemed to have gained the Mandate of Heaven. Under vigorous new emperors, administration and taxation were restored. After some generations, though, the new dynasty fell prey to the old ills, and people, especially the literate, thought the emperor had lost his heavenly mandate; the cycle started over.

> **Mongol**   Central Asian dynasty, founded by Genghis Khan, that ruled China as the Yuan dynasty in thirteenth and fourteenth centuries.
>
> **Manchu**   Last imperial dynasty of China, also known as *Qing;* ruled from 1644 to 1911.
>
> **steady-state**   A system that preserves itself with little change.

Two millennia of empire still mark China today. Not a feudal system like Japan, China was unified and centralized. (The defining characteristic of a feudal system is an autonomous aristocracy, which Japan had and China did not.) In China, an emperor at the top set the direction and tone, Mandarins carried out Beijing's writ, gentry ran local affairs, and peasants—the overwhelming majority of the population—toiled in the fields. For centuries China was the world's greatest civilization and biggest economy, far ahead of Europe. By around 1500, however, Europe began surging ahead (for some of the factors, see page 3) while China stagnated. One prominent factor: China was one state when Europe was many states. Europe's monarchs competed with each other for wealth, power, and new territories, whereas huge, unified China faced no competition. Soon expansionist European empires controlled much of the world, including China. Chinese today are well aware that China was a great civilization, one humiliated by the West.

With little new territory to expand into, Chinese society evolved **steady-state** structures aimed at stability and making peasants content with what they had rather than encourage them to pioneer and innovate. Labor-saving devices would render peasants jobless and were not encouraged. China's achievements in science and technology—far ahead of medieval Europe's—remained curiosities instead of contributions to an industrial revolution. Commercial expansion was also discouraged. Instead of a Western mentality of reinvestment, growth, and risk-taking, Chinese merchants sought only a steady-state relationship with peasants and government officials; they depended heavily on government permits, monopolies, and set prices.

China took little interest in anything foreign. The Middle Kingdom was surrounded by barbarians who should be walled out or bought off. Chinese culture could uplift the near barbarians

Geography

RAINFALL

A focus on Europe may cause us to overlook one of the most basic physical determinants of a politico-economic system. Rainfall in Europe is generally sufficient and predictable, but in much of the world it is not. There is plenty of land in the world; water for humans and crops is the limiting factor. Over one billion humans do not have clean drinking water, a number that is growing rapidly. Per capita, China has less than a third the water of the global average. With water tables dropping rapidly, many warn that China's water supplies will soon reach dangerous levels. Massive industrial pollution makes matters worse.

Irrigation and conservation can compensate for lack of rain, but they require a high degree of human organization and governmental supervision. This may explain why high civilizations arose early in China and Iran. Large desert or semi-desert areas of our four Third World examples—China, Mexico, Nigeria, and Iran—cannot sustain much development.

kow-tow Literally, head to the ground; to prostrate oneself.

Ming Han Chinese dynasty between Mongols and Manchus, ruled 1368–1644.

(Koreans and Vietnamese), who could then **kow-tow** and pay tribute to the emperor. This was called the *tributary system* and was quite different from the diplomacy developed in Europe. China never had the European concept that other lands were sovereign and should be treated diplomatically as equals. They should simply pay tribute. China's superiority complex poorly equipped it to handle European penetration.

China was centuries ahead of Europe in naval technology, including the compass and watertight compartments. From 1405 to 1433 the **Mings** sent huge naval expeditions under Admiral Zheng He, a Muslim eunuch (eunuchs were common among court officials) all around the Indian Ocean. Some of Zheng's ships were 400 feet long, many times bigger than any ship Europeans would build for centuries. If the Chinese fleets had rounded Africa or crossed the Pacific, China would have discovered Europe and the Americas. Would that have mattered? Could we now be

Political Culture

CONFUCIANISM: GOVERNMENT BY RIGHT THINKING

Confucianism is not a religion but a philosophy of governance. It was much more influential than Buddhism in Chinese political culture. The scholar Confucius (551–479 B.C.) advised rulers of the small Zhou kingdom (before China unified) that the key to good, stable government lay in instilling correct, moral behavior in ruled and rulers alike. People can be improved, but they must understand their roles and perform them obediently. Sons are subservient to fathers, wives to husbands, younger brothers to elder brothers, and subjects to rulers. The ruler sets a moral example. Pure spirit and careful manners create a conservative political culture more effective and durable than mere laws. Japan copied Confucianism from China (see page 339).

Confucianism emphasized that good government starts with thinking correct thoughts in utter sincerity. If things go wrong, it indicates rulers have been insincere. The system did not depend on Confucianism alone; it also had strong police controls that permitted no dissent. Mao Zedong hated everything old China stood for, but he could not help picking up the Confucian stress on right thinking. Adding a Marxist twist, Mao taught that one was a proletarian not because of blue-collar origin but because one had revolutionary, pure thoughts. Confucius would have been pleased.

Statue of Confucius at Beijing Temple.

Curiously, Confucianism died out in China but survives in Japan, often the case when ideologies are transplanted from their country of origin. Japanese are still inculcated with politeness and decorum, of bowing and obedience. Such patterns have disappeared in China, the result of more than a century of revolution and war. Mao Zedong finished off Confucianism with his "destroy the four olds" campaign, part of the Cultural Revolution of the late 1960s. Political cultures are not fixed in concrete; they change under the pressure of events and regimes.

speaking Chinese? Probably not, as old China had no thirst for imperial expansion or colonization of distant barbarian lands. Instead,
Ming officials decided the expeditions were too expensive and China
had everything it needed. For centuries, China remained a stay-at-
home country.

> **Opium Wars**   Nineteenth-century British (and French) campaigns to keep China open to opium imports.

The Long Collapse

For some 2,000 years China absorbed invasions, famines, and new dynasties. The old pattern always reasserted itself because it was the most rational way to rule the Middle Kingdom. But as the
modern epoch impinged on China, the system could not handle two new factors: population growth
and Western penetration. In 1741, China's population was 143 million; just a century later, in 1851,
it had become an amazing 432 million, the result of new crops (corn, potatoes, and sweet potatoes
from the Americas), internal peace under the Manchu dynasty, some new farmland, and just plain
harder work on the part of the peasants. Taxation and administration lagged behind the rapid population growth, which hit as the Manchus were going into the typical decline phase of their dynastic cycle in the nineteenth century.

At about the same time the West penetrated and disoriented China. In a clash of two cultures—
Western dynamism and greed versus Chinese stability—China was no match. Over roughly a century, old China went into convulsions and breakdowns, which, some suspect, still lurk under the
surface.

The first Westerners to reach China were daring Portuguese navigators in their tiny caravels in
1514. Gradually, they and other Europeans gained permission to set up trading stations on the coast.
For three centuries the Imperial government disdained the foreigners and their products and tried
to keep both to a minimum. In 1793, for example, in response to a British mission to Beijing, the
emperor commended King George III for his "respectful spirit of submission" but pointed out that
there could be little trade because "our celestial empire possesses all things in prolific abundance."

But the West, especially the British, pushed on, smelling enormous profits in the China trade.
Matters came to a head with the First **Opium War** of 1839 to 1842. Opium smoking was illegal and
unknown in China, but for over a century, the British imported more and more opium from the

Key Concepts

CYCLICAL VERSUS SECULAR CHANGE

China illustrates the two kinds of change that social
scientists deal with. Cyclical change is repetitive; certain familiar historical phases follow one another like
a pendulum swing. China's dynastic cycles are examples of cyclical change; there is change, but the overall pattern is preserved.

Secular change means a long-term shift that does
not revert back to the old pattern. China's population

growth, for example, was a secular change that
helped break the stability of traditional China. One
of the problems faced by historians, economists, and
political scientists is whether a change they are ex-
amining is secular—a long-term, basic shift—or
cyclical—something that comes and goes repeatedly. (Discussions of global warming face the same
problem.)

treaty ports   Areas of China coast run by European powers.

extraterritoriality   Privilege of Europeans in colonial situations to have their own laws and courts.

poppy fields of British-held India. The British flouted China's law and popularized opium smoking. When a zealous Imperial official tried to stop the opium trade, Britain went to war, invoking the principle of "free trade," to keep the lucrative commerce open. Britain easily won, but the Chinese still refused to admit that the foreigners were superior. Moaned one Cantonese: "Except for your ships being solid, your gunfire fierce, and your rockets powerful, what good qualities do you have?" For the Chinese, war technology was not as important as moral quality, a view later adopted by Mao Zedong.

The 1842 Treaty of Nanjing (Nanking in Wade-Giles) wrested five **treaty ports** from the Chinese. Britain got Hong Kong as an outright possession. In the treaty ports the foreigners held sway, dominating the commerce and governance of the area, and enjoying **extraterritoriality**, meaning they were not subject to Chinese law but had their own courts, a point deeply resented by both Chinese and Japanese. In the Second Opium War of 1856–1860 an Anglo-French expedition occupied Beijing, burned the Summer Palace, and forced China to add nine more treaty ports. China called the imperialist land-grabs "unequal treaties."

THE UNITED STATES AND CHINA: THE CHINA TIE

The United States has had long and deep ties to China. Some of Boston's leading families profited early from the China trade (including the sale of Turkish opium). While the British carved up China's coast, we prided ourselves on being above that sort of imperialism (but we did use the British treaty ports). In 1900 Secretary of State Hay issued the Open Door notes (see page 347) to stop the dismemberment of China. We saw ourselves as China's "big brother" and were happy to note that Chinese called us their "favorite people," who were only there to help and seized no territory.

American churches sent hundreds of missionaries to China in the nineteenth and early twentieth centuries to make the Chinese Protestant and prosperous. The Boxers killed American missionaries and their converts. Henry Luce, born in China in 1898 the son of a Presbyterian missionary, arrived at Yale speaking Chinese. All his life Luce carried the missionary view that we can and must uplift China, and working with the Chinese Nationalists was the way to do it. Luce founded *Time* magazine in 1923 and put Nationalist chief Jiang ten times on its cover. Opinionated and influential, Luce used *Time* to rail against Chinese Communists and U.S. Democrats (he conflated the two).

U.S. support for China had to bring us into war with Japan. When Japan conquered Manchuria in 1931, Secretary of State Stimson issued his *non-recognition doctrine*. When Japan began its conquest of all of China in 1937, we increasingly embargoed trade with Japan, and this led to Pearl Harbor. China could not be more than a minor theatre of operations for the U.S. war effort. The Japanese occupied the entire China coast, so only a trickle of U.S. supplies could reach Jiang's armies by air and by the Burma Road from India. During the war U.S. officials attempted to get Chinese Nationalists and Communists to work together against the Japanese, but their alliances were fleeting because the two sides distrusted each other.

When the Communists took over China in late 1949, U.S. Republicans like Luce intoned "Who lost China?" and blamed the Democrats. The "Old China Hands" of U.S. diplomats were purged from the State Department for letting the Communists take over China—they could not have done anything about it—leaving Washington for decades without experts who knew China first-hand. Washington broke all ties with mainland China in 1949 and did not resume them until Nixon's visit in 1972. We fought China in Korea. The twenty-three years of U.S.-China hostility, however, was an aberration in a history of two centuries of good ties.

Around the treaty ports grew **spheres of influence**, understandings among the foreign powers as to who really ran things there. The British, French, Germans, Russians, and Japanese in effect carved up the China coast with their spheres of influence, in which they dominated trade. Foreign powers turned the treaty port of Shanghai into a major and modern trading center. Then and now, Shanghai was China's leading city both in size and commercial importance. China was reduced to semicolonial status.

sphere of influence Semicolonial area under control of major power.

Taiping Religion-based rebellion in nineteenth-century China.

Boxer Chinese antiforeigner rebellion in 1900.

warlord Local military chief who runs province.

◼ From Empire to Republic

Internally, too, the Empire weakened. Rebellions broke out. From 1851 to 1864, the **Taipings**—espousing a mixture of Christianity (picked up from missionaries), Confucianism, and primitive communism—baptized millions in South China and nearly overthrew the Manchu (Qing) dynasty. In 1900, with the backing of some reactionary officials and the empress dowager, the antiforeign **Boxer** movement, based on traditional temple-boxing exercises, killed missionaries and besieged Beijing's Legation Quarter for fifty-five days. What the Chinese call the "Eight Powers Expedition" of British, French, German, Russian, American, Japanese, Austrian, and Italian troops broke through and lifted the siege. The foreigners then demanded indemnities and additional concessions from the tottering Imperial government.

Could the Qing (pronounced "Ching") dynasty have adapted itself to the new Western pressures? The Japanese had; with the 1868 Meiji Restoration (see pages 343–344) they preserved the form of empire but shifted to modernization and industrialization with spectacular success. Many young Chinese demanded reforms to strengthen China, especially after their humiliating defeat by Japan in 1895. In 1898 the young Emperor Guangxu gathered reformers around him and in the famous Hundred Days issued more than forty edicts, modernizing everything from education to the military. Conservative officials and the old empress dowager would have none of it; they carried out a coup, rescinded the changes, and put the emperor under house arrest for the rest of his short life. (He was probably poisoned.)

A system that cannot reform is increasingly ripe for revolution. Younger people, especially army officers, grew fed up with China's weakness and became militant nationalists. Many Chinese studied in the West and were eager to modernize China. Anarchist, socialist, and Marxist ideas from Europe intrigued Chinese intellectuals. Under an idealistic, Western-trained doctor, Sun Yixian (Sun Yat-sen in Wade-Giles), disgruntled provincial officials and military commanders overthrew the Manchus in 1911. It was the end of the last dynasty but not the beginning of stability. In the absence of central authority, so-called **warlords** fragmented China from 1916 to 1927.

Japan took advantage of China's weakness. Every Japanese grab generated passionate nationalism in China. In 1894 Japan started a war with China and took Taiwan and made it a Japanese province from 1895 to 1945. In 1915 Japan issued a far-reaching Twenty-One Demands on China that would have turned it into a Japanese protectorate. Chinese were furious. On May 4, 1919, the Versailles peace conference decided to allow Japan to keep the former German concessions in Shandong Province, the seizure of which had been Japan's tiny contribution to the Allied side in World War I. Beijing students protested and rioted, and anti-Japanese demonstrations broke out in many Chinese cities. The May Fourth Movement that followed was the training ground for young Chinese Nationalists and Communists. In a parallel to the German invasion of Russia in World War I,

Nationalist   Chiang Kai-shek's party that unified China in late 1920s, abbreviated KMT.

Japanese incursions into China led to the Communist takeover in 1949. It was foreign invasion rather than mass uprising that brought communism to both Russia and China.

The **Nationalist** party, or Guomindang (in Wade-Giles, Kuomintang, KMT), gradually overcame China's chaos. Formed by Sun Yatsen shortly after the Manchu's overthrow, the Nationalists were guided by intellectuals (many of them educated in the United States), army officers, and the modern business element. Their greatest strength was in the South, in Guangzhou (Canton), especially in the coastal cities where there was the most contact with the West. It was no accident that they made Nanjing their capital; it means "southern capital." (North-South tension still exists in China.)

After Sun died in 1925, General (later Generalissimo) Jiang Jieshi (Chiang Kai-shek) took over the Nationalists, who by 1927 controlled most of China after a series of military expeditions. While many Americans hailed Jiang as the founder and savior of the new China, in reality Nationalist rule was weak. The Western-oriented city people who staffed the Nationalists did not reform or develop the rural areas where most Chinese lived, often under the thumb of rapacious landlords. Administration became terribly corrupt. And the Nationalists offered no plausible ideology to rally the big majority of Chinese, who were peasants.

Still, like Kerensky's provisional government in Russia, the Nationalists might have succeeded were it not for war, in this case a Japanese invasion. In 1931 the Japanese army seized Manchuria and in 1937 began the conquest of the rest of China. By 1941 they had taken the entire coast, forcing the Nationalists to move their capital far up the Yangzi River from Nanjing to Chongqing. Jiang's forces preferred fighting Communists to Japanese, while waiting for a U.S. victory to return them to power.

Mao Zedong proclaims the founding of the People's Republic of China at Beijing's Tiananmen Square on October 1, 1949.

◼ The Communist Triumph

One branch of Chinese nationalism, influenced by Marx and the Bolshevik Revolution, decided that communism was the only effective basis for a nationalist revolution. The Chinese Communists have always been first and foremost nationalists, and from its founding in 1921 the Chinese

Communist party (CCP) worked with the Nationalists until Jiang, in 1927, decided to exterminate them as a threat. The fight between the KMT and CCP was a struggle between two versions of Chinese nationalism.

> **mass line**   Mao's theory of revolution for China.

Stalin, who knew nothing about China, mistakenly advised the Chinese Communists to base themselves on the small proletariat of the coastal cities; however, Mao Zedong rose to leadership of the Party by developing a rural strategy that he called the *mass line*. Mao concluded that the real revolutionary potential in China, which had little industry and hence few proletarians, was among the poorest peasants. It was a major revision of Marxist theory, one that Marx probably would not have recognized as Marxism. Mao, considered a maverick in the CCP, in 1931 organized peasants in the Jiangxi province (Kiangsi in Wade-Giles) into a small Chinese Soviet Republic.

In 1934, with KMT forces surrounding their "Jiangxi redoubt," some 80,000 began their incredible Long March of 5,000 miles (8,000 km) to the relative safety of Yenan (Yan'an in Wade-Giles) far to the north in Shaanxi Province. The march took over a year and led across mountain ranges and rivers amidst hostile forces. Only 6,000 survived. The Long March became the epic of Chinese Communist history. Self-reliant and isolated from the Soviets, the Chinese Communists developed their own strategy for survival, including working with peasants and practicing guerrilla warfare.

China's war against Japan drained and demoralized the Nationalists, but it gave the Communists a chance to seize power. Besides stocks of captured Japanese weapons from the Russian takeover of Manchuria in 1945, the Chinese Communists got little but bad advice from the

Key Concepts

MAO AND GUERRILLA WAR

In what became a model for revolutionaries the world over, the Chinese Communists swept to power in 1949 after a decade and a half of guerrilla and civil warfare. During these years, Mao Zedong, often in his Yenan cave, developed and taught what he called the **mass line**. His lessons included the following:

1. Take the countryside and surround the cities. While the enemy is stuck in the cities, able to venture out only in strength, you are mobilizing the masses.

2. Work very closely with the peasants, listen to their complaints, help them (for example, getting rid of a landlord or bringing in the harvest), propagandize them, and recruit them into the army and Party.

3. Do not engage the enemy's main forces but rather probe for his weak spots, harassing him and wearing him out.

4. Do not expect much help from the outside; be self-reliant. For weapons, take the enemies'.

5. Do not worry about the apparent superior numbers and firepower of the enemy and his imperialist allies; their strength is illusory ("paper tigers") because it is not based on the masses. Willpower and unity with the masses are more important than weaponry.

6. At certain stages guerrilla units come together to form larger units, until, at last, as the enemy stumbles, your forces become a regular army that takes the entire country.

Soviets and felt they never owed them much in return. In 1947 full-scale civil war resumed between the KMT and CCP, which the Communists won in late 1949. Mao and the CCP came to power largely on their own, through their peasant and guerrilla strategies, a point that contributed to the later Sino-Soviet split.

After World War II, the Nationalist forces were much larger than the Communists' and had many U.S. arms. Nationalist strength, however, melted away as hyperinflation destroyed the economy, corrupt officers sold their troops' weapons (often to the Communists), and war weariness paralyzed the population. The Nationalists had always neglected the rice roots of political strength: the common peasant. The Communists, by cultivating the peasantry (Mao himself was of peasant origin), won a new Mandate of Heaven. In 1949, the disintegrating Nationalists retreated to the island of Taiwan while the Communists restored Beijing ("northern capital") as the country's capital and proceeded to implement what is probably the world's most sweeping revolution. On that occasion, Mao, reflecting his nationalistic sentiments, said: "Our nation will never again be an insulted nation. We have stood up." China today, in its race for respect and prestige, is still putting Mao's words into action.

Key Terms

Boxer (p. 417)

Bronze Age (p. 410)

civilization (p. 410)

dynastic cycle (p. 412)

extraterritoriality (p. 416)

Han (p. 410)

kow-tow (p. 414)

Manchu (p. 413)

mass line (p. 419)

Middle Kingdom (p. 410)

Ming (p. 414)

Mongol (p. 413)

Nationalist (p. 418)

Neolithic (p. 410)

Opium Wars (p. 415)

Pinyin (p. 412)

sphere of influence (p. 417)

steady-state (p. 413)

Taiping (p. 417)

treaty ports (p. 416)

warlord (p. 417)

Warring States (p. 410)

Further Reference

Antony, Robert J., and Jane Kate Leonard, eds. *Dragons, Tigers, and Dogs: Qing Crisis Management and the Boundaries of State Power in Late Imperial China*. Ithaca, NY: Cornell University Press, 2002.

Fairbank, John King. *China: A New History*. Cambridge, MA: Harvard University Press, 1994.

Hutchings, Graham. *Modern China: A Guide to a Century of Change*. Cambridge, MA: Harvard University Press, 2001.

Morton, W. Scott, and Charlton M. Lewis. *China: Its History and Culture*, 4th ed. New York: McGraw-Hill, 2005.

Mungello, D. E. *The Great Encounter of China and the West, 1500–1800*, 2nd ed. Lanham, MD: Rowman & Littlefield, 2005.

Spence, Jonathan. *Mao Zedong*. New York: Viking, 2000.

———. *The Search for Modern China*. New York: Norton, 1990.

Terrill, Ross. *China in Our Time*. New York: Simon & Schuster, 1992.

Chapter 29

CHINA:
THE KEY INSTITUTIONS

In our first five countries, we had to do a little detective work to find out what the key institutions were. Parliaments, executives, political parties, interest groups, and bureaucracies all had a role, some more important than others. We generally concluded that chief executives—prime ministers in Britain and Germany, presidents in France and Russia—held the most power. China, one of the few remaining Communist dictatorships, is a bit different. Here a president and a prime minister (as in France and Russia) run things but only because the Chinese Communist party (CCP) has put them into power.

▪ The Importance of the Party

China is still a party-state. China's 1982 constitution repeatedly specifies that everything runs "under the leadership of the Communist Party of China." As in all Communist countries, neither competing parties nor factions within the CCP are permitted. One can find informal cliques based on geography, such as the "Shanghai clique," who went on to occupy top positions in Beijing. Allowing either other parties or open splits within the Party would be a major step to Chinese democracy. So far, either is out of the question.

China may be a dictatorship, but it is now the dictatorship of a small Party elite, rather different from Stalin's or Mao's one-man rule. After Mao and Deng died, China's rulers have adhered to fixed term limits—two five-year terms—and do not stay in power forever. China has evolved a method for the orderly and regular change of top personnel, something the Soviet Union never did. Most Soviet chiefs simply died in office, as did Mao. The lack of a succession mechanism produced at least two problems: (1) rule by the elderly (*gerontocracy*), and (2) messy succession crises, as the contenders for top power had to battle each other (for example, Stalin and Trotsky after Lenin's death). In this and other ways, China has been cleverer than the Soviet Union.

Questions to Consider

1. How close a parallel were the Soviet and Chinese institutional structures?
2. If China now has a mostly market economy, how can a Communist party lead it?
3. What are the perils of indirect analysis of closed systems?
4. What is a *cadre* in Asian Communist parties?
5. What and where is the *Zhongnanhai*?
6. What role has the Chinese army played?
7. Is China a unitary or federal system? How organized?
8. How would we characterize the fourth generation of China's leadership?
9. What kind of regional resentments does China have?

■ The Soviet Parallel

Kremlinology   Noting personnel changes to analyze Communist regimes.

Zhongnanhai   Walled compound for China's top leaders next to Forbidden City in Beijing.

In a parallel with the Soviet Union/Russia, we must also specify a "before and after" in dealing with political institutions. The break in China was not as sharp as the one that came with the collapse of the Soviet Union in late 1991, but we must remember that Russia has turned part-way *back* to authoritarianism. China had no comparable interlude of Russia's attempted democracy; it merely shifted into a lighter authoritarianism. The original Communist institutions Mao set up after taking power in 1949 were closely modeled after Stalin's Soviet system. Now they are somewhat changed, and the system as a whole is much looser and freer. Indeed, tourists intent on simply viewing the sights (both ancient and modern) and sampling the cuisine (good and cheap) might not notice they are in a Communist country. Mao's portrait on Tiananmen Square and all paper currency are among the few reminders of his rule.

Key Concepts

INDIRECT ANALYSIS OF AUTHORITARIAN SYSTEMS

Democracies are easier to study than authoritarian systems. In democracies you can get a variety of data, much of it quantified, on public opinion, party positions, election results, legislative votes, and policy shifts. With authoritarian systems you can get only the last policy shifts, and they are veiled by obscure wording. It may take a while to figure out what has changed.

During the Cold War, academics and journalists developed indirect techniques to study Soviet politics. Dubbed derisively "**Kremlinology**," they focused on who in the Kremlin got promoted, demoted, or executed. By associating these personnel shifts with their positions and statements, observers attempted to infer the direction of Kremlin politics. Stalin's dismissal of Foreign Minister Maxim Litvinov in 1939, for example, and his replacement by Vyacheslav Molotov signaled a major shift in Soviet foreign policy, from trying to gain Western allies to making a deal with Hitler. Even who stood next to whom atop Lenin's tomb could be significant. In 1953, after Stalin's death, Kremlinologists noted that secret-police chief Lavrenti Beria was missing from the reviewing stand. "Maybe he had a cold," scoffed one American editor. Actually, Beria had already been shot as a threat to other Politburo members. In Kremlinology, little things mean a lot.

The equivalent, dubbed "China watching" (much of it from Hong Kong) during the Cold War, applies similar techniques to China. Who is under whose protection? Did Premier Zhou Enlai quietly protect Deng Xiaoping from the ravages of the Cultural Revolution? (Likely he did, in order to ensure a pragmatic successor.) Did Deng fire Party General Secretary Zhao Ziyang in 1989? (Clearly he did, because of Zhao's soft line on the Tiananmen demonstrators.) If, after a series of engineers in top positions, a U.S.-trained economist (and there are several in China) joins their ranks, what could it indicate about China's direction?

Indirect analysis, based on fragmentary evidence, guesswork, and faulty analogies, can lead to mistakes. A bright young Harvard China specialist took at face value an unverified (and probably fake) report that Mao on his deathbed in 1976 handed Premier Hua Guofeng a note saying, "With you in charge I am at ease." From such dubious indicators, the Harvard professor concluded that Hua was indeed Mao's successor. But behind the scenes Deng Xiaoping still pulled the strings. He gradually sidelined Hua and kicked him out of the Politburo in 1981. The Harvard professor was denied tenure. Don't bet the farm on indirect analysis. Unfortunately, until the politics of the **Zhongnanhai** opens up, indirect analysis is all we have.

The institutions of China's government are similar to what the Soviet Union had: interlocking state and Party hierarchies (see Chapter 19). For example, what is supposed to be the top Party body, the National Party Congress, has many of the same members as the top legislative body, the National People's Congress. (The two are easy to confuse. Just remember one is Party, the other state.) Typically, a Chinese leader first climbs into the upper ranks of the Party and then assumes high government jobs as well. In Communist systems generally, position in the Party determines who also gets governing power within the state structure. China's current chief, Hu Jintao, became Party general secretary a few months before getting named president.

China, however, adds a Third-World twist to Communist governance: The army has also been quite important, at times intervening directly into politics, as happens in other developing countries. China, no less than Nigeria (see Chapter 34), has experienced upheaval and chaos, which has led to army participation in politics, the mark of a Third-World country. Typically, the army intervenes not merely to grab power but to save the country from disorder and breakdown. Until China is no longer vulnerable to upheaval, we cannot be sure the army will not intervene again.

As in the old Soviet model, each state and Party level ostensibly elects the one above it. In practice, the Party handpicks delegates to be elected from the lower to the higher congresses. In China, townships elect congresses every two years, which then elect some 2,800 county congresses every three years, which in turn choose provincial and big-city People's Congresses every five years. In the old days of Mao, factories were main base units of political organization; now it is townships. The provincial People's Congresses then elect the unicameral National People's Congress (NPC) of nearly 3,000 delegates—some 70 percent of them government officials—for a five-year term.

As in the ex-Soviet Union, this parliament is too big to do much at its ten-day annual sessions. Recent NPC sessions, however, have featured hundreds of motions from the floor, lively debate, contested committee elections, and negative votes—possibly indications that it may gradually turn into a real parliament with some checks on the executive. This would be a major step to democracy, but it would require letting NPC delegates form links with outside groups and other members, whom they could mobilize and represent—in a word, parties. An individual NPC delegate introducing a bill is fine but no substitute for pluralism. Standing alone, the delegate is nothing; with groups behind them they are the building blocks of democracy. A faint beginning could be seen in the growing number of NPC joint motions and bills, each of which requires the signatures of at least thirty delegates. If this were to expand and solidify, the NPC would have the making of parliamentary parties (but not yet mass parties). Long ago such groupings in Britain's House of Commons marked the beginning of parties.

The NPC Standing Committee of about 155 is theoretically supreme, but it too does not have much power to oversee the executive branch. The chairman of the Standing Committee is considered China's head of state or president. As is usual in Communist countries, Party General Secretary Hu Jintao became president in 2003. The top of the executive branch is the State Council, a cabinet of approximately forty ministers (specialized in economic branches) and a dozen vice-premiers led by a premier, China's head of government, since 2003 Wen Jiabao. China, therefore, has both a president and a premier and superficially resembles the semipresidential system de Gaulle devised in France. In practice, China is more like the Russian system, in which the president is much more powerful than the premier. Almost all of China's current top leaders graduated in engineering or science and worked in those fields. In terms of education, China's governing elite is now among the world's brainiest and most technocratic, which tends to make them self-assured.

The formal structure of China's executive may not always correspond to the real distribution of its power. In 1976, after the death of both Party Chairman Mao and Premier Zhou, a relative unknown, Hua Guofeng, was installed in both their offices. On paper, Hua appeared to

Beida   Short name for Beijing University, long China's best (equivalent to Japan's *Todai*).

Comintern   Short for Communist International; the world's Communist parties under Moscow's control.

be the most powerful figure in the land, but an elderly, twice-rehabilitated Party veteran, Deng Xiaoping (see box on page 428), who took the modest title of senior vice-premier in 1977, was in fact more powerful than his nominal boss, Hua. When Deng toured the United States in 1979, he acted like a head of state. Deng's power grew out of his senior standing in the Party and the army. In 1980, he demoted Hua and assumed power himself, still without taking over the job titles, which he left to others. By 1982, Hua was out of the Politburo and out of sight.

Personalities

TANDEM POWER: MAO AND ZHOU

For over a quarter of a century, until both died in 1976, power in Beijing was divided between Party Chairman Mao Zedong and Premier Zhou Enlai. This set a Chinese pattern of tandem power that still operates and may now be sufficiently *institutionalized* (see page 491) to continue into the future.

Both were of rural backgrounds, but Mao was born in 1893 into a peasant family in inland Hunan Province, while Zhou was born in 1898 into a gentry family in coastal Jiangsu Province. Mao's father had worked his way up from poverty to property and was counted as a better-off peasant, exactly the kind Mao ordered tried and executed by the million in the early 1950s. Mao said his background let him understand China's peasants, but his cold-blooded policies showed no sympathy for them.

Mao went away to school but in late 1911 became a soldier briefly in the revolution against the dying Manchu dynasty. Mao never attended a university but graduated in 1918 from Hunan's teacher-training school. Already a radical nationalist, while there he organized the New People's Study Society, a precursor of the CCP. Mao briefly worked as a library assistant at Beijing University, the famous **Beida**, where he was caught up in the anti-Japanese May Fourth Movement of 1919. In 1921, when Chinese Marxists with **Comintern** help organized the Chinese Communist party (CCP) in Shanghai, Mao was one of its founding members.

Zhou went to a top middle school and then to Japan in 1917 to study. Japan, having beaten the

Russians in 1904–1905 (see Chapters 18 and 23), was then an example and magnet for nationalists throughout Asia, including Chinese and Vietnamese. The 1919 May Fourth movement brought an exodus of Chinese students from Japan, and Zhou returned to China. Already a student radical, Zhou was jailed briefly in 1920. Upon release, Zhou went to France in 1920 to study, but with the founding of the CCP he worked at recruiting Chinese students in Europe to join the Communists. Zhou returned to China in 1924 to participate in Sun Yat-sen's Nationalist revolution. Mao had no experience outside of China.

As was often the case with young Chinese early in the twentieth century, Mao and Zhou were passionate Chinese nationalists before they turned to Marxism. Neither of them went much further than high school in formal education, although both studied, debated, and published in Chinese leftist circles.

Under Moscow's orders, the young Chinese Communist party worked in alliance with the Nationalists. Zhou, for example, was in charge of political education at the Nationalist military academy at Whampoa, where Nationalist Jiang Jieshi was commandant. In 1927, Zhou became CCP military director. As KMT forces approached Shanghai that year, Zhou organized workers to seize the city. But Jiang, suspicious that the Communists were disloyal to the Nationalist cause, massacred them by the thousands, and both Mao and Zhou barely escaped with their lives. (Zhou was the model militant Chinese revolutionary

The Party

Like the old Soviet Communist party, the Chinese Communist party (CCP) is constitutionally and in practice the leading political element of the country. With 70 million members, the CCP is large, but relative to China's population it is proportionately smaller than the CPSU was in the Soviet Union. As China's economy decentralized and marketized, the Party began admitting private businesspeople, provided they are patriotic and follow the Party line. Many business people see Party membership as a way to get government permits, loans, and contracts. Perhaps some day these capitalist Communists will introduce pluralistic perspectives into the Party's upper ranks, but so far the

for French writer André Malraux's novel *Man's Fate,* set in 1927 Shanghai.)

The next decade set the Mao-Zhou relationship. Mao concluded from his work with peasants that they were the means to China's revolution. Zhou initially remained loyal to Stalin's "proletarian line," which argued for a series of worker uprisings in China's coastal cities. Stalin knew little about the world and nothing about China. By 1931, after all uprisings had failed, Zhou changed his mind and joined Mao in his Jiangxi redoubt. From there, the two led the arduous Long March to the north. By the time they arrived in Yenan, Mao was clearly the leader of the CCP, and his "mass line" of basing the revolution on the peasantry prevailed.

Mao dominated mainly by force of intellect. Other CCP leaders respected his ability to theorize in clear, blunt language. Mao became the Party chief and theoretician but did not supervise the day-to-day tasks of survival, warfare, and diplomacy. These became Zhou's jobs; he was the administrator of the revolution. Never bothering to theorize, Zhou was a master at shaping and controlling bureaucracies, clever compromise, and political survival amidst changing lines. Asked for his views on the French Revolution, the cagey Zhou replied, "One should not comment on such a recent event."

There was some tension between the two, but Zhou never showed it. Publicly Zhou dedicated himself to fulfilling Mao's policies, although at times, in the shambles of the Great Leap Forward (1958–1960) and

Beijing's Military Museum displays figures of Mao and Zhou at Communist headquarters during the war against Japan.

the Cultural Revolution (1966–1969), he tried to stabilize things and limit damage. Mao was the abstract thinker, Zhou the pragmatic doer. This made Mao more radical and Zhou more conservative. Mao could spin out his utopian dreams, but Zhou made the bureaucracy, military, and economy function. Zhou's pragmatic views won out; all China's top leaders since 1977 have been Zhou's ideological descendants. Mao's radicalism has disappeared.

Personalities

THE INVISIBLE PUPPETEER: DENG XIAOPING

Deng Xiaoping followed a strange path to power. He had been purged from Chinese politics twice before becoming "senior vice-premier" in 1977, a deliberately deceptive title to cover the fact he was China's undisputed boss. And Deng sought no fame or glory; unlike Mao, he built no personality cult. Deng seldom appeared in public or in the media but governed in the ancient Confucian tradition: quietly, behind the scenes, chiefly by picking top officials. MIT political scientist Lucian Pye called him the "invisible puppeteer." This former protégé of Zhou Enlai—who, like Zhou, was a pragmatic administrator rather than a theorizer—set China on its present course and gave China its current problems.

Deng was born in 1904 into a rural landlord family. Sent to study in France, Deng was recruited there by Zhou Enlai and soon joined the Chinese Communists. As a political commissar and organizer of the People's Liberation Army, Deng forged strong military connections. Rising through major posts after 1949, Deng was named to the top of the Party—the Politburo's Standing Committee—in 1956.

Deng was not as adroit as Zhou and kept getting into political trouble. An outspoken pragmatist, Deng said after the Great Leap: "Private farming is all right as long as it raises production, just as it does not matter whether a cat is black or white as long as it catches mice." During the Cultural Revolution this utterance was used against Deng to show he was a "Capitalist Roader." Although not expelled from the Party, Deng dropped out of sight and lost his official position. His son was crippled by a mob during the Cultural Revolution.

But the little man—Deng was well under five feet tall—bounced back in 1973 when moderates regained control. In 1975, he seemed to be ready to take over; he spoke with visiting U.S. President Ford as one head of state to another. But just a month later Deng was again in disgrace, denounced by the radicals of the **Gang of Four** as anti-Mao. Again, he was stripped of his posts, but an old army buddy gave him sanctuary in an elite military resort. The adaptable Deng bounced back yet again. With the arrest of the Gang of Four in 1976, moderates came back out of the woodwork, among them Deng. In July 1977, he was reappointed

Deng Xiaoping

to all his old posts. Many Chinese state, Party, and army leaders, badly shaken by the Cultural Revolution, looked to old comrade Deng to restore stability.

In 1978 Deng, then already seventy-four, proclaimed his famous "Four Modernizations" of agriculture, industry, science, and defense. Typical of the veiled language of authoritarian regimes, Deng included permitting "side-occupations," which turned out to mean individuals could work growing, making, and selling things for personal profit. Thus a few words triggered a massive shift, as now city streets are lined with shops and restaurants run by individual entrepreneurs. Deng also urged "adaptation to local conditions," which meant the provinces and localities were freed from lock-step central direction. This was the starting signal for the rapid industrialization of the southern coastal regions.

Deng started China on its present course by splitting economics from politics. He in effect offered Chinese a new deal: Work and get rich in a partly market economy but leave politics to the Communist party. This started China's amazing economic growth. But will not massive economic changes eventually influence politics? How much inequality can China take without unrest? Could provinces go off in their own directions? Apparently Deng never gave much thought to the contradictions he was creating, and they are now China's chief problems.

Deng was no "liberal." He encouraged economic reform but blocked any moves toward democracy, as have his successors. In 1989, Deng brutally crushed the prodemocracy movement in Beijing's Tiananmen Square. Although weak and reclusive in the 1990s, Deng still quietly controlled Beijing's top personnel and main policy lines until he died in 1997 at age ninety-two.

Party *co-opts* (see page 501) them as another device to control the economy and society. CCP leaders no longer wear military-style Mao suits. Instead, in coat and tie (usually red) they look like business executives, which some of them are.

With the economic changes since the late 1970s, the CCP has lost authority and sense of mission. Said one longtime Party member: "What does the Communist party stand for now? Nothing. Stability, maybe. But really no ideals at all." In today's China, lust for money trumps all else. Some Communist officials now use their positions for personal gain; massive corruption has set in. If not revitalized, the

Gang of Four Mao's ultraradical helpers, arrested in 1976. (See page 428.)

Forbidden City Emperor's walled palace complex in Beijing.

geomancy Divinely correct positioning of structures.

Tiananmen Gate of Heavenly Peace, Beijing's main square.

Geography

HEAVENLY GOVERNMENT: CONCENTRATED AND ISOLATED

The Mongols who founded the Yuan dynasty first made Beijing China's capital in 1267 and it mostly stayed that way. The first two Ming emperors in the fourteenth century set up their capital in Nanjing ("Southern Capital," although it is actually in the middle of China's coast), but the third Ming emperor returned it to Beijing ("Northern Capital"). The southern-facing Nationalists restored Nanjing as their capital from 1928 to 1949, but to escape the Japanese they had to flee far up the Yangzi River to make Chongqing their wartime capital.

The Mings also founded the **Forbidden City** as the divine center of Beijing in the early fifteenth century on a strict north-south axis; the main entrance is the Meridian Gate, so named because it is directly aligned with heaven. **Geomancy** was always important in traditional China. Only the emperor, his family, and a relatively few officials and servants were allowed to enter the walled, 178-acre City, which contains numerous halls and temples. The Forbidden City aimed to show Chinese (and later foreigners) by awe and magnificence that the emperor was the center of the universe. Unfortunately, it was also a huge, costly, extravagant tax drain, which isolated the emperor and absurdly overconcentrated power at a site too far north to be China's original core area, which is to the south, in the Yellow and Yangzi River valleys.

The Communist regime has at great expense elaborately restored the Forbidden City and made it the country's number-one public museum and tourist attraction. It is designed to show how the Communists

The Gate of Heavenly Peace to the south of the Forbidden City still bears Mao's portrait, one of the last few public signs of his influence.

have returned China to its deserved status at the center of heaven. Mao gave his 1949 "China has stood up" speech from the huge Gate of Heavenly Peace overlooking the wide-open **Tiananmen** Square, at the southern end of which sits Mao's mausoleum (officially called a "memorial hall"). Some wonder if the current leaders' isolation and the concentration of power in the adjacent top government offices of the *Zhongnanhai* spell similar trouble for the Communist regime.

CCP could implode, leaving China without a backbone. Such revitalization would have to include, at a minimum, (1) a new, realistic statement of mission, of where the Party wants China to go; and (2) open disagreements among Party factions that media and citizens could discuss publicly. Allowing factions to publicly develop inside the Party could be a major step to eventual democratization, but nothing of the sort has been hinted at.

In organization, the CCP parallels the defunct CPSU. Hierarchies of Party congresses at the local, county, provincial, and national levels feed into corresponding Party committees. At the top is the National Party Congress; composed of some 2,100 delegates and supposed to meet at least once in five years, this congress nominally chooses a Central Committee of about 200 members. Since both bodies are too big to run things, real power is in the hands of a Politburo of about twenty Party chiefs. But this too is not the last level. Within the Politburo is a Standing Committee, now with nine members who really decide things. Power in China is highly concentrated.

The CCP's structure used to be a bit different from the classic Soviet model. Instead of a general secretary at its head, the CCP had a Party chairman, Mao's title, which he passed on to the short-term Hua Guofeng. By then, however, the office was robbed of meaning, and Hua was eclipsed by Senior Vice-Premier Deng Xiaoping, who, to be sure, also held important Party and army positions. Under Deng's guidance, the Party abolished the chairmanship—part of a repudiation of Mao's legacy—and upgraded the position of general secretary (*gensek*), so that now the CCP structure more closely matches that of the old CPSU. Since 2002 Hu Jintao has been CCP general secretary.

Geography

SOUTH VERSUS NORTH CHINA

The way South Chinese see it, they do all the work and make tremendous economic strides while North China, home of the Beijing bureaucrats, just spends their taxes propping up dinosaur industries mostly in the North: "We earn it, they waste it." South Chinese officials proudly show off their instant high-rise cities and industries, implying superiority over North China. Such regional economic resentments are found worldwide—they trouble Italy and ripped apart Yugoslavia—but tend to be especially dangerous in the developing lands, where they can lead to breakaway movements and even civil war. (See the Nigeria chapter for an example of angry tension between the region with oil and the regions without it.)

There is no easy fix for regional economic disparities. If you shrug them off and say the market will take care of these things—capital will be drawn automatically to low-cost areas—you let wide areas of your country stay poor, weak, and resentful. Even the United States set up the Tennessee Valley Authority to remedy such a disparity.

On the other hand, if you set up a fund—as many countries have done—to develop poorer provinces, the richer provinces (who pay the biggest taxes) resent their extra tax burden. They further argue (often correctly) that investments in backward areas are less efficient than in the already more developed areas, which have the infrastructure and trained people. In the poor area, you have to start from scratch. A government fund can make foolish, costly investments in unsuitable regions—"cathedrals in the desert," as Northern Italians say of their Fund for the South.

China, in the name of regional imbalances, is now extending its industrial zones deep inland, along the Pearl and Yangzi Rivers. Startup and shipping costs are higher than in the southern coastal provinces, but Beijing feels it must be done, and in the long run they are probably right. China cannot have hundreds of millions of its people leave poor inland provinces moving to the southern coast. Better to bring jobs to them in their home provinces.

Generations of Chinese Communist Rulers			Accomplishments
First	Mao and Zhou	1949–1976	Won revolution, brutally communized, destructive upheavals
Second	Deng	1977–1989	Calmed China, allowed private enterprise, crushed Tiananmen
Third	Jiang, Li, Zhu	1989–2002	Foreign investment, rapid growth
Fourth	Hu and Wen	2002–	

Deng arranged to have his protégé Hu Yaobang named general secretary. Hu, however, proved to be too liberal and unpredictable. He also failed to win approval of the army and was dropped in 1987. His place was taken by another Deng protégé, Zhao Ziyang, who in turn was ousted in 1989 for siding with student demonstrators. Replacing him was the hard-line mayor of Shanghai, Jiang Zemin, who retired as head of the Party in 2002 but retained important positions for a while afterwards, just as Deng Xiaoping did. In China, one man no longer rules; a handful of the Party elite does.

cadre French "framework," used by Asian Communists for local Party leader.

China's nervous system is its Party **cadres**. There are 30 million CCP cadres, and whoever controls them controls China. In 1979, Deng Xiaoping began the ticklish job of easing out both the incompetent old guard—whose only qualification, in many cases, was having been on the Long March—and the extreme leftists who wormed their way into the cadre structure during the tumultuous Cultural Revolution. Quietly, Deng brought in younger, better-educated cadres dedicated to his moderate, pragmatic line.

The Army

Until recently, all top figures in the Chinese elite held both high state and high Party offices, as in the old Soviet Union. In China, though, they also held high positions atop the military structure, through the important Central Military Commission, which interlocks with the CCP's Politburo. Mao, Hua, Deng, and Jiang were all chairmen of the Military Commission, as is Hu now. In addition, the CCP Standing Committee usually has a top general.

From the beginning, the People's Liberation Army (PLA), earlier known as the Chinese Red Army and Eighth Route Army, has been so intertwined with the CCP that it is hard to separate them. Deng named an active-duty general to the elite Politburo Standing Committee, and several on the Central Committee are PLA. Fighting the Nationalists and the Japanese for at least a decade and a half, the CCP became a combination of Party and army. The pattern continues to this day. Political scientist Robert Tucker called the Chinese system "military communism."

Mao wrote, "Political power grows out of the barrel of a gun," but "the Party commands the gun, and the gun must never be allowed to command the Party." Where the two are nearly merged, however, it is hard to tell who is on top. As the Communists took over China in the 1940s, it was the PLA that first set up their power structures. Until recently, China's executive decision makers all had extensive military experience, often as political commissars in PLA units. Said Zhou Enlai, who had been involved in military affairs since the 1920s: "We are all connected with the army."

When the Cultural Revolution broke out in 1966, as we shall see, the army first facilitated, then dampened, and finally crushed the Red Guards' rampages. By the time the Cultural Revolution sputtered out, the PLA was in de facto control of most provincial governments and most of the Politburo. Several Politburo members are still active military men. At various times during mobilization campaigns, the army is cited as a model for the rest of the country to follow, and heroic individual soldiers are celebrated in the media.

What does PLA influence mean for the governance of China? Armies, as guardians of their countries' security, define whatever is good for them as good for the country. Anyone who undermines their power earns their opposition. During the Cultural Revolution, for example, Defense Minister Lin Biao fanatically supported Mao's program to shake up the Party and state bureaucracy. (The army was not touched.) As the chaos spread, however, military commanders worried that it was sapping China's strength and military preparedness. Lin became increasingly isolated within the military. In 1971 Beijing released the amazing story that Lin had attempted a coup and tried to assassinate Mao. The official story was that Lin fled to the Soviet Union in a plane that crashed. Outside observers accept the attempted-coup story but think that Lin was executed. Mao's bodyguard, the secretive Unit 8341, foiled the Lin plot, making China at that point literally praetorian. Lin's supporters were purged from the military. The PLA thus helped tame Maoist radicalism.

Personalities

HU IS NEXT, AND WEN

Hu Jintao

Wen Jiabao

In 1989, when Deng Xiaoping at age eighty-five gave up his last formal post—chairman of the powerful Central Military Commission—he made sure two protégés took over: Party General Secretary Jiang Zemin (who also took on the title of president) and Premier Li Peng. They were, respectively, sixty-three and sixty-one years old, the "third generation" of Beijing's Communist rulers. In 1998, when Li's two five-year terms were up, he was replaced as premier by Zhu Rongji, then seventy.

All three of these leaders kept firm central control of politics while encouraging the growth of a market economy. All silenced troublesome intellectuals. All were graduate engineers—still the case today—giving their rule a technocratic bent. None were popular, nor did they seek popularity. None returned to the visions of Mao, but all were cautious about major change. None suggested democracy in China's future. In late 2002, Jiang gave up his Party position, and in 2003 Premier Zhu retired.

China obtained its "fourth generation" of Communist leaders at the Sixteenth Communist Party conference in late 2002. Succeeding Jiang was Vice President Hu Jintao, then fifty-nine, picked by Deng Xiaoping before he died. An engineer, Hu was typed as an obedient technocrat. He was formally elected China's president by the National People's Congress in March 2003. Jiang tried to stay influential, as chair of the Central Military Commission, but in 2004, at age 78, he reluctantly stepped down, and President Hu became China's military chief, thus completing the triple transfer of power—head of party, of executive, of military. Succeeding Premier Zhu in 2003 was Deputy Premier Wen Jiabao, then sixty. Wen trained as a geologist but is experienced in finance and agriculture; he is reputed to be extremely bright. We do not know who will replace them, or when.

China's attempted coup revealed a latent *praetorianism* that marks it as a Third World country (see our Nigeria chapter).

China's leaders seem to have decided that the army is not a good way to control domestic unrest. (They are right.) The PLA did not like mowing down students in Tiananmen in 1989. To deal with such situations, Beijing built up the People's Armed Police (PAP), now over 1 million strong. These **paramilitary** police, believed to be under PLA control, are sometimes called *internal security forces*. In addition, in 2005, riot police and anti-terrorist squads were merged into "special police," probably in preparation for the 2008 Olympics.

China's leaders pay special attention to the PLA and are now increasing its budget, but the PLA, with 2.3 million soldiers, is still poor and underequipped. Trying to supplement its meager budget, the PLA went massively into private industry, running some 15,000 businesses. Worried about the PLA's corruption, smuggling, and loss of mission, President Jiang ordered the army to get out of business and get back to soldiering. They complied, indicating that the Party still commands the gun. In general, the PLA has been a conservative force in Chinese politics, for almost axiomatically, an army stands for order and sees disorder as a security problem. In China, when chaos threatens, the army moves.

In 2005 U.S. Defense Secretary Donald Rumsfeld expressed apprehension over China's rapidly growing defense budget, which probably understates actual expenditures. He asked what is China going to use its modernized forces for? The obvious answer is to take Taiwan, either by amphibious invasion across the Formosa Strait or, more likely, by intimidation that will frighten Taiwan into a mainland takeover without military resistance. Recovery of the "renegade province" of Taiwan burns brightly in the PLA, but it is not clear if the PLA sets Taiwan policy or has a deadline in mind. A top PLA general in 2005 warned bluntly of something nasty and nuclear if the United States interferes in the return of Taiwan to China. The PLA is still a major player in Chinese politics.

paramilitary National police force organized and equipped like a light army, such as French *CRS*.

autonomous region Soviet-style home area for ethnic minority.

■ A Unitary System with Chinese Characteristics

China, like most countries in the world, is organized on a unitary rather than federal pattern. China has twenty-three provinces, five autonomous regions, and four huge cities—Beijing, Chongqing, Shanghai, Tianjin—which count as provinces. In China, a "small" city like Xian, capital of Shaanxi Province, has 7 million people. China has 200 cities with populations of over 1 million. China lists Taiwan as its twenty-third province, something many Taiwanese do not wish to happen. Hong Kong and Macau—recently taken over from, respectively, Britain and Portugal—are designated *special administrative regions* and are allowed to preserve local laws and economic systems (capitalist) for several decades.

The concept of an **autonomous region** was borrowed from Stalin's organization of the Soviet Union, where large nationalities got their own *Soviet republics* and smaller ones got autonomous regions within those republics. In practice they were not very autonomous, and neither are China's. China's purpose here is the same as Stalin's: to give possibly troublesome ethnic groups use of their language and the feeling that they run local affairs.

The most troublesome are the 8 million Turkic-speaking Muslim Uygurs of Central Asia in Xinjiang (literally "new frontier," named by the Manchu Qing dynasty). Some Uygurs, radicalized by Islamic fundamentalism elsewhere, have set off bombs in China. Tibet has a distinctive Buddhist culture and long ago was independent. First acquired by the Mongols in the thirteenth century as part of their Yuan dynasty, Tibet (*Xizang*) has been claimed by China ever since. The PLA crushed a major Tibetan independence uprising in the 1950s. Another potential troublesome area, Inner Mongolia (*Nei Mongol*), home of nomadic Buddhist herders, covers a huge swath along China's northern border. Stalin set up Outer Mongolia as independent Mongolia, a buffer on Russia's underbelly. China's autonomous regions have been gradually brought under Beijing's control by settling millions of Han Chinese in them.

Although a unitary system, Chinese administration is almost dangerously decentralized. Most national laws are written very generally and let provinces devise their own laws. Chinese lawyers advising foreign investors must now know the laws and usages of each province (and implicitly, whom to bribe). In China, one law does not fit all. Deng's administrative decentralization opened the gates to massive corruption as local officials seek cash incentives to interpret laws in the needed fashion. In a minor 2003 case about the price of seeds, a young woman judge in Henan Province ruled that national law overrides provincial law. Chinese jurists hoped it would modernize the unprofessional and corrupt court system and lead to judicial autonomy. "It may not be *Marbury v. Madison*," said a Chinese constitutional scholar, "but it is a very important case."

Key Terms

autonomous region (p. 433)
Beida (p. 426)
cadre (p. 431)
Comintern (p. 426)
Forbidden City (p. 429)
Gang of Four (p. 429)

geomancy (p. 429)
Kremlinology (p. 424)
paramilitary (p. 433)
Tiananmen (p. 429)
Zhongnanhai (p. 424)

Further Reference

Chang, Jung, and Jon Halliday. *Mao: The Unknown Story.* New York: Knopf, 2005.
Dreyer, June Teufel. *China's Political System: Modernization and Tradition,* 5th ed. New York: Longman, 2006.
Gilley, Bruce. *China's Democratic Future: How It Will Happen and Where it Will Lead.* New York: Columbia University Press, 2004.
Gittings, John. *The Changing Face of China: From Mao to Market.* New York: Oxford University Press, 2005.
Gries, Peter Hays, and Stanley Rosen. *State and Society in 21st Century China: Crisis, Contention, Legitimacy.* New York: Routledge, 2004.
Howe, Christopher, Y. Y. Kueh, and Robert Ash, eds. *China's Economic Reform: A Study with Documents.* New York: Routledge, 2003.

Kuhn, Robert Lawrence. *The Man Who Changed China: The Life and Legacy of Jiang Zemin*. New York: Crown, 2005.

Li, Cheng. *China's Leaders: The New Generation*. New York: Rowman & Littlefield, 2001.

Lü, Xiaobo. *Cadres and Corruption: The Organizational Involution of the Chinese Communist Party*. Stanford, CA: Stanford University Press, 2000.

Nathan, Andrew J., and Bruce Gilley. *China's New Rulers: The Secret Files*. New York: New York Review of Books, 2002.

Saich, Tony. *Governance and Politics of China*, 2nd ed. London: Palgrave, 2004.

Chapter 30

CHINESE
POLITICAL CULTURE

One of the problems of the Third World countries is that few have a consistent political culture that has grown slowly over time. Instead—as we will also see in Mexico and Iran—they have imported and distorted waves of outside ideas that rarely blend into a coherent whole. And each wave of ideas is overthrown, often violently, by the next. We can see, for example, at least three layers in Chinese political culture. They sometimes reinforce and sometimes contradict one another.

Traditional Culture

Mao used to say that his countrymen were "firstly poor, secondly blank," meaning that the Communists could start with a clean slate and create the Chinese citizens they wished. Mao was wrong. Many values deeply engrained over two and a half millennia of Chinese civilization have carried over into the People's Republic. No one, not even Mao, could wipe them clean. Indeed, even Mao's vision of perfecting human nature by thinking right thoughts is a Confucian notion. Even after a century of upheaval, Chinese are still basically polite and deferential, testimony to the staying power of Confucianism.

When the Communists restored Beijing as the capital in 1949, they were restoring an old symbol, because Jiang's Nationalists had moved the capital to Nanjing (Southern Capital). Many traditionalists felt Beijing (Northern Capital) was the legitimate one. Top government offices and elite living quarters are in the Zhongnanhai, across the street from the old Forbidden City of the emperors. Tiananmen (Gate of Heavenly Peace) Square is still Beijing's parade and demonstration area, much like Red Square is in Moscow.

Another major symbol carried over from China's history is the deeply held conviction that China is one country and must never be divided, first articulated by Confucian intellectuals in reaction to the time of the Warring States. The Qing (Manchu) dynasty annexed Taiwan only in 1683 (to stop Taiwanese pirates and a Dutch takeover), but Chinese still feel strongly it is an eternal part of China and must soon reunify with the motherland. They are not adverse to using force to this end. We feel that Beijing exaggerates the Taiwan question, but it is part of Chinese political culture.

Questions to Consider

1. Could any country be culturally "blank," as Mao said?
2. How much of traditional China lingers under the surface?
3. How does the regime now use China's history?
4. Is China now more nationalist or Communist? How can you tell?
5. Compare the three layers of China's political culture with Iran's.
6. Why does Beijing inflict periodic upheavals on China? What were the big ones?
7. What is "voluntarism" and how did Mao exemplify it?
8. How does China's political culture resemble Russia's?
9. Could nationalism turn aggressive in China?

The Communists' bureaucrats and cadres perform much the same function as the old Mandarins and gentry. Reciting the latest Party line instead of Confucius, the new elites strive to place a huge population under central control and guidance. Their aim now, to be sure, is growth and modernization, but still under a central hand. Mao himself recognized the similarity of old and new when he denounced the bureaucrats as the "new Mandarins" during the Cultural Revolution. Deng Xiaoping governed in the old Confucian style.

Another carryover from Old China: Age confers special qualities of wisdom and leadership in the People's Republic. Mao died at eighty-two and Zhou at seventy-eight, both in office. When he returned to power in 1977, Deng Xiaoping was seventy-three. In his early nineties he was still politically influential although weak and deaf. Former President Jiang and Prime Minister Zhu still governed in their seventies. Trying to break the tendency to gerontocracy, the Party now does not appoint anyone over seventy to a new position.

Geography

PEASANTS IN THE CITIES

One of the characteristics of the Third World is rapid urbanization. Unemployed or underemployed rural people flock to cities looking for jobs and improved standards of living. The trend is strong in China, where the urban-rural gap is huge. Historically, some 90 percent of Chinese lived in the countryside, and over 60 percent—some eight-tenths of a billion people—still do. They are not all peasant farmers; some pursue other rural trades, such as construction and vehicle repair. But in the last quarter-century a quarter-million rural Chinese have left for the cities (some illegally), making China nearly 40 percent urban, an incredible change with many ramifications.

Back in the village, discontent is no worse than it has always been. Most peasants are wretchedly poor, with some families living on around $1 a day. They can feed themselves, but any medical expense leaves them destitute. There are no health plans in rural China: no money, no treatment. When peasants have gone to a city to look for work—at 30 yuan ($3.60) a day in pick-and-shovel construction—they often become discontented. They see the vastly better life of the emerging urban middle class—apartments, cars, money to spend—and resent their lowly status. They also resent the regime spending billions to redo Beijing to impress foreigners for the 2008 Olympics. The games are prestigious but do nothing for them.

There is still a carryover of peasant mentality in the willingness to work hard for one's family and not ask for much. Earthy peasant humor and folkways and frugal personal habits are found not only in villages today but in cities and industries. Many urban and educated Chinese remember growing up poor in a village. Unfortunately, newly arrived peasants in the cities also take a while to learn elementary sanitation and politeness. Spitting on the sidewalks and reckless driving are standard.

Peasants in the cities represent a huge problem for the regime. On the one hand, they know they have to get Chinese out of peasant farming. There is simply not enough land, and ignorant, uneducated peasants do not move China ahead. Unrest is growing in rural China as peasants protest land seizures and local officials who pocket fake taxes. On the other hand, the regime knows its cities cannot absorb additional hundreds of millions of rural newcomers, even if they are willing to live in shacks. They fear a large, angry urban underclass might lend their numbers to protests started by students and intellectuals. (There are, however, few such contacts across social classes, and the regime aims to keep it that way.)

Beijing's current "fourth generation" leaders claim they are fighting rural poverty by spreading rapid industrialization inland, up the great river valleys, and into towns and smaller cities. They are trying to bring jobs to the peasants rather than peasants to the cities. If they can do this, they may succeed in bringing China's rural people up to a level of education and sophistication that could sustain democracy.

■ Nationalism

Overpowering traditional Chinese values is a more recent one, the nationalism that has dominated China's intellectual life for more than a century. Chinese nationalism, like Third World nationalism generally, is the result of a proud and ancient civilization suffering penetration, disorientation, and humiliation at the hands of the West and Japan. This can induce explosive fury and the feeling that the native culture, although temporarily beaten by foreigners, is morally better and more enduring. In our day, Chinese, Russians, and Iranians still act out their resentment of the West, especially of America. Most of what Beijing does today—from economic growth to space launches to hosting the 2008 Olympics—is out of a sense of nationalism. For the sake of Chinese power, Beijing has even accepted capitalism. Chinese communism is at heart Chinese nationalism.

In Asia, Chinese and Japanese nationalists vowed to beat the West at its own game, building industry and weaponry but placing them at the service of the traditional culture. The Japanese modernizers, starting with the 1868 *Meiji Restoration* (see pages 343–344), were able to carry out their designs; the Chinese are still caught up in this process, which from time to time leaps out in self-destructive campaigns. All of the founding generation of Chinese Communist leaders, including Mao and Zhou, began as young patriots urging their countrymen to revitalize China and stand up to the West and to Japan.

As in the old Soviet Union, the prevailing Chinese attitude is the nationalist drive to catch up with the West. During their good economic-growth years—the mid-1950s and since 1980—Chinese leaders were proud of their rapid progress. The Great Leap Forward and the Cultural Revolution ruined the economy. A pragmatic moderate such as Zhou or Deng always had a powerful argument against such disruptions: They harm growth and weaken China. Basically, this is a nationalist argument and one used by pragmatists today.

Chinese are deeply patriotic, sometimes in a negative way. Anti-U.S. Chinese nationalism is growing. Part is deep and genuine, part is hyped by the regime. Chinese do not like any foreigners pushing them around. Tension with the United States over Taiwan and American pressures regarding human rights and copyright violations spark government-approved anti-U.S. campaigns. A popular book (modeled on an earlier Japanese book), *China Can Say No*, portrayed a vast conspiracy led by America to keep China down (the same line put out by extreme Russian nationalists). Well, America better watch out, the book said, because China will defend itself. Chinese got angry when U.S. jets mistakenly bombed the Chinese embassy in Belgrade in 1999 and a U.S. surveillance plane entered Chinese airspace in 2001.

Anti-U.S. feelings are nothing compared to anti-Japanese feelings in China. Chinese deeply remember how the Japanese army butchered Chinese civilians, even babies, during World War II. The 1937 Japanese "Rape of Nanjing"—with an estimated 20,000 female victims—is especially remembered. In 2005 Beijing again sponsored anti-Japanese protests. Emperor Akihito and some Japanese prime ministers, after a delay of several decades, have apologized for Japan's World War II crimes against China, but Japanese textbooks increasingly minimize or fail to mention the crimes, and Tokyo politicians still visit the Yasukuni Shrine, which honors war criminals among Japan's dead soldiers.

Beijing turns on and off anti-U.S., anti-Japanese, or take-over Taiwan demonstrations to deflect mass discontent, a very old governing technique. These outpourings are partly government-contrived but have strong roots in Chinese nationalism, especially against Japan. The trouble is, once the protests get rolling, the protesters become too eager and use the demonstrations to vent displeasure at the Communist regime. Without exception, the regime gets frightened and abruptly calls off the protests as "an evil plot to undermine the Communist party" and warns citizens to behave. Especially enthusiastic protesters are jailed. "Look at how worried they are," grinned one Beijing businessman at the 2005 anti-Japan demonstrations. "They lit a spark and set off a wildfire."

Maoism   Extreme form of communism, featuring guerrilla warfare and periodic upheavals.

Qin   First dynasty to unify China, 221–206 B.C.

Taiwan   Large island off China's southern coast, ruled by Nationalists since 1945.

Korean War   1950–1953 conflict involving North and South Korean, U.S., and Chinese forces.

Anti-Japanese War   Chinese name for World War II in China, 1937–1945.

Maoism

China's constitution still proclaims **Maoism**, or Mao Zedong Thought as Beijing calls it, as one of the bases of modern China, but in practice it has faded to empty recitation. Maoism draws from both traditional and nationalistic values, despite its claim to be totally new and revolutionary. From traditional China, it takes the Confucian emphasis on thinking right thoughts, based on the idea that consciousness determines existence rather than the reverse: Willpower is more important than weaponry in wars; willpower is more important than technology in building China. The unleashed forces

Political Culture

HOW CHINA USES ITS PAST

Mao hated old China and denounced it as feudal and reactionary. During the Cultural Revolution he encouraged Red Guards to "destroy the four olds." Zhou Enlai quietly ordered the army to protect important sites from their rampages. Since Mao's death in 1976, the regime has rediscovered—much as Stalin did—the utility of history: The past, artfully interpreted, makes it easier to rule the present. Beijing now uses old China to deliver lessons for today.

In 1974—fortunately after the worst of the Cultural Revolution—a farmer digging a well in the inland Shaanxi Province found the terra-cotta soldiers of **Qin** Shihuang, the emperor who first united China in 221 B.C. Archeologists unearthed thousands of fragments—there could be well over 7,000 figures all together—and from them reconstructed hundreds of the life-size soldiers. Each one is different, apparently modeled on strapping individual soldiers of that day. To protect Qin in the afterlife, all were equipped with weapons (looted very early) and drawn up into companies of pikemen, archers, cavalry, and so on. They were originally painted in lifelike colors. Chinese and foreign tourists now swarm to see them at a major pilgrimage site near the city of Xian. The message: China's unity is eternal. You got that, **Taiwan**? (Actually, the pirate sanctuary of Taiwan was taken over by the Qing dynasty only in 1683.)

Likewise Beijing's Military Museum (which has its own subway stop) now devotes much space to a historical review of all China's dynasties, emphasizing that each had to be very strong in the face of peasant uprisings, breakaway provinces, and Mongol or Manchu invasions. No dynasty enjoyed tranquil times; all had to be prepared. If they weakened, they perished. Attempts to undermine or overthrow the emperor were punished by torture and dismemberment. You got that, intellectuals and troublemakers? Also in the Military Museum (but without English captions) is how the heroism of the PLA won the **Korean War**, which China fought to block U.S. aggression. You got that, Americans?

The strongest use of the past in today's China is the **Anti-Japanese War** of 1937–1945. (Remember, World War II began in China earlier than in Europe.) Beijing, in addition to the Military Museum, has a separate Anti-Japanese War Museum that stresses the atrocities the invaders committed. Television series show how China "fought bravely against Japan under the leadership of the Communist party." With communism no longer a usable ideology, the regime hypes hatred of Japan to deflect discontent and hold China together. The regime thunders against Japan getting nuclear weapons or a permanent seat on the UN Security Council, and all Chinese agree. You got that, Tokyo?

of the masses, guided by Mao Zedong Thought, can conquer anything. This extreme form of **voluntarism** comes from China's past.

From nationalism, Mao took the emphasis on strengthening and
rebuilding China so that it could stand up to its old enemies and become a world power. The trouble is that these two strands are partly
at odds with each other. Traditional values call for China to ignore the
West and its technology, but nationalistic values call for China to
learn and copy from the West. The continuing, unresolved conflict of these two streams of thought
spells permanent trouble for China.

Maoism is an outgrowth of Mao's thoughts on guerrilla warfare (see page 419). According to
Maoist doctrine, what the PLA did to beat the Nationalists, China as a whole must do to advance
and become a world leader: Work with the masses, be self-reliant, and use more willpower than

voluntarism Belief that human will
can change the world.

Century of Humiliation China's term
for its domination by imperialists from
first Opium War to Communist victory,
1839–1949.

Beijing often invokes its "**Century of Humiliation**"
and sees its every move as erasing the humiliations and
restoring China to its rightful place in the world. Mao's
mausoleum is perfectly on-axis with the Meridian Gate
of the Forbidden City across Tiananmen Square, just
where the old geomancers would have sited it. Mao's
continuity with the past he hated is now for all Chinese
to see. In 2005 archeologists unearthed a 4,000-year-
old bowl of petrified noodles, proving that China invented pasta. You got that, Italians?

*The terra cotta soldiers of Emperor Qin, who first united China in 221 B.C., remind Chinese of the unity
and strength of their country.*

technology to overcome obstacles. Mao can be seen as a theorist of guerrilla warfare who continued to apply his principles to governance—with catastrophic results.

In the Great Leap Forward from 1958 to 1960, Mao tried guerrilla warfare tactics on the economy, using raw manual labor plus enthusiasm to build earthen dams and backyard blast furnaces. Engineers, experts, and administrators were bypassed. The Soviets warned Mao it would not work and urged him to follow the Soviet model of building the economy by more conventional means; Mao refused. In 1960, unhappy with Mao's radicalism, the Soviets withdrew their numerous foreign-aid technicians, and the Sino-Soviet split became public.

For the Soviet Communists, the revolution was over; the proletariat triumphed in 1917 and moved Russia into the most advanced stage of history. For Mao, the revolution never ends. Mao held that at any stage there are conservative tendencies that block the path to socialism: bureaucratism, elitism, and opportunism. Mao resolved to combat these tendencies by means of "permanent revolution," periodic upheavals to let the force of the masses surge past the conservative bureaucrats.

Socialism and bureaucratism are closely connected—as Max Weber saw long ago—but Mao thought he could break the connection. He saw China settling into the bureaucratic patterns he hated and was determined to reverse it by instituting a permanent revolution. The result was the Great Proletarian Cultural Revolution from 1966 to 1976, during which young people were encouraged to criticize, harass, and oust all authority except the army. Chaos spread through China, the economy slumped, and the army took over. Shortly after Mao's death, power returned to the bureaucrats; they won and Mao failed.

Mao refused to recognize the unhappy truth that if you want socialism you must accept the big bureaucracy that comes with it. By trying to leap directly into a sort of guerrilla socialism without bureaucrats, Mao nearly wrecked China. On balance, Mao Zedong Thought is inherently inapplicable, and in today's China Mao is quoted little and out of context. Such vague homilies as "Get truth from facts" lets leaders claim they are following Mao even as they repudiate him. Mao's picture is on Tiananmen and *all* paper currency, but he has become a meaningless symbol used to try to hold together a decaying Party.

Key Concepts

DEFLECTING DISCONTENT

Yale's Harold Lasswell (1902–1978) helped define American political science with his 1936 classic *Politics: Who Gets What*. In that and other works Lasswell claimed that psychology explains much of politics. He argued, among many other points, that a nervous regime will try to deflect discontent away from itself, its problems and shortcomings, and onto allegedly threatening foreign powers; in a word, nationalism.

China's current rulers behave as if they have read Lasswell, cranking up (and then cranking down) anti-U.S. and anti-Japanese campaigns at periodic intervals. Many Chinese are tired of these campaigns and ignore them. The U.S. Congress is not bad at this game either, blaming China for everything from loss of jobs to oil prices. Twenty years earlier, they blamed Japan.

■ Crouching Anger, Hidden Dissent

Protests and demonstrations are increasing in China—among rural people, unemployed rust-belt workers, and Muslim **Uygurs** in **Xinjiang** Province in the west. Security officials admit there are tens of thousands of "mass incidents" every year, some of them ending in police gunfire. So far, protests have been purely local and unorganized; most seem to be spontaneous and related to specific grievances, such as evictions, land seizures, pollution, and corrupt officials. Local democracy would let angry people vote out crooked officials, but the regime is cautious about even small-scale democracy. Instead, it crushes protests, jails leaders, and smothers news reports. Brave souls who criticize corruption and incompetence—journalists, lawyers, medical doctors, and academics—are fired, harassed, and arrested. The doctor and editor who first reported the SARS virus were jailed. Workers who try to organize labor unions languish in prison. A nervous regime and Party, afraid that criticisms undermine their rule, deny and cover up problems.

One may find reasoned criticism and intellectual calls for reforms in China's cities, which have always been the sparkplugs of dissent. Although a small minority, the urban educated classes have often taken the lead in changing China. Student protests in Beijing, for example, go back more than a century; Mao himself as a young man participated in the student May Fourth Movement of 1919. Such protests contributed much to the overthrow of the Empire and the rise of first the Nationalists and then the Communists.

During the twentieth century, educated Chinese generally had a cause to believe in. At first it was building a new republic that would not be carved up by foreigners. Then it was in repelling the

Uygur   Muslim, Turkic-speaking ethnic group bordering ex-Soviet Central Asia; sometimes spelled *Uighur*.

Xinjiang   China's northwesternmost province, home of *Uygurs*.

Political Culture

BEIJING RULES

Much can be learned from a taxi ride in Beijing. (Under no circumstances drive yourself.) Streets are crowded, sometimes clogged. Drivers dodge, weave, force their way, even drive on the wrong side of the street. They nearly run over bicyclists, pedestrians, and three-wheeled cargo motorcycles. A left turn into oncoming traffic is like a video game. But there are few collisions. Drivers are skilled and miss each other by inches. Car drivers yield only grudgingly to big trucks and buses. Beijing Rules are basically: "There are no rules." Actually, there are plenty of rules, but they are not enforced or even understood, so people do whatever they can get away with. In fairness, this lawless culture is standard throughout the Third World. Mexicans and Nigerians understand it perfectly; only Americans are shocked by it.

This "no-rules" rule seems to apply to China's laws, government regulation, diplomacy, corruption, shopping, and much else. It may be illegal in some law book, but one does whatever it takes to get ahead in business or traffic. The Chinese fighter pilot who clipped a U.S. surveillance plane in 2001 (he died) was flying by Beijing Rules. The massive pirating of foreign DVDs and sneaker and handbag labels are Beijing Rules. No accounting and banking standards are Beijing Rules. Beijing Rules exemplify the lack of civil society, of the usages and interactions that over time build up into polite, predictable behavior. Beijing Rules make China colorful but lawless. Eventually, China will have to evolve some rules.

Daoism (From Dao, "the way") old Chinese religion originally based on nature; earlier spelled *Taoism*.

Jesuit Society of Jesus, Catholic religious order once especially active in converting Asians.

Japanese invaders. With the Communist takeover, many Chinese idealistically believed that Mao offered them a blueprint for a prosperous, socialist China. After Mao, Deng Xiaoping offered the image of a prosperous, semicapitalist China. After the June 1989 massacre of prodemocracy students in Tiananmen Square, many Chinese fell into despair. For most, Marx, Mao, and Deng have been discredited, and the Party now has nothing to offer except a better job for some.

What then do Chinese have to believe in? Make money, that's all. Chinese now display an almost complete lack of values. Confucian values are erased, bourgeois

Political Culture

CHRISTIAN CHINA?

China appears even more irreligious than Japan. Nowadays money seems to be China's only religion. Buddhism in China was historically less important than Confucianism (which, strictly speaking, is not a religion). Buddhism (see page 444) never rooted itself in China as deeply as in Tibet, Japan, or Vietnam. Traces of **Daoism** survive only in the cult of luck, which many Chinese are still obsessed with as the way to win money. The number nine, for example, is especially lucky and desirable. Muslims, both the Central Asian Uygurs of Xinjiang and the Chinese Hui Muslims in several pockets throughout China, may total 2 percent.

Nobody knows how many Chinese are Christians, as many attend "home churches" outside of the few state-supervised churches. Estimates put Christians at 3 to 6 percent of China's people, a number believed to be quietly growing. Because other religions are so weak, Christians by default form China's biggest group of believers. The Communists (and long ago the Boxers) always regarded Christianity as an unwelcome foreign import that missionaries used to subordinate China to the imperialists. Foreigners with known church connections are watched like hawks as possible secret missionaries.

There has been a Catholic presence in China for centuries—first brought to China, as to Japan, by brilliant **Jesuits**—but the Communists in the 1950s ordered the Catholic Church to break with Rome and become a state-supervised "national" church, which includes a large cathedral in Beijing. The regime does not permit Rome to appoint bishops—foreign influence again—so there can be no ordination of new

priests. Ordination of priests by Communist-appointed bishops does not count as Catholic, says Rome. Since 1980 there have been a few cautious contacts between Rome and Beijing, but these are slow to develop for at least two good reasons. The Vatican insists on the right to appoint bishops—which in effect means taking back the church from regime hands—and Beijing insists on Rome breaking with Taiwan.

Some Chinese intellectuals, including a few at the official Academy of Social Sciences, note that Protestant Christianity first appeared in northwest Europe and made it capitalist, rich, and strong (a theory advanced a century ago by German sociologist Max Weber). Accordingly, it might not be a bad thing for China. On this basis, some Chinese intellectuals could be potential converts to Christianity. They, however, have little or no contact with the broad masses of Chinese and are unlikely to link up with underground churches. Christian intellectuals combined with broad masses of believers could produce a major Christian interest group in China, which is why the regime prevents it.

The regime fears any alternate organization that could challenge or ignore the Party. If Beijing permitted it, Christianity could spread rapidly in China, making the missionaries' old dream of a prosperous and democratic Christian China come true. Chinese badly need something to believe in, and Chinese society badly needs the pluralism that comes with churches. Allowing the free exercise of religion would mark a major step toward pluralism and democracy in China.

values never took hold, and Maoist values are discarded. As in Russia after the collapse of communism, China has an "anything goes" mentality in which everyone is out for themselves with no notion of a common good. This is partly the fault of the CCP's power monopoly: It alone is allowed to define the common good, and it fails to do so. Chinese live in a spiritual vacuum, which may be communism's saddest legacy. The regime does not mind the lack of values because it makes Chinese easier to govern. In the long run, though, something will fill the vacuum. We can only guess what it might be.

Tibet   Himalayan region of China with distinct language and culture.

Putonghua   "Common language" of China, now standard; used to be called Mandarin.

Missing in China is the *civil society* that is also weak in Russia (see Chapter 20). As Alexis de Tocqueville observed in *Democracy in America*, these are the autonomous associations bigger than the family but smaller than the state—churches, labor unions, business firms, bicycle clubs, voluntary groups—and the habits and usages that come with them. Such associations are the basis of pluralism and a prerequisite of stable democracy. There are growing numbers of business people and homeowners in China and some of them form associations. But the regime supervises and controls these associations and does not permit them to challenge or demand much from the regime. The key to pluralism is *autonomous* organizations, those outside of state control. (A few business people are co-opted into the CCP.) This has several negative ramifications. No organized group can put leverage on the regime to clean up China's horrendous air and water pollution. Individuals may make environmental statements from time to time, and provided they do not push it too hard may get away

Geography

REGION AND LANGUAGE

China illustrates the close connection—and problems—between a country's languages and its regions. All but small countries have regions, often based on language. In some cases, as between Serbs and Albanian-speaking Kosovars, the country splits apart. China is populated mostly by Han Chinese (there are important non-Han minorities in **Tibet**, Xinjiang, and elsewhere), but Han are divided into several languages.

China's rulers have always proclaimed the unity of China, but China is the world's most linguistically complex country with eight main language groups—mutually unintelligible—and hundreds of dialects. The biggest language by far is Mandarin, dialects of which are spoken by 800 million in a broad swath from north to south, but not in the important southern coastal provinces, where 90 million speak some form of the Wu language (including Shanghai) and 70 million speak Cantonese.

China's rulers have always feared that separate languages could lead to breakaway tendencies. Since

1913 under the KMT, the regime has tried to make Mandarin standard and universal. The Communist regime has largely succeeded with the modified Beijing dialect of **Putonghua**, now the language of government and education. Putonghua has been the classroom language starting in elementary school for some time, so now most Chinese who have been educated in the last quarter-century can speak it, sometimes along with the local language. A Shanghai professional, for example, might speak the Shanghai language for daily life but switch to Putonghua to communicate with non-Shanghai Chinese. (In addition, the Shanghai professional is likely to know English, needed for international business.) Unfortunately, some Chinese children get little schooling, and in the countryside local dialects are still used, especially by old people. The new prosperity in China's southern coastal provinces has actually boosted the use of their local dialects. Beijing is not pleased.

blog From "web log"; self-published reviews and comments on Internet.

with it. No group can organize an environmental protest—any who try are quickly arrested—or support elected representatives. No pluralism means no inputting devices from masses to rulers.

Religion, both old (including Christianity) and new, is growing rapidly despite the arrest, imprisonment, and torture of believers. The sudden rise in the 1990s of a new religion, *Falun Gong* (Buddhist Law), illustrates what happens to a spiritual vacuum: Dubious faiths rush in to fill it. Falun Gong attracted all kinds of Chinese with faith healing and traditional exercises. As we saw in Japan, Buddhism generates offshoots without limit. Beijing understands that religion can bring upheaval—the Taipings and Boxers in the nineteenth century—and in 1999 denounced Falun Gong as a brainwashing cult, outlawed it, and arrested thousands of its followers. This is the reaction of a nervous regime. The chief commandment of Communist regimes: Thou shalt have no autonomous associations outside the control of the Party. The result is a yet-deeper vacuum where there should be a political culture.

Some educated Chinese have rediscovered classic liberalism—the philosophy of freedom and small government of Locke, Adam Smith, and Jefferson—that was popular a century ago among Chinese intellectuals. Now young Chinese returning with American MBAs understand the free markets extolled by Hayek and Friedman. This could challenge the stale Marxism of the regime and lead to democracy, but discussions are low key and among friends. Open advocacy of liberalism could get you in trouble.

Over the decades, Chinese became politically numb. They had to mouth slogans and participate in mass campaigns—one year anti-Confucius, the next anti-capitalist roaders, then anti-Gang of Four, then anti-"spiritual pollution," then anti-"bourgeois liberalization"—without end. Chinese are fed up with this nonsense and mentally tune out. They become apolitical.

The great hope for Chinese students is to go abroad. Many study English and dream of joining the thousands of Chinese students already in the United States, many of whom do not return to China. The regime, aware of this brain drain, now restricts their numbers. Chinese university graduates are supposed to first work five years before they can apply for graduate study overseas. The great prize: a graduate degree, often an MBA, from a prestigious U.S. university. Some high-ranking Chinese get their children into such programs.

The Chinese way of handling the latest government crackdown on freedom and democracy is called *biaotai,* "to express an attitude." Chinese know how to crank out the current line while concealing their true feelings. This leads to what Chinese call *nei jin, wai song,* "tranquility outside, repression within." Everything looks calm, but only because people know they are being carefully watched. Just below the surface, though, repressed anger waits to erupt. Some of this shows up in the constant flow of nasty rumors about repression, economic incompetence, and the corruption of officials. This has been called a struggle between the Big Lie and Little Whisper: The government tries to fool people with big lies, but the people fight back with little whispers. Chinese, knowing that contacts with foreigners may be monitored, are reluctant to discuss anything political (or religious) with visitors.

Electronic media now provide an outlet for discontent. China has an estimated 100 million Internet users, a number sure to increase. Thousands of censors supervise China's Net, filtering e-mails for key words such as "democracy," "Tiananmen," and "Taiwan." The regime jails some **bloggers** for "subverting state power," but hundreds evade identification and ridicule the regime indirectly to a booming audience. Great subversive potential comes with cellphones, used by over 350 million Chinese and impossible to monitor. (You can text message in Chinese, using the keypad to enter brushstrokes.)

Such a controlled system is frightened and unstable. Most Chinese are apolitical, but a small fraction dislikes and distrusts the regime. They are more prevalent in the South, which has long resented rule by the North. Many Chinese are frustrated with a Party elite that simply wants to cling to its power and good jobs and hinders China's progress. They know that in the southern coastal zones, where capitalism and foreign investment began, the economy is booming. Why then not just expand free enterprise until it covers all of China? They also know that Taiwanese enjoy five times the per capita income and far more freedom than mainlanders. Some Chinese students speak with shame that they did not have the guts to do what the Romanians did in 1989: stand up to the government's guns and overthrow the regime. In time, Chinese student frustration could boil over again.

bourgeoisie   French for middle class; adjective *bourgeois*.

Qinghua   China's top technological university, in Beijing (still often spelled in Wade-Giles, *Tsinghua*).

Key Concepts

A BOURGEOIS CHINA?

One of the contradictions now troubling China is the fact that a Marxist country is rapidly creating a middle class, precisely the class it claims to staunchly oppose. Anti-bourgeois ideology is woven into Marxism. Even as a student Marx hated the bourgeoisie; he later developed his complex theories to prove that they were doomed. Actually, they were and still are the most successful social class in history. The **bourgeoisie** rose with the modern state and created the modern economy. They also brought democracy, personal freedom, education, and mass communications. Marxists are loath to admit that middle classes do anything good. They may be a temporary necessity but only in the march to a proletarian paradise.

Now China is creating a new middle class at a record-setting rate by expanding its universities. The regime, itself run by engineers, educates massive numbers of engineers and scientists to push China's economic growth. The portion of young Chinese attending college shot up from 1.4 percent in 1978 to about 20 percent in 2005. (Over 40 percent go to college in the United States.) Students who test well get into one of a dozen prestige universities. China's Harvard is (and for a century has been) Beijing University (*Beida*); its MIT is the nearby **Qinghua**. China has many lesser institutions with lower standards for

admission. A problem for the regime: More students can lead to more student protests.

A major definitional problem appears: What, exactly, makes one middle class? A certain level of income? Of education? Of material possessions? There is no standard definition, at least not one that can be used transnationally. A definition of the Spanish middle class would be useless applied to China. The urban Chinese who dwell in shabby apartments or traditional crowded alleyways (called *hutongs* in Beijing), are poor by our standards but middle-class by Chinese standards. They own televisions and electric fans. What we see as middle class—nice but small apartments with air conditioners (necessary for China's summers)—in China is probably upper-middle class. The few who can afford large, modern housing—most with California-type names—constitute an upper class for China but would be just middle class in America.

The more important question: Does becoming bourgeois make one interested in politics and in favor of democracy? Or can the regime forever feed the material cravings of the middle class and keep it quiet and disorganized? Virtually all industrializing countries show that as middle classes grow they demand responsive political systems and increasingly voice their discontent. They turn from passive to active.

Solidarity Huge Polish labor union which ousted Communist regime in 1989.

In the right situation—for example, a split in Beijing leadership over personnel and policies—China's peasants, workers, and students could make common cause and challenge the regime. Needless to say, the police work hard to prevent a Chinese equivalent of Poland's **Solidarity**. Political repression, of course, solves nothing; it merely postpones the day of reckoning. What happened in East Europe could happen in China.

◼ Proud China

How can a regime handle the several and contradictory impulses of Chinese political culture? Uncontrolled, they could be dangerous. Beijing's answer seems to be to cultivate nationalistic pride. Almost everything the regime does goes toward demonstrating China's greatness. In 2003 China, bursting with pride, sent an astronaut into earth orbit, the third country to do so. China's motive was the same as the earlier U.S. and Soviet space programs: to show the world that it is a great nation. In 2008, Beijing will host the Olympics, which China will use to showcase how modern and powerful it is.

China is quite open about its aim to become once again the leading power in Asia and the second power globally, after the United States. In economics, China has already done this.

Will China's policy of national pride ease China through to becoming a normal, prosperous, and respected country? Or could national pride run out of control and turn aggressive and expansionist? This could be the great question of the twenty-first century.

Key Terms

Anti-Japanese War (p. 440)	Qin (p. 440)
blog (p. 446)	Qinghua (p. 447)
bourgeoisie (p. 447)	Solidarity (p. 448)
Century of Humiliation (p. 441)	Taiwan (p. 440)
Daoism (p. 444)	Tibet (p. 445)
Jesuit (p. 444)	Uygur (p. 443)
Korean War (p. 440)	voluntarism (p. 441)
Maoism (p. 440)	Xinjiang (p. 443)
Putonghua (p. 445)	

Further Reference

Aikman, David. *Jesus in Beijing: How Christianity Is Transforming China and Changing the Global Balance of Power.* Washington, D.C.: Regnery, 2003.

Chang, Maria Hsia. *Falun Gong: The End of Days.* New Haven, CT: Yale University Press, 2004.

Chase, Michael S., and James C. Mulvenon. *You've Got Dissent! Chinese Dissident Use of the Internet and Beijing's Counter-Strategies.* Santa Monica, CA: RAND, 2002.

Chen, Jie. *Popular Political Support in Urban China.* Stanford, CA: Stanford University Press, 2004.

Goldman, Merle. *From Comrade to Citizen: The Struggle for Political Rights in China.* Cambridge, MA: Harvard University Press, 2005.

Gries, Peter Hays. *China's New Nationalism: Pride, Politics, and Diplomacy.* Berkeley, CA: University of California Press, 2004.

King, Ambrose. *Chinese Society and Politics.* New York: Oxford University Press, 2005.

Perry, Elizabeth, and Mark Selden, eds. *Chinese Society: Change, Conflict and Resistance,* 2nd ed. New York: Routledge, 2003.

Qing, Dai. *Tiananmen Follies: Prison Memoirs and Other Writings.* Norwalk, CT: EastBridge, 2005.

Starr, S. Frederick, ed. *Xinjiang: China's Muslim Borderland.* New York: M. E. Sharpe, 2004.

Tang, Wenfang. *Public Opinion and Political Change in China.* Stanford, CA: Stanford University Press, 2005.

Tyler, Christian. *Wild West China: The Taming of Xinjiang.* London: John Murray, 2003.

Ye, Sang. *China Candid: The People on the People's Republic.* Berkeley, CA: University of California Press, 2006.

Zhao, Suisheng. *A Nation-State by Construction: Dynamics of Modern Chinese Nationalism.* Stanford, CA: Stanford University Press, 2004.

Chapter 31

CHINA:
PATTERNS OF INTERACTION

Since the Communists came to power in 1949 there have been three major upheavals plus several smaller ones. Among major upheavals are the "agrarian reforms" (that is, execution of landlords and redistribution of land) of the early 1950s, the **Great Leap Forward** from 1958 to 1960, and the **Cultural Revolution** from 1966 to 1976. Smaller upheavals include the brief Hundred Flowers liberalization of 1956, the antirightist campaigns of 1957 and the early 1970s, the crushing of the Gang of Four and their supporters in the late 1970s, and the 1989 repression of alleged "counterrevolutionary rebellion" of prodemocracy students.

Questions to Consider

1. Why does China undergo periodic upheavals?
2. Why would Mao harm China's prosperity and strength?
3. How can we define liberals and conservatives in China?
4. Is it possible to govern without bureaucracy?
5. What would it take to make China pluralistic?
6. What is the "peaceful rise" theory?
7. What is a "technocrat" in the Chinese context?
8. What are the macroeconomy and microeconomy?
9. Why doesn't Beijing crack down on corruption?

Cycles of Upheaval

The big upheavals and most of the smaller ones can be traced to the same underlying problem: Beijing's leaders, having inherited a poor and backward land, want to make China rich, advanced, and socialistic. Mao Zedong Thought taught that everything is possible: China can leap into the modern age and even beyond it. But the old, stubborn, traditional China does not yield; it frustrates the bold plans and tugs the system back toward the previous patterns and problems.

Observers used to label CCP figures as "radicals" or "moderates" according to their willingness to support the upheavals Mao periodically decreed. China's moderates were and still are those high up in the Party, government, or army. Almost axiomatically, anyone who is part of the establishment will not be a radical. Mao was right: Bureaucrats are by nature conservative. China's radicals were drawn largely from those peripheral to power but ambitious for it: students, junior cadres, and some provincial leaders. The old radical-moderate split faded with the death of Mao, replaced with a conservative-liberal split.

One of the prime motivations for radicals, especially during the Cultural Revolution, was the scarcity of job openings in Party, state, army, industrial, and other offices. For the most part, positions until recently were staffed by aging Party comrades who go back to the 1949 liberation or even the Long March. They never retire, and their longevity in office breeds impatience and resentment among younger people with ambitions of their own. A further element fueling youthful discontent was the difficulty of getting into a university. Such tensions underlay the radical outburst of the Cultural Revolution. Those who aspired to power enthusiastically attempted to carry out

Mao's designs. Those who held power pretended to go along with it, often by mouthing the correct slogans and self-denunciations. In Mao's words, they "waved the red flag to oppose the red flag." When the campaign burned itself out, the bureaucrats and cadres took over again, and it appeared that the moderates had won.

Chinese Liberal and Conservative Politics

With the Maoist demon back in the bottle, a gradual split between liberal and conservative forces appeared, similar to what the Soviets went through before their system collapsed. Conservatives tend to be older people, with secure positions in the Party, army, and bureaucracy, much like Soviet *apparatchiks*. They want socialism on the Soviet model, with centralized control over the economy, politics, and cultural life.

Great Leap Forward   Mao's failed late 1950s effort to industrialize China overnight. (See page 451.)

Cultural Revolution   Mao's late 1960s mad effort to break bureaucracy in China. (See page 451.)

Red Guards   Radical Maoist youth who disrupted China during *Cultural Revolution*. (See page 453.)

Liberals, usually younger people, see the unfairness and inefficiency of central control. They point to the record-setting growth in output that came with private, cooperative, and foreign enterprises. "All we have to do is expand the market system until it covers the whole Chinese economy," they say in effect. Some also hint at Western-style political democracy and cultural freedoms. Chinese conservatives, just like their old Soviet counterparts, fear that such a system would no longer be socialist, would collapse into chaos (a possibility) and, worst of all, would cost them their jobs.

Key Concepts

THE GREAT LEAP FORWARD

In 1958 Mao Zedong launched one of the strangest efforts in the Third World's struggle to move ahead: the Great Leap Forward. Vowing to progress "twenty years in a day" and "catch up with Great Britain in fifteen years," all of China was urged to "walk on two legs" (use all possible means) to industrialize rapidly. Most peasants—then a majority of Chinese—were herded into gigantic communes, some with as many as 100,000 people. Deprived of their private plots, they were ordered to eat in communal dining halls, leave their children in nurseries, and even sleep in large dormitories.

The communes were ordered to participate in engineering and industrial projects. Relying on "labor-intensive" methods to compensate for lack of capital, millions were turned out to move earth with baskets and carry poles to build dams and irrigation works. Backyard blast furnaces were ordered built so that every commune could produce its own iron.

Within a year the failure was plain for all to see. Even Mao had to admit it; he resigned as president of the PRC but kept his chairmanship of the CCP. Peasants—as in the Soviet Union—failed to produce without private incentives. Labor was wasted in foolish projects. Major food shortages developed, and over 30 million Chinese died of malnutrition. To meet Party quotas, peasants melted down their good tools to produce implements of miserable quality. The communes were phased out, broken first into "production brigades" and then into "production teams," which were in fact the old villages. Private farming was again permitted. Mao lost; old China won.

Key Concepts

THE GREAT PROLETARIAN CULTURAL REVOLUTION

If the Great Leap Forward was strange, the Great Proletarian Cultural Revolution was downright bizarre. In it, an elderly Mao Zedong tried to make his revolution permanent by destroying the very structures his new China had created. Of the many slogans from the Cultural Revolution, "bombard the command post" perhaps best summarizes its character. Mao encouraged young people, who hastily grouped themselves into ragtag outfits called **Red Guards**, to destroy most authority, even the CCP. They did, and Chinese progress was set back years. Some of their slogans, many of them quotes from Mao:

- "Put destruction first, and in the process you have construction."
- "Destroy the four olds—old thought, old culture, old customs, old habits."
- "Once all struggle is grasped, miracles are possible."
- "Bombard the command post." (Attack established leaders if they are unrevolutionary.)
- "So long as it is revolutionary, no action is a crime."
- "Sweep the great renegade of the working class onto the garbage heap!" (Dump the moderate chief of state, Liu Shaoqi.)
- "Cadres step to the side." (Bypass established authorities.)
- "To rebel is justified."

The Cultural Revolution began with a 1965 flap over a Shanghai play some radicals claimed criticized Mao by allegory. Mao turned a small literary debate into a mass criticism that led to the ouster of several Party officials. Then university and high-school students were encouraged to air their grievances against teachers and school administrators. Behind their discontent was a shortage of the kind of jobs the students thought they deserved upon graduation. Some young people saw a chance to cut loose and have fun destroying things.

By the fall of 1966, most schools were closed as their students demonstrated, humiliated officials, wrote wall posters, and traveled to "share revolutionary experiences." China was in chaos. Hundreds of thousands of victims of the Red Guards committed suicide. A much larger number were "sent down" to the countryside to work with the peasants and "learn from the people." This included physical abuse and psychological humiliation. An unknown number were murdered. Worried officials set up their own Red Guard groups to protect themselves. Different Red Guard factions fought each other.

Even Mao became concerned, and in early 1967 he ordered the army to step in. By the end of 1967 the People's Liberation Army pretty much ran the country. To replace the broken governmental structures, the army set up "revolutionary committees" on which sat PLA officers, Red Guard leaders, and "repentant" officials. By 1969, the worst was over, although officially the Cultural Revolution did not end until 1976 when Mao died and the ultra-radical Gang of Four (headed by Mao's wife, Jiang Qing), was arrested.

The effects of the Cultural Revolution were all bad. Industry suffered. Education, when it resumed, was without standards, and students were chosen on the basis of political attitudes rather than ability. The more moderate and level-headed officials, whom the Red Guards sought to destroy, laid low and pretended to go along with the Cultural Revolution. When it was over, they reasserted themselves and made sure one of their own was in charge: Deng Xiaoping.

And what became of the Red Guards? Claiming their energy was needed on the farm, the army marched more than sixteen million young city people to rural communes for agricultural labor and forbade them to return to their cities. By hook or by crook, many of them managed to get back to their homes to try to continue their studies. Some, utterly disillusioned with the way they had been used, turned to petty crime or fled to the British colony of Hong Kong. Some eventually became capitalist millionaires in China's new market economy.

CONSERVATIVES AND LIBERALS IN CHINESE POLITICS	
Conservatives	Liberals
selectively quote Mao	forget about Mao
keep Party Communist	admit business people
control media closely	freer media
demand purity	demand modernization
central economic controls	largely market economy
oppose foreign influence	open to foreign influence
minimize mass input	expand local elections
take over Taiwan	tolerate Taiwan
ideological	empirical

microeconomics Close-up picture of individual markets, including product design and pricing, efficiency, and costs.

macroeconomics Big picture of a nation's economy, including GDP size and growth, productivity, interest rates, and inflation.

As we discussed in connection with the old Soviet Union, ideology is often a mask for self-interest. The people who have the cushy jobs warn that democracy and liberalization mean "abandoning socialism." In analyzing Communist (and many other) systems, take ideology with a grain of salt; follow the jobs. (Think the jobs explanation is an exaggeration? What motivates you?)

The liberal-conservative split caused Deng and his successors much grief. They are prepared to liberalize cautiously, hoping to confine it to the economic sector. But demands keep bubbling up to go farther and faster. In the spring of 1989, tens of thousands of Chinese university students staged giant protests and hunger strikes in favor of democracy. Deng fired his handpicked and liberal-minded successor, Zhao Ziyang, and had the PLA mow down the students in Tiananmen Square. Several hundred died, and some ten thousand were imprisoned. A chill settled over Chinese life. Conservatives also launched anti-Western campaigns (see box on page 455). The conservatives had one serious drawback: Most were elderly. Time seemed to be on the side of the liberalizers, but not without rearguard conservative actions.

■ Rule by Engineers

We mentioned *technocrats* in connection with French governing style (and will consider it again in the Mexico chapter), but the term applies much more to China. The fourth generation of China's rulers—the nine current members of the Party's Standing Committee, which really rules—are all graduate engineers. In most of the world, technocrat means a high unelected official who governs by economic and financial skills, often the case in France. In China it means top unelected officials with engineering backgrounds. To be sure, China's engineers often know a good deal about economics, but it is focused on building dams and factories rather than on the bigger questions of where China should go and how to get there. Engineers are more trained in **microeconomics** than in **macroeconomics**.

What does rule by engineers do for China? They are quite bright, and their emphasis on rationality generally means they minimize ideological considerations, a welcome change for a China that was drenched in and ruined by Maoism. In most cases they will allow the growth of a market economy in China, so long as it builds a richer, stronger China, as they are also very nationalistic. They beam with pride at China's economic growth and the world political clout that comes with it.

But technocrats—whether in France, Mexico, China, or even the United States—have a huge weakness that often dooms their efforts: They expect quick, right answers and pay little or no attention to the human factor and to long-term consequences. They are cool, distant, rational numbers-crunchers. As we discussed in Chapter 10 on France and in Chapter 17 on the European Union, the decisions of distant bureaucrats, even if they are the correct economic decisions of very bright people, rub citizens the wrong way. Thus the French are permanently angry at their own government in Paris and at the EU in Brussels. In 2005 they voted down the new EU constitution. More than a century ago in Mexico, Díaz's *científicos* (an early form of technocrat) thought they were developing Mexico's economy, but they were just making the vast majority of Mexicans poorer and poorer (see page 488).

America has its own painful example of a technocrat in Robert McNamara, Johnson's brilliant secretary of defense (he had a Harvard MBA), who assured us in 1962 that "every quantitative measurement we have shows we're winning the war" in Vietnam. He overlooked the human factor that the enemy was willing to take enormous casualties to expel the Americans and unify their country. The human factor did not compute, so he missed it. You begin to see why "technocrat" is often preceded by an unprintable adjective.

China's technocrats operate along similar lines: Numbers matter, people do not. The technocrats argue that at this stage of China's economic takeoff, they are precisely the right people to run things. The quicker they can industrialize China, the sooner they can start spreading the prosperity. No country has industrialized in an even, fair, and balanced way. The beginnings of capital accumulation are rough in any country, characterized by inequality and bad working conditions. That is why labor unions formed in Western countries. China, like all Communist countries, has official unions (under the control of the All-China Federation of Labor Unions), but they do not complain or strike, even over the most wretched and dangerous working conditions. China permits no independent unions and jails anyone who tries to organize one. Unions just get in the way of rapid

Political Culture

ANTI-WESTERN CAMPAIGNS

Every few years China is hit with a campaign aimed at making the Chinese pull away from the Western model of economic and political freedom. The work of conservatives within the CCP, these campaigns warned that decadent Western ideas such as free enterprise, open discussion, and a loosening of Party control would mean the end of socialism in China.

In late 1983, the catchword was "spiritual pollution," meaning that Western styles in clothes, music, and thought were ruining China. Deng, fearing the campaign was being used to block his economic liberalization, called it off after only four months.

In 1986, a somewhat longer campaign against "bourgeois liberalization" appeared, ruling out any discussion of ending the CCP monopoly on power and replacing it with Western-style liberalism. After the 1989 Tiananmen Square massacre, conservatives charged that it was a "counterrevolutionary rebellion" inspired by Western influences, which had to be curbed. We have not seen the last anti-Western campaign.

think tank   Research organization that analyzes problems and advocates policies.

Hainan   Large island province in the very south of China.

R & D   Research and development of new technologies.

growth—an old capitalist argument. Even worse, unions (along with churches) would be organizational alternatives that could rally opposition to Communist rule.

Furthermore, China's technocrats could point out, Japan also industrialized on a top-down basis, first with the Meiji modernizers (see pages 343–344) and after World War II with MITI (see page 362). China should do the same. Beware of analogies between countries; they can deceive. Meiji central control of Japan's rapid modernization relied on brutal suppression of common people and paved the way to Japan's aggressive militarism. (Some see parallels between this and China's current industrialization.) MITI influence after the war—and some say MITI was never really that important—took place in a democratic context with few state enterprises that had to be privatized. One point in common: Both Japanese and Chinese banks lent foolishly and recklessly, and both refused for years to admit they were insolvent. The Japanese banks, however, are privately held and accountable to shareholders; the Chinese banks are state-owned and little accountable to anyone. The MITI analogy applies poorly to China.

China's current technocrats must be given some credit for trying to correct the imbalances. They recognize that extreme economic unevenness is dangerous and are now spreading investment to the north and west of the country to industrialize China's vast interior. There is even talk of modest welfare programs for the poorest rungs of Chinese society. We will see how clever China's technocrats really are. Will they be smart enough to head off trouble before it gets explosive?

Emerging Pluralism?

One difference between the China of Mao and the China of now is the growth of a few different viewpoints. This represents the shift of China from totalitarianism to authoritarianism (see page 312), a hopeful sign. None of the views are really radical, and no one is allowed to organize a pressure group; all operate within the system, and most are Party members. These discussions take place at the elite level in several state-linked **think tanks**, mostly in Beijing and Shanghai (the two cities are sometimes intellectual rivals). They would have to be state-linked; the many private research and advocacy groups one finds in Washington would not be allowed in China. Here are some of the views one can encounter among educated Chinese:

Peaceful Rise of China   This school of thought, found heavily in Shanghai university circles, argues that China should keep doing what it has been doing: Take high-tech products developed elsewhere and use China's massive labor advantage to manufacture them so cheaply that China becomes a leading economic power. And all this without lifting a hostile finger, hence the name "peaceful rise." Historically, many fast-rising powers have turned aggressive (Germany and Japan), but war is bad and unnecessary for China, argue the peaceful risers. Shanghai has been the epicenter of China's spectacular economic growth, so it is not surprising this view is rooted there. Advocates of this view are sometimes called "liberal internationalists."

Critics in other schools argue that "peaceful rise" makes China sound militarily uncertain of itself and suggests to Taiwan that it could declare independence with impunity. In response, the term "peaceful rise," which first appeared in 2003 at an international forum on **Hainan**, has been diluted to "peaceful development" and "peaceful coexistence." Other problems: If China simply manufactures high-tech products developed in Japan and the United States, it will remain permanently behind more advanced countries. China must get its own **R & D** capacity, something that comes with free societies, not supervised ones. Cheap labor is not necessarily the best kind; China needs better trained workers and has a serious shortage of skilled managers.

neo-cons Short for neo-conservatives; originally U.S. liberals who turned to conservative and power-oriented approaches.

Realists   China's realists are sometimes called in jest **"neo-cons"** because they resemble the tough-minded U.S. intellectuals who did not shy away from the use of military power. Found in Beijing universities, especially Qinghua (see page 447), realists argue that China needs military modernization to contain the threats posed by Japan, Taiwan, and the United States. A weak China will be pushed around, as it was during the Century of Humiliation (see page 441). Chinese realists are not personally hostile to Americans, provided we respect them as equals. They may be personally hostile to Japanese, especially if Japan does not acknowledge its war guilt and gives way to Chinese dominance of Asia.

The danger of this view is it parallels the American neo-cons, who now warn in sinister terms of a China threat. Two sides seeing the other as threats means hostility and tension. Likewise some Japanese hard-liners resent being pushed around by China and urge a tighter U.S.-Japan alliance to offset Chinese power. Mutual fears often precede wars. As Thucydides famously observed about the cause of the Pelopponesian War that devastated Athens in the fifth century B.C.: "War became inevitable with the growth of Athenian power and the fear this caused in Sparta."

Middle Ground   Between these two views, many Chinese diplomats want to pursue a middle course: peaceful, but with sufficient armed strength. Accordingly, China's military should get major funding increases even as China stresses world cooperation. Taiwan, for example, must be won over with one hand but threatened with invasion by the other. Middle grounders like capitalism and the growth it brings and are delighted to have China buy more foreign firms. It makes China stronger.

New Left   Maoism is dead, but there are still some Chinese Marxists—at Qinghua University, for example—who try to keep the equality issue alive. Differences of wealth were supposed to disappear under socialism, but in China now they are growing rapidly. Chinese incomes by some measures are more unequal than American incomes. For Deng Xiaoping this was not a problem. He observed (correctly) that "some people must get rich first." In China, differences are stark between the urban middle class and people either still in the villages or recently arrived in a city to seek work. You do not have to be a Marxist to see the unfairness in this. China, which still calls itself socialist, treats its workers and poor worse than any capitalist system.

China's New Left would channel funds from rich to poor by government programs funded by higher taxes on the latter. They argue that China should not be so focused on exports but should let poorer Chinese consume more. For example, export tax credits—which allow firms producing for foreign markets to avoid some taxes—should be dropped. The New Left also likes cooperative enterprises that give all members shares rather than capitalist enterprises owned by a few. Their ideal would be a social-democratic welfare state such as Germany (see Chapter 16). The regime claims to be interested in this viewpoint and mindful of rural poverty, which it hopes to correct under the name "harmonious society."

Incremental Democrats   Little has been said of democracy since Tiananmen in 1989 (see page 460), but at least one Beida academic, reportedly well connected to the regime, urges baby steps to greater mass participation. Overthrowing the regime is not the goal, reconnecting the CCP to the masses is. This was always Mao's chief approach, so incremental democrats can invoke Mao's name for essentially non-Maoist purposes. In elections at lower levels—some are already happening—Party members could rededicate themselves to the people instead of using their connections to get rich.

What do we call these several views? Latent pluralism? Some Soviet specialists claimed to see a variety of views emerging in the late Soviet Union, but they led to collapse rather than reform. By themselves, the existence of several viewpoints in a few universities or research organizations means little. What makes *pluralism* (see page 72) is the autonomous interactions of many groups, not just abstract notions discussed by a few elites. If the regime let public groups form to support these and other ideas, then you would have pluralism. There is no sign of this in China yet.

Comparison

EQUALITY AND GROWTH

Do big income differentials spur economic growth? Ronald Reagan, George W. Bush, and Margaret Thatcher thought so; under them, incomes in America and Britain grew more unequal. The reasoning: If people can make a lot of money, they will have a greater incentive to work hard and get rich. And rich people invest more. According to this theory, inequality and growth are twins. Data are not so clear; some may even point in the opposite direction. The data in the table on the right are from the 2005 United Nations Development Program. Careful here; data from the Third World are approximations, so take them with a grain of salt. The first column shows the ratio of the top fifth of incomes to the bottom fifth. The lower this number, the more equal that country is. The second column shows the average annual growth in per capita GDP from 1975 to 2003.

China has great income inequality—its top 20 percent rake in almost eleven times what the poorest 20 percent get. China is more unequal than the United States and is a growth demon. That supports the theory. But none of the other high-inequality countries do; some scored negative growth. Latin America has both some of the sharpest inequality and weakest growth rates. Japan, with the world's most equal income distribution, turned in better growth than other most developed countries.

The theory that inequality accompanies growth is much too simple. There are many factors that make economies grow. Government policies have a lot to do with it. Government—through corruption, high taxes, and state ownership—may discourage private investment. Some cultures have an internalized work ethic or nationalistic pride. Japanese chief executives, who work like maniacs, receive on average only eleven times what their factory workers get; their American counterparts take home a staggering 475 times as much as their workers. Another point: Poor people have no money to save; middle-class people do. The most equal countries on the list, Japan and Germany, are the biggest savers, and savings mean investment. Beware of one-cause theories.

	Top/Bottom Fifths Ratio	GDPpc Growth Average 1975–2003
Japan	3.4	2.4%
Germany	4.3	2.0
Russia	4.8	−2.1
France	5.6	1.7
Canada	5.8	1.6
Britain	7.2	2.1
United States	8.4	2.0
Iran	9.7	−0.3
China	10.7	8.2
Nigeria	12.8	−0.5
South Africa	17.9	−0.6
Mexico	19.3	0.9
Brazil	26.4	0.8
Sierra Leone	57.6	−3.3

Source: UNDP, 2005

Comparison

Should political scientists attempt to prognosticate, to foretell what will happen in a given country? The profession is divided. Some argue that there are simply too many **variables**, most of which are hard to define, measure, and weigh. How could one untangle the complex interactions of economic growth, regional tensions, ideology, personalities, and institutions? Everything matters, but we do not know which matters most. Others argue that prediction, or at least anticipation, concentrates the mind on the variables that are relevant. If one variable predicts moderately well, we focus on it and ignore variables that predict nothing. In doing this, we begin to theorize. If we stay only in the present, describing but refusing to predict, we proclaim that we really do not know much. Predicting, at least approximately, tests whether we have mastered our area of study.

Next we ask which is the best way to predict or anticipate. Political scientists who specialize in one country or region immerse themselves in it and accumulate vast data and details about it. They usually know the language and write their dissertations and articles about the area. Many have spent time as researchers in one country and personally know many of its citizens. From talking to them, they are able to delineate the varieties of opinions in that country, as we have done briefly in this chapter. Their books and articles are crammed with endnotes, many of them from original-language publications.

Their expertise is impressive, but they are frequently wrong. Many Soviet specialists were unable to detect the collapse of their subject matter (see page 325). They were too optimistic that Gorbachev's reforms would work. And afterwards, many Russia specialists confidently portrayed the establishment of democracy in Russia. They were again too optimistic in assuming that ending a dictatorship brings democracy. (Is there a built-in human tendency toward optimism? If so, we must be careful of optimistic analyses of China.) The Soviet/Russia area experts' mistaken predictions suggest they were following the wrong variables.

Part of the problem is knowing too much about one country. Specialists often collect masses of details, supposing that the data put them "inside" the system and able to anticipate its evolution. The Kremlinologists and China watchers (see page 424) knew a lot about the Politburo personalities whose rise and fall they charted. Some scholars closely studied city or regional councils or specialized agencies. But such studies assumed *unilinear* (see page 82) development and could not anticipate sudden breaks or **discontinuities**. Due to the inherent delays of publishing, some of their detailed studies appeared after the Soviet Union had ceased to exist. Soviet specialists got so deeply into the box that they could not think outside of it. We may legitimately fear that China specialists are doing the same. How do we know which details are relevant?

In contrast, comparativists have broader perspectives but bring problems of their own. A comparativist might have less language or area expertise but be able to compare and contrast the country under consideration with similar cases across a continent or even the globe. They might find, for example, that democratization in many Latin America countries at about the same time were similar to one another, almost like a contagious illness spreading. It does not necessarily follow, however, that this pattern transfers to democratization in Central Europe or the Soviet Union. This was the problem with *transitology* (see page 319). They tried to make an **analogy** between Latin America and Central Europe and then between Central Europe and the Soviet Union. Many, however, failed to note the elements of **dysanalogy** between the cases. The Soviet Union, for example, had nothing remotely resembling Poland's Solidarity, and neither does China today.

Comparing is good because it requires its practitioners to ask which are the relevant facts and variables we should be studying; in effect, it forces one to theorize and then test these theories against reality. Single-country experts rarely do this. They assume that the accumulation of many facts will point to obvious conclusions without having to structure the facts into a theoretical framework that makes sense and works in more than one country. It is the contention of this book that it is better to err on the side of being too broad (comparative politics) than being too narrow (country expertise). Just make sure you have the right analogies.

■ Rice-Roots Democracy

variable   Factor that changes and is related to other factors. (See page 459.)

discontinuity   A break and new direction in the expected course of events. (See page 459.)

analogy   Taking one example as the model for another. (See page 459.)

dysanalogy   Showing that one example is a poor model for another. (See page 459.)

With the new millennium, scattered across China thousands of village-level competitive elections appeared, like rice shoots just poking out of the soil. Such things cannot happen without Party approval. Some believe it is the work of liberalizers in the Party ever-so-slowly introducing democracy. Others say it comes from the bottom up, from villagers' anger at corrupt local officials who demand arbitrary "taxes." In some villages and townships, the Party candidate loses.

So far, the scope of these elections is limited. Elected village and township chiefs are still controlled by local Party secretaries. But gradually, local Party secretaries are also chosen by more open methods among Party members. Since 1999, a few urban neighborhoods have had direct, competitive elections for minor offices. Some

Democracy

THE TIANANMEN MASSACRE

During the early morning of June 4, 1989, more than 100,000 Chinese troops opened fire on young demonstrators camped out in Beijing's Tiananmen Square, killing hundreds and injuring thousands. (The regime never released figures, so the number of dead is guesswork.) Much of the killing, including tanks crushing protesters and bicyclists shot at random, took place outside the Square, but the horror went down in history as "Tiananmen."

Tiananmen marked the point at which China's Communist chiefs choked over letting China's 1980s experiment with a partially free market economy spill over into political democracy, never the intention of Beijing's rulers. The massacre illustrates the danger of halfway reform: It gets people thinking of democracy.

Trouble began with the death of the liberal ex-Party chief Hu Yaobang in April 1989. Students began mourning him and protesting the current CCP leadership. On April 18, thousands began to occupy the Square. While the regime pondered how to handle the demonstration, the students organized, gave speeches, and built a Goddess of Democracy statue that resembled New York's Statue of Liberty. Around the country, many sympathized with the demonstrators, and criticism of the regime mounted.

If prodemocracy demonstrations had kept going, the regime would have been in trouble. The regime knew that and struck back. Zhao Ziyang, who succeeded Hu in 1987, went out to talk with the students and took their side. Politburo hardliners immediately ousted Zhao from office. (Zhao was under house arrest until his death in 2005, and his funeral was nearly secret so as not to give mourners another occasion to demonstrate for freedom. Even funerals are touchy events in China.) Deng Xiaoping, still the real power at age 84, ordered the army to crush the demonstrators. "We do not fear spilling blood," he said.

Troops and tanks poured into Beijing. The soldiers, mostly simple country boys, felt little in common with the urban students. In one memorable videotaped confrontation, a lone protester blocked a tank column; when the tanks tried to go around him, he quickly stepped in front of them again. It seemed to symbolize the individualism of democracy standing up to the coercion of dictatorship. Many ordinary Beijingers sided with and helped the students. After the bloodbath, thousands were arrested. The top protest figures received sentences of up to thirteen years, less for those who "repented." Hundreds were held for years without trial. China's elite decided to keep going with economic change but to keep the lid on political change. The ingredients for new upheavals in China are already present.

Chinese political scientists predict the level of elections will climb to include mayors and provincial and eventually even national office. A clever regime could expand democratic elections as a way to defuse anger, but if it does not let democracy go all the way to top national offices it could end up increasing mass anger. There could be other Tiananmens.

coercion   Government by force.

There are basically two ways to gradually introduce democracy into China: (1) Let pluralistic groups form in the society at large and voice their views and demands; or (2) let views that are quietly voiced within the CCP establish factions that they then present to the citizenry at large. In a nutshell: Either let it happen inside the Party or outside of it. Best bet for a smooth transition to democracy in China: Let Party factions form first and then go public. Once they have to present divergent views to win votes, the factions will in effect become separate parties but preserve continuity by claiming they are just pursuing "socialism with Chinese characteristics." Gradual change is better than tumultuous change. The regime, however, so far has not allowed either path.

■ Coercion in Reserve

China's regime retains authority by means of patriotism and performance-based legitimacy. **Coercion** has receded into the background, but everyone knows it is still available. The regime's achievements are impressive and appreciated by average citizens. For a time, that might suffice to keep the regime halfway legitimate. Most Chinese now can speak a common language (*Putonghua*). There has been no famine since 1959–1961 (the Great Leap Forward). Since 1980 a considerable urban middle class has emerged.

Coercive tools are close at hand but needed only occasionally. The Tiananmen area of Beijing is laced with plainclothes police who are trained to instantly pounce on any protest group that might form. Any group of three or more that lingers too long in one spot could get spoken to. Security police remember how Falun Gong used e-mails to quietly organize a large and sudden gathering in Tiananmen Square. That will not happen again. There is unrest, especially in the countryside, but with no organizational alternatives discontent is unfocused and free-floating. And the regime takes elaborate precautions against the formation of civil society—especially churches and labor unions—that might provide organizational alternatives.

Law can powerfully boost civil society. China claims to have rule of law, but it is selective. Some cases relating to economic efficiency—fraud and corruption—are handled fairly. But cases related to Party control are likely to be smacked down. Lawyers defending church and union organizers risk disbarment and arrest. Some go into hiding. A 1989 law is supposed to give citizens the right to sue state agencies, but only a handful succeed. Western freedoms owe much to courageous lawyers who insisted that even the powerful be bound by rule of law. One hopes that China is slowly moving in this direction.

The 2008 Olympics are a mixed blessing for China. It showcases the modern face of China, but preparations involve displacing tens of thousands of farmers and *hutong* (alleyway) dwellers. By law they are supposed to be compensated but are not. No one owns land in China. The urban underclass feels the games do nothing for them and resents their costs. Students might think the Olympics are the perfect time to make a statement the whole world will see. The regime, of course, will permit no such protests. We could see something similar to the police massacres of Mexican student protesters on the eve of the 1968 Mexico City Olympics (see page 502).

One point should puzzle us. If the authoritarian regime has great powers of coercion, why does it not use some to fix problems, for example, cleaning up corruption, which most Chinese citizens detest? Singapore imposed tough rules against corruption (or any form of misbehavior) and now ranks as one of the cleanest countries in the world (see the Transparency International ratings on page 537). Why could not Beijing have a hundred or so of the most corrupt officials tried and speedily executed to get the message out to the thousands of others? (Actually, China already does execute some egregiously corrupt characters and has the most capital punishment in the world.) You've got the coercive tools; why not use them?

The only reasonable explanation is that China's top leaders recognize that corruption is so widespread and tolerated that cleaning it up would cost them the support of precisely the Party cadres (see page 537) it relies upon to govern. If you shoot all your helpers, you will be helpless. The United States faces the same problem in Afghanistan. We are reluctant to crack down on the warlords and drug lords who make Afghanistan ungovernable because they are precisely the locally powerful people we used to overthrow the Taliban and still need to hold the country halfway together. They are unsavory but necessary allies. China will be stuck with massive corruption for a long time, until rising economic, social, and education levels enable Beijing to do what Singapore did.

Key Terms

analogy (p. 460)

coercion (p. 461)

Cultural Revolution (p. 452)

discontinuity (p. 460)

dysanalogy (p. 460)

Great Leap Forward (p. 452)

Hainan (p. 456)

macroeconomics (p. 454)

microeconomics (p. 454)

neo-cons (p. 457)

R & D (p. 456)

Red Guards (p. 452)

think tank (p. 456)

variable (p. 460)

Further Reference

Buruma, Ian. *Bad Elements: Chinese Rebels from Los Angeles to Beijing.* New York: Random House, 2001.

Dickson, Bruce J. *Red Capitalists in China: The Party, Private Entrepreneurs, and Prospects for Political Change.* New York: Cambridge University Press, 2003.

Ding, Yijiang. *Chinese Democracy after Tiananmen.* Vancouver: University of British Columbia Press, 2001.

Fewsmith, Joseph. *China since Tiananmen: The Politics of Transition.* New York: Cambridge University Press, 2001.

Finkelstein, David M., and Maryanne Kivlehan, eds. *China's Leadership in the 21st Century: The Rise of the Fourth Generation.* Armonk, NY: M. E. Sharpe, 2003.

Gamer, Robert E., ed. *Understanding Contemporary China,* 2nd ed. Boulder, CO: L. Rienner, 2003.

Huang, Jing. *Factionalism in Chinese Communist Politics.* New York: Cambridge University Press, 2000.

Naughton, Barry J., and Dali L. Yang, eds. *Holding China Together: Diversity and National Integration in the Post-Deng Era.* New York: Cambridge University Press, 2004.

Wang, Chaohua, ed. *One China, Many Paths*. New York: Verso, 2003.

Wang, Hui, and Theodore Huters. *China's New Order: Society, Politics, and Economy in Transition*. Cambridge, MA: Harvard University Press, 2003.

Wright, Teresa. *The Perils of Protest: State Repression and Student Activism in China and Taiwan*. Honolulu: University of Hawaii Press, 2001.

Zhao, Dingxin. *The Power of Tiananmen: State-Society Relations and the 1989 Beijing Movement*. Chicago, IL: University of Chicago Press, 2001.

Chapter 32

WHAT CHINESE
QUARREL ABOUT

China's economy has been roughly doubling every seven years, a spectacular rate. From poverty, China has vaulted to the world's second largest economy (but not per capita). Urban China now shows off its middle-tech industries, modern downtowns, and traffic-clogged streets. And China did it without following the Japanese economic model, which kept out foreign firms and imports and pushed technology and innovation under MITI guidance (see page 396). In contrast, China welcomes foreign investment, technology, and (partial) ownership and has no equivalent of MITI. China is actually more open and easier to do business with than Japan. All of China's advanced industries are foreign imports. Beijing saw this as the fastest way to industrialize.

Questions to Consider

1. What accounts for China's rapid economic growth? Is it like Japan's?
2. What could go wrong with China's rapid growth?
3. What is a "soft landing" in the Chinese context?
4. How does the U.S. economy depend on China (and Japan)?
5. What problems have come with China's economic growth?
6. Is there a middle way between capitalism and socialism?
7. What are second- and third-order effects?
8. Do market systems always lead to democratization?
9. What should the United States do if China takes Taiwan by force?

The reasons for China's growth are several. Unlike Latin America, China has no old dominant class that invests little. Mao had China's old landowners and capitalists shot, so China started capitalism with a clean slate. Unlike Muslim countries, Chinese have no cultural or religious problems with rapid modernization and copying from the West. China has vast supply of cheap labor plus plentiful capital (much of it foreign) plus a regime that pushes economic growth. A Chinese auto worker earns about $1.50 an hour in wages and benefits (triple the Chinese average); his U.S. counterpart costs $55 an hour. General Motors is expanding rapidly in China even as it declines in the United States. With plentiful cash, China has become the second-largest holder of U.S. debt (after Japan).

But there are several things that could go wrong with China's economic miracle. No economy—neither Germany's (see Chapter 16) nor Japan's (see Chapter 27)—goes up forever. Factors limiting China include dependency on imported technology—China invests minimally in R & D—and on the world market staying open for Chinese goods. China has shortages of *skilled* labor and, more importantly, skilled managers. Much Chinese investment is politically influenced, incoherent, short-term, and wasted—a mess **masked** by low labor costs. Eventually, bad investments hurt economic growth. A crisis of China's banks threatens optimistic projections of growth without pause.

■ It Only Looks Capitalist

The streets of China's cities are lined with small shops and restaurants and clogged with hawkers and hustlers. ("You want buy T-shirt? Special price for you.") It looks like a capitalist boomtown, and, at the micro level, it is indeed one. But virtually all large economic entities are controlled or partially owned by the state and have government or Party officials on their boards of directors with right of veto. Until recently, all of China's large banks were state-owned and are now only partly private. Many "capitalist" firms are actually branches of China's **state-owned enterprises** (SOEs). For example, the Chinese National Overseas Oil Company (CNOOC), which claims to be a commercial operation, is 70 percent owned by China's petroleum ministry. China's market sector produces two-thirds of its GDP, but the state is still in overall control.

mask   To cover over a problem. (See page 465.)

state-owned enterprises (SOEs) Firms still owned by the Chinese government, mostly older and money-losing.

yuan   China's currency (symbol ¥), worth 13 U.S. cents; officially called *renminbi* (RMB, people's money).

insolvent   Owes more than it owns.

Other Communist countries have tried such mixtures. Tito's Yugoslavia and Gorbachev's Soviet Union suggest that such third-way economies are unstable. They tend to turn more and more into market economies until the regime, afraid of losing control, retightens central supervision and discipline. Seeking faster growth, however, after a while the regime loosens controls again. The economy moves in a zig-zag, never finding stability. \

Amid incoherence, economic errors grow. Vast sums are invested foolishly, mistakenly, or ⚹ crookedly. Government control has forced some well-run and rapidly growing firms to make bad business decisions. Peasants fleeing rural unemployment keep labor costs cheap—as low as 30 **yuan** ($3.90) per unskilled worker a day—and lets developers overbuild. The state-owned banks loan generously for modern buildings because they impress everyone, especially foreigners. Builders, all aiming for the top of the rental market, constructed too many glitzy high-rise buildings, which now are only partially occupied money-losers. Shanghai alone has twice as many skyscrapers as New York City. Beijing has the world's biggest shopping mall, but it is nearly empty of customers because it is too expensive and inconveniently located. China's building boom is a bubble that could pop.

After years of bad loans to state-owned enterprises (SOEs), Party officials, and just plain crooks, all of China's banks are technically **insolvent**. Beijing requires banks to lend to SOEs, which rarely repay the loans. With weak (but rising) accounting standards, the banks

A Beijing welding shop makes and repairs three-wheeled cycles that dog the streets.

carry on as if they will be repaid, much like Japan's banks did for years. Massive savings and rapid industrial growth mask the underlying problems. There is no requirement to **write off nonperforming loans**, for that would force many banks and SOEs to admit they are bankrupt. Fears of a Chinese banking crash are widespread and justified.

Virtually all educated professionals, many with U.S. university degrees, understand China's economic imbalances and dislocations, and most say the regime understands them too. All nine members of the Party's Standing Committee, China's real governing body, are well-educated engineers. But views on them diverge. Chinese professionals connected to the establishment claim the regime knows what it is doing in bringing the situation under control. "We are well governed by very bright technocrats," is their message. China's leaders avoided the currency and banking crises that swept East Asia in 1997 and 1998, and they will bring China's overheated economy in for a "**soft landing.**" China's reserves are so huge they can cover any banking problems. Furthermore, China is now spending billions to prepare several of its biggest banks to sell shares to private investors, and this will induce discipline throughout the banking system, regime defenders claim. All will be well.

Professionals not dependent on state connections, on the other hand, fear the regime does not know what to do and, paralyzed by indecision, lets the banking sector rumble on to a crash. Some of the big banks that China privatizes are to be listed on the New York Stock Exchange, where they will come under tough U.S. financial and accounting rules. When American banks open in China they will draw customers who appreciate the greater security. In these ways, Chinese banks will come under pressure to adopt tougher banking rules. But tougher scrutiny could uncover incomplete or inaccurate accounting and cause a Chinese banking crisis. Insiders worry about Chinese banks.

write off Lender admits that a *nonperforming loan* will never be repaid.

nonperforming loan One that is not being paid back.

soft landing Gradual calming of destabilizing economic shifts.

devalue To change the worth of a currency downward in relation to other currencies (opposite of *revalue*).

peg To fix one currency at an unchanging rate to another.

revalue To change the worth of a currency upward in relation to other currencies (opposite of *devalue*).

float To allow a currency to find its own level based on supply and demand.

■ Yuan and Dollars

China's currency situation is not closely parallel to the late 1990s banking problems elsewhere in East Asia, where some countries' currencies were suddenly **devalued**. China's yuan is undervalued and likely to rise. If such a rise is big and sudden, however, it could disrupt China's rapid growth of exports. Accordingly, Beijing wants to keep such changes under control. From 1995 to 2005, partly to avoid what was hitting other East Asian currencies, China **pegged** the yuan to the dollar. At the time it was applauded by all, including the United States, as a stabilizing device. For years, one dollar bought a nearly constant eight yuan.

Over time, however, America, which imports more and more Chinese goods, complained that the fixed rate was unfair; it kept the yuan too low and allowed China to gain at the expense of U.S. factory jobs. The U.S. Congress thundered that this had to change. Some urged China to **revalue** the yuan 20 to 30 percent. Most economists say an undervalued yuan is not the root of America's trade problems with China (the extremely low U.S. savings rate is the chief culprit). China, due to its low wages (and high savings rate), is just a super competitor, and its inexpensive goods hold down U.S. inflation and lets Americans consume more.

A country with a trade surplus could let its currency **float** to a higher value. The market would in effect revalue the currency. But China, like many countries, wanted to keep the yuan cheap to support its rapid growth of exports. If the yuan gets too high, China could lose some of its export advantage. To keep the yuan low and stable, in the 1990s China began buying massive amounts of U.S. Treasury securities (Japan does the same). This has intertwined the Chinese and U.S. economies in strange ways. Rich America is now deeply indebted to poor China. Chinese purchase of U.S. notes kept our interest rates low and underwrote our real-estate boom. If China were to sell—or simply stop purchasing—U.S. bonds and notes, our interest rates would climb and housing prices fall. The dollar would weaken around the world. On the other hand, a sudden major Chinese pullout of the U.S. debt market would also decrease the value of China's huge dollar holdings. Would China take a financial hit in order to oppose U.S. policy? In a showdown over Taiwan, it surely would.

In 2005 Beijing gave in a little and slightly unpegged the yuan by switching its peg from the dollar to a basket of currencies that includes dollars, euros, Japanese yen, and South Korean won. The yuan initially went up a trivial 2.1 percent against the dollar. Instead of letting let the yuan float freely, China carried out a "controlled managed float" in line with its *dirigiste* (see page 143) economy. The modest move did suggest further revaluations of the yuan, which, if done gradually, could correct the yuan-dollar imbalance with harm to neither country. Perhaps China really is governed by brilliant technocrats.

Comparison

BIG MAC INDEX

As we discussed in Japan (page 399), traditional per-capita GDP (GDPpc) figures that use the "market exchange rate" are deceptive because they do not figure in prices in each country. China's GDPpc at exchange rate, for example, is only about $1,300. But exchange rates overvalue or undervalue currencies and change rapidly. To correct for this, economists now calculate GDPpc in *purchasing power parity* (PPP) by measuring what it costs to live in each country. This makes Chinese a lot richer, about $5,000 GDPpc.

PPP is hard to calculate because economists must find a market basket of goods and services that is the same in each country. A quick and cheeky way to approximate PPP was devised by the British newsweekly *The Economist:* Compare the price of a Big Mac sandwich at the local McDonald's with its U.S. (big-city) price. Since a Big Mac requires the same ingredients, labor, and overhead wherever it is produced, it is actually a mini-market basket that reflects local costs fairly accurately. A Big Mac that is more expensive than the U.S. price indicates the local currency is overvalued, the case with the euro and the British pound. A cheaper Big Mac indicates the local currency is undervalued, the case in Japan, China,

and Russia. The Big Mac Index is a quick way to check currency parities, which can change rapidly as the dollar rises and falls. These Big Macs are big-city prices in January 2006. You can do your own field research the next time you travel overseas.

	GDPpc at PPP	Big Mac price
United States	$37,800	3.15
France	27,600	3.51*
Germany	27,600	3.51*
Britain	27,700	3.32
Canada	29,800	3.01
Mexico	9,000	2.66
Japan	36,000	2.19
Russia	8,900	1.60
Iran	7,000	—
China	5,000	1.30
Nigeria	900	—

*average of euro-area prices.

Sources: First column column CIA, second column *The Economist.*

■ A Market Economy for China?

guanxi   Chinese for connections (do not confuse with Guangxi Province).

Will China become a fully market economy? Starting in 1978, the Chinese economy grew at amazing rates. China, like all Communist countries, faced the question of how centralized the economy should be and decided on decentralization while retaining central political control. This, as in other countries that tried it, is an unstable combination.

Key Concepts

THE TROUBLE WITH MARKETS

The trouble with bringing a market economy into Communist countries, such as Yugoslavia, Hungary, or China, is that it runs out of control and destabilizes. China has seen major increases in the following:

Too-Rapid Growth   China's infrastructure cannot keep up with its industrial and urban growth, which creates problems in transportation, water supply, land, housing, you name it. Beijing is one permanent traffic and subway jam. The regime tries to fix the immediate problem but does not plan long-term.

Unemployment   Communist systems disguised unemployment by gross labor inefficiency, but once China's firms had to make profits, they let go millions of workers. Urban unemployment is estimated at 8–10 percent. Rural joblessness is much higher, and some 200 million rural Chinese, most without permission, have left to seek work in the Special Economic Zones (SEZs). More are ready to do the same.

Inequality   Some individuals and provinces got rich; others lagged far behind. With FDI, the SEZs of the southern coast got rich fast while inland provinces stayed poor. Skilled and educated Chinese became a new middle class, leaving their rural cousins far behind.

Worker Protest   Faced with low wages and bad working conditions—especially miners—some Chinese workers attempt to form unions, but they are jailed. Beijing denies that unions even exist. Ironically, a Communist regime that turned anti-labor and pro-capitalist has created the basis of a Marxist revolution.

Currency Distortion   Beijing fixed the yuan too low in relation to the dollar (¥ 8 to $1) and has revalued it only a little. Most other countries let their currencies float. The cheap yuan helped China become the "workshop of the world" but caused a property bubble and foreign resentment.

Corruption   Corruption grows at the interface of the private and governmental sectors. Economic liberalization multiplies such interfaces as entrepreneurs need permits from government officials, obtained by under-the-table payments. China has become one of the world's most corrupt countries. Most Chinese business is based on **guanxi**.

Crime   With all the above plus weakened social controls, crime grows, along with campaigns to stop it. Firing squads execute thousands each year. China leads the world by far in capital punishment (Iran is second). Counterfeiting is widespread; banks check U.S. currency, and businesses check larger yuan bills.

Pollution   Focused only on economic growth, China has the world's worst environmental problems. City air is foul, ground water and rivers are contaminated, and diseases spread rapidly. Officials cover up the problems and jail environmental and health activists for revealing them. Intolerable pollution sparks riots and may limit growth.

How to solve these problems? A start is democracy, which permits people to organize interest groups and parties and holds officials accountable.

Special Economic Zones   Areas
originally on China's southern coast
where capitalist economic development
was encouraged.

foreign direct investment   (FDI)
Foreign firms setting up operations in
other countries.

The earliest changes came in the countryside, where some 70 percent of China's population still lives. Collectivized farms were broken up, and families were permitted to go on the "responsibility system," a euphemism for private farming. Peasants lease land from the state for fifteen years or more—still no private owners—and must deliver a certain quota to the state at set prices. Beyond that, they can sell their produce on the free market for the best price they can get. They can choose their own crops and decide how to use fertilizer and farm machinery, which they buy at their own expense. Farm production soared, Chinese ate better, and farmers' incomes went up; some even got rich.

By the 1990s, things were not going so well in the countryside. With substantially all peasants now producing for the market, competition held farm prices and profits down, and farm incomes declined. In many rural areas, order broke down as villagers rioted and attacked local authorities, who extort fake "taxes" from them. In a pattern very typical of the Third World, millions of rural Chinese leave every year for jobs in the coastal cities where market economies flourish, a destabilizing tide the regime cannot control. To calm growing rural discontent—and diminish the flow of peasants to the cities—in 2005 Beijing ended millennia-old taxes on harvests and even offered peasants some financial aid. The regime fears that peasant anger could turn into the sort of uprising that has punctuated China's history.

A partly free market was allowed to spread to the cities. Faced with growing unemployment, the regime let individuals open small stores, restaurants, repair shops, and even manufacturing facilities. It was even permissible to hire workers, something Marxists used to call capitalist exploitation. But it worked. The Chinese applied individual hustle to produce and sell more and better products than the indifferent state factories and stores ever could. Hole-in-the-wall "department stores" had customers waiting in line to buy the fashionable clothing and footwear Mao used to scorn. People swarmed to outdoor markets to buy home-produced chairs and sofas. Restaurants grew like weeds.

Starting with the Shenzen area around Hong Kong, parts of coastal China were declared "**Special Economic Zones**," open to private and **foreign direct investment** that was invited to turn China into a modern, market economy. FDI is extremely important in the developing world. Marxists and nationalists hate and fear it as a form of capitalist takeover, but it is the key to rapid economic growth. Over half a trillion dollars of FDI poured into China (much of it from Taiwan and Hong Kong) to take advantage of low Chinese wages (for unskilled, 40 cents an hour, but rising), and production soared. These firms compete in a world market to make profits. Because of these firms—which now account for half of China's economy—in a quarter century China's GDP grew at an amazing average of 9.5 percent a year to become the world's second largest overall economy (but not per capita) and third biggest exporter (after America and Germany). China's economy was twenty times bigger in 2002 than it had been in 1980. By comparison, one-third of some 100,000 state-owned enterprises (SOEs) lose money and have to be propped up by subsidies and loans that will never be repaid. At least half the SOEs are reckoned to be hopeless. Whether to close them and create unemployment is one of the great questions facing Beijing. The fact that the Standing Committee keeps stalling on this important decision suggests uncertainty and paralysis: They simply don't know what to do.

As modern, high-rise boomtowns sprang up on the coast, some Chinese business people became millionaires, and a substantial middle class began to form. Most Chinese liked their taste of the free market, but many cadres did not. If you really go to a market system, what do you do with the cadres who make a good living by supervising a controlled economy? They dig in their heels and try to block major change. Deng purged or retired the old guard and replaced them with young technocrats—such as current Party chief Hu and Premier Wen—who pursue capitalist-style economic growth and call it "socialism with Chinese characteristics." Nobody knows what that means.

> **yuppy**   Short for "young urban professional."

But market economies produce problems of their own (see box on page 469) and awaken resentments and jealousies. China's leaders fear the economy is careening out of control and attempted to slow it, aiming for a "soft landing." In the longer term, the system needs democracy, but Beijing vows China will have only one party. What will happen when a destabilizing economic system escapes the bonds of a dictatorial political system? Think: Bucking bronco (China's economy) throwing its rider (the Party).

Key Concepts

SECOND- AND THIRD-ORDER EFFECTS

China's program to limit population growth shows what can go wrong with coercing society into what the government has decided is desirable. It also illustrates the problem of second- and third-order consequences—sometimes called "unforeseen consequences"—namely, how hard it is to predict the longer-term effects of a policy.

In the early 1980s China carried out a ferocious program to curb births. Women were ordered to have only one child and were fined and lost benefits if they had more. Many women were forced to have abortions. The first-order consequence, as might be expected, was to bring down China's rate of population increase to under 1 percent a year, similar to Europe but very low for the Third World, much of which grows at 3 percent.

A second-order effect, however, was a large excess of boy over girl babies, both by abortion and female infanticide. About 5 percent of the girls expected to be born from 1979 to 1995 are missing, 10 percent in the 1990s. In 2000, 118 males were born for 100 females. Cheap ultrasound scans permit selective abortions. Like many Third World cultures, Chinese value boys above girls, both to work on the farm and to support the parents in old age. So, if they are allowed only one child, many Chinese strongly prefer a son. This is not the case with educated urban Chinese, who welcome daughters.

Third-order effects flow from the second. The surplus of males over females mean that millions of Chinese men will never find brides. Further, the drastic restriction in fertility rates—from 2.29 births per average woman in 1980 to 1.69 in 2004—means that China's retired generation—now much bigger and living much longer, thanks to improved nutrition and health care—will not have nearly enough working Chinese to support it. In 2030 one-fourth of Chinese will be over sixty-five. Chinese speak of "4-2-1": four grandparents and two parents supported by only one child, the logical result of the one-child policy. China, still a poor country, will thus face exactly the same problem as the rich countries. China's State Family Planning Commission, which now emphasizes education and contraception, did not consider the second- and third-order consequences.

How then to handle the serious Third World problem of too-rapid population increases? Economic growth solves the problem without coercion, as Chinese **yuppies** already demonstrate. They have few children (and are happy to have daughters). As the economy grows, more people become urban and middle class and decide for themselves to limit their number of children, as Japanese have done. As more women are educated they postpone marriage in favor of career, a strong trend among Chinese yuppies, who work so long and hard they may not have time for marriage. No rich country has a problem of too many babies (in fact, it is just the opposite), and newly industrializing lands show a dramatic falloff in births. China's demographic debacle is one example of Mao's (and, earlier, Stalin's) thinking that society can be forced into any shape the Party decrees.

■ A Middle Way for the Middle Kingdom?

The basic supposition of Beijing's recent and current rulers is that there is a middle way between capitalism and communism, between a controlled and a free-market economy, between the Soviet and American models. (Soviet President Gorbachev entertained similar notions, and you know what happened to him.) By bringing in elements of a market economy while keeping overall control in state hands, they suppose they have found a middle way. Is there one? Not really, and some observers think the Chinese elite quietly admit it among themselves.

When a Communist country introduces a bit of market economics—supply and demand, competing producers, profits, family farming, prices finding their own level—the first few years are usually good. Farm output especially grows, and people eat well. Consumer goods become far more available, and people live and dress better. New industries produce clothing and consumer electronics for the world market. Statistically, growth rates shoot up. It looks like they found the happy balance: a market economy at the *micro* level to produce consumer goods under the benevolent guidance of a state-run economy at the *macro* level (see page 396 for the distinction). Food, clothing, consumer electronics, and much else are produced by private firms, much of them with FDI, but some big industries as well as banking and planning systems are still state-owned and under Party control.

But after a few years things start to go wrong. Shortages, distortions, and bottlenecks appear. China's growth has slowed compared to the early 1990s. The private sector keeps bumping into the state sector. Every time it does, there is a "crisis" that can be resolved only by expanding the private sector and shrinking the state sector. After some years of this, there is little socialism left, and this Beijing's rulers do not like.

Democracy

DO MARKETS LEAD TO DEMOCRACY?

Economic liberalization tends to encourage political participation. You cannot reform the economy alone, for economic reform generates demands for political reform, namely, democracy. As political scientist Peter Berger put it: "When market economies are successful over a period of time, pressure for democratization inevitably ensues." A market economy generates a large, educated middle class and interest groups. People start resenting a corrupt government treating them like small children. They want democracy. If the regime is intelligent and flexible, it gradually opens up, usually by permitting a critical press, then opposition parties, and finally free and fair elections.

Taiwan is the textbook example of this transition from authoritarianism to democracy. Some argue that China will follow a similar path, but there are differences. First, Taiwan is small, making it easier to control. Taiwan's elites, many of them educated in the United States, led the way to democracy in the late 1970s. One of their motives: Show the Americans they are a democracy in order to win U.S. support against Beijing's demands to take over Taiwan. Remembering our warning about *dysanalogies,* the Taiwan model does not fit mainland China. China's elite is still firmly Communist, has no desire for democracy, and is not trying to please the Americans. Much of China's economy that looks private is actually still controlled by the state or army. China's leaders are not planning for capitalism; they are planning for Chinese power. China's middle class is rapidly growing, but it is tied to the state, which also blocks the growth of *civil society,* the autonomous groups that underlay pluralist democracy. Calls for democracy are ruthlessly crushed. Do not count on China moving to democracy automatically or peacefully, no matter what its economic growth.

The Chinese—like the Yugoslavs and Hungarians—found that a little bit of capitalism is like being a little bit pregnant. The choice Communist countries faced was difficult. If they went part of the way to a market economy, they experienced a few years of growth followed by dangerous distortions. If they called off the liberal experiment, they returned to the centralized, Stalinist system that was slowly running down, leaving them further and further behind the capitalist world. If they went all the way to a market system, they admitted they had been wrong all these decades.

Another problem cropped up with the financial problems that hit other East Asian lands in 1997: China's banks also loan recklessly and crookedly; the banking system, until recently entirely state-owned, is fragile. Some loans are under government orders, to prop up money-losing state industries. The central government itself was deeply in debt from subsidizing too much and collecting too little in taxes. With a faulty and foolish financial system, China's growth is threatened. Like America, China has a debt bomb ticking away.

Some observers argue that China's reforms were far more clever than the Soviet Union's and have a much better chance to succeed. First, China permitted private farming. The Soviet Union was still debating private farming when it collapsed. Then China permitted small businesses. Next, China designated SEZs for foreign investment. Missing in China is the political liberalization that blew up in Gorbachev's face. All Beijing's rulers know how Gorbachev inadvertently collapsed the Soviet Union, and all fear becoming China's Gorbachev, so they tolerate no democracy, competing parties, or free press, precisely the reforms that Gorbachev did first. Did the Chinese do it right, sequencing their reforms so as to build an economic basis for democracy before reforming their political system?

Other observers fear that China could collapse, that its economic reforms without political reforms will blow up. With increasing corruption and inequality (see box on page 469) there is increasing mass unrest. So far, the only successful transitions from communism to free-market capitalism have come in Central Europe—Poland, the Czech Republic, and Hungary—where anticommunists completely threw out the communist regimes. No controlled, middle-way transition has worked.

■ Enraging the Dragon

Some Americans feared an aggressive China was buying up the United States, an almost exact replay of the 1980s, when Americans were convinced Japan would soon own us. America seems to need an Asian country to bash. It is more like us selling the United States because we would rather consume than save. The Chinese (and Japanese) do the opposite, and that gives them a lot of spending money.

Reinforcing a sinister view of China was the 2005 offer by the Chinese National Overseas Oil Company (CNOOC) to buy a U.S. oil company, Unocal, for $18.5 billion. Unocal is not large but owned Asian oilfields that China wants to secure its growing energy needs. CNOOC, however, is a branch of China's petroleum ministry, and that made the offer something different than a purely commercial transaction. Remember, China only looks capitalist; much is still state-owned. China is now the world's second largest oil consumer (after the United States) and lines up oil deals worldwide to secure its energy supplies. The U.S. Congress howled in nationalistic anger at the CNOOC bid, much like Mexico or Nigeria do at mention of foreigners buying their oilfields. CNOOC withdrew its offer, and Chevron bought Unocal. Americans can be economic nationalists too.

Some observers were bothered by the implications of the failed deal. Were we discriminating against China, creating the very hostility we do not want to happen? How might China react to Congress's economic nationalism? Starting with President Nixon in 1972, we urged China to come out

World Trade Organization   120-plus members open selves to trade and investment; has quasi-judicial powers.

into the world market and make money. China followed our advice and now has a lot of dollars. Why should it not be free to spend them on a U.S. firm—whose main holdings were in Asia anyway? Some worried that America—which continually faults China on trade, currency, and copyright questions—was enraging the Chinese dragon. The road to Pearl Harbor was paved with U.S. trade restrictions on Japan, especially on oil.

■ China and the World

Several destabilizing forces are hitting China at the very time it will host the 2008 Olympics, of which it is very proud. The easy economic reforms—allowing a capitalist microeconomy—have been done. The really tough parts remain: dangerous government, banking, and state-industry debts; inefficient agriculture; and the need to add some nine million new jobs every year. Any global economic slowdown cuts China's export-led growth. As Japan discovered in the 1990s, exports cannot be the sole basis of an economy.

Another factor will have consequences that are hard to predict. In 2001 China won membership in the **World Trade Organization** (WTO), which it had long sought in order to boost China's exports. But in joining the WTO, China also had to open up its own economy to all manner of foreign investments and companies, including hitherto protected sectors like banking. Many weak Chinese firms will fall. They might include major banks. Imported grains may be cheaper than Chinese rice and wheat.

Membership in the WTO did not calm China's trade relationships with other lands. At the end of 2004 an agreement to regulate the world textile and clothing trade expired, leaving China free to export without limit. China, with plant overcapacity and abundant cheap labor, looked like

Geography

THE HONG KONG EXAMPLE

In 1997 the British colony of Hong Kong reverted back to China. Most of Hong Kong actually consisted of leased territory on the mainland—the source of the colony's water supplies—and the lease was up in 1997. Britain decided to give the whole package back to Beijing. Many prosperous and hardworking Hong Kongese did not want to be part of China (some took their money and fled to Vancouver, Canada). Beijing guaranteed, under the formula "one nation, two systems," that Hong Kong could keep its autonomy for fifty years. Beijing's intention, many believed, was to show Taiwan that it could rejoin the mainland and still keep its political and economic system. Few Taiwanese are buying.

Beijing slowly introduced new laws in Hong Kong on "security" and "information" to punish dissent.

Beijing court decisions eroded Hong Kong's special status. Critical Hong Kong editors lost their jobs. Corruption grew, as certain cooperative Hong Kongese got special deals. Beijing favors Shanghai as China's financial hub, as it once was before World War II. Prime Minister Zhu—like President Jiang, a former mayor of Shanghai—said in 1999, "Shanghai will be China's New York." Hong Kong will be its "Toronto." Hong Kong, one of the world's great financial centers, did more and more business with mainland China and less and less with other Pacific Rim countries. As Hong Kong lost its glitter, Singapore tried to move into its place as the great trading post of the Pacific Rim.

it would take over the world textile and clothing market, where it already had a major share. (Thought your $5 T-shirt was a bargain? In China they are three for $1. But careful, a Chinese XL is more like our medium.) Other countries screamed "unfair" and invoked emergency WTO provisions to limit imports from China. China reacted angrily, complaining of unfair treatment of its exports. Such trade lockouts fuelled Japanese nationalism before World War II.

Much could happen in relation to the 2008 Beijing Olympics. As noted, preparations are displacing and angering many Chinese. If students and dissidents try to use the Olympics to voice demands, they will be quickly crushed. Warned the *People's Daily*, the official CCP newspaper: "Protecting stability comes before all else." One good point: Beijing will likely not have a serious showdown over Taiwan until the games are over. The regime will let nothing mar their Olympics. The games themselves could make athletes and tourists very unhappy at the heat, humidity, and poisoned air of Beijing in August. The Olympics may not turn out to be the showcase China was hoping for.

Could China seize Taiwan by force or intimidation? Definitely, and we should decide now how to react. By early 2009, after the Olympics, the question may no longer be hypothetical. U.S. military intervention could turn into war, even nuclear war. A U.S. trade embargo would not frighten China. China could inflict great economic damage on the United States simply by selling its Treasury notes. China would also take a hit but would not hesitate to do so. Do not underestimate Chinese nationalism.

Key Concepts

ANTICIPATING CHINA CHANGE

One technique of anticipating change (see box on page 459) is to draw up several scenarios and state which you think are most probable. My list:

1. *No change.* The regime continues doing what it has done since about 1980: steady as she goes with a series of minor reforms backed up by coercion when needed. In the near term this is clearly Beijing's choice, but it may not work much longer, as many problems are coming to a head.

2. *Major reforms.* The technocrats of the Standing Committee see unrest coming and move to head it off by a series of major reforms. No one wants to move too fast and cause system breakdown, as Gorbachev did in the Soviet Union. This scenario is moderately probable.

3. *Panicked reforms.* If unrest gets big the regime could panic and offer hasty and sweeping reforms—even ones leading to democracy—while trying to keep a lid on discontent by coercion. (An analogue to this might be Mexico's "desperate priísmo" discussed on page 490. But remember, be careful with analogies.) It

might also attempt to deflect discontent with nationalism by taking over Taiwan while denouncing U.S. and Japanese pleas not to. Reforms in a panic are often bad reforms, coming too late and revealing regime weakness and fear. This scenario too is moderately probable. A hint of it came in 2005 when Beijing ended agricultural taxes, both to mollify peasants and to encourage them to stay on the farm and not leave for the cities.

4. *System change.* Facing massive unrest and a Taiwan crisis, the regime steps down. This would be the Gorbachev scenario and is improbable. In the absence of a Chinese civil society it would also have a chaotic aftermath and not guarantee a democratic outcome.

5. *Overthrow.* This is an unlikely scenario because it supposes Beijing would let discontent get sufficiently organized to challenge the regime in the streets. This could happen only with a drastic slowdown of China's economy that dashes citizen expectations of material improvement. If Beijing lost its performance-based legitimacy it would more likely revert to heavy coercion.

China has not really been stable in more than a century and could go off the tracks again. China, hard to govern in good times, now has a split and uncertain Party, corrupt local officials, weakening central authority, and growing regional disparities and discontent. Some observers fear Beijing is deflecting discontent outward by promoting an angry nationalism, a common practice of nervous regimes, and this is a very nervous regime.

China is already the number-one military power of East Asia, eclipsing Japan. Said former Party chief Jiang: "There will only be two superpowers by around 2020—China and the United States." One of China's priorities is its navy, with which it has claimed and fortified islets far from its shores in the East and South China Seas. This angers other countries in the region—Japan, the Philippines, Malaysia, Indonesia, and Vietnam. And Beijing proclaims the right to seize Taiwan, which it regards as a renegade province, at any time. By a 1979 law, the United States is committed to a peaceful, voluntary reunification. If Beijing applies force or intimidation to Taiwan, how should we react?

Underlying everything is China's deep craving for dignity and respect for what was once the world's greatest civilization but one that was brought low by Western and Japanese imperialists. How China achieves this recognition will be one of the great chapters of twenty-first century history.

Key Terms

devalue (p. 467)

float (p. 467)

foreign direct investment (p. 470)

guanxi (p. 469)

insolvent (p. 466)

mask (p. 466)

nonperforming loan (p. 467)

peg (p. 467)

revalue (p. 467)

soft landing (p. 467)

Special Economic Zones (p. 470)

state-owned enterprises (p. 466)

World Trade Organization (p. 474)

write off (p. 467)

yuan (p. 466)

yuppy (p. 471)

Further Reference

Chang, Gordon G. *The Coming Collapse of China*. New York: Random House, 2001.

Economy, Elizabeth C. *The River Runs Black: The Environmental Challenge to China's Future*. Ithaca, NY: Cornell University Press, 2004.

Fishman, Ted C. *China, Inc.: How the Rise of the Next Superpower Challenges America and the World*. New York: Scribner, 2005.

Greenhalgh, Susan, and Edwin A. Winckler. *Governing China's Population: From Leninist to Neoliberal Biopolitics*. Stanford, CA: Stanford University Press, 2005.

Huang, Yasheng. *Selling China: Foreign Direct Investment during the Reform Era*. New York: Cambridge University Press, 2003.

Hughes, Neil C. *China's Economic Challenge: Smashing the Iron Rice Bowl*. Armonk, NY: M. E. Sharpe, 2002.

Johnson, Ian. *Wild Grass: Three Stories of Change in Modern China*. New York: Pantheon, 2004.

McGregor, James. *One Billion Customers: Lessons from the Front Lines of Doing Business in China.* New York: Free Press, 2005.

Terrill, Ross. *The New Chinese Empire: And What It Means for the United States.* New York: Basic Books, 2004.

Tsai, Kellee S. *Back-Alley Banking: Private Entrepreneurs in China.* Ithaca, NY: Cornell University Press, 2002.

Wedeman, Andrew H. *From Mao to Market: Rent Seeking, Local Protectionism, and Marketization in China.* New York: Cambridge University Press, 2003.

Wu, Hung. *Remaking Beijing: Tiananmen Square and the Creation of a Political Space.* Chicago, IL: University of Chicago Press, 2005.

Zheng, Yongnian. *Globalization and State Transformation in China.* New York: Cambridge University Press, 2004.

Part VII

THE THIRD WORLD

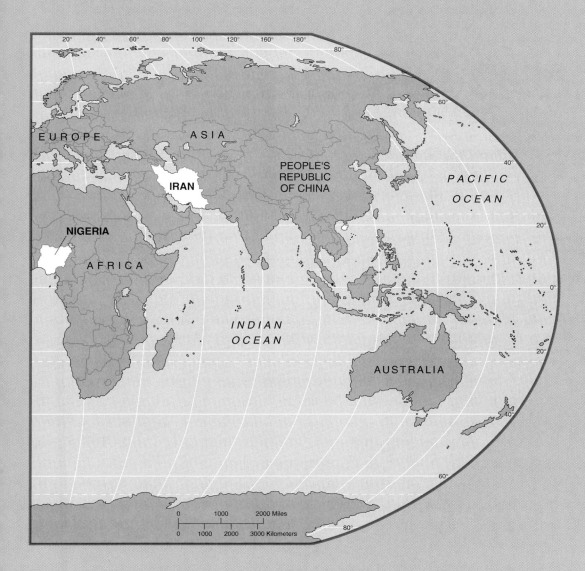

EUROPE

ASIA

IRAN

NIGERIA

AFRICA

PEOPLE'S
REPUBLIC
OF CHINA

PACIFIC
OCEAN

INDIAN
OCEAN

AUSTRALIA

20° 40° 60° 80° 100° 120° 160° 180°

80°

60°

40°

20°

0°

20°

40°

60°

80°

0   1000   2000 Miles

0   1000   2000   3000 Kilometers

Geography

WHAT IS THE THIRD WORLD?

Coined by French writers in the 1950s, *le Tiers Monde* (**Third World**) referred to the majority of humankind that was in neither the Western capitalist First World nor the Communist Second World. It is an awfully broad term that permits few firm generalizations. Now, with the collapse of communism in East Europe and the ex-Soviet Union, the Third World is simply everything that is not "the West," meaning Europe, the United States, Canada, Australia, and now Japan. Some say the only meaningful dividing line is now "the West and the rest."

The Third World is mostly poor, but some oil-producing countries are rich, and some of its lands have industrialized so fast that they are already affluent. China is trying to do this now. It is mostly nonwhite. Almost all of it was at one time or another a colony of a European imperial power. Most of it is hot and closer to the equator than the rich countries, so some writers call it the Global South. The U.S. State Department and some international banks call it the LDCs (less-developed countries). The ones making fast economic progress, such as China and India, are called NICs (newly industrializing countries). Business calls them the "emerging markets."

Call it what you will, one generalization stands up fairly well: It is politically unstable. The political institutions of almost all of its 120-plus countries are weak, and this is their chief difference from the West. Most Third-World lands are wracked by political, social, and economic tensions that sometimes explode in revolution, coups, and upheavals, and often end in dictatorship. Crime and **corruption** penetrate most Third World lands; rule of law is usually weak. In some countries, crime replaces politics. Few Third World countries have yet made it into the ranks of stable democracies, the characteristic now of all the West. Some developing lands are unstable democracies; **demagogues** gull unsophisticated voters with deceptive promises and turn themselves into dictators, something now happening in Venezuela.

Scholars find an imperfect correlation between economics and democracy. Most countries with per capita GDPs above $6,000 (middle-income countries and higher) are able to found stable democracies that do not revert to authoritarianism. Countries with per capita GDPs below $5,000 have trouble establishing and sustaining democracy; they often revert to authoritarianism. India is an amazing exception to the wealth-democracy link—although it too went through a bout of authoritarian rule under Indira Gandhi. Pakistan is more typical: unstable elected governments alternating with military rule. Notice how some of the countries discussed here are in this borderline area. Per caps above $6,000 do not guarantee democracy; much depends on the size, education levels, and pluralistic organization of the country's middle class.

We should really come up with a better name than Third World to describe the complexity of the lands that are home to five-sixths of the human race, but until such a term has become standard, we use Third World.

Geography

We understand much about Third World countries by knowing who were their former imperial masters, who left behind borders (most of them artificial), languages, legal codes, transportation lines, and styles of governance. Notice how few non-European lands stayed free of imperial rule: Afghanistan, Ethiopia, Japan, Thailand, and Turkey. China and Iran were reduced to semi-colonial status.

Much has been written about Europe's imperial impulse. Marxists see it as a race for riches, but in the long run administering and defending colonies cost the imperial powers more than they gained. Europe's richest countries never had colonies, but its poorest, Portugal, was drained by colonial expenses. Private interests, to be sure, profited from the colonial trade. Some see imperialism as a race for security: "If we don't take it, someone else will." Spain, Britain, France, and others competed for colonies out of fear they would be at a strategic disadvantage if they had none. A "contagion" or "copy-cat factor" was also at work: Colonies brought prestige. Only powers with colonies were respected. This helps explain the U.S. push for colonies in 1898. Roughly, here is who had what:

Spain, starting with Columbus, had most of Latin America (almost all of it lost in the 1820s) and the Philippines (lost to the United States in 1898).

Portugal's was the longest-lived empire. Portugal had Brazil (independent in 1822) but kept Goa until India took it in 1961; Angola, Mozambique, and Guinea-Bissau in Africa until 1975; East Timor until invaded by Indonesia in 1975; and Macau (near Hong Kong), ceded to China in 1999.

Britain's was the biggest empire—"The sun never sets on the British Empire"—and included Canada, Australia, New Zealand, India (which then included Pakistan and Bangladesh), Sri Lanka, Burma, Malaya, South Yemen, much of Africa below the Sahara (including Kenya, South Africa, and Nigeria), and Hong Kong, plus temporary arrangements in Egypt, Israel, Jordan, and Iraq.

France's was the second-biggest empire, including Vietnam, Laos, Cambodia, most of North and Equatorial Africa, and bits of the Caribbean and South Pacific. France and Britain gave up their colonies from 1947 to 1964.

The Netherlands held the rich Dutch East Indies from the seventeenth century to 1949 and South Africa's Cape area in the eighteenth century, plus specks on the Caribbean.

Belgium brutally exploited the vast Congo from 1885 to 1960, initially as the personal property of King Leopold.

Latecomer Germany in 1885 got some leftover pieces of Africa (Tanganyika, Namibia, Cameroon) and half of Samoa but lost them all at the close of World War I.

Italy, another latecomer, took Somalia in 1889, Eritrea in 1890, Libya from the Ottomans in 1912, and Ethiopia in 1935 but lost everything in World War II.

Imperialism was not solely a European thing. The Ottoman Turkish Empire took the Balkans in the late fourteenth century and held parts of it until the early twentieth. They also took the Middle East in the sixteenth century until pushed out by Britain in World War I.

Japan took Taiwan in 1895, Korea in 1910, and Manchuria in 1931 but lost them all in 1945.

And let us not forget that the United States had an empire too. In 1898 America took the Philippines (independent since 1946), Puerto Rico, Hawaii, Midway, and Guam.

Chapter 33

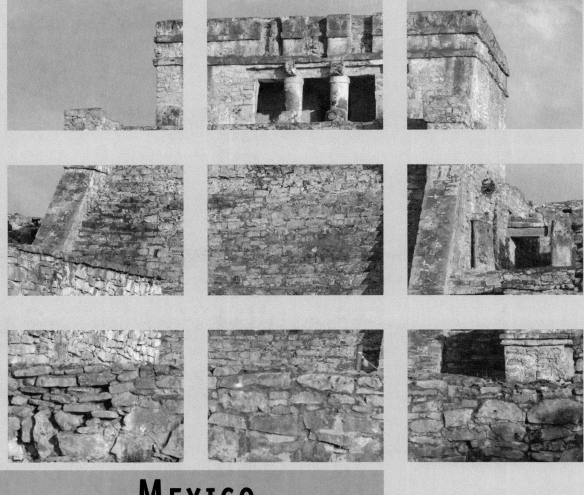

MEXICO

THE IMPACT OF THE PAST

Roughly 15,000 years ago hunter-gatherers, probably pursuing game, walked across the Bering Strait from Asia into North America. The ice age had lowered the sea level and formed ice bridges across the Strait. In a few millennia the hunter-gatherers spread the length of the Western Hemisphere. Some of them founded civilizations, but several thousand years later than the first civilizations of the Middle East. The domesticated plants and animals that spread from Mesopotamia to Europe and Asia never crossed the Bering Strait. The Americas had few domesticable plants (corn and potatoes in Peru) or animals (llamas in Peru), so their civilizations lagged behind Europe's, leaving them easy prey for the greedy Europeans.

Several civilizations rose and fell in Mexico long before the Spaniards arrived. The first, the Olmec, flourished around present-day Veracruz a thousand years before Christ and set the pattern for subsequent **Mesoamerican** civilizations. In the first centuries A.D. the Zapotec and Teotihuacán constructed palaces and pyramids tourists visit today. During the first millennium the Mayas built a high civilization in the Yucatán. From the tenth to twelfth centuries the Toltec held sway in Central Mexico until destroyed by nomadic invaders, the Aztecs among them.

Questions to Consider

1. What are the difficulties with the term *Third World*?
2. What countries did the main European empires rule over?
3. How did Mexico's colonial period differ from ours?
4. Why were Calles and Cárdenas so important?
5. In what ways was the PRI reign undemocratic?
6. What ideologies did Mexico import? Do any fit Mexico?
7. Was the breakdown of PRI accidental or necessary?
8. What role did the Catholic church play in Mexico?
9. Why do elections not equal democracy?
10. What is the impact of globalization on Mexico?
11. Has Mexico become a true democracy? How can you tell?

The Aztecs or Mexica, who originated in the northwest of Mexico, pushed into the Valley of Mexico around 1300. They made their capital on an island where they had sighted a prophetic eagle with a snake in its beak, later the symbol of Mexico. In 1376 the first Aztec king was crowned. Aztec kings had absolute power and ran their empire through a huge bureaucracy. The Aztecs kept expanding because they needed more land, serfs, and captured warriors to sacrifice to their deities. As a result, subordinate peoples did not love the Aztecs. The Aztec kingdom was complex and highly developed but not terribly old by the time Columbus sailed.

New Spain

Portugal actually started the voyages of discovery, initially aimed at direct access to the wealth (especially spices) of the "Indies" and a route that bypassed the Arab traders and the Moors, whom Spain and Portugal had just expelled. Prince Henry the Navigator saw himself as a religious crusader against

Third World   Most of Asia, Africa, and Latin America. (See page 480.)

corruption   Use of public office for private gain. (See page 480.)

demagogue   Manipulative politician who wins votes through impossible promises. (See page 480.)

Mesoamerica   (Spanish for Middle America) Southern Mexico and northern Central America. (See page 483.)

cacique   (Originally Indian chief) local political boss.

Muslims. For over half a century, Portuguese navigators worked their way down Africa's west coast until they rounded the Cape of Good Hope, Africa's southern tip, in 1488. They quickly crossed the Indian Ocean and set up forts and trading posts in Asia. Spain's Ferdinand and Isabella, aware that Portugal was far ahead in opening the Asia trade, accepted Columbus's argument that Spain could reach Asia directly across the Atlantic. (Yes, even then, educated people understood—from the ancient Greeks—that the world was round.) Columbus's 1492 voyage was to be a quick way to catch up with Portugal.

Columbus thought he had nearly reached India and called the inhabitants of Hispaniola "Indians." The name stuck, although some now prefer Native Americans, Amerindians, First Nations (Canada), or *índigenas* (Latin America). The Spaniards charged quickly into the New World for "gold, God, and glory," serving respectively the royal treasury, the Catholic church, and the *conquistadores*, who had just won a struggle of nearly eight centuries to expel the Arabs from Spain. They treated the Indians with the same contempt they held for the Moors. Indian lives meant nothing to them.

The Aztecs had a large population—their capital was probably larger than any European city at that time—and were well organized into a bureaucratic empire. Why could they not send the Spaniards packing? Several factors doomed the Aztecs. First, the Spaniards brought with them smallpox, against which Native Americans had no immunity. Mexico's population plunged from about 20 million at the time of the conquest to barely 1 million by 1600. Only in 1940 did Mexico reach the population it had under the Aztecs. Next, the Spaniards had steel; their swords sliced up the Aztecs (and later the Incas) as steel armor minimized their own casualties. They also had horses and guns, which the Aztecs had never seen before. Many of the peoples the Aztecs had subjugated aided the Spaniards. Finally, the Aztecs had a legend that the white god Quetzacóatl would return from the east and destroy them.

Geography

MEXICO'S MOUNTAINS

Mexico's geography is distinctive and helped mold its current politics, which is highly regional. Two mountain chains, the Sierra Madre Oriental on the east and Sierra Madre Occidental on the west, connect at Mexico's narrow neck, forming a kind of Y. Between the Y's two arms is the Mesa Central, an upland that includes the Valley of Mexico with its rich volcanic soil and abundant rainfall. Mexico City, at 7,500 feet (a mile and a half), is one of the highest capitals in the world.

Like other mountainous areas (Spain, Colombia, and the Caucasus), mountains can make a country hard to unify. With communication slow and difficult, some tribes and ethnic groups live in *patrias chicas* (little countries) outside central control. As the West Virginia motto says, *Montani Semper Liberi* (Mountaineers are always free). Mexico was never well integrated—neither by the Aztecs nor Spaniards—and still retains important regional differences and politics. In remote mountain villages, many still speak Indian languages. Mexico's crumpled geography forced any national government to work through and with **caciques.** Current Mexican voting patterns (and cuisine) are still regional.

Initially based in Cuba, Spanish ships explored Mexico's coast and brought back news of fabulous wealth in the interior. Partly at his own expense, Hernán Cortés equipped eleven ships and sailed from Havana in late 1518. After founding the city of Veracruz, he pushed inland with a force of 500 Spanish soldiers and several thousand Indians. The Aztec emperor Moctezuma (known to Americans as Montezuma) at first welcomed the Spaniards to his capital of Tenochtitlán, but they soon arrested him, and fighting broke out. Cortés retreated from the city but returned in 1521 after smallpox had killed much of its population. After three weeks of fierce battle, the Spaniards captured and killed the last emperor, Cuauhtémoc (a name that reappears with a current Mexican politician). Mexico today celebrates Aztec heroes but no Spanish ones, and many **pre-Columbian** traditions remain in Mexican culture.

pre-Columbian   The Americas before Columbus arrived.

creole   Spaniard born in the New World.

On the ruins of Tenochtitlán the Spaniards built a new capital and called it Mexico. Upon the ruins of the main Aztec temple they built a huge cathedral. With little resistance, they soon took over most of Southern Mexico. Rich silver mines moved the Spaniards to expand over Central Mexico, but takeover of Northern Mexico, arid and thinly populated, was not completed until about 1600. North of the present U.S.-Mexico border Spanish occupation was sparse and late—Texas in 1716 and California in 1769—which ultimately led to war with the United States and loss of the vast territories that became the Southwest United States.

To control what they called New Spain, Spain used a Roman institution, *encomiendas*, grants of land and the people who worked on it, to Spanish soldiers and settlers. In the feudal manner, the *encomendero* was the lord and master of Indian serfs. They worked for him, and he looked after their welfare and Christianized them. Actually, the setup was not much different than what the Indians were used to under the Aztecs. The *encomienda* system soon produced a feudal type of social stratification. At the top were those born in Spain, *peninsulares*, who held both all administrative positions and a social edge over *criollos* (**creoles**). Persons of mixed parentage, *mestizos*, became artisans and foremen, often in competition with poor Spaniards. The Indians worked the land on the *encomiendas* or stayed up in the mountains out of Spanish control.

The Spanish Habsburgs ran out of heirs; in 1707 a French Bourbon became king. (Spain's present monarch, Juan Carlos, is a Bourbon.) The Spanish Bourbons improved administration by dividing New Spain into twelve *intendencias*, each supervised by a French-style *intendente*, who reported to a central authority. Economic liberalization boosted Mexico's economy, and more Spaniards settled there. Bourbon reforms thus helped wake up Mexico.

Mexican Independence

The late eighteenth century brought new ideas to both Spain's and Portugal's Latin American colonies. The Enlightenment and the U.S. and French Revolutions inspired some to seek independence. A parish priest, Miguel Hidalgo, on September 16, 1810, proclaimed Mexico's independence. It got nowhere but is still commemorated as Mexico's Independence Day. Hidalgo led a strange uprising of Indians that presaged the turmoil of the Mexican Revolution a century later. On the one hand, Hidalgo demanded equality of all Mexicans and the redistribution of land for the Indians. But he also fought against French-style atheism and for Catholicism. Hidalgo's band ran out of control and massacred Spaniards and Creoles. Royalist forces soon captured and executed Hidalgo. Another priest of similar persuasion, José Maria Morelos, in 1814 and 1815 led a widespread guerrilla uprising in Southern Mexico until he too was caught and shot. Hidalgo and Morelos are

considered revolutionary heroes who founded the populist nationalism still very much alive in Mexican politics. Mexico's states of Hidalgo and Morelos are named after them.

caudillo Military chief or strongman, specifically one who takes over government.

Central America Countries between Mexico and Colombia.

South America Continent south of Panama.

Latin America All countries south of the United States.

Perhaps the real trigger to Mexico's independence was Napoleon's occupation of Spain in 1808. Spanish King Ferdinand VII was imprisoned, and Spain's Cortes (parliament) passed the liberal 1812 constitution, which Mexico's elite feared would spread French atheism and liberalism into their realm. In 1814 Ferdinand rejected the 1812 constitution, but an uprising of Spanish liberals got him to reinstate it in 1820. Again, Mexican conservatives feared it threatened their privileged status. To preserve it, they reasoned, they must declare independence from Spain, which they did, in 1821. The impulse to Mexico's independence was conservative, not liberal as in the United States. Mexican independence was an elite thing with no mass participation and no fighting with Spain to achieve it. Only Brazil's 1822 independence from Portugal was as painless.

Between Monarchy and Republic

Mexico, like Brazil, began as a conservative monarchy, but that lasted only a year and a half (Brazil's lasted until 1889). Immediately Mexico's elite—and politics was an exclusively elite thing—split into two camps: conservative centralizers and liberal federalists, a split that has never fully healed. For much of the nineteenth century Mexico, like most of Latin America, was led by **caudillos**.

The key figure in the first decades of the Republic of Mexico was Antonio López de Santa Anna, Mexico's off-and-on president, general, and dictator who played both sides of every conflict and continually broke his word. Santa Anna's big problem was Texas. To populate huge, thinly populated Texas, Mexico in 1821 gave American settlers land there, but they soon outnumbered Mexicans. To discourage further American immigrants—who brought slaves with them—Mexico outlawed slavery in 1828. (Texas was later a slave state and joined the Confederacy.)

By 1833 Texas had some 30,000 American settlers who demanded state's rights to govern themselves (and their slaves) within a Mexican federation. Santa Anna rejected the demand, the Republic of Texas declared independence in 1836, and Santa Anna marched north to reclaim it. He took the Alamo but was captured by the Texans. The United States annexed Texas in 1845, but Mexican and U.S. forces

Geography

BOUND MEXICO

Mexico is bounded on the north by the United States;
on the east by the Gulf of Mexico and the Caribbean;
on the south by Belize and Guatemala;
and on the west by the Pacific.

Geographically, Mexico is considered part of North America. To its south is **Central America**, consisting of Belize, Guatemala, Honduras, El Salvador, Nicaragua, Costa Rica, and Panama. **South America** is south of that. Everything south of the United States, including Mexico, is called **Latin America**.

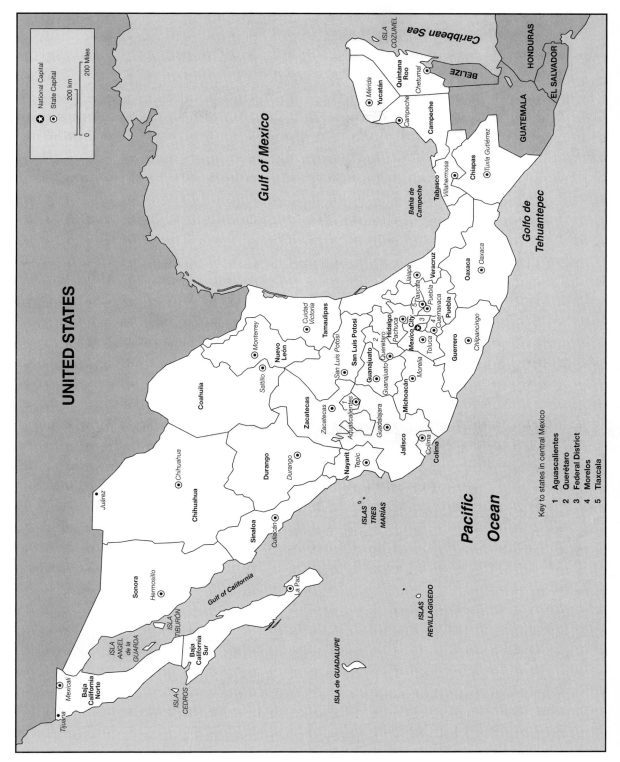

UNITED STATES

Gulf of Mexico

Caribbean Sea

ISLA COZUMEL

HONDURAS

BELIZE

GUATEMALA

EL SALVADOR

Mérida
Yucatán
Quintana Roo
Chetumal
Campeche
Campeche

Chiapas
Tuxtla Gutiérrez
Tabasco
Villahermosa

Bahía de Campeche

Golfo de Tehuantepec

Oaxaca
Oaxaca

Ciudad Victoria
Tamaulipas

Jalapa
Veracruz
5 Tlaxcala
Puebla
4 Cuernavaca
3 Puebla
Mexico City
Hidalgo
Pachuca
Toluca
Chilpancingo
Guerrero

Monterrey
Nuevo León
Saltillo

San Luis Potosí
San Luis Potosí
Coahuila
Zacatecas
Zacatecas
Guanajuato
Guanajuato
2 Querétaro
Morelia
Michoacán
1 Aguascalientes
Guadalajara
Jalisco
Colima
Colima
Durango
Durango
Nayarit
Tepic

Chihuahua
Chihuahua
Juárez
Sinaloa
Culiacán

ISLAS TRES MARÍAS

Pacific Ocean

Sonora
Hermosillo

Gulf of California

La Paz

ISLA ÁNGEL de la GUARDA
ISLA TIBURÓN

Baja California Sur

ISLAS REVILLAGIGEDO

ISLA de GUADALUPE

ISLA CEDROS

Baja California Norte
Mexicali
Tijuana

Key to states in central Mexico
1 Aguascalientes
2 Querétaro
3 Federal District
4 Morelos
5 Tlaxcala

National Capital
State Capital

200 Miles
200 km
0

Positivism Philosophy, originally French, of applying scientific methods to analyze and improve society.

soon clashed, leading to the 1846–1848 War with Mexico. The United States, after occupying Mexico City, took the southwest states and paid Mexico $15 million. Mexico was permanently humiliated.

An especially strange interlude in Mexico's history was its brief occupation by France, 1861–1867. Mexican conservatives in exile convinced Napoleon III that he could reconstruct a Catholic monarchy in Mexico. The ambitious Napoleon III thought Mexico would be the base for a French-led "Latin America" (the first use of that term). With the U.S. Civil War giving Napoleon III a window of opportunity, he used the pretext of Mexico's big European debts to send French troops to install the Austrian Habsburg Maximilian as his puppet emperor of Mexico. The effort found little support in Mexico and collapsed. It cost Paris too much money, and the U.S. Civil War was over. The French left, and Maximilian was shot. The French had committed the common mistake of supposing that Mexico was more or less like orderly Europe, where rational authority is obeyed. Latin America is quite different, more chaotic and rebellious. Few obey and plans seldom work right. The only remnant of the French in Mexico is the word *mariachi*, from the French hiring musicians for a *mariage*.

The iconic figure of nineteenth-century Mexican politics was Benito Juárez (1806–1872), who was remarkable on several counts. First, he was born of Indian parents (who died when he was three) at a time when all power was in Creole hands. Educated in law, Juárez rose in state and national politics and became president in 1858. A classic nineteenth-century liberal, Juárez saw a stagnant Mexico dominated by the old aristocracy and a conservative Catholic church. He wanted to redistribute their lands and institute a market economy, federalism, and separation of church and state. Juárez did not invent Mexican *anti-clericalism* (see page 91) but gave it a powerful boost. Conservatives forced Juárez to spend 1853–1855 in New Orleans, and in the 1860s the French forced him to withdraw to the U.S.-Mexico border, to a city later renamed after him. Although not long in power, Juárez set standards of modesty and honesty that few other Mexican leaders have met.

Porfirio Díaz (1830–1915) followed in Juárez's footsteps but turned himself into a harsh dictator. Like Juárez, Díaz was born in the southern state of Oaxaca (pronounced: wha-haw-ka), but of a mestizo family. Díaz studied law, fought the French, but turned against Juárez. Díaz was "elected" president seventeen times between 1877 and 1910, personally centralizing control over all branches of government. With the **Positivism** then popular in Latin America, Díaz's top bureaucrats, *los científicos*, pushed economic growth, but profits and land ownership went to a wealthy few and to foreign investors. Peasants were forced by debt to sell their land and grew poorer. By 1910 perhaps 95 percent of rural Mexican families were landless and eager to follow Zapata, who preached returning land to them. Díaz's long stay in power, called the Porfiriato, offered Mexicans *pan y palo* (bread and bludgeon), prominent in Mexico's governing philosophy ever since.

Political Culture

POOR MEXICO!

¡Pobre Mexico! Tan lejos de Dios, tan cerca de los Estados Unidos. "Poor Mexico!" exclaimed President Porfirio Díaz. "So far from God, so close to the United States." He voiced the widespread Mexican view that just sharing a long border with us condemns them to be dominated by the powerful United States. Díaz had seen the U.S. invasion of 1846–1847 that robbed Mexico of its northern half in 1848. The sad exclamation also indicates Mexican resentment of their rich, well-run neighbor, a sentiment found throughout Latin America.

■ The Mexican Revolution

Compared to Mexico's 1910–1920 upheaval, the Russian and Chinese revolutions are clear and easy to understand. They had only two sides; Mexico's had several, and they changed allegiances during the course of it. Mexico's is one of Latin America's few genuine revolutions. Latin America, to be sure, has had scores of military coups and "palace revolutions," but they were among elites. Mexico and much later Cuba and Nicaragua had armies fighting for years to overthrow regimes and replace them with totally different ones. (Castro's Cuban revolution, however, was conducted by law graduates plus one medical graduate, Che Guevara from Argentina.) A revolution is seldom caused by just one problem. It takes a series of mutually reinforcing, insoluble problems. Mexico had been storing up its contradictions until they erupted in the Revolution of 1910.

Under the long Porfiriato, discontent increased at the unfairness and cruelty of the Díaz regime. Anarchist and socialist ideas crept in from Europe. Juárista liberals who organized clubs, parties, and newspapers were jailed; many fled to the United States. Labor unrest was crushed by government troops. Influenced by Russian revolutionary Mikhail Bakunin, in 1906 the Mexican group Regeneration published a manifesto calling for one term for a president, civil rights, public education, land reform, improved pay and working conditions, and ending the power of the Catholic Church. These eventually became the program of the party that ruled Mexico for most of the twentieth century.

The trigger for the Mexican Revolution was Díaz having the obedient Chamber of Deputies "re-elect" him once again. Presidential candidate Francisco Madero, from a wealthy family that owned much of Northern Mexico, proclaimed from San Antonio, Texas, that the election was illegal and urged Mexicans to revolt on November 20, 1910, now celebrated as the start of the Revolution. Madero used his own fortune to supply rebels such as Pancho Villa. Díaz's decrepit Federalist army fell back, and Díaz resigned and left for Paris. Mexico's Congress proclaimed Madero the new president. If things had stopped there, Mexico would have had another of its many irregular changes of power.

But Federalist General Victoriano Huerta, encouraged by the U.S. ambassador, had President Madero arrested and shot. Huerta assumed the presidency himself, and full-fledged revolution broke out. Angered by the assassination and believing America could put things right in Mexico, President Woodrow Wilson had the Navy occupy Veracruz in 1914 and sent General Pershing after the bandit and guerrilla chief Pancho Villa in 1916. Wilson announced that America "went down to Mexico to serve mankind," but the effort solidified Mexican opposition to U.S. intervention, and U.S. forces had to fight Mexican guerrillas. (Sound familiar?)

Huerta fell in 1914, but at least four armies then battled for control of the country. Two of them were genuinely revolutionary, that of peasant leader Emiliano Zapata in the south and Pancho Villa in the north. The other two, under moderates Venustiano Carranza and Álvaro Obregón, sought to establish a stable order. The four sometimes collaborated but sometimes fought each other. Zapata was assassinated in 1919, Carranza in 1920, Villa in 1923, and Obregón in 1928. Revolution is a dangerous business. Mexicans still celebrate the revolutionary tradition of Zapata and Villa.

■ The Revolution Institutionalized

With the 1917 constitution, Mexican generals and state political bosses started what Peruvian novelist Mario Vargas Llosa called "the perfect dictatorship"—perfect because it looked like a democracy. Others have called it a series of six-year dictatorships because of limits on the presidential term. It was impressive and lasted about as long as Lenin's handiwork in Russia. The system grew out of a deal between Obregón and Calles.

ejido   Land owned in common by villages.

priísmo   Ideology and methods of PRI.

sexenio   (from *seis años*) Six-year term of Mexico's presidents.

austerity   Drastically holding down government expenses.

Obregón became president in 1920 and began to implement rural education and land reform, including the granting of **ejidos** to poor villagers. In 1924 he arranged the election of his collaborator, Plutarco Elías Calles, who in turn got Obregón reelected in 1928. But just then a Catholic fanatic assassinated Obregón, part of the bloody 1927–1929 Cristero Rebellion. Calles had implemented the anticlericalism of the 1917 constitution by banning foreign priests and clerical garb. With the cry, "*¡Viva Cristo Rey!*" (Long live Christ the King), militant Catholics rebelled, and government troops crushed them. Mexico's

Political Culture

MEXICO'S POLITICAL ERAS

Few countries have gone through such radical and bloody changes as Mexico. Most political cultures develop slowly and gradually. Mexico's developed in sudden shifts, each jerked back and forth by the introduction of new cultures and ideas, which never blended into a coherent whole.

The three phases of **priísmo** summarize the thrust of the presidents of each period. The four **sexenios** of the conservative period mark PRI's turning away from the Revolution and from *Cárdenismo,* giving lip service to labor and peasants but shifting to business and to stability. The three destabilizing *sexenios* mark the oil boom and government debt plus the 1968 massacre of students in Mexico City and psychological breakdown of President Echevarría. The desperate phase marks the recognition by Presidents de la Madrid, Salinas, and Zedillo that Mexico's economy is in shambles, and the whole system is losing legitimacy. U.S.-trained economic technocrats try to stabilize it with policies of **austerity** to reign in Mexico's runaway economy, but average Mexicans are hurt by it. Two political assassinations under Salinas turn many Mexicans against PRI. Panismo, never really implemented under Fox, faced an uphill struggle.

Era	Years	Remembered for
Aztec	1325–1521	High civilization, bureaucratic empire, human sacrifice.
New Spain	1521–1821	Colonialist exploitation, Catholicism.
Empire	1821–1823	Conservative independence.
Santa Anna	1830s–1850s	Erratic leadership, lost Texas and U.S. war.
Juárez	1850s–1860s	Equality, federalism, anticlericalism.
Porfiriato	1877–1911	Dictatorship, economic growth, poverty.
Revolution	1910–1920	Complex multisided upheaval.
Maximato	1924–1934	Calles, *el jefe máximo,* founds single six-year term and PNR.
Cárdenismo	1934–1940	Cárdenas makes PRI socialistic and corporatistic; nationalizes oil.
Conservative Priísmo	1940–1964	Favors business and foreign investment; crackdown on leftists.
Destabilizing Priísmo	1964–1982	Oil, overspending, and inflation spur unrest; massacre of students.
Desperate Priísmo	1982–2000	Technocrats calm economy, promote NAFTA, clean up elections; assassinations.
Panismo	2000–	First non-PRI president; attempts free-market reforms.

Church-anticlerical split began to heal only with the election of the conservative and Catholic Vicente Fox in 2000.

Calles, still running things from behind the scenes, decided in 1928 on a law making Mexico's presidency a single, non-renewable six-year term, something Mexicans had wished since Díaz kept reelecting himself. To perpetuate his hold on power, in 1929 Calles organized a coalition of state political bosses, generals, union chiefs, and peasant leaders into the National Revolutionary party (PNR), renamed in 1946 the Institutional Revolutionary party (Partido Revolucionario Institucional, PRI).

The remarkable politician is one who builds lastingly, and Calles did. He founded the political party that brought stability and led Mexican politics for the rest of the twentieth century. It could not, however, last forever. (Well, what can?) The Calles system masked contradictions and concentrated power in the presidency. From its founding until 2000, PRI never lost an election, which, to be sure, were less than democratic. Still, considering what much of Latin America went through

> **political institution**   Established and durable relationships of power and authority.
>
> **institutionalize**   To make a political relationship permanent.

Key Concepts

INSTITUTIONS AND INSTITUTIONALIZATION

Obviously, politics depends on power (see page 4). Power is not necessarily force, which is a subset of power, a coercive one best used sparingly. Reason: If you use a lot of force, people will hate you and be eager for your overthrow. You will build little legitimacy. Political power is temporary unless it is turned into **political institutions**.

Mexico has had plenty of strong leaders, who concentrated a great deal of power into their hands, but it vanished when they left office. Then the new leader had to amass power into his hands. Political power must not be too personal. Franco ruled Spain, sometimes by jail and firing squad, from 1939 to his death in 1975. He built what looked like a stable regime, but it was too much based on his one-man rule and quickly unraveled upon his death. Dictators rarely **institutionalize** their power. Within two years there was essentially nothing left of the Franco setup.

No country is born with functioning institutions; they have to evolve over time, usually in a series of accommodations among groups. An institution is not just an impressive building—although often they are housed in them to foster respect—but relationships of power that have solidified or congealed into understandings—sometimes written into constitutions or statutes, sometimes just traditions (as in Britain)—over who can do what.

Political scientists speak of Third World governments as "poorly institutionalized," characterized by irregular or extra-legal changes of leaders (such as revolutions and coups) and no clear boundaries as to who can do what. There are no rules; many try to seize power. Long ago, all countries were like that. We admire British government as "well-institutionalized," but centuries ago it suffered conquest, massacre, civil war, a royal beheading, a temporary Commonwealth, and attempts at absolutism. British institutions evolved and did not reach their modern form until the nineteenth century. Go back far enough and Britain resembled Mexico. Thanks to several historical factors, Britain institutionalized out of its tumultuous phase a couple of centuries earlier.

Accordingly, let us not ask too much of countries like Mexico too soon. They are bound to be messy and chaotic. Mexico did not begin political institutionalization until the 1920s, with Calles, and has not yet completed the process. (It will be complete when power alternates democratically among Mexico's parties.) Americans often wonder why Mexico cannot be like us—with democracy and rule of law—but Americans too spilled rivers of blood, first for independence, then to hold the country together. And America is no stranger to gangsters, drug traffickers, and crooks in high places.

corporatism Direct participation of interest groups in politics.

clientelism Government favors to groups for their support.

in the twentieth century—numerous military coups—the "soft authoritarianism" of the Mexican system was not bad.

Calles was basically a conservative, and his PNR made only moderate reforms until the 1934 election of Lázaro Cárdenas, who took Mexico on a radical path by implementing what the Revolution and 1917 constitution had promised. When Calles opposed him, Cárdenas had Calles exiled to California. Cárdenas was of mestizo descent and had little formal education but joined Carranza in the Revolution, becoming a general in 1920. Cárdenas was one of the PNR's founders and its first president, transforming it from a loose coalition to a cohesive and well-organized nationwide party. Upon taking office, President Cárdenas implemented a serious leftist program, including nationalization of U.S.-owned oil industries, which he turned into Petróleos Mexicanos (Pemex). In doing this, Cárdenas connected to an old Latin American pattern, *statism*, that Mexico has been reluctant to shed. Cárdenas carried out massive land redistribution and organized peasants and workers, making their unions constituent groups of the renamed Party of the Mexican Revolution. He left office on schedule, in 1940, but kept a watchful leftist eye on the government until his death to make sure it did not drift under *yanquí* influence. Cárdenas remains a legend of Mexican nationalist radicalism, something that helped his son, Cuauhtémoc Cárdenas, later head of the leftist Party of Democratic Revolution.

Cárdenas also made the party into a corporatist one. **Corporatism**, which brings interest groups directly into parties and parliaments, was riding high at the time. Initially a device of Mussolini's fascism, Brazil's Vargas also adopted corporatism into his New State in 1935. Cárdenas organized the PNR with peasant, labor, military, and "popular" sectors. The last included small businesses, later expanded to include big businesses. He built a large bureaucracy to mediate demands among groups and allocate funds to them, what is called **clientelism**. Initially, they seem to solve the problems of

Key Concept

CLIENTELISM

How can a society as badly fractured as Mexico's hold together? Why is it not stuck in civil wars, upheavals, and coups (which it was until the 1920s)? Clever political leaders, such as Calles and Cárdenas in Mexico, may calm such situations by making sure important groups have a share not only of seats in parliament but of favors, such as development projects, rigged contracts, subsidies, or just plain cash. In a clientelistic situation, the elites of each major group strike a bargain to obtain resources and restrain their followers from violence. Most major groups get something; no one group gets everything. Clientelism is widely practiced in the Third World (heck, maybe in the First as well), as in the Persian Gulf oil sheikdoms and in Nigeria (see next chapter).

Clientelism has at least three problems. First, it may be fake, with only small payouts to labor and agrarian sectors, which PRI kept in line with the traditional *pan y palo*. Second, it may exclude important groups. In Mexico, the Catholic church got no part of the deal, and big businessmen got little until some were co-opted into PRI during World War II. (The Catholic church and business are among the groups that brought Vicente Fox to power in 2000.) A third problem is rigidity. The allocation of which group gets how much help and money cannot be frozen; it has to change as society and the economy evolve. Village land held in common and state-owned industries can retard economic growth, but the Mexican groups who benefit from these institutions fight change. Fortunately, Mexico loosened up its system in time to avoid an explosion.

participation, power-sharing, and allocation of resources in chaotic situations. They are, however, not really democratic and over time become rigid and unstable. They are contrived and temporary fixes and leave the system saddled with an overlarge bureaucracy.

constitutionalism Degree to which government limits its powers.

THE KEY INSTITUTIONS

The first thing you notice about Mexico's political history is that, prior to 1924, few Mexican presidents either came to power or left office in a regular, legal way. Most were installed and/or ousted on an ad hoc basis by a handful of elites or military coups, sometimes with violence. Mexico has had four constitutions since independence but not much **constitutionalism**. Once in office, Mexico's presidents observed few limits on their powers and tended to construct personalistic dictatorships. This is true of much of the Third World, where politics consists of strong personalities making their own rules.

Comparison

TERM LENGTHS

Some American critics of our two four-year presidential terms say we should consider a single six-year term. The theory here is that presidents are so concerned with reelection that they accomplish little their first term and then do irresponsible things their second term, because they do not have to worry about reelection. It is not clear that term lengths cause anything very specific. Both limited and unlimited terms have lent themselves to mistakes and corruption. The table below shows how our nine countries' terms for chief executives compare:

Remaining too long in office can lead to corruption, but not if chiefs of government must face an informed electorate at regular intervals. Margaret Thatcher served eleven years through three elections until her party dumped her over policy questions and slumping popularity. Term limits in Nigeria, on the other hand, did nothing to curb corruption. A limited term may even encourage officials to grab more sooner. By themselves, term limits do little; it all depends on the institutional and cultural context.

Britain	prime minister	Unlimited terms, each for up to five years (but usually four).
France	president	Unlimited five-year terms.
Germany	chancellor	Unlimited terms, each for up to four years (but sometimes shorter).
Japan	prime minister	Unlimited but usually short.
Russia	president	Two four-year terms.
China	president	Two five-year terms (but this is recent).
Mexico	president	One six-year term.
Nigeria	president	Two four-year terms (barring overthrow).
Iran	president	Two four-year terms (but real power in hands of Islamist Guide).

That changed—but not completely—with the beginning of the single, six-year presidency in 1928 and the 1929 founding of what became PRI. A contrived stability settled over Mexico for the rest of the century. There were no more upheavals because all the major reins of power—including the military—passed through PRI into the hands of the president. The personality of the president still counted—some, such as Cárdenas, were radical, others conservative—but the system counted more. Mexico was an example of what political scientists call a *clientelistic* system in which most major groups have been *co-opted* (see page 501) into cooperation. They feel they have a stake in the system and minor input into government policy. Peasants get land reforms and ejidos; workers get unions; and bureaucrats get jobs.

■ The Six-Year Presidency

Latin America generally has modeled its institutions on the U.S. pattern, preferring presidential to parliamentary systems (see page 38). Mexico's presidential system, like that of the United States, combines head of state and chief of government. For most of the twentieth century it was even more powerful than the U.S. presidency. We must qualify that statement by noting that it was powerful when a PRI president dominated a Congress with a big PRI majority. The 2000 election of Vicente Fox of PAN did not give PAN a majority in the Congress, making Fox much less powerful than his PRI predecessors. Starting in 2000 Mexico tasted the "divided government" that often prevails in the United States, when a president of one party faces a Congress dominated by another. Likewise, the French system devised by de Gaulle made the president very powerful, but these powers shrank

Democracy

MEXICO'S CLOSE 2006 ELECTION

At the time that this textbook went to press, Mexico's 2006 presidential election was too close to call and, regardless of who declared himself the winner, the final verdict had to work through recounts, court challenges, and charges of rigging. The big question: If the leftist PRD lost, would it abide by the decision or turn to violence? A rigged election in 1910 triggered the Mexican Revolution.

The good news is that the 2006 election showed a real Mexican democracy. Mexicans now could choose among left, right, and center, something PRI had not allowed. The closeness of the election indicated competition, the crux of democracy. It was a dirty campaign, but slinging mud is better than buying votes.

On the left, the populist ex-mayor of Mexico City, Andrés Manuel López Obrador of the PRD, promised money for the poor and curbs on NAFTA (see page 509). On the right, Felipe Calderón of the PAN, which

had won in 2000 with Vicente Fox, urged a market economy within NAFTA. He also called López Obrador a radical demagogue like Venezuela's Hugo Chávez. In the center, Roberto Madrazo of the PRI ran third; PRI's old base had collapsed amid corruption.

Middle-class voters liked the PAN for its free-market growth plans. Those worried about Mexico's huge inequality voted PRD. Poor and rural people liked the PRD's promise of welfare. Government employees went PRI.

The winner of the 2006 Mexican election will take office knowing that many Mexicans voted against him, and he will face a Congress still badly divided among three parties (see page 495). If Calderón is the winner, he—like Fox—would not have a legislative majority, and he has vowed to build a coalition across party lines. The world holds its breath, waiting to see if Mexican democracy is rooted enough to calmly accept the 2006 electoral results.

when opposition parties won a majority of the National Assembly. Then French presidents had to practice *cohabitation* with prime ministers of opposition parties.

dedazo   (From *dedo,* finger) Tapped for high office.

Since 1928 Mexico has not deviated from the single, six-year term, although it might have been otherwise. One of the Revolution's goals was "no reelection"—to prevent another Díaz from monopolizing power. Obregón, who already had served from 1920 to 1924, won reelection in 1928, with Calles's support, but was assassinated before taking office. That decided Calles to support the *sexenio* without reelection, even after an interval.

Under the long PRI reign, succession was actually in the hands of the president, who was also party chief. In consultation with past presidents and other PRI leaders, the current president would name his successor, who became the party's nominee for the next election. Once nominated, of course, until 2000 no PRI candidate lost, and many won by 90 percent. Presidents would pick their successors—not necessarily well-known persons—with an eye to preserving stability and the power of PRI. The process was called half in jest **dedazo**. It may also have included understandings that the new president would not look into corruption. No choice was absolutely predictable and, once in office, presidents often departed from previous policies. Calles did not know, for example, how far left Cárdenas would veer. When his term was ending, Cárdenas picked an obscure military officer, Manuel Ávila Camacho, who was more conservative.

■ Mexico's Legislature

Mexico's bicameral Congress (Congreso de la Unión) has been much less important than its presidency. Díaz was famous for simply putting obedient supporters into the legislature, and PRI did much the same. Legislative elections changed with the 1986 Electoral Reform Law, induced by uproar over PRI's habitual election frauds. Inspired by Germany's *mixed-member* system, Mexico (like Italy) now fills most seats from single-member districts, Anglo-American style, but allocates additional seats based on each party's share of the popular vote, that is, by proportional representation (PR).

Mexico's upper house, the Senate (Cámara de Senadores), now has 128 seats and six-year terms. Ninety-six of the seats are filled from single-member districts, 32 by PR. The lower house, the Federal Chamber of Deputies (Cámara Federal de Diputados), now has 500 seats with three-year terms. Three hundred seats are filled by district voting, 200 by PR in five regions. In 2005, PRI was the biggest party in both chambers but no longer a majority:

	Senate	Chamber of Deputies
PRI	60 seats	222 seats
PAN	46	151
PRD	16	95

Some smaller parties such as the Greens and Workers parties held a few seats.

Since 1997, after several electoral reforms, PRI lost its majority in the Congress. PAN and PRD together could outvote PRI, but they are from opposite ends of the political spectrum and agree only in their dislike of PRI. Conservative PAN favors a free-market economy and curbs on spending, radical PRD the opposite. That kind of legislative deadlock persuades some voters to return to

populist Claims to be for common people and against elites.

PRI as the only party that can run the country. Unless PAN can achieve majority status (unlikely) or get cooperation from some PRI senators and deputies (difficult), it can do little in Congress. This deadlock hamstrung the Fox *sexenio*.

■ Mexico's Dominant-Party System

We mentioned that Britain is a "two-plus" party system: two big parties and several small ones. Some countries might be called "one-plus" party systems, for they are dominated by parties so big that they seldom lose. Mexico's PRI, Japan's Liberal Democrats, and Putin's United Russia are examples. India, under the long reign of the Congress party, used to be, but has since experienced electoral alternation.

In a dominant-party system (see page 358), other parties are perfectly legal, but the dominant party is so well-organized and has so many resources that upstart parties seldom have a chance. In some cases, the party founded the country, as the Congress party under Ghandi did in India. The big parties dominate the media and civil service. Voters may acknowledge that the dominant party is corrupt, but they may also like the stability and prosperity it has brought. Many Japanese voters see the Liberal Democrats in this light. When the dominant party can offer neither, as PRI discovered, it may cease to be dominant.

PRI, founded by Calles in 1929, is Mexico's oldest party. As its name attests, it billed itself as revolutionary and socialist long after it abandoned such policies. PRI presidents such as Cárdenas and Luis Echevarría Álvarez took leftist—especially anti-U.S.—stances, but most have been

Key Concepts

THE DEMAGOGUERY TENDENCY

Conservatives feared that if the **populist** López Obrador of the PRD were elected president he would follow radical leftist policies like Venezuela's demagogic Hugo Chávez and bring economic disaster. *Demagogue* has the same root as democrat—*demos,* the people—but demagogues use issues in a manipulative and self-serving way to erase democracy. The populist demagogue or "rabble rouser" whips up poor or frightened masses with promises of jobs, welfare, or law and order, and once in office becomes dictatorial. Classic demagogues include Robespierre (page 94), Hitler (page 175), Perón of Argentina, and Vargas of Brazil.

Demagoguery tends to appear in poor countries that are only recently democratic, such as much of the Third World today. Desperate people confuse democracy with prosperity, and the populist demagogue helps in this confusion: "The people cry out for

bread, and I shall give them bread!" When the country reaches middle-income levels and has a large, educated middle class, demagoguery fades; few people swallow the populist promises.

Latin America has been fertile ground for populist demagoguery. It appears now in Venezuela, where Chávez—a former paratroop officer who earlier attempted a coup—was twice elected president. Chávez's line: Venezuela is rich with oil but has been robbed by the United States, rich Venezuelans, and corrupt officials. Most Venezuelans are below the poverty line and believed him. Chávez's "Bolivarian" revolution (nobody knew what it meant), took over industry and distributed oil wealth to the poor. This was made possible by the big runup in oil prices but is unlikely to last. Mexico's López denied he was anything like Chávez.

moderate centrists. Calles and Cárdenas designed the party well, with its four sectors and strong patronage network, but as Mexico gained a large middle class, these sectors became less and less important, making PRI out-of-date. Some Mexican commentators call the PRI sector chiefs "dinosaurs." PRI's share of the vote has shrunk, but it still wins in a broad belt across Central Mexico. PRI victories in many state gubernatorial elections did not carry over into the 2006 presidential contest.

bilateral opposition Centrist governments undermined from both sides.

PAN was founded in 1939 to oppose PRI on religious grounds. PAN was a Catholic reaction to Calles's anticlericalism. Mexico's church-state relations have been bloody at times, and serious Catholics felt martyred by the PRI government. In the 1980s, the modern business community, which disliked state-owned industries and economic instability, found PAN a useful vehicle for their discontents. The two strands, Catholic and business, coexist uneasily within PAN and could pull it apart. PAN makes its best showings in Northern Mexico, where proximity to the United States has contributed to prosperity and a capitalist orientation. PAN, still dominated by Catholic militants, is not nearly as well organized as PRI. Mexicans' big 2000 Fox vote did not indicate that they had become conservative Catholics but that they were fed up with PRI. Although many were disappointed with Fox, Felipe Calderón of PAN came from behind in the 2006 elections.

The south of Mexico is the poorest and most radical part of the country. Zapata, a local boy, is remembered. It is here that the new PRD makes its best showing. In 2005 the PRD won the governorship of the southern state of Guerrero (and of Baja California Sur). Cuauhtémoc (the Aztec name won him some votes) Cárdenas, son of the oil-nationalizer, might have won the 1988 presidential election if not for PRI rigging. Cárdenas, along with a leftist chunk of PRI, split from PRI in 1988 over its turn to free-market policies. PRI had to split; it had abandoned revolution in favor of business. With some Socialists and Communists, Cárdenas in 1989 formed the leftist PRD, which claims to be true to the ideals of his father, anticapitalist and anti-United States. With a much weaker organization and base of support than PRI or PAN, PRD, too, has an uphill struggle. The PRD's Andrés Manuel López Obrador (known as AMLO), the popular former mayor of Mexico City, was initially the leading presidential contender for 2006. Mildly leftist parties have won elections in Argentina, Brazil, Chile, and Venezuela. Mexico could one day elect a PRD president.

At this point some might call Mexico a "former dominant-party system," as the PRI has weakened and now faces **bilateral opposition**, that is, both on its left (PRD) and right (PAN). The key factor in PRI's decline: its corruption and the growth of an educated middle class that no longer stands for it. Mexico may be on its way to becoming a multiparty or two-plus party system. The United States is no stranger to dominant-party systems: Most U.S. congressional districts reliably return the same party to Congress, sometimes without opposition.

■ Mexican Federalism

Most countries are unitary systems, but the Western Hemisphere boasts the largest number of the world's federal systems, partly due to the U.S. model and partly to the sprawling geography of many countries. Argentina, Brazil, Canada, and Mexico are federal systems, some more federal than others. Mexico consists of thirty-one states and the Federal District (Distrito Federal, DF, the equivalent of our D.C.) of Mexico City. Each state has a governor elected for a single six-year term but only a unicameral legislature.

In actuality, Mexican federalism concentrates most power in the center, a bit like Soviet federalism. For most of the twentieth century PRI presidents handpicked state governors, who then

mercantilism   Originally French theory that a nation's wealth is the gold and silver in its treasury.

egalitarian   Dedicated to equality.

used the office as a tryout for federal positions. As in the United States, many Mexican presidents first served as governors, including President Fox. The states get much of their revenue from the national government and then dispense it to the municipalities, a food chain that keeps subordinate levels of government loyal and obedient.

MEXICAN POLITICAL CULTURE

Mexican political culture—and this is true of much of Latin America—is hard to comprehend because it is a dysfunctional pastiche of several cultures and ideologies: Indian passivity, Spanish greed, Catholic mysticism, populist nationalism, and European anticlericalism, liberalism, anarchism, positivism, and socialism. Unsurprisingly, these many strands never blended. Mexico is regionally, socially, and culturally badly integrated, never forming a coherent whole. Mexican political culture did not grow slowly and locally over time but was imported in waves, mostly from Europe, none of which really sank in enough to create a coherent Mexican political culture. In comparison, most elements of American political culture blend and reinforce each other: freedom, equality, Protestantism, individualism, pragmatism, materialism, market economics, and rule of law. The U.S. creeds that did not easily blend—slavery, Catholicism, and welfarist liberalism—formed America's political divides for several generations.

Comparison

MEXICO AND AMERICA AS COLONIES

The Spanish colonies of the New World resembled the declining feudal system of Europe. Society was rigidly stratified by birth and race into privileged and lower ranks. The Catholic church, supervised by Rome, tried to calm Mexico's Indians by both material help and spiritual uplift. Madrid's chief interest in New Spain was in the amount of gold and silver it could ship to the royal treasury. For this, Spain set up Mexico (indeed, all of its Latin American holdings) as vast bureaucracies, which plague the region to this day. Latin America was born bureaucratic. Mexico was Spain's richest colony; its gold and silver funded the giant Habsburg military effort in the Thirty Years War. Under the mistaken doctrine of **mercantilism**, Spain reckoned it was rich, but gold and silver produce neither crops nor manufactured goods. Ironically, as Spain stole the vast wealth of the New World it grew poorer. The extractive industries impoverished Mexico, too.

The English colonizers of Virginia and New England arrived a century after the Spaniards did in Mexico.

By the early seventeenth century the feudal age was over in England, and the immigrants carried little feudal baggage or bureaucracy. The colonies largely ran themselves. No one expected quick gold or silver, either for themselves or for London. Although the English brought ranks of nobility with them, most settlers were farmers or merchants with an **egalitarian** ethos. They concentrated on agricultural production. Their several varieties of Protestantism—none of which had Catholicism's central control—taught hard work, delayed gratification, equality, and individuality. They pushed the Indians westward but did not turn them into serfs.

Samuel Huntington's latest controversial book, *Who Are We?*, posits religion as the biggest determinant of political culture. If French, Spanish, or Portuguese Catholics had originally settled the United States, he argues, we would today resemble, respectively, Quebec, Mexico, and Brazil. The fact that we were first settled by Anglo-Protestants has made all the difference.

Mexico's Indian Heritage

Mexico looks Spanish but, many scholars argue, beneath the surface remains very Indian. Indian cultures and languages still survive in isolated villages. Mexico's cuisine is basically Indian. Mexico's spirituality is a blend of pre-Columbian religions and Spanish Catholicism, which was always dipped in blood. The Indians, of course, were used to blood sacrifice at the hands of the Aztecs and took easily to the blood emphasis of Spanish Catholicism. The Spanish Inquisition, which traveled to Mexico and even to New Mexico, also utilized human sacrifice. Since the Spaniards built their great cathedral on the ruins of the main Aztec temple, it is hard to tell the precise reason why it is a pilgrimage site. Is the impulse purely Christian or an echo of pre-Christian religion?

hacienda Large country estate with Spanish owner (*hacendado*) and Indian serfs.

mestizaje Intermingling of Spanish and Indian.

norteamericanos "North Americans"; U.S. citizens.

personalismo Politics by strong, showoff personalities.

machismo Strutting, exaggerated masculinity.

The Aztecs and earlier Mexican societies were strongly hierarchical. Those at the base, peasants, were taught to defer to their social superiors. Social-class distinctions come with civilization. When the Spanish took over from the Aztecs, Indian peasants were used to subordinate behavior; most accommodated to the forced labor of **haciendas** and silver mines. (In contrast, the Indians of the present-day United States had no cities and were highly egalitarian.) The Spanish, of course, brought their own feudal society with them and imposed it on the Indians.

One important demographic point about Mexico is that its Spanish conquerors were exclusively males; Spanish women did not arrive until much later. (The English settled whole families in America.) Very quickly, a new class of persons appeared in Mexico, mestizos, those of mixed descent. **Mestizaje** was also a cultural and social thing, contributing to Mexican Catholicism and the beginnings of a middle class between the Spaniards (later creoles) and the Indians.

Latin Americans boast, especially to **norteamericanos**, that they are free of racial prejudice. In Latin America, they say, money and manners count for more than skin color in deciding race. A person with the right culture and language is accepted as essentially European. As they say in much of Latin America, "Money lightens" (one's skin color). There is some truth to it, but money and life chances tend to come with racial origin in Latin America. Whites have a much better chance of going to a university, entering a profession, making lots of money, and living in a nice house. Mexicans of Indian descent run a high risk of infant death, malnutrition, poverty, and the lowest jobs or unemployment.

Political Culture

PERSONALISMO AND MACHISMO

Latin American politicians frequently rely on **personalismo** in politics rather than on parties, ideologies, or laws. Said one Mexican diplomat, "In Mexico we have egos, not institutions." Most Latin Americans like to be perceived as having a strong personality, the men especially as *macho* (male), leading to **machismo**. Latin American leaders traditionally combine personalismo and machismo to gain mass support.

After Cárdenas, Mexican presidents of the PRI era, selected by *dedazo,* did not much utilize these qualities because they did not need them. With the recent arrival of competitive politics, however, personalismo and machismo appeared in Mexico. Vicente Fox and López Obrador ran on their colorful and outspoken personalities, and other Mexican politicians must do the same.

Still, Mexico has done a better job historically than the United States at letting at least some nonwhites rise to the top. Juárez, of Indian descent, led Mexico in the mid-nineteenth century. Cárdenas and several other presidents were of mestizo descent. The United States has not yet had a comparable racial breakthrough. Most of Mexico's top leaders, in the economy and politics, to be sure, have been white, a point true of Latin America generally. Because few Mexicans are of purely European descent, all Mexican politicians celebrate the country's Indian heritage. There are no statues of Cortés in Mexico, and the quincentennial of Columbus's 1492 voyage was little noticed.

◼ Imported Ideologies

Latin America is noted for picking up ideas invented elsewhere, warping them, and then trying to apply them where they do not fit. One Latin America expert called the continent a *reliquiario*, a place for keeping old relics of saints, a piece of the true cross, and so on. Now it is a reliquary for old ideas long passé in the rest of the world. This makes Latin American political thought a sort of remainder sale of old ideologies. Here are some notions still or recently alive in Latin America:

Liberalism here means the original, nineteenth-century variety that rejected monarchy and opened society to new forces. The United States, with its large middle class, took naturally to this philosophy of freedom, but Latin America, encumbered by inherited social positions, big bureaucracies, and state-owned industries, did not. No middle class, no liberalism. Juárez and Díaz could not make liberalism work in Mexico. Some Latin American countries have recently turned to economic "neoliberalism" by trying to build free markets.

Positivism, as discussed earlier, proposed that experts should improve society through science. It died out in Europe but caught on in Latin America, especially Brazil, where its motto, "Order and Progress," is in the flag. In Mexico, Díaz's *científicos* typified the positivist spirit, which conflicts with the hands-off philosophy of liberalism.

Socialism in Europe made sense, as Europe had much industry and a large working class that was amenable to unionization and social-democratic parties, such as Britain's Labour and Germany's

Democracy

CAUTIOUS DEMOCRATS

Latin America (except Cuba) turned democratic in the 1980s, but Latins have embraced democracy slowly and cautiously. Like Russians, they expected democracy to bring prosperity; both were slow in coming. Half of Latin Americans tell pollsters that democracy is always preferable, but a considerable percent still say that an authoritarian government can sometimes be preferable.

Democratic feeling rises and falls with the economy, as most Latins worry about unemployment and poverty. Latin America's economies have been up lately, and so has democratic support. In a downturn,

many say a dictatorship that puts food on the table is not so bad. Many Latin Americans perceive all government, democratic or not, as essentially rigged to favor a few powerful interests. Mexico's numbers are typical: The percent preferring democracy barely climbed from 53 percent in 1996 to 59 percent in 2005. During the same period, however, the percent saying authoritarian rule can be preferable dropped from 23 to 13 percent. Democracy is not yet fully rooted in Latin American political culture, but authoritarianism has been largely uprooted.

Social Democrats. Latin America, however, until recently had little industry and only a small proletariat; it was precapitalist. No
working class, no socialism. Governments such as Mexico's and
Brazil's invented and coddled unions to make it look like they had
a working-class base. Some idealists still see socialism as the answer
to Mexico's vast poverty, but they offer no successful examples of
it. Chile prospered after it overthrew the Socialist government of
Salvador Allende.

> **quixotic**   (From Don Quixote) Roman-
> tic, unrealistic efforts to achieve
> mistaken goals.
>
> **co-opt**   To enroll other groups in your
> cause, rendering them harmless.

 Rural socialism rejects industry in favor of small farms. It proposes returning to a rural idyll of
equality and sufficiency based on family farming. Zapata was its hero. It idealizes a past that never
existed and cannot be: There is simply not enough land for exploding populations. Peasant farming
equals poverty. Zapatista guerrillas in Chiapas state in Mexico's south, however, still pursue this
quixotic vision.

 Anarchism is a sort of primitive socialism that argues the end of national government will erase
class differences. A small political movement, it appeared in the late nineteenth century in Russia
and in Spain, where it became anarcho-syndicalism: no government needed because trade unions
will run things. Several Mexican revolutionaries were influenced by anarchism.

 Anticlericalism, founded by French writer Voltaire (see page 91), caught on strongly in Spain and
then spread to Latin America. Anticlericalists such as Calles claim the Catholic church has too
much political power, favors the rich, and keeps Mexico backward. Few scholars think the Catholic
church in Latin America really had much power. Now the shortage of priests has marginalized it.

 Fascism, founded by Mussolini and copied by Hitler, briefly influenced some Latin American
countries, especially those with many German and Italian immigrants. It combines nationalism,
corporatism, and fake socialism under a charismatic leader. Vargas's Brazilian New State drew the
quip "fascism with sugar." Perón's Argentina was not as sweet and welcomed Nazi war criminals.
Cárdenas's nationalism and socialism hinted at national socialism.

 Communism, revolutionary Marxist socialism under Moscow's control, was for decades popular
among Latin American intellectuals. It proposed to cure the continent's drastic inequality and poverty by the state taking over production and ending U.S. exploitation, a permanent and popular theme.
Some of Mexico's leading artists, such as Diego Rivera and David Siqueiros, were Communists. Castro's Cuba and Che's icon drew much support until Latin intellectuals noticed that Cuba is a stagnant tyranny. Although largely defunct, Marxism lingers in *dependency theory* (see page 502).

 Latin American intellectuals have been so addicted to one ideology after another that they fail
to notice the rest of the world has already discarded them. Communism, for example, collapsed in
East Europe and the Soviet Union and is meaningless in China but is still alive in Cuba, which will
likely be the last Communist country in the world, the reliquary of Marx's bones.

PATTERNS OF INTERACTION

Calles and Cárdenas devised a system of **co-optation** that gave the Mexican government control over groups that might otherwise cause them trouble. They promised peasants and labor a
good deal but rarely gave them much in return. When rural and worker unions got demanding,
the government crushed them. The large Mexican Workers Confederation, for example, was
under the thumb of PRI through its chief, who served fifty-six years. While professing "socialism," Mexican presidents tolerated no competition from Communists, especially after Stalin

dependency theory   Radical theory that rich countries exploit Third World lands and keep them poor.

had Trotsky assassinated in Mexico in 1940. Even "leftist" presidents such as López Mateos had no trouble arresting Communists and breaking strikes. There was a large element of fakery in PRI governance. Chiefly, they served themselves.

For decades, the Mexican government tried to co-opt students by giving them a nearly free education and then employing them as civil servants. (Saudi Arabia attempted to do the same.) This cannot work forever; there is simply not enough money. Student numbers and discontent grew. Many turned radical and accused PRI of abandoning its commitments to social justice. President Gustavo Díaz Ordaz was obsessed with order and tolerated no criticism. With the 1968 Mexico City Olympics just weeks away, he feared student protests would mar his picture of a modern, happy Mexico. In October at the Plaza of the Three Cultures in Mexico City, police gunned down as many as 400 student protesters. What PRI could not co-opt it crushed. Some mark this as a turning point in PRI rule, the point at which it visibly began to destabilize.

Key Concepts

DEPENDENCY THEORY

During much of the Cold War, many Latin American intellectuals subscribed to fashionable leftist views that their region's poverty was the result of exploitation by wicked capitalists, especially by *norteamericanos*. After World War II, radicals worked this up into what they called **dependency theory**, that the Third World is economically dependent on the capital, products, and policies of the First World, especially the United States. (Think: U.S. "shark" feeding on Latin American "sardines.") Only by getting out from under the control of U.S. corporations—who dictated what Latin American lands would produce (bananas and coffee) and what they would consume (Chevrolets and Coca-Cola)—would Latin America eliminate poverty. Accordingly, radical regimes such as Cuba, Nicaragua, and currently Venezuela are praiseworthy, because they broke their dependency on the Yankees and instituted independent economic development that would benefit their own peoples.

Dependency theory contains several disputes. It is a type of Marxist theory, but some orthodox Marxists disliked it. Marx saw class conflict *within* a country as the key to its economic and political development. Many Latin American critics blame their continent's poverty on its "predatory class structure," where a few rich families own everything and there is not much of an industrial proletariat. Latin America's problem, in

their view, is that it is still saddled with a feudal social structure. Marx had little to say about relations among countries. Lenin made that leap (see page 268) with his claim that some imperialist countries have redone the globe to suit themselves by exploiting their colonial areas. Dependency theory partakes more of Lenin than of Marx. Mexican dependency theorists use Cárdenas as an exemplar of Mexico's efforts to break *dependencia*.

By the 1990s, many dependency theorists came to doubt the theory. Brazilian President Fernando Henrique Cardoso (1995–2002), for example, had been a radical sociologist and promoter of dependency theory, but by the 1980s had abandoned it. A famous Latin American saying: "If you are not a Communist when you're twenty, you have no heart. If you're still a Communist when you're forty, you have no head." Aging wises you up. The demise of Communist regimes in East Europe and the Soviet Union made many wonder if "socialism" really worked. The economic success of Chile, where a military dictator enforced capitalism, made many appreciate market systems and foreign trade. Other Latin American countries restructured their economies in the early 1990s. The results were generally unimpressive, and we may expect a new wave of Latin dependency theory.

■ Politics inside PRI

Any party as big as PRI is bound to have factions. The two most relevant are the *políticos* and *técnicos*, politicians and technicians. The *políticos* are populists seeking elected office; they pay heed to mass needs and demands. As such, they pay little heed to economics and are not averse to running up huge deficits. This pleases the crowd but leads to inflation and outcries from foreign investors and international banks for Mexico to get its economic house in order. Presidents Díaz Ordaz (1964–1970), Echevarría (1970–1976), and López Portillo (1976–1982) typify the *político* approach. They relied too much on Mexico's new oil finds and overspent. Eventually, Mexico's economy crashed.

Democracy

ELECTIONS AND DEMOCRACY

Americans are given to the notion that elections equal democracy. PRI won fourteen presidential elections in a row, illustrating that democracy is more complex than just balloting. As we considered in Russia (Chapter 20), it involves a great deal of philosophical, moral, social, and legal underpinning, and these tend to come with a large middle class. Elections are just the visible parts and can mislead foreign election monitors, who see little more than the physical balloting on election day and miss the longer-term and less-visible problems. Monitors are getting better, though, and in 2004 called Ukraine's elections rigged, forcing a repeat. Few elections in the Third World are completely free and fair. There are several ways to rig them:

Media Dominance   The big problem is what happens in the weeks and months before the election. To a considerable extent, he who controls television rules the country, as Putin showed in Russia. A country with one or two government-controlled channels will give much news coverage to the ruling party and little to opposition candidates. Paid-for TV advertising may give opposition parties a chance to reach a broad public, so beware any country that bans it. Newspapers can suffer distribution problems and shortage of newsprint.

Bribery   Poor people are often so desperate for money or jobs that they vote for the party that provides them. Mexico's PRI was notorious for rewarding voters. In the 2000 elections in Yucatán PRI gave voters thousands of washing machines, no doubt to ensure a clean election.

Ballot Security   Voting is supposed to be secret, but there are techniques to figure out who voted how. Actually, just telling people you know how they voted is often enough to scare them into compliance. This is especially a problem in unsophisticated rural areas. If a whole village does not vote for the party in power, it may miss out on next year's road-repair hires. Ballot boxes can be stuffed in advance. As they used to say in Chicago: "Vote early and often!"

Ballot Counting   Opposition parties may not have enough poll watchers and counters to insure honest counts. They may be barred from watching. Computers do not necessarily make tabulating votes honest. In the 1988 elections, with Cuauhtémoc Cárdenas mounting a major challenge, Mexico's computers tabulating the vote crashed; when they were back up PRI won with a bare 50.4 percent. Over the sixty previous years PRI had never won less than 70 percent.

Amid major complaints of PRI fraud, especially from PAN and PRD, to its credit the PRI government of Salinas in 1990 abolished the Federal Electoral Commission, widely believed to be crooked. In its place, the Federal Electoral Institute (IFE), autonomous and supervised by representatives of all parties, greatly cleaned up Mexican voting at all levels. Immediately, non-PRI parties started winning more votes. IFE demonstrates that Mexico is getting modern and democratic. Recent problems in U.S. vote counts suggest we could use an IFE.

peso (Spanish for "weight") Mexico's currency, fluctuates at around ten U.S. cents.

The *técnicos* (known in much of the world as *technocrats*—see pages 107 and 455) try to fix economic instability. They are more likely to staff appointive positions and worry less about mass demands. Many have studied modern *neo-classical* economics in the United States and see a free market and fewer government controls as the path to prosperity. They urge for Mexico what much of the world calls *neoliberalism* (see page 62), the return to Adam Smith's original economic ideas. This confuses Americans, as we call it *conservatism*. For Europeans and Latin Americans, however, Britain's Margaret Thatcher instituted a neoliberal economic program. In Chile under Pinochet, the "Chicago boys" (who studied neo-classical economics at the University of Chicago) put neoliberalism into practice with good results.

Presidents Miguel de la Madrid Hurtado (1982–1988) and Carlos Salinas de Gortari (1988–1994) gave technocrats a chance to stabilize the fiscal chaos wrought by the overspending of their predecessors. Actually, these fiscal technicians in PRI implemented some of the free-market reforms that PAN also sought. But reforms provided insufficient regulation, and Mexico's newly freed banks made bad and even crooked loans. Mexico's financial sector crashed in 1995. The **peso** lost most of its value against the dollar, Mexico's GDP declined by 6.2 percent in 1995 alone, and Mexicans grew poorer. (In 1997, Asian banks folded from exactly the same sort of *crony capitalism*.) The problem is not a lack of bright, well-educated economists. Both PRI and PAN have plenty. The problem is part-way economic reforms that provide freedom without rule of law. These tend to set up wild expansion followed by crashes. Many Mexican groups fight thorough reform, though, and President Fox could accomplish little.

Mexican Catholicism

The real sleeper in Mexican politics has been the Roman Catholic church. More than 90 percent of Mexicans are professed Catholics, some of them quite serious. Since independence, however, the spirit of the Mexican Republic has been generally secular. The church was never happy with Mexico's break from Spain and tilted strongly conservative. It was conservative Mexican Catholics who convinced Napoleon III that France could take Mexico. The republic tilted in an anticlerical direction, which became especially pronounced in the 1910–1920 Revolution. Its leaders saw the church as a bastion of upper-class conservatism and reaction. The 1917 constitution imposed limits on church lands, educational institutions, and religious orders. Detectives ferreted out secret convents and closed them. Priests had to travel in ordinary clothing, without clerical collar. Calles's anticlericalism provoked the Cristero Rebellion. For much of the twentieth century, the Mexican church was on the defensive.

But the church never gave up. Through Catholic teachings, lay organizations, schools and universities, and the 1939 founding of PAN, it methodically set the stage for the return of Catholic politics. These are not the politics of a reactionary past but of a modern, business-oriented future. PAN resembles Italy's postwar Christian Democrats, a catchall party that is Catholic but not pietistic.

Crime and Politics

We have mentioned several Mexican interest groups—labor unions, peasant associations, business, the Catholic Church—but Mexico's most powerful interest group is crime. (Actually, looking at the world as a whole, crime of all sorts is humankind's biggest economic activity.) This is nothing new. Early in human history, the state gave birth to twins—politics, the means of influencing the state, and crime, the means of avoiding the state. Politics and crime know and understand each other quite well, forming an almost symbiotic relationship, one especially clear in a country like

Geography

BOUND BRAZIL

Brazil is bounded on the north by Venezuela, Guyana, Suriname, and French Guiana;

on the east by the Atlantic Ocean;

on the south by Uruguay, Argentina, and Paraguay;

and on the west by Bolivia, Peru, and Colombia.

Bounding Brazil enables us to locate all South American countries except Chile and Ecuador.

Mexico. Politics needs money to win elections and pays little attention to the sources of this money (for example, Japanese Liberal Democratic politicians and *yakuza* gangsters). And crime needs the protection of politics to continue its enterprises (for example, the inability of the Russian police to solve a single assassination). Corruption occurs at the triple interface of the state, politics, and crime. In a weak state, politics, because it is unrestrained, easily turns violent. Crime, because it has little to fear from the state, ignores state power.

Justice has always been weak in Mexico. Pancho Villa seamlessly blended banditry and revolution. As we noted, starting with Madero in 1914, assassination of top leaders was common. Assassinations continue in our day. Nosy journalists, zealous prosecutors, and aides to Cuauhtémoc Cárdenas have been gunned down. A hit on a rival drug lord in 1993 by mistake killed a Mexican cardinal in his vestments. Mexicans were outraged. Frustrated at police corruption, in 2004 a Mexico City mob lynched two cops. In Mexico, rapists, murderers, and kidnappers are rarely arrested, but police beat innocent people until they confess. Perhaps 20 percent of Mexico's crimes are reported; people feel it is useless. As in Russia, the inability of police to solve crimes suggests they are in on the deal.

Two killings in 1994 shocked the world and paved the way to Fox's 2000 victory. Luis Donaldo Colosio, PRI's own presidential candidate handpicked by President Salinas, was shot dead at an election rally in Tijuana. Who ordered the hit is unclear. Later PRI party secretary general José Ruiz Massieu was shot dead. President Salinas's brother Raúl, who got very rich with drug connections during the *sexenio* of his brother, got fifty years for ordering the killing (but was freed in 2005). Massieu's own brother, a deputy attorney general, was assigned to investigate but resigned, accusing PRI bosses of complicity and coverup. President Salinas, who worked his way up as a brilliant U.S.-educated economist, ended his term in disgrace and went into exile in Ireland. In 2004 the youngest Salinas brother, Enrique, suspected of laundering money in France for Raúl, was strangled to death in Mexico City. An interviewer asked Colosio shortly before his death about the Salinas family. He replied, "Have you seen *The Godfather?*"

Some good came of the horrors. The 1994 contract killings brought together two trends that had been growing over the years: (1) PRI was stinking more and more, and (2) Mexicans were sufficiently educated and sophisticated to see the government for what it was. A system of control and co-optation that could work amid ignorance and poverty could not work amid a substantial middle class, and Mexico by now had one. Even top *Priístas*, many with U.S. graduate degrees, were ashamed, and embarrassment can be a powerful motivator. It was almost as if PRI knew the game was up. It implemented serious electoral reforms and, to its credit, lost. In 2000 Mexico got its first turnover in power since the Revolution. A second turnover could mark a stable Mexican democracy.

WHAT MEXICANS QUARREL ABOUT

▎ Population and Jobs

Mexico's population exploded from 16 million in 1935 to 34 million in 1960, a growth rate of 2.8 percent a year. The population is now more than triple that but growing at a reasonable 1.2 percent a year. This itself is testimony to the power of economic development to solve the population explosion. Middle-class people turn naturally and with no coercion to small families. Mexico's rate of population increase is not much bigger than the U.S. rate. The difference is that the Mexican rate is held down by emigration while the U.S. rate grows from immigration, much of it from Mexico.

Mexicans do not quarrel about birth rates—Catholic countries seldom do—but they do quarrel about how to create jobs for the millions of unemployed and underemployed. Mexico's institutions and economy simply cannot keep up with its population growth. The Zapatista dream of land for the poor cannot work because there is simply not enough land to redistribute. State-owned industries grow too slowly and employ too few. A state-owned oil industry like Pemex needs only a few trained technicians. It generates a lot of money but not a lot of jobs. (The same is true of Nigeria and the Persian Gulf petrostates.)

The gap between rich and poor in Mexico is huge, as it is throughout Latin America. Economists estimate that the top 4 percent of Mexicans own half of Mexico's wealth while 40 percent of Mexicans live below the poverty line, which is not very high. (Brazil has even greater inequality of wealth and incomes.) With no land or jobs, millions of Mexicans stream to the cities, where they live in shanties and eke out a living selling small items or stealing. Some 22 million Mexicans work off the books, in the "informal economy" (black market), and pay no taxes, contributing to Mexico's chronic federal budget deficits. Mexico City, with a population of over 10 million, is one of the biggest cities in the world, and with some of the world's worst air pollution.

Poverty is especially horrible in the interior south of Mexico, precisely where the Zapatista rebellion started in 1994. Although the Mexican army quickly drove the guerrillas from the towns of Chiapas, they still operate in the mountainous jungles of the region, where they are very hard to catch. Their leader, "Subcomandante Marcos," who always wears a ski mask when interviewed, speaks eloquently and accurately about Mexico's history of exploitation and poverty and of PRI's betrayal of its promises to uplift the poor. Marcos, however, has no feasible program of his own. He imbibes of the romanticism of the Revolution, as do many Mexicans.

In addition to its obvious injustice, maldistribution of income has several other negative consequences. Some Mexicans go hungry, and many do not earn even the minimum daily wage of $4.50. Poor people have no money to save, which means insufficient capital for investment and growth. Middle-class people save, generating ample capital for investment, as in Germany and Japan. Without domestic capital, Latin American lands must depend on foreign capital, which not everyone likes. (The U.S. middle class also saves little, and the same thing happens: massive inflows of foreign capital, much of it from China and Japan.) The very poor have trouble acquiring the skills needed to lift themselves into the middle class. Schools

Shown here is a "shantytown" built on a hillside on the outskirts of Mexico City.

gringo (From the Spanish for "gibberish.") Foreigner, specifically *norteamericano,* pejorative.

are inadequate in rural Mexico and in the vast shantytowns around Mexico's cities. The high crime rate frightens away foreign business- es, whose executives are often kidnapped for ransom. Poverty leads to more poverty until it becomes almost endemic. One of the few escape hatches is *el Norte*, sneaking into the United States.

The cures proposed relate to the neoliberal economics mentioned earlier. Populists, leftists, trade unionists, and nationalists—many now clustered in the PRD—want to keep or restore state- owned industries. Privatization of national treasures such as Pemex is deemed a sellout to the for- eign capitalists. Mexico's constitution prohibits any private ownership—foreign or domestic—of the country's energy industry. This means lack of investment and shortages; Mexico, which has vast fields of natural gas, must import it from the United States. Young, U.S.-trained economists, on the other hand, recognize that state-owned industries are stagnant, inefficient, corrupt, and employ too few Mexicans. Such people are Panistas or PRI técnicos. Recent PRI presidents have gingerly lib- eralized Mexico's economy, and Fox wished to go much further.

Oil is an unreliable fix for Mexico's economic problems. Indeed, some Arab intellectuals now speak of their petroleum as a "curse": It skews development away from long-term and balanced growth, employs few, concentrates wealth, and makes the country dependent on the rise and fall of oil prices. (See the Nigeria chapter for further discussion.) When new oilfields were discovered in the south in the 1970s, Presidents Echeverría and López Portillo went crazy with spending. For a while, some Mexicans felt rich, but inflation and the 1995 crash of the peso soon ended that. Mex- ico, in effect, followed the path of the oil sheiks in squandering new oil revenues to produce a tem- porary and unsustainable illusion of wealth. Oil is a kind of drug that induces fantasies of grandeur.

If Pemex is ever privatized and foreign firms allowed to develop Mexico's oil—both very hot po- litical issues—it will mark the coming of Mexican economic maturity. Yes, the **gringos** want your oil, Mexico, but they pay good money for it and bring badly needed technological improvements. The untouchable status of Pemex as a fountain of corruption does no good for Mexico's economy or political culture.

Geography

SHANTYTOWNS

The Third World is characterized by shantytowns, vast tracts of squatter housing that surround most cities, called *barrios coloniales* in Spanish and *favelas* in Por- tuguese. Many houses are just shacks, but over time some turn into modest homes. Nearly all occupants do not own the land under their dwellings, so they have no legal claim to them and can't use them as collateral for loans. One Peruvian economist proposes that giving legal title would yield loans and rapid economic growth.

Some inhabitants of Mexico's *colonias* hold regular jobs, others sell things on the street, and some steal. Crime bosses hold sway in the *colonias*. Mexico's crime rates are astronomical. PRI claims to look out for the poor, but urban poor are neither farmers nor, for the most part, organized workers. No one represents them.

If life is so wretched in the *barrios*, why do Mexi- cans move there? Because it is even worse in the countryside. Moving to a city for many is a step up, for there they have access to more education and health services and may even find a job. If the Mexican econ- omy worked right, more businesses would start up in the *barrios*, taking advantage of the low rent and cheap labor. Historically, cities are the incubators of economic growth, even if they are not pretty.

The NAFTA Question

globalization   The world becoming one big capitalist market.

Globalization has been a buzzword for some years. Whole books are written either praising it or denouncing it. We need to ask at least two questions about **globalization**: (1) Does it really exist? (2) Does it uplift the poor countries? Basically, globalization is nothing more than trade, and that has been going on for millennia. World trade increased dramatically with Portugal and Spain's voyages of discovery and their trade with, respectively, Asia and Latin America. World trade grew quickly with the steamship and the British Empire, "Victorian globalization." Current globalization, aided by instant communication and rapid transport, just accelerates earlier upward trends.

But globalization does not really cover the globe. Wide areas—especially the Middle East and Africa—are little involved. Globalization extends in a band across North America and Europe, falls off, and picks up again in East Asia. Some developing countries benefit enormously from free trade, namely the "growth dragons" of East Asia. We could nearly cross out "globalization" and put in "Made in China."

Latin America plays a relatively minor role and is not sure about globalization, because so far it has enjoyed few of its benefits. Some critics cite Latin America's slow or stagnant economic growth as proof that globalization either does not work at all or at least does not work in Latin America, where a rigid class structure stifles growth. China zooms along at nearly 10 percent growth a year, Latin America at a couple percent. Leftists point out that Latin America's gaps between rich and poor are getting bigger, and this helped produce the leftist electoral victories in Argentina, Brazil, Chile, Bolivia, and Venezuela.

NAFTA was both hailed and feared. American fear-mongers said U.S. jobs would make a "vast sucking sound" as they drained down to Mexico. Nothing of the sort happened; U.S. employment reached record heights in the late 1990s. Canadian and Mexican nationalists feared the U.S. economy would dominate their two countries. Free-market optimists foresaw economic growth for all.

Actually, not much happened, and that is the trouble. Mexican trade with the United States, which had been growing for years before NAFTA, slowed. The first three years of the Fox administration saw feeble GDP growth (but it was up to 4 percent in 2005) and the loss of 2.1 million jobs. The problem was so obvious that few saw it coming: No one can compete with China. No one. What we thought would be produced in Mexico is produced in China, because it is much cheaper. The globalization paradigm did not ask what would be the effects of free trade when one large producer has incredible advantages over all the others. How many giant, low-cost producers can the world take? Will China's productive capacity snuff out all others? Mexicans might paraphrase Díaz and exclaim, "Poor Mexico! So close to the United States, so far from China."

Much of Mexican politics revolves around NAFTA. The left, including PDR people, want to either scrap the whole thing or seriously modify it. PAN is solidly for it; Vicente Fox, with his Coca-Cola background, exemplifies and celebrates globalization as Mexico's way out of poverty. PRI negotiated and ratified NAFTA but has some doubts. It has not produced its expected effects, but home-made Mexican economic instability ruined its first few years. Give it some time, they say, and NAFTA will work. Mexico does not have much time. Its growing population coupled with slow economic growth spells increased poverty and unemployment. To escape them, Mexicans have two poor choices, both related to the United States: illegal immigration and drug smuggling.

◼ Drugs: A Mexican or U.S. Problem?

Mexico grows marijuana, but most cocaine and heroin come from Colombia, Peru, and Bolivia. Farmers who grow no drugs stay poor. Mexico is the most important way-station. Its long border with the United States makes smuggling relatively easy. By air, tunnels, trucks, or "mules," drugs pour into an eager U.S. market. For every kilo found, perhaps twenty or more get through. For several years, drugs on America's streets have gotten cheaper and purer, indicating an excess of supply over demand. We are not staunching the flow.

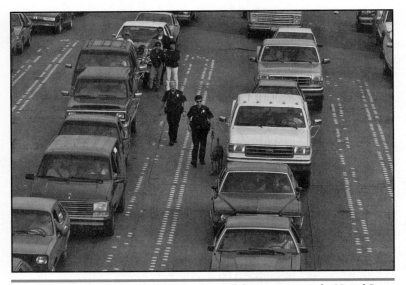

Two border patrol officers with a sniffing dog walk by cars entering the United States through San Diego, California.

Drugs are both a Mexican and a U.S. problem. For Mexico, drugs have led the penetration of crime into the highest levels of power. Mexico's police, judicial system, and army have all been corrupted by drug money. Even President Salinas had a brother in the drug trade. In 2005 a spy for a drug cartel was found in President Fox's office. One of the characteristics of the weak state is its penetration by crime. In Mexico, crime and politics depend on each other; drug money helps politicians, and politicians help the traffickers, a difficult cycle to break.

The real problem is the lucrative U.S. drug market. If no Americans took illicit drugs, a wide layer of Latin American crime would disappear. But there are drug users in every town, campus, and walk of life in America. Some think it's cool. They might consider that the **narcotraficantes** murder hundreds and harm the stability and growth of several Latin American lands. Drugs finance the decades-long guerrilla war in Colombia. Catching traffickers and checking border crossings has little impact on overall U.S. drug consumption. The profits from feeding the U.S. drug market are so great that many gladly join. In the words of Walt Kelly's Pogo, "We have met the enemy, and he is us."

narcotraficante   Drug trafficker.

◼ Illegal or Undocumented?

We call them "illegal immigrants"; Mexicans call them "undocumented workers." An estimated 11 million illegals are in the United States. The Mexico-U.S. border is the only place on earth you can walk from the Third World into the First. For the millions of Mexicans who have made the risky walk, they merely relocated to the northern portion of their republic that the United States seized in 1848. Many die every year, but few worry about breaking the law. The U.S. Border Patrol arrests over 1 million a year and sends them back. Many immediately try again. Probably more than 1 million a year get through.

remittance   Money sent home.

The problem of the *indocumentados* parallels the drug problem. There is both a push and a pull. Unemployment and poverty push Mexicans to leave, and jobs and the opportunity to give their families a decent life pull. And Americans do hire Mexicans (and others from further south) with little thought to their immigration status. Many businesses, especially in the U.S. Southwest, depend on cheap Mexican labor. "Heck, he gave me a Social Security number," say many employers. (True, but it's probably the same number used by dozens of illegals.) Few U.S. families could afford household help—maids and gardeners—if they had to hire Americans. This, however, depresses the wages of Americans who might otherwise take these jobs.

Again, this is not really a Mexican problem; it's an American problem. The Mexican government, as a humanitarian service, puts out a comic book showing how to survive the dangers and deserts of crossing the border. Mexico wants a better deal from the U.S. administration to accept more immigrants, as either legal or temporary immigrants, and grant amnesty to illegals already here. Americans do not want a flood of Hispanic immigrants, but employers in clothing, manufacturing, meatpacking, and agriculture like the cheap labor and make campaign contributions. Their payoff: Fewer than 100 U.S. investigators nationwide enforce laws against hiring illegals. Illegal immigration became a hot issue within the U.S. Republican party. One of President Fox's biggest defeats was in not getting President Bush to make legal Mexican immigration easier. His PRI and PRD opponents sneered, "Thought you were going to get something from your gringo friend? Ha!" But when in power they try to do exactly the same thing.

Going to the United States is both an escape valve for Mexican unemployment and source of **remittances** from those already working here, who sent back $19 billion in 2005. Remittances are the best form of foreign aid; they bypass corrupt officials and go right to the families who use them to raise children and start businesses. The best thing we could do for Mexico's development is to make remittances safe and cheap.

Modern Mexico?

Can Mexico serve as an example of modernization for a continent where it seems that nothing works right? Compared to most of the rest of Latin America, Mexico is a model of growth and prosperity. With the right policies it might become the "Latin tiger," rivaling the growth dragons on the other side of the Pacific.

And what is the right policy for growth? The record of the postwar world shows one combination works: low wages and good productivity. When labor costs—and they include taxes and pensions as well as hourly wages—lag behind productivity growth you can produce more and better and earn a share of the world market. Labor costs over time, of course, rise. The trick is to keep productivity rising even faster. You do this through more technology and higher worker skills. The models for the combination of low wages and high productivity: postwar Germany and Japan and present-day China. When German and Japanese labor costs became some of the world's highest, their economic growth flattened. Negative examples include postwar Britain and present-day Mexico.

How can you tell if a country's labor costs are too high and its productivity too low? You do not need elaborate economic calculations. Just note whether foreign or domestic businesses invest there. If domestic businesses park their money overseas—"flight capital," as we saw in Russia—you know there are problems. Other factors that foster a "hostile business climate" include too many regulations, high taxes, state takeovers, strike-happy unions, crime, and corruption. Clean these up, and you can have rapid growth. Milton Friedman, winner of a Nobel Prize in economics, long extolled the free market as the basis of economic growth. Asked recently if he still thought so, he said he now realizes it is not; the real basis, he said, is rule of law. He might have been speaking of Mexico.

Key Terms

austerity (p. 490)
bilateral opposition (p. 497)
cacique (p. 484)
caudillo (p. 486)
Central America (p. 486)
clientelism (p. 492)
constitutionalism (p. 493)
co-opt (p. 501)
corporatism (p. 492)
corruption (p. 484)
creole (p. 485)
dedazo (p. 495)
demagogue (p. 484)
dependency theory (p. 502)
egalitarian (p. 498)
ejido (p. 490)
globalization (p. 509)
gringo (p. 508)
hacienda (p. 499)
institutionalize (p. 491)

Latin America (p. 486)
machismo (p. 499)
mercantilism (p. 498)
Mesoamerica (p. 484)
mestizaje (p. 499)
narcotraficante (p. 510)
norteamericano (p. 499)
personalismo (p. 499)
peso (p. 504)
political institution (p. 491)
populist (p. 496)
Positivism (p. 488)
pre-Columbian (p. 485)
priísmo (p. 490)
quixotic (p. 501)
remittance (p. 511)
sexenio (p. 490)
South America (p. 486)
Third World (p. 484)

Key Web Sites

History
mexconnect.com
Biographies
cidob.org/bios/castellano/lideres
Documents
uwaterloo.ca/~aLópez-o/polind.html
University of Texas Latin American Studies
lanic.utexas.edu/la/mexico/
Chiapas Rebellion
flag.blackened.net/revolt/mexico/html#Chiapas
News Sources
mexidata.info

El Norte
elnorte.com
El Universal
el-universal.com/mx/noticiash.html
The Herald (English)
el-universal.com/mx/pls/impreso/ol_miami.html
Reforma
reforma.com

Further Reference

Ai Camp, Roderic. *Politics in Mexico: The Decline of Authoritarianism,* 4th ed. New York: Oxford University Press, 2001.

Babb, Sarah. *Managing Mexico: Economists from Nationalism to Neoliberalism.* New York: Routledge, 2001.

Brading, David. *Mexican Phoenix, Our Lady of Guadalupe: Image and Tradition across Five Centuries.* New York: Cambridge University Press, 2001.

Chand, Vikram. *Mexico's Political Awakening.* Notre Dame, IN: University of Notre Dame Press, 2001.

Crandall, Russell, Guadalupe Paz, and Riordan Roett, eds. *Mexico's Democracy at Work: Political and Economic Dynamics.* Boulder, CO: L. Rienner, 2005.

Davidow, Jeffrey. *The U.S. and Mexico: The Bear and the Porcupine.* Princeton, NJ: Markus Wiener, 2004.

Eisenstadt, Todd A. *Courting Democracy in Mexico: Party Strategies and Electoral Institutions.* New York: Cambridge University Press, 2004.

Krauze, Enrique. *Mexico: Biography of Power: A History of Modern Mexico, 1810–1996.* New York: HarperCollins, 1997.

Mann, Charles C. *1491: New Revelations of the Americas before Columbus.* New York: Knopf, 2005.

Merrell, Floyd. *The Mexicans: A Sense of Culture.* Boulder, CO: Westview, 2003.

Mizrahi, Yemile. *From Martyrdom to Power: The Partido Acción Nacional in Mexico.* Notre Dame, IN: University of Notre Dame Press, 2003.

Needler, Martin C. *Mexican Politics: The Containment of Conflict,* rev. ed. Westport, CT: Greenwood, 1995.

Peeler, John. *Building Democracy in Latin America,* 2nd ed. Boulder, CO: L. Rienner, 2004.

Preston, Julia, and Samuel Dillon. *Opening Mexico: The Making of a Democracy.* New York: Farrar, Strauss & Giroux, 2004.

Rubio, Luis, and Susan Kaufman Purcell, eds. *Mexico under Fox.* Boulder, CO: L. Rienner, 2004.

Salinas de Gortari, Carlos. *Mexico: The Policy and Politics of Modernization.* New York: Random House, 2002.

Shirk, David A. *Mexico's New Politics: The PAN and Democratic Change.* Boulder, CO: L. Rienner, 2005.

Tulchin, Joseph S., and Andrew D. Selee, eds. *Mexico's Politics and Society in Transition.* Boulder, CO: L. Rienner, 2003.

Youngers, Coletta A., and Eileen Rosin, eds. *Drugs and Democracy in Latin America: The Impact of U.S. Policy.* Boulder, CO: L. Rienner, 2004.

Chapter 34

NIGERIA

Nigeria is important. It has the largest population in Africa—one fifth of Africans south of the Sahara are Nigerians—and is larger than any European country. It is the world's seventh largest oil producer and the fifth largest oil supplier to the United States, so we often treat it as little more than a gas station, like we did the Persian Gulf. Such places do not stay gas stations but turn into zones of chaos and conflict. Nigeria has much influence in Africa and, along with South Africa, has led peacekeeping operations in several African countries. Nigeria is also attempting, for the third time, to establish democracy in a situation that could explode at any time. Nigerian democracy deserves our support.

Questions to Consider

1. What and where are Nigeria's religions?
2. What and where are Nigeria's main ethnic groups?
3. What were colonialism's effects on Africa?
4. Nigeria modeled its institutions after which country's?
5. How does Nigeria illustrate *praetorianism*?
6. What do the Igbo and Biafra illustrate?
7. Does colonialism explain poverty?
8. What did oil do to Nigeria's economic development?
9. Why does not fragmented Nigeria just fall apart?
10. Can corruption be measured objectively?
11. Could Nigeria's PDP become like Mexico's PRI?

THE IMPACT OF THE PAST

Nigeria, like Mexico, was home to civilizations long before the coming of Europeans. The Nok culture, adept at grain farming and iron smelting, created an inland kingdom around the time of Christ at the southern end of the trade route from North Africa. Starting in the eleventh century A.D., the Yoruba built a series of city-states in the southwest under a king in the city of Ife. Only the Igbo (also known as Ibo) appear to have been stateless; they lived in egalitarian, self-contained villages in the southeast. There was never a single kingdom of Nigeria.

Islam from the Sudan region arrived in the Sahel of northern Nigeria in the ninth century A.D. and converted the Hausa and Fulani peoples, who are often known as the Hausa-Fulani. The Borno kingdom and later Songhai empire were seats of Islamic learning and culture. Islam also meant that Nigeria would inherit a tragic split between a Muslim north and a largely Christian south, the source of much conflict today.

515

◼ The Coming of the Europeans

Nigeria, like Mexico, was launched by the voyages of discovery. Portuguese navigators, in their effort to round Africa to tap the wealth of Asia, in 1471 were the first Europeans to reach what was much later called Nigeria. The Portuguese began a pattern later followed by other Europeans. They did not venture far inland—climate and disease made that unpleasant—but set up trading forts along the African coast.

jihad Arabic for "struggle," also Muslim holy war.

caliphate Islamic dynasty.

desiccation Drying out.

sub-Saharan Africa south of the Sahara.

Sahel Narrow band south of Sahara, arid but not yet desert.

aquifer Underground water-bearing layer.

savanna Tropical grasslands south of Sahel.

They soon found their chief item of trade: slaves. Slavery had always been practiced in Africa; most were used locally, but some were exported to North Africa. Starting with the Portuguese, local African chiefs, by raiding and kidnapping, delivered slaves to the burgeoning European slave trade on the coast, which became known as the "slave coast." Portugal's colony of Brazil and Spain's colony of Cuba needed labor for their sugarcane fields. England's American colonies needed labor for their cotton and tobacco fields. From the 1530s to the 1850s Portuguese, Spanish, French, English, and later Americans shipped over 3.5 million Africans across the Atlantic, chiefly to Brazil (which took perhaps six times as many as the United States did). Due to this brutal trade, many Americans, Brazilians, and Cubans are of Yoruba or Igbo ancestry.

An Islamic **jihad** from 1804 to 1808 in the northern region was little noticed by Europe but contributed to Nigeria's current difficulties. Islamic scholars, in a familiar pattern, found the Muslim kingdoms there insufficiently pure and demanded their overthrow. That done, they set up what was known as the Sokoto **Caliphate**, a single political system much more powerful than any other in the region, and one motivated by Islamic fundamentalism. In less than a century, it collided with British colonialism.

Geography

SAHARA, SAHEL, SAVANNA

African geography can be looked at as climate bands running east to west. The northernmost of these bands, the Sahara, is very dry, and the south, close to the equator, is very rainy. The Sahara was not always a desert, but about 5,000 years ago its **desiccation** began, making it difficult to traverse and leaving **sub-Saharan** Africa semi-isolated.

Traders, raiders, and Muslim armies occasionally crossed from North Africa into the **Sahel**, which includes northern Nigeria. With uncertain rainfall, the Sahel can be used for little more than cattle grazing, so human populations are thin. The Sahara has been expanding southward as the Sahel gets drier. Some blame this on global warming, others on ice ages, and still others on growing populations of cattle growers for drawing too much water from its very limited **aquifer**.

South of the Sahel are Africa's vast **savannas**, characterized by hot wet summers and hot dry winters. Much of Nigeria, indeed much of Africa, is savanna. Here rainfall permits farming. Only the south of Nigeria, along the coast of the Gulf of Guinea, has the lush rain forest that some suppose covers most of Africa. Actually, this region of year-round rainfall occupies only the equatorial band of Africa.

Famed Scottish explorer Mungo Park, often wracked with fever, explored the Niger River from 1795 to 1806 until he drowned while trying to canoe down it. Few ventured after him until quinine was developed for use against malaria in the 1850s. Christian missionaries arrived to work among the Yoruba, Igbo, and others, setting up missionary posts on the coast. Missionaries were often the advance element of imperial expansion, as protecting them soon required a military presence.

colonialism Gaining and exploitation of overseas territories, chiefly by Europeans, related to *imperialism*.

It was Britain's suppression of the slave trade that led to the establishment of Nigeria. Under pressure from British Christians, Parliament in 1807 outlawed the shipping of slaves (but not slavery itself, which Parliament ended in the British Empire in 1834). To enforce the ban, the Royal Navy stationed a squadron in the Gulf of Guinea. To replace the slave trade, Britain encouraged trade in palm oil, used for soaps and lubricants. An example of "unforeseen consequences," the move stimulated the capture of more slaves, who were needed to produce and transport the palm oil. To suppress this internal trade, Britain first shelled Lagos, the Yorubas' island capital, in 1851 and then annexed it in 1861.

Key Concepts

COLONIALISM

Colonialism means several things. From the legal point of view, a colony lacks sovereignty; ultimate lawmaking authority resides in a distant capital. London controlled the laws governing Nigeria, Paris those of Senegal, and Brussels those of the Congo. For the most part, the "natives" were kept politically powerless, as the imperial power deemed them too backward and ignorant. The British in Nigeria and other colonies gave chiefs some local responsibility.

From the economic point of view, **colonialism** involved exploitation by the imperial country. The colonies supplied cheap agricultural and mineral raw materials, which the imperial country manufactured into industrial products that it sold back to the colonies. Marxists argue that colonies were captive markets that were kept poor in order to enrich imperialists. Actually, most colonies cost imperial governments more to administer and defend than they earned. Individual firms, to be sure, often made lush profits in the colonial trade.

Racially, colonies were governed on the basis of skin color on the principle that "the lowest of the Europeans is higher than the highest of the natives." A French policeman directing traffic in Algiers was superior to an Algerian doctor. A Dutch clerk in Jakarta was the social better of an Indonesian professor. Racism was an important part of colonialism; it psychologically enabled the imperialists to govern millions of unlike peoples who did not want them there. It also contributed to the rage felt by educated subjects, some of whom became leaders of independence movements: "You treat me like dirt in my own country. Well, that will stop!"

In hindsight, colonialism stands condemned as brutal and evil. But it was the unavoidable outcome of the restless, dynamic West encountering the traditional areas of the globe that looked like easy pickings. The imperial powers had no right to conquer and govern others; they simply had guns. Of course, without colonialism there would be no United States. "Colonial" has a nice sound to Americans, connoting hardy settlers, Thanksgiving, and pretty landscapes. It has a bitter ring for most other peoples. Colonialism left a chip on the shoulders of the Third World and helps explain lingering anti-West feelings.

■ The Scramble for Africa

The Niger (from the Latin for *black*) River, the greatest river of West Africa, rises far to the west, in Guinea, only 150 miles from the Atlantic, and makes a 2,600-mile semicircle, at first north through Mali, then turning south through Niger and finally Nigeria. During the nineteenth century, trade

Geography

BOUND NIGER

Bounding Niger (a former French colony easy to confuse with Nigeria) teaches us more African geography than bounding Nigeria.

Niger is bounded on the north by Algeria and Libya;

on the east by Chad;

on the south by Nigeria (a former British colony), and Benin;

and on the west by Burkina Faso (formerly Upper Volta) and Mali.

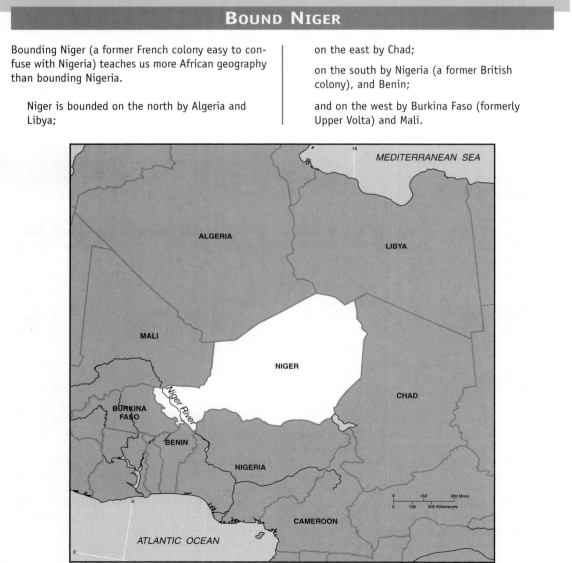

along the Niger, much of it in cocoa, became more profitable. In response to calls from missionaries, a Scottish explorer made monthly steamboat runs up the lower reaches of the Niger.

British businessman George Goldie, the "father of Nigeria," set up the United Africa Company in 1879 and turned it into the chartered Royal Niger Company in 1886, after the Berlin Conference (see box below) had carved up Africa and assigned borders to European imperial powers. The conference stated, however, that no power could claim what it did not occupy, setting off a race to turn vague claims into colonies. This "scramble for Africa" prompted the British to grab Nigeria before the French could.

indirect rule   British colonial governance through native hereditary rulers.

divide and rule   Roman and British imperial ruling method of setting subjects against each other.

■ The Colonial Interlude

In 1894 real British colonialism took shape with the arrival of Fredrick Lugard, one of a remarkable handful of energetic Englishmen who dedicated their lives to the British colonial service and the vision of a British Empire that brought peace and prosperity to the world. To do this, they often used their new Maxim gun on the natives, as Lugard did in many colonial battles around the world. Lugard consolidated the areas of the Yoruba and Igbo—who fought a guerrilla war against him—into two British protectorates and in 1900 moved into the Muslim north with a military force. By 1903 he had captured Kano and Sokoto to form the Protectorate of Northern Nigeria. In 1914 Sir Frederick (he was knighted) combined Southern and Northern Nigeria into nearly its present form under a governor-general in Lagos. (A piece of the German-ruled Cameroon was added on the east after World War I.) In classic imperial fashion, Lugard invented Nigeria, and his wife, a journalist, invented the name Nigeria.

Lugard used two British colonialist styles, the twin policies of **indirect rule** and **divide and rule**. With only a few hundred white men the British ran colonies as vast as India by working with and

Geography

BOUNDARIES IN AFRICA

The boundaries of Africa are especially artificial. Notice how several of Africa's borders are straight lines, a sure sign that a border is artificial. Many of the ones for Central Africa were settled at a conference in Berlin in 1885, the great "carve-up" of Africa to settle overlapping claims of imperial powers. The British envisioned owning a band of Africa running the entire length of the continent, "from Cairo to the Cape." After pushing the Germans out of Tanganyika in World War I, they achieved this. Their great competitors, the French, turned a great swath of Africa running east-west across the continent's great bulge into French West Africa and French Equatorial Africa. Portuguese, Germans, and Belgians took smaller areas of Africa.

The imperialist-imposed, artificial boundaries cut through tribes and forced together unworkable combinations of tribes. A river in Africa is a poor border because typically people of the same tribe live along both banks. In 1963, however, with most of Africa independent, the new Organization of African Unity (renamed African Union in 2002) decided not to change the Berlin borders and even put them in its charter. The new leaders were both afraid of unleashing chaos and of losing their governing jobs. Best to leave these artificial borders alone, they figured. In Africa, the imperialists' land grabs became permanent boundaries.

through local chiefs and princes, who were bought off with titles and honors. The French, who practiced a much more direct rule and were reluctant to turn over local responsibilities to natives, needed thousands of Frenchmen to staff their colonies. The British were far more efficient.

Geography

BOUND THE DEMOCRATIC REPUBLIC OF CONGO

The Democratic Republic of Congo (formerly Zaire, earlier the Belgian Congo), is bounded on the north by Central African Republic and Sudan;

on the east by Uganda, Rwanda, Burundi, and Tanzania;

on the south by Zambia and Angola;

and on the west by the Atlantic, the Angolan exclave of Cabinda, and (the formerly French) Congo-Brazzaville.

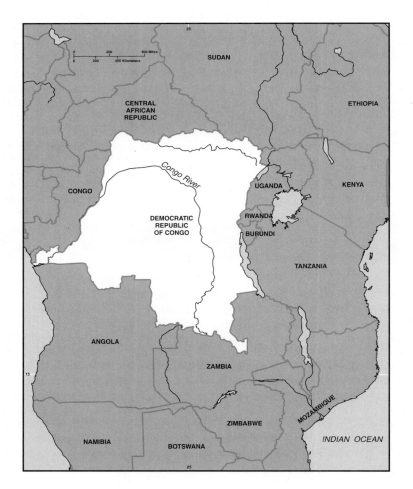

Divide and rule is an old technique of the Roman Empire: *divide et impera* in Latin. Its logic: "If you keep them divided you can easily rule them. United they could throw you out." Under this policy colonialist officials emphasized the distinctiveness of cultures, powers, and

pan-Africanism   Movement to unite all Africa.

territories of existing tribes to set them against each other. There were always tribes in Africa, but some scholars claim the Europeans hyped tribalism to facilitate their rule. The often-murderous tribalism found today owes something to colonialist manipulations.

Colonialism, however, is a wasting asset. The more you organize and educate the natives, the more they want to throw you out. Missionary activity ensured a growing number of educated Africans, some through college level. In the 1920s, especially in the British colonies of Africa, intellectuals developed **pan-Africanism** to liberate the continent from European domination. They argued that without the imperialists to divide them, Africans of all tribes could get along in a united Africa. The British strategy for handling growing political claims from Africans was to cede them local and partial political power in small steps. In 1914 the British established a Nigerian Legislative Council in Lagos and enlarged it with elected members in 1922. It had limited powers and did not include the north. Actually, Britain pursued fairly enlightened colonial policies that may have prevented the worst violence during and after independence. The Belgians, on the other hand, gave the Congolese nothing, trained them for nothing, prepared them for nothing. Result: When Belgium, after some riots, hastily granted the Congo independence in 1960, it erupted into civil war and is still strife-torn.

◾ Independence

World War II weakened the European empires both materially and psychologically. They could no longer afford or justify ruling distant, unlike peoples. Decolonization came first as a trickle and then as a flood: India and Pakistan in 1947, Israel (formerly Palestine) in 1948, Indonesia (Dutch East Indies) in 1949, Ghana (Gold Coast) in 1957, then, in 1960, seventeen countries, mostly British and French colonies in Africa. Where there were many European settlers—Algeria, Kenya, and Rhodesia—decolonization was long, hard, and violent, as the settlers wanted to keep their privileged status. Where there were few settlers—West Africa in general, including Ghana, Sierra Leone, and Nigeria—decolonization was easy. By the mid-1960s, all the old African colonies had been liquidated except for Portugal's Angola, Mozambique, and Guinea-Bissau. The first European empire was also the last. In 1975, Lisbon too gave way. After white-ruled Rhodesia became black-ruled Zimbabwe in 1980, South Africa was the last white-ruled country in Africa, and this ended in 1994 with the election of a black government under Nelson Mandela. Africa returned to African hands.

To work for independence, the first Nigerian political party was founded in 1923. Herbert Macaulay, grandson of a prominent African Christian minister, founded the Nigerian National Democratic party. Macaulay, whom the British fought, is now called the father of Nigerian independence. The Nigerian Youth Movement was founded as a nationwide party in 1934. Macaulay and Nnamdi Azikiwe ("Zik"), a U.S.-educated Igbo, in 1944 brought together more than forty groups to form the National Council of Nigeria and the Cameroons (NCNC). World War II, in which Nigerian soldiers served in the British army, made subject peoples ask what the struggle against fascism meant when they still lived under authoritarian colonial regimes. The British had no good answer. By now many Nigerians were calling for independence.

The British strategy was to give way piecemeal. In 1947 they set up a federal system—the only plausible solution to Nigeria's regional differences—with Northern, Western, and Eastern regions, corresponding, respectively, to the three largest ethnic groups, the Hausa-Fulani, the Yoruba, and the Igbo. (It is now divided into smaller states.) In 1951 they set up a national House of Representatives, but it fell apart over the question of who represented what, a harbinger of the Nigerian fragmentation that would later wreck the country. In 1954 they made the Nigerian federation self-governing with a Muslim prime minister from the north. Western and Eastern regions got internal self-government, the Eastern under Azikiwe and the NCNC and the Western under Chief Obafemi Awolowo, a lawyer who founded the Action Group, a party for Yoruba. Parties in Africa tend to form along tribal lines.

Nigeria's big problem was clear: how to make the huge Muslim Northern province and the two mostly Christian Southern provinces into one Nigeria. They do not go together easily or naturally. The chief party of the North was the People's Congress, which was always wary that the mostly Christian Eastern and Western peoples and parties would dominate the region. Muslims do not like being ruled by non-Muslims. A parallel happened earlier in India, where in 1906 the Muslim League split off from the Indian National Congress and eventually got a separate Pakistan in 1947.

Britain left Nigeria with a federal constitution and a prime minister that looked pretty good on paper. As in India, the British political position in Nigeria had become impossible to sustain; they had to leave and planned it for years. On October 1, 1960, Britain granted Nigeria independence. It had been a formal colony less than sixty years but had experienced European imperialism for much longer. The imperialists take much blame for Nigeria's troubles. They deranged it with a massive slave

Political Culture

NIGERIA'S POLITICAL ERAS

Even more than Mexico, Nigeria is badly fragmented and lacks a unifying political culture. Consciousness focuses on religions, tribes, and regions. The brief British colonial period had given some Nigerians a modern education and a semblance of unity to Nigeria's elites but was not nearly enough to psychologically unify Nigeria as a nation. Nigeria's elites mostly know each other, but they look out more for their tribes than for Nigeria as a whole, as the tribes are their supporters.

Era	Years	Remembered for
Slave trade	1530–1820	Massive export of humans.
Pre-Colonial	1820–1894	Suppression of slave trade; British explorers and missionaries.
Colonial	1894–1960	By 1914 Lugard consolidates regions into one colony named Nigeria.
Independence	1960–1963	Commonwealth member, falls apart.
First Republic	1963–1966	Becomes republic.
Military rule	1966–1979	Coups, Biafra War.
Second Republic	1979–1983	Presidential system, corrupt civilian rule.
Babangida	1983–1993	Long military dictatorship.
Third Republic	1993	Abortive transition to democracy.
Abacha	1993–1998	Cruel and corrupt military dictatorship.
Fourth Republic	1999–	Another attempt at democracy under Obasanjo.

trade, took it over at gunpoint, cobbled together an artificial country composed of tribes who disliked each other, and then left. Thus it was not surprising that Nigeria, weak from the start, should collapse into military dictatorships. Nigeria is not unique; it is the story of many nations created by the imperialists (example: Iraq).

THE KEY INSTITUTIONS

In the first forty-five years of independent Nigeria, civilians ruled only sixteen years, little more than a third of the time. The other two-thirds of the time were military rule under six different generals, some more brutal and greedy than others. The current period of civilian rule, starting in 1999, is the longest one. We hope it will continue but must be forever mindful that Nigeria is still an unstable country with strong tendencies to fall apart. When breakup threatens, the military takes over.

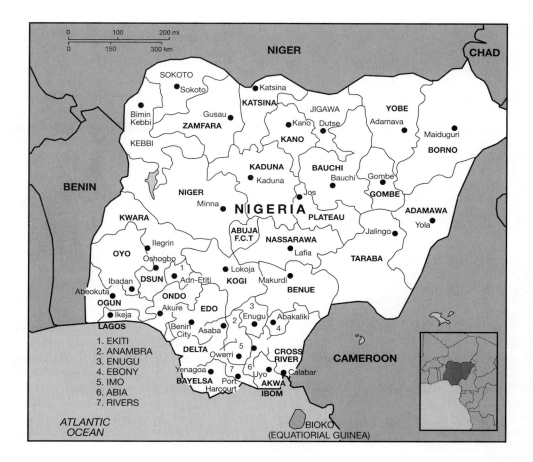

From British to U.S. Model

The British set up Nigeria on the Westminster model with a prime minister as chief of government, but the 1979 constitution, now somewhat modified, turned Nigeria into a U.S.-style presidential system, and for a good reason. The British system depends on one party winning a majority of seats in Commons, which almost always happens in Britain. But if the legislature is fragmented into many parties, as it was in Nigeria's earlier years, the government must form multiparty coalitions and can "fall" easily on votes of no-confidence.

A U.S.-type presidential system avoids this, as the president can govern with or without majority support in the legislature. Presidents stay until the end of their terms and cannot easily be ousted. Nigeria's president, like the U.S. president, combines head of state with chief of government (see page 31) for a maximum of two four-year terms. Olusegun Obasanjo the current and first president of Nigeria's Fourth Republic that emerged after dictator Sani Abacha died, tried to change the constitution so he could have a third term. Many were suspicious of his motives.

Nigerian federalism also resembles the U.S. variety. Nigeria's rulers, some of them military dictators, progressively increased the number of states, from twelve, to nineteen, to thirty-one, to the present thirty-six. Every few years the map of Nigeria is redrawn. This is done to calm Nigeria's many ethnic groups, who often feel trapped in a state dominated by another group. When they turn violent, which is often, Nigeria is inclined to carve out a new state for them. It may have worked, as there is less violence between ethnic groups now but never zero. Critics complain that Nigerian federalism is less than genuine, that the center has far too much power (especially over oil revenues) and runs Nigeria more like a unitary state.

In 1991 the military dictator Ibrahim Babangida (1985–1993) moved the capital from the old colonial capital of Lagos on the coast to Abuja, a new capital in the precise center of the country. The move resembled Brazil's shift of capital from Rio de Janeiro to Brasilia in 1960 to open up the interior. The purpose of the move in Nigeria was to take the capital out of Yoruba hands and put it in more neutral territory. Abuja is now designated the Federal Capital Territory, rather like the District of Columbia. Like Brasilia, Abuja is in the middle of nowhere and has been costly and inefficient.

The National Assembly

The U.S. model is again evident in Nigeria's legislative branch, the bicameral National Assembly, which meets in Abuja. The Senate has 109 seats; each of the thirty-six states has three Senate seats plus one for the Federal Capital Territory. The House of Representatives has 360 seats, ten for each state, each representing a single-member district. Both houses are elected for four-year terms at the same time.

The Nigerian setup departs from its U.S. model, because its states get the same ten seats regardless of population. It would be like the United States having two Senates. Nigeria feels it must do this to appease smaller ethnic groups with their own states. Appeasing the smaller groups, however, creates resentment in the more populous states that they are underrepresented. The U.S. solution—a Senate to represent states on the basis of equality and a House to represent districts on the basis of population—strikes us as a good compromise, but we do not have Nigeria's touchy ethnic situation. The danger in Nigeria is *hyperfederalism*, a system that tries too hard to represent ethnic groups. It seems to work for a while but can lead to the country falling apart, as it did in Yugoslavia.

Nigeria's Parties

Freedom House is skeptical about democracy in Nigeria and rates it only 4, "partly free," but better than Russia (which earned a 5.5). The 2003 Nigerian elections were rigged by registration only for favored parties, missing ballots, stuffed boxes, intimidation, and violence, but most Nigerians, remembering the years of Abacha's brutal military rule, accepted the officially reported results:

Party	Senate		House	
	Vote	Seats	Vote	Seats
PDP	53.7%	76	54.5%	223
ANPP	27.9	27	27.4	96
AD	9.7	6	8.8	34

The PDP bills itself as a centrist party, but to a considerable extent it is the *personalistic* vehicle of President Obasanjo. The smaller ANPP gets its strongest following among Northern Muslims; some of its leaders earlier supported the brutal dictatorship of Sani Abacha (1993–1998) and got rich during it. The Alliance for a Democracy (AD) is a Yoruba party that does well on its southwest home turf but weaker elsewhere. There are other smaller parties, some of them militant Northern Muslim parties, which win one or two seats in the House.

The evolution of Nigeria's party system is a hopeful sign. From many parties—nearly one per tribe—Nigeria seems to have evolved into a "two-plus" party system, a bit like Mexico's. The PDP is a well-funded and well-organized nationwide party and draws votes from all ethnic groups, including many Muslims. The big question: Could the PDP become Nigeria's PRI? Whatever negative one might say about Mexico's dominant party (see the Mexico chapter), it got Mexico out of *praetorianism* (see page 533) and held it together during times of rapid change and modernization. The PRI analogy may not fit Nigeria, as most Northern

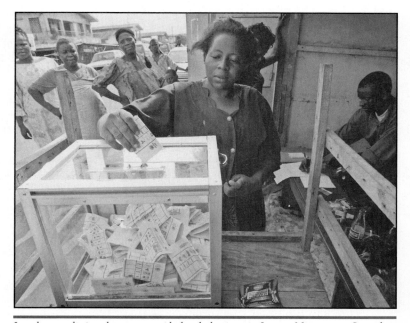

Locals vote during the countrywide local elections in Lagos, Nigeria, on Saturday, March 27, 2004.

Muslims do not support the PDP; some vote for regionalist and Islamist parties. Mexico has troublesome regions, but none with different religions. Nigeria parallels Iraq in its fragmentation. Like Iraq, Nigeria has three major ethnic groups that British imperialists forced into a single artificial state. Some suggest that letting Nigeria and Iraq fall apart into their three main components might not be the worst solution.

Personalities

OLUSEGUN OBASANJO

Curiously, elected President Olusegun Obasanjo had earlier (1976–1979) been an unelected military president. In 1999 he was elected president and re-elected in 2003 as candidate of the centrist People's Democratic party (PDP) on a platform of reducing poverty and corruption and restoring dignity to much-maligned Nigeria.

A Yoruba Christian born north of Lagos in 1937, Obasanjo was educated at the Baptist Boys' High School and worked as a teacher for a year before joining the army in 1958. With further training in England and military cadet school, Obasanjo moved up quickly as an officer and headed an elite commando unit that helped end the Biafra War.

In 1975, when Brigadier Murtala Ramat Mohammed seized power in a coup, Obasanjo was deputy. When Mohammed was assassinated in 1976, Obasanjo become military president. He established a good reputation by appointing to his cabinet representatives of all major tribes and leaving power voluntarily to an elected civilian president in 1979, the first time for such a handover in Nigerian history. The 1979 U.S.-style constitution was drafted under Obasanjo.

Obasanjo became a top Nigerian diplomat and at one point was even mentioned as a possible UN Secretary General. Dictator Sani Abacha (1993–1998), suspecting Obasanjo of plotting a coup, had him imprisoned. When Abacha died (the "coup from heaven"), Obasanjo was released and ran for the presidency for the PDP, which became Nigeria's biggest and best-organized party. He won in 1999 with 63 percent of the vote and was reelected in 2003 with 62 percent, indicating his ability to attract

Olusegun Obasanjo

voters from all regions. His chief opposition in 2003 was another former general who had pulled a coup in 1983, Muhammad Buhari, a Muslim from the North and candidate of the All Nigeria People's party (ANPP), who won 32 percent. Nigeria's civilian government has military roots.

Like Fox in Mexico, Obasanjo can not get nearly the reforms he wants, even though his PDP has a comfortable majority of seats in both houses of Congress. Every Nigerian group that lives well because of the present corrupt setup—state governors, unions, executives of the many state-owned corporations, and the bureaucracy—resists reforms. In another parallel to Mexico, Obasanjo works with a team of young technocrats, many educated in the United States, who understand the urgent need for reforms to the economy. Many think Obasanjo is a genuine patriot and the best president Nigeria has ever had, even though he has not accomplished much in office. Many fear what will come after Obasanjo's second term ends in 2007. Changing the Constitution to permit him a third term was proposed but rejected.

NIGERIAN POLITICAL CULTURE

■ Nigerian Fragmentation

cross-cutting cleavages Multiple splits in society that make group loyalties overlap.

cumulative Reinforcing one another.

Half of Nigerians are Muslim; another 40 percent are Christian, and 10 percent practice indigenous faiths, for example, the Yoruba religion. Nigeria is also ethnically fragmented. Of Nigeria's approximately 250 ethnic groups, these are the largest: 29 percent Hausa-Fulani, 21 percent Yoruba, 18 percent Igbo, and 10 percent Ijaw. In Mexico we spoke of regionalism, but Nigeria's problem is far worse and tends to fragment along religious and regional lines. Eastern, Western, and Northern regions have trouble living together and exist within Nigeria only because the British colonialists set up an artificial country.

The North is especially different—poor, isolated, traditional, and Muslim. It has never liked being ruled by Christians, either British or southern Nigerians. If they had to be in a single country, the northerners always sought to be its rulers. Many especially dislike President Obasanjo for being a born-again Christian who supports the U.S. war on terror. The fundamentalist Islamic Movement of Nigeria has al Qaeda and Iranian ties and is believed to recruit terrorists.

Islam has been the chief religion in Northern Nigeria for a millennium, and, like Islam elsewhere in Africa, has been spreading south by vigorous proselytizing. African Muslims argue that Islam is

Key Concepts

CROSS-CUTTING CLEAVAGES

One of the puzzles of highly pluralistic or multiethnic societies is why they hold together. Why do they not break down into civil strife? One explanation, offered by the German sociologist Georg Simmel early in the twentieth century, is that successful pluralistic societies develop **cross-cutting cleavages**. They are divided, of course, but they are divided along several axes, not just one. When these divisions, or cleavages, cut across one another, they actually stabilize political life.

In Switzerland, for example, the cleavages of French-speaking or German-speaking, Catholic or Protestant, and working class or middle class give rise to eight possible combinations (for example, German-speaking, Protestant, middle class). But any combination has at least one attribute in common with six of the other seven combinations (for example, French-speaking, Protestant, working class). Because most Swiss have something in common with other Swiss, goes the theory, they moderate their conflicts.

Where cleavages do not cross-cut but instead are **cumulative**, dangerous divisions grow. A horrible case is ex-Yugoslavia, where all Croats are Catholic and all Serbs are Eastern Orthodox. The one cross-cutting cleavage that might have helped hold the country together—working class versus middle class—had been outlawed by the Communists. The several nationalities of Yugoslavia had little in common.

Many of Africa's troubles stem from an absence of cross-cutting cleavages. Tribe counts most, and in Nigeria this is usually reinforced by religion. Nigeria does have some cross-cutting cleavages. Not all Nigerian Muslims, for example, are Hausa-Fulani of the North; some are Yoruba in the Southwest, others are Ijaw in the Delta. Social class may also cut across tribal lines, as when a Yoruba businessman knows he has much in common with an Igbo businessman. Nigeria, indeed all of Africa, needs more such connections across tribal lines.

sharia Muslim religious law based on the Koran.

the natural religion for Africa because it pays no attention to skin color and has deep roots in Africa, whereas Christianity is a recent arrival brought by Europeans with an implicit racism.

Islam can be rigid and intolerant. Some insist on a strictly religious education of Arabic and memorizing the Koran. Muslim preachers insist on Islamic purity, sometimes for all of Nigeria. In the North now a strong fundamentalist movement demands making **sharia**

Geography

BOUND GUINEA

Guinea, a former French colony in West Africa not to be confused with Guyana in South America, is bounded on the north by Guinea-Bissau, Senegal, and Mali;

on the east by the Ivory Coast;
on the south by Liberia and Sierra Leone;
and on the west by the Atlantic Ocean.

state law, and several Northern states have done so. This does not sit well with Nigerian Christians and federal authorities, because it means states can override national laws. Christians living in the Northern states would also come under *sharia*, which, for example, punishes adulterous women (but rarely men) by stoning to death and thieves by chopping their hands off. A country with two very different legal systems is a house that cannot stand. Compromise might be possible—*sharia* for family law in the North, Nigerian secular law for everything else—but Islamists insist that *sharia* is God's law and must not be mixed with other legal systems.

Fundamentalist Muslim clerics in the North denounced a World Health Organization project to immunize all children against polio. The clerics preached that it was to sterilize Muslim children. Vaccinations were stopped in three Northern states, and polio cases climbed. Muslims took offense at the 2002 Miss World pageant, which was to be held in Abuja, Nigeria. Riots broke out, and the pageant was hastily relocated to London. The smallest incident can touch off Christian-Muslim riots in Northern Nigeria, and thousands have been killed.

Other regions also present problems. The worst was the bitter Biafra War of 1967–1969, in which the Igbo of Eastern Nigeria attempted to break away with their own country, Biafra. In the Niger Delta, well-armed Ijaw and Itsekiri tribesmen fight government soldiers for control of the oil terminals. The Movement for the Emancipation of the Niger Delta (MEND), demanding compensation for the massive environmental damage the oil industry has caused, sabotages pipelines and kidnaps foreign oil workers. Violence in the Delta takes over a thousand lives a year and can explode any time into civil war.

To put things into perspective, though, we might consider what happened in tiny Rwanda, a former Belgian colony east of the Congo. Belgium played classic divide and rule by setting up one tribe, the Tutsis, to be aristocratic masters and another tribe, the Hutus, to be underlings. After the Belgians left in 1962, Hutu-Tutsi fighting and massacres became intermittent and exploded in 1994 as Hutu *genocidaires* massacred an estimated 800,000. The conflict spilled over into eastern Congo where it took an estimated 1.7 million lives, most from starvation and disease. The combined Rwanda-Congo deaths of 2.5 million is the world's worst since World War II. Nigeria has not had anything that bad, but it could.

■ The Igbo and Biafra

Nigeria's prime example of interethnic violence is what happened with the Igbo people of southeastern Nigeria in the late 1960s. British explorers and colonial officials noted long ago that the Igbo lacked the cities and culture of the Yoruba of the southwest or the Hausa-Fulani of the north. The Igbo, who lived in scattered villages in the rain forest and Niger Delta, seemed rather primitive in comparison. But the Igbo (also spelled Ibo) harbored a competitive and hustling culture that was not noticed until later. Under the British, the Igbo eagerly took to self-advancement through business, education, the civil service, and military. Igbo, nearly all Christian, also scattered throughout Nigeria. Igbo merchants dominated much of the commercial life of Northern Nigeria, where they were despised for both their wealth and their religion. Some observers called them the "Jews of Nigeria" because they were hard-working, dispersed, better-off, and of a different faith. The Igbo were the most modern and educated Nigerians but were culturally at odds with more traditional Nigerians.

Independent Nigeria started destabilizing almost immediately; unrest and disorder broke out early and often. In response to the fraudulent elections of October 1965, in January 1966 a group of army officers, mainly Igbo, attempted a coup. Prime Minister Abubakar Tafawa Balewa, a Northern

developmentalism Early 1960s theory that we could develop Third World lands.

Muslim, was assassinated. General Johnson Aguiyi-Ironsi, an Igbo, took over with a plan to save Nigeria by turning it from a federal to a unitary system. Especially to the Muslims of the North, this looked like an Igbo conspiracy to seize the entire country. In July 1966 another coup, under Colonel Yakubu Gowon, a Christian from a small tribe in the center of Nigeria, the Anga, overthrew Ironsi, who was killed.

Nigeria's ethnic pot boiled over. In October 1966 murderous riots against Igbo merchants and their families in the North killed some 20,000 and sent perhaps a million Igbos streaming back to Igboland. After some futile efforts to hold Nigeria together, a consultative assembly of three Eastern states, knowing that they had Nigeria's oilfields, authorized an Igbo colonel, Odumegwu Ojukwu, to set up a separate country. On May 30, 1967, Ojukwu proclaimed the Republic of Biafra. The federal government also knew where the oil was and therefore had to get back the breakaway area. Much of the Biafra War was about oil. At first the Biafran army did well, almost reaching Lagos, until the Nigerian army under Gowon threw them back. For two painful years, the Biafra fighters held out, improvising munitions within a shrinking perimeter, until they finally collapsed in December 1969. Igbo deaths, most from starvation, are estimated at half a million.

Gowon was actually quite magnanimous in victory and brought back the Eastern states into Nigeria as equals within the federation, which he had divided into twelve states. It helped that he

Democracy

THE DEVELOPMENTALIST IMPULSE

In the late 1950s the Cold War refocused from Europe to the Third World. Academics and the U.S. government were fascinated with the emphasis on the developing areas, where the big showdown with communism was to come. Many universities offered "area studies" of Southeast Asia, Africa, Latin America, and every other part of the globe. In a parallel to the academic misperceptions of the Soviet Union (see page 325), political scientists were much too optimistic in supposing the Third World would achieve stable democracy and economic growth. Some developing countries, mainly on the rim of Asia, did achieve both, but few academics predicted these success stories in advance. As Princeton economist Paul Krugman points out, no one has successfully predicted the next country or region of rapid economic growth; it always surprises us.

The academics' poor predictions grew out of the pervasive American fear that the Soviets would take over most of the Third World. Cuba and the 1962 Missile Crisis were frightening warnings. Kennedy's advisors wrote urgently that either we develop the Third World or the Communists will. The newly independent lands were in a shaky, vulnerable transition, but U.S. help could guide them through it and put them on the path to free-market democracy. This came to be called **developmentalism**. The Kennedy administration responded with the Agency for International Development, the Peace Corps, and Vietnam.

The U.S. Agency for International Development (AID), the CIA, and the Ford Foundation funded studies on implementing developmentalist strategies, and academics won grants and built theories to support them. Improving communications was touted as an important technique. But Third World countries developed along the lines of their own internal logic, not ours. Some received lots of U.S. money and advice and bombed. Others received little and prospered. The theories underestimated the impact of culture by assuming that all peoples are culturally ready for development. One key topic was almost totally overlooked: corruption. In an echo of the 1960s, new alarms now urge us to democratize the Middle East before radical Islam takes it over. Review the mistaken developmentalism of the 1960s before you sign up.

was from a small tribe that posed no threat to other ethnic groups. The oil boom that soon followed in the 1970s brought jobs and prosperity. Gowon was overthrown by a coup in 1975 by Brigadier Murtala Ramat Mohammed, a Hausa Muslim from the North, who was himself assassinated in 1976. The Biafra War serves as a reminder of just how ethnically fragile Nigeria is and how risky it is to be a Nigerian head of state.

> **cleft country**   In Huntington's theory, a country split by two civilizations.
>
> **torn country**   In Huntington's theory, one with a Westernizing elite but traditional masses.

■ The Trouble with Nigeria

Nigeria has no shortage of smart, educated people. Two-thirds of Nigerians are literate, not bad for a still-poor developing country. Nigeria has considerable numbers of college graduates, some from British or U.S. universities. Many of its army officers were trained in British military academies.

Nigeria, in the theory of Samuel Huntington (see pages 298 and 552), is a **cleft country**, that is, it is split between Islam and Christianity, displaying what he calls "intercivilizational disunity." The two civilizations rarely live peacefully within one country. Muslims especially tend to break away from such countries. Upon independence in 1947, Muslim Pakistan split from India, which is a majority Hindu. In Yugoslavia, Muslims in Bosnia and Kosovo refused to be ruled by Serbs. The Muslim Central Asian republics of the Soviet Union separated from it in late 1991. Muslim Turks broke away the north of Cyprus in 1974 from the Christian Greeks who held the reins of government. In a parallel with Nigeria, Christians in the south of Sudan—where oil has been discovered—tried to break away from the Muslims of the north. (Do not confuse "cleft countries" in Huntington's terms with **torn countries**, such as Turkey and Mexico, whose leaders wish to make them modern and Western despite mass reluctance.)

Nigeria is not unique in this regard. Most of the coastal nations of West Africa have a Muslim interior and a Christian coastal region. The reason: Islam came by land from the north and from Sudan; Christianity came by ship from Europe. East Africa, on the other hand, has a Muslim coast and a heavily Christian interior, as in Kenya and Tanzania. Some countries with the two faiths manage to get along tolerably well if they can keep religion in the personal sphere and have adherents of the two faiths dispersed enough to make it hard for either to claim a special area as theirs. The overlap of religion with politics in ethnically specific territories, though, can produce breakaway movements.

Political scientists have long celebrated "pluralism" (see page 72) as the basis of modern government and democracy. This is true but only within limits. There must be widespread agreement among groups to not take things too far and to live within certain rules and bounds. Lebanon and Nigeria have plenty of interactions among their many groups, but rules to limit the interactions are weak, so they turn competitive and violent, and the country breaks down. Pluralism without restraint leads to civil war.

■ Democrats without Democracy

A majority of Nigerians want democracy. In a 2000 poll, 81 percent expressed support for democracy, a number that, amidst continuing corruption, ethnic strife, and poverty, has since dropped lower. Just wanting democracy does not necessarily make it happen. The problem is not that insufficient numbers

praetorianism Tendency for military takeovers.

of Nigerians understand and desire democracy; there are more than enough educated Nigerians who do. If they were not divided by tribe and religion, Nigerians might have achieved stable democracy. The terrible dilemma for Nigerian democrats is that they know that whenever Nigeria attempts democracy—as it is doing now—it can easily fail amidst tribal and religious animosities, corruption, and military power-grabs. Still, most Nigerians have not given up on democracy.

PATTERNS OF INTERACTION

Russia and Mexico are weak states, characterized by the penetration of crime deep into politics. Nigeria is even weaker but is not yet a *failed state* (see page 2) such as Somalia or Afghanistan, where national government effectively ceased. Nigeria has a central government and a strong incentive for most of Nigeria's elites to keep the country intact: graft from the lush oil revenues. If Nigeria fell apart, only the Niger Delta would have the oil. This was one of the roots of the Biafra War.

■ Count the Coups

Weak states often experience repeated military coups, a condition known as **praetorianism** (see box on page 533). It indicates that the normal institutions of government—parliaments, parties, and presidents—have too little legitimacy and authority to stand up in times of stress. Most coups are easy and involve little fighting, because the government has no mass support. Let us count Nigeria's military coups:

Year	Ousted	Installed
1966 (Jan.)	Balewa (Hausa) killed	Ironsi (Igbo)
1966 (July)	Ironsi killed	Gowon (Anga)
1975	Gowon deposed	Mohammed (Hausa)
1976	Mohammed killed	Obasanjo (Yoruba)
1983	Shagari (Fulani) deposed	Buhari (Hausa)
1985	Buhari deposed	Babangida (Gwari)
1993	Babangida deposed	Abacha (Hausa)

The best of the lot was Obasanjo, who returned to office as the current president of Nigeria, but now democratically elected. In 1979 he turned power over to a civilian government. The worst was Sani Abacha, a cruel supercrook who, with his family to help him, looted at least $3 billion of Nigerian oil money and stashed it in Swiss, British, and U.S. banks. Oil revenues give a great incentive for Nigerian generals to think about coups. Another cause of Nigeria's coups is apparent: disputes among ethnic groups, a reflection of Nigeria's fractured political culture. Northern Muslims especially bristle at rule by Southern Christians and vice-versa.

Nigeria still seethes with poverty and violence and could have another coup. Praetorianism tends to become a self-reinfecting illness endemic in the Third World. A country that has had a coup will likely have others. Bolivia has had dozens of coups since independence. Brazil last had a coup in 1964 and was ruled by generals until 1985. Mexico during the nineteenth century was praetorian, but Calles ended it by bringing Mexico's main political forces into one party, the PRI. Nigeria's problem is that it never developed the equivalent of PRI, a dominant nationwide party.

patronage   Giving government jobs to political supporters.

The praetorian tendency raises the question: If these countries slide so easily into military rule, why do they ever slide out? Why does a military dictator ever leave power? The material rewards from control over natural resources could be ample incentives to stay in office forever. The means for staying in power are well known and widely practiced in the Third World: **patronage** and *clientelism* (discussed in the Mexico chapter). Mobutu seized power in a 1965 coup and ruled and looted the Congo (which he renamed Zaire) until 1997, with the flimsy cover story that he was the only one who could keep the country together. His real strength was the patronage and clientelistic networks he developed. Sani Abacha of Nigeria set up similar networks and died in office of a heart attack in 1998.

But other forces work against permanent military government. Military officers overthrow governments that have little *legitimacy*, but the military regime then has even less legitimacy. The military rulers know they are unpopular. A few heads of military regimes may be genuine patriots and professional soldiers who recognize that military government soon turns rotten. Obasanjo in 1979 handed power over to a civilian government. The Brazilian generals who seized power in 1964 boasted how they would end inflation and modernize the Brazilian economy. By the 1980s they were embarrassed as their economic miracle stalled; they left power in 1985.

A more persuasive motive for dictators to leave is their recognition that an angry mob or their own officers could overthrow them. Every general who has seized power in a coup knows that there are several colleagues waiting to do the same to him. With no legitimacy to rely on, the dictator may for a time buy support with pieces of graft, but sooner or later those bought off ask, "Why settle for a piece?" Praetorian systems are rife with conspiracies. The dictator may sense when the time has come to flee with his life and his offshore bank accounts.

Key Concepts

THE PRAETORIAN TENDENCY

As the Roman Empire ossified and crumbled, the emperor's bodyguard, the Praetorian Guard, came to play a powerful role, making and unmaking emperors, some of them their own officers. Political scientists now use praetorianism for a situation where the military feels it must take over the government in order to save the country from chaos.

Praetorianism is not just a problem of power-hungry generals but reflects deep conflict in the whole society. In praetorian societies, it is not only the generals who want to take power, but many other groups as well: Students, labor unions, revolutionaries, and demagogic politicians would like to seize the state machinery. Institutional constraints and balances have broken down; nobody plays by the rules. In such situations of chaos and breakdown, it is the army among the many power contenders that is best equipped to seize power, so praetorianism usually means military takeover, the case in Nigeria.

WHAT NIGERIANS QUARREL ABOUT

Upon independence in 1960, Nigeria had roughly the same per capita GDP as several East Asian countries. Forty years later, most of these Asian lands were many times richer than Nigeria, even with Nigeria's major oil revenues. Political scientists and economists have sought explanations at several levels for this growing gap. They divide into two great camps: explanations from the physical and material world, and explanations from the cultural and psychological realm. The two, of course, are not exclusive; it is likely that one feeds into the other.

The most obvious explanation—that the poor countries have few natural resources—does not hold up. Nigeria and Indonesia have great mineral wealth but are poor. Japan, South Korea, Taiwan, Hong Kong, and Singapore have almost no natural resources and are rich. There may even be an inverse relationship between natural resources and prosperity. Oil may be a curse, its revenues a prize for corruption. With few natural resources, Asian Rimland countries had to get clever, competitive, and productive. It is not natural resources but incentivized humans that really matter.

Another culprit is imperialism, but it does not provide a complete explanation. In some countries there was a great deal of imperialist exploitation; others, where there was not much to exploit, were left largely alone. The imperialists did not do nearly enough to get their colonies ready for independence. They should have provided more education and training.

But colonialism does not explain success stories in some ex-colonies. Consider what Hong Kong and Singapore had working against them. Both had been British colonies for more than a century. Both are small islands with zero natural resources; they were economically important only for their locations. Both were destroyed in World War II and occupied by the Japanese. That should predict poverty, but now both are thriving economies at the First World level.

In explaining such apparent anomalies, cultural factors loom large. Some cultures take quickly to economic development, others do not. Those who believe that the future can be formed by one's own activities generally do well. Fatalism, on the other hand, keeps people passive; all is God's will. Cultures that instill discipline and a work ethic can grow rapidly. So far, the winners in this cultural race seem to be the Confucian-influenced lands of East Asia, although few predicted their growth. Indeed, some decades ago scholars attributed Asia's

Nigerians understand markets, as in this crowded street market in Lagos.

backwardness to its Confucian heritage. In the right circumstances, a seemingly sleepy culture can wake up and produce an economic miracle. In Nigeria, the Igbo are an example of this; what was latent in their culture became manifest under the British. Do not write off Africa as forever poor. Cultures change.

strategic variable   Factor you can change that makes a big improvement.

policy   The specific choices governments make.

Some social scientists seek a **strategic variable**, and that is usually in the area of **policy**, a regime's decisions, laws, and programs that may either push or retard

Geography

BOUND KENYA

Kenya is bounded on the north by Sudan and Ethiopia;

on the east by Somalia and the Indian Ocean;

on the south by Tanzania;

and on the west by Uganda.

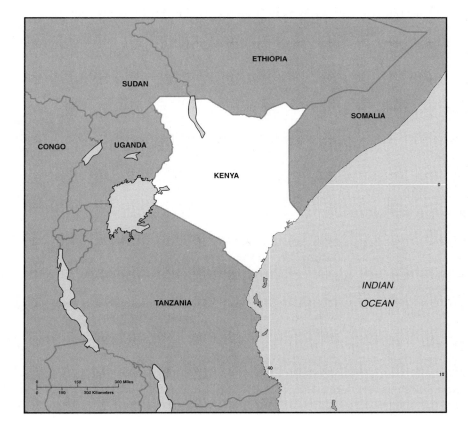

growth. Governments have two types of economic policy tools, macroeconomic and microeconomic. Some economists urge governments to get the *macroeconomy* (see page 396), sometimes called "the fundamentals," in order—little public debt, plentiful savings, low inflation, sufficient investment capital—and then stand back and let the market do its stuff. The German "economic miracle" followed this pattern. Third World technocrats—who are now as prominent in Nigeria as they are in Mexico—tend, however, to get into the microeconomy by choosing which industries to foster or phase out. Postwar Japan used considerable microeconomic management (as well as getting its fundamentals right).

Nigeria shows signs of both macro- and microeconomic mismanagement. The president and finance minister currently propose major reforms, but that means inflicting some of the pain of austerity, at least for the short term. (For the pain of austerity in Mexico, see page 490.) Such reforms could also help clean up corruption. Nigeria's inflation, debt, and unemployment suggest poor choices at the macro level. And the oil industry, in Nigeria as in Mexico, is a constant temptation for microeconomic meddling. Leaving it to market forces would likely produce the best growth. In both countries, that is improbable. Economic rationality often conflicts with political expediency.

The impact of a given policy is hard to judge in advance; you have to see how it works out. Generous public spending (a macroeconomic policy) may keep Nigeria's state governments compliant but unleash inflation, currently around 20 percent a year in Nigeria. Nigeria keeps fuel prices low, because Nigerians demand a special deal on the gasoline they produce. Nigerian subsidies for fuel (a microeconomic policy) mean less to sell on the world market. Nigeria's technocrats understand that the subsidies must be cut, but then you get riots.

■ The Corruption Factor

One factor trips up the best-laid plans for Third World development: corruption, which makes foreign investors keep away. Corruption can be divided into petty and grand. The petty is the small demands for cash—called "dash" or "sweetbread" in West Africa. A friend of the author once flew into Lagos (then the capital of Nigeria) on an assignment for the World Bank. An airport "health officer" stopped him, saying his inoculation record (often required for travel in the tropics) was missing a stamp (it wasn't), but he could fix it for $20. My friend refused, arguing that he was there to help Nigeria. A higher official came and urged him to pay: "You are a rich man, and he is a poor man." My friend finally paid. Such holdups are still standard at Lagos airport and show the logic of petty corruption. Any time you need a stamp, permit, license, or help from the police—even driving or parking a car—in the Third World, be prepared to pay sweetbread, *la mordida*, or *baksheesh*. It is a normal part of daily life. In Nigeria, police set up road blocks and demand 15 cents per car.

Some see petty corruption as an unofficial welfare system to redistribute wealth from the better off to the poor, but it seldom goes to the truly needy and does not spare those with little money. Petty corruption is the demands of underpaid policemen and bureaucrats who are in a position to help or hurt. The historical root of Third World corruption is a less-developed country acquiring a large bureaucracy before it was ready for one. Spain set up Latin America with a giant bureaucracy to supervise its extractive economy, and it has been the source of corruption there ever since. One solution is to pay civil servants more, but Third World countries can seldom afford to. Another is to cut the number of regulations and the bureaucrats needed to enforce them. Chile got a lot less corrupt after it did both.

Petty corruption is a minor annoyance compared to grand corruption, the use of official positions to siphon money wholesale—called "eating" in Nigeria. There is no clear dividing line between petty and grand corruption, but if the money goes into overseas accounts you can be sure it is the grand variety. The governor of oil-rich

transparency Exchanges of money open to public scrutiny. (Opposite: *opacity*.)

Bayelsa state stashed millions abroad and was arrested in Britain in 2005 but slipped out disguised as a woman. Back in Nigeria he enjoyed immunity as a governor. Transparency International's CPI (see box below) does not distinguish between the two levels. Theoretically, a country could have grand corruption at the highest levels and still have an honest civil service, and vice versa. But it is unlikely, for one is usually a reflection of the other. If a postal clerk steals your stamps, chances are the minister of communications is stealing far larger amounts. The grand variety does far more damage than the petty variety of corruption, for it eats capital that should go for economic growth, health, and education. It is a major factor in keeping the Third World poor. Nigeria received $3.5

Comparison

CORRUPTION INTERNATIONAL

Corruption is nearly everywhere, finds Transparency International, a Berlin-based organization that polls business people on their perceptions of having to pay off government officials. TI ranks countries on a ten-point scale, ten being totally clean, one totally corrupt. Some of their 2005 Corruption Perception Index (CPI) findings are shown in the table at the right.

TI founder Peter Eigen was a World Bank official in charge of loans to East Africa but concluded that so much was skimmed off in graft that the loans did little good. To call attention to the massive problem—and to put pressure on governments for **transparency** in their financial dealings—he formed TI in 1993. A poor TI ranking chastises a corrupt country by scaring away business and aid donors, hopefully pushing it to get clean.

Skeptics doubt the accuracy of the CPI (not to be confused with the U.S. Consumer Price Index), because it is just a compilation of subjective perceptions. These change from year to year—depending on which businessmen are interviewed—and countries often trade positions on the TI rankings even though little in their behavior has actually changed. That weakness is built into TI's methodology, but there is no other way to measure corruption, even approximately. Corruption (along with drugs and crime) does not show up in GDP calculations, and crooked officials do not list "earnings from kickbacks" on their income tax. TI's CPI is the best measure we have. The big question is, will TI's efforts over time increase rule of law and boost economic growth?

Iceland	9.7
Singapore	9.4
Britain	8.6
Canada	8.4
Germany	8.2
United States	7.6
France	7.5
Japan	7.3
Portugal	6.5
Israel	6.3
Italy	5.0
South Africa	4.5
Brazil	3.7
Mexico	3.5
China	3.2
Iran	2.9
Russia	2.4
Nigeria	1.9
Bangladesh	1.7

Source: Transparency International

kickback Payoff to government official for a contract.
absolute poverty Living on $1 a day or less.

billion in foreign aid from 1980 to 2000, but far more than that was looted by corrupt officials. No Nigerian has been publicly tried for corruption, suggesting that other officials fear what might come out in a trial.

Grand corruption is not simply a matter of crooks in government but of foreign businesses willing to pay them—usually by **kickbacks**—for profitable contracts. Many corporations that would never kick back on contracts in their home countries reckon it is normal in the Third World: If they do not pay, a competing firm that does pay will get the contract. There is no quick, simple cure for corruption, which sometimes feels as if it is rooted in the soil. Some countries have developed an ethos of clean administration, but this may take centuries. A nobleman developed the Swedish civil service in the seventeenth century and hired other aristocrats, thereby stamping the Swedish bureaucracy with traditions of honor and service. Looking at the TI rankings (see box on page 537), we might all wish to become Icelanders or Singaporeans. There is a hopeful sign here, as Singapore is a new country (independent only in 1965) that started poor but cultivated, under draconic penalties, an ethos of clean administration in a part of the world known for the opposite. With enough will at the top, it can be done.

■ Oil and Democracy

There is an unhappy correlation between petroleum wealth and nondemocratic government. One of the few democratic oil-producing countries is Norway, but it has many other industries and a long history of democracy. Note how the four major oil-producing countries of this book—Russia, Mexico, Nigeria, and Iran—are (or recently were) nondemocratic. Russia attempted democracy but slid back to authoritarianism. Mexico, we hope, is coming out of a long period of one-party domination. Nigeria at this moment has an elected government but for two-thirds of its history did not. And Iran overthrew one tyrant but now has worse ones.

What is there about oil that works against democracy? True, it produces vast wealth, but the wealth is terribly concentrated, mostly in government hands, and seldom benefits the whole society. Oil becomes the great prize of politics in that country, for he who controls the oil monopolizes power. One of Putin's main efforts (successful) was to bring back most petroleum production into state hands. The oil industry employs relatively few, and its wealth is squandered in corruption, overlarge bureaucracies, showcase projects, and rewards for supporters of the regime. The oil bonanza lets rulers avoid investing in infrastructure, industry, and other long-term growth mechanisms. The petrostates' vast incomes have netted them little that can be sustained after the oil runs out. When that happens, the elites will still have their secret overseas bank accounts to live well forever. Their citizens will be poor.

Such is the story of Nigeria, a country with major oil revenues where a majority of the people live in **absolute poverty**. And even with its oil wealth, Nigeria still has an international debt of $30 billion. Some oil was found long ago in the Niger Delta around Port Harcourt, but major oilfields came on line in the 1970s, just as oil prices were quadrupling. Like Iran, Nigeria is a member of OPEC (see page 549), which assigns quotas to member states to keep oil production down and its price up. The good thing about Nigeria here is that it is one of the easiest OPEC members to bribe to get officials to (secretly) produce above Nigeria's quota.

What to do with the oil has thus become one of Nigeria's most difficult political problems: How to make sure oil serves the long-term good of all Nigerians? Most Nigerian oil is produced through joint ventures between foreign firms and the Nigerian National Petroleum Corporation (NNPC), which gets most of the revenues. Like Mexico's Pemex, the NNPC is corrupt, but nationalizing all Nigerian oil production would simply concentrate more wealth and encourage more corruption. Privatizing Nigeria's oil might help, but only if it were total, that is, with oil companies able to buy the oilfields outright. No Nigerian government is likely to sell the fields; that would eliminate the kickbacks that come from leases. The stated reason for rejecting any such sales, as in Mexico, will always be: "What? Sell Nigeria's sacred patrimony to greedy foreign capitalists? Never!" Nationalism cloaks corruption.

One possibility is a joint Nigerian-international board of supervisors (perhaps staffed by Icelanders and Singaporeans) with power of oversight and audit. Such a board would make Nigeria's oil deals transparent and take them out of government hands. The oil revenues should not go to Nigeria's federal treasury, where they could be disbursed to favored tribes and officials, but into an internationally supervised bank to make loans for infrastructure, education, and founding and expanding

Democracy

CORPORATE SOCIAL RESPONSIBILITY

A current business buzzword is "corporate social responsibility" (CSR). According to CSR doctrine, large firms must recognize that they owe more than profits to shareholders; they owe fairness and justice to "stakeholders"—their workers, the community, and the environment. Now most corporations' annual reports trumpet their CSR activities, although critics charge they are little more than public relations.

Nigeria offers a good example of CSR—or lack of it—in action. Shell, Chevron, and other oil companies make immense profits from the Niger Delta, but their operations pollute soil and water. Some local people get good jobs in the oilfields, but greater numbers of fishermen and farmers have lost their livelihood. Poverty feeds rising ethnic tensions in the Delta, where well-armed Ijaw gangs demand "self-determination," that is, control of the oil. The oil companies pay them protection money. Strikes and sabotage are common, and violence, some involving the Nigerian army, takes an estimated thousand lives a year in the Delta. Ken SaroWiwa, a writer and environmental activist from the small Ogoni tribe in the oil region, was hanged in 1995 on trumped-up murder charges. His real crime was calling attention to the ecological damage uncontrolled oil pumping had done to his people. The Nigerian government depends on oil revenues and did not like that kind of criticism.

Most agree that the oil companies have a responsibility, but carrying it out is difficult. The oil companies pay the Nigerian government billions a year in taxes and royalties, but much of it disappears into private pockets; little gets back to the Delta. Trying to practice CSR, the oil companies have also given millions to the Niger Delta Development Commission, but it too is corrupt and inefficient. The companies, aware of the poverty and resentment, also build health clinics in the Delta, but many of them are either empty (because the government will not staff them) or burned down by neighboring tribes who are jealous that they did not get a clinic.

There is no way CSR can deliver help to poor Nigerians; it will always get skimmed. The best thing would be to get the Nigerian government to adopt accountability and transparency standards, but the oil companies have no leverage for this. Said one Chevron executive in Nigeria: "It's very difficult for the private sector to replace government. It's not our role." Some economists argue that corporations should just produce income, out of which come wages and taxes. Stakeholders have real grievances, but they must act through democratic governments to obtain pollution laws, fair wages, public health, and so on. These things need force of law, not corporate generosity. Do not expect CSR to solve vast problems of poverty and corruption.

micro-loan   Small unsecured loan (of a few hundred dollars) to beginning businesses.

valid enterprises. **Micro-loans** have been effective in encouraging thousands of start-up businesses—sometimes just one woman with a sewing machine—at low cost in developing areas. If done well and honestly, oil could give Nigeria a growing economy that would use but not depend on petroleum.

We sometimes forget that there are African success stories. Senegal, Mali, and Botswana are examples of positive development. Effective leadership, sound policies, and the promotion of a national political culture make a difference. Remember, we used to write off Asia as hopeless.

Key Terms

absolute poverty (p. 538)

aquifer (p. 516)

caliphate (p. 516)

cleft country (p. 531)

colonialism (p. 517)

cross-cutting cleavages (p. 527)

cumulative (p. 527)

desiccation (p. 516)

developmentalism (p. 530)

divide and rule (p. 519)

indirect rule (p. 519)

jihad (p. 516)

kickback (p. 538)

micro-loan (p. 540)

pan-Africanism (p. 521)

patronage (p. 533)

policy (p. 535)

praetorianism (p. 532)

Sahel (p. 516)

savanna (p. 516)

sharia (p. 528)

strategic variable (p. 535)

sub-Saharan (p. 516)

torn country (p. 531)

transparency (p. 537)

Key Web Sites

University of Pennsylvania African Studies Center
sas.upenn.edu/African_Studies/Country_Specific/Nigeria.html

U.S. Department of Energy
eia.doe.gov/emeu/cabs/Nigeria/html

News Sources
Guardian Newspaper
ngrguardiannews.com

nigeria.com

nigeriadaily.com

Against Nigerian Scams
home.rica.net/alphae/419coal/

Further Reference

Apter, Andrew H. *The Pan-African Nation: Oil and the Spectacle of Culture in Nigeria*. Chicago, IL: University of Chicago Press, 2005.

Bah, Abu Bakarr. *Breakdowns and Reconstruction: Democracy, the Nation-State, and Ethnicity in Nigeria*. Blue Ridge Summit, PA: Lexington Books, 2005.

Coleman, James S. *Nigeria: Background to Nationalism*. Berkeley, CA: University of California Press, 1963.

Farris, Jacqueline W., and Mohammed Bomoi, eds. *Shehu Musa Yar'Adua: A Biography*. Boulder, CO: L. Rienner, 2004.

Howe, Herbert M. *Ambiguous Order: Military Forces in African States*. Boulder, CO: L. Rienner, 2004.

Laitin, David D. *Hegemony and Culture: Politics and Religious Change among the Yoruba*. Chicago, IL: University of Chicago Press, 1986.

Larémont, Ricardo René, ed. *Borders, Nationalism, and the African State*. Boulder, CO: L. Rienner, 2005.

Osaghae, Eghosa. *Crippled Giant: Nigeria since Independence*. Bloomington, IN: Indiana University Press, 1998.

Paden, John N. *Muslim Civic Cultures and Conflict Resolution: The Challenge of Democratic Federalism in Nigeria*. Washington, D.C.: Brookings, 2005.

Rotberg, Robert I., ed. *Crafting the New Nigeria: Confronting the Challenges*. Boulder, CO: L. Rienner, 2004.

Schwarz, Frederick A. O., Jr. *Nigeria: The Tribes, the Nation, or the Race: The Politics of Independence*. Cambridge, MA: MIT Press, 1965.

Chapter 35

Iran

THE IMPACT OF THE PAST

Much of Iran is an arid plateau around 4,000 feet above sea level. Some areas are rainless desert; some get sufficient rain only for sparse sheep pasture. In this part of the world, irrigation made civilization possible, and whatever disrupted waterworks had devastating consequences. Persia's location made it an important trade route between East and West, one of the links between the Middle East and Asia. Persia thus became a crossroads of civilizations and one of the earliest of the great civilizations.

The trouble with being a crossroads is that your country becomes a natural target for conquest. Indo-European-speaking invaders took over Persia about the fifteenth century B.C. and laid the basis for subsequent Persian culture. Their most famous kings: Cyrus and Darius in the sixth century B.C. The invasions never ceased, though: the Greeks under Alexander in the third and fourth centuries B.C., the Arab-Islamic conquest in the seventh century A.D., Turkish tribes in the eleventh century, Mongols in the thirteenth century, and many others. The repeated pattern was one of conquest, the founding of a new dynasty, and its falling apart as quarrelsome heirs broke it into petty kingdoms. This fragmentation set up the country for easy conquest again.

Iran, known for most of history as Persia (it was renamed only in 1925), resembles China in that it is heir to an ancient and magnificent civilization that, partly at the hands of outsiders, fell into "the sleep of nations." When it awoke, it was far behind the West, which, like China, Iran views as an adversary. If and how Iran will move into modernity is one of our major questions.

Although it does not look or sound like it, Persian (*Farsi*) is a member of the broad Indo-European family of languages; the neighboring Arabic and Turkic tongues are not. Today, Farsi is the mother tongue of about half of Iranians. Another fifth speak Persian-related languages (such as Kurdish). A quarter speak a Turkic language, and some areas speak Arabic and other tongues. The non-Farsi speakers occupy the periphery of the Farsi-speaking heartland and have at times been discontent with rule by Persians. In Iranian politics today, to be descended from one of the non-Persian minorities is held against politicians.

Questions to Consider

1. What has geography contributed to Iran's development?
2. How does Iran differ from Arab countries?
3. What is a *modernizing tyrant*? Why do they fail?
4. What factors brought Iran's Islamic Revolution?
5. Explain Iran's dual executive. Who is more powerful?
6. Does secularization always come with modernization?
7. What kind of Iranians wish to liberalize their system?
8. Explain the power struggle in Iran.
9. How is attire a political debate in Iran?
10. How have America and Iran misunderstood each other?
11. Why is the Persian Gulf region strategic?

■ The Arab Conquest

Allah's prophet Muhammad died in Arabia in 632, but his religion spread like wildfire. **Islam** means "submission" (to God's will), and this was to be hastened by *jihad*. Islam arrived soon in Iran by the sword. The remnant of the Sassanid empire, already exhausted by centuries of warfare with Byzantium, was easily beaten by the Arabs at Qadisiya in 637 and within two centuries Persia was mostly Muslim. Adherents of the old religion, Zoroastrianism, fled to India where today they are a small, prosperous minority known as Parsis.

Islam   Religion founded by Muhammad.

Shia   Minority branch of Islam.

The Arab conquest was a major break with the past. In contrast to the sharp social stratification of Persian tradition, Islam taught that all Muslims were, at least in a spiritual sense, equal. Persia adopted the Arabic script, and many Arab words enriched Persian. Persian culture flowed the other way, too, as the Arabs copied Persian architecture and civil administration. For six centuries, Persia was swallowed up by the Arab empires, but in 1055 the Seljuk Turks invaded from Central Asia and conquered most of the Middle East. As usual, their rule soon fell apart into many small states, easy prey for Genghis Khan, the Mongol "World Conqueror" whose horde thundered in from the east in 1219. One of his descendants who ruled Persia embraced Islam at the end of that century. This is part of a pattern Iranians are proud of: "We may be conquered," they say, "but the conqueror ends up adopting our superior culture and becomes one of us."

The coming of the Safavid dynasty in 1501 boosted development of a distinctly Iranian identity. The Safavids practiced a minority version of Islam called **Shia** (see box below) and decreed it

Geography

SUNNI AND SHIA

Over 80 percent of the world's Muslims practice the mainstream branch of Islam, called Sunni. Scattered unevenly throughout the Muslim world, however, is a minority branch (of 100 million) called Shia. The two split early over who was the true successor (*caliph*) of Muhammad. Shias claim the Prophet's cousin and son-in-law Ali has the title, but he was assassinated in 661. Shia means followers or partisans, hence Shias are the followers of Ali. When Ali's son, Hussein, attempted to claim the title, his forces were beaten at Karbala in present-day Iraq (now a Shia shrine) in 680, and Hussein was betrayed and tortured to death. This gave Shia a fixation on martyrdom; some of their holidays feature self-flagellation.

Shia also developed a messianic concept that was lacking in Sunni. Shias in Iran hold that the line of succession passed through a series of twelve *imams* (religious leaders) of whom Ali was the first. The twelfth imam disappeared in 873 but is to return one day to "fill the world with justice." He is referred to as the Hidden Imam and the Expected One. Such believers are sometimes called "Twelver" Muslims.

Shias are no more "fundamentalist" than other Muslims, who also interpret the Koran strictly. Although the origin and basic tenets of the two branches is identical, Sunnis regard Shias as extremist, mystical, and crazy. Some 60 percent of Iraqis are Shia, but only in Iran is Shia the state religion. With their underdog status elsewhere, sometimes Shias rebel (with Iranian money and guidance), as in Lebanon, southern Iraq, and eastern Arabia. Shia imparts a peculiar twist to Iranians, giving them the feeling of being isolated but right, beset by enemies on all sides, and willing to martyr themselves for their cause.

Persia's state religion. Most of their subjects switched from **Sunni** Islam and are Shias to this day. Neighboring Sunni powers immediately attacked Safavid Persia, but this enabled the new regime to consolidate its control and develop an Islam with Persian characteristics.

Sunni   Mainstream Islam.

Geography

BOUND IRAN

Iran is bounded on the north by Armenia, Azerbaijan, the Caspian Sea, and Turkmenistan;

on the east by Afghanistan and Pakistan;

on the south by the Gulf of Oman and the Persian Gulf;

and on the west by Iraq and Turkey.

◼ Western Penetration

It is too simple to say Western cultural, economic, and colonial penetration brought down the great Persian empire. Safavid Persia was attacked from several directions, mostly by neighboring Muslim powers: the Ottoman Turks from the west, Uzbeks from the north, and Afghans from the northeast. In fighting the Ottomans, Safavid rulers made common cause with the early Portuguese, Dutch, and English sea traders in the late sixteenth and early seventeenth centuries. As previously in the region's history, the outsiders were able to penetrate because the local kingdoms had weakened themselves in wars, a pattern that continues in our day.

Majlis   Arabic for assembly; Iran's parliament.

shah   Persian for king.

In 1722, Afghan invaders ended the Safavid dynasty, but no one was able to govern the whole country. After much chaos, in 1795 the Qajar dynasty emerged victorious. Owing to Persian weakness, Britain and Russia became dominant in Persia, the Russians pushing in from the north, the British from India. Although never a colony, Persia, like China, slid into semicolonial status, with much of its political and economic life dependent on imperial designs, something Persians strongly resented. A particularly vexatious example was an 1890 treaty giving British traders a monopoly on tobacco sales in Persia. Muslim clerics led mass hatred of the British tobacco concession, and the treaty was repealed.

At this same time, liberal, Western ideas of government seeped into Persia, some brought, as in China, by Christian missionaries (who made very few Persian converts). The Constitutional Revolution of 1906–1907 (in which an American supporter of the popular struggle was killed) brought Persia's first constitution and first elected parliament, the **Majlis**. The struggles over the tobacco concession and constitution were led by a combination of two forces: liberals who hated the monarchy and wanted Western-type institutions and Muslim clerics who also disliked the monarchy but wanted a stronger role for Islam. This same combination brought down the **Shah** in 1979; now these two strands have turned against each other over the future of Iran.

Notice how at almost exactly the same time—1905 in Russia, 1906 in Persia—corrupt and weak monarchies promised somewhat democratic constitutions in the face of popular uprisings. Both monarchies, dedicated to autocratic power and hating democracy, only pretended to deliver, a prescription for increasing mass discontent. A new shah inherited the throne in 1907 and shut down the Majlis with his Russian-trained Cossack bodyguard unit. Mass protest forced the last Qajar shah to flee to Russia in 1909; he tried to return in 1911 but was forced back as Russian troops occupied Tehran. The 1907 Anglo-Russian treaty had already cut Persia in two, with a Russian sphere of influence in the north and a British one in the south. During World War I, Persia was nominally neutral, but its strategic location turned into a zone of contention and chaos. Neighboring Turkey allied with Germany, and Russia and Britain allied with each other. Russian, British and German agents tried to tilt Persia their way.

◼ The First Pahlavi

As is often the case when a country degenerates into chaos, military officers see themselves as saviors of the nation, the *praetorianism* that we saw in Nigeria. In 1921 an illiterate cavalry officer, Reza Khan, commander of the Cossack brigade, seized power and in 1925 had himself crowned shah, the founder of the short-lived (1925–1979) Pahlavi dynasty. The nationalistic Reza took the pre-Islamic surname Pahlavi and told the world to start calling the country by its true name, Iran, from the word *aryan*, indicating the country's Indo-European roots. (Nazi ideologists also loved the word aryan, which they claimed indicated genetic superiority. Indeed, the ancient Persian Zoroastrians preached racial purity.)

Like Atatürk, Reza Shah was determined to modernize his country (see box below). His achievements were impressive. He molded an effective Iranian army and used it to suppress tribal revolts and unify Iran. He created a modern, European-type civil service and a national bank. He replaced traditional and Islamic courts with civil courts operating under Western codes of justice. In 1935 he founded Iran's first Western-style university. Under state supervision and fueled by oil revenues, Iran's economy grew. Also like Atatürk, Reza Shah ordered his countrymen to adopt Western dress and women to stop wearing the veil. But Reza also kept the press and Majlis closely obedient. Troublemakers and dissidents often died in jail. Reza Shah was a classic **modernizing tyrant**.

World War II put Iran in the same situation as World War I had. It was just too strategic to leave alone; it was a major oil producer and conduit for U.S. supplies to the desperate Soviet Union. As before, the Russians took over in the north and the British (later the Americans) in the south. Both agreed to clear out six months after the war ended. Reza Shah, who tilted toward Germany, in September 1941 was exiled by the British to South Africa, where he died in 1944. Before he left, he abdicated in favor of his son, Muhammad Reza Pahlavi.

The Americans and British left Iran in 1945; the Soviets did not, and some argue this incident marked the start of the Cold War. Stalin claimed that Azerbaijan, a Soviet *republic* in the Caucasus, was entitled by ethnic right to merge with the Azeris of northern Iran and refused to withdraw Soviet forces. Stalin set up puppet Communist Azeri and Kurdish governments there. In 1946 U.S. President Truman delivered some harsh words, Iran's prime minister promised Stalin an oil deal, and Stalin pulled out. Then the Majlis canceled the oil deal.

modernizing tyrant   Dictator who pushes country ahead.

secular   Nonreligious.

mosque   Muslim house of worship.

Ottoman   Turkish imperial dynasty, fourteenth to twentieth centuries.

Comparison

ATATÜRK AND REZA SHAH

During the 1920s, two strong personalities in adjacent Middle Eastern lands attempted to modernize their countries from above: Kemal Atatürk in Turkey and Reza Shah in Iran. Both were nationalistic military officers and Muslims but **secular** in outlook; both wished to separate **mosque** and state.

In economics, both were statists (see page 118) and made the government the number-one investor and owner of major industries. Both pushed education, the improved status of women, and Western clothing. As such, both aroused traditionalist opposition led by Muslim clerics. Both thundered "You will be modern!" but religious forces opposed their reforms, and do to this day.

Their big difference: Atatürk ended the **Ottoman** monarchy and firmly supported a republican form of government in Turkey. He pushed his reforms piecemeal through parliament, which often opposed him. Reza Shah rejected republicanism and parliaments as too messy; he insisted on an authoritarian monarchy as the only way to modernize his unruly country, as did his son. Although Turkey has had plenty of troubles since Atatürk, it has not been ripped apart by revolution. Atatürk built some political institutions; the Pahlavi shahs built none.

■ The Last Pahlavi

Oil determined much of Iran's twentieth-century history. Oil was the great prize for the British, Hitler, Stalin, and the United States. Who should own and profit from Iran's oil—foreigners, the Iranian government, or Iranians as a whole? Major oil deposits were first discovered in Iran in 1908 and developed under a British concession, the Anglo-Persian (later Anglo-Iranian) Oil Company. Persia got little from the oil deal, and Persians came to hate this rich foreign company in their midst, one that wrote its own rules. Reza Shah ended the lopsided concession in 1932 and forced the AIOC to pay higher royalties.

The AIOC still rankled Iranians, who rallied to the radical nationalist Prime Minister Muhammad Mossadeq in the early 1950s. With support from Iranian nationalists, liberals, and leftists, Mossadeq nationalized AIOC holdings. Amidst growing turmoil and what some feared was a tilt to the Soviet Union, Shah Muhammad Reza Pahlavi fled the country in 1953. The British urged Washington to do something, and President Eisenhower, as part of U.S. **containment**, had the CIA destabilize the Tehran government. It was easy: The CIA's Kermit Roosevelt arrived with $1 million in a suitcase and rented a suitable mob. Mossadeq was out, the Shah was restored, and the United States won a battle in the Cold War. We thought we were very clever.

containment   U.S. Cold War policy of blocking expansion of communism.

Like his father, the Shah became a modernizing tyrant, promoting what he called his "White Revolution" from above (as opposed to a red revolution from below). Under the Shah, Iran had excellent relations with the United States. President Nixon touted the Shah as our pillar of stability in the Persian Gulf. We were his source of money, technology, and military hardware. Some 100,000 Iranian students came to U.S. universities, and 45,000 American businessmen and consultants surged into Iran for lucrative contracts. (This point demonstrates that person-to-person contacts do not always lead to good relations between countries.)

The United States was much too close to the Shah. We supported him unstintingly and unquestioningly. The Shah was Western-educated, anti-Communist, and was rapidly modernizing Iran; he was our kind of guy. Iranian unrest and opposition went unnoticed by the U.S. embassy. Elaborate Iranian public relations portrayed Iran in a rosy light in the U.S. media. Under Nixon, U.S. arms makers sold Iran "anything that goes bang." We failed to see that Iran and the Shah were two different things, and that our unqualified backing of the Shah was alienating many Iranians. We ignored how the Shah governed by means of a dreaded secret police, the SAVAK. We failed to call a tyrant a tyrant. Only when the Islamic Revolution broke out did we learn what Iranians really thought about the Shah. We were so obsessed by communism penetrating from the north that we could not imagine a bitter, hostile Islamic revolution coming from within Iran.

Geography

CRUISING THE PERSIAN GULF

The countries bordering the Persian Gulf contain two-thirds of the world's proven petroleum reserves. Some of you may do military service in the Gulf, so start learning the geography now. Imagine you are on an aircraft carrier making a clockwise circle around the Gulf. Upon entering the Strait of Hormuz, which countries do you pass to port?

Oman, United Arab Emirates, Qatar, Saudi Arabia, Bahrain (an island), Kuwait, Iraq, and Iran.

What finally did in the Shah? Too much money went to his head. With the 1973 Arab-Israeli war, oil producers worldwide got the chance to do what they had long wished: boost the price of oil and take over oil extraction from foreign companies. The Shah, one of the prime movers of the Organization of Petroleum Exporting Countries (**OPEC**), gleefully did both. What Mossadeq attempted, the Shah accomplished. World oil prices quadrupled. Awash with cash, the Shah went mad with vast, expensive schemes. The state administered oil revenues for the greater glory of Iran and its army, not for the Iranian people, creating resentment that hastened the Islamic Revolution. Oil led to turmoil.

> **OPEC**   Cartel of oil-rich countries designed to boost petroleum prices.
>
> **mullah**   Muslim cleric.
>
> **ayatollah**   "Sign of God," top Shia religious leader.

The sudden new wealth caused great disruption. The Shah promoted education, but the more education people got, the more they could see the Shah was a tyrant. Some people got rich fast while most stayed poor. Corruption grew worse than ever. Millions flocked from the countryside to the cities where, rootless and confused, they turned to the only institution they understood, the mosque. In their rush to modernize, the Pahlavis alienated the Muslim clergy. Not only did the Shah undermine the traditional cultural values of Islam, he seized land owned by religious foundations and distributed it to peasants as part of his White Revolution. The **mullahs** also hated the influx of American culture, with its alcohol and sex. Many Iranians saw the Shah's huge military expenditures—at the end, an incredible 17 percent of Iran's GDP—as a waste of money. As Alexis de Tocqueville noted in his study of the French Revolution, economic growth hastens revolution.

One of Iran's religious authorities, **Ayatollah** Khomeini, criticized the Shah and incurred his wrath. He had Khomeini exiled to Iraq in 1964 and then forced him to leave Iraq in 1978. France allowed Khomeini to live in a Paris suburb, from which his recorded messages were telephoned to cassette recorders in Iran to be duplicated and distributed through mosques nationwide. Cheap cassettes bypassed the Shah's control of Iran's media and helped bring him down.

In the late 1970s, matters came to a head. The Shah's overambitious plans had made Iran a debtor nation. Discontent from both secular intellectuals and Islamic clerics bubbled up. And, most dangerous, U.S. President Jimmy Carter made human rights a foreign-policy goal. As part of this, the Shah's dictatorship came under U.S. criticism. Shaken, the Shah began to relax his grip, and that is precisely when all hell broke loose. As de Tocqueville observed, the worst time in the life of a bad government is when it begins to mend its ways. Compounding his error, Carter showed his support for the Shah by exchanging visits, proof to Iranians that we were supporting a hated tyrant. In 1977, Carter and the Shah had to retreat into the White House from the lawn to escape the tear gas that drifted over from the anti-Shah protest (mostly by Iranian students) in Lafayette Park.

By late 1978, the Shah, facing huge demonstrations and (unknown to Washington) dying of cancer, was finished. Shooting into the crowds of protesters just made them angrier. The ancient Persian game of chess ends with a checkmate, a corruption of the Farsi *shah mat* ("the king is trapped"). On January 16, 1979, the last Pahlavi left Iran. *Shah mat.*

THE KEY INSTITUTIONS

A Theocracy

Two and a half millennia of monarchy ended in Iran with a 1979 referendum, carefully supervised by the Khomeini forces, that introduced the Islamic Republic of Iran and a new constitution. As in most countries, the offices of head of state and head of government are split. But

theocracy   Rule by priests.

velayat-e faqih   "Guardianship of the Islamic jurist," theocratic system devised by Khomeini.

canon law   Internal laws of Roman Catholic Church.

Islamist   Someone who uses Islam in political way.

instead of a figurehead monarch (as in Britain) or weak president (as in Germany), Iran now has two heads of state, one its leading religious figure, the other a more standard president. The religious chief is the real power. That makes Iran a **theocracy** and a dysfunctional political system.

Theocracy is rather rare and tends not to last. Even in ancient times, priests filled supporting rather than executive roles. Russia's tsar, officially head of both church and state, was way over on the state side; he wore military garb, not priestly. Iran (plus Afghanistan and Sudan) attempted a theocratic system. The principle of political power in Iran—in the system devised by Khomeini—is the **velayat-e faqih**. This leading Islamic jurist, the *faqih*, serves for life. "Jurist" means a legal scholar steeped in Islamic, specifically Shia, religious law. (The closest Western equivalent is **canon law**. In medieval Europe, canon lawyers were among the leading intellectual and political figures.) Allegedly the *faqih*, also known as the "Spiritual Guide" and "Supreme Leader," can use the Koran and related Islamic commentaries to decide all issues, even those having nothing to do with religion. (An **Islamist**, of course, would say everything is connected with religion.)

Khomeini, the first and founding *faqih*, died in 1989. He was nearly all-powerful. Successors are chosen by an Assembly of Experts of eighty-six Muslim clerics elected every eight years, who are supposed to choose from among the purest and most learned Islamic jurists. The man they elect (Islam permits no women religious leaders) is not necessarily an ayatollah, one of the wisest Shi'ite jurists. In 1989 the Experts chose Ali Khamenei, a Hojatollah, the rank just below, but he was immediately promoted to ayatollah. Khamenei, expected to serve for life, lacks Khomeini's (do not confuse the two names) charisma and Islamic authority but is still the real power. He names the heads of all major state and religious organizations and may declare war. He controls the judiciary, armed forces, security police, intelligence agencies, radio, and television. He is much more powerful than Iran's president and continually blocks any reform efforts.

■ Iran's Legislature

Iran has a unicameral (one-house) legislature, the Islamic Consultative Assembly (*Majlis*), consisting of 290 deputies elected for four-year terms. Iran uses single-member districts, like Britain and the U.S. Congress. Iran is divided into 265 constituencies, and each Iranian sixteen and older can vote. Additional seats are reserved for non-Muslim deputies: five each for Assyrian Christians, Jews, and Zoroastrians, two for Armenian Christians, none for Baha'is. The Speaker of parliament is a major position. The constitution guarantees MPs immunity from arrest, but the conservative judiciary still jails MPs who call too loudly for reforms.

Electoral balloting is free and fair, but permission to run is totally rigged. The Council of Guardians (see next paragraphs) must approve all candidates, and they disqualify thousands who might be critical. Out-and-out liberals are thus discouraged from even trying to run. The low-turnout 2004 parliamentary elections gave the Majlis to conservatives because no openly liberal or reformist candidates were allowed, so only half of Iranians bothered to vote.

More powerful than the Majlis is the Council of Guardians, a strange institution combining features of an upper house, a supreme court, an electoral commission, and a religious inquisition. Its twelve members serve six years each, half of them changed every three years. The *faqih* chooses six Islamic clerics; Iran's supreme court (the High Council of Justice) names another six, all Islamic lawyers, who are approved by the Majlis.

The Council examines each Majlis bill to make sure it does not violate Islamic principles. If a majority decides it does, the bill is returned to the Majlis to be corrected. Without Council approval, a bill is in effect vetoed. All bills aiming at reform are blocked in this way. To settle conflicts between the Majlis and the Council, an "Expediency Council" appointed by the Leader, has become like another legislature. In 2005 the Expediency Council—chaired by Rafsanjani, the very man Ahmadinejad had beaten in elections—was given additional powers to oversee the president. Iran's conservative religious establishment does not really like the rambunctious Ahmadinejad.

Democracy

IRAN'S 2005 PRESIDENTIAL ELECTION

The surprise winner of Iran's 2005 presidential election was the populist mayor of Tehran, Mahmoud Ahmadinejad, age forty-nine. The radical Ahmadinejad, now seen as an extremist, sought to restore the original Islamist and socialist goals of the 1979 revolution, in which he was a student leader. The expected winner, Ayatollah Ali Akbar Hashemi Rafsanjani, who had earlier been president (1989–1997), talked a pragmatic and reformist line but was disliked as corrupt and part of the establishment.

The election was not democratic. The Council of Guardians screened out hundreds of candidates deemed liberal or insufficiently Islamic. Only eight were allowed to run, and one dropped out. Many charged the 2005 balloting was rigged; they were silenced. Two critical newspapers were closed. Iran's religious hard-liners backed Ahmadinejad and ordered the army and the fanatic *Basij* militia to turn out and bring their relatives to vote for Ahmadinejad, who was in the Basij and Pasdaran Revolutionary Guards. Iran elects presidents with a French-style two rounds, the first for the two biggest winners, the second a runoff between them. Rafsanjani edged Ahmadinejad 21–19.5 percent in the first round, but Ahmadinejad won the second round 62–36 percent over Rafsanjani, with a reported (but probably inflated) 60 percent turnout, much lower than the 83 percent turnout in 1997. Many liberal Iranians did not vote in 2005.

Ahmadinejad won chiefly with the vote of poor Iranians, to whom he promised welfare. There was a social-class element to the 2005 election. Rafsanjani ran an aloof campaign based on his religious rank and

political experience (he had also been Majlis speaker). He and his relatives became very wealthy. Ahmadinejad ran as a man of the people who lived modestly and looked after Tehran's poor in his two years as mayor. Ahmadinejad, the first Iranian president to hold no religious rank, was an engineering professor. Some may have voted for him just to protest Iran's corrupt establishment.

Ahmadinejad's victory was, in a way, a mirror image of Muhammad Khatami's, who won in a surprise landslide in 1997. Unknown before the election, Khatami hinted at reform and suddenly became a symbol of change. With no liberals allowed to run, Iranians turn to any outsider candidate as a protest. Khatami in office was blocked by Khamenei and the hard-liners and reformed nothing. Ironically "conservative" Ahmadinejad was a bigger threat to Iran's establishment than "liberal" Khatami.

Ahmadinejad, fanatic in religion and populist in economics, fired many officials as corrupt. This angered establishment conservatives, who blocked his policies and ministerial nominations and his efforts to redistribute oil revenues to low-income Iranians. Ahmadinejad played the nationalist card by openly defying the West on Iran's "peaceful" nuclear program, widely suspected as a cover for building nuclear weapons. Many Iranians liked his defiance. He thundered that "Israel must be wiped off the map" and that the Holocaust was a "myth," comments which further isolated Iran in the world. Ahmadinejad, who claimed mystical experiences, made Ayatollah Khamenei, Iran's Leader, seem moderate and stable in comparison.

More important, the Council of Guardians examines all candidates for the Majlis and has the power to disqualify them without explanation. The Council scratches a large fraction of Majlis candidates. In 2002 President Khatami and the Majlis tried to take this power away from the Council of Guardians, but the Council vetoed the bills. At present, the Council of Guardians makes the Iranian system unreformable.

Political Culture

Is Islam Anti-Modern?

Most Middle East experts deny there is anything inherent in Islamic doctrine that keeps Muslim societies from modernizing. Looking at cases, though, one finds no Islamic countries that have fully modernized. Under Atatürk, Turkey made great strides between the two wars, but Islamic militants still try to undo his reforms. In Huntington's terms (see page 531), Turkey is a *torn country*, pulled between Western and Islamic cultures. Recently Malaysia, half of whose people are Muslim, has scored rapid economic progress. Generally, though, Islam coincides with backwardness, at least as we define it. Some Muslim countries are rich but only because oil has brought them outside revenues.

By itself Islam probably does not cause backwardness. The Koran prohibits loaning money at interest, but there are ways to work around that. Islamic civilization was for centuries far ahead of Christian Europe in science, philosophy, medicine, sanitation, architecture, steelmaking, and more. Translations from the Arabic taught Europe classic Greek thought, especially Aristotle, which helped trigger the Renaissance and Europe's modernization. A millennium ago you would find Muslims concluding that Christianity kept Europe backward.

But Islamic civilization faltered and European civilization modernized. By the sixteenth century, when European merchant ships arrived in the Persian Gulf, the West was ahead of Islam. Why? According to some scholars, early Islam permitted independent interpretations of the Koran (*ijtihad*), but between the ninth and eleventh centuries this was replaced by a single, orthodox interpretation (*taqlid*); intellectual life atrophied. Islam has never had a reformation.

The Mongol invaders of the thirteenth century massacred the inhabitants of Baghdad and destroyed the region's irrigation systems, something the Arab empire never recovered from. (The Mongols' impact on Russia was also devastating.) Possibly because of this Islam turned to mysticism. Instead of an open, flexible, and tolerant faith that was fascinated by learning and science, Islam turned sullen and rigid. When the Portuguese opened up direct trade routes between Europe and Asia, bypassing Islamic middlemen, trade through the Middle East declined sharply and with it the region's economy.

Islam has a structural problem in its combining of religion and government, making it difficult to split mosque and state. Those who try (such as Atatürk) are resisted. Even today, many Muslims want *sharia* (see page 528) to be the law of the land. This creates hostility between secular modernizers and religious traditionalists, who compete for political power, a destructive tug-of-war that blocks progress.

A major factor was the domination of European (chiefly British) imperialists starting in the nineteenth century. This created the same resentment we saw in China, the resentment of a proud civilization brought low by unwelcome foreigners: "You push in here with your guns, your railroads, and your commerce and act superior to us. Well, culturally and morally we are superior to you, and eventually we'll kick you out and show you." With this comes hatred of anything Western and therefore opposition to modernity, because accepting modernity means admitting the West is superior. Islam teaches it is superior to all other civilizations and will eventually triumph worldwide. Devout Muslims do not like evidence to the contrary.

If Islamic countries do not discard their cultural antipathy to modernity—which need not be a total imitation of the West—their progress will be slow and often reversed. Millions of Muslims living in the West are modern and still Islamic. Ideas for religious modernization are already afoot in Islam with, ironically, Iranian intellectuals in the lead. Eventually, we could see societies that are both modern and Muslim. One of the best ways to promote this: Educate women.

■ Emerging Parties?

Parties are legal under Iran's constitution, but the government does not allow them; only individual candidates run. Even Khomeini dissolved his own Islamic Republic party in 1984. Lack of party labels makes Iranian elections less than free, for without them voters cannot clearly discern who stands for what. It is difficult to count how many seats each of the several "tendencies" control; they have to be estimated. In practice, candidates are linked with informal parties and political tendencies. Eventually these may turn into legal parties. Observers see four main political groupings plus many factions and individual viewpoints.

Radicals, the most extreme supporters of the Islamic Revolution—such as President Ahmadinejad—want to adhere to what they perceive as Khomeini's design for an Islamic republic. Socialist in economics, they also favor state control over the economy. They wish to keep out Western influences and continue Islamic supervision of society, such as squads who dictate women's attire.

Conservatives, calmer than the radicals, want a nonfanatic Islamic Republic with special consideration for the economic needs of small merchants. They still oppose any liberalization.

Reformists tend to cluster in the educated middle class. They favor privatization of state enterprises, less Islamic supervision of society, elections open to most candidates, fewer powers for the Council of Guardians, and dialogue with the United States. In the late 1990s they held a majority in the Majlis and formed a sort of party called the Participation Front. With most of their candidates disqualified by the Council of Guardians in 2004, the Front resigned from the Majlis and boycotted elections.

Liberals would go farther. Popular among Iranian students, they emphasize democracy and civil rights and want totally free elections. They want to end all social controls imposed by the Islamists. In economics, however, they are a mixed bag, ranging from free-marketers to socialists. Knowing the Council of Guardians would reject them, no liberals run for office. In effect, there is no longer opposition in Iran's parliament.

■ An Unfree System

Iran could be described as a political system waiting to be free. The potential is there, but important institutional changes would have to be made. First, the power of the Leader would have to be reduced to that of a purely spiritual guide with few or no temporal powers. Next, the Council of Guardians would have to be abolished. If these two things happened, Iran's institutions could quickly turn it into a democracy, with a real executive president, a critical Majlis, multiparty elections, and a free press. Iran has the greatest democratic potential of any Persian Gulf country.

IRANIAN POLITICAL CULTURE

As in much of the Third World, many Iranians do not want their traditional culture erased by Western culture. "We want to be modern," say many citizens of the Third World, "but not like you. We'll do it our way, based on our values and our religion." Whether you can be a modern, high-tech society while preserving your old culture is a key question for much of the globe today. Will efforts to combine old and new cultures work or lead to chaos? In some cases, like Japan, it has worked. For Islamic nations, so far it has not. The key factor may be the flexibility and adaptability

Koran   Muslim holy book.

secularization   Cutting back role of religion in government and daily life.

of the traditional culture, which is very high in the case of Japan. Japan learned to be modern but still distinctly Japanese. Can Muslim countries do the equivalent?

Beneath all the comings and goings of conquerors and kingdoms, Persian society kept its traditions for centuries. As in China, dynastic changes little disturbed the broad majority of the population, poor farmers and shepherds, many of them still tribal in organization. As in much of the Third World, traditional society was actually quite stable and conservative. Islam, the mosque, the mullah, and the **Koran** gave solace and meaning to the lives of most Persians. People were poor but passive.

Then came modernization, mostly under foreign pressure, starting late in the nineteenth century, expanding with the development of petroleum, and accelerating under the two Pahlavi shahs. Iran neatly raises the question of whether you can modernize and still keep your old culture. According to what political scientists call *modernization theory*, a number of things happen more or less simultaneously. First, the economy changes, from simple farming to natural-resource extraction to manufacturing and services. Along with this comes urbanization, the movement of people from country to city. At the same time, education levels increase greatly; most people become literate and some go to college. People consume more mass media—at first newspapers, then radio, and finally television—until many people are aware of what is going on in their country and in the world. A large middle class emerges along with a variety of interest groups. People now want to participate in politics; they do not like being treated like children.

It was long supposed that **secularization** comes with modernization, and both Atatürk and the Pahlavis had tough showdowns with the mullahs. But Iran's Islamic Revolution and other religious revivals now make us question the inevitability of secularization. Under certain conditions—when things change too fast, when the economy declines and unemployment grows, and modernization repudiates traditional values—people may return to religion with renewed fervor. If their world seems to be falling apart, church or mosque give stability and meaning to life. This is as true of the present-day United States as it is of Egypt. In the Muslim world, many intellectuals first passionately embraced modernizing creeds of socialism and nationalism only to despair and return to Islam. (Some intellectuals are now interested in free-market capitalism, which had been unpopular because it was associated with the West.)

The time of modernization is a risky one in the life of a nation. If the old elite understands the changes that are bubbling through their society, they will gradually give way toward democracy in a way that does not destabilize the system. A corrupt and foolish elite, on the other hand, that is convinced the masses are not ready for democracy (and never will be), hold back political reforms until there is a tremendous head of steam. Then, no longer able to withstand the pressure, they suddenly give way, chaos breaks out and ends in tyranny. If the old elite had reformed sooner and gradually, they might have lowered the pressure and eased the transition to democracy. South Korea and Taiwan are examples of a favorable transition from dictatorship to democracy. Iran under the Shah is a negative example.

The Shah was arrogant: He alone would uplift Iran. He foresaw no democratic future for Iran and cultivated no important sectors of the population to support him. When the end came, few Iranians did support him. Indeed, the Shah scorned democracy in general, viewing it as a chaotic system that got in its own way, a view as old as the ancient Persian attack on Greece. The mighty Persian empire, under one ruler, could surely beat a quarrelsome collection of Greek city-states. (Wrong!) The Shah supposed that Iran, under his enlightened despotism, would soon surpass the decadent West. A journalist once asked the Shah why he did not relinquish some of his personal power and become a symbolic monarch, like the king of Sweden. He replied: "I will become like the king of Sweden when Iranians become like Swedes."

The answer to this overly simple view is that, yes, when your people are poor and ignorant, absolute rule is one of your few alternatives. Such a country is far from ready for democracy. But after considerable modernization—which the Shah himself had implemented—Iran became a different country, one characterized by the changes discussed earlier. An educated middle class resents one-man rule; the bigger this class, the more resentment builds. By modernizing, the Shah sawed off the tree limb on which he was sitting. He modernized Iran until it no longer wanted him.

Islamism· Islam turned into political ideology.

■ Islam as a Political Ideology

Ayatollah Khomeini developed an interesting ideology that resonated with many Iranians. Traditionally Shia Islam kept away from politics, waiting for the return of the Twelfth Imam to rule (see box on page 544). Khomeini and his followers, departing from this old tradition, decided that while they wait the top Shia religious leaders should also assume political power. Called by some **islamism**, it was not only religious but also social, economic, and nationalistic. The Shah and his regime, held Khomeini, had both abandoned Islam and turned away from economic and social justice. They allowed the rich and corrupt to live in Westernized luxury while most struggled in poverty. They sold out Iran to the Americans, exchanging the people's oil for U.S. weapons. Tens of thousands of Americans lived in Iran, corrupting Iran's youth with their "unclean" morals. By returning to the Koran, as interpreted by the mullahs, Iranians would not only cleanse themselves spiritually but also build a just society of equals. The mighty would be brought low and the poor raised up by welfare benefits administered by mosques and Islamic associations. Like communism, Islamism preaches leveling of class differences, but through the mosque and mullahs rather than through the Party and *apparatchiks*.

Islamism is thus a catchall ideology, offering an answer to most things that made Iranians discontent. It is a potent mix, but can it work? Probably not. Over time, its several strands fall apart, and its factions quarrel. Islamism's chief problem is economics (as we shall consider in greater detail later). As Islamism recedes as a viable ideology, look for the reemergence of other ideologies in Iran.

Key Concepts

IS "ISLAMIC FUNDAMENTALISM" THE RIGHT NAME?

Some object to the term "Islamic fundamentalism." Coined in the early twentieth century to describe U.S. Bible-belt Protestants, fundamentalism stands for inerrancy of Scripture: The Bible means what it says and is not open to interpretation. But that is the way virtually all Muslims view the Koran, so Muslims are automatically fundamentalists. Some thinkers propose we call it *Islamic integralism* instead, indicating a move to integrate the Koran and sharia with government. *Integralism* too is borrowed, from a Catholic movement early in the twentieth century whose adherents sought to live a Christ-like existence. The Sunni Muslim movement for returning to the pure Islam of the founders is *salafiyya*, which has been around for centuries in several forms. The Wahhabi Islam of Saudi Arabia and al Qaeda are *salafi*.

Some political scientists use the term *political Islam*, indicating it is the political use of religion to gain power. The term *Islamism*, a religion turned into a political ideology, won favor for the simple reason that it is short (not a bad reason).

■ Democracy and Authority

Many observers think rule by the mullahs will be overturned. Western diplomats estimate that only a minority of Iranians support the current regime. But can Iranians then establish a stable democracy, or was the Shah right—do Iranians need a strong hand to govern them? There were two impulses behind the 1979 revolution: secularist intellectuals seeking democracy and Islamists seeking theocracy. The secular democrats, always a small minority, threw in with the more numerous Islamists, figuring they would be an effective tool to oust the Shah and that the two would form an equal partnership. But the Islamists, better organized and knowing exactly what they wanted, used the secular democrats and then dumped them (in some cases, shot them). Many fled to other countries. Learning too late what was happening to them, some democratic supporters of the Revolution put out the slogan: "In the dawn of freedom, there is no freedom."

But these secular democrats did not disappear; they simply laid low and went along outwardly with the Islamic Revolution. To have opposed it openly could have earned them the firing squad. Among them are the smartest and best-educated people in Iran, the very people needed to make the economy grow. With Iran's drastic economic decline, many lost their jobs and became private consultants and specialists, working out of their apartments. Tens of thousands emigrate each year, preferably to the United States and Canada. Many of them—once they are sure you are not a provocateur for the regime—speak scathingly in private of the oppression and economic foolishness of the mullahs. "I believe in Islam, but not in the regime of the mullahs," said one Iranian.

People like these—who voted for Khatami in 1997 and 2001—believe Iranians are capable of democracy. They argue that the anti-Shah revolution was hijacked by the Islamists but that its original impulse was for democracy, not theocracy, and this impulse still remains. Especially now that people have tasted the economic decline, corruption, and general ineptitude of the mullahs, they are ready for democracy. If the regime ever opens up, the secular democrats will go public to demand open elections with no parties declared ineligible. For now, they lay low and aim their TV satellite dishes to pick up critical views from the large (800,000) Iranian community in the United States.

Political Culture

ARE IRANIANS RELIGIOUS FANATICS?

Only a minority of Iranians are Muslim fanatics. Not even the supposed Islamic fundamentalists are necessarily fanatic. Many Iranians are perfectly aware that religion is a political tool (more on this in the next section) and are fed up with it. Massive regime propaganda depicts the United States as the "Great Satan," but most Iranians are very friendly to the few Americans who visit. Some have been in the United States or have relatives there; many remember that when Iran was allied with America, Iraq did not dare invade. Iran was the only Muslim country where tens of thousands spontaneously showed sympathy with Americans after 9/11. Do not confuse regime propaganda with the attitudes of ordinary citizens.

Ironically, Iranians pointed to the now defunct Taliban government of neighboring Afghanistan as *salafi* extremists. Far stricter than Iranian Islamists, the Taliban confined women to the home and required all men to have beards. Why the conflict with Iran? Like most of Afghanistan, the Taliban were Sunni and attacked the Shia minority, some 1.5 million of whom fled to Iran. The Taliban killed Iranian intelligence agents who were aiding Afghan Shias. Dangerous stuff, this religious extremism.

■ Iranian Nationalism

Nationalism, always strong in Iran, is coming back. Some analysts hold that Iran today is more motivated by nationalism than by any religious fervor. (Notice how nationalism also grows in China.) Islam was imposed on Persia by Arab swords, and Iranians to this day harbor folk memories of seventh-century massacres by crude, barbaric invaders. Iranians do not like Arabs and look down on them as culturally inferior and lacking staying power. By adopting Shia, Iranians were and are able to distinguish themselves from their mostly Sunni neighbors. "Yes, of course we are Muslims," is the Iranian message, "but we are not like these other Muslim countries." Accordingly, not far under the surface of Iranian thought is Persian nationalism, affirming the greatness of their ancient civilization, which antedates Islam by a millennium.

The Shah especially stressed Persian nationalism in his drive to modernize Iran. The Shah was Muslim and had himself photographed in religious devotion, as on his **hajj**, required of all Muslims who can afford it once in their lifetime. But the Shah's true spirit was secular and nationalistic: to rebuild the glory of ancient Persia in a modern Iran. If Islam got in the way, it was to be pushed aside. The Shah was relatively tolerant of non-Muslim faiths; Baha'is (a universalistic and liberal offshoot of Islam), Jews, and Christians were unharmed. Since the Islamic Revolution, non-Muslims have been treated harshly, especially the 300,000 Baha'is, Iran's largest minority religion, who are regarded as dangerous **heretics**. For centuries, Iran's sense of its unique Persianness coexisted uneasily with its Islam. The Shah's modernization program brought the two strands into open conflict.

The Islamic Revolution of 1979 did not totally repudiate the nationalist strand of Iranian thought. It put the stress on the religious side of Persianness, but the long and horrible war with Iraq, 1980–1988, brought out the regime's Persian nationalism. They were fighting not only for their

hajj   Muslim pilgrimage to Mecca.

heretic   Someone who breaks away from a religion.

Democracy

IRAN'S ANGRY STUDENTS

In the late 1970s, Iranian students, most of them leftists, battled to overturn the old regime. Now Iran's students—whose numbers have exploded to close to two million—again demonstrate for civil rights. Many students are outspoken liberals and want to push for pluralism, a free press, and free elections. They also worry about the serious lack of jobs for graduates.

Every year hard-line courts—especially the Revolutionary Court—close liberal newspapers and block web sites. Between 2,000 and 4,000 Iranian editors, writers, professors, public-opinion pollsters, student leaders, and politicians are in jail. Some of them fought in the 1979 Revolution and in the long war against Iraq. At least a hundred dissidents were mysteriously killed. In protest, students demonstrate—

chanting "Death to dictatorship"—which leads to arrests and violence. In 2002 Professor Hashem Aghajari, who lost a leg and a brother in the war against Iraq, was sentenced to death (never carried out) for advocating an Islamic Protestantism to separate mosque and state. Massive pro-Aghajari student demonstrations swept Iranian campuses.

Could students and intellectuals one day lead the way to democracy? By themselves, probably not. They are not organized and lack ties to the broad masses of Iranians, few of whom are openly discontent. But if they could organize in combination with other groups, they could destabilize the clericalist regime. In many countries, students have been the spark plugs of revolution.

faith but for their country and against Iraq, a savage, upstart Arab country that did not even exist until the British invented it in the 1920s. Iran celebrates two types of holidays, Persian and Muslim. The Persian holidays are all happy, such as New Year (*Now Ruz*). The Islamic holidays are mostly mournful, such as the day of remembrance of the martyrdom of Hussein at Karbala, during which young Shia men beat themselves until they bleed.

PATTERNS OF INTERACTION

Religion as a Political Tool

Manipulate, use, discard. This is how Khomeini's forces treated those who helped them win the Revolution. Like turbaned Bolsheviks, the Islamists in the late 1970s hijacked the Iranian revolution as it unfolded. First, they captured the growing discontent with the Shah and his regime. By offering themselves as a plausible and effective front organization, they enlisted all manner of anti-Shah groups under their banner—the democratically inclined parties of the National Front, the Iran Freedom Movement, the Marxist (and Soviet-connected) Tudeh party, and Islamic guerrilla movements. They had these groups do their dirty work for them, and then got rid of them, sometimes by firing squad. The flowering of democratic, Islamic, secular, and socialist parties that accompanied the Shah's overthrow was crushed within three years. As an example of revolutionary technique, Lenin would have admired their skill and ruthlessness.

In doing all this, the Islamists used their religion much as the Bolsheviks used Marxism, as a tool, a recruiting and mobilizing device, a means of gaining authority and obedience, and a way to seize and consolidate power. This is not to say they were not serious about Islam, but rather that in a revolutionary situation the instrumental uses of their faith predominated over the devotional. If you want to seize state power, you cannot be otherworldly; you must be very shrewd and practical. There is

Political Culture

DOES ISLAM DISCRIMINATE AGAINST WOMEN?

Iran is one of the better Muslim countries in the treatment of women. Unlike the Arab kingdoms on the southern shore of the Gulf, Iranian women drive cars, go to school, work outside the home, and participate in politics. But even in Iran there are tough restrictions on dress, contact with males, and travel.

Devout Muslims swear women are deeply honored in their societies, but their place is in the home and nowhere else. Women are kept at a subservient status in most Islamic countries; often they get little education, cannot drive a car, and their testimony is worth half of men's in courts of law. But such discrimination does not always come from the Koran. In some Muslim countries (not Iran), such customs as the seclusion of women, the veil, and female genital mutilation are pre-Islamic and were absorbed by Islam (much as Europeans adopted for Christmas the pagan worship of trees). These non-Koranic imports can therefore be discarded with no harm to the faith, maintain Muslim feminists. Yes, there are such people, and increasingly they are speaking out and organizing. If they succeed, they will greatly modernize their societies. The widespread education of Iranian women predicts social and legal change.

nothing "crazy" about the Islamists who run Iran; they are perfectly capable of calm and rational decisions calculated to benefit themselves. In our eyes, to be sure, some look crazy.

After some time immersed in politics, the power side takes over and the original religious (or ideological) side takes a back seat. As with the Bolsheviks, this soon leads to opportunism and cynicism among the politically involved and ultimately to regime decay. The ruling group turns into a self-serving new class. This is why regimes that base themselves on ideology or religion (Islamism combines both) have finite life spans. After a while, everyone notices the power and greed of the ruling class, and mass disillusion sets in; the regime loses legitimacy. This is happening in Iran. Iran's Islamic revolution will burn out.

An example of this was the seizure of the U.S. embassy in Tehran by student militants in November 1979, which brought American cries of outrage and a complete break in relations. The embassy takeover and holding of fifty-two American officials for 444 days indeed broke every rule in the diplomatic book and seemed to prove that mad fanatics governed Iran.

Looked at more closely, though, the incident was a domestic Iranian power play, cynically manipulated by the Khomeini forces. The ayatollah had no further use for the prime minister he had appointed early in 1979, Mehdi Bazargan, a moderate. How to get rid of him and other moderates? The occasion was the admission of the ailing Shah to the United States for cancer treatment. Khomeini's cadres whipped up mass rage in Iran, claiming that medical help for the Shah proved the United States still supported the ousted regime. Then they had a group of student militants invade and take over the U.S. embassy, which had already been reduced to a skeleton staff. No shots were fired; the U.S. Marine guards were ordered not to shoot. The militants took sixty-six Americans prisoner—but killed none and released fourteen—and published classified embassy documents (pieced together from the shredder) purporting to show how dastardly the Americans were.

The Islamic activists, using anti-American hysteria ("Death to USA!"), consolidated their hold on the country. Humiliated and powerless, Bazargan resigned. Anyone opposed to the embassy takeover was fired or worse. One foreign-ministry official (who had dropped out of Georgetown University to promote revolution) helped some Americans escape via the Canadian embassy. He was tried and shot. Khomeini's followers seemed to enjoy watching President Carter squirm, especially after the aborted U.S. rescue mission in April 1980. Carter's apparent weakness on Iran hurt him in the 1980 election, which he lost to Reagan.

At that point, the holding of U.S. diplomats had exhausted its utility for Khomeini. Knowing Reagan was not averse to military measures, Tehran released the diplomats just as he was inaugurated. The militants who had seized and held the Americans had also served their purpose. Considered unreliable, some were arrested and executed. Others were sent to the front in the war with Iraq, where they died in the fighting. As a historian of the French Revolution observed, the revolution devours its children.

▮ Moderates and Islamists in Iran

After the 1986 Iran-Contra fiasco, in which White House aides attempted to secretly sell U.S. missiles to Iranian "moderates," the term "Iranian moderate" disappeared from Washington's vocabulary. The U.S. officials fell for a sucker play by Iranian leaders, who set up the deal and then leaked word that the United States was trading with Iran, illegal under U.S. law. These people never miss a chance to embarrass the United States. There are Iranian moderates, but they have learned to keep their mouths shut and do nothing stupid, like having contact with Americans. Instead, the Iranians who fit under the labels "moderates" and "liberals" discussed earlier play a cautious game, not

Moderates	Islamists
end Islamic revolution	maintain it
shift power to Majlis	preserve power of *faqih*
permit many parties	ban non-Islamic parties
free press	censored press
permit Western women's attire	Islamic attire only (veil)
improve relations with West	keep distant from West
dialogue with America	hate America
end nuclear programs	build nuclear bombs
liberalize economy	keep economy statist

directly opposing the Islamic revolution while trying to tone it down. They are in a permanent power struggle with conservative forces.

The strongest and most dangerous conservative force is the Islamic Revolutionary Guards (*Pasdaran*). Originally formed in 1979 to support Khomeini, they took many casualties in the war with Iraq and now, with 150,000 members, are separate from and higher than the regular army, rather like the SS under Hitler. They get the best weapons, dominate the defense and intelligence ministries, and supervise Iran's nuclear-bomb program, arguing that only with nukes can Iran stand up to America. They are the "muscle" of the conservative clerics and likely more influential than them. Former Pasdaran hold about a third of Majlis seats and set the agenda and dictate policy to the president. President Ahmadinejad was in the Pasdaran in the war with Iraq. Direct military influence in politics, *praetorianism*, as we considered in Nigeria, is a hallmark of the Third World. A Pasdaran general could take over Iran's presidency, making Iran a truly praetorian system.

Those who fit under the labels "radicals" and "conservatives" described earlier, want a truly Islamic republic, one based on religious law and presided over by the *faqih*. Anything else means giving in to Iran's enemies—the West in general, the United States in particular—with eventual loss of Iran's independence, culture, and religion. They block any liberalizing reforms, from closing newspapers to voting out ministers to putting political opponents on trial.

In a parallel with what we did earlier for Russia and China, we can construct a list of Iranian moderate and Islamist views (see table above). On at least a couple of points there is no clear divergence between moderates and Islamists. First, both groups are Muslim and want to preserve a generally Islamic emphasis in public life, including the judicial system. Second, both groups want economic growth, both for the sake of Iran's national power and to improve the lot of its people. How to do this is the issue: free market or state controlled? In elections no one runs on an opposition platform; all seem to be supporting at least a version of the Islamic revolution. In Iran, direct opposition could be hazardous to your health. It is in the nuances among groupings that differences begin to appear.

There are some Iranians, both inside and outside the country, who would like to get rid of the whole Islamic revolution. A few monarchists would like to restore the son of the last Pahlavi, a young man now living in the West, to the throne, but even Iranians who think the Shah's rule was not so bad give this option no chance. The times are against monarchy; every decade there are fewer and fewer ruling (as opposed to figurehead) monarchs.

On the other side, some Marxist-type revolutionaries, the *Mujahedin-e Khalq* (Fighters for the People), who earlier worked with the Islamists to overthrow the Shah now try to overthrow the

Comparison

IS SAUDI ARABIA NEXT?

The 9/11 attacks suggested that the Kingdom, as Saudis call their country, is lurching into instability. Fifteen of the nineteen hijackers were Saudis. Al Qaeda terrorists set off bombs in the Kingdom. Islamists such as Osama bin Laden, son of a Saudi billionaire, represent the same kind of forces that overthrew the Shah in Iran. The Saudi regime is almost paralyzed by fear of this. It tries to buy off threats and deflect discontent by funding extremist religious schools (many in Pakistan) and minimizing Islamist recruitment.

The House of Saud conquered the country in the 1920s based on the austere Wahhabi creed of salafi Islam and is highly vulnerable for the same reasons as the Shah of Iran. Saudi Arabia is less democratic than Iran is now, and the legitimacy of the royal family has eroded amidst charges of abandoning Wahhabism in favor of Western pleasures. Of the five thousand Saudi princes, more than five hundred are eligible to become king, an invitation for a succession struggle.

Oil created some very rich Saudis, including the princes, but left many poor Saudis far behind. Earlier, the oil revenues allowed the regime to buy loyalty with subsidies for thousands of Saudis. But oil prices fluctuate, and the population exploded from 7 million in 1980 to 20 million in 2004, cutting per capita Saudi income in half. Forty percent of the population is under fourteen. Cushy jobs no longer await young Saudis; many are unemployed and discontent. Shia Saudis from the oil-producing Eastern Province carry out bombings (with Iranian backing), including American targets.

News from the Kingdom is rigorously censored—nothing negative is allowed—and until 9/11 Washington never criticized "our good friends," the House of Saud. It was the same way we treated the Shah. After 9/11 some Americans called Saudi Arabia a false friend and supplier of money and personnel for Islamist terrorism. Dozens of young Saudis cross into Iraq for jihad against the Americans and Shia. A succession struggle over the new king could destabilize the Kingdom. It may be too late to do anything to prevent a Saudi revolution.

Reforms can hasten revolution, as we saw in Iran. Controlled moves to democracy, such as these, might stabilize the Kingdom.

- Allow some opposition parties. Make sure they are moderate, and let them criticize the regime in a constructive way. Make sure there are several parties (some conservative, some liberal, none radical) to divide public discontent.
- Permit a semifree press along the same lines as parties: limited criticism only.
- Crush and suppress Islamists. Do not ease up on them. These people are out to destroy you, and if they take over they will not be moderate or democratic.
- Hold legislative elections but among parties ranging from conservative to moderate. Gradually, you can let other parties participate.
- Have the new legislature redistribute wealth in the form of heavy taxes on the rich, especially on members of the royal family, who must be seen taking a financial hit. This is to defuse mass anger over the royals' great and unfair wealth.
- Do not automatically follow U.S. policy in the region, as that delegitimizes your regime. Limit any American presence; it is a cultural irritant and natural fodder for Islamic extremists. (Saudi leaders did not support our 2003 invasion of Iraq and had U.S. troops leave. They are not stupid.)
- Crack down on corruption, especially among the highest officials and princes. Show that you mean business here, and that the crackdown will be permanent.

Have we learned anything from Iran? Would any of this work to head off a revolution? Maybe, but it would require the willingness of the House of Saud to cut its own wealth and power, and that is something ruling classes rarely do. But if Saudi Arabia cannot transition to some kind of democracy, revolution and then U.S. military involvement is likely. The Persian Gulf and its oil is one place we do not walk away from.

Islamists. Among them were some of the young militants who seized the U.S. embassy. Subsequently, it is estimated that over 10,000 Mujahedin were executed by the Khomeini forces. Their survivors were sheltered in and sponsored by Saddam Hussein's Iraq, which invaded and massacred Iranians (sometimes with poison gas), during the 1980s, so these Mujahedin have little resonance among Iranians. Even Washington now considers them a crazy cult.

Change may come from the struggle between Iranian militants and moderates, not the influence of outside forces. Some of the regime's sharpest critics were leaders of the 1979 revolution, including Grand Ayatollah Hossein Ali Montazeri, one of the most senior figures of Shia Islam, now held in house arrest in the holy city of Qom for denouncing repression and demanding reform. "Either officials change their methods and give freedom to the people, and stop interfering in elections, or the people will rise up with another revolution," he warned. Another voice is that of 2003 Nobel Peace Prize winner Shirin Ebadi, a lawyer and regime opponent who defends Iranians' human rights. She also cites the Koran to show Islam should not discriminate against women, a view shared by many Iranian women. Iran could be the birthplace of Islamic feminism.

■ The Revolution Burns Out

Iran fits Crane Brinton's classic theory of revolution (see page 93). To recapitulate: The Shah's regime loses its legitimacy. Antiregime groups form, rioting breaks out, and the Shah leaves. Initially moderates take power, but the ruthless Khomeini forces soon dump them and drive the revolution to a frenzied high point. But this burns itself out; eventually a *Thermidor*, or calming down, arrives. It was almost as if Iranians had read Brinton. Every stage, that is, except the last, and even that seems to be have happened without a clear-cut Thermidor. Instead, there may be a low-key, rolling Thermidor that led to Khatami's election in 1997.

No revolution lasts forever. In Iran we see an effort to become stable and normal, opposed by Islamic conservatives. Time is probably on the side of the normalizers. Many mullahs have corrupted themselves; some do not go onto the street in clerical garb. Mullahs run the *bonyads*, foundations originally set up to redistribute the wealth of the Shah and his supporters. These *bonyads* now control billions of dollars and much of Iran's industry. They are supposed to be run for the good of all, a sort of Islamic socialism, but in practice they have made

The spirit of Iran's Islamic Revolution lives on in this Tehran cemetery memorial to the fallen of the Iran-Iraq war of 1980–1988. Iranian losses were horrifying—at least half a million killed, many of them boys. Note the women in chadors in the foreground.

their mullahs rich, powerful, and corrupt while their industries are run poorly. As Lord Acton observed (see page 25), power corrupts.

Aware of this, many Iranians want the mullahs to return to the mosque and get out of government and the economy. Even some mullahs wish it, as now they see that running a country ruins their reputation and their spiritual mission. Chant Iranian demonstrators: "The mullahs live like kings, while the people are reduced to poverty." Another factor is that now over half of Iranians were born after the Shah and have no personal commitment to the Islamic revolution. They want jobs and more freedom, and they can vote at age sixteen.

Will there be a point at which we can say the Iranian revolution is finally over? The reestablishment of diplomatic ties between the United States and Iran—something many Iranians want to happen soon—would indicate that point had passed some time earlier. There were hopes of this with former President Khatami, who mentioned "dialogue" with Americans (but not with Washington) but pulled back when conservative forces objected. Current President Ahmadinejad initially disdained any contact with America. Other indications would be the mullahs giving up control of the *bonyads* and the *faqih* becoming a figurehead or *dignified* office.

hezbollahi "Partisan of God," fanatic supporter of Islamism.

WHAT IRANIANS QUARREL ABOUT

■ Which Way for Iran's Economy?

Iran has changed rapidly, partly under the Shah and partly under the Islamic Revolution. The countryside has received schools, electricity, health care, and tractors. Infant mortality, a key measure of health care, fell from 169 per 1,000 births in 1960 to 40 in 2006. Average life expectancy jumped twenty years, from 50 to 70. Literacy has climbed from less than half to three-fourths. More Iranian women than ever are in schools and universities (segregated from males, of course).

The Iranian economy was hurt by revolution, war, isolation, and mismanagement. Although total oil income has increased, per capita GDP has barely recovered to pre-1979 levels. Iran depends far too much on the 2004 and 2005 runup in world oil prices. If oil prices fall, Iran is in trouble (as are Russia and Nigeria). There is some growth, but inflation is still hefty, and unemployment (estimated at 20 percent) and poverty are worse than under the Shah. Iran needs some 1.5 million new jobs a year. Pay is low so people hold two and three jobs to make ends meet. Many jobs and business dealings, as in Russia, are off the books. The oil industry, still the pride and basis of the Iranian economy, needs replacement parts and up-to-date technology. Its productivity is miserable. U.S. pressure has kept most oil companies from cooperating with Iran. The *bonyads* are run badly and corruptly, and increasingly Iranians notice this.

By giving all Iranians a welfare floor (including subsidized food and gasoline) while simultaneously damaging Iran's great source of revenue (its petroleum connection with the West), Tehran has made itself vulnerable. Iran has run large annual budget deficits, which translate into persistent inflation. The Shah left a foreign debt of $8.4 billion, which the Khomeini regime, amid great hardship, repaid, swearing Iran would never fall into imperialist clutches again. But by 1996, Iran's foreign debt was a dangerous $33 billion. Under worsening material conditions, many of the early adherents of Islamism have dropped out or even come to oppose it. The **hezbollahis** still try to supervise much of Iranian society, but they are an increasingly resented minority, the functional equivalent of the old Soviet Communist party. And you recall what happened to them.

The Islamic Revolution did not dismantle the Shah's *statist* economy. The state still controls 60 percent of Iran's economy (biggest part: the oil industry). The *bonyads* control another 10 to 20 percent. Only about 20 percent of Iran's economy is in private hands. Theoretically, foreigners can invest in Iran, but most are scared off by the many and tangled limits and regulations. Investors must pay numerous bribes. Iran's is not a free-market economy. The big question: Should it become one?

Opposing arguments show up in Majlis debates over economic policy, which have become thinly disguised battles over the future of strict Islamic rule. As we have considered, Islamism is a surrogate socialism; that is, it blends Islamic correctness with collectivist economics. In the minds of many Islamists, socialism is the logical extension of Islam, for Islam preaches equality and leveling of class differences. Thus, they claim, Islam is the true and only path to a just society of equal citizens, where no one is either rich or poor. What the Marxists, Socialists, and Communists talked about, they say, we can deliver.

Most moderates respond that socialism and/or statism is not the way to go, that they just keep Iran poor and backward. The collapse of the Soviet system demonstrates socialism does not work, and the decline of Iran's economy demonstrates statism does not work. Besides, they note, there is no Koranic basis for government control of the economy. It is perfectly feasible to combine free-market capitalism with the alms-giving required of Muslims and achieve social justice. If we keep declining economically, moderates also worry, we will never be able to build a first-class army and so will be vulnerable to hostile outside forces. And if our towering unemployment problem is not solved soon, the whole Islamic revolution could be doomed. The best and quickest way to solve these problems is the free market. State ownership of major industries, especially petroleum, is what the Shah tried, and we certainly do not want to follow in his footsteps. Such are the arguments of Iranian moderates. Notice that outright rejection of the Islamic revolution is not one of their points.

Geography

HOW MANY IRANIANS?

Islam traditionally frowns on family planning: The more babies the better. After the revolution, Iran's mullahs urged women to produce a generation of Muslim militants; subsidized food helped feed them. Iran's rate of population growth averaged 3.5 percent a year during the 1980s, one of the world's highest. Despite the murderous war with Iraq, since the 1979 Revolution Iran's population doubled from 34 million to 68 million.

By the early 1990s, though, the government, realizing it could not subsidize or employ the vast numbers of young Iranians—two-thirds were born after the Revolution—reversed the high-births policy. Amid economic decline, families now can afford fewer children. Clinics offer all manner of contraception free of charge (but not abortions). Women agents go door-to-door to promote family planning. Food and other family aid is decreased after a family has three children. One Muslim cleric even issued a *fatwa* in favor of smaller families. From an average 7 births per woman over her life in 1986, the fertility rate plunged to 1.8 in 2005, lower than in the United States. By 2005, the rate of population growth was down to a modest 0.86 percent. The turnaround on births is an indication the revolution is over.

The Veiled Debate on Islam

Iran will always be a Muslim country, but what kind of Islam will it have? A moderate kind that keeps out of most direct political involvement or a militant kind that seeks to guide society by political means? Judging by the Khatami landslides in 1997 and 2001, most opt for the first kind. The 2005 elections of Ahmadinejad makes one wonder.

Because the Council of Guardians bars openly liberal candidates, public debate on the religion question is muted. No one risks being branded "anti-Islamic." Still, one can infer that such a debate is taking place. One of the stand-ins for a discussion of Islam in public life is the debate on what kind of clothing is admissible, especially for women. Even for men, though, blue jeans were frowned upon, partly because they represent American culture. Liberals say they do not; jeans are simply a comfortable and international garment with no political connotations.

Before the Islamic revolution, urban and educated Iranian women dressed as fashionably as European women. Then suddenly they could not use makeup and had to wear the veil and *chador*, the single-piece head-to-toe garment designed to cover feminine attractiveness. Devout Muslims, including many women, say this attire is better than Western clothing as it eliminates lust, vanity, and distinctions of wealth. (Notice how some U.S. schools are coming to similar conclusions about school uniforms.) Western clothes and makeup are the first steps toward debauchery and prostitution, they argue. But in subtle ways urban Iranian women dress in a manner that pushes to the limit of the permissible in public (and in private dress as they wish). The veil and *chador* are no longer mandatory on the street, so long as a woman is dressed very modestly without makeup and with hair and forehead covered by a kerchief. Women still risk Islamic *komitehs* (morals police) stopping them on the street and sending them home or to jail. Young people suspected of having a good time may be beaten by *basij* (militia). These volunteer squads are some of the most obnoxious features of the Islamic regime and have alienated urban and educated Iranians.

What Kind of Foreign Policy?

The guiding lights of the Islamic revolution had aspirations beyond Iran. Some still have. They saw themselves as the revitalizers of the entire Islamic world and tried to spread their revolution, not only among Shias but among Muslims in general. They were immediately concerned with the Shias of southern Iraq, long a suppressed 60 percent of Iraq's population. The Sunni Arabs of the middle of Iraq are only about 20 percent, but they monopolized political power. Many of the main Shia shrines are in southern Iraq, where Khomeini was exiled in 1964. Upon taking power in Tehran, the Khomeini people propagandized Iraqi Shias and urged them to join the Islamic revolution. This was one of the irritants—but hardly a sufficient excuse—for Iraqi dictator Saddam Hussein to invade Iran in 1980. Now Iranian arms, agents, and money operate freely inside Iraq, encouraging its Shias to build a second Islamic republic.

Wherever there are Shias, Iranian influence turned up: southern Lebanon, Kuwait, Bahrain, and Saudi Arabia. Funds, instructions, and explosive devices flowed through this connection. Iran, along with Iraq, Syria, and Libya, were placed on the U.S. State Department's list of countries sponsoring terrorism. Iran feels it must take a leading role in destroying Israel, which it depicts as a polluter of Islamic holy ground (Jerusalem is also sacred to Muslims) and outpost of Western imperialism. Under the Shah, Tehran had good (but informal) relations with Israel and quietly sold it most of its oil. Suddenly that totally changed, and Iran supports Lebanon's *Hezbollah* (Party of God), which harasses Israel's northern border. (One of the best information sources for critical Iranians is Israeli radio, which broadcasts to Iran in Farsi.)

Political Culture

THE UNITED STATES AND IRAN

A culture gap hinders Americans and Iranians from understanding each other. We have not been clever in dealing with the Iranian Revolution. Part religious, part nationalistic, part cultural, and part antityranny, it defied our predictions and efforts to tame it. When we tried to deal with "Iranian moderates" in 1986, we got humiliated. When we tilted toward Iraq in its war against Iran, we supported a fiendish dictator (Saddam Hussein) whom we twice fought ourselves. In 1988 a U.S. destroyer mistook an Iranian jetliner for an attacking fighter, shot it down with a missile, and killed all 290 aboard. Iran, and indeed the whole Persian Gulf, is a tar baby: Once you punch it, you get stuck worse and worse.

But if we are calm and clever, things may work out. Iran's Islamic revolution is over, and relations could eventually improve. Many Iranians want contact and dialogue with the United States. In the long term, Iran needs us. We can provide the petroleum technology and other means to modernize the country. If an aggressive Russia starts rebuilding its Caucasus empire, Iran would need U.S. support. Historically, Russia always had territorial designs on Persia; the United States never did.

Anthropologists point out that when two Iranian *bazaaris* quarrel, by long tradition they simply shun and ignore each other for some years. Gradually, the quarrel fades and they cautiously reestablish relations with each other. After a while, the quarrel is forgotten. It is a civilized way to handle a quarrel. We might take a leaf from Persian folkway in dealing with Iran.

Iranians do not understand American culture. Americans are in many ways the opposite of Iranians; we are direct, unsubtle, and prone to violence: cowboys. Americans like guns and military solutions, even though most see America as good and trying to do good in the world. We are poorly informed about the Gulf region. Few Americans know as much about Iran as the student who has just read this chapter. To win mass support our presidents use simplified rhetoric—"axis of evil"—and notice only later that it sets back quiet efforts to improve U.S.-Iranian relations (desired by two-thirds of Iranians). Loose talk about knocking out Iran's nuclear facilities may make matters worse. U.S. threats lead to Iranian counterthreats.

Iranians must watch their rhetoric too. Your mass chanting of *Marg bar Amrika!* ("Death to America!") sounds like a direct threat when Iran is working on nuclear bombs. Do you really want to kill us? Then you'd better stop saying so. After 9/11, we take these things very seriously. The U.S. commitment to making sure the oil of the Persian Gulf flows in a friendly fashion is one point Americans agree on in foreign policy. No amount of bombings can persuade us to abandon this policy. And we can "make your economy scream." Those were Kissinger's words describing what we did to Chile when it came under Marxist rule. (We are probably doing it to you now.)

So stop sponsoring or encouraging terrorism. When a bomb goes off in Beirut, we smell Iranian money funneled through Syria. Do not develop nuclear weapons, which are more likely to provoke than deter the United States. Turn to your own tradition and simply shun America, doing nothing against us. And when you are ready to resume contact and economic growth, let us know in a public way. We understand that you are in a long struggle against an odious theocracy and cannot move prematurely. Eventually, the rule of the mullahs will pass and relations will thaw. We were friends once and can be again. Foolish moves on either side could lead to a war neither wants.

Iran isolated itself. Iran created not only U.S. hostility but angered the Sunni-ruled lands of the Persian Gulf (and Afghanistan), who still do not trust Iran's intentions. Iran's stonewalling on its nuclear program alienated Britain, France, and Germany, who had sought a diplomatic solution to ensure that Iran does not build nuclear weapons. Tehran says it seeks only nuclear power generation—in a country with massive oil and natural gas reserves—but no one trusts it. In 2006 the International Atomic Energy Agency (IAEA), no longer allowed to inspect Iran's nuclear labs, referred the matter to the UN, where few supported Iran. Iran's isolation harms its economic growth and requires it to maintain armed forces it cannot afford.

Many thinking Iranians want to improve relations with the West, even with America. Hostility brings nothing but trouble and no rewards. A few militant mullahs want to keep up the hatred, no matter what it costs the country. Revolutionary Iran has been both the victim and practitioner of terrorism. Antiregime forces, particularly the nutty Mujahedin-e Khalk, assassinated several Iranian leaders, including one prime minister. In return, Iranian hit squads in Europe took out several regime opponents, including a former prime minister and the leaders of a breakaway Kurdish movement. Bombs in Iran's Arab-majority province of Khuzistan were planted by Iraqi Sunnis, charged Tehran.

Tehran tries to wiggle out of its isolated status. It has major influence among Shias in Iraq, some of whom aim to set up an Iranian-style Islamic republic. If they succeed, Iran could get its first and only ally. Tehran also uses commercial deals to break out of isolation. It purchases nuclear technology from Russia, builds a gas pipeline to India, and sells oil to China.

Geography

STRATEGIC WATERWAYS

These are mostly narrow choke points connecting two bodies of water. Hostile control of them causes one or more countries discomfort or fear. Here are the main ones:

Turkish Straits (Dardanelles and Bosporus), connecting the Black and Mediterranean Seas.

Strait of Gibraltar, connecting the Atlantic and the Mediterranean.

Suez Canal, connecting the Mediterranean and Red Seas.

Bab al Mandab, connecting the Red Sea and Indian Ocean.

Strait of Hormuz, connecting the Persian Gulf and Indian Ocean.

English Channel, connecting the Atlantic Ocean and North Sea.

Skagerrak, connecting the Baltic and North Seas.

North Cape, dividing the Atlantic from the Barents Sea.

Cape of Good Hope, where the Atlantic and Indian Oceans meet off the southern tip of Africa.

Strait of Malacca, connecting the Indian Ocean and South China Sea, East Asia's oil lifeline.

Korea (Tsushima) Strait, connecting the East China Sea and Sea of Japan.

Panama Canal, connecting the Atlantic and Pacific Oceans.

You are the captain of a small tanker that has just loaded oil in Kuwait for delivery in Umea, Sweden. Which bodies of water—including seas, oceans, straits, and canals—do you pass through? (Note: Supertankers are too big for Suez; they have to go around Africa. But small tankers still pass through Suez.)

■ Do Revolutions End Badly?

Burke (see box on page 26) was right: Revolution brings in its wake tyranny far worse than that of
the regime it toppled. Iran is a good example: The Shah was a dictator, but rule of the mullahs is worse.
Only in America did revolution lead to the establishment of a just, stable, democracy—and the
American revolution was a very special, limited one, aimed more at independence than at revolu-
tion. The twentieth century is littered with failed revolutions: fascist, communist, and now Islamist.
The few remaining Communist countries that still celebrate and base their legitimacy on an alleged

Geography

BOUND ISRAEL

Israel is bounded on the north by Lebanon;   on the south by Egypt;
on the east by Syria and Jordan;   and on the west by the Mediterranean Sea.

revolution, Cuba and North Korea, are hungry and isolated. Communist China and Vietnam, by partly integrating their economies with world trade, have so far been spared this fate.

| **fatwa** | Ruling by Islamic jurist. |

Why do revolutions end badly? Several writers have attempted to answer this question. Burke argued that the destruction of all institutional and political structures leaves people confused and ripe for dictatorial rule. François Furet wrote along similar lines that the French Revolution unleashed such chaotic forces that it had to "skid out of control." Crane Brinton wrote that revolutions fall into the hands of their most ruthless element, who then proceed to wreck everything until they are replaced in a Thermidor. Hannah Arendt wrote that revolution goes astray when revolutionists try to solve the "Social Question" (how to bring down the rich and help the poor); to do this they must institute a tyranny. It is interesting to note all these writers were, to some extent, conservatives. Radicals and leftists often refuse to admit revolutions end badly; if something goes wrong they tend to blame individuals for "betraying" the revolution.

The unhappy revolution is something Iranians ponder. Although few want a return of the Pahlavis, many Iranians know the Islamic revolution has turned out wrong. At least under the Shah there was economic growth, however unfairly distributed, and modernization. Now there is economic decline and unemployment. Most Iranians live more poorly than before. Certain mullahs and their friends, those in charge of the *bonyads*, do well. Given a chance, most Iranians would throw these rascals out. The mullahs and their security and judicial forces try to make sure this never happens. They have some bases of support—more than the Shah had—among the religious and the poor who have benefited from Islamic handouts.

Iran is now caught in a stalemate between reformist and conservative forces. Eventually, reform will come to Iran; the status quo is unsustainable. The longer the conservatives stonewall, the greater the danger of political violence, fueled by millions of angry, unemployed young Iranian males. What can the United States do? U.S. threats just play into the hands of hardliners, but the right combination of firmness (over Iran's uranium enrichment efforts) and carrots (trade) could start a dialogue. Time and economic difficulties will calm the Iranian revolution. I am convinced that Iran will one day be free and we will be friends again.

Political Culture

A FATWA ON RUSHDIE

One of the more horrifying examples of the Iranian revolution was the turning of a **fatwa** into an international death warrant. In 1989 Khomeini issued a *fatwa* ordering the execution of British author Salman Rushdie, a lapsed Muslim of Indian origin. Rushdie had just published his *Satanic Verses,* a fantasy on the life of Muhammad that was extremely offensive to devout Muslims. A semiofficial Tehran foundation offered a reward of $1 million (later raised to $2.8 million) for killing Rushdie, who went into hiding for years. Even now, he appears rarely and cautiously; he knows they mean it.

The Western world was aghast at this order to kill someone in a faraway country for writing a book. The entire concept of the *fatwa* underscores the cultural differences between Islamic and Western civilizations. (In 1993, the top Saudi cleric issued a *fatwa* that the earth is flat and anyone claiming it round should be punished as an atheist.) Iran's relations with most of Europe deteriorated. Even many Iranians are embarrassed and apologetic over the *fatwa* and wish it rescinded. Khomeini's successors claim that he is the only one who can rescind it, and he died a few months after issuing it. Even though the Tehran government says it has dissociated itself from the *fatwa* on Rushdie, it harms Iranian relations with other countries.

Key Terms

ayatollah (p. 549)
canon law (p. 550)
containment (p. 548)
fatwa (p. 569)
hajj (p. 557)
heretic (p. 557)
hezbollahi (p. 563)
Islam (p. 544)
Islamism (p. 555)
Islamist (p. 550)
Koran (p. 554)
Majlis (p. 546)

modernizing tyrant (p. 547)
mosque (p. 547)
mullah (p. 549)
OPEC (p. 549)
Ottoman (p. 547)
secular (p. 547)
secularization (p. 554)
shah (p. 546)
Shia (p. 544)
Sunni (p. 545)
theocracy (p. 550)
velayat-e faqih (p. 550)

Key Web Sites

Country Study
lcweb21.loc.gov/frd/cs/irtoc.html
Government in General
netiran.com
Presidency
www.president.ir
News Sources (None Independent)
Iran Daily
www.iran-daily.com
National News Agency
www.irna.com/en
Iran News
www.irannews.freeservers.com

Further Reference

Abdo, Genieve, and Jonathan Lyons. *Answering Only to God: Faith and Freedom in Twenty-First Century Iran*. New York: Henry Holt, 2003.
Adelkhah, Faribah. *Being Modern in Iran*. New York: Columbia University Press, 2000.
Beeman, William O. *The "Great Satan" vs. the "Mad Mullahs": How the United States and Iran Demonize Each Other*. Westport, CT: Praeger, 2005.

Crone, Patricia. *God's Rule: Government and Islam*. New York: Columbia University Press, 2004.

Diamond, Larry, Marc F. Plattner, and Daniel Brumberg, eds. *Islam and Democracy in the Middle East*. Baltimore, MD: Johns Hopkins University Press, 2003.

Jahanbegloo, Ramin, ed. *Iran: Between Tradition and Modernity*. Lanham, MD: Lexington, 2004.

Keddie, Nikki R. *Modern Iran: Roots and Results of Revolution*. New Haven, CT: Yale University Press, 2003.

Mackey, Sandra. *The Iranians: Persia, Islam, and the Soul of a Nation*. New York: Dutton, 1996.

Menashri, David. *Post-Revolutionary Politics in Iran: Religion, Society, and Power*. Portland, OR: F. Cass, 2001.

Moin, Baqer. *Khomeini: Life of the Ayatollah*. London: I. B. Tauris, 1999.

Schirazi, Asghar. *The Constitution of Iran: Politics and the State in the Islamic Republic*. London: I. B. Tauris, 1998.

Sciolino, Elaine. *Persian Mirrors: The Elusive Face of Iran*. New York: Free Press, 2001.

Yaghmaian, Behzad. *Social Change in Iran: An Eyewitness Account of Dissent, Defiance, and New Movements for Rights*. Albany, NY: SUNY Press, 2002.

Yu, Dal Seung. *The Role of Political Culture in Iranian Political Development*. Brookfield, VT: Ashgate, 2002.

Zahedi, Dariush. *The Iranian Revolution Then and Now: Indicators of Regime Instability*. Boulder, CO: Westview, 2000.

Chapter 36

LESSONS
OF NINE COUNTRIES

1. States often precede and create nations. Countries are rather artificial things, the product of governments instilling a common culture over many generations. A working, effective government is the crux of nationhood; those without one are *failed states*.

2. The modern state has existed only about half a millennium and is not necessarily the last word in political organization. The emergence of the *European Union* suggests a new entity beyond the nation-state.

3. Most *boundaries* are artificial. Where one country ends and another begins is a political decision, often contested. The expansion and contraction of Germany is an example of how fluid some boundaries can be.

4. Most countries have *core areas*, often where the state began, that are still home to the country's capital. Outside of these core areas, in the *periphery*, regionalism and resentment at being governed by a distant capital often grow. Thus peripheral areas often vote differently than core areas.

5. The past is alive and well in current politics. The past forms a country's political institutions, culture, and quarrels. The past is especially lively in the resentments of aggrieved people, for example among regions and social groups that feel they have been shortchanged.

6. War can wreck political systems. War, said Marx, is the midwife of revolution. Several of our countries have undergone total system change as a result of war.

7. Economic growth is destabilizing, especially rapid growth. Economic growth and change bring new people into politics, some of them bitterly discontent. Do not think economic growth solves political problems; it often makes them worse. Democracy must accompany economic growth in order to head off revolution.

8. A system that cannot change to meet new challenges is doomed. Wise rulers make gradual and incremental changes in order to avoid sudden and radical changes. Rulers who wait to reform until revolution is nigh may actually fan its flames by offering concessions. All regimes tend to petrify; the good ones stay flexible.

9. Solid, time-tested *institutions* that people believe in are a bulwark of political stability. No political leader, however clever, has pulled functioning institutions out of a hat. They require time, intelligence, and continual modification.

10. Constitutions rarely work the way they are intended and written. Many factors modify the working of *constitutions*: popular attitudes, usages that change over time, powerful parties and interest groups, and behind-the-scenes deals.

11. Everywhere, *parliaments* are in decline. Some have become little more than ritual, under such tight executive and/or party control that they have lost their autonomy, and only a few are fighting to regain it. As governance becomes more complex and technical, power flows to bureaucrats and experts.

12. Everywhere, *bureaucracies* are in the ascendancy. In some systems, the permanent civil service is already the most powerful institution. Bureaucrats tend to see themselves as the indispensable saviors of their countries. No country has yet devised a way to control its bureaucracies.

13. Multiparty systems tend to be less stable than two-party systems. Much depends on other factors, such as the rules for forming a cabinet or choosing the executive. Reforms can stabilize *multiparty* systems so that their behavior is not much different from two-party systems.

14. Electoral system helps determine *party system.*.Single-member districts with a simple plurality required to win tend to produce *two-party systems* because third parties have difficulty surviving in such systems. *Proportional representation* tends to produce many parties.

15. There are no longer purely *federal* or purely *unitary* systems. Instead, the trend is for federations to grant more and more power to the center, while unitary systems set up regional governments and devolve some powers to them.

16. Most cabinets consist of about twenty ministers. By American standards, other cabinets are large and their portfolios rather specialized. In most countries (but not the United States), ministries are added, deleted, combined, or renamed as the prime minister sees fit; the legislature automatically goes along.

17. In some ways, *prime ministers* in parliamentary systems are more powerful than *presidents* in presidential systems. If they have an assured and disciplined majority in parliament, prime ministers can get just about whatever they want with no deadlock between executive and legislative. Prime ministers who have to rely on *coalitions*, of course, are weaker.

18. Most people, most of the time, are not much interested in politics. As you go down the socioeconomic ladder, you usually find less interest in political participation. More-educated people participate more. Mass participation in politics tends to be simple and episodic, such as voting every few years.

19. Democracy does not grow everywhere and is not everyone's chief desire. In countries without a history of democratic rule, most people prefer law and order, jobs, and food on the table to democracy. This makes it hard to implant democracy in countries like Russia and Iraq.

20. Political culture is at least as much a reflection of government performance as it is a determinant of the workings of government. *Political culture* can be taught—intentionally or inadvertently—by a regime. Countries with a cynical, untrusting political culture have usually earned it with decades of misrule. By the same token, a democratic regime that does a good job over many years firms up democratic attitudes.

21. Social class is only one factor in establishing political orientations. Often other factors, such as religion and region, are more important. Usually these three—*class, religion,* and *region* in varying combinations—explain a great deal of party identification and voting behavior.

22. Religion is important in politics. In Iran, the two merge. More typical are political parties based on religion, as in Nigeria, or religiosity (degree of religious feeling), as in France and the United States.

23. Political systems are rarely totally ideological, but neither are they totally pragmatic. Parties and regimes usually talk some *ideology* to justify themselves, but rulers tend to *pragmatism* in making decisions. Ideology as window dressing is a common political device.

24. Every country has its *elites*, the few people with much influence. Depending on the system, party elites, labor elites, business elites, military elites, even religious elites may assume great importance. Elites pay attention to politics, usually battling for the groups they lead. Elites rather than masses are the true political animals.

25. Elites, especially intellectual elites, create and articulate political ideas (ideologies, reform movements, media commentary), something the masses rarely do. Elite attitudes tend to be more democratic than mass attitudes.

26. Education is the gateway to elite status. Except in revolutionary regimes, most elites now have university educations. Elite higher education produces some elites, as in Britain and France. Educational opportunity is never totally equal or fair; the middle class usually benefits most from it.

27. Much of politics consists of competition and bargaining among elites. Occasionally elites, in order to gain leverage on competing elites, refer questions to the masses in elections or referendums and call it democracy. Of all the political interactions discussed in this book, notice how relatively few of them involve mass participation.

28. Mass politics is easier to study than elite politics. With *mass politics*—elections, voter alignments, public opinion—political scientists can get accurate, quantified data. Since much of elite politics is out of the public eye, we have to resort to fragmentary anecdotal and journalistic data. This means that some of the most crucial political interactions are hard to discern and even harder to document.

29. Democracy grows when elites open their decisions and deals to public scrutiny and approval. Typically, bargains are struck among elites and then presented to parliament and the public. Much legislative and electoral behavior is in ratifying decisions made earlier among elites.

30. Politicians are endlessly opportunistic. Most will do whatever it takes to get, keep, or enhance their power. To this end, they will change their views and policies. This is not necessarily deplorable, however; it lets democracy work because it makes politicians bend to the popular will.

31. Politicians are addicted to money. They need it for election campaigns and sometimes to make themselves rich. Countries with very different institutions and political cultures thus often have similar scandals over money.

32. Parties are balancing acts. Parties are invariably composed of different groups, factions, and wings. Some *parties* split apart over personal and ideological differences. To hold the party together, politicians dispense favors, jobs, and promises to faction leaders. This holds for both democratic and authoritarian parties.

33. Once the army has taken over a government, there is an increased probability it will do so again. Democracy and reformism are often short-lived phenomena between periods of military rule. Countries can grow out of *praetorianism* with economic growth, increased education, and stable governance.

34. Most of humanity lives in the *Third World*, roughly defined as Asia, Africa, the Middle East, and Latin America. Some are making good progress to prosperity and democracy; others, encumbered by institutional, ideological and cultural rigidity, are not.

35. The Third World is trying to get into the First. One of the big problems of the rich world is the foreign workers—Pakistanis in Britain, Algerians in France, Turks in Germany, Mexicans in America—who come for jobs and stay. Given the differential rates of birth and economic growth, the trend is increasing and has become a major political issue worldwide.

36. Within Third-World countries, people are flocking to the cities. Overpopulation and few jobs in the countryside push people to the cities, where many live in *shantytowns*. The Third World already has the globe's biggest cities, most surrounded by shantytowns.

37. Racism can be found nearly everywhere. Most nations deny it, but discrimination based on skin color, religion, or ethnic group is widespread. When asking if there is *racism*, look to see what a country does, not what it says. Underdog racial and ethnic groups are locked out of economic and political power.

38. Cutting *welfare* benefits is extremely difficult; recipients take them as a right and protest angrily. Conservatives often come to power with promises to end the welfare state, but they seldom touch the problem. Once a benefit has been extended, it is almost impossible to withdraw it. The most conservatives can do is restrain expansion of the welfare system.

39. Likewise, cutting state sectors of an economy is difficult. Most countries have state ownership, control, or guidance over the economy (the United States relatively little). In countries as

diverse as Russia, Mexico, Nigeria, and Iran, those who have something to lose oppose ending *statism*. Many governments talk about privatization but delay doing it.

40. Much of what people and politicians quarrel about is economic. Some economists claim that economics is the content of politics. There are important political conflicts that are not directly economic, such as questions of region, religion, and personality. Still, most of the time people argue over who should get what. Study economics.

41. At almost the same time, countries rediscovered the market economy. Most found that statist control retards growth. Markets are now the intellectual trend, but not everyone likes them.

42. Democracy depends a great deal on economic development. Poor countries rarely sustain democracy. Middle-income and richer countries are mostly democracies. The likely reason: Economic growth generates a large, educated, pluralistic, and moderate middle class that starts insisting on political participation.

43. Inflation is easy to ignite, but it hurts growth, sours attitudes, and can even bring down governments. In several of our countries, inflation destroyed people's means of making a living and their confidence in government.

44. Unemployment is a problem everywhere and one few governments solve. Worldwide, there is a struggle for jobs, ranging from difficult in West Europe to desperate in the Third World. The Soviet Union was able to provide jobs but only because its industry and agriculture were grossly inefficient.

45. Many political issues are insoluble. They are the surfacing of long-growing economic and social problems that cannot be "fixed" by government policy. Time and underlying economic and social change may gradually dissolve the problem. Politics has been overrated as a way to cure problems. Often the best politics can do is keep things stable until time can do its work.

46. Things get more political, not less. As government takes on more tasks, what were previously private interactions become political interactions with all the quarreling that entails. No country ever runs out of political problems. As soon as one is solved, new ones appear, usually over the administration of the problem-solving mechanism.

47. Things do not always get better. Some political systems are unable to handle massive and multiple stresses; they turn into *weak states*, characterized by crime, corruption, and insecurity.

48. Political movements, parties, ideologies, and regimes are hard to judge by a priori criteria. We seldom know how something will work until we see it in practice for a while. We learn what is good and bad by studying results.

49. Whenever you look closely at political phenomena, you find they are more complicated than you first thought. You discover exceptions, nuances, and differentiations that you did not notice at first. You can modify and sometimes refute generalizations—including the ones offered here—by digging into them more deeply.

50. Ultimately, in studying other countries we are studying ourselves. One of the lessons that should have emerged from this book is that neither our country nor we as citizens are a great deal different from other countries and peoples. When you compare politics, be sure to include your own system.

GLOSSARY

Following are some frequently used words or technical terms from the field of comparative politics. Each is defined here in its political sense. The country where the term originated or is most commonly used is given where appropriate, but often the word is now used worldwide.

absolute decline   Growing weaker economically compared to one's own past.
absolute poverty   Extremely low income, defined by World Bank as living on under $1 a day.
absolutism   Royal dictatorship in which king amasses all power.
affect   Individual citizens' feelings of fondness toward political system.
affluence   Having plenty of money.
African National Congress   South Africa's largest and oldest party, formerly vehicle for black liberation.
Afrikaners   White South Africans of mostly Dutch descent, speak *Afrikaans*.
agitprop   (Soviet Union) Combination agitation and propaganda; mass-mobilization arm of Soviet Communist party.
alienated   Psychologically distant and hostile.
Allies   World War II anti-Axis military coalition.
alternation in power   Overturn of one party by another in elections.
aggregate   Items or persons taken together.
anachronism   Something from past that does not fit present times.
anarchism   Radical ideology seeking to overthrow all conventional forms of government.
analogy   Taking one example as the model for another.
ancien régime   French for old regime, monarchy that preceded Revolution.
Anglican   Church of England, Episcopalian in America.
anglophile   Someone who loves England and the English.
anticlerical   Favoring getting Roman Catholic church out of politics.
Anti-Japanese War   Chinese name for World War II in China, 1937–1945.
antithetical   Ideas opposed to one another.
apparatchik   "Man of the apparatus," full-time CPSU functionary.
arable   Useable for agriculture.
archipelago   Chain of islands.
aristocrat   Person of inherited noble rank.
Article 9   No-war clause in Japan's constitution.
aryan   (Iran) Old Persian name for Iran; used by Nazis as alleged superior branch of white race.
asset-stripping   Selling off firm's property and raw materials it controls for short-term profit.
austerity   Cutting government expenditures, belt-tightening.
aquifer   Underground, water-bearing layer.
authoritarian   Nondemocratic or dictatorial politics.

authority   Power of political figure to be obeyed.
Autobahn   German express highway, like U.S. interstate.
autocracy   Absolute rule of one person in centralized state.
autonomous region   Soviet-style home area for ethnic minority.
autonomy   Partial independence.
ayatollah   (Iran) "Sign of God," top Shia religious leader.
baccalauréat   Exam by which French finish high school.
backbencher   (Britain) Ordinary MP with no executive responsibility.
bashing   Criticizing another country for alleged unfair trade practices.
Basic Law   Germany's constitution.
Bastille   Old and nearly unused Paris jail, storming of which started French Revolution in 1789.
Beida   Short name for Beijing University, China's best.
belle époque   "Beautiful epoch," France around 1900.
Berlin airlift   U.S.-British supply of West Berlin by air in 1948–1949.
Berlin Republic   Reunified Germany, with capital in Berlin.
bicameral   Legislature that has two houses.
Big Mac Index   Quick estimate of purchasing power parity by comparing world prices of well-known hamburger.
bilateral opposition   Centrist parties or governments being undermined from both sides.
bimodal   Two-peaked distribution.
bloc   Grouping or alliance.
blog   from "web log"; self-published reviews and comments on Internet.
blocked society   One in which interest groups prevent major, necessary change.
Bolshevik   "Majority" in Russian; early name for Soviet Communist party.
Bonn Republic   West Germany 1949–1990, with capital in Bonn.
bounce-back effect   Tendency of trends and values to reverse.
bound   To name bordering countries.
Bourbon   French dynasty before Revolution.
bourgeois   Middle-class (pronounced "boozh-wah").
bourgeoisie   French for middle class; adjective *bourgeois*
Boxer   Major Chinese antiforeigner rebellion in 1900.
Bronze Age   Beginning of metal-working and cities.
Buddhism   Asian religion that seeks enlightenment through meditation and cessation of desire.
Bundesrat   Literally, federal council; upper chamber of German parliament, represents states.
Bundestag   Lower house of German parliament.
bunyad   (Iran) Islamic foundation that owns and runs parts of Iran's economy.
bureaucracy   Civil service; connotes rigid, hierarchical administration.
bureaucratized   Heavily controlled by civil servants.
burghers   Originally, town dwellers; by extension middle class; French *bourgeoisie*.
by-election   Midterm election for vacant seat in Parliament.
cabinet   Group of ministers or secretaries who head executive departments of government; in Europe, synonymous with government.
cacique   (Originally Indian chief) local political boss.
cadre   French "framework," used by Asian Communists for local Party leader.
caesaropapism   Combining top civil ruler (caesar) with top spiritual ruler (pope), as in Russia's tsars.
caliphate   Islamic dynasty.
canon law   Internal laws of Roman Catholic Church.
capital   Accumulated wealth, either money or goods, that is used to produce more goods.
capital flight   Tendency of businesspersons in countries with shaky economies to send their money out of country.
capital goods   Implements used to make other things.
carpetbagger   In U.S. usage, outsider attempting to run in different constituency.

Cartesian After French philosopher René Descartes, philosophical analysis based on pure reason without empirical reference.

caste Hereditary social stratum or group.

catchall Parties that welcome all and offer little ideology.

Caucasus Mountainous region between Black and Caspian Seas.

caudillo Military chief or strongman, specifically one who takes over government.

causality Proving that one thing causes another.

Celts Pre-Roman inhabitants of Europe.

censure Condemnation of executive by legislative vote.

center Politically moderate or middle-of-the-road, neither left nor right. In federal systems, powers of nation's capital.

center-peaked Distribution with most people in middle, a bell-shaped curve.

center-periphery tension Resentment of outlying areas at rule by nation's capital.

center-seeking Parties trying to win big vote in center by moderate programs.

Central America Countries between Mexico and Colombia.

Central Asia Region between Caspian Sea and China.

Central Committee Large, next-to-top governing body of most Communist parties.

centralization Concentration of administrative power in nation's capital, allowing little or no local autonomy.

central office London headquarters of British political party.

Century of Humiliation China's term for its domination by imperialists from first Opium War to Communist victory, 1839–1949.

chancellor German prime minister.

charisma (pronounced "kar-isma"; Greek for gift) political drawing power.

chauvinism After Napoleonic soldier named Chauvin; fervent, prideful nationalism.

chief of government Country's top political executive, either prime minister or president, who engages in day-to-day political affairs; also called head of government.

civility Keeping reasonably good manners in politics.

Civilization City-based Culture with writing, social classes, and complex economic and political organization.

civil society Humans after becoming civilized. Modern usage: associations larger than family but not part of government.

class bias Slanting of jobs, schools, and political power to favor one class at expense of another.

class struggle Basic tenet of Marxism that social classes, especially the working class and the rich, are of necessity antagonistic toward each other's interests.

clientelism Government favors to groups for their support.

class voting Tendency of given class to vote for party that claims to represent its interests.

cleft country In Huntington's theory, a country split by two civilizations.

coalition Multiparty alliance to form government.

coercion Government by force.

cohabitation French president forced to name premier of opposing party.

Cold War Period of armed tension and competition between United States and Soviet Union, approximately 1947–1989.

colonialism Gaining and exploitation of overseas territories, chiefly by Europeans.

Comecon Trading organization of Communist countries, defunct.

Comintern Communist International, world's Communist parties under Moscow's control.

Common Agricultural Program EU program to subsidize farmers; biggest single part of EU budget.

Common Law System of judge-made law developed in England.

Common Market Now European Union; grouping of West European nations that eliminated tariffs and trade and labor restrictions between members.

Commons (Britain) Lower, popularly elected, and more important house of Parliament.

commonwealth A *republic*.

communism   Economic theories of Marx combined with organization of Lenin.

compartmentalization   Mentally separating and isolating problems.

comprehensive school   Publicly funded British secondary school, equivalent to U.S. high school.

Confederation of British Industry   Leading British business association.

Confucianism   Chinese philosophy of social and political stability based on family, hierarchy, and perfection of manners.

consensus   Agreement among all constituent groups.

conservatism   Ideology aimed at preserving existing institutions and usages.

consociation   Sharing of political power at executive level, giving all major parties cabinet positions.

Constantinople   Capital of Byzantium, conquered by turks in 1453.

constituency   District or population that elects legislator.

constitution   Written organization of country's institutions.

constitutional monarchy   One whose powers are limited.

constructed   Deliberately created but widely accepted as natural.

constructive no-confidence   Requires parliament to vote in new cabinet when it ousts current one.

consumer goods   Things people use, such as food, clothing, and housing.

consumption   Buying things.

containment   U.S. policy throughout Cold War of blocking expansion of communism.

Continent, the   British term for continent of Europe, implying they are not part of it.

co-opt   To enroll other groups in your cause, rendering them harmless.

core   Region where state originated.

corporatism   Representation by branch of industry, device of Mussolini.

Cortes   Spain's parliament.

corruption   Use of public office for private gain.

counterculture   Rejection of conventional values, as in 1960s.

coup   Extralegal seizure of power, usually by military officers.

courtier   Person who hangs around royal court.

CPSU   Communist Party of Soviet Union.

Creole   Spaniard born in the New World.

cross-cutting cleavages   Multiple splits in society that make group loyalties overlap.

Crown   Powers of British government.

CRS   Republican Security Companies, French riot police.

culmination   Logical outcome or end.

cult of personality   Dictator who has himself worshiped.

Cultural Revolution   Mao's late 1960s mad effort to break bureaucracy in China.

cumulative   Reinforcing one another.

Current-account balance   A country's exports minus its imports.

cynical   Untrusting; belief that political system is wrong and corrupt.

Cyrillic   Greek-based alphabet of Eastern Slavic languages.

daimyo   Feudal Japanese regional lords.

Daoism   (From Dao, "the way") old Chinese religion originally based on nature; earlier spelled Taoism.

deadlock   U.S. tendency for executive and legislature, especially when of opposing parties, to block each other.

dealignment   Voters losing identification with any party.

debt   Sum total of government *deficits* over many years.

decentralization   Diffusion of administrative power from nation's capital to regions, localities, or economic units.

decolonization   Granting of independence to colonies.

dedazo   (From *dedo*, finger) Tapped for high office.

de facto   In practice although not officially stated.

default   Not being able to pay back loan.

deferential   Accepting leadership of social superiors.

deficit   Government spends more in a given year than it takes in.

deflation   Overall decrease in prices, opposite of inflation.

deification   Glorification of leader into artificial god.

deindustrialization   Decline of heavy industry.

demagogue   Manipulative politician who wins votes through impossible promises.

democracy   Political system of mass participation, competitive elections, and human and civil rights.

demography   Study of population growth.

denazification   Purging Nazi officials from public life.

département   (Department) French first-order civil division, equivalent to British county.

dependency theory   Radical theory that rich countries keep poor countries poor by siphoning off their wealth.

depoliticization   Either loss of political involvement or turning political issues into neutral administrative matters.

deputy   Member of French and many other parliaments.

deregulation   Cutting governmental rules on industry.

desiccation   Drying out.

destalinization   (Soviet Union) Criticism and downgrading of Stalin that occurred under Khrushchev.

deutsche Mark   German currency 1948–2002.

devalue   To change the worth of a currency downward in relation to other currencies (opposite of *revalue*).

developmentalism   Early 1960s theory that we could develop third world lands.

devolution   Central government turning some powers over to regions.

Diet   Name of some parliaments, such as Japan's and Finland's.

dignified   In Bagehot's terms, symbolic or decorative offices.

diplomatic recognition   One state announces it is ready to do business with another.

direct democracy   One in which citizens vote on many issues, by passing elected representatives.

dirigiste   Bureaucrats directing industry, closely connected to French *statism*.

discontinuity   A break and new direction in the expected course of events.

dissident   Person who openly criticizes his or her political system.

divide and rule   Roman and British imperial ruling method of setting subjects against each other.

division   Vote in House of Commons.

Dolchstoss   German for "stab in the back."

dominant-party system   One in which one party is much stronger than all others and stays in office very long time.

Dreyfus Affair   French trial in late nineteenth century over alleged treason by Jewish officer; split France badly.

dries   In Thatcher's usage, Tories who shared her *neoliberal* vision.

Duma   Russia's national parliament.

dynastic cycle   (China) Rise, maturity, and fall of imperial family.

dysanalogy   Showing that one example is a poor model for another.

eclectic   Drawn from variety of sources.

Ecole Nationale d'Administration   (ENA) France's school for top bureaucrats.

efficient   In Bagehot's terms, working, political offices.

egalitarian   Dedicated to equality.

Eire   Republic of Ireland.

ejido   Land owned in common by villages.

electoral alignment   Temporary coalition of parties in order to win elections.

electoral franchise   Right to vote.

electoral system   Laws structuring manner in which persons are elected to office, such as from single- or multimember districts, and by proportional representation or simple plurality.

electorate   That part of population entitled to vote.

elites   The top or most influential people.

Elysée   Presidential palace in Paris, equivalent to U.S. White House.

embargo   Not selling certain goods to disfavored country.

emergency powers   Clause in most constitutions permitting chief executive to take on extraordinary powers under certain circumstances.

emigration   Moving out of your native country.

endemic   Persistent, seemingly permanent problem.

Enlightenment   Eighteenth-century philosophical movement advocating reason and tolerance.

enryo   (Japan) Nonpresumptuousness, not asking for too much.

entitlement   Spending programs citizens are automatically entitled to, such as Social Security.

entrepreneurial   Starting your own business.

environmentalism   Political movement addressing industrial, chemical, and nuclear dangers to the environment.

equalitarian   Policy aiming at making persons more equal in income, political power, or life opportunities; a leftist political viewpoint.

Establishment   Half in jest, supposed monopoly of clubby social elite in British politics.

Estates-General   Old, unused French parliament.

étatisme   (French "statism") Government ownership of major sectors of nation's economy.

ethnicity   Cultural characteristics differentiating one group from another.

euro   (symbol: €) Currency for most of West Europe since 2002; value fluctuates around $1.

Eurocommunism   Move in 1970s by Italian Communists away from Stalinism and toward democracy.

European Central Bank   Supervises interest rates, money supply, and inflation in the euro area.

European Union (EU)   Federation of most West European states; began in 1957 as *Common Market*.

Euroenthusiast   Likes EU and wishes to strengthen it.

Euroskeptic   Does not wish to strengthen EU at expense of national sovereignty.

Events of May   Euphemism for riots and upheaval of May 1968.

excess liquidity   Too much money floating around.

Exchequer   Britain's treasury ministry.

exclave   Part of country separated from main territory.

extraterritoriality   Privilege of Europeans in colonial situations to have separate laws and courts.

extreme multipartism   Too many parties in parliament.

faction   Party within a party.

factious   Tending to break up into quarreling *factions*.

failed state   Collapse of sovereignty, essentially no national governing power.

fatwa   Ruling by Islamic jurist.

Federal Constitutional Court   Germany's top court, equivalent to U.S. Supreme Court.

federalism   System in which component areas have considerable autonomy.

Federal Republic of Germany   Originally West Germany, now all of Germany.

fertility rate   How many children average woman bears.

feudalism   Political system of power dispersed and balanced between king and nobles.

fiefdom   Land granted by king to noble in exchange for support.

Fifth Republic   French regime devised by de Gaulle, 1958 to present.

Final Solution   Nazi program to exterminate Jews.

first-order civil division   Main units countries are divided into, such as departments in France.

fiscal   Related to taxes and public spending.

Five-Year Plans   Stalin's forced industrialization of Soviet Union starting in 1928.

flash party   One that quickly rises and falls.

flight capital   Money owner sends out of country in fear of losing it.

float   To allow a currency to find its own level based on supply and demand.

Forbidden City   Emperor's walled palace complex in Beijing.

foreign direct investment   Foreign firms setting up operations in other countries.

Fourth Republic   1946–1958 French regime.

Four Tigers   South Korea, Taiwan, Hong Kong, and Singapore.

FPTP   "First past the post," short way of saying "single-member districts with plurality win."

fragmented   Marked divergence of views among subgroups and little or no consensus.

franchise   Right to vote.

francophobe   Someone who dislikes France and the French.

Free French   De Gaulle's World War II government in exile.

French Revolution   1789 popular ouster of monarchy.

fusion of powers   Combination of executive and legislative as in parliamentary systems; opposite of U.S. separation of powers.

gaiatsu   Japanese for foreign pressure.

gaijin   Japanese for foreigner.

Gang of Four   Mao's ultraradical helpers, arrested in 1976.

Gastarbeiter   "Guest workers," temporary labor allowed into Germany.

Gaullism   Policies of de Gaulle aimed at making France stable, unified, prosperous, strong, and independent.

GDP   Gross Domestic Product, sum total of goods and services produced in country in one year.

general election   British for nationwide vote for MPs.

generalization   Finding of repeated examples and patterns.

general will   Rousseau's theory of what whole community wants.

genocide   Murder of an entire people.

geomancy   Divinely correct positioning of structures.

gensek   Russian abbreviation for "general secretary," powerful CPSU head.

geopolitics   Influence of geography on politics and use of geography for strategic ends.

gerontocracy   Rule by elderly.

gerrymander   Drawing electoral-district boundaries to favor one party.

Gini Index   Measure of inequality of incomes, with 0 being totally equal.

glasnost   Gorbachev's policy of media openness.

Gleichschaltung   Nazi control of Germany's economy.

globalization   World becoming one big capitalist market.

Good Friday agreement   1998 pact to share power in Northern Ireland.

Gosplan   Soviet central economic planning agency.

government   A particular cabinet, what Americans call "the administration."

grand coalition   Coalition of two or more large parties who previously opposed each other.

grande école   French for "great school," elite, specialized institution of higher education.

Grands Corps   Top bureaucrats of France.

Greater East Asia Coprosperity Sphere   Asia run by Japan, Tokyo's World War II propaganda line.

Great Leap Forward   1958–1960 failed Chinese effort at overnight industrialization.

Great Purge   Stalin's murder of thousands of Communist party members from 1936 to 1938 on faintest suspicion of disloyalty.

Greens   In Europe, environmentalist parties.

gringo   Foreigner, specifically *norteamericano*, pejorative. (From the Spanish for "gibberish")

Grundgesetz   Basic Law, Germany's constitution.

guanxi   Chinese for connections.

guided capitalism   State supervision but not ownership of economy, as in Japan.

guilt   Deeply internalized feeling of personal responsibility and moral failure.

Gulag   Soviet central prisons administration.

Guomindang   Chinese Nationalist party ousted from mainland in 1949; earlier spelled Kuomintang and abbreviated KMT.

Habsburg   Leading Catholic dynasty that once held Austria-Hungary, Spain, Latin America, and Netherlands.

hacienda   Large country estate with Spanish owner and Indian serfs.

Hainan   Large island province in the very south of China.

hajj   Muslim pilgrimage to Mecca.

Han   Original and main people of China.

hard currency   Noninflating, recognized currencies used in international dealings, such as dollars and euros.

head of state   Symbolic national leader, either monarch or president, who normally stands above political fray.

heckling   Interrupting a speaker.

hegemony   Being the top or commanding power.

Helsinki Final Act   1975 agreement to make Europe's borders permanent.

heretic   Someone who breaks away from a religion.

hezbollahi   "Partisan of God," fanatic supporter of Islamism.

Holocaust   Nazi genocide of Europe's Jews during World War II.

home rule   Giving region some autonomy to govern itself.

hooliganism   Violent and destructive behavior.

Huguenots   French Protestants.

human capital   Education, skills, and enthusiasm of nation's work force.

Hundred Flowers   1956 Chinese campaign to encourage different views; crushed when views grew critical.

hyperinflation   Very rapid inflation, more than 50 percent a month.

hypermarché   French for "hypermarket," store that sells everything.

ideal-typical   Distilling social characteristics into one example.

identity   Recognition by people of their nationality, ethnic group, region, or party.

ideology   Belief system to improve society.

IMF   International Monetary Fund, grants loans to promote economic stability.

immigration   Resettling into new country.

immobilisme   Inability of government to solve big problems.

imperialism   Powerful countries turning other lands into colonies.

indicative planning   (France) Governmental economic research and suggestions for business expansion.

indigenous   Home-grown, rooted in the local soil.

indirect rule   British colonial governance through native hereditary rulers.

Indochina War   First Vietnam war, 1946–1954, between French and Communist Viet Minh.

industrialization   Shifting country's economy from agriculture to industry.

inequality   Degree of difference in wealth, income, social status, or political power among individuals.

infant mortality rate   Number of live newborns who die in their first year, per thousand; standard measure of nation's health.

inflation   Systematic rise of almost all prices.

informal economy   Under-the-table transactions to avoid taxes and regulations.

infrastructure   Network of highways, railroads, electricity, and other basic prerequisites of economic growth.

input-output table   Spreadsheet for economy of entire nation.

insolvent   Owes more than it owns.

Inspection   Short for General Finance Inspection, very top of French bureaucracy, with powers to investigate all branches.

institution   Established rules and relationships of power.

institutionalize   To make a political relationship permanent.

intelligentsia   Russian (from Italian) for "educated class."

intendants   French provincial administrators, answerable only to Paris; early version of *prefects*.

interested member   MP known to represent interest group.

interest group   Association aimed at getting favorable policies.

interior ministry   In Europe, department in charge of local administration and national police.

Irish Republican Army   Anti-British terrorists who seek unification of all Ireland.
iron triangle   Interlocking of politicians, bureaucrats, and business people to promote flow of funds among them.
Islam   Religion founded by Mohammed.
Islamism   Islam turned into political ideology.
Islamist   Someone who uses Islam in political way.
-ism   Suffix indicating ideology.
Jacobins   Radical clubs in revolutionary France.
Jesuit   Society of Jesus, Catholic religious order once especially active in converting Asians.
jihad   Muslim holy war.
jihadi   From *jihad*; Muslim holy warrior.
junior minister   MP with executive responsibilities below that of cabinet rank.
Junker   (Pronounced "yoon care") Prussian nobility.
junta   (Pronounced Spanish-style, "khun-ta") group that pulls military coup.
Jusos   Short for Young Socialists, radical youth wing of SPD.
jus sanguinis   Latin for "right of blood," citizenship based on descent.
jus soli   Latin for "right of soil," citizenship given to those born in the country.
Kaiser   German for Caesar; emperor.
karoshi   (Japan) Death by overwork.
keiretsu   (Japan) Industrial conglomerates, new name for prewar *zaibatsu*.
Kempeitai   Japan's army-run security police before and during World War II.
kickback   Payoff to government official for a contract.
knighthood   Lowest rank of nobility, in Britain carries title of "Sir."
kleptocracy   Rule by thieves.
Komsomol   (Soviet Union) Communist youth organization.
Koran   Muslim holy book.
Korean War   1950–1953 conflict involving North and South Korean, U.S., and Chinese forces.
kow-tow   (China) Literally head to ground; to prostrate oneself.
Kremlin   Moscow fortress, center of Russian government.
Kremlinology   Noting personnel changes to analyze Communist regimes.
kulaks   (Soviet Union) Class of better-off peasants Stalin ordered liquidated as part of farm collectivization.
Kulturkampf   Culture struggle, specifically Bismarck's with Catholic Church.
labor-force rigidities   Unwillingness of workers to take or change jobs.
Land   (plural *Länder*) Germany's first-order civil division, equivalent to U.S. state.
landlocked   Country with no seacoast.
Landtag   German state legislature.
Latin America   All countries south of United States.
Law Lords   Britain's top judges, members of Lords.
Lebensraum   German for "living space" for entire nation.
left   Politically more radical; aiming at greater equality.
legitimacy   Mass perception that regime's rule is rightful.
Levellers   Radicals during English Civil War who argued for equality and "one man, one vote."
liberal   European and Latin American for unrestrained capitalism (Note: approximately opposite of U.S. meaning.)
liberal democracy   System that combines tolerance and freedoms (liberalism) with mass participation (democracy).
Liberal Democrats   LDP, Japan's dominant party, a catchall.
liberalism   Originally ideology to minimize government supervision of economy and society; current U.S. usage, welfare measures and greater equality.
life peers   Distinguished Britons named to House of Lords for their lifetimes only, does not pass on to children.

Lockean   Following thoughts of John Locke, who emphasized natural right to "life, liberty, and property."

Long March   (China; 1934–1935) Exodus of Chinese Communist party from southern to northern China to escape *Guomindang*.

Lords   (Britain) Upper, originally aristocratic house of Parliament; less important than Commons.

lycée   French academic high school.

Maastricht   1992 treaty setting up EU.

MacArthur Constitution   Japan's U.S.-drafted postwar constitution.

machismo   Strutting, exaggerated masculinity.

Machtpolitik   Power politics.

macroeconomics   Big picture of nation's economy, including GDP and its growth, productivity, interest rates, and inflation.

mafia   Criminal conspiracy.

Maginot Line   Supposedly unbreachable French defenses facing Germany before World War II.

Magna Carta   1215 agreement to preserve rights of English nobles.

Majlis   Arabic for assembly; Iran's parliament.

majoritarian   Electoral system that encourages dominance of one party in parliament, as in Britain and United States.

Malthusian   View that population growth outstrips food.

Manchu   Last imperial dynasty of China, also known as *Qing*; ruled from seventeenth century to 1911.

Manchukuo   Japanese puppet state set up in Manchuria.

Manchuria   Northeasternmost area of China.

Mandarin   (China) Traditional administrator, schooled in *Confucian* classics.

man-land ratio   How much *arable* land per person.

Maoism   Extreme form of communism, featuring guerrilla warfare and periodic upheavals.

Marseillaise   French national anthem.

Marshall Plan   Massive U.S. financial aid for European recovery.

Marxism-Leninism   Communism, ideology combining Marx's economic and historical theories with Lenin's organizational techniques.

Marxist   Follower of socialist theories of Karl Marx.

mask   To cover over a problem.

mass   Most of citizenry, everyone who is not *elite*.

mass line   Mao's theory of revolution for China.

Medef   French Business Association

Meiji   Period starting in 1868 of Japan's rapid modernization.

Menshevik   Russian for "minority"; less-radical faction of Russian Social Democrats, which Lenin repudiated.

mercantilism   Theory that nation's wealth is its gold and silver, to be amassed by government controls on economy.

Mercosur   "Southern market"; free-trade area covering southern part of South America.

meritocracy   Advancement based only on intellectual ability.

Mesoamerica   (Spanish for Middle America) Southern Mexico and northern central America.

mestizaje   Intermingling of Spanish and Indian.

METI   Japan's powerful Ministry of Economy, Trade, and Industry (formerly MITI).

Metternichian   Contrived conservative system to restore pre-Napoleon European monarchy and stability.

microeconomics   Closeup picture of individual markets, including product design and pricing, efficiency, and costs.

micro-loan   Small unsecured loan to beginning businesses.

middle class   That of professionals or those paid salaries, typically educated beyond secondary school.

Middle Kingdom   China's traditional name for itself.

middle way   Supposed blend of capitalism and socialism; also called "third way."

Midi   (French for "noon") South of France.

Ming   Han Chinese dynasty between Mongols and Manchus, ruled 1368–1644.

minister   Head of major department (ministry) of government.

Mitbestimmung   German for "codetermination," unions participating in company decisions.

Mitteleuropa   German for Central Europe.

mixed-member   Electoral system that combines single-member districts with proportional representation.

mixed monarchy   King balanced by nobles.

Modell Deutschland   German economic model.

modernization   Becoming modern; also theory that this process follows certain known paths.

modernizing tyrant   Dictator who pushes country ahead.

monetarism   Friedman's theory that rate of growth of money supply governs much economic development.

money politics   Lavish use of funds to win elections.

Mongol   Central Asian dynasty, founded by Genghis Khan, that ruled China in thirteenth and fourteenth centuries.

monocolor   In parliamentary systems, cabinet composed of just one party.

mosque   Muslim house of worship.

MP   Member of Parliament.

mullah   Muslim cleric.

multiculturalism   Preservation of diverse languages and traditions within one country.

multinational   Country composed of several peoples with distinct national feelings.

multiparty   Party system of three or more competing parties.

Muslim   Follower of Islam, also adjective of *Islam*.

NAFTA   1994 North American Free Trade Agreement, among the United States, Canada, and Mexico.

Narodniki   From Russian "people," *narod*; radical populist agitators of late nineteenth century.

narcotraficante   Drug trafficker.

nation   Cultural element of country; people psychologically bound to one another.

National Assembly   France's parliament.

National Front   French anti-immigrant party.

national interest   What is good for country as a whole in international relations.

nationalism   Belief in greatness and unity of one's country and hatred of rule by foreigners.

Nationalist   Chiang Kai-shek's party that unified China in late 1920s, abbreviated KMT.

nationality   Belonging to nation or, in East Europe and ex-Soviet Union, to ethnic group.

nationalization   Governmental takeover of private industry.

near abroad   Non-Russian republics of old Soviet Union.

nemawashi   Japanese for "root-binding," as in gardening; formation of group consensus.

Neo-cons   Short for neo-conservatives

neo-Gaullist   Chirac's revival of Gaullist party, Rally for the Republic (RPR).

neoliberalism   Revival of free-market economics.

Neolithic   New Stone Age, beginning of agriculture.

NEP   Lenin's New Economic Policy that allowed private activity 1921–1928.

New Class   Djilas's description of new Communist elite of party leaders, bureaucrats, and security officials.

New Labour   Tony Blair's name for his very moderate Labour party.

nihonjinron   (literally Japan person-ness) Japaneseness.

no-confidence   Parliamentary motion to oust current cabinet.

nomenklatura   Lists of sensitive positions and people eligible to fill them, the Soviet elite.

nonaggression pact   Treaty to not attack each other, specifically 1939 treaty between Hitler and Stalin.

nonperforming loan   One that is not being paid back.

Normans   Vikings who settled in and gave their name to Normandy, France.

norte americano   North Americans; U.S. citizens.

North caucasus   Mountainous region north of Georgia and Azerbaijan; includes Chechnya.

objective   Judged by observable criteria.

October Revolution   1917 Bolshevik seizure of power in Russia.

Okurasho   Japan's finance ministry.

old boy   Someone you knew at boarding school.

oligarchy   Rule by a few.

omnipotent   All-powerful.

on   Japanese for duty or debt of honor.

OPEC   Cartel of oil-rich countries designed to boost petroleum prices.

Open Door   U.S. policy of protecting China.

Opium War   1839–1842 British-Chinese war to enable Britain to sell opium to Chinese.

opportunist   Unprincipled person out for self.

opposition   In parliamentary systems, parties in parliament that are not in cabinet.

Orangemen   After King William of Orange (symbol of Netherlands royal house), Northern Irish Protestants.

Ossi   Nickname for East German.

Ostpolitik   Literally "east policy"; Brandt's building relations with East Europe, including East Germany.

Ottoman   Turkish imperial dynasty, fourteenth to twentieth centuries.

output affect   Attachment to system based on its providing material abundance.

Oxbridge   Slang for Oxford and Cambridge universities.

Pahlavi   Iranian monarchy 1925–1979, overthrown by Islamic revolution.

Palais Bourbon   Paris building of French National Assembly.

Pan-Africanism   Movement to Unite all Africa.

paramilitary   National police force organized and equipped like a light army.

paranoia   Unreasonable suspicion of others, not same as fearful.

parliament   National assembly that considers and passes laws. When capitalized, Britain's legislature, specifically its lower chamber, *Commons*.

Parliamentarians   Supporters of Parliament in English Civil War.

parliamentary system   Political system in which cabinet is responsible to, and can be ousted by, parliament; chief executive is prime minister who is not elected directly.

Paris Commune   Takeover of Paris government by citizens during German siege of 1870–1871.

participation   Citizen involvement in politics such as voting, helping party or candidate, or contacting officials.

particularism   Region's sense of its difference.

party identification   Psychological attachment of voter to particular political party.

party image   Way electorate perceives given party.

party list   Party's ranking of its candidates in PR elections; voters pick one list as their ballot.

party system   Number and competitiveness of parties in given country; five general types: no-party, one-party, two-party, dominant-party, and multiparty systems.

passé   Outmoded, receded into past.

patrie   French for fatherland.

patronage   Using political office to hire supporters.

peerage   British Lord or Lady, higher than *knighthood*.

peg   To fix one currency at an unchanging rate to another.

per capita   GDP divided by population, giving approximate level of well-being.

periphery   Nation's outlying regions.

perestroika   Russian for "restructuring," Gorbachev's proposals to reform Soviet economy.

permanent secretary   Highest British civil servant who runs ministry, nominally under a minister.

personalismo Politics by strong, show-off personalities.

personality cult Adulation and deification of political leaders, such as Stalin and Mao.

peso (Spanish for "weight") Mexico's currency, fluctuates at around ten U.S. cents.

petit bourgeois Small shopkeeper.

pietà Italian for "pity"; artistic representation of Mary cradling body of Jesus.

Pinyin Current system of translating Chinese into English.

plebiscite *Referendum*, mass vote for issue rather than for candidate.

pluralism Autonomous interaction of social groups with each other and government.

pluralistic stagnation Thesis of Beer that interest groups out of control produce policy log jam.

plurality Largest quantity, even if less than majority.

polarized pluralism Sick multiparty system that produces two extremist blocs with little in center.

Policy The specific choices government makes.

Politburo "Political bureau," small, top governing body of most Communist parties.

political culture Values and attitudes of citizens in regard to politics and society.

political generation Theory that age groups are marked by great events of their young adulthood.

political geography Ways territory and politics influence each other.

political institution Established and durable relationships of power and authority.

Popular Front Coalition government of all leftist and liberal parties in France and Spain in 1930s.

populist Claims to be for common people and against elites.

pork barrel Government projects that narrowly benefit legislators' constituencies.

portfolio Minister's assigned ministry.

Positivism Philosophy of applying scientific method to social problems and gradually improving society.

postmaterialism Theory that modern culture has moved beyond getting and spending.

power Ability of A to get B to do what A wants.

praetorianism Tendency for military takeovers.

pragmatic Without ideological considerations, based on practicality.

precedent Legal reasoning based on previous cases.

pre-columbian The Americas before Columbus arrived.

prefect (French *préfet*) administrator of department.

prefecture First-order Japanese civil division, like French department.

premier French for prime minister.

president Elected head of state, not necessarily powerful.

presidential system Political system in which powerful president is elected directly and separately from parliament and cannot be ousted by parliament.

prime minister Chief of government in parliamentary systems.

pritsmo Ideology and methods of PRI.

privatistic Tending to purely private and family concerns.

privatization Selling state-owned industry to private interests.

production Making things.

productivity Efficiency with which things are produced.

proletariat Marx's term for class of industrial workers.

proportional representation Electoral system that assigns parliamentary seats in proportion to party vote.

protective tariff Tax on imported goods to prevent them from undercutting domestic products.

protectionism Keeping out imports by tariffs and regulations so as to aid domestic producers.

Protestant ethic Theory of Max Weber that hard work and capitalist reinvestment originated in Protestant Christianity.

protest vote Ballot cast against existing regime.

Prussia Powerful North German state, Berlin its capital.

pseudo- Prefix for "fake."

public finances What government takes in, what it spends, and how it makes up difference.

public corporation   Special-purpose economic unit owned in whole or in part by government.

public school   In Britain, private, boarding school, equivalent to U.S. prep school.

purchasing power parity   Way of comparing cross-nationally how well people live based on how much they can buy rather than on how much currency they earn.

purge   Stalin's "cleansing" of suspicious elements by firing squad.

Putonghua   "Common language" of China, now standard; used to be called Mandarin.

Qin   First dynasty to unify China, 221–206 B.C.

Qing   Last Chinese dynasty, Manchu in origin, 1636–1912.

Qinghua   China's top technological university, in Beijing.

quarrels   As used here, important, long-term political issues.

Question Hour   Time reserved in British Commons for MPs to question members of cabinet.

quixotic   (from Don Quixote) Romantic, unrealistic efforts to achieve mistaken goals.

R & D   Research and development of new technologies.

reactionary   Seeking to go back to old ways, extremely conservative.

Realpolitik   Politics of realism.

recession   Economy going downward.

Rechtsstaat   Literally, state of laws; state based on written rules and rights.

redbrick   British universities other than *Oxbridge*.

red-brown   Possible combination of Communists and Fascists, brown standing for Hitler's brownshirts.

Red Guards   Radical Maoist youth who disrupted China during *Cultural Revolution*.

redistribution   Taxing better off to help worse off.

referendum   Mass vote on issue rather than on candidates, same as *plebiscite*.

Reform Acts   Series of laws expanding British electoral franchise.

reformism   Political movement aiming at change and improvement in moderate and noncoercive way.

regency   Council that runs state until king comes of age.

regierungsfähig   German for "able to form a government," party that has matured and shown itself capable of ruling.

regionalism   Political movement that emphasizes regional autonomy and distinctiveness.

regional nationalism   Particularist and separatist movements in some peripheral areas.

regressive tax   Tax that is lighter on rich than on poor.

Reich   German for empire.

Reichstag   Pre-Hitler German parliament; its building now houses *Bundestag*.

reify   From Latin *res*, thing; to take theory as reality.

Reign of Terror   Robespierre's 1793–1794 rule by guillotine.

relative decline   Failing to keep up economically with other nations.

remittance   Money sent home.

renminbi   China's currency, also called *yuan*; worth about 12 U.S. cents.

reparations   Paying back for war damages.

representative democracy   One in which citizens do not rule directly but through elected and accountable representatives.

republic   Country not headed by monarch. Also civil division of Communist federal systems and now of Russia.

republican   In its original sense, favoring getting rid of monarchy.

Résistance   Underground French anti-German movement of World War II.

revalue   To change the worth of a currency upward in relation to other currencies (opposite of *devalue*).

revisionism   Rethinking of ideology or reinterpretation of history.

revolution   Sudden and complete overthrow of regime.

Rhodes scholarship   Founded by South African millionaire, enables top English-speaking students to attend Oxford.

right   Politically more conservative, favoring preservation of or return to previous status quo.

romanticism   Hearkening to ideal world or mythical past.

Roman law Legal system in most of Europe and Latin America based on relatively fixed codes, as opposed to judge-made common law.

Royalists Supporters of king in English Civil War.

rule of anticipated reactions Friedrich's theory that politicians plan moves in anticipation of how public will react.

rump state Leftover portions of country after dismemberment.

runaway system Influential people use their powers to amass more power.

russification Making non-Russian nationalities learn Russian.

safe seat Constituency where voting has long favored given party.

Sahel Narrow band South of Sahara, arid but not yet desert.

samizdat (Soviet Union) Russian for "self-published"; manuscripts, often by dissidents, circulated underground.

samurai Literally, "those who serve"; Japanese knights.

sararimen Japanese for "salary men," mid-level employees.

Savanna Tropical grasslands south of *Sahel*.

scandal Corrupt practice publicized by news media.

scapegoating Unfairly blaming persons or groups for ills of political or economic system.

Schengen 1990 treaty ending passport controls in most of west Europe

seat Membership in legislature.

secular Long-term, irreversible trends; also nonreligious.

secularization Cutting back role of religion in government and daily life.

select committee Specialized committee of Commons focusing on a ministry.

semipresidential System with features of both presidential and parliamentary systems.

Sexenio (From *seis años*) Six-year term of Mexico's presidents.

shadow shogun Unofficial term for top faction chief who names and controls Japan's prime minister.

shame Feeling of incorrect behavior and violation of group norms.

shah Persian for king.

sharia Muslim religious law.

Shia Minority branch of Islam.

shin jinrui (Japan) new human race, the younger generation.

Shinto Japan's original religion; the worship of nature, of one's ancestors, and of Japan.

shock therapy Sudden replacement of socialist economy with free-market one.

shogun Feudal Japanese military chief who ruled in name of emperor.

shogunate Political system with *shogun* at its head.

Siberia From Russian for "north"; that part of Russia east of Ural Mountains but not including Central Asia.

single-member district Sends one representative to parliament.

skinheads Racist youth, begun in England, with shaved heads and quasi-military attire.

Slavophiles Nineteenth-century Russians who wished to develop Russia along native, non-Western lines.

sleaze factor Public perception of politicians on the take.

snap election One called on short notice, ahead of schedule.

Social European for welfare state ("liberal" in U.S. terms).

social class Layer or section of population of similar income and status.

social cleavages Division of society along class, regional, religious, or ethnic lines or over important issues.

social costs Taxes for medical, unemployment, and pension benefits.

socialism Political movement aiming at greater equality by means of welfare measures and/or nationalization of industry.

socialize To teach political culture, often informally.

social mobility Movement of individuals from one class to another, usually upward.

soft landing   Gradual calming of destabilizing economic shifts.

soft money   In U.S. politics, funds given to parties and other groups rather than to candidates in order to skirt restrictions.

Solidarity   Huge Polish labor union that ousted Communist regime in 1989.

Sorbonne   Main branch of University of Paris.

South America   Continent south of Panama.

sovereignty   Last word on law in given territory; boss on your own turf.

soviet   Russian for "council"; name of 1917 revolutionary bodies and of legislatures in Soviet Union.

sovkhoz   (Soviet Union) State farm where workers were employees.

Sozialmarkt   "Social market," Germany's postwar capitalism aimed at reconstruction and welfare floor.

SPD   German Social Democratic party.

Special Economic Zones   Areas originally on china's southern coast where capitalist economic development was encouraged.

sphere of influence   Semicolonial area under control of major power.

stalemate   Politically stuck among competing groups.

Stalinist   Brutal central control over Communist party.

state   Institutional or governmental element of country.

state-owned enterprises   Firms owned by chinese government.

State Duma   Lower house of Russia's parliament.

state-led modernization   Government pushes change and growth.

state of nature   Humans before civilization.

statism   Idea that strong government should run major industries.

statute   Ordinary law, usually for specific problem.

steady-state   System that preserves itself with little change.

strategic   Important to life of nation.

strategic variable   Factors you can change that make a big improvement.

structure   Institutions of government such as constitution, laws, and branches.

structured access   Permanent openness of bureaucracy to interest-group demands.

subject   Originally, subject of the Crown; now another term for British citizen.

subjective   Judged by feeling or intuition.

Sub-Saharan   Africa south of Sahara.

Subsidiarity   Letting smaller government units decide most questions (equivalent to U.S. tenth Amendment, "reserved to the states.")

subsidy   Government financial help to private individual or business.

Sunni   Mainstream branch of Islam.

Supra national   Organizations that group together several Countries; literally "above national."

Supreme Soviet   National legislature of Soviet Union, defunct.

swing   Those voters who change party from one election to the next.

system affect   Attachment to system for its own sake.

system change   Displacement of one set of political institutions by another.

Taiping   Major religion-based rebellion in nineteenth-century China.

Taiwan   Large island off China's southern coast, ruled by Nationalists since 1945.

Tatar   Mongol-origin tribes who ruled Russia for centuries.

technocrat   Official, usually unelected, who governs by virtue of economic and financial skills.

temporal   Of this world, opposite of spiritual.

tendency   In France, generally favoring either left or right parties.

terrorism   Use of violence and fear thereof for political ends.

Thatcherite   Free-market, anti-welfarist ideology of former British Prime Minister Margaret Thatcher.

theocracy   Rule by priests.

theory   Firm generalizations supported by evidence.

Thermidor   Month when Robespierre fell, calming down after revolutionary high.

think tank   Research organization that analyzes problems and advocates policies.

Third Estate   Largest chamber of *Estates-General*, representing commoners.

Third Republic   France's democratic regime from 1871 to 1940.

Third World   Most of Asia, Africa, and Latin America.

Thirty Years War   1618–1648 Habsburg attempt to conquer and Catholicize Europe.

threshold clause   Minimum percent party must win to gain any seats.

Tiananmen   Literally "Gate of Heavenly Peace"; main square in central Beijing, site of 1989 massacre.

Tibet   Himalayan region of China with distinct language and culture.

-to   Japanese suffix for party.

Todai   Short name for Toyko University

Tokugawa   Dynasty of *shoguns* who ruled Japan from 1600 to 1868.

Tories   Faction of British Parliament that became Conservative party; now their nickname.

torn country   In Huntington's theory, one with a Westernizing elite but traditional masses.

totalitarian   Political system that attempts total control of society, as under Stalin and Hitler.

Trades Union Congress   TUC, British labor federation equivalent to U.S. AFL-CIO.

trade surplus   Exporting more than you import.

traditional Tory   Moderate or centrist Conservative, not follower of Thatcher.

transparency   Making public political and economic information.

Treasury   British ministry that supervises economic policy and funding of other ministries.

treaty ports   Areas of China coast run by European powers.

Trotskyist   Follower of Marxist but anti-Stalin theories of Leon Trotsky.

Tsar   From "caesar"; Russia's emperor. Sometimes spelled *Czar*.

turnout   Percentage of those eligible who vote in given election.

tutelle   French for tutelage; bureaucratic guidance.

"two-plus" party system   Two big parties and several small ones.

tyrannical   Coercive rule, usually by one person.

Ukraine   From Slavic for "borderland"; region south of Russia, now independent.

underclass   Permanently disadvantaged people.

unicameral   Parliament with only one chamber.

unification   Process of pulling nation together out of diverse regions.

unimodal   Single-peaked distribution of political attitudes or opinions; a bell-shaped curve.

unilinear   Progressing evenly and always upward.

unimodal   Single-peaked distribution.

unitary   System in which power is centralized in capital and component areas have little or no autonomy.

unit labor costs   What it costs to manufacture same item in different countries.

unit veto   Ability of one component to block laws or changes.

urbanization   Shift of population from countryside to city.

Utilitarian   Promotes material payoffs; "useful."

Uygur   Muslim, Turkic-speaking ethnic group bordering ex-Soviet Central Asia; sometimes spelling *Uighur*.

value-added tax   Large, hidden national sales taxes used throughout Europe.

variable   Factor that changes and is related to other factors.

Vatican   Headquarters of Roman Catholic church.

Vatican II   Short name for *Second Vatican Council*.

velayat-e faqih   (Iran) "Guardianship of the religious jurist," theocratic system devised by Khomeini.

Vergangenheitsbewältigung   Literally, "mastery of the past," coming to grips with Germany's Nazi past.

Versailles   Palace and estate on outskirts of Paris built by Louis XIV.

Versailles Treaty   1919 treaty ending World War I.

vice-minister   Top bureaucrat in Japanese ministry.

Vichy   Nazi puppet regime that ran France during World War II.

volatile   Rises and falls quickly.

Volksgeist   German for "spirit of the people," has racist connotations.

voluntarism   Belief that human will can change world.

vote of no confidence   Parliamentary vote to oust cabinet.

wa   Japanese for social harmony.

wage restraint   Unions holding back on compensation demands.

Waldsterben   German for death of forest from pollution.

walking-around money   Relatively small payments by politicians to buy votes.

war communism   Temporary strict socialism in Russia 1918–1921.

warlord   In 1920s China, general who ran province.

Warring states   China's early period (475–221 B.C.), before unification.

Warsaw Pact   Soviet-led alliance of Communist countries, defunct.

weak state   One unable to govern effectively; corrupt and crime-ridden.

Weimar Republic   1919–1933 democratic German republic.

welfare   Redistributive measures that provide health care, food, housing, and insurance to poorer classes.

welfare state   Political system that redistributes wealth from rich to poor, standard in West Europe.

Weltanschauung   German for "world view"; parties offering firm, narrow ideologies.

Wessi   Nickname for West German.

Westernizers   Nineteenth-century Russians who wished to copy West.

Westphalia   Treaty ending Thirty Years War.

wets   In Thatcher's usage, Tories too timid to apply her militant neoliberalism.

Westminster   British Parliament building.

whig democracy   Democracy with limited participation, typical of democracy's initial phases.

Whigs   Faction of British Parliament that became Liberal party.

whip   Parliamentary party leader who makes sure members obey party in voting.

Whitehall   Main British government offices.

Wirtschaftswunder   German for "economic miracle."

working class   That of those paid hourly wage, typically less affluent and educated.

World Trade Organization   120-plus members open selves to trade and investment; has quasi-judicial powers.

write off   Lender admits that a *nonperforming loan* will never be repaid.

xenophobia   Fear and hatred of foreigners.

Xinjiang   China's northwesternmost province, home of *Uygurs*.

¥   Western symbol for yen, Japan's currency, and for yuan, China's currency (not used in those written languages).

Yalta   Town in Soviet Crimea where in 1945 U.S., British, and Soviet leaders decided postwar status of Germany and East Europe.

yuan   China's currency, worth 12 U.S. cents; officially called *renminbi* (RMB, people's money).

yuppy   Short for "young urban professional."

zaibatsu   Prewar Japanese industrial conglomerates headed by samurai clans.

zemtsvo   Local parliaments in old Russia.

Zhongnanhai   Walled compound for China's top leaders next to Forbidden City in Beijing.

Zionism   Jewish nationalist movement, founded Israel.

PHOTO CREDITS

CHAPTER 1

p. xxxvi: top two rows, Michael G. Roskin; bottom row left, Keith Levit/www.indexopen.com; bottom row middle, "General and Officers," from Benin, c. 1550–1650 (Middle Period). Bronze. 21″ (53.5 cm) H. National Museum, Lagos, Nigeria/Dirk Bakker; bottom row right, © Werner Forman/Corbis, All Rights Reserved. (These credits also apply to p. 572 in Chapter 36.)

CHAPTER 2

pp. 16, 18: Michael G. Roskin; p. 26: top row left, Library of Congress; top row right, The Granger Collection; bottom row, Lebrecht Music & Arts Photo Library.

CHAPTER 3

p. 30: Michael G. Roskin; p. 32: Central Office of Information, London; pp. 36, 39: British Information Service.

CHAPTER 4

p. 46: Michael G. Roskin.

CHAPTER 5

p. 58: Michael G. Roskin.

CHAPTER 6

pp. 70, 76, 79: Michael G. Roskin; p. 80: British Information Service.

CHAPTER 7

pp. 84, 86: Michael G. Roskin; p. 91: top row left, Library of Congress; top row right, Lebrecht Music & Arts Photo Library; bottom row, Archive Icongrafico, S.A./Corbis/Bettmann.

CHAPTER 8

p. 100: Michael G. Roskin; p. 106: French Embassy Press and Information Division.

CHAPTER 9

p. 116: Michael G. Roskin.

CHAPTER 10

p. 132: Michael G. Roskin.

CHAPTER 11

p. 146: Michael G. Roskin.

CHAPTER 12

pp. 160, 162, 175: Michael G. Roskin; p. 171: Corbis/Bettmann.

CHAPTER 13

pp. 180, 182, 187, 188: Michael G. Roskin; p. 186: CDU.

CHAPTER 14

pp. 196, 199, 201, 203: Michael G. Roskin.

CHAPTER 15

pp. 210, 220: Michael G. Roskin.

CHAPTER 16

p. 226: Michael G. Roskin; pp. 231, 233, 235: German Information Center.

CHAPTER 17

p. 240: © Rolf Haid/dpa/Corbis, All Rights Reserved; p. 246: UPI/Corbis/Bettmann.

CHAPTER 18

pp. 260, 262, 264: Michael G. Roskin; p. 268: Corbis/Bettmann; p. 271: Dagli Orti/Picture Desk, Inc./Kobal Collection; p. 275: top, Corbis/Bettmann; bottom, Michael G. Roskin.

CHAPTER 19

pp. 278, 289: Michael G. Roskin; p. 287: National Academy of Sciences.

CHAPTER 20

p. 294: Michael G. Roskin; p. 303: Ashley Barnes.

CHAPTER 21

pp. 308, 317: Michael G. Roskin; p. 311: Getty Images, Inc./Hulton Archive Photos; p. 313: Sergei Grits/AP Wide World Photos; p. 318: ITAR-TASS, Presidential Press Service/AP Wide World Photos.

CHAPTER 22

pp. 322, 326, 327: Michael G. Roskin.

CHAPTER 23

pp. 336, 338, 344: Michael G. Roskin.

CHAPTER 24

pp. 352, 357: Michael G. Roskin; p. 354: Japan Information Center; p. 356: Viktor Korotayev, Pool/AP Wide World Photos.

CHAPTER 25

pp. 366, 369, 371: Michael G. Roskin.

CHAPTER 26

pp. 380, 382, 389: Michael G. Roskin.

CHAPTER 27

pp. 392, 400, 402: Michael G. Roskin.

CHAPTER 28

pp. 406, 408, 414: Michael G. Roskin; p. 418: Xinhua.

CHAPTER 29

pp. 422, 427, 429: Michael G. Roskin; p. 428: Keystone_Paris/Getty Images, Inc./Hulton Archive Photos; p. 432: left, Xinhua, Fan Rujun/AP Wide World Photos; right, Xinhua/AP Wide World Photos.

CHAPTER 30

pp. 436, 441: Michael G. Roskin.

CHAPTER 31

p. 450: Michael G. Roskin.

CHAPTER 32

pp. 464, 466: Michael G. Roskin.

CHAPTER 33

p. 482: Keith Levit/www.indexopen.com; p. 507: Paul Conklin/PhotoEdit, Inc.; p. 510: A. Ramey/PhotoEdit, Inc.

CHAPTER 34

p. 514: "General and Officers," from Benin, c. 1550–1650 (Middle Period). Bronze. 21″ (53.5 cm) H. National Museum, Lagos, Nigeria/Dirk Bakker; p. 525: Saurabh Das/AP Wide World Photos; p. 526: Martial Trezzini/Keystone/AP Wide World Photos; p. 534: © Daniel Laine/Corbis, All Rights Reserved.

CHAPTER 35

p. 542: © Werner Forman/Corbis, All Rights Reserved; p. 562: Mehrdad Madresehee.

INDEX